ERA'S OF HUMANITY BY GENEALOGY

Author

Brian Daniel Starr

ERA'S OF HUMANITY BY GENEALOGY

ISBN-13:
978-1535343930

ISBN-10:
1535343931

Printed in the United States of America

To

Lovely Daughter

Gabriella Maria Starr

And My Loving Fiancée

Lindsay

Who have given me the

Patience and fortitude to

Complete this work

Also Dedicated to the cause for

Sainthood for

Blessed Ermengard

and

Venerable Servant of God

Father Michael McGivney

Founder of the Knights of Columbus

- Authors Disclosure: As the author of this work I humbly beg the readers pardon as to the validity of the material. Most of the research that has taken place in the last 15 years was done with the aid of a computer and is based on peoples uploads to the intenet. I have an honorable discharge from the US Navy elite branch of the US Marine Corp and at the time of service was given a bible that contained the New Testament, Psalms, and Proverbs. At the time of service the only religious courses I have had numbered three, Understanding the New Testament taught by Professor James (not his surname) at University of North Carolina State where the bible we had to buy as a text book was later lost in Okinawa Japan and was a New International Version NIV Translation that I smuggled into the country and the officers looked the other way when the book pasted thru customs. Religions of Man taught by a Professor at NCSU authored by Hustin Smith that covered the seven major religions in use on the planet today. Ancient Civilizations until 180 AD. That covered the Greeks, Persians, Chinese, etc... also taught at NC State. This text was written after the civilization attempt of the present Pope Emeritus Benedict XVI after a mass I attended after the beativication ceremony of Pope John Paul II in Saint Peters Square. The mass was offered by Cardinal Bertotti and I religiously buy that brand of Olive Oil. I was commissioned as a Notary Public for the State of Tennessee and owned and still own Starr Books, a sole proprietorship in Tennessee and now an LLC in Ohio as well. I was employed on assignment however not earning money on that companies clock. I had spent years doing research practicing Engineering, {My Bachlawarette Major} and am still a member of Mensa as I was in the Vatican, which some contries around the world use as either intelligence or intelligence consulting. Some of my works were printed before the trip to the Vatican in an attempt to prove I personally had some of this knowledge before my scaling the walls of Rome, but I in no attempt claim any religious or holy vow to the Pope, or any other religious body other than the defense of his holiness as member of the Roman Order of the Knights of Columbus, Knighted to the fourth degree, and a descendent of real Marines of the Kingdom of Britain with arms in the College of Arms recognized with a Lion Couchan and other markings as posted in Burke's Armory and Reinstats International Armory. I am more of a curious visitor to the laws of divinity, with no title past Lance Corporal or Knight in a country whose Constitution says the Civil Law cannot recognize any title of nobility but does recognize the division of Church and State and the surnames of people like Mr. Knight, Mr. Prince, Mr. King, etc... as well as Mr. Pope, Mr. Lord, Mr. Prayer, Mr. Law etc.

As well as the humble Einhard, a learned scholar of the years around the time of the Carolingian Empire to write the Life of Charlemange, and the learned Rynsvarch who wrote the Life of Saint Dewi about 800 years after his life, I humbly ask the reader to forgive misspellings and any false truths that might result from this work or the readers interpretation of this work. Other works or volumes of Religious Literature I have completed include John Paul Getty's translation of the Roman Catholic Bible with many of the commentary's there, My Bible issued by a Church subject to the Crown of England, that I lost when loaned to the State School in a play and used as a prop. Some of the Writings of Flavius Josephus including the Antiquieties of the Jews, The War of the Jews, Against Apion, and The Extract out of Josephus' Discourse To The Greeks

Concerning Hades. I have read the Tao Ta Ching, the Bhavada Gita, the first verse of the Koran concerning Abraham, and other works considered Sacred. I have read Ravi Berg's Zohar and the Zohar of Daniel Matt Volume 7 concerning Leviticus at the time of this writing, as well as Kaballah from Daniel Matt, a gentile covert to Judaism, and am almost complete with the Kabtallah from David Aaron. I have read about 80 percent of ChrIstian Literature of the early church that existed before the canon was approved by Saint Ireaneus. I am from the same Starr lineage as Eliza Allen Starr and Ellen Gates Starr who were involved with Christian literature about 1850 to 1905 and some of their scribblings are available today and part of many rare book stores. I believe Eliza was know to help the Sisters of the Holy Cross. I do believe in common sense when interpreting works and hope the reader will understand just because it is in print doesn't make it true and that Freedom of the Press is part of the Bill of Rights which is a collection of additions to the constitution. I therefore humbly ask to reader to take all this with a grain of salt, and ignore Paul who seems to refute all genealogy as worthless. Rather help the Law convict Paul of harvest in a Monastery. Special thanks to all the Brothers, Sisters, Mothers, Fathers, Monsiguiers, Bishops, Cardinals, and of course those who have served as Pope and have occupied the Chair of Peter. May Our Lady of the Lake bless all the Knighted of Christianity in the past and the present including those and especially those who have taken a holy vow to the Lord. May God have mercy on their souls when they become angels.

Table of Contents

DEDICATION **4**

- **Authors Disclosure:** **6**

SECTION ONE : INTRODUCTION **19**

KNIGHTHOOD, THE CHALLENGE **19**

Saint Mary Magdalene 22
The Secrets of the Knight 23

ERA OF EARLY CHRISTIANITY THE MAKING OF A LORD **25**

SECTION TWO : THE PRIEST **25**

Time of the Crucifixtion and the Ministry of the Lord. 25
BRANCHES FROM JERUSALEM AROUND THE FIRST CENTURY 25
BISHOPS OF JERUSALEM AND POPES OF ROME 25

The Five Generation Genesis of God **26**

SECTION THREE: THE FIVE GENERATION GENESIS OF GOD **29**

The First Generation **29**
The Davidic 29
The Aaronic Levitical 29

The Second Generation **30**
The Davidic 30
The Aaronic Levitical 30

The Third Generation **30**
The Davidic 30
The Aaronic Levites 30

The Fourth Generation **31**
The Davidic 31
The Gamalas 31
The Arimathea 31
The Aaronic Levitcal. 31

The Fifth Generation **32**

The Davidic....32
The Arimathea....32
The Gamala....32
Aaronic Levitical....32
SECTION FOUR: Time of the Crucifixion and the Ministry of the Lord....33
BRANCHES FROM JERUSALEM AROUND THE FIRST CENTURY....33

Section on the Time of the Cruxifiction of the Lord and the Era of Christianity....33
The Sons of Mary....37
THE DAUGHTERS OF MARY....40
The Sisters of Mary....41
The Brothers of Mary....42
The Mothers of Mary....42
The Fathers of Mary....43
Husbands of Mary....43
The Many Named Ann in the Biblical Period....44
The Many Named Salome in the Biblical Period....45
The Many Named Joseph....48
in the Biblical Period....48
The Many Named the Same As the Lord Jesus in the Biblical Period....49
ROLE CALL OF NAMES IN THE FIVE GENERATION GENESIS OF GOD....54
The Many Named James in the Biblical Period....56
The Many Named Simon in the Biblical Period....57
The Many Named John in the Biblical Period....60
The Many Named Judas or Jude in the Biblical Period....61
The Many Named Eleazar or Lazarus in the Biblical Period....65
The Many Named Alexander or Alexandra in the Biblical Period....67
Alternative Use of Single Alexandra by a theology found on the internet....68
The High Priest of Israel....69

ERA OF THE EARLY CHURCH, THE FIRST FEW GENERATIONS....70

SECTION FIVE: EARLY CHRISTIAN HOUSES....70

Houses and Surnames....70

THE KNIGHT ORDERS OF KNIGHTS....72
Illustrious Royal Order of Saint Januarius....72
House of the Cross....73

House....75

Of Eleazar....75

House of Elizabeth **76**
HOUSE OF MARY 78
HOUSE OF SIR JOHH or SAINT JOHN or JOHNSON 78
HOUSE OF SIMON 78
HOUSE OF JUDE 78

House of Don Verch Mathonry **79**

HOUSE OF JAMES **80**

HOUSE OF JOSE **80**

HOUSE OF PRAYER **81**

HOUSE OF HORSE OR ALPHAEUS **81**

HOUSE OF THOMAS **82**

HOUSE OF THE LAKE **82**

House of Herod **83**

HOUSE OF JACOB **84**
DAVIDIC AND LEVITICAL LINES 89
Rule of Divinity after the Cruxifiction 92
Chart of the First 37 Bishops of Jerusalem and Their Ascent 93

ERA OF THE TIME OF BABYLON COMING TO THE ERA OF CHRISTIANITY **98**

ERA OF THE TIME OF ABRAHAM TO DAVID, THEN THE TIME OF DAVID TO BABYLON, THEN THE TIME OF BABYLON TO THE ERA OF CHRISTIANITY **101**

SECTION SIX: THE AARONIC HIGH PRIEST **101**
THE AARONIC PRIEST 101
THE HIGH PREIST OF ISRAEL 101
Aaaronic High Priest 102

HIGH PRIEST **104**

OF ISRAEL **104**

High Priest of **105**

Aaron **105**
CHART DESCENDENTS OF MATTATHIAS 106

HIGH PRIEST AND THE BETRAYER 107

ERA OF CHRISTIANITY TO THE EARLY SAINTS, BEFORE 1000 AD. 108

SECTION SEVEN: CHRISTIAN SAINTS AND THEIR LINEAGES 108

ADDITIONAL SAINTS FROM EARLY CHRISTIANITY 108
The Gospel Writer Saint Mark 108
Saint Judicael 109
JUDICAEL 111
Saint King Ethelbert 112
Saint Bertha of Paris 113
The CAESAR 114
ETHELBERT 115
ETHELBERT AND BERTHA 116
SAINT ETHELBERT 117
Saint Raymond Berenger 118
BERENGER RAYMOND
..... 120
CLOTIDE 122
Saint Dewi 123

March 1 Saint Dewi 123
Direct Descendants of Levi to The Saint Dewi 124
SAINT DEWI 126
THE ARMENIAN SAINTS 126
Saint Gregory the Enlightened 127
Saint Narses Pahlav 129
Saint Isaac Pahlav 130

ERA OF THE TIME OF BABYLON TO THE ERA OF CHRISTIANITY 135
ERA OF THE TIME OF DAVID TO THE TIME OF BABYLON 137
SECTION EIGHT: THE KINGDOM AND KINGS 137
DAVID ANCESTORS 138

ANCESTORS OF DAVID 139
The Kingdom of David, How it evolved with his descendents line of Kings. 140

.HIGH PRIEST 140

EZRA 141

PRIEST LINE AND DAVID 142

MARY **143**

HIGH PRIEST **144**

ISRAEL **144**

HIGH PRIEST **145**

ISRAEL **145**
KINGS AND ISRAELITES 146
KINGS 147
HOUSE OF DAVID 148
KINGS OF JUDAH MARRIAGES OR HOUSE OF KINGS 149
KINGS 151
KINGS 152
Lines from Ahab and Jehoikim and the ArchAngel Michael. 153
Commentary on Kings 155
KINGS AND ISRAEL 158

ERA OF BABYLON **160**

SECTION NINE: DANIEL THE PROPHET AND PERSIA **160**
DANIEL OF THE HOFNAI 162

ERA OF ISRAEL, A FEW GENERATIONS AFTER ABRAHAM **165**

SECTION TEN: ISRAELITES AND MAJOR FIGURES OF ISRAEL **165**
HOUSE OF ROETHEUS 166
HOUSE OF RACHEL 167
TEN 169
ISRAELITES 169
House of Jacob's Brother Esau 173
HOUSE OF JOSEPH THE ISRALEITE 174
HOUSE OF BENJAMIN 175
HOUSE OF DAN AND NAPTALI ISRAELITES 176
HOUSE OF REUBEN AND ZEBULON AND ISAAC-HAR ISRAELITES 177
HOUSE OF ASHER AND GAD ISRAELITES 178
HOUSE OF SIMEON THE ISRAELITE 179
ASCENT OF ISRAELITES WIVES 181

ERA OF NOAH TO ABRAHAM. **182**

SECTION ELEVEN: EGYPT **182**
THE LINE TO SARAH, ABRAHAM, AND SOLOMONS WIFE THE QUEEN FROM EGYPT. 182
THE SARAI 183
SARAI 184
THE SARAI 185
ANCESTORS OF NICOLE 190
JEREBOAM AND KARAMAT 192
Shealtiel and Scota 193

ERA OF BEFORE ADAM AND EVE AND BETWEEN ADAM AND NOAH **194**

SECTION TWELVE: ANCIENT CIVILIZATIONS WHAT LINEAGE STILL EXISTS. **194**
ANCIENT LINES 195
EBER FATHER OF 196
AABRAHAM's SON ISHBAK AND INDIA 199
ADAM AND EVE 202

THE ANCIENT **203**

CHINA **204**

Sumatria **206**

ERA OF ISRAELITES TO BABYLON IN GREECE **209**

SECTION THIRTEEN: THE GREEK **209**

THE ANCIENT LINES OF ZEUS **209**

NOTE ON LINEAGES **209**

LINEAGE OF AENEAS **212**

LINEAGE OF **214**

IULUS **214**

LINEAGE OF SIR HECTOR **215**

Lineage of Hyllus and Hercules **216**
KING PHILLIP 217
ANCESTORS OF HELEN OF TROY 218

FAMILY OF ZEUS........221

TABLE OF WIVES OF ZEUS AND THEIR CHILDREN........222

Zeus Line........224

to Bran........224

Zeus and His Family........225

Zeus and His Family........226

Zeus and His Family........227

SECTION FOURTEEN :ROMAN AND RANKS........228
The Law related to Military Rank, Greek, Roman, and Hebrew Saints and Gods.........228
NOBLE MILITARY DIETY IMPORTANCE RANK AND SIMILARITIES........232

THE APOSTLES GUARDIANSHIP........233

LAW In the Lord.........233

LAW In the Knight........233

THE CRIMES AND THEIR PREVENTION........235

SECTION FIFTEEN: PHILOSOPHIES........237
The Great Clan Battle........237
Wisdom of the Clan Battle........238
After Genesis........242
Philosphy of the Aaronic Priest........243
Consider King David.........244
Building the Justice........244
Master and Man........246
The last Master.........247
Lot From Nahor And the Precedent........248
Lot........249
Lot........250
From Abraham and Sari to Noah.........250
COUSINS........252
Rebecca's Cousins........253

ERA OF ABRAHAM A FEW GENERATIONS UP AND A FEW DOWN.........254

ERA OF CHRISTIANITY **256**

SECTION NINETEEN: TIME LINE **256**

Time in History **256**

Davids Mighty Men **262**
HOUSE OF DAVID 263
HOUSE OF REUBEN AND 264
ZEBULON AND ISAAC-HAR ISRAELITES 264
HOUSE OF DAN AND NAPTALI ISRAELITES 265
KINGS 266
KINGS 267
HOUSE OF JOSEPH THE ISRALEITE 268
HOUSE OF BENJAMIN 269

HIGH PRIEST **270**

ISRAEL **270**
HOUSE OF ASHER AND GAD ISRAELITES 273

HAM **274**

SARIYA **275**

RAHAB **277**

THE BIG SUR **279**

The Ladies of the Tribe of Jacob. **280**

SECTION ONE : INTRODUCTION

Knighthood, the Challenge

This book is about the secrets of the Christian/Judea religion that are not apparent to the average Christian that has not studied genealogy and knighthood. All the secrets of the religion are no doubt in the Vatican and are known to different families and orders. To think that any book of less than 400 pages could contain all the secrets of Knighthood would be ridiculous, so if the reader of this book learns only one secret, that would be good. If the reader does not learn anything new at least the secrets he already knows have been reviewed.

A Christian Knight should know many secrets about the Christian Religion. To list all that a Knight might come to know would be very difficult.

Some claim divinity of veneration of the time of Galilee as a divinity. Others claim divinity only comes from Zeus. Possibly veneration of Abraham is a divinity. He is the God of three religions. Therefore there must be different kinds of Divinity. Christian Divinity is likely different from Judaic and Islam Divinity.

The relationships to the Lord must be defended from Heresy and his divinity must be recognized at all times according to the Christians, but the Jews call him a Josh or a Joke, and the Islamic recognize him as a prophet.

Since the beginning of the Christian Religion there has been armed conflict with factors opposed to the Kingdom the Lord would create. These warriors have become Knights and other noble ranks in order to further the Kingdom of the Lord.

The papacy has been defended and many arguments among the nobility have resulted in the Chair of Peter to be in conflict with other factors, or anti-popes. However, the true Pope has always come back to own the papal seat.

There is a concept called nobility where the Knights Charity has been used to bless his fellow Knights, his King, his Emperor, and his foot soldiers and the people in the Kingdom where the Knight resides. There is a ranking to the nobility that a Knight should know.

The first noble rank is Lord. The second Knight, the third Barron, the fourth Count, the fifth Earle, the sixth Duke, the seventh Prince, the eighth King and the last Emperor. There are also noble ranks of Squire, Page, etc.... that are in truth part of the house of the Lord.

Many of these titles have become hereditary, such as Prince and King. It seems in the subject of these noble ranks there is not much violence at the rank of Lord. A little more at Knight, and at Barron (who holds land) some more. Finally at King and Emperor the violence becomes wars and conquests, and defense of the Pope.

Therefore since these titles have become hereditary the lineage idea has taken more significance in Christianity. Certainly more would be expected of someone descended from an Earle than from a Lord. Only a King or Queen in times past could bestow the advancement of these ranks. Therefore the noble would keep these ranks and houses would become known by these ranks.

A noble would be expected to try to attain more rank and success and so would strive to serve their King, (the term Christ in the Greek Language means King) and so advance their house.

To do this a Knight, or Page, or Squire, would expected to practice study and exercise and be ready to defend the Church and his liege lord or King. The exercise would include war practice but the study would be about the Christian Religion, its Saints, and its previous Warriors.

There was a ranking of the Nine most worth Warriors of All time. This could be disputed by anyone however the list contains three Warriors from the Christian era, three warriors of the Hebrews (biblical figures) and three warriors from other cultures including the Roman, Greek and Macedonian. The three warriors from the Christian error are Duke Godfrey of Bouillion, Emperor Charlemange, and King Arthur of the Knights of the Round Table. The three warriors from the Hebrew (Old testament) would be Joshua son of Nun, King David of Judea and Israel, and Judas Maccabeus. The three warriors from other cultures would be Alexander the Great from Macedonia, Hector from Greece, and Julius Ceasar from Rome. All nine of these warriors are significant to the study of Knighthood. In this book the author will show the ancestry of each of these warriors, and their descendents if any are known. (Judas Maccabeus did not leave descendents, however his brother Simon called Thassi did).

Also involved in the Study of Knighthood is the subject of Saints. Many of these Saints are involved with the royalty, or were in fact the royalty, and their lineage, ancestry, and descendents become important to the Knight.

More important to the Knight is the subject of the Saints who are involved with the canon of the bible, their relationships, their lineage and their descendents. Many of these lines have been kept secret by the church, not because the church has a motive to keep secrets, but rather that the lines may not have any factual documentation or may have caused heresies or disputes. The church primarily concerned with the Lord, would keep harmful doctrine away from the innocent, so that the innocent would not be harmed. However as a Christian Knight becomes more knowledgeable with the doctrines and history of the Church and Knighthood in general more knowledge could be trusted with the Knight.

A Duke, Count or Baron would only allow his most trusted Knights in on some of these biblical secrets, and that knight would then advance the country, fief or Kingdom.

A Question comes up with the intent of writing the bible. Most scholars agree the New Testament Gospels were written years after the passion of the lord (the cruxifixtion) by apostles, a scribe, and a physician. The letters of the bible concern the early church and were written as well. There were many gospels however, many of them have survived to this present time and were not included in the canon. Certainly a party that was not interested in Christianity would come to a few meetings, attend a few church gatherings, and then leave it alone. They would not be in on the relationships of the apostles, the study of the Saints, the secrets that only come thru years of study to the Christian. Why then were these secrets hidden in the canon? Was the divine intent that the family, the father, and other important aspects of society be protected? Was the intent that only the intelligent enough to see the secrets be allowed to keep them? The ideas could be easily presented to the reader of the canon but they were not. Possibly the ideas need to be arrived at by the individual, not presented in a way that could be rejected.

Some of these ideas come from the study of genealogy. Ancestry of biblical figures like the Israelites would be held by the families of the Jewish people so that they can claim they are Jews. Without the documentation the claim is not as strong as a converted jew. Ancestry and descendents of the Greeks and Macedonians would be also kept by those people, because that is what makes those nations great. Lineage to Ancestors who were knighted, had a coat of arms, etc... would also become important to a Christian. With the invention of the internet the study of Genealogy has advanced from a trip, and consulting texts and records in librarys to simply sitting in the easy chair and surfing the net. This book and the information collected would not be possible without the internet. The author hopes he is the first to compile this information and present it in book form, however the internet is open to all.

Biblical figures whose ancestry is examined in this book is Saint Joseph of Arimathea, the Apostles John and James Zebedee, the apostles James the lesser, Simon, and Judas. Saint Mary Magdalene would also be examined. The lineage of the apostle Paul is examined. Saint Mary the Virgin is examined, and Saint Joseph the carpenter is shown. Saint James the brother of the lord is examined, and Saint Joseph Barabas is shown. Saint Anne and Saint Joachim would be found. There are many people named Mary found in the lineages. From the old testament, King David, the prophets Jeremiah, Isaiah, Obadiah, the Israelites Joseph, Levi, Benjamin, Zebulon, and Judah. The lineage of the Prophet Samuel is examined. Simon and his brother Judas Maccabeus's lineage is examined. The merging of the lines of David with Levitical lines (lines from Levi the Israelite) are examined. There are many ideas covered in this book. Many of them may not be agreeable to common conventions and may be considered preposterous. The intent is to present a secret and hope it opens the eyes and stimulates the passion of the reader. Almost all of the content of the book is from the internet, so the ideas may or may not be true. Heresy is a part of the Christian religion, and there has been an effort made to keep the information in this book apart from heresy.

Saint Mary Magdalene

The relationship between the Lord and Saint Mary Magdalene is very interesting. After the crucifixion Saint Mary Magdalene met the Lord. This is in the canon of the bible. There is much speculation about the relationship and many of the ideas have been branded heretical. The author of this work does not wish to be branded a heretic, so the reader may have to go elsewhere to find more information about this classically heretical idea. There has been speculation about the Mary the sister of Martha and Lazarus if she was Mary Magdalene, and also the Women with the Alabaster Jar who anointed the Lord if she was Mary Magdalene. The speculation is good and causes one to think, however there is no exact evidence of this so the ideas may present themselves but the early authors of the Gospel may have left this information out for a reason. Possibly because Rome was besieging Jerusalem and the Kingdom of Judea and Israel was in conflict with Rome.

Now Mary Magdalene was possessed by seven demons according to the scriptures. These demons may be presented in the Gospel of Mary Magdalene that was found in the late 19th Century. These demons were darkness, Craving, ignorance, Lethal Jealousy, enslavement to the body, intoxicated wisdom, and guileful wisdom. There is a genealogy that explains the heresy and the truths and parallels that the heretical take advantage of.

The Holy Bible is the most important part of the knowledge of the Knight. Some of the law the Knight must use is hidden in Hebrew texts like the Book of Jubilee and the Zohar. The problem is that the Knight is usually law enforcement for the country he is presently in, so depending on the resources of that particular country the Christian Law of the Knight is based on the Bishops or Archbishop is there is one. At any rate it is based on the Strength of the Papacy, and regulated by the Father of the local parish. With the Chaos that resulted from the posting of the Thesis on the Church in Germany by the adulterer Martin Luther and the schism that resulted in the English Church as well as other Churches, the Papacy was considerably weakened, not the mention the beheadings that took place in England when King Henry VIII killed two Roman Bishops and declared the supremacy of the Crown. This is reminiscent of the early Emperors of the Roman Empire. At the time of the Roman Empire the writings of Flavius Josephus, including the Antiquieties of the Jews, the War of the Jews, etc.... related the history of the Hebrew People to a people that did not have any idea of the people who lived in the area called the Holy Land. Unfortunately some of what was written by Flavious Josephus may not have been accurate, at least most of it gets refuted. In this book I quote the Aaronic Priest section and give a summary of the Priesthood in graphic format. Knight hood then becomes a quest for holiness and law that is usually written in holy books. Most religions have holy books and the reasons they are sacred to a people is that they relate ancestry and lessons that allow people to live better, which is what people want.

It is thought that the Hebrew hold the texts and attempts at what is Law that is much older than the other lawful religions on the planet, including the religion that was practiced by Alexander the Great who made the Roman Empire.

Certainly humanity has progressed further from conquest by champion and sword and the greatest warrior. The advent of nuclear weapons in World War II and their use makes up an end to war as Civilization understands war. Humanity can certainly destroy itself.

So other than holy books, common sense and study of other religions other than Christianity what would make a Knight progress in the Law? Possibly study of existing genealogies and how they relate to other religions etc...

This book attempts to take all the genealogies that are found on the internet and make a complete sense of them. Many cannot be taken seriously that are found on the internet and there are two or more conflicting genealogies for some of them. It would depend on what the theology that was used at the creation or birth of the individual would have believed.

The reason this book is Law of the Past is because of just that. The Knight knows about it and does not bring it to the light of day. The Father gestures and the Knight comes forward and the neophyte or young child remains in Innocence. For example it is referenced in the bible that Joshua Son of Nun was a great warrior. Where in the sacred does it mention he was the husband of Rahab the Harlot and had children that married the Aaronic Priest. Of course this would be hidden. So the Knight crucifies the neophyte, he or she runs off and back to his mother or father and all is well. The mean old Knight carries the Guilt, the Father smiles on the Knight, the Knight knows he blessed the Innocent, and the Mother and Father put their offering in the plate and all is well. In previous works the author has presented the charts, In this work the author will attempt to relate them to the sacred scripture and other writings.

So the Law becomes that which the nobility enforces. A small tribe of Israelites began with a certainly difficult father to reproduce, where the father is actually the cousin of his daughter, and there are a lot of conflicts, where the son of twins that are brother and sister kills people. So how did all the civilizations handle the making of the law. Certainly the Law of the Past Kings of the Kingdom of Israel deserves an analysis, due to the reestablishment of the Kingdom in 1948. The jewish people were in exile for almost 2000 years since the temple was destroyed, and somehow came back into the world order. So how did these people exist, how was the conquered people able to resurrect themselves thru the Roman Empire, and how were these people so misunderstood that a kingdom of peace and harmony could exist where the world was ruled by the sword and the legions. The Law of the Past examines these laws and how their influence has continued throughout the world, with each civilization alive in the year 33 AD when the Lord was crucified and the Knight, Soldier, King, Emperor and other nobility took little notice. Did these people understand how the human was resurrected and how the laws are enforced by the innocent and the leaders alike?

The laws that were written in the blood shed by the Kings of Israel and Judah, the Greek Gods, the

Chinese and other lines that go back such as the Egyptian civilization. What secrets are hidden by the priest that these people did then in order that the ways of the people who are named after the spirit of these people whp have a part to play, if properly instructed in the laws and acts of their spirit they can do to bless other people who may be in error or who may not be getting the maximum of their station in life or of their situation. Because other people are either related thru blood, altar, church, institution membership, or ability, these people can enhance everyone's life because they know the Law of the Past, or better enjoy themselves in application of the Law of the Past.

In all there are only about 40 to 50 people whose existence is known that were alive in the year 33 AD when the Lord crucified himself. The people are found in France, Ireland, England, the Holy Land, China, and Rome Italy, Armenia, and other places. There are only three lines from the Ancient Greeks, thru Helen, Hercules, and Aenas. The lines from the wives Sarah, the Queen of Sheba Nicole, Karamat the wife of Jeroboam, and the Scota the wife of Shealtial of Persia are all Egyptian based and are part of everyone's past. How then is the Law of the Past still in rule today. Please read on.

SECTION TWO : THE PRIEST

Time of the Crucifixtion and the Ministry of the Lord.

BRANCHES FROM JERUSALEM AROUND THE FIRST CENTURY

It seems there are more than one line that leaves the Holy Land and branches to other parts of the world. The line from James the Just son of Saint Joseph leads directly to Conan, who marries the line from Anna of Arimathea in Saint Dareca. This line continues to Saint Judicael thru one branch and to Saint Brychan's wife Prawst thru another branch. Actually Saint Brychan is directly descended from Joseph Ha Rama Theo the son on Saint Joseph thru Siaclotus who marries Eurgain the descendent of Saint Joseph of Arimathea. These lines all contribute to the English Kings that show descent from James the Just, Saint Joseph of Arimathea, and Joseph Ha Rama Theo.

Another branch that springs from the area around Jerusalem is the lines from Judas of Gamla that lead to Meroveous who is the father of the Merovian Dynasty. (The kings and queens of France.) This line is from Judas of Gamla thru Joseph of Gamla father of Jesus of Gamla who marries Saint Mary Magdalene, father of Jesus Justus father of Joseph. This line leads to the Franks, whose line is joined by a long line from Joseph the Israelite and eventually becomes the Roman Emperor the seven foot tall Charlemagne.

Finally a third branch that leads to the other parts of the world is the line from Joseph Ha Rama Theo who was the son of Saint Joseph. Siaclotus marries Eurgen and has descendents who are Saint Helen of the Cross and the Emperor Saint Constantine who changes the religion of Rome to Christianity. Eurgen was of the lines of the British Kings (Beli the Druid King was an ancestor) and thru a female branch Numerius Julius Caesar can be found as well as Tiberius Nero Caesar as ancestors of Eurgen.

BISHOPS OF JERUSALEM AND POPES OF ROME

The lines from Simon, son of Saint Joseph contain many Bishops of Jerusalem. (See charts in this book). There is also the line from John the son of James the Just (son of Saint Joseph) that has many Bishops of Jerusalem in them. Also in this line is Saint Pius the 10th Pope. Simeon the son of Cleopas the brother of Saint Joseph was the second Bishop of Jerusalem. The line from Joseph Ha Rama Theo has Josue as a son and this line contains Mark the 16th Bishop of Jerusalem. The line from James the Lesser who was an apostle contains two Popes, Evaristus the 5th Pope and Hyginus the 9th Pope. Linus the Second Pope was descended from Saint Joseph of Arimathea (See chart) and

Pius the 10th Pope was descended from John the son of James the Just who was the first Bishop of Jerusalem.

So the Church in Jerusalem had the first 16 Bishops all descended from Saint Joseph or Cleopas (All descended from Jacob) as well as three of the Popes in Rome, with the fourth pope descended from Saint Joseph of Arimathea.

The Five Generation Genesis of God

The Davidic Line as it Merges with the Levitical Line at the Time of the Crucifixion.

The Davidic line starts with Eleazar, and the Levitical Line starts with John Hyrancus. Saint Joseph is four generations from Eleazar, and Mary the Virgin is four generations from John Hyrancus.

Janna the sister to Judas Macabee and Simon Thassi married Eliub and had Eleazar. This is the first marriage the author at this time knows between the Levitical line of Aaron and the line of David from Solomon.

Eleazor married Salome Maccabee. They had a son and two daughters. The son was Mathan, and the daughters were Rachel and Alexandra . Antigonus was of the line of Simon Thassi who was the brother of Judas Maccabee and brother to Janna Maccabee who married Eliud the father of Eleazor. Antigonus had sons Judas of Gamla and Joidiah. (Jeshus III) The line of Nathan also is Davidic and Mathat was of the same generation as Mathan, Rachel, Alexandra, Judas of Gamla and Joidiah. Mathat married Alexandra who was the daughter of Hyracanus II who was the son of Alexander Yanni and brother to Salome Maccabee.

Rachel was the mother of Joseph of Arimathea and Bianca. Rachel married Mathat, and so Mathan and Mathat were brothers in law. Mathat was the father of Joaichim and Zacharia with Alexandra. Joaichim was the father of Mary the Virgin and Salome with Anne. Because Joadiah the father of Anne was called Jeshua III the son of Mary had the same name as his great grandfather. The Virgin Mary would have to be the oldest daughter and was dedicated to the temple in the same manner as Samuel was. Anne was a daughter of Bianca and Joidiah. Bianca married Joidiah the son of Antigonus, who was of the Levitical Line. Joidiah's brother Judas of Gamla the elder was the father of Zebedee and Eucharia. Eucharia was the mother of Saint Mary Magdalene. Saint Mary Magdalen was the sister to Lazaris the son of Eucharia and Mathew and Lazaris, Mary, and Martha was the grandchildren of Judas of Gamla the son of Antigonus. Joidiah was the son of Antigonus and was the father of Anne, who married Joachim. Anne the daughter of Lazaris and Salome married Joseph of Arimathea. Thus there are two Anne's, one the daughter of Joaidiah and one the daughter of Lazaris. Lazaris also has a line that continued thru his son Eurgen.

Alexandra married Mathat. She was thus the mother of Zacharia and Joachim, and so the grandmother of the Virgin Mary and Saint John the Baptist. Now Eleazar's daughter Rachel was the mother to Bianca, who was the mother to Elizabeth who married Zachariah and had Saint John the Baptist. So Rachel would be the Great Grandmother of Saint John the Baptist.

Now Jacob who was father to Saint Joseph also had a son Cleopas. And Cleopas had a wife Mary Alphaes who was the daughter of Saint JoAnne who was the daughter of Bianca. They had sons Saint James the Lesser, Saint Simon , Saint Jude, and Saint Joseph Barabas. Cleopas was a twin to Ptolas, who may have been the Apostle Thomas.

Saint JoAnne married another Joaichim who was the son of Alymos whose line ascends to Zerrubabel thru Meshasllum and contains Sirach and Haggai. Now Biancha married Jeshua II the son of Panthera as well as Joidaiah or Jeshua III. Jeshua's line is the Panthira's line that also rises to Zerrubabel thru Meshallum. This line contains Tobit and Jose and merges at Tobit's father Anani who is father of Onaid, Tobits brother. Onaid's line is the line mentioned that contains Sirach and Haggai.

Mathan had three sons, Jacob who married Cleopatra, Judas of Gamla, and Hizikiah the Zealot. Jacob was the father of Saint Joseph who married the Virgin as a widower. Judas of Gamla was the father of another Joseph whose son married Saint Mary Magdalene. Saint Mary Magdalene's brother Lazaris married Salome the younger sister of the Virgin Mary and had Eugen. Eugen's line continues to Wales.

It is interesting to note there are two Alexandra's, Alexandra the daughter of Eleazar and Alexandra the daughter of Hyrancus II one of the sons of Alexander Yanni, the son of John Hyrancus. One Alexandra married Matthan, and the other married Mattat. Now Matthan was the husband of Alexandra the daughter of Hyrancus II and so married the Levitical line of Aaron. Mathat married the daughter of Eleazar, and so married the Davidic lineof Eleazar.

It is obvious that with two Alexandra's it becomes somewhat confusing. Now let's examine some other possibilities. There were 12 people alive at the time who had the name of the lord in some form. There were 9 number of people alive who bore the name of Joseph, 9 number of people alive that bore the name of Mary, 8 number of people alive that bore the name of James, 15 number of people alive that bore the name of Judas, 12 number of people alive that bore the name of Simon, 6 people alive that bore the name of Jacob. All of these people are examined in this book and their relationships mentioned. Charts and text are the primary ways to relate to these people. The interesting thing is that there is conflicting relationships that are defined for the same characters. Now of course one way is right, the truth, and that is what happened about two thousand years ago. However there is so much disagreement that the author has decided to present what makes sense and is most often found, and the remainder of the relationships are not here refuted, but may have been left out. In some cases two or three possibilities are presented for the same people. This presents the idea of different theologies, and a study of any or all of them could only benefit the reader.

Of all these that are presented in the book there were likely very many more that were alive and lost to history. All these names were common names for the Hebrew people. Now consider that the war with the Romans was alive during the Maccabees at the time of John Hyrancus's father Simon Thassi who was the brother to the famed warrior Judas Maccabee. There were different opinions of how to defeat the Romans.

The Romans knew the Hebrew were ruled by a priest, and the House of David was something they also knew about. Bands of what the Romans considered Outlaws formed, Athongones and Hizikiah both Zealots were of these bands. The Romans had to stay in camps and fortifications to stay alive. Hebrews that were captured did not give them any information. To the Hebrew this information was considered sacred. The fact is this information was part of a breeding project that took place after many generations. Priests were heretical offices, inherited from parents. The House of David was a dynasty that was based on heretical ownership. The defeat of the Hebrew was not something that would happen over night !!

The ruling class of the Roman knew this, and were not that concerned about what happened in the frontier of the east. The Hebrew were also not that worried about losing their sovereignty. It had happened before and the philosophies and ways of life that were recorded in the scriptures always seemed to bring the Hebrew back. The Persians and the Egyptians were always the allies of the Hebrew. The Romans were the new world power, that did not last, but at least organized the religions and was the first empire.

What then were the Hebrews after that made this breeding project of the last four hundred years of history? They were after the one philosophy that would end up ruling the world. A world of peace, love, justice, and equality based on the sufferings of the one son was the objective. A way to rule capital punishment, someone who could survive the pains of death, and yet not die, but rather give his life to those who demanded it, in order to correct and teach their wrongs. A world of justice where those who were guilty paid for it, and then after payment were forgiven. A world were love was the objective, ruled by the most prolific race the world had ever known, a race that was ruled by strength of its people, from building the pyramids of Egypt to occupying and holding the trade routes of Africa, Europe, and Asia for many and most generations.

Now these people did not give away their secrets easily, and many peoples and Knighthoods have arisen and tried to oppress or conceal the secrets that are associated with this Hebrew religion, and its branch of Christianity. Of course secrets of the religion are based on occupation as well. It is complicated enough that the priest is not easily taught, so you have to become a full time priest in order to do it right. The same with the healing, a full time doctor is required to heal one, not a part time jack of all trades. The same is true of the law, a full time lawyer, detective or reformer, the same as for a teacher, the same for a soldier, the same for an engineer. How then is this done that one is made to occupy the post of the most high? It would have to be the royalty from all the dynasties, and major civilizations at the time. The Lord is shown in this book to be from the royal line of the Hebrew, the Egyptian, and the Roman.

Also the secrets of the religion that are revealed to each person that studies the religion are also only revealed when one gets the fundamentals correct. The elementary teachings are found in the new testament, which refers to the old testament. The more difficult truths and teaching are in the old testament. Further teachings are found in books that are not canonical, however very much related to the new testament as well as the old testament. Truths found in other religions are also found in Christianity. Therefore the truths that are more difficult may never be understood by some. Many may not want to understand them and this is alright as well. Christianity is not a religion that says that I am right and your way is wrong, it is a religion that says that this way will work if you want to try it. Other ways may work fine, and even better for some peoples, and Christianity does not condemn those ways, it merely presents its part that mirrors and duplicates the parts that are found in the other religions.

Another thing to consider is that in life if you can do more you will get rewarded for doing more. If the religious side of life is such that supplements all aspects of life the more understanding of religious subjects will help one succeed in life. This is especially true if the proper training and attention is granted to the subjects. I would not be in the least surprised if one reader picked up this book and said, this is so complicated I will leave it to the priest, pastor, reverend and I will go on with my life and forget about this. Another reader may say this is something that is true and I will study it in order to be able to communicate with the priest and reverend. Another reader will utterly reject the entire topic and say it is all false and anything this complicated will never be true. Finally the truly gifted reader will read this and say yes, it is not so difficult, I really understand this, and I would like to follow this up with more thought.

Different areas of the book are outlined below. First the presentation of all the names. Second the charts that show how these names are related to each other. Finally how after the genesis of god the lines continued and formed the modern world.

SECTION THREE: THE FIVE GENERATION GENESIS OF GOD

The First Generation

The Davidic

Eleazar was the son of Eliub and Janna. Eliub was from the Davidic line of Solomon, thru the Male line. Janna was a daughter of the Levitical priest of Aaron, Mathias. Eleazar married Salome Maccabee. Salome was the daughter of Alexander Yanni and Alexandra. Alexander Yanni was of the Aaron ic line of Mathias and Alexandra was the daughter of Shetah, who was of the line of Jose and Tobit. This line was also from Solomon. This line continues to both the Virgin Mary and also thru to the husband of the Virgin, the Saint Joseph.

The Aaronic Levitical

Simon Thassi was the father of John Hyrancus. Simon Thassi had many brothers. Judas Maccabeus as a great Warrior. Eleazar Avaram is mentioned in the book of Macabeus. His line continues thru Jason of Idumea and Antipater. Johnathon Macabeus was also a brother of Simon Thassi. These lines continue to join with the Davidic to make the line that is the Gamala (also called the Magadan). This is thru Judas of Gamala of the Third Generation. Also this line continues to the Mother of the Virgin Mary who is in Generation third.

The Second Generation

The Davidic

Eleazar and Salome had three children. Mathan, Alexandra, and Rachel. Matthan was the husband of another Alexandra, yet not his sister. This Alexandra was from Hyrancus the son of Alexander Yanni. Now Alexandra the sister to Mathan married Levi of the line of Nathaniel who was the Father of Mathat who was the Father of the Virgin Mary. Rachel the sister of Mathan was of Arimathea and she was the mother of Joseph of Arimathea. Now Joseph of Arimathea was the brother of Mathat of the line of Nathaniel. It is true then that Mathan married Alexandra, and Mathat married Alexandra. It is possible that Alexandra who married Mathan was widowed when she married Mathat.

The Aaronic Levitical

John Hyrancus was the father of Alexander Yanni and also of Antigonus. Antigonus was the father of a Judas of Gamala who was the ancestor of Saint Mary Magdalene. Alexander Yanni's line continues to Miriam who married Herod the King. Alexander Yanni was the father of Aristobulus II. Antigonus was also the father of Joidiah who was the father of Saint Ann the mother of the Virgin Mary.

The Third Generation

The Davidic

Matthan was the father of Jacob. Jacob had two brothers, Judas of Gamala and Hizikiah. Jacob also had a sister Don. Jacob married Cleopatra of Jerusalem, who was the Mother of Joseph. Jacob also had a wife Eucharia who was the mother of Miriam. Now Jacob's brother Judas of Gamala was the father of Joseph of Gamala. This is the region of the Dan or Magadan. Hizikiah was the father of Judas the Zealot, and also Jacob. HIzkiah's line did not continue as far as is known past about four or five further generations.

Don the sister to Jacob married the British King Beli. She was the mother of Caswallon, Lldwiath, Affalach, and Llud. These four lines continue to the present day. Caswallon's line continues to Wales, Affalach continues to Brychienog, and Lldwiath line continues to Bran who married Anna of Aramathea. Llud's line continues to Julia of Iceni and thru to the roman.

The Aaronic Levites

Here Alexander Yanni was the father of Salome Macabee. Judas of Gamala was the father of Judas Zebedee, whose sons were the apostles Zebedee. Judas of Gamala was father of Menehem and Menechem. Menehem was the father of Eucharia and Menechem was the father of Mathew Syrus.

Alexander Yanni was also the father of Aristobulus II who was of the line of Miriam, who married Herod.

Alexander Yanni was also the father of Antigonus who was the father of Joaidiah.

Hyrancus II the son of Alexander Yanni was the father of Salome Alexander. She was the wife of Jonathan Alexander and the mother of Miriam who married King Herod. Jonathan Alexander was the son of Aristobulus II the son of Yanni. Hyrancus II is also the father of Alexandra that married Mathan the son of Eleazar.

The Fourth Generation

The Davidic

Jacob was the father of Saint Joseph. Saint Joseph had many sons and daughters before his wife died. As a widower he became the husband of the Virgin Mary. He had a brother Cleopus who married Mary Alphaeus. Now Cleopus and Mary Alphaeus had many sons and daughters three of these became Apostles of the Lord. Cleopus and Joseph had a brother Ptolas. He was the twin of Cleopas and may have been an Apostle of the Lord. (Thomas)

Heli or Joachim was the brother to Joseph of Arimathea. He was the son of Mathat. Mathat was the father of Joachim who married Saint Ann by Alexandra. Mathat was the father of Joseph of Armimathea by the sister to Alexandra Rachel of Arimathea. Rachel of Arimathea is also called Escha or Esmiralda.

The Gamalas

Judas of Gamala son of Mathan son of Eleazar was the father of Joseph of Gamala, and also Tolmai. Tolmai became the father of the apostle Bartholomew. Joseph of Gamala from the Davidic had a son who married Mary Magdalene. This son was not the Christ, however he had the name of Jesus. This is a union between the levitical and the Davidic line. The line from this union continues to both Wales and also to Spain and France.

The Arimathea

Rachel of Arimathea was the mother of Joseph of Arimathea. Joseph of Arimathea was the father of Anna of Arimathea. She married Bran of the line of Don verch Mathonway. (thru Lledwiath) This line continues to the present day. Joseph of Arimathea was also the father of Josephes of Arimathea the father of Alain. This line continues thru to Wales. Bran also may have had Bennardum for a mother, (not Lledwiath) the daughter of Ann the daughter of Josephes the Rama Theo the son of Joseph the husband of Mary the Virgin who was the son of Jacob. This Ann may have married Manogan, who was the father of Beli and had Bennardum. The line from Bran continues thru to Julia of Iceni.

The Aaronic Levitcal.

In the Gamala

Eucharia was the father of the Saint Lazarus, Saint Martha, and Saint Mary Magdalene. These three were the son and daughters of Mathew Cyrus who was son of Menechem.

In the Jerusalem

Joidiah was the father of Saint Ann who was mother of the Virgin.

In the levitical line Miriam was the wife of Herod. She was the daughter of Salome Alexander and Jonathon Alexander. Miriam was the mother of Aristobulus and Alexander.

The Fifth Generation

The Davidic

The Virgin Mary was the mother of the Lord Jesus the Christ. Also in this generation was the sons of Cleopas, James the Lesser, Judas Thadeus, Simon, and Joseph Barsabbas. In this generation was the son of Ptolas Jacobus, who was father of Justus. Now Joseph had a daughter by his first wife, Mary, who had sons Amana, Ptolo, and Masen. Joseph has an eldest son by his first wife, James, who became the First Bishop of Jerusalem. His brother Joses line continues to Wales, and his brother Simon had many sons who became bishops of Jerusalem. James the Bishop line continues thru to Saint Judacael . The lines from Caswallon, Afallach, Bran, and Josephes of Arimathea can also be shown to go to Saint Jucacael.

The Arimathea

The son of Joseph of Arimathea was Josephes of Arimathea whose line continues. Josephes of Arimathea had a sister Anna the "Prophetess" who were progenetors of three lines.

The Gamala

Saint Mary Magdalene married the son of Joseph of Gamala, Jesus, who was the father of Justus who Married Marcella. Marcella was the daughter of a son who was the son of Rabbi Nicodemus the Pharisee mentioned in the canonical scriptures. Thus Nicodemus was of the third or fourth generation.

Saint Lazarus married Salome the sister to the Virgin Mary and had Ann and Eurgen whose line continues thru to Wales. This line can also be shown to lead to Saint Judicael.

Aaronic Levitical

Herod had the sons Alexander and Aristobulus IV by Mariam. Herod was of the levitical line of Eleazar Avaram. Aristobulus was the father of another Miriam who was the mother of the Scribe John Mark. Aristobulus as also the father of Barnabas and Perpetua. Perpetua married Simon called Peter the son of Jonas who was also father of Andrew.

SECTION FOUR: Time of the Crucifixion and the Ministry of the Lord

BRANCHES FROM JERUSALEM AROUND THE FIRST CENTURY

It seems there are more than one line that leaves the Holy Land and branches to other parts of the world

Section on the Time of the Cruxifiction of the Lord and the Era of Christianity

This next section shows why the Hebrew people will always be studied and never conquered. There are 200-300 people all involved in the area called Galilee, in Bethsaida, Arimathea, the Gamala and in the surrounding areas. Not only does the names differ, and yet are the same, the purpose of each part can be determined.

The Christian religion has its basis in the lord, however where it came from is the Judasic religion, so the study leads to study of more than one religion, which leads to how all the religions have worked for each type of people. Of course there is one central figure, but study of the central figure leads to study of the surrounding figures, his allies, the war with Rome at the time, the hidden alliance with one of the emperors, not all of the emperors, and the philosophies of humble figures that were really generals, and kings disguised as paupers.

Knowledge of this makes it difficult to understand why a religion, based on one individual, cannot be ruled or influenced by any one individual, an emperor, soldier, governor, or king, and if an individual attempts it the errors will be pointed out and the individual is shown why the many people involved keep the status quo.

The next section could be used to form monasteries based on the Sisters of Mary, Brothers of Mary, On the Holy Name of the Lord, etc...or the order of James, etc. because of the duplicity of names. In fact if about 300 people all changed there names to interact in the relationships shown in the genealogies in the charts, these relationships would endure forever, and be alive to the people who practive the religion of Christianity.

Let the reader enjoy the charts and the many mirrors of Galilee, and learn who he/she was if the reader has a name similar to one of the pages mentioned!!

The Confusion of Mary or the Many Mary's of the Biblical Period

During the time of the ministry of the Lord, there existed a number of women named Mary

First, and possibly the greatest Saint is Mary the Virgin Mother of God. She is likely the daughter of Ann and Joachim There is a legend that she was given to the temple to be raised, similar to Samuel of the old testament who was also raised in the temple.

Second, and also a Saint is Mary Magdalene, who was mentioned in the scripture. Her lineage is very interesting There is some evidence that she is descended from the Priestly line of Levi the Israelite This line includes Simon Thassi who is mentioned in the old testament book of Maccabees

The third Mary in the same time and story is Mary Alpheaws, who was the mother of the apostles James the Lesser, Jude, Joseph Barsabas, and Simon One Theology says she was the daughter of Cleopas, who was the son of Saint Joseph of Arimathea Another Theology says she married Cleopas the brother of Saint Joseph Both Theologies agree on her children

One Theology has the fourth Mary in the same time and story is Mary who was the mother of John and James who were from the Zebedee This Mary was the daughter of Salome, who was the daughter of Saint Joseph of Arimathea Another Theology has Salome the sister of Mary who married Cleophas the brother of Saint Joseph and the Mary here is listed as the Sister to John and James son of Zebedee

The brother of Joseph Cleophas the father of Simeon may have been married to a women named Mary (Likely Mary Alphaeus)

The sister to James the brother (or half brother of Jesus the Christ) was named Mary or Miriam

The sister to Saint James the Lesser was named Mary or Miriam She would be the daughter of Mary Alpheus

There is another Mary mentioned in the War of the Jews by the Historian Josephus She is possibly one of the Women named Mary mentioned above

Saint Joseph the foster father of the lord Jesus the "Christ" was son of Jacob who married Cleopatra of Jerusalem Jacob also had another wife Eucheria who had a daughter by Jacob named Mary or Miriam She was the half sister to Saint Joseph, Cleophas and Ptolas sons of Jacob by Cleopatra

Mary Sta Da was the wife of Panthera and the mother of Jeshua III who was father of JoAnne

List of Mary's of the biblical period

1) Saint Mary the Virgin
2) Saint Mary Magdalene
3) Mary Alphaeus
4) Mary Half Sister to Saint Joseph
5) Mary the sister to Saint James and Saint John sons of Zebedee
6) Mary the daughter of Mary Alphaeus sister to Saint James the Lesser mother of John Mark the Gospel Writer
7) Mary the sister to Saint James Bishop of Jerusalem son of Saint Joseph
8) Miriam the daughter of Salome Alexander Wife of King Herod the Great
9) Miriam the daughter of Miriam and King Herod the mother of the Scribe John Mark
10) Miriam the daughter of Miriam, twin to Phillip, and sister to the Scribe John Mark
11) Miriam Sta Da the wife of Panthera
12) Miriam Maccabeus sister to Judas Maccabeus

Additional notes

Now Saint Joseph of Arimathea was the son of the daughter of Eleazor (possibly Rachel) Eleazar was the father of Mathan and the sister of Mathan may have been Rachel Mathan was the father of Jacob, the father of Joseph, who raised the Lord Joseph mentioned in the New Testament is most likely the father of James, who is mentioned as a brother to the lord It is likely that Joseph was a widower, and had a family before his marriage to Mary It is likely then that James was considered the brother of the Lord, although he was not the son of Mary He may have been a half brother

Therefore the relationship from the Lord to five of the apostles was a sort of Kinship From Eleazor to Saint James the brother of the Lord there was four generations

From Eleazor to the five Apostles mentioned above there was five generations

Also the ancestry of Saint Dewi thru Sant his father is from a Sister of Mary (not necessarily named Mary but worth a mention)

Confusion about the genealogies found about Mary Alphaews

There is one genealogy about Mary Alpaews that says she is the daughter of Saint Joseph of Arimathea There is agreement in all genealogies found so far that she is the mother of Saint James the Lesser, Saint Jude, and Saint Joseph Barabbas One genealogy has her the daughter of Cleopus, who is a son of Saint Joseph of Arimathea Another genealogy has her the daughter of JoAnne who married Joachim, and JoAnne is the daughter of Bianca, the sister to Saint Joseph of Arimathea The first genealogy mentioned does not list her husband The second genealogy lists her husband as Cleopas the brother to Saint Joseph The second genealogy adds Simeon the son of Cleopas to the brothers of Saint James the lesser The first genealogy list the Apostle Simon as a brother to Saint James the lesser Possibly Simon is the same as Simeon The major difference would be the relationship to Saint Joseph Either the Apostle James the Lesser and his brothers are cousins to Saint Joseph's descendents, (Saint James the Just etc...) or they are related by going up the tree to Eleazar (four generations above Saint Joseph) and down thru Rachel who was the daughter of Eleazar and the mother of Bianca Another difference would be if Simeon is the apostle Simon, or if he is not related to Saint James the Lesser

Saint Mathew the apostle was a publican This means the Hebrew did not recognize him socially Therefore he may have been considered a bad influence on his fellow Jews He was the son of Alphaeus, however his is not considered by most scholars the brother to Saint James the lesser This may because he was a publican, or this may be because he was descended from another Alphaeus With as many duplications of names found at the time of the crucifixion there is no reason to say there can be only one Alphaeus There is no mention in the scripture either way, but it is possible that he was the brother to Saint James the Lesser. Another possibility is that Mathew is the son of a brother of the Virgin Mary. Joachim and Ann were older when they started with children. A Sister Salome may be the next child and a brother Alphaeus may be the next. This makes Saint Mathew the closest relationship to the Lord.

CHART OF THE MANY NAMED MARY

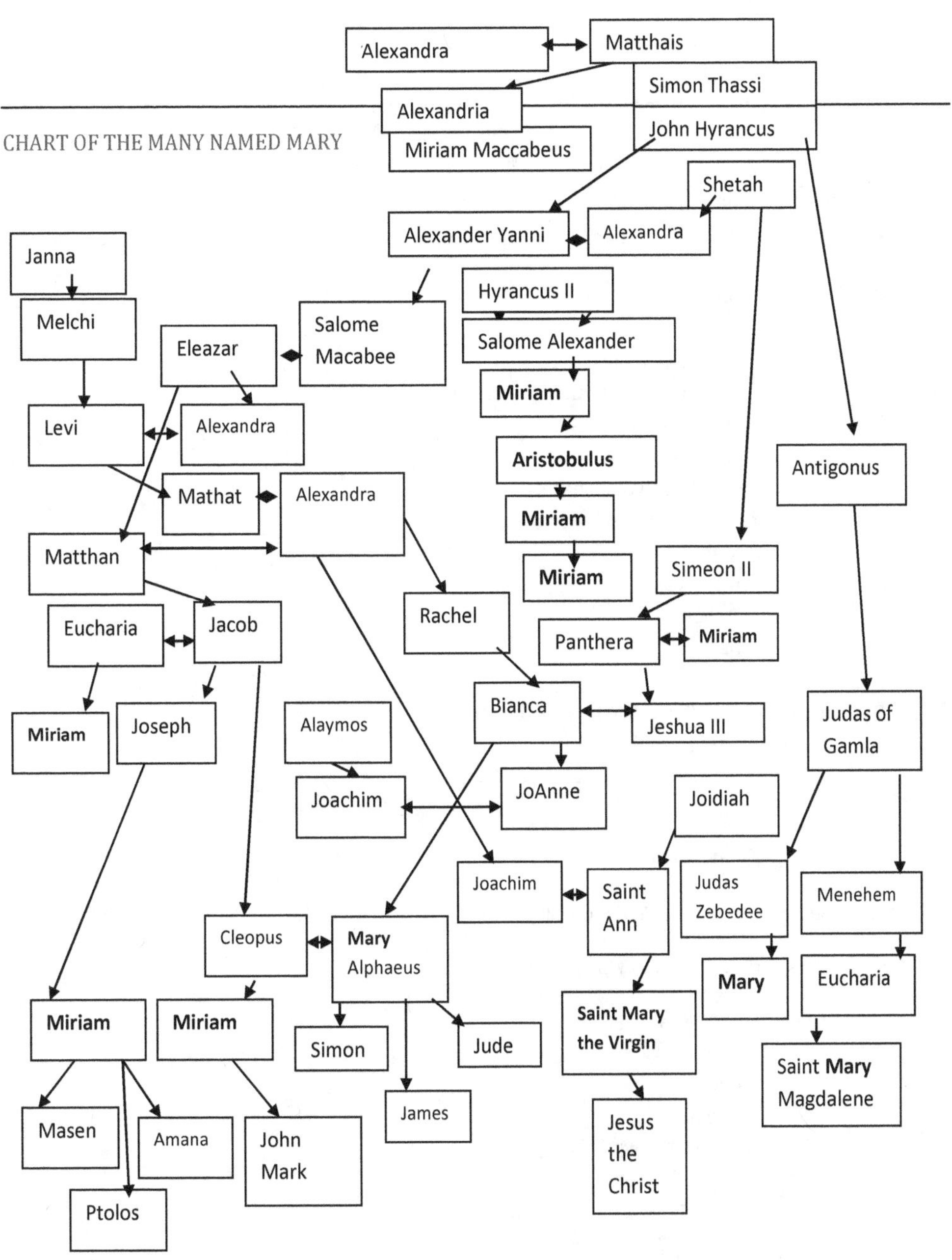

1. The son of the Virgin
2. The three sons of the daughter of Joseph
    a. Masen
    b. Amana
    c. Ptolo
3. The four sons of the wife of Cleopas
    a. Saint James the Lesser Apostle
    b. Saint Jude the Apostle
    c. Saint Simon the Apostle
    d. Saint Joseph Barabbas
4. The five sons of Miriam who married Theudas
    a. Addia James
    b. Andronicus
    c. Theboutis
    d. Mathias
    e. James
5. The son of the Sister of Saint James the Lesser
    John Mark
6. The son of Miriam the daughter of Aristobulus IV
    a. John Mark
    b. Phillip the Apostle
7. The son of Miriam the Twin to Phillip
    a. Arrius Antonius Calpernius Piso
8. The sons of Saint Mary Magdalene
    a. Jesus Justus
    b. Jude
    c. Joseph
9. The sons of Miriam the wife of King Herod
    a. Aristobulis IV
    b. Alexander of Judea
10. The son of Miriam Sta Da and Panthera
    Jeshua III

CHART THE SONS OF MARY

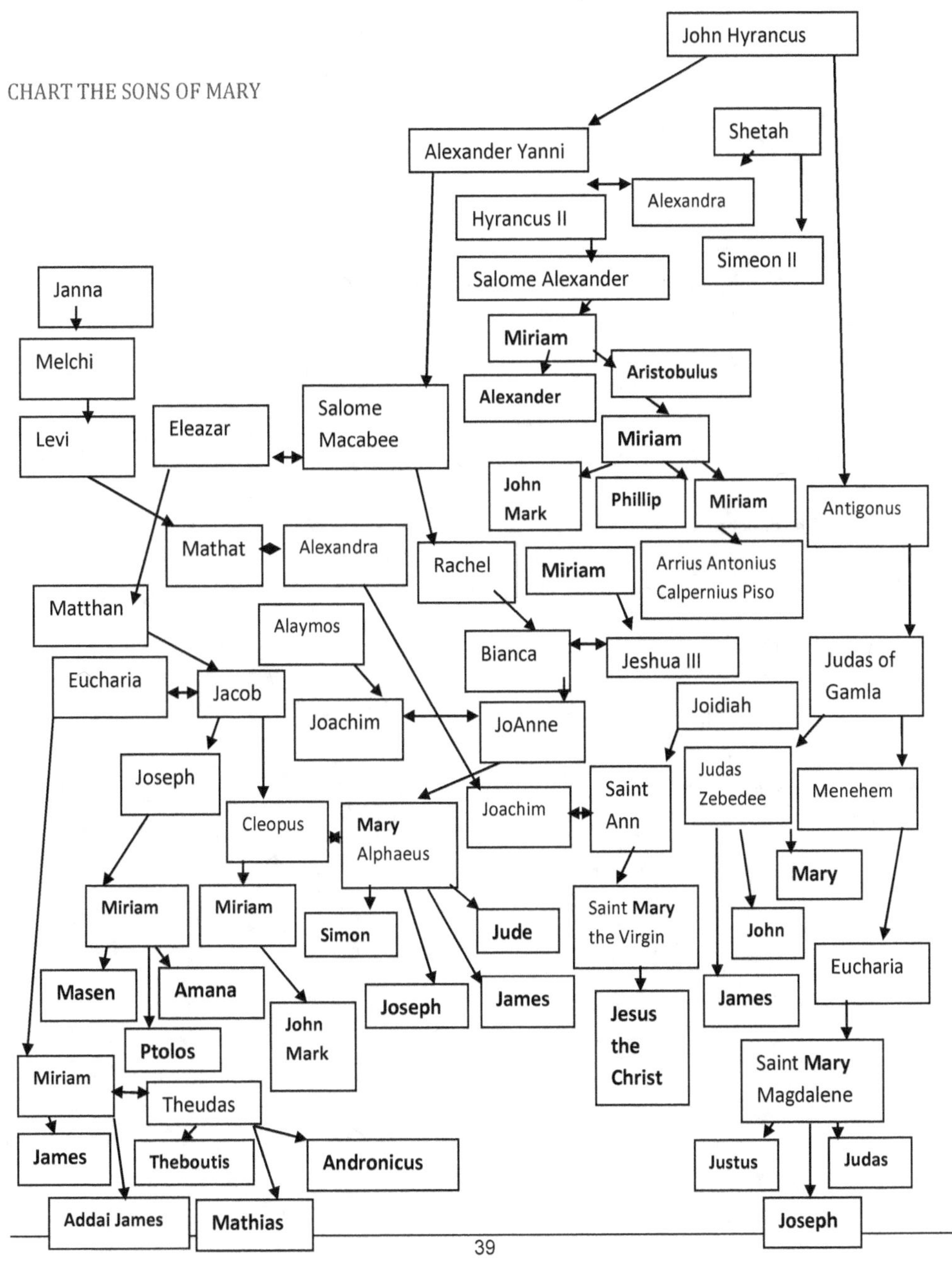

THE DAUGHTERS OF MARY

1. The daughters of Mariam the wife of Theboutis

    Lydia of Judah
    Lysia of Judah
    Assia of Judah

2. The daughters of the wife of Cleopus and Mary Alphaeus

    Cyrian
    Lillian
    Salome
    JoAnne
    Miriam
    Dinah

3. The daughters of Saint Mary Magdalene

    Phoebe
    Damaris
    Tamar
    Sarah

4. The daughters of Miriam the wife of King Herod the Great

    Cypros III
    Salampsio

CHART THE DAUGHTERS OF MARY

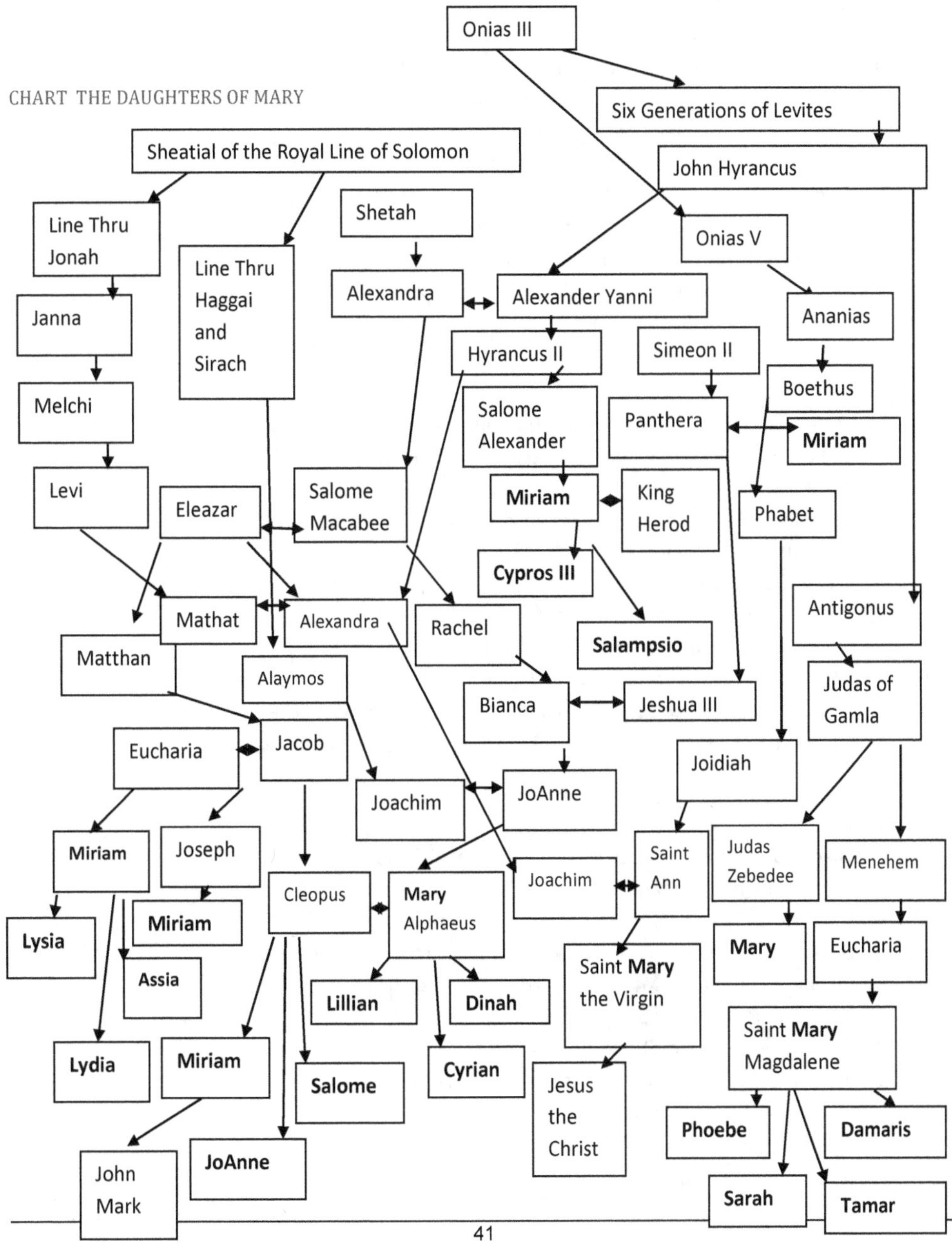

The Sisters of Mary

1. Salome Sister of Mary Alphaeus
2. Escha Sister of Mary Alphaeus
3. Cyria Sister of Miriam the daughter of Mary Alphaeus
4. Lillian Sister of Miriam the daughter of Mary Alphaeus
5. Salome Sister of Miriam the daughter of Mary Alphaeus
6. Johanne Sister of Miriam the daughter of Mary Alphaeus
7. Dinah Sister of Miriam the daughter of Mary Alphaeus
8. Salome Sister of Mary the daughter of Saint Joseph
9. Anne Sister to Mary the daughter of Saint Joseph
10. Saint Martha the sister of Saint Mary Magdala
11. Salome the Sister to Saint Mary the Virgin

The Brothers of Mary

1. James the Lesser Brother of Miriam the daughter of Mary Alphaeus
2. Jude Apostle Brother of Miriam the daughter of Mary Alphaeus
3. Simeon Apostle Brother of Miriam the daughter of Mary Alphaeus
4. Joses Barsabbas Brother of Miriam the daughter of Mary Alphaeus
5. Simon the son of Saint Joseph
6. James the Just the son of Saint Joseph
7. Jude of Galilee the son of Saint Joseph
8. Saint Lazarus the brother of Saint Mary Magdala
9. Alphaeus the brother to Saint Mary the Virgin the father of Saint Mathew
10. Saint John Zebedee the brother to Mary the daughter of Judas Zebedee
11. Saint James the Greater the brother to Mary the daughter of Judas Zebedee

The Mothers of Mary

1. Saint Ann the mother of the Virgin Mary
2. Mary Alpheus the mother of Miriam the mother of John Mark
3. JoAnne or Jane the mother of Mary Alpheus
4. Eucharia the Mother of Miriam who married Theudas
5. Salome Alexander the mother of Miriam who married Herod the Great
6. Salome the mother of Mary who married Judas Zebedee
7. Eucharia the Mother of Saint Mary Magdalene
8. The mother of Miriam Sta Da is unknown
9. The mother of Miriam the daughter of Saint Joseph is unknown

The Fathers of Mary

1. Cleopas the Father of Miriam mother to John Mark
2. Saint Joseph Father of Miriam the mother to John Mark
3. Jacob the father of Miriam who married Theudas
4. Mathew Syro the Father of Mary of Magdala
5. Jonathan Alexander the Father of Miriam the wife of Herod the Great
6. Judas Zebedee the Father of Mary the sister to the sons of thunder
7. Joachim the Father of the Virgin Mary

Husbands of Mary

1. Panthera Husband of Miraim Sta Da
2. Cleopas husband of Mary Alphaeus
3. Theudas the husband of Miriam daughter of Jacob
4. Jesus Bar-Joseph of Gamala the husband of Mary of Magdala
5. Herod the Great the husband of Miriam
6. Saint Joseph husband of the Virgin Mary

There was first the Mother of the Virgin Mary who was named Ann. She married Joachim or Jeshua II and the two dedicated their daughter Mary to the temple and she became a Virgin.

There was the daughter of Ptolas the twin of Clopas and his wife Salome.

The daughter of Joseph of Arimathea was named Anna the Prophetess.

The wife of Joseph of Arimathea was named Ann

The daughter of Salome and Lazaris was named Ann

The wife of Jeshua III was named JoAnne.

1. The daughter of Bianca who married Joachim and had the Virgin Mary
2. The daughter of Ptolas the twin of Clopas and Salome
3. The daughter of Joseph of Arimathea and his wife Anne
4. The wife of Joseph of Arimathea
5. The daughter of Salome and Lazaris
6. The daughter of Joseph the mother of Belus
7. The daughter of Joseph the Rama Theo the son of Joseph the Carpenter

CHART THE MANY NAMED ANN

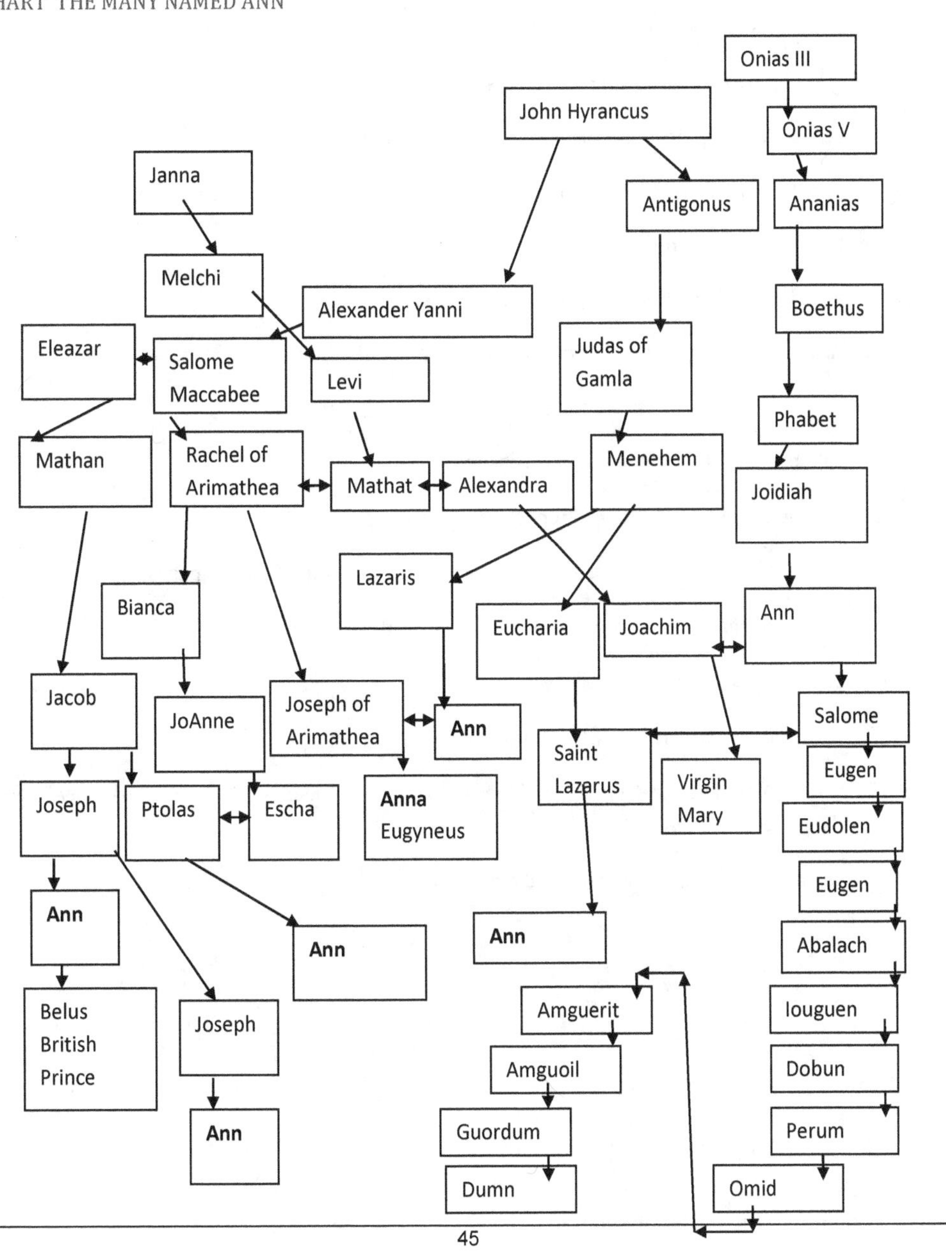

The wife of Ptolas was named Salome

The wife of Judas of Zebedee was name Salome

The daughter of Joseph of Arimathea was named Salome

The daughter of Mary Alphaes and Cleopas was named Salome

The daughter of Joseph the son of Jacob the Husband of the Virgin Mary was named Salome

Salome Maccabee who married Eleazar

Salome of Judea married Aristobulus son of Alexander Yanni

Salome Alexxandra the daughter of Hyrancus II son of Alexander Yanni married Jonathon Alexander

1. Salome the mother of the Apostles Zebedee
2. Salome the sister to Anna the Prophetess
3. Salome the sister to the Apostles James, Simon, Jude the sons of Mary Alpaeus
4. Salome the daughter of Joseph and sister to James the First Bishop of Jerusalem
5. Salome Macabee who married Eleazar
6. Salome of Judea married Aristobulus son of Alexander Yanni
7. Salome Alexandra the daughter of Hyrancus II son of Alexander Yanni married Jonathon Alexander the father of Miriam
8. Salome the daughter of Cleopus and Mary Alphaeus

CHART THE MANY NAMED SALOME

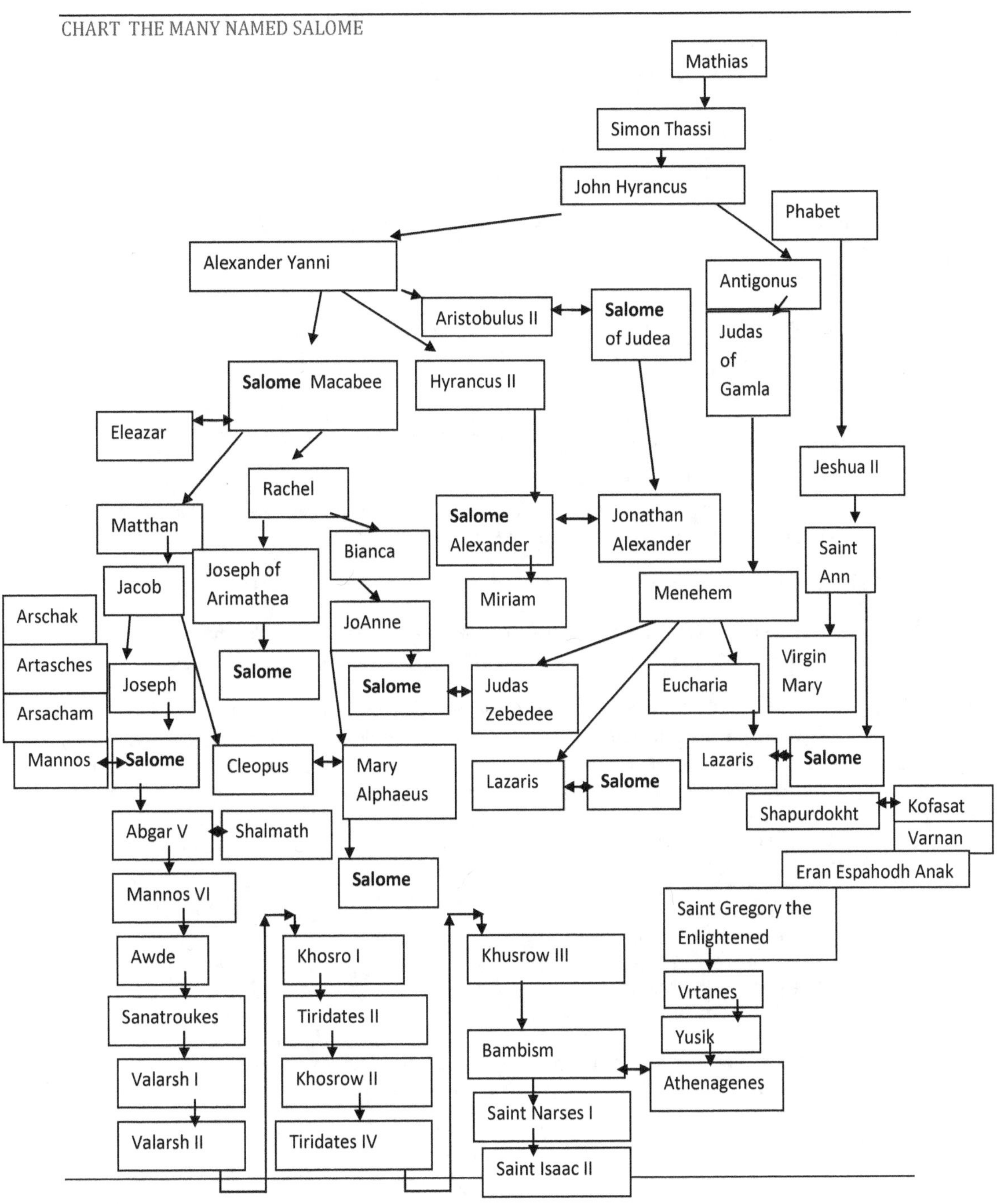

The Many Named Joseph

in the Biblical Period

The Saint Joseph is considered the foster father of the Lord Jesus Christ He was the son of Jacob who married Cleopatra of Jerusalem

Jacob had a brother named Judas of Gamla Judas of Gamla had a son Joseph of Gamla who had a great grandson Joseph bar Jesus the Rama Theo This is in the line that goes to the founder of the French Merovian Kings Merovious

Saint Joseph of Arimathea was the son of Mattat and brother to Heli (Heli was mentioned in the Gospel of Luke in the Genealogy of Jesus Chapter) Saint Joseph married Rachel the sister to Mathan the father of Jacob who married Cleopatra

Saint Joseph of Arimathea had a son Josephes who was the ancestor of the Grail Kings

Saint Joseph the son of Jacob Foster Father of the Lord was the father of Joseph Ha Rama Theo This Joseph the Rama Theo was the brother to James the First Bishop of Jerusalem These lines from Saint Joseph thru his son Joseph go to Saint Helen of the Cross, Saint Brychan, and Saint Patrick

Saint Joseph the Foster Father of Jesus the Christ had a brother Cleopas He had a son Joses or Joseph

There is also Saint Joseph Barabas, brother to Saint James the Lesser Apostle who is mentioned in the scripture He was not chosen by lot to become the 12th disciple, however he was considered

The Line from Simon the son of Saint Joseph contains after four generations Joseph This may have been the Josephus who wrote the only History Book that has mention of Jesus the Christ in it The complete works consist of the Antiquities of the Jews, The War of the Jews, Against Apion, and other exerpts and dissertations about the time and the writings as they have existed since biblical times

List of those bearing the name Joseph in the Biblical Period

1) Saint Joseph Foster Father of the Lord
2) Joseph of Gamla the son of Justus of Gamala
3) Joseph bar Jesus the Rama Theo
4) Saint Joseph of Arimathea
5) Josephes of Arimathea son of Joseph of Arimathea
6) Joseph Ha Rama Theo son of Saint Joseph
7) Joseph the son of Cleopas
8) Joseph the 14th Bishop of Jerusalem (May have been the Historian Josephus)
9) Joseph of Gamala the son of Saint Mary Magdalene

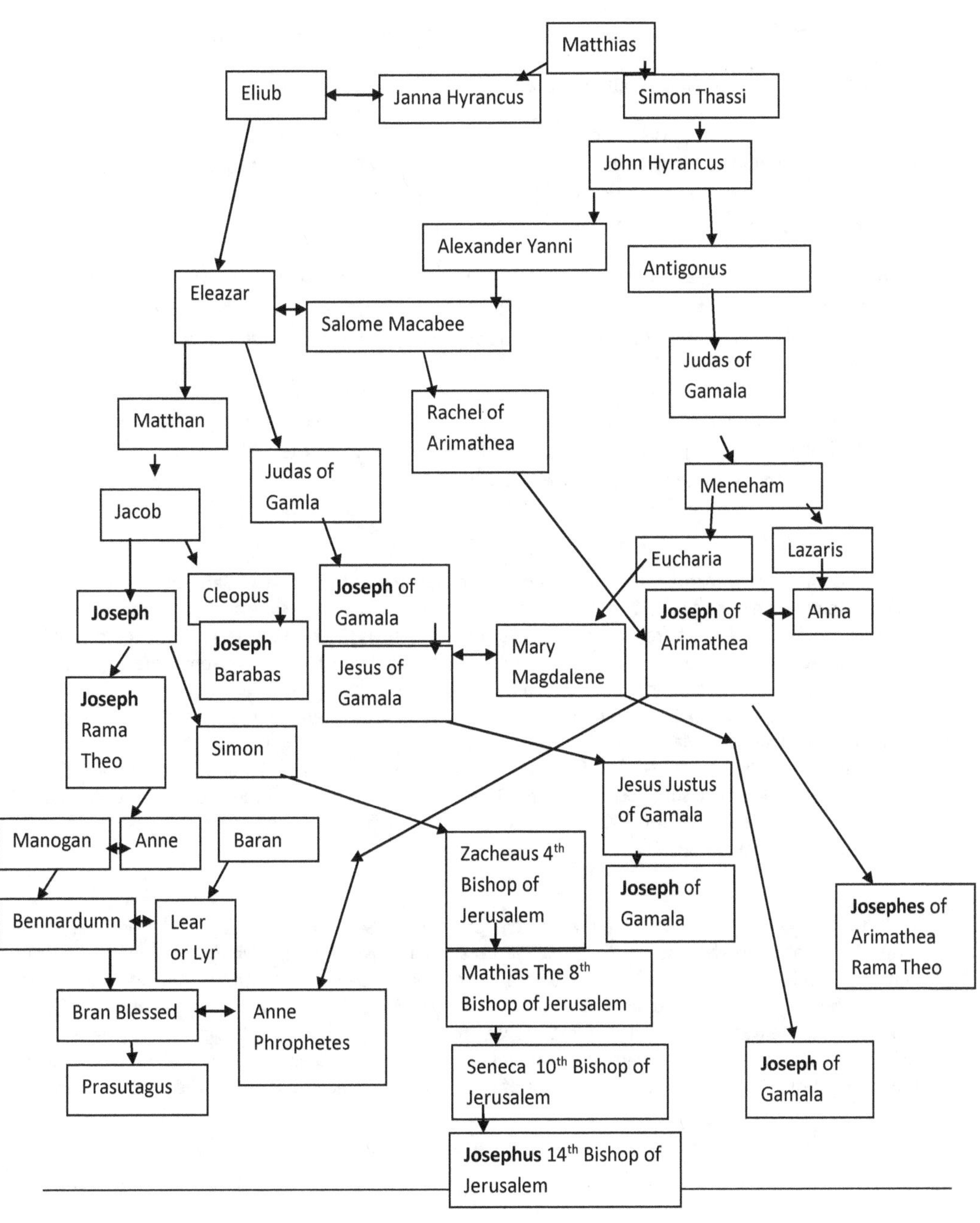
Matthias
Eliub
Janna Hyrancus
Simon Thassi
John Hyrancus
Alexander Yanni
Antigonus
Eleazar
Salome Macabee
Judas of Gamala
Matthan
Rachel of Arimathea
Judas of Gamla
Meneham
Jacob
Eucharia
Lazaris
Cleopus
Joseph of Gamala
Joseph
Joseph of Arimathea
Anna
Joseph Barabas
Jesus of Gamala
Mary Magdalene
Joseph Rama Theo
Simon
Jesus Justus of Gamala
Manogan
Anne
Baran
Zacheaus 4th Bishop of Jerusalem
Joseph of Gamala
Josephes of Arimathea Rama Theo
Bennardumn
Lear or Lyr
Mathias The 8th Bishop of Jerusalem
Bran Blessed
Anne Phrophetes
Seneca 10th Bishop of Jerusalem
Joseph of Gamala
Prasutagus
Josephus 14th Bishop of Jerusalem

The secrets here are the many named Jesus (and the marriage of Saint Mary Magdalene)

The scripture is very concerned about the Lord, who is called Jesus the Christ

His is considered the Son of Mary and is of the house of David Mary's Ascent (or Lineage) is listed in the Gospel of Luke Jesus the "Christ's" father is considered the "Holy Spirit", and Joseph of the house of David is considered his "Foster Father" and the man who raised the Lord However there are many more names of Jesus at the time that were in use

There has been some confusion about the Saint Joseph and his descendents First, One cannot claim Jesus the Christ as a descendent because he was conceived by the "Holy Spirit", so Saint Joseph is not recognized as the biological father Joseph had many sons and daughters, but nowhere did the name of Jesus come up as a descendent

Joseph had a father named Jacob Jacob was the son of Mathan, and Jacob was brother to Judas of Gamla and to Hizkiah the Zealot Hizkiah had sons, one of these sons was Judas the Zealot His son Saphath was the father of Jesus (This Jesus was not the Christ but had the same name)

Judas of Gamla, son of Mathan, was the father of Tolmai who was the father of Bartholomew or Nathaniel (one of the twelve disciples or apostles) Judas of Gamla was also the father of Joseph of Gamla who was the father of Jesus of Gamla So here it is accurate to say that Joseph is the father of Jesus, however it would not be accurate to say the Joseph is the father of Jesus the one called Christ who is the son of the Virgin Mary It would be accurate to say that Joseph of Gamla is the father of Jesus of Gamla and that Jesus of Gamla was not necessarily Crucified or the one called Christ Now Mary Magdalene married Jesus of Gamla, so it is accurate to say that Saint Mary Magdalene is the wife of Jesus however she would not be the wife of Jesus the Christ, but rather Jesus of Gamla Saint Mary Magdalene and Jesus of Gamla had a son named Jesus Justus of Rome, who had a son Joseph the Rama Theo This line will eventually lead to Merovius founder of the Merovian Kings and ancestor of Charlemagne who at one time saved the Pope So Judas of Gamla has two descendents named Jesus

Jacob the brother to Judas of Gamla married Cleopatra of Jerusalem and was father to Saint Joseph the Foster Father of Jesus who was called "Christ" Jacob also had a wife Eucheria who was the mother of Mary This Mary would have been a half sister to Saint Joseph, Judas of Gamla, and Hizikiah She married Theudas and had five sons and three daughters One of the sons, Addai James was the father of a son (Name Unknown) and he was the father of Soter Soter was the father of Jesus of Lydda Again, this was not Jesus the "Christ" but named Jesus nevertheless Another of Mary and Theudas sons was Thebouthis whose son was named Jesus Thus Jacob was the ancestor of two descendents named Jesus, neither of them being the "Christ"

The order of the use of his name might be considered. The order that would be best would be the Son of Mary, the most powerful first, then the son of Soter and then the Son of Thebouthis. This would be protected by Athrongenes the father of Theudas. Next the half brother of Doris, because everything going up in his name would not be the same legitimate family, but a group of all families, as the brother of Doris was not a legitimate son. Next the son of Panthera to straighten out the illegitimate son. Following this the illegitimate must be worked out (the familes or sirs involved) so the son of Panthera is used, who would be the father of Doris's half brother. Note that now everything going up would not be based on a name or lineage but only on the blessing of this name. Next the son of Mary Magdalene, the Justice of the world and then his father the son of Joseph of Gamla. Next is the release of the innocent if no injustice was found and approved by the father (Jesus Barabbas was released from the crucifixion). Next would be the zealot the son of Saphia, Finally the son of Antigonus because this would naturally follow thru to Ann, then Mary, and back then to the son of Mary and start all over again.

1) The son of Mary (the most powerful).
2) The son of Soter (protected by Athongones and Theudas).
3) The son of Theboutis (Protected by Athongones and Theudas).
4) The half brother to Doris (every thing above an illegitimate tie).
5) The son of Panthera, who fathers and straightens out the illegitimate.
6) The son of Saint Mary Magdalene the Justice of the world.
7) The son of Abbas Jesus Barabbas the release of the innocent.
8) The son of Joseph of Gamla, the father of the Justus.
9) The zealot son of Saphira, with no possessions.
10) The son of Antigonus who fathers Ann who leads to the Son of Mary back to 1.

There is a son of Jeshua III who was the father of Bianca. He was Bar Jesus the Sorceror and also bore the name of Jesus

The person released in place of the lord was Barabas This person is listed as Jesus called Barabas He was descended from Judas of Gamla

King Herod had many wives One of these, Doris had Jesus Panthera as a father

List of Those bearing the name Jesus of the Biblical period

1) Jesus the Christ
2) Jesus the son of Soter
3) Jesus the son of Thebouthis
4) Bar-Jesus who was the son of Jeshua III and half brother to Jo-Anne.
5) Jesus Justus of Rome the son of Jesus of Gamla and Saint Mary Magdalene
6) Jesus of Gamla the son of Joseph the son of Judas of Gamla
7) Jesus the son of Saphia the son of Judas the Zealot the son of Hizkiah
8) Jesus Barabas released by the crowd at the Crucifixion the son of Abbas the son of Judas of Gamla.
9) Jesus Panthera the father of Doris who married Herod the Great is also Jeshua III who married Bianca and had Saint Jo Anne.
10) Jeshua who was known as Joidiah and fathered Saint Anne who was the mother of the Virgin Mary. There is a tradition he was the son of Antigonus and another tradition the son of Phabet.
11) Justus the son of Jacobus the son of Ptolas
12) Josue the son of Joseph of Gamla the son of Saint Mary Magdalene
13) Jeshua IV the 81st High Priest son of Gamaliel (see High Priest Chart)
14) Yeshua IV 64th High Priest son of Sethus (see High Priest Chart)
15) Jeshua the son of Perachiah of the lineage of Tobit whose descendent is Saint Isaac Pahlav (see charts of the Virgin Mary)
16) Jesus the Grandson of Sirach who wrote the book of Sirach. (see chart of the Lines of the Virgin Mary)

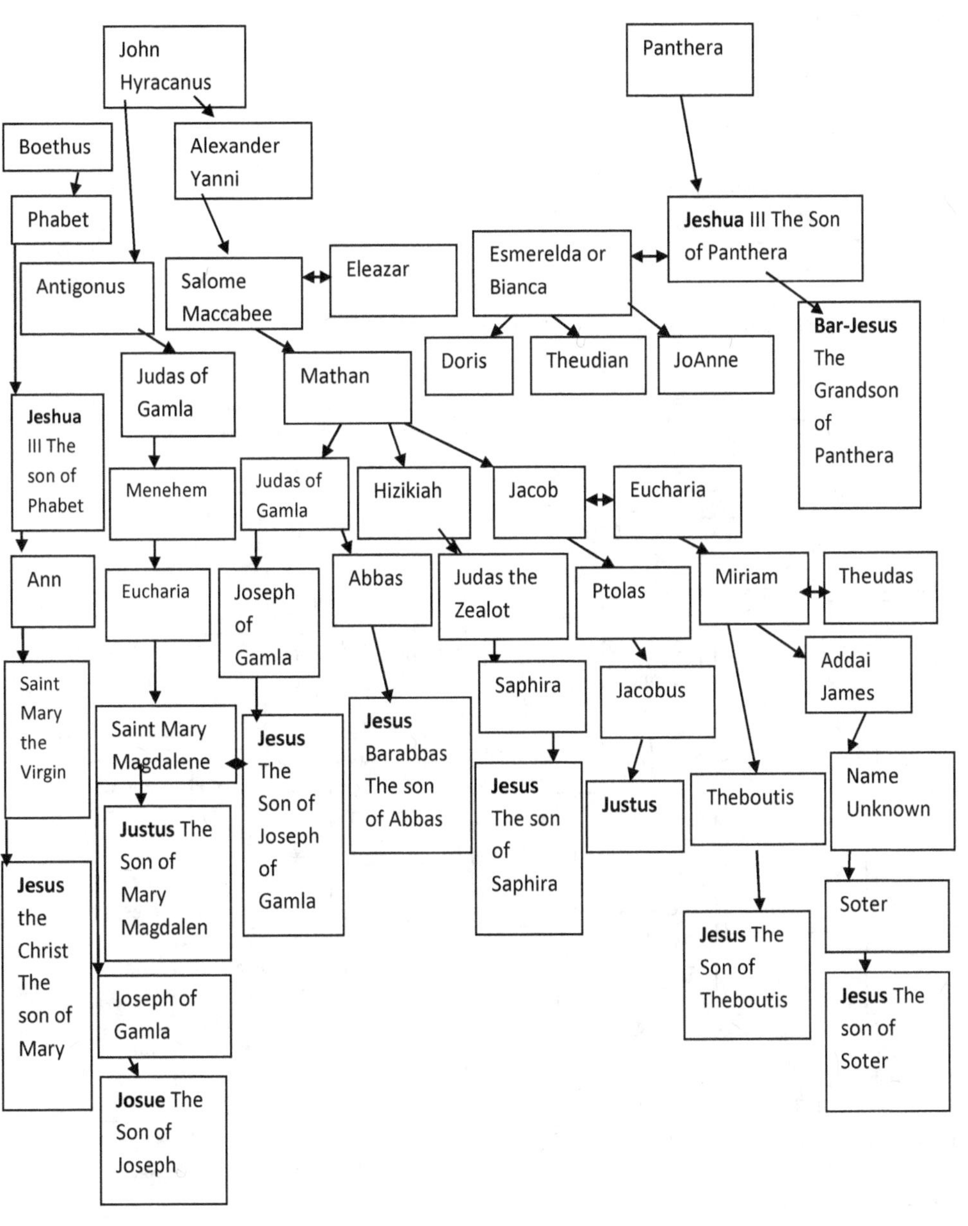

John Hyracanus
Panthera
Boethus
Alexander Yanni
Phabet
Jeshua III The Son of Panthera
Antigonus
Salome Maccabee
Eleazar
Esmerelda or Bianca
Bar-Jesus The Grandson of Panthera
Doris
Theudian
JoAnne
Judas of Gamla
Mathan
Jeshua III The son of Phabet
Menehem
Judas of Gamla
Hizikiah
Jacob
Eucharia
Ann
Eucharia
Joseph of Gamla
Abbas
Judas the Zealot
Ptolas
Miriam
Theudas
Addai James
Saint Mary the Virgin
Saphira
Jacobus
Saint Mary Magdalene
Jesus The Son of Joseph of Gamla
Jesus Barabbas The son of Abbas
Name Unknown
Jesus The son of Saphira
Justus
Theboutis
Justus The Son of Mary Magdalen
Jesus the Christ The son of Mary
Soter
Jesus The Son of Theboutis
Jesus The son of Soter
Joseph of Gamla
Josue The Son of Joseph

To state this in another way His name was used as (Please note that this order of the names leads from the son of Mary all the way around and ends with the father of Mary.)

1) The son of Mary
2) The son of Soter
3) The son of Thebouthis
4) The half brother to Doris
5) The son of Panthera
6) The son of Abbas
7) The son of Mary Magdalene
8) The son of Joseph of Gamla the son of Judas of Gamla
9) The son of Saphia
10) The son of Antigonus
11) The son of Jacobus
12) The son of Joseph of Gamla the son of Saint Mary Magdalene

CHART NAME OF THE SON

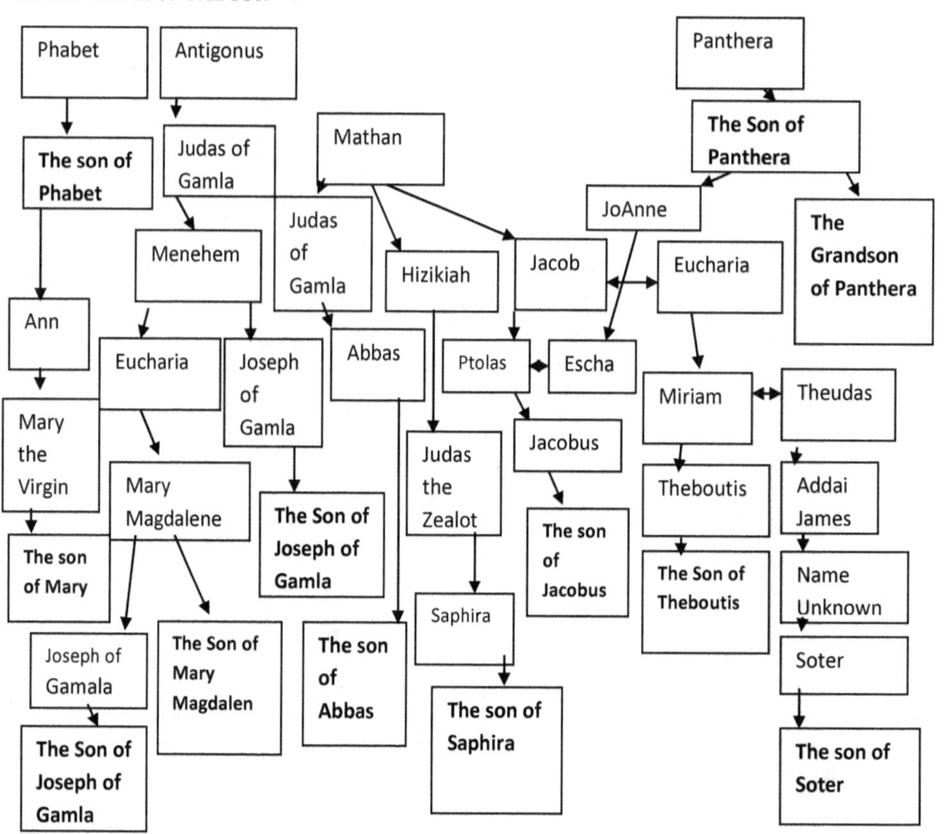

Here is a list of the names in the above text and charts and a population of each of the names

Mary	9
Ann	6
Salome	8
Joseph	9
Jesus	12
Simon	12
Judas	15
James	8
John	9
Eleazar	9
Alexander or Alexandra	7
Jacob	6
Total in Charts	110

There are a considerable number of other people shown in the charts that are not part of the names that are duplicated or the same in different places.

Consider that there are 110 people who are mirrored with the same name occurring 7 to 15 times with 12 of these multiple names. Now also consider there are quite a few others whose names and places are important, however not duplicated to such an extent. So about 200 - 250 people are involved in the Five Generation Genesis of God, or the making of the High Priest of Christianity, and royalty from David, Cleopatra, and Rome are in the direct blood lines of many of the characters.

There are two apostles that bore the name James in the biblical period

These are James Zebedee who was the brother to John Zebedee, and James the Apostle called the lesser to distinguish him from the Zebedee

There is also James the Just who was the son of Saint Joseph

Of the Marriage between Jacob the father of Saint Joseph and Eucheria who was not mother of Saint Joseph however was the Mother of Mary (Miriam) there is a grandson James This James was the son of Mary the daughter of Eucheria who was one of the wives of Jacob This James was the father of Evodius who was the father of Hero III

In the descent from Jacob by Eucheria there is an Addai James who was the grandfather of Soter who was the father of Jesus of Lydia Addai James sons name is not known

The son of Saint Joseph Jude of Galilee had a son James who was the father of another James who had a brother Zoker

There is a James the son of Simon who was the son of Jude of Galilee He had a brother also named Simon

List of James in the biblical Period

1) James Zebedee Apostle and Saint
2) James the Lesser Apostle and Saint
3) James the Just Bishop and son of Saint Joseph
4) James the son of Theudas and the father of Evodius
5) Addai James the Grandfather of Soter
6) James the son of Jude of Galilee
7) James the brother of Zoker
8) James the brother of Simon and the Son of Simon

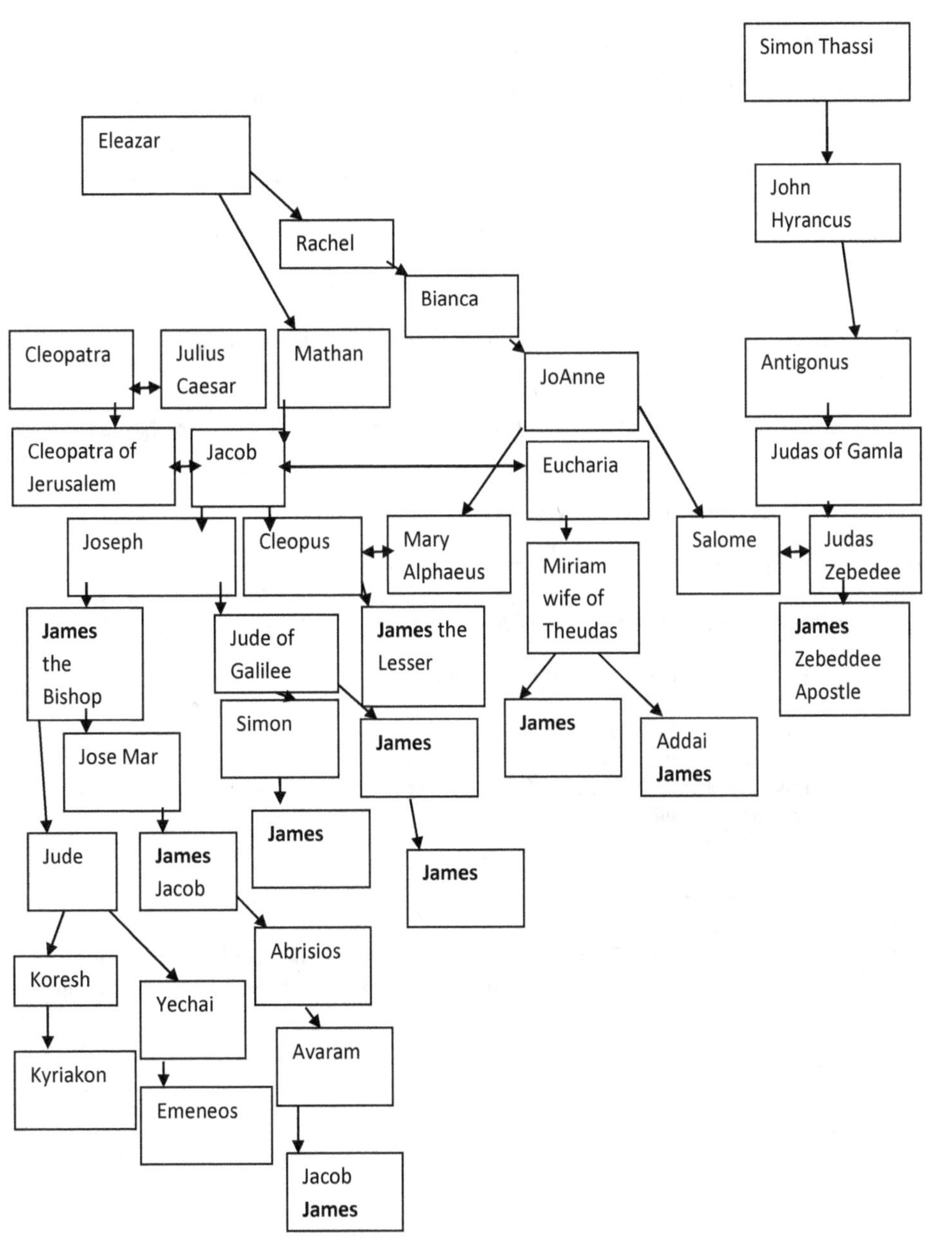
Simon Thassi
Eleazar
John Hyrancus
Rachel
Bianca
Cleopatra
Julius Caesar
Mathan
JoAnne
Antigonus
Cleopatra of Jerusalem
Jacob
Eucharia
Judas of Gamla
Joseph
Cleopus
Mary Alphaeus
Miriam wife of Theudas
Salome
Judas Zebedee
James the Bishop
Jude of Galilee
James the Lesser
James Zebeddee Apostle
Simon
James
James
Addai **James**
Jose Mar
Jude
James Jacob
James
James
Abrisios
Koresh
Yechai
Avaram
Kyriakon
Emeneos
Jacob **James**

There is Simon the Apostle Brother to Saint James the Lesser

There is also Simeon who may be the same as Simon the Apostle however most scholars agree there is a difference

There is a Simon who was the Son of Saint Joseph and brother to James the Just, first Bishop of Jerusalem

There is a Simon who was the son of Jude of Galilee who was the son of Saint Joseph

The Simon who was the son of Jude of Galilee had a son named Simon

Of the descendents of Hizkiah the Zealot who was the brother to Jacob and Judas of Gamla there is a son named Judas the Zealot who had a son named Simon

Simon the son of Judas the Zealot had a son Hyrancus who was a Grandfather to another Simon the son of Eleazar "Ha-Gadol"

Judas the Zealot has another son Jair who was the father to Simon

Judas the Zealot has another son Judas who as the father to Simon

List of the Many who bore the Name Simon in the Biblical Period

1) Simon Apostle and Saint the brother to Saint James the Lesser
2) Simeon the son of Cleopas
3) Simon the son of Saint Joseph
4) Simon the son of Jude of Galilee
5) Simon the son of Simon the son of Jude of Galilee
6) Simon the son of Judas the Zealot
7) Simon the son of Eleazar "Ha-Gadol"
8) Simon the son of Jair
9) Simon the son of Judas
10) Simon the Son of Kathla of Gamla
11) Simon V bar Kosevah the Son of Kosevah the son of Simon the son of Judas the Zealot
12) Simon the son of Kozevah the son of Joseph Barsabbas the son of Cleopas and Mary Alphaeus

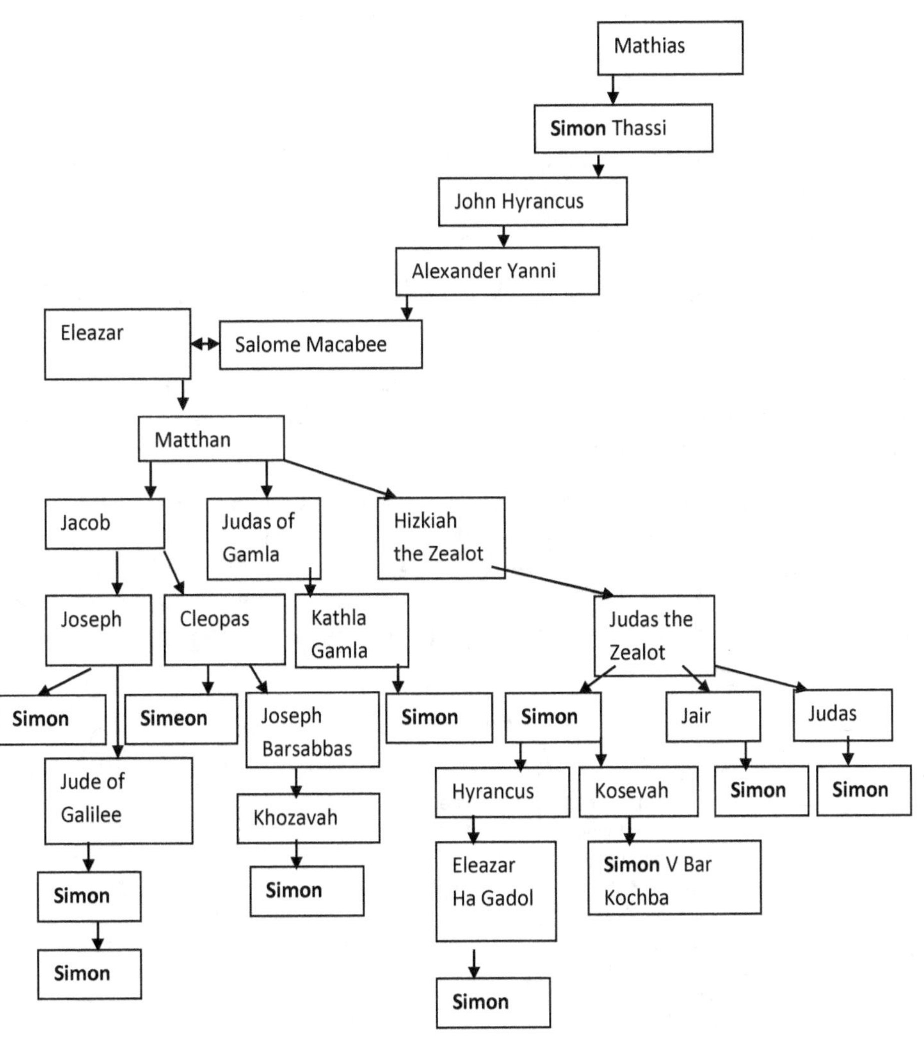
Mathias
Simon Thassi
John Hyrancus
Alexander Yanni
Eleazar
Salome Macabee
Matthan
Jacob
Judas of Gamla
Hizkiah the Zealot
Joseph
Cleopas
Kathla Gamla
Judas the Zealot
Simon
Simeon
Joseph Barsabbas
Simon
Simon
Jair
Judas
Jude of Galilee
Khozavah
Hyrancus
Kosevah
Simon
Simon
Simon
Simon
Eleazar Ha Gadol
Simon V Bar Kochba
Simon
Simon

The Many Named John in the Biblical Period

The first and possibly the greatest called John would be John the Baptist, son of Zechariah and Elizabeth

Second would be John Zebedee, the son of Zebedee the apostle

There is a John of Giscala who is the son of Judas the son of Judas the Zealot the son of Hizkiah the brother of Jacob

There is John Mark who was the scribe of the Gospel the son of Mariam. Mariam was the sister to James the Lesser Apostle and the daughter of Mary Alphaeus.

There is a John the son of James the Just the son of Saint Joseph

There is a John the 7th Bishop of Jerusalem the son of Benjamin the 6th Bishop of Jerusalem the son of John the son of James the Just the son of Saint Joseph

An important figure in the Gospel was John Mark who was the son of Miraim (Mary) His mother was the sister to James the Lesser. He is credited as writing the Gospel of Mark many years after the crucifixion and resurrection. His name was John so is included.

John of Emesa the son of Joseph of Gamla, who was the son of Marcella who married Justus the son of Mary Magdalene was John of Emessa. His son Anicetus was a Saint and Pope. The interesting thing about this line is that it continues until Johannes in 423 who became Emperor of Rome. Considering that Constantine was the first Roman Empire who legalized Christianity, The Emperor's seat was held by a descendent of David from 423 to 425, Although after Constantine he would have had the ancestor of Saint Mary Magdalene that the other emperors may not have had.

List of the Many who bore the Name John in the biblical Period

1) John the Baptist son of Zechariah and Elizabeth
2) John the son of Judas Zebedee Apostle
3) John of Giscala who is the son of Judas
4) John the son of James the Just
5) John the 7th Bishop of Jerusalem the son of Benjamin the 6th Bishop of Jerusalem
6) John Mark the son of Mary who was the sister to James the Lesser.
7) John of Emesa the son of Joseph of Gamla the son of Marcella and Justus.
8) John Gaddi the son of Matthias
9) John Hyrancus the son of Simon Thassi
10) John Mark the son of Miriam the daughter of Aristobulus

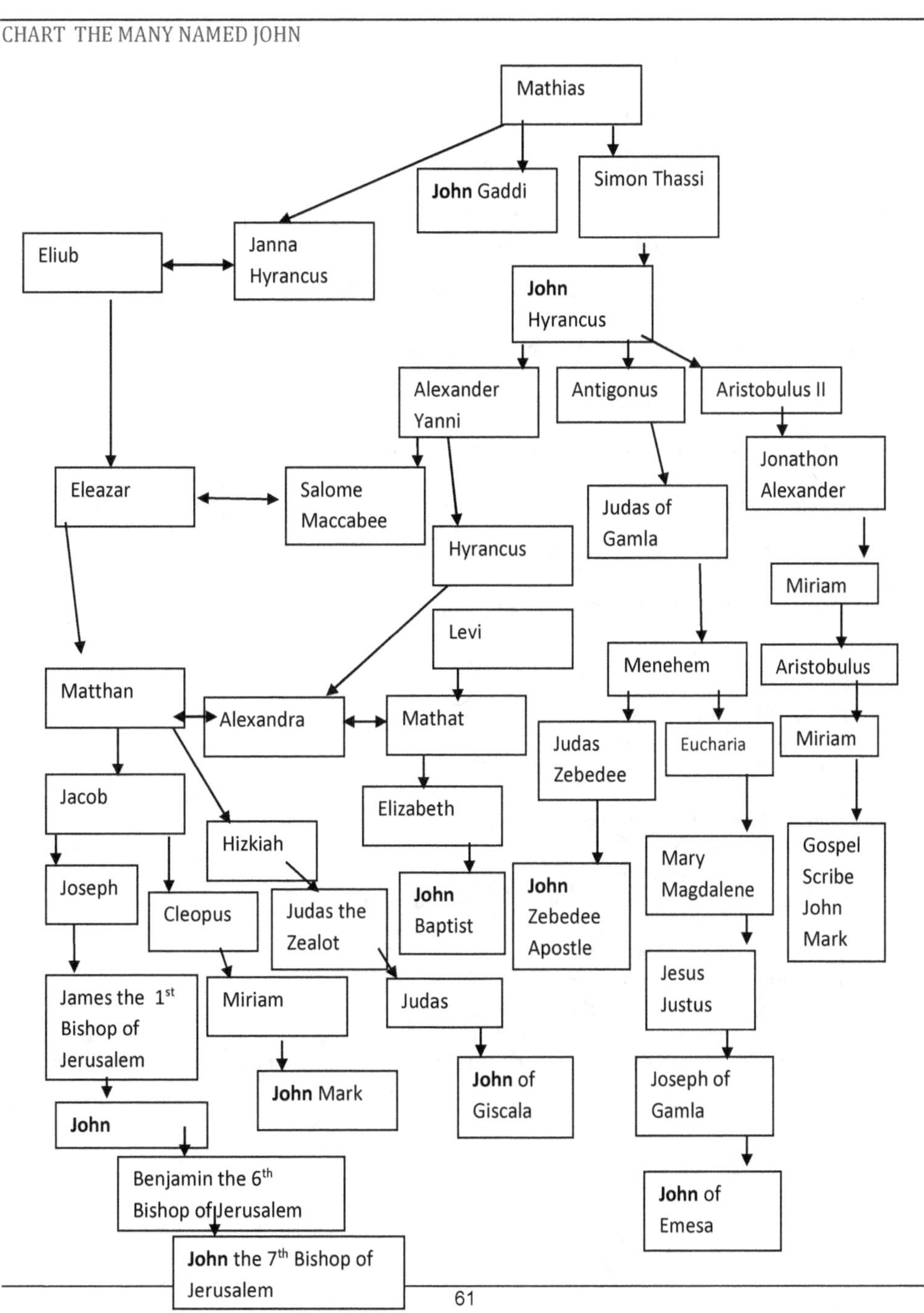
Mathias
John Gaddi
Simon Thassi
Eliub
Janna Hyrancus
John Hyrancus
Alexander Yanni
Antigonus
Aristobulus II
Jonathon Alexander
Eleazar
Salome Maccabee
Hyrancus
Judas of Gamla
Miriam
Levi
Menehem
Aristobulus
Matthan
Alexandra
Mathat
Judas Zebedee
Eucharia
Miriam
Jacob
Elizabeth
Hizkiah
Gospel Scribe John Mark
Mary Magdalene
Joseph
Cleopus
Judas the Zealot
John Baptist
John Zebedee Apostle
Jesus Justus
James the 1st Bishop of Jerusalem
Miriam
Judas
John Mark
John of Giscala
Joseph of Gamla
John
Benjamin the 6th Bishop of Jerusalem
John of Emesa
John the 7th Bishop of Jerusalem

The Many Named Judas or Jude in the Biblical Period

Saint Jude the Apostle brother to James the Lesser Apostle

Jude of Galilee the son of Saint Joseph

Jude or Gaiso the son of James the Just the son of Saint Joseph

Jude the 15th Bishop the Father of Pope Pius of Rome and also the son of Benjamin the 6th Bishop of Jerusalem the son of John the son of James the Just

Jude the son of James the Lesser the Apostle the father of Evaristus the 5th Bishop of Rome Pope

Judas of Gamla the father of Joseph of Gamla and Brother to Jacob and Hizkiah the Zealot

Judas the Zealot the son of Hizkiah the Zealot

Judah Ben Hur (the son of Hur) the son of Jacob the son of Hizkiah the Zealot

Judas of Gamla the ancestor of Saint Mary Magdalene

Judas Zebedee was the father of John and James Zebedee

Jude of Gamla the brother to John of Emesa and Great Grandson of Saint Mary Magdalene.

1) Saint Jude the Apostle brother to James
2) Jude of Galilee
3) Jude the son of James the Just
4) Jude the 15th Bishop of Jerusalem
5) Jude the son of Saint James the Lesser Apostle
6) Judas of Gamla
7) Judas the Zealot the son of Hizkiah the Zealot
8) Judah Ben Hur
9) Judas of Gamla the ancestor of Saint Mary Magdalene
10) Judas Zebedee the father of John and James Zebedee
11) Jude of Gamla the Great Grandson of Saint Mary Magdalene
12) Jude the Son of Saint Mary Magdalene
13) Judas the son of Judas the Zealot
14) Jude the Son of Saint Bartholomew the Apostle
15) Judas Macabees the Son of Matthais
16) Judas Kyrikos the son of James the son of James the son of Jude of Galilee the son of Jospeh

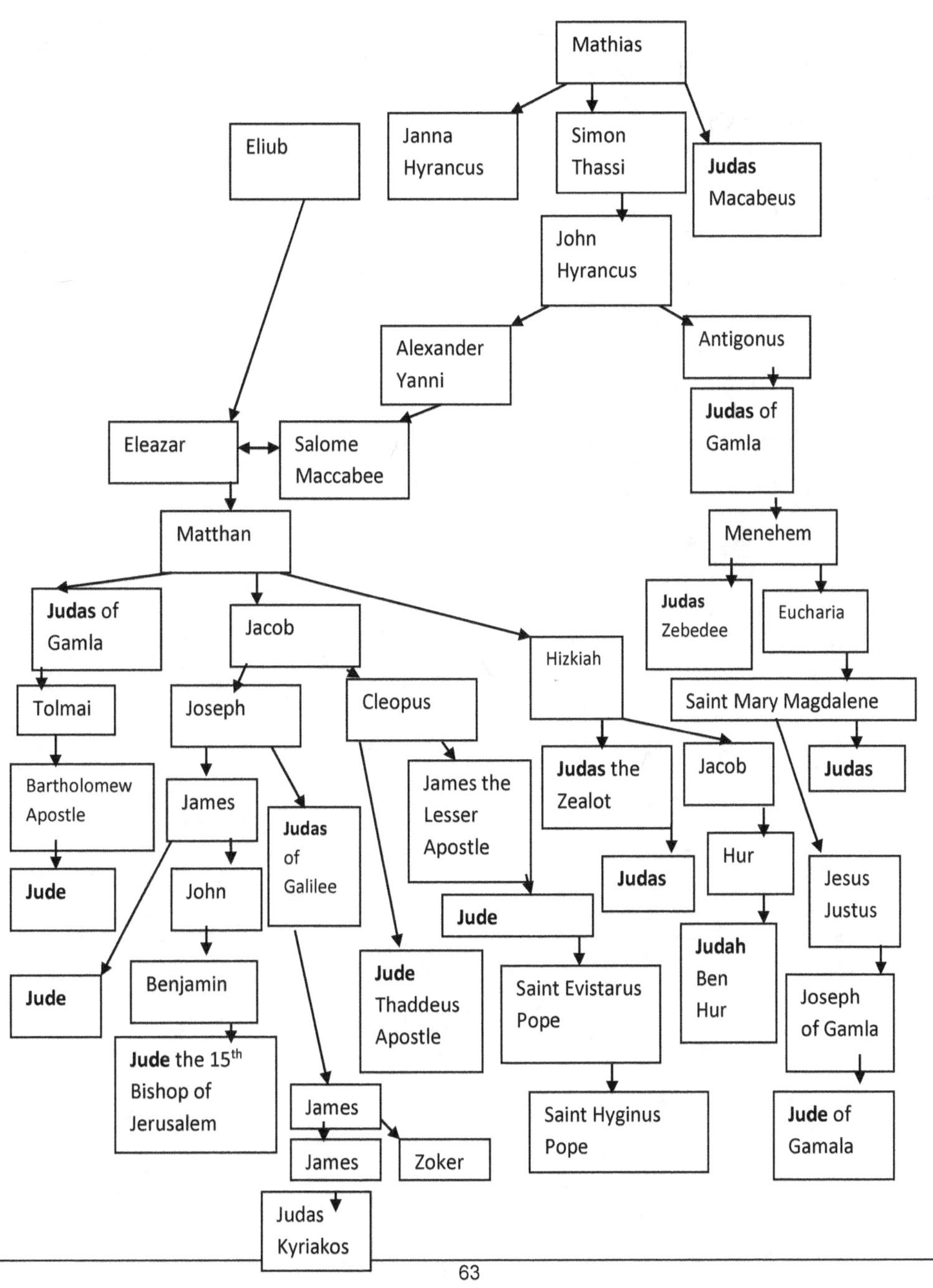
Mathias
Janna Hyrancus
Simon Thassi
Judas Macabeus
Eliub
John Hyrancus
Alexander Yanni
Antigonus
Judas of Gamla
Eleazar
Salome Maccabee
Matthan
Menehem
Judas Zebedee
Eucharia
Judas of Gamla
Jacob
Hizkiah
Saint Mary Magdalene
Tolmai
Joseph
Cleopus
Judas the Zealot
Jacob
Judas
Bartholomew Apostle
James
Judas of Galilee
James the Lesser Apostle
Hur
Jesus Justus
Jude
John
Judas
Jude
Judah Ben Hur
Jude
Benjamin
Jude Thaddeus Apostle
Saint Evistarus Pope
Joseph of Gamla
Jude the 15th Bishop of Jerusalem
James
James
Zoker
Saint Hyginus Pope
Jude of Gamala
Judas Kyriakos

Jacob Giacomo the son of Jude of Gamala who was the great grandson of Saint Mary Magdalene

Jacob the son of Mathan the father to Saint Joseph

Jacob the son of Hizkiah father to Hur

Jacobus the son of Ptolas

James Jacob the son of Jose Mar

Jacob James the son of Avaram

1) Jacob Giacomo the son of Jude of Gamala
2) Jacob the father of Saint Joseph
3) Jacob the son if Hizkiah the zealot the father to Hur.
4) Jacobus the son of Ptolas
5) James Jacob the son of Jose Mar
6) Jacob James the son of Avaram

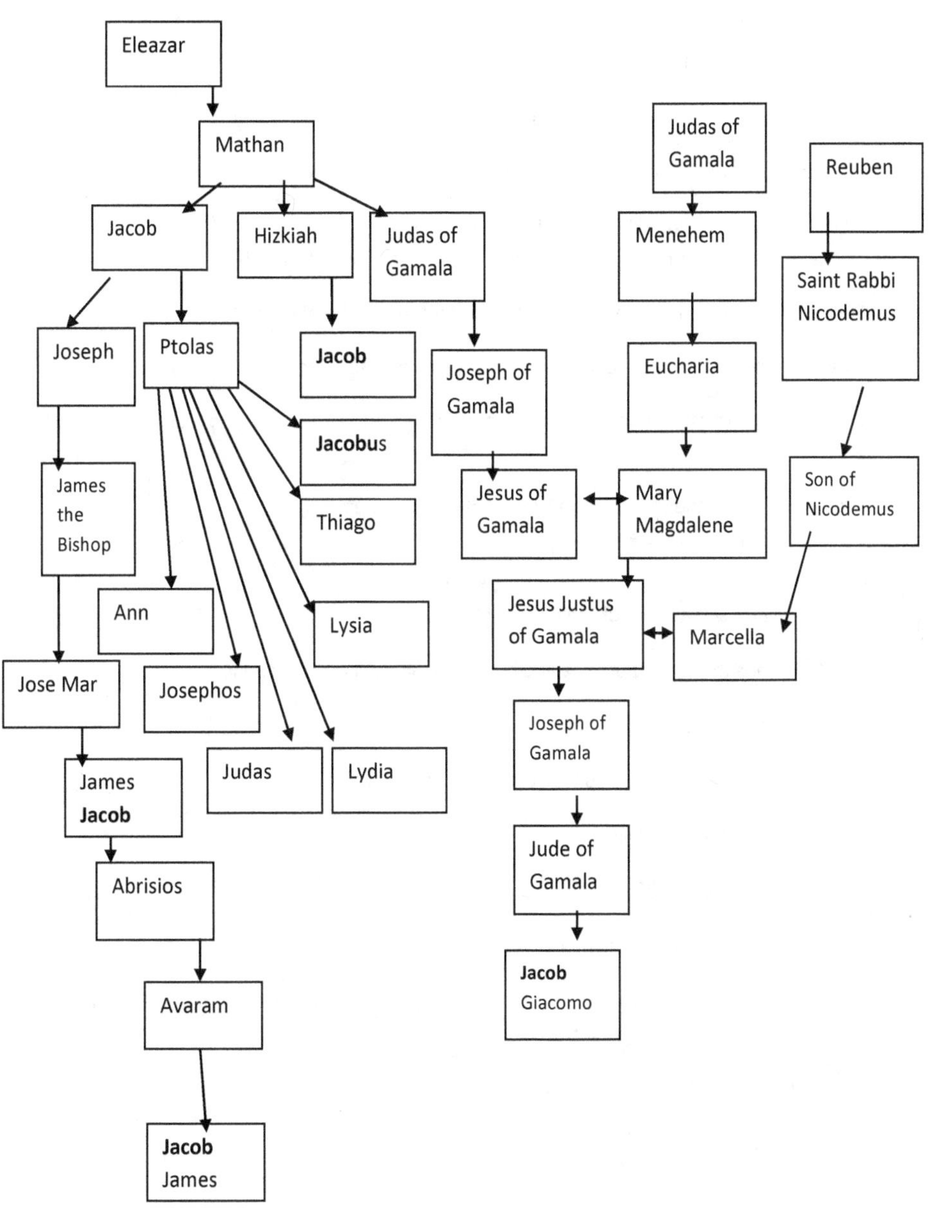
Eleazar
Mathan
Jacob
Hizkiah
Judas of Gamala
Joseph
Ptolas
Jacob
Joseph of Gamala
Jacobus
Thiago
James the Bishop
Ann
Lysia
Jose Mar
Josephos
Judas
Lydia
James Jacob
Abrisios
Avaram
Jacob James
Judas of Gamala
Reuben
Menehem
Saint Rabbi Nicodemus
Eucharia
Jesus of Gamala
Mary Magdalene
Son of Nicodemus
Jesus Justus of Gamala
Marcella
Joseph of Gamala
Jude of Gamala
Jacob Giacomo

Eleazar the son of Eliub

Lazaris the son of Eucharia and Mathew the Syrus

Eleazar the son of Ananiah the son of Menaham the son of Hizkiah

Eleazar the son of Jacob the son of Hizkiah
Eleazar the son of Simon the son of Judas the Zealot the son of Hizkiah

Eleazar the son of Jair the son of Judas the Zealot the son of Hizkiah

Eleazar Avaran the brother to Simon Thassi and Judas Maccabee

Lazaris the son of Menahem the husband of Salome the father of Ann who married Joseph of Arimathea

Eleazar the Zealot the son of Dinah the son of Athrongones

1. Eleazar son of Eliub of the house of David
2. Lazaris the son of Eucharia and brother to Saint Mary Magdalene
3. Eleazar the son of Ananiah
4. Eleazar the son of Jacob the son of Hizkiah
5. Eleazar the son of Simon
6. Eleazar the son of Jair
7. Eleazar Avaran the brother to Judas Maccabee
8. Lazaris the son of Menahem the husband of Salome who was the mother to Ann who married Joseph of Arimathea
9. Eleazar the Zealot the son of Dinah

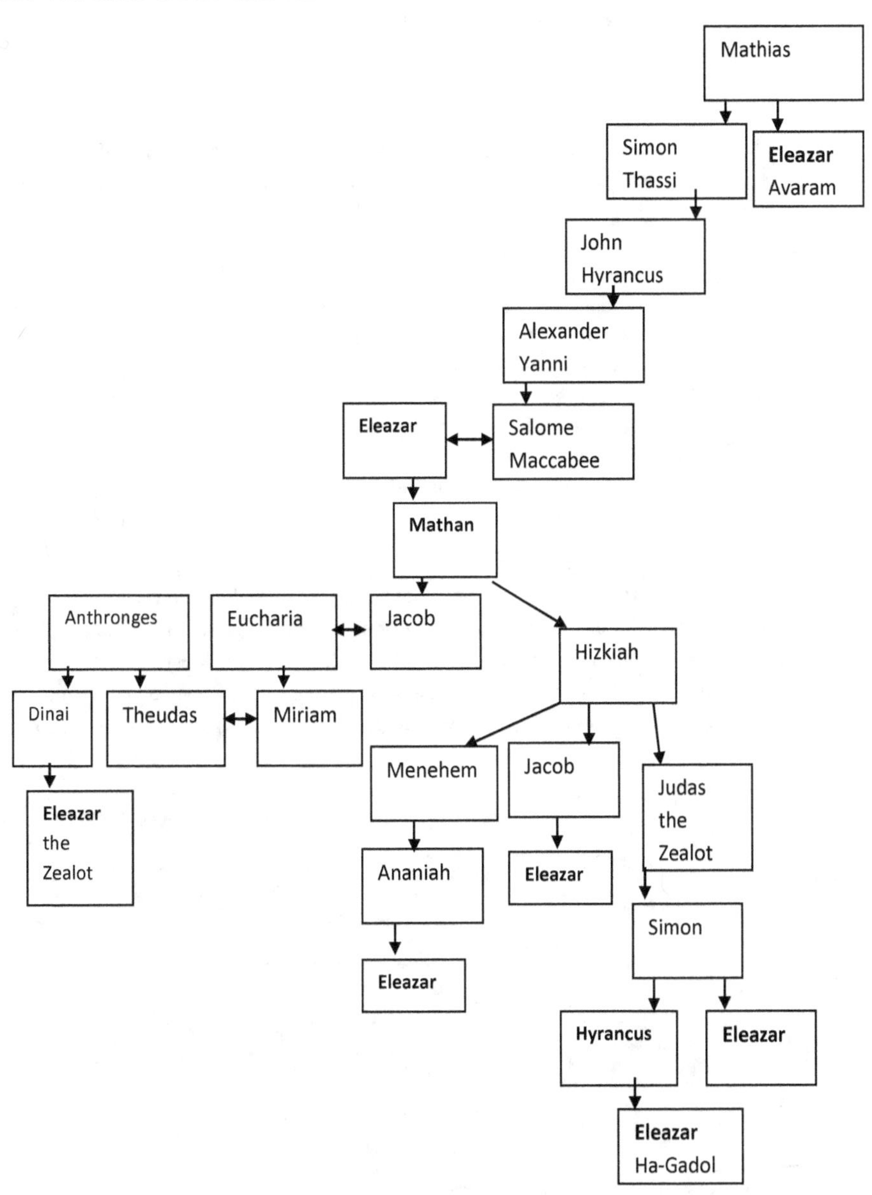
Mathias
Simon Thassi
Eleazar Avaram
John Hyrancus
Alexander Yanni
Eleazar
Salome Maccabee
Mathan
Anthronges
Eucharia
Jacob
Hizkiah
Dinai
Theudas
Miriam
Menehem
Jacob
Judas the Zealot
Eleazar the Zealot
Ananiah
Eleazar
Simon
Eleazar
Hyrancus
Eleazar
Eleazar Ha-Gadol

The Many Named Alexander or Alexandra in the Biblical Period

Alexander of Judea the son of Herod the Great and Cleopatra of Jerusalem

Jonathon Alexander the son of Arisobulus

Alexander Yanni the son of John Hyrancus

Alexandra the daughter of Eleazar

Salome Alexandra married Jonathan Alexander and were parents of Miriam wife of King Herod

Alexandra II married Mathan and was daughter of Hyrancus II who was son of Alexander Yanni

1. Alexander of Judea
2. Jonathon Alexander the son of Aristobulus
3. Alexander Yanni the son of John Hyrancus
4. Alexandra the daughter of Eleazar married Levi Father of Mathat
5. Salome Alexandra married Jonathon Alexander
6. Alexandra II married Mathan and Mathat
7. Alexander the Zealot the son of Amram the brother to Theudas
8. Alexandria the daughter of Matthais married Ptolomy line continues to Armenia
9. Alexandra the wife of Matthais
10. Alexander the son of Miriam the daughter of Jonathan Alexander

Alternative Use of Single Alexandra by a theology found on the internet.

This idea that the daughter of Hyrancus II was the mother of both Jacob and Joachim is an interesting idea. With as many mirrors existing for all the other names, the idea there was one Alexandra is possible, however another genealogy shows two Alexandra's. I leave it for the reader to decide. It was certainly not lawful for a woman to have two husbands unless widowed, which is also possible. It is also found in the genealogy files that Eleazar was the father of an Alexandra different from the daughter of Hyrancus that married Mathat.

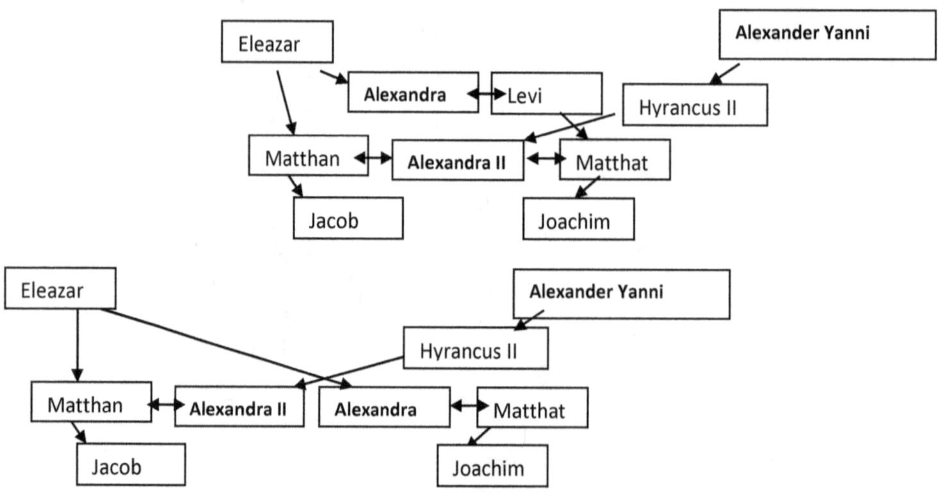

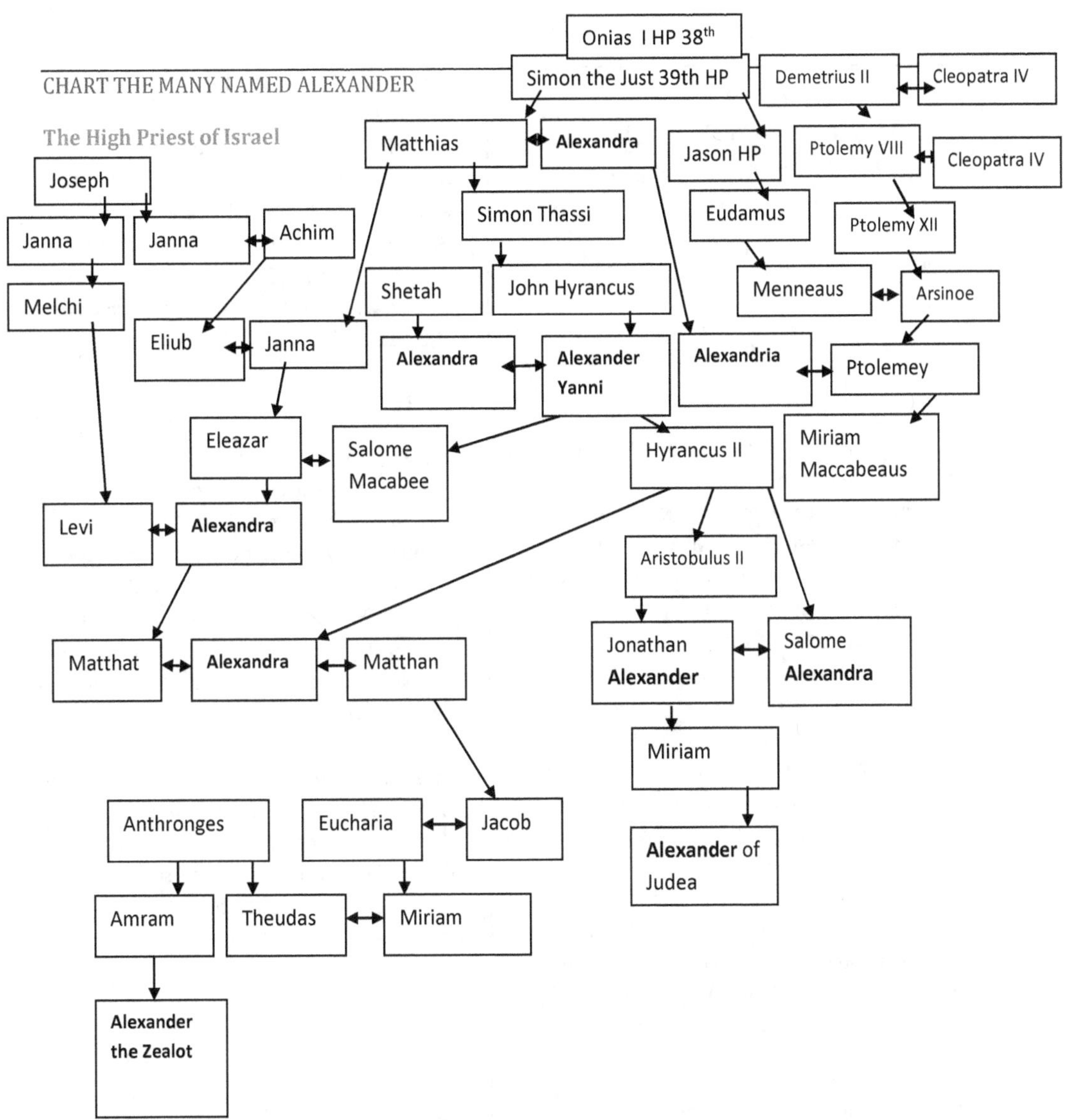
CHART THE MANY NAMED ALEXANDER
The High Priest of Israel
Onias I HP 38th
Simon the Just 39th HP
Demetrius II
Cleopatra IV
Matthias
Alexandra
Jason HP
Ptolemy VIII
Cleopatra IV
Joseph
Janna
Janna
Achim
Simon Thassi
Eudamus
Ptolemy XII
Melchi
Shetah
John Hyrancus
Menneaus
Arsinoe
Eliub
Janna
Alexandra
Alexander Yanni
Alexandria
Ptolemey
Eleazar
Salome Macabee
Hyrancus II
Miriam Maccabeaus
Levi
Alexandra
Aristobulus II
Matthat
Alexandra
Matthan
Jonathan Alexander
Salome Alexandra
Miriam
Alexander of Judea
Anthronges
Eucharia
Jacob
Amram
Theudas
Miriam
Alexander the Zealot

ERA OF THE EARLY CHURCH, THE FIRST FEW GENERATIONS.

SECTION FIVE: EARLY CHRISTIAN HOUSES

Houses and Surnames

There are many houses and Sirnames that exist today that are related to the people of Galilee. The Christian houses are the relationhips that exist in the new testament. Many houses exist in the old testament times (B.C.) Take for example Saint Joseph. The house or Surname of James or Jameson would then be the eldest son of Joseph or the Bishop of Jersusalem James. The house of John or Sir John would be the son of James (Jameson) and his descendents. The Johnson sirname or house could be different from Sir John but be the son of James the bishop named John and his descendents. Thus Johnson would be a part of James that would be a part of Joseph would be a part or Jacob etc.. All of these would check on each other and make sure that the law and the relationships were followed. Utilization of the Charts in this book can lead to many ideas about how the charts are related to the houses, and whose spirits are in each house.

Many surnames such as Lord are related to the sacred gospels. In this case possibly the Lords Prayer found in Mathew or Luke. The Star of Bethlehem house is related to breeding, Christmas, the three wise Kings and the Shepards. Many houses are nalmed after church offices or appointments like Priest, Bishop, Cardinal, and Pope. Surnames like Prayer and Church are also related to the Christian Religion.

Many houses are houses that are simply a cross of a name such as Brian or Scott. Now Scott would also refer to Scotland and the Scotti dog, while Brian would refer to the King of Ireland. Baldwin would refer to the King of Jerusalem, such as also Godfrey, Brienne, Fowlkes Le Jeune de Anjou. Note that Godfrey and Fowlkes are French while Brienne would be British, while Baldwin would also be French.

Many surnames where Knighted in History and each country has an armoury of arms, the most famous being Cantebury of Kent, the Burkes Armoury. The Reinstap European Armory is the more prominent International Armoury for Europe. Many laymen have been honored with Knighthood and the blessing of the Bishop, with divine knowledge of the area of Galilee, and the common knowledge that the whole of Galilee is completely honorable in all its relationships, and that there could be no reason for any Emperor to order a takeover of the Holy Land except to defend it from ignorant pagans. This was proven when the Roman Empire attempted to subdue the Hebrew who patiently thru 2000 years showed their belief to be honorable and so a 63 year independent peace exists today in the Holy Land.

THE KNIGHT OR OF THE GOOD SHEPARD ATHRONGONES

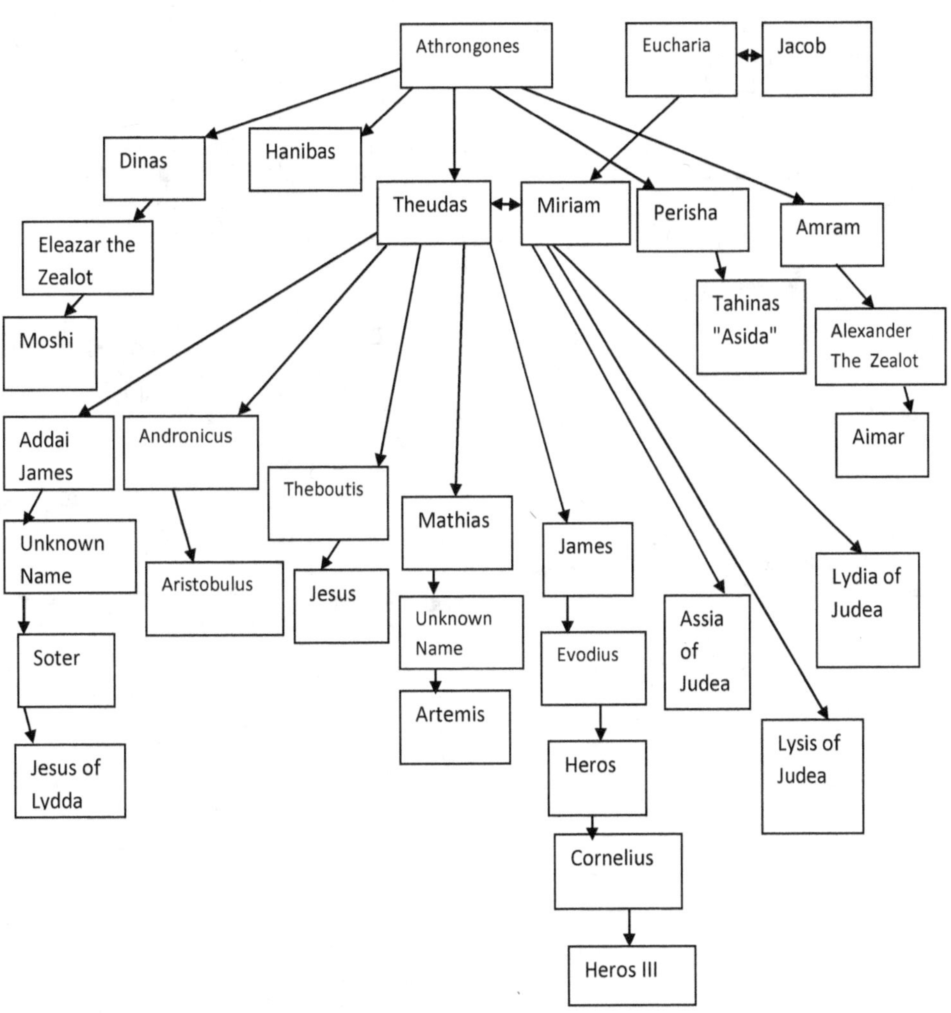

THE KNIGHT ORDERS OF KNIGHTS	***The Masonic order (US)***	***Equestrian Order of the Holy Sepulcher.***
The Knights of St John of Jerusalem: AD 1113-1291	***The Knights of Columbus (founding in US by Father Michael McGivney, International Order)***	***The Sacred Military Constantinian Order of Saint George***
The Knights Templars: AD 1120-1291	***The Knights of Pythias***	***Four Spanish Military Orders of Santiago, Calatrava, Alcántara and Montesa***
The Teutonic Knights: AD 1191	***The Knights of Columba***	***Royal Order of Saint George for the Defense of the Immaculate Conception***
The Order of the Garter: AD c.1347	***The Knights of Saint Peter Claver***	***Order of the Golden Fleece***
The Knighthood of Caltrava (Saint Raimond from Spain)	***Vatican Orders.***	*Illustrious Royal Order of Saint Januarius*
	Sovereign Military Hospitaller Order of Malta,	

There were many people alive during the Passion of Christ. Most of the records of these people are lost, however some still survive. These people would have been alive when Christ conquered death, and a record of some kind exists that shows their lineage to the ancients. Here are 49 such people from all over the world. Many other people from other religions were alive as well and could be added to the list. The author is almost certain in the other religions these people would now be deified.

Christmas Crosses

Those Alive During the Time of Christ's Passion

	Ireland
1	Feardach and Mar Fath
	Father Crimthann Niadhnair
	Line of Ishmael
2	Layla and Ilyas (Inki)
	Father Amr Mudrika and Salma
	Edessa
3	Abgar and Shalmath
	Father Mannos
	Rome
	Marcus Antonius Gnaeus Piso d 20 ad
4	Gaius Calpernius Piso and Mariamne Caecina Arria Sabinus
	Arrius Antonius Calpernius Piso
5	Tiberius Claudius Nero and Julia Agrippa Minor or Messalina Valeria
	Father Appius Claudius Nero
	Descent of the Franks
6	Halfida Rugij, Clodimir
7	Antenor and Bran
	Father Clodomir
	Line of Kent
8	Beaw and unknown wife
	Father Skyjod Syjbold
	Lazarine
9	Lazarus and Salome
	Father Mathew the Cyrus
	Region of Gamala
10	Mary Magdalene and son of Joseph of Gamla
	Marcella and son of Mary Magdalene
	Region of Arimathea
11	Bran and Prophetess Anna of Aramathea
	Father Lyr
	The Knight
12	Theudas and Miriam
	Father Athrongones
	Region of Israel
13	Bishop James
14	Jose
15	Jude
16	Simon
17-32	12 Apostles
	From Beli and Don Verch Mathonry
33	Mandabratus
34	Aflach
35	Llud Law
36	Father Beli
	Armenia
37	Vonores from Mamokonian and Armenia
38	Vologaesus
39	Sanatroukes (Sanstruk)King of Armenia
40	Mithradates from Mamokonian and Aramathea
41	Amazaspus I
42	Sames II Theoseves Dikaios
	Ptolas or Thomas
43	Jacobus
44	Justus son of Jacobus
	Father Ptolas
	High Priest
45	Caiaphas and daughter of Ananus son of Sic
	Ka'yefes (Caiaphas)
	Wessex
46	Hezekiah married Akkub daughter of Elionoei
	From Bustani
	Nasi
47	Gamaliel I "The Elder", "Nasi"
	China
48	Otyura
49	Dao Gao

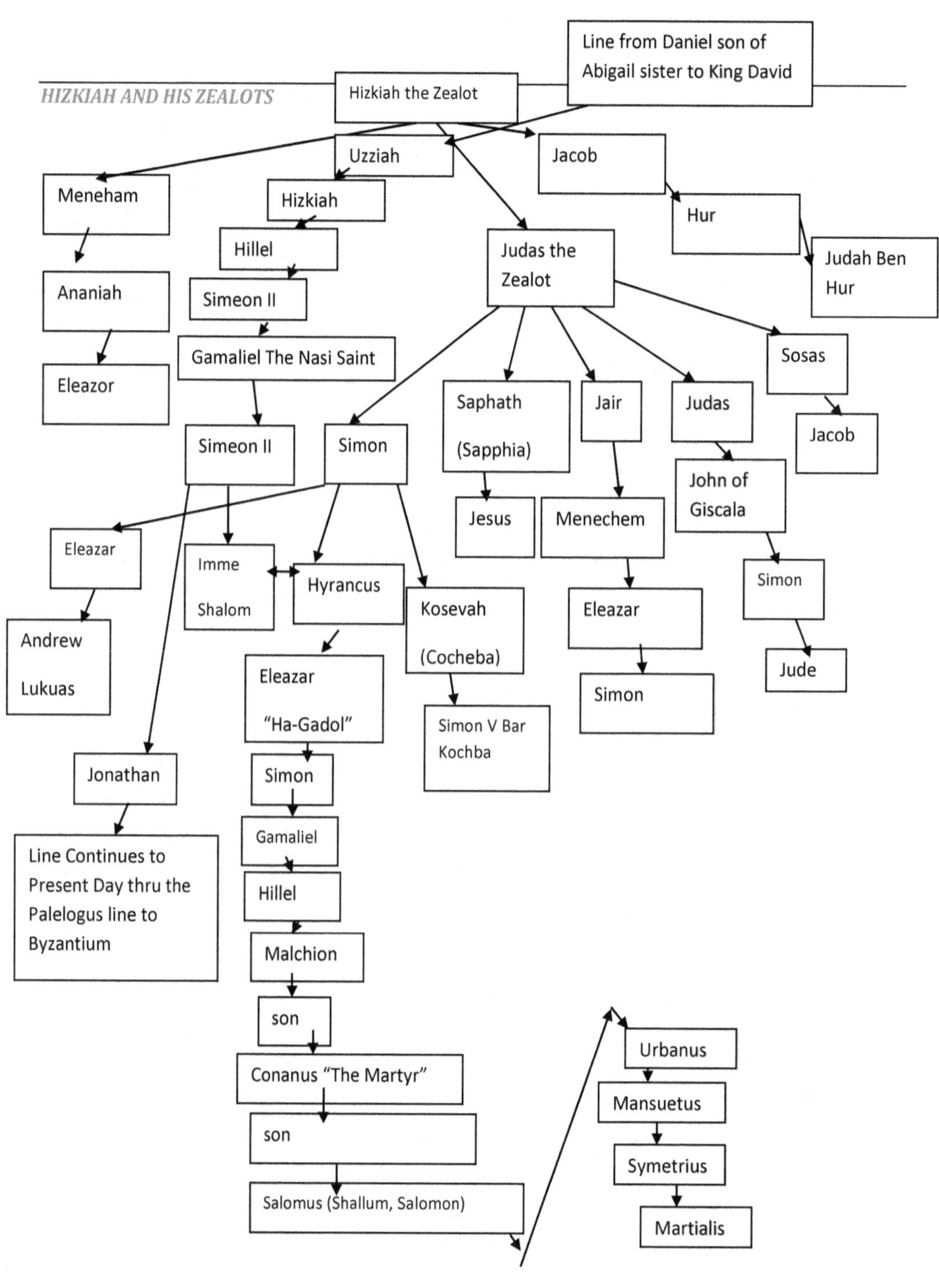
Line from Daniel son of Abigail sister to King David
Hizkiah the Zealot
Uzziah
Jacob
Meneham
Hizkiah
Hur
Hillel
Judas the Zealot
Judah Ben Hur
Ananiah
Simeon II
Gamaliel The Nasi Saint
Sosas
Eleazor
Saphath (Sapphia)
Jair
Judas
Jacob
Simeon II
Simon
John of Giscala
Jesus
Menechem
Eleazar
Imme Shalom
Hyrancus
Kosevah (Cocheba)
Simon
Eleazar
Andrew Lukuas
Jude
Eleazar "Ha-Gadol"
Simon
Simon V Bar Kochba
Jonathan
Simon
Gamaliel
Line Continues to Present Day thru the Palelogus line to Byzantium
Hillel
Malchion
son
Urbanus
Conanus "The Martyr"
Mansuetus
son
Symetrius
Salomus (Shallum, Salomon)
Martialis

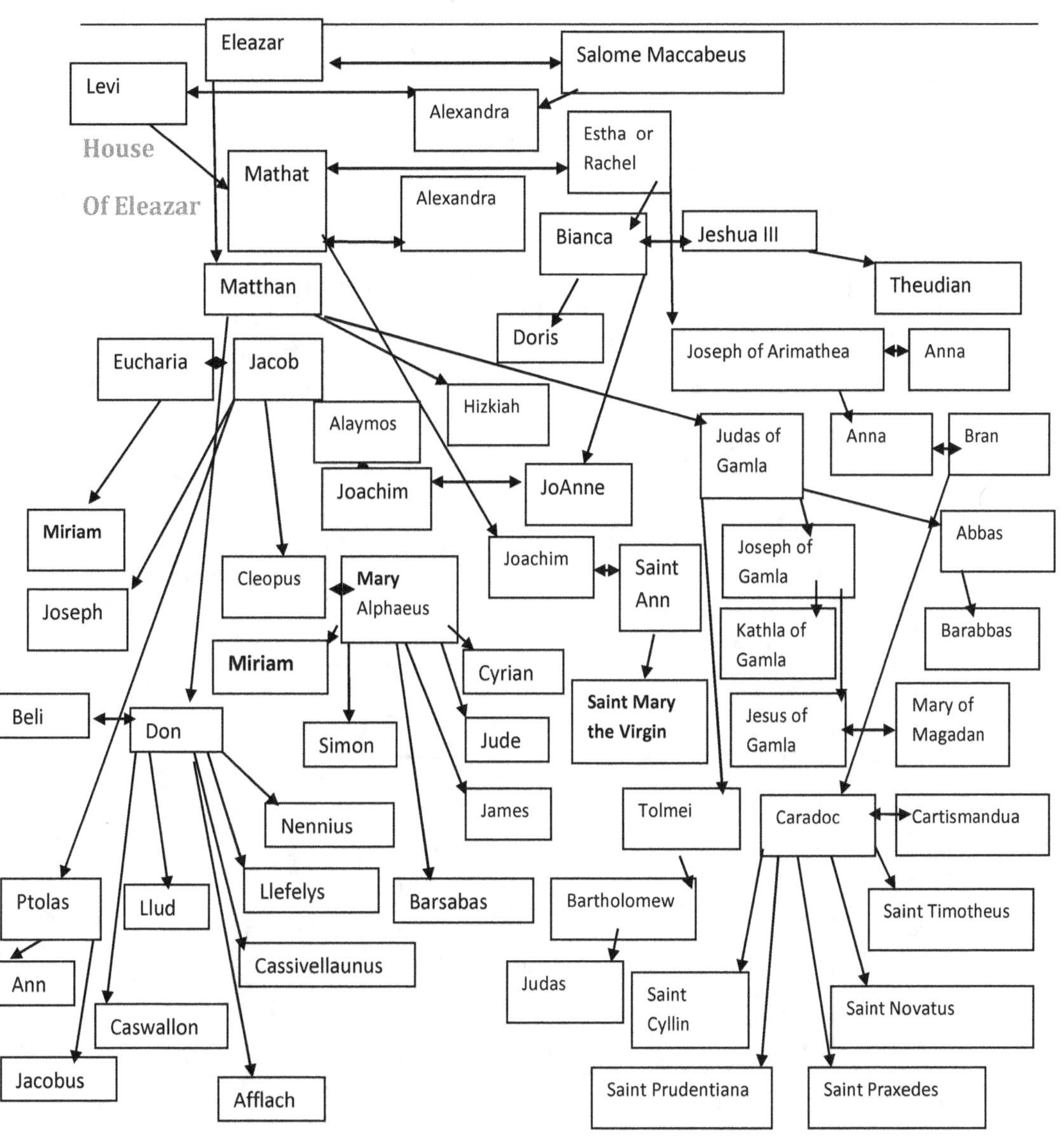

Eleazar
Salome Maccabeus
Levi
Alexandra
House
Of Eleazar
Mathat
Estha or
Rachel
Alexandra
Bianca
Jeshua III
Matthan
Theudian
Doris
Joseph of Arimathea
Anna
Eucharia
Jacob
Hizkiah
Alaymos
Judas of
Gamla
Anna
Bran
Joachim
JoAnne
Miriam
Joseph of
Gamla
Abbas
Joachim
Saint
Ann
Cleopus
Mary
Alphaeus
Joseph
Kathla of
Gamla
Barabbas
Miriam
Cyrian
Saint Mary
the Virgin
Jesus of
Gamla
Mary of
Magadan
Beli
Don
Simon
Jude
Nennius
James
Tolmei
Caradoc
Cartismandua
Ptolas
Llud
Llefelys
Barsabas
Bartholomew
Saint Timotheus
Ann
Cassivellaunus
Judas
Saint
Cyllin
Saint Novatus
Caswallon
Jacobus
Afflach
Saint Prudentiana
Saint Praxedes

House of Elizabeth

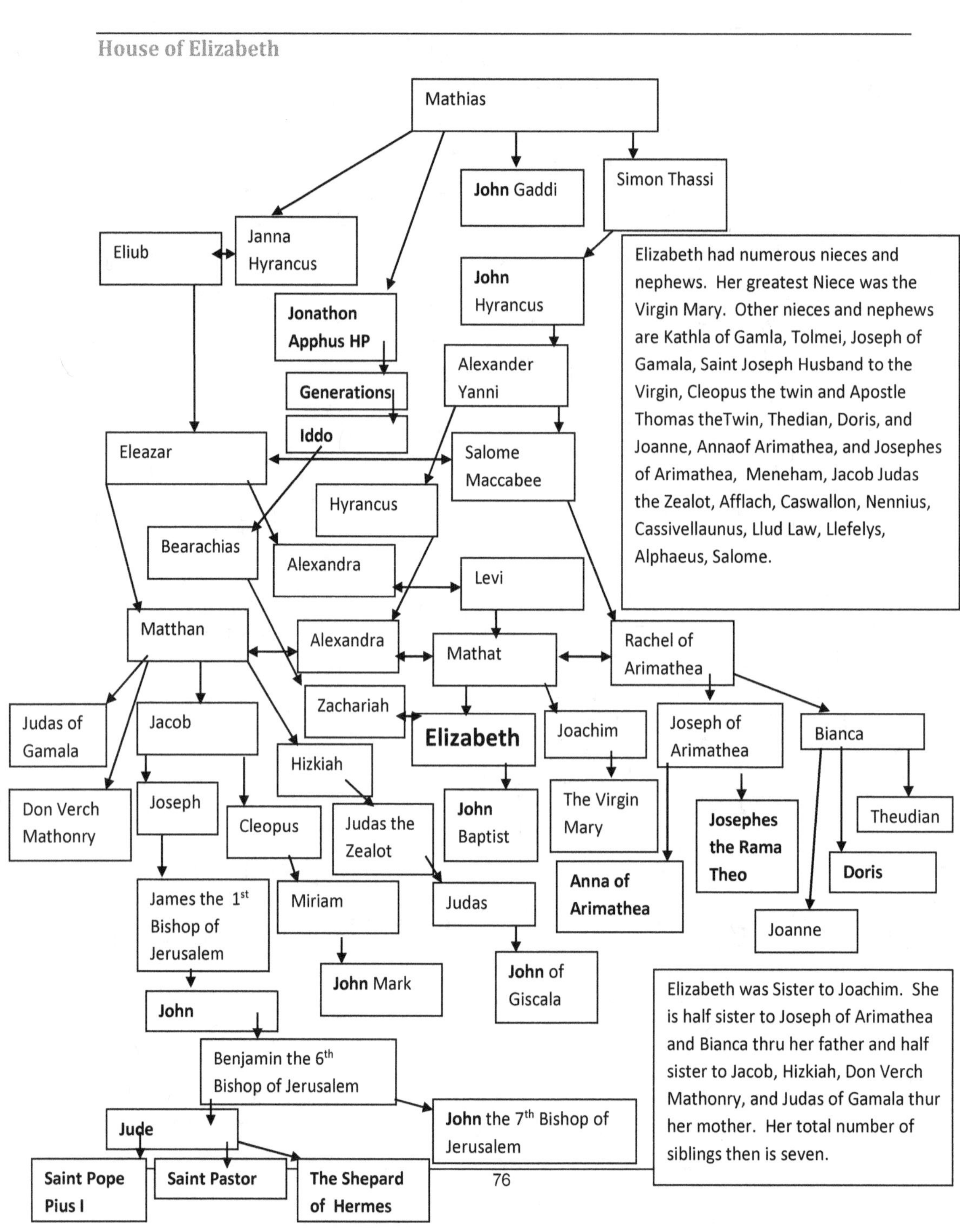

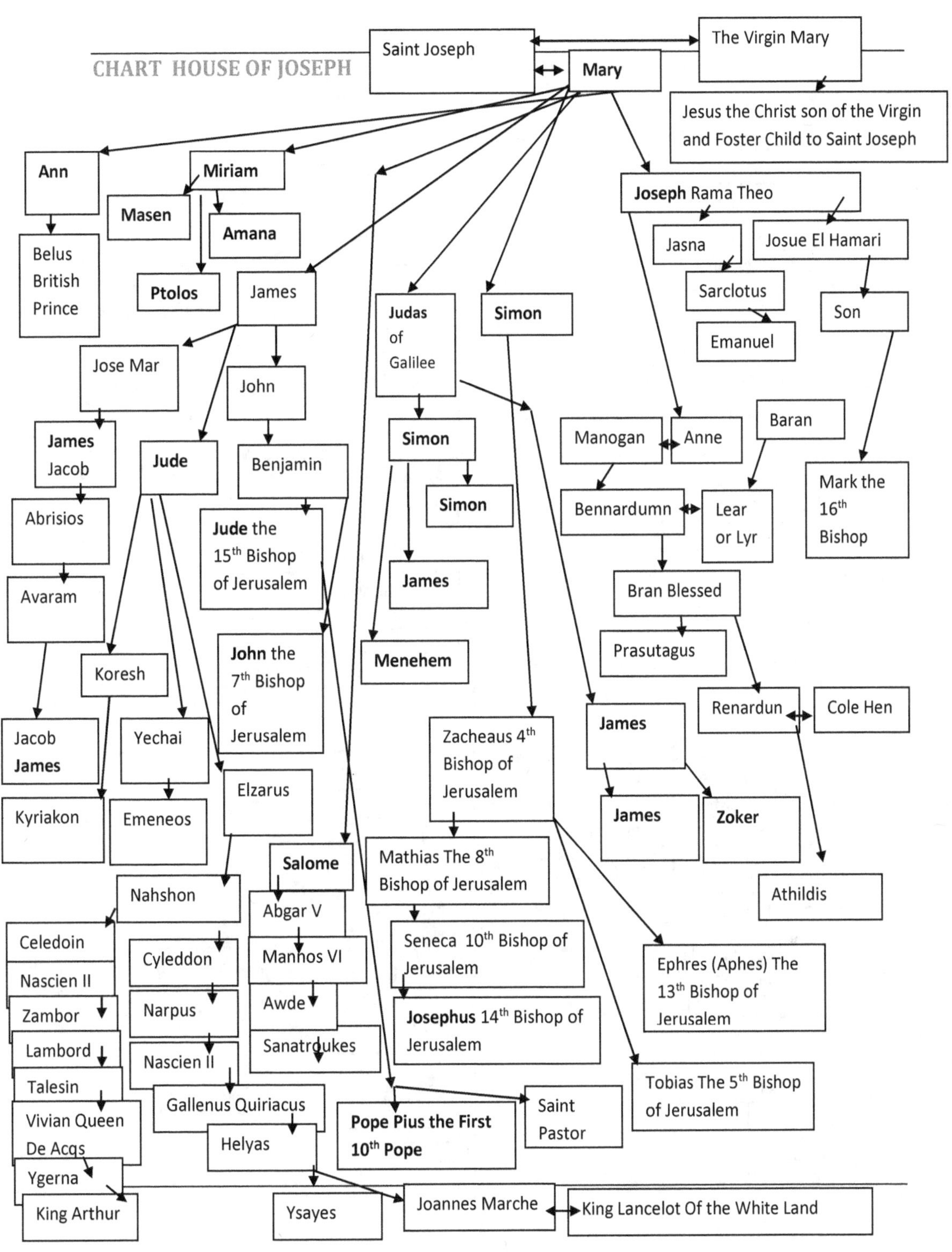
CHART HOUSE OF JOSEPH
Saint Joseph
The Virgin Mary
Mary
Jesus the Christ son of the Virgin and Foster Child to Saint Joseph
Ann
Miriam
Masen
Amana
Belus British Prince
Ptolos
James
Joseph Rama Theo
Jasna
Josue El Hamari
Sarclotus
Emanuel
Son
Judas of Galilee
Simon
Jose Mar
John
James Jacob
Jude
Benjamin
Simon
Simon
Manogan
Anne
Baran
Mark the 16th Bishop
Abrisios
Jude the 15th Bishop of Jerusalem
Bennardumn
Lear or Lyr
James
Avaram
Bran Blessed
John the 7th Bishop of Jerusalem
Menehem
Prasutagus
Koresh
Renardun
Cole Hen
Jacob James
Yechai
Zacheaus 4th Bishop of Jerusalem
James
Kyriakon
Emeneos
Elzarus
James
Zoker
Salome
Mathias The 8th Bishop of Jerusalem
Athildis
Nahshon
Abgar V
Celedoin
Cyleddon
Manhos VI
Seneca 10th Bishop of Jerusalem
Ephres (Aphes) The 13th Bishop of Jerusalem
Nascien II
Narpus
Awde
Zambor
Josephus 14th Bishop of Jerusalem
Lambord
Nascien II
Sanatrukes
Tobias The 5th Bishop of Jerusalem
Talesin
Gallenus Quiriacus
Saint Pastor
Vivian Queen De Acqs
Helyas
Pope Pius the First 10th Pope
Ygerna
King Arthur
Ysayes
Joannes Marche
King Lancelot Of the White Land

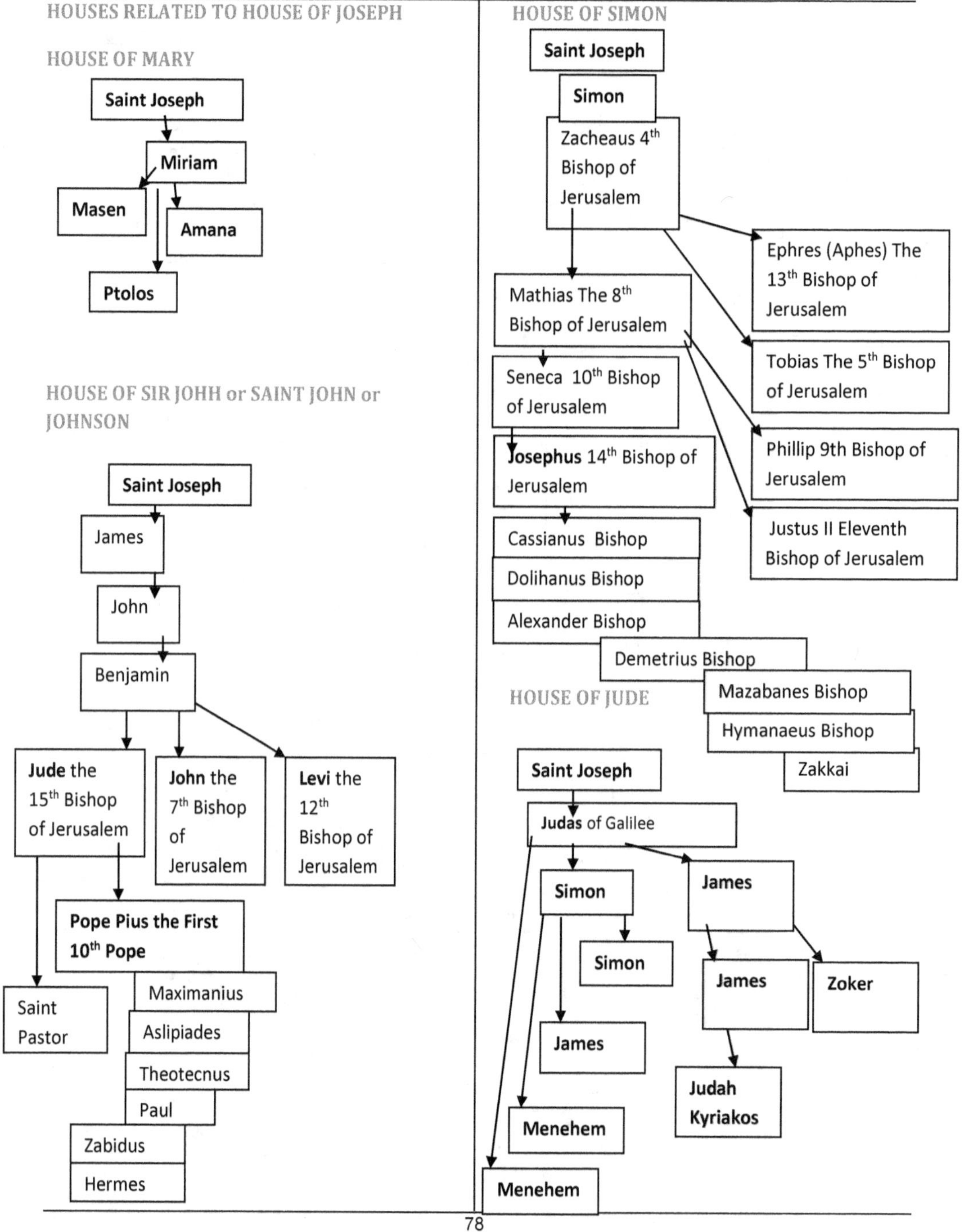
HOUSES RELATED TO HOUSE OF JOSEPH
HOUSE OF MARY
Saint Joseph
Miriam
Masen
Amana
Ptolos
HOUSE OF SIR JOHH or SAINT JOHN or JOHNSON
Saint Joseph
James
John
Benjamin
Jude the 15th Bishop of Jerusalem
John the 7th Bishop of Jerusalem
Levi the 12th Bishop of Jerusalem
Pope Pius the First 10th Pope
Saint Pastor
Maximanius
Aslipiades
Theotecnus
Paul
Zabidus
Hermes
HOUSE OF SIMON
Saint Joseph
Simon
Zacheaus 4th Bishop of Jerusalem
Ephres (Aphes) The 13th Bishop of Jerusalem
Mathias The 8th Bishop of Jerusalem
Tobias The 5th Bishop of Jerusalem
Seneca 10th Bishop of Jerusalem
Phillip 9th Bishop of Jerusalem
Josephus 14th Bishop of Jerusalem
Justus II Eleventh Bishop of Jerusalem
Cassianus Bishop
Dolihanus Bishop
Alexander Bishop
Demetrius Bishop
Mazabanes Bishop
Hymanaeus Bishop
Zakkai
HOUSE OF JUDE
Saint Joseph
Judas of Galilee
Simon
James
Simon
James
Zoker
James
Judah Kyriakos
Menehem
Menehem

House of Don Verch Mathonry

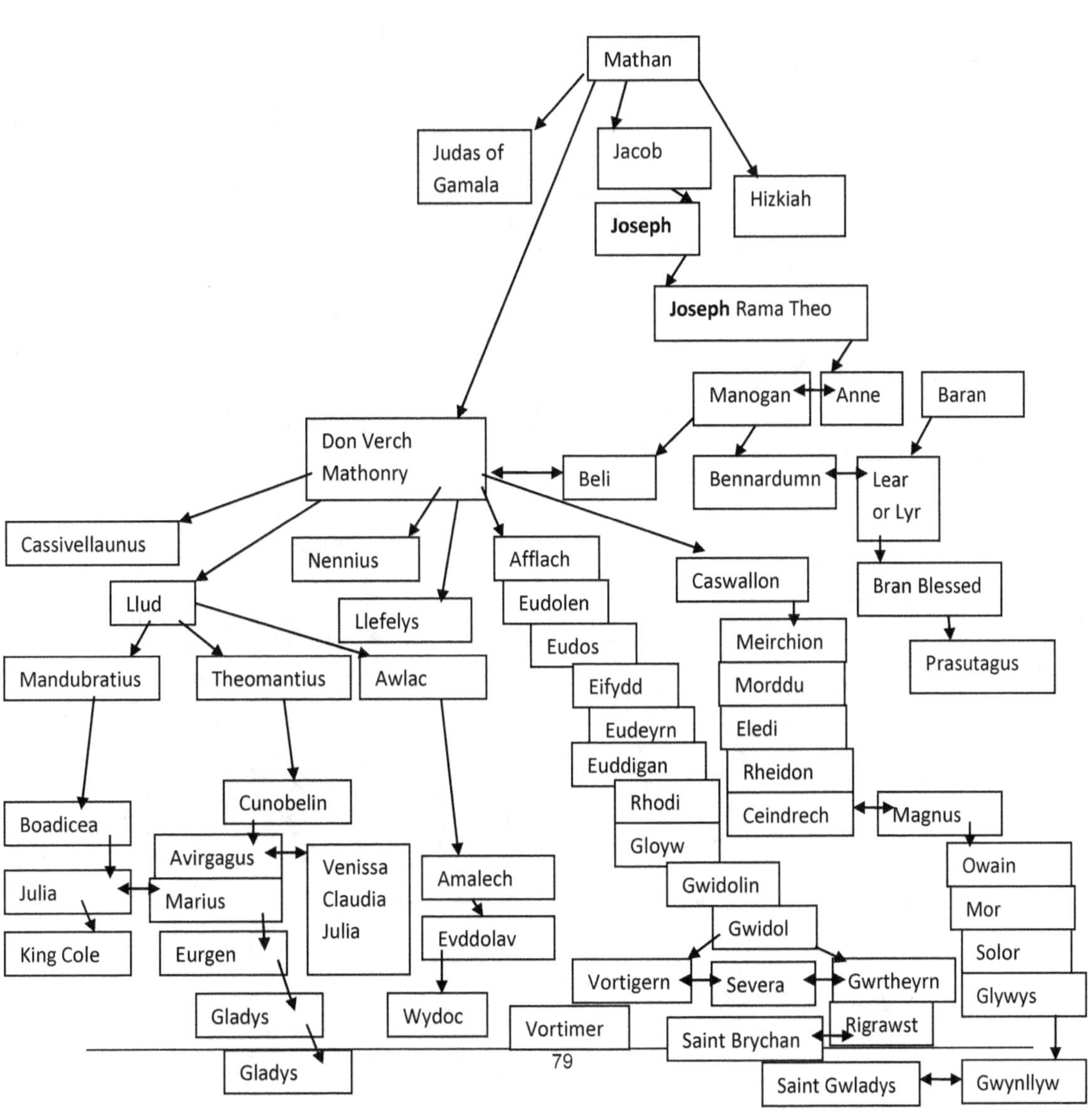

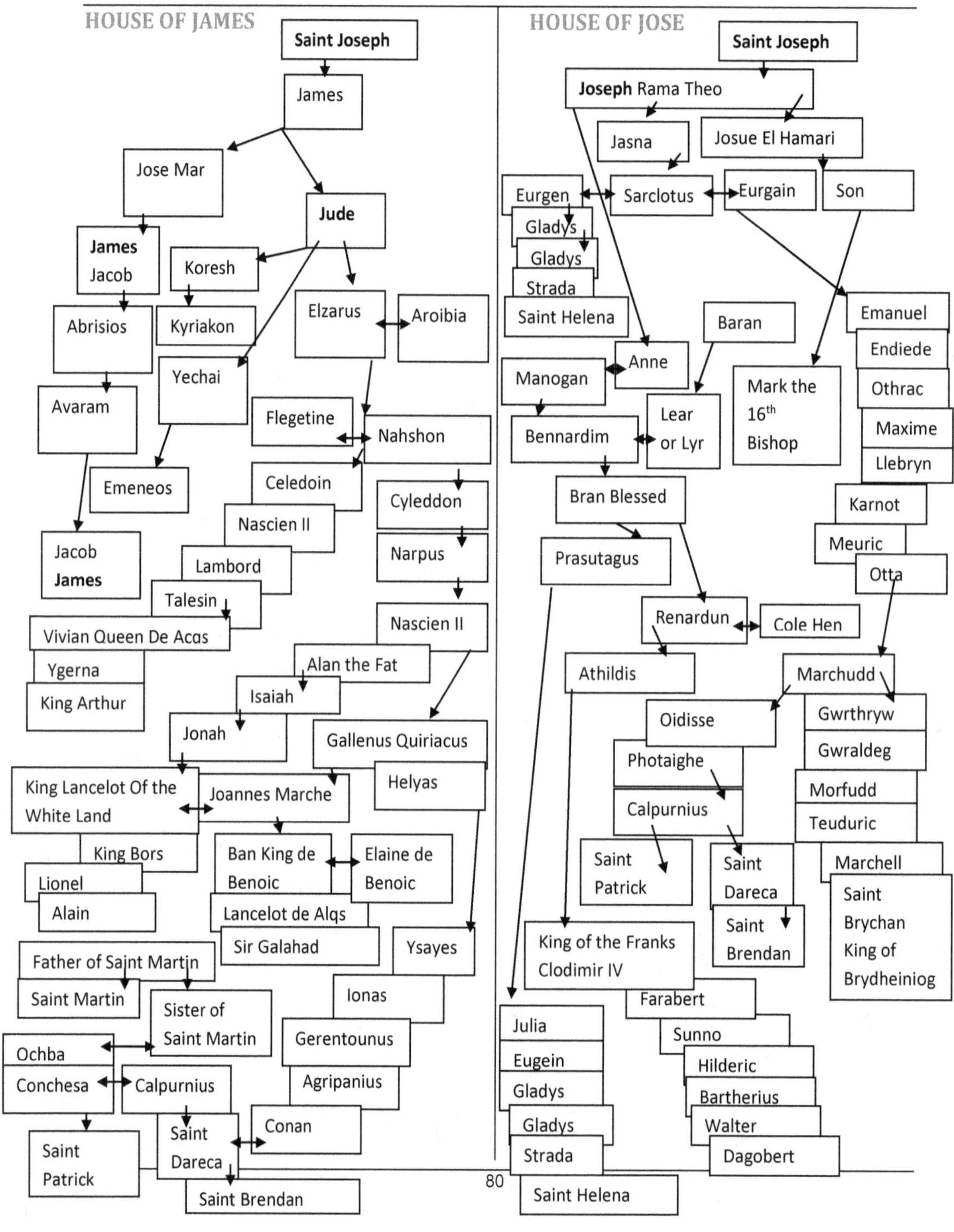
HOUSE OF JAMES
Saint Joseph
James
Jose Mar
Jude
James Jacob
Koresh
Elzarus
Aroibia
Abrisios
Kyriakon
Yechai
Avaram
Flegetine
Nahshon
Emeneos
Celedoin
Cyleddon
Nascien II
Jacob James
Lambord
Narpus
Talesin
Vivian Queen De Acqs
Nascien II
Ygerna
Alan the Fat
King Arthur
Isaiah
Jonah
Gallenus Quiriacus
King Lancelot Of the White Land
Joannes Marche
Helyas
King Bors
Ban King de Benoic
Elaine de Benoic
Lionel
Alain
Lancelot de Alqs
Sir Galahad
Ysayes
Father of Saint Martin
Saint Martin
Sister of Saint Martin
Ionas
Gerentounus
Ochba
Conchesa
Calpurnius
Agripanius
Saint Dareca
Conan
Saint Patrick
Saint Brendan
HOUSE OF JOSE
Saint Joseph
Joseph Rama Theo
Jasna
Josue El Hamari
Eurgen
Sarclotus
Eurgain
Son
Gladys
Gladys
Strada
Saint Helena
Baran
Emanuel
Endiede
Anne
Manogan
Mark the 16th Bishop
Othrac
Lear or Lyr
Bennardim
Maxime
Llebryn
Bran Blessed
Karnot
Meuric
Prasutagus
Otta
Renardun
Cole Hen
Athildis
Marchudd
Gwrthryw
Oidisse
Gwraldeg
Photaighe
Morfudd
Calpurnius
Teuduric
Saint Patrick
Saint Dareca
Marchell
Saint Brychan King of Brydheiniog
Saint Brendan
King of the Franks Clodimir IV
Farabert
Julia
Sunno
Eugein
Hilderic
Gladys
Bartherius
Gladys
Walter
Strada
Dagobert
Saint Helena

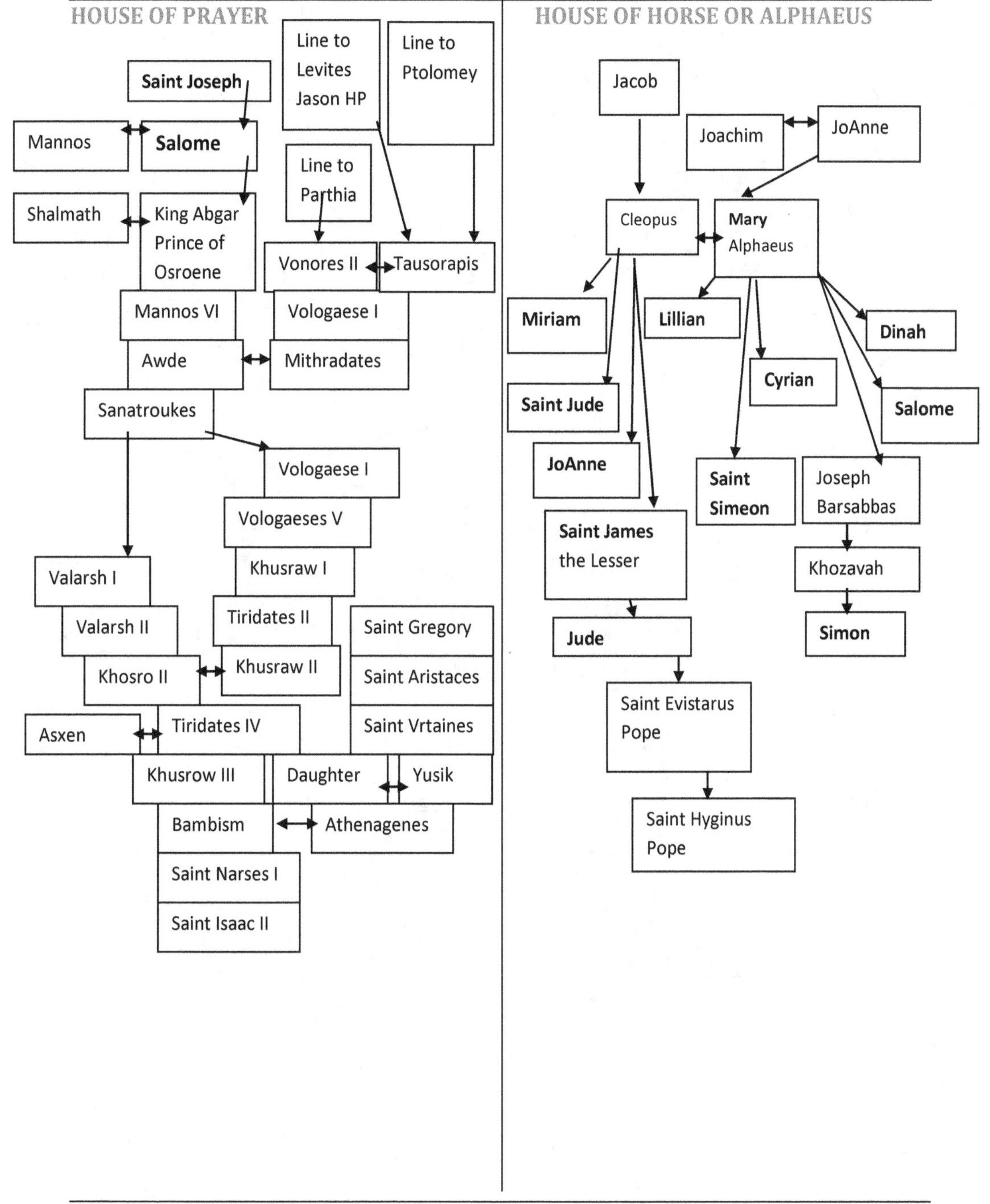
HOUSE OF PRAYER
Line to Levites Jason HP
Line to Ptolomey
Saint Joseph
Mannos
Salome
Line to Parthia
Shalmath
King Abgar Prince of Osroene
Vonores II
Tausorapis
Mannos VI
Vologaese I
Awde
Mithradates
Sanatroukes
Vologaese I
Vologaeses V
Valarsh I
Khusraw I
Valarsh II
Tiridates II
Saint Gregory
Khosro II
Khusraw II
Saint Aristaces
Asxen
Tiridates IV
Saint Vrtaines
Khusrow III
Daughter
Yusik
Bambism
Athenagenes
Saint Narses I
Saint Isaac II
HOUSE OF HORSE OR ALPHAEUS
Jacob
Joachim
JoAnne
Cleopus
Mary Alphaeus
Miriam
Lillian
Dinah
Cyrian
Saint Jude
Salome
JoAnne
Saint Simeon
Joseph Barsabbas
Saint James the Lesser
Khozavah
Jude
Simon
Saint Evistarus Pope
Saint Hyginus Pope

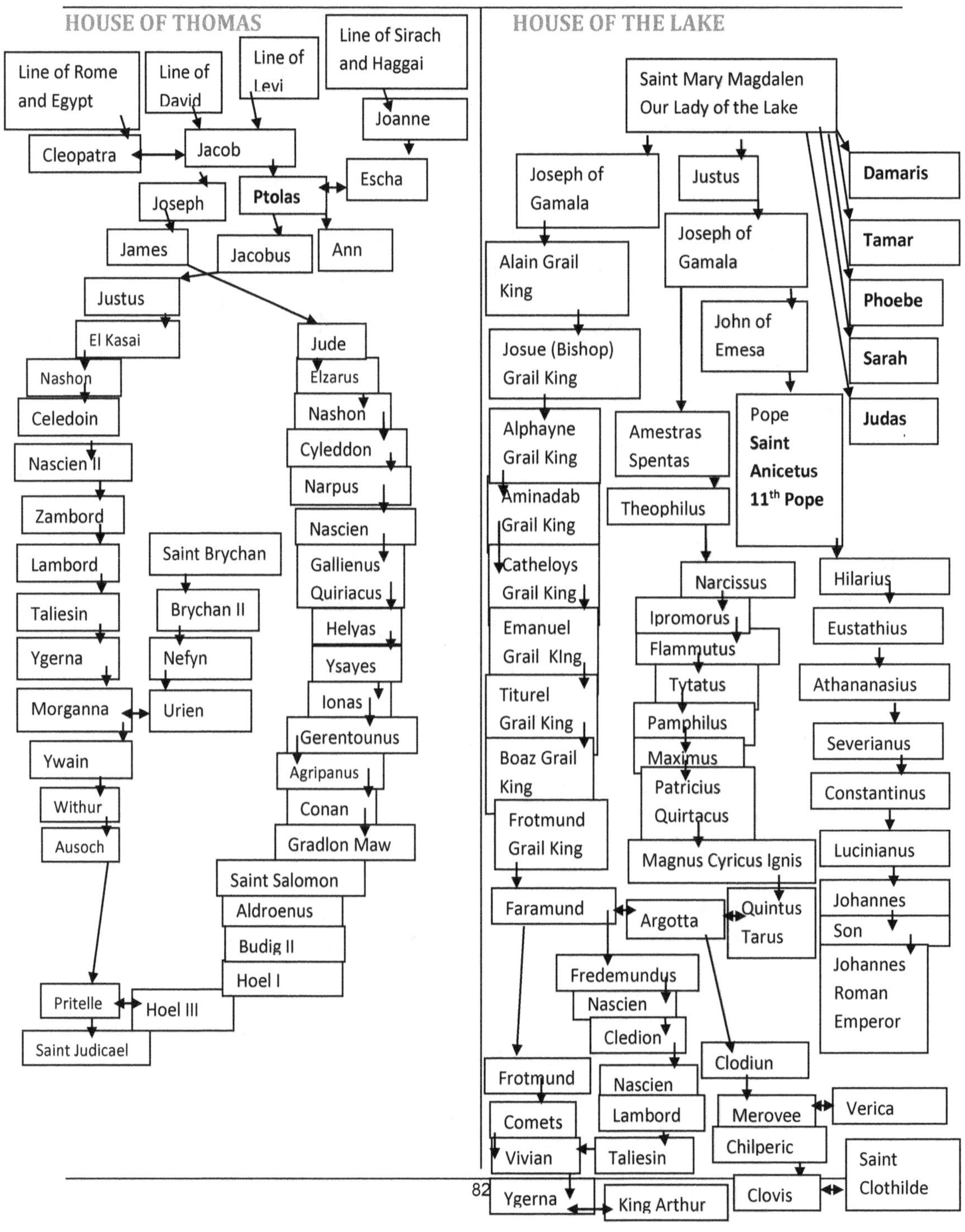
HOUSE OF THOMAS
Line of Rome and Egypt
Line of David
Line of Levi
Line of Sirach and Haggai
Joanne
Cleopatra
Jacob
Escha
Joseph
Ptolas
James
Jacobus
Ann
Justus
El Kasai
Jude
Nashon
Elzarus
Celedoin
Nashon
Cyleddon
Nascien II
Narpus
Zambord
Nascien
Lambord
Saint Brychan
Gallienus Quiriacus
Taliesin
Brychan II
Helyas
Ygerna
Nefyn
Ysayes
Morganna
Urien
Ionas
Gerentounus
Ywain
Agripanus
Withur
Conan
Ausoch
Gradlon Maw
Saint Salomon
Aldroenus
Budig II
Hoel I
Pritelle
Hoel III
Saint Judicael
HOUSE OF THE LAKE
Saint Mary Magdalen Our Lady of the Lake
Joseph of Gamala
Justus
Damaris
Joseph of Gamala
Tamar
Alain Grail King
Phoebe
John of Emesa
Sarah
Josue (Bishop) Grail King
Pope Saint Anicetus 11th Pope
Judas
Alphayne Grail King
Amestras Spentas
Aminadab Grail King
Theophilus
Catheloys Grail King
Narcissus
Hilarius
Ipromorus
Eustathius
Emanuel Grail King
Flammutus
Tytatus
Athananasius
Titurel Grail King
Pamphilus
Severianus
Boaz Grail King
Maximus
Patricius Quirtacus
Constantinus
Frotmund Grail King
Magnus Cyricus Ignis
Lucinianus
Faramund
Argotta
Quintus Tarus
Johannes Son
Johannes Roman Emperor
Fredemundus
Nascien
Cledion
Clodiun
Frotmund
Nascien
Lambord
Merovee
Verica
Comets
Chilperic
Vivian
Taliesin
Saint Clothilde
Ygerna
King Arthur
Clovis

House of Herod

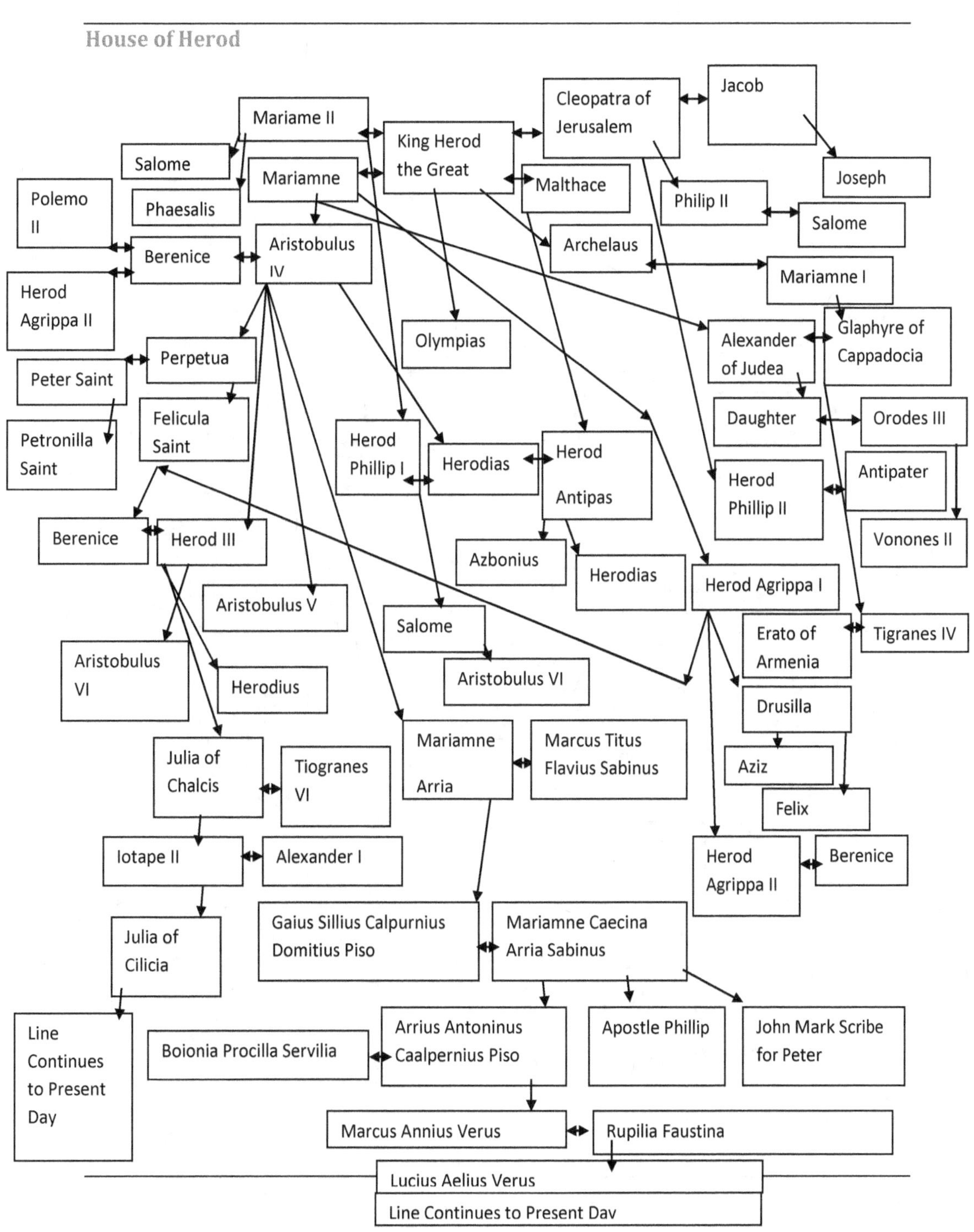

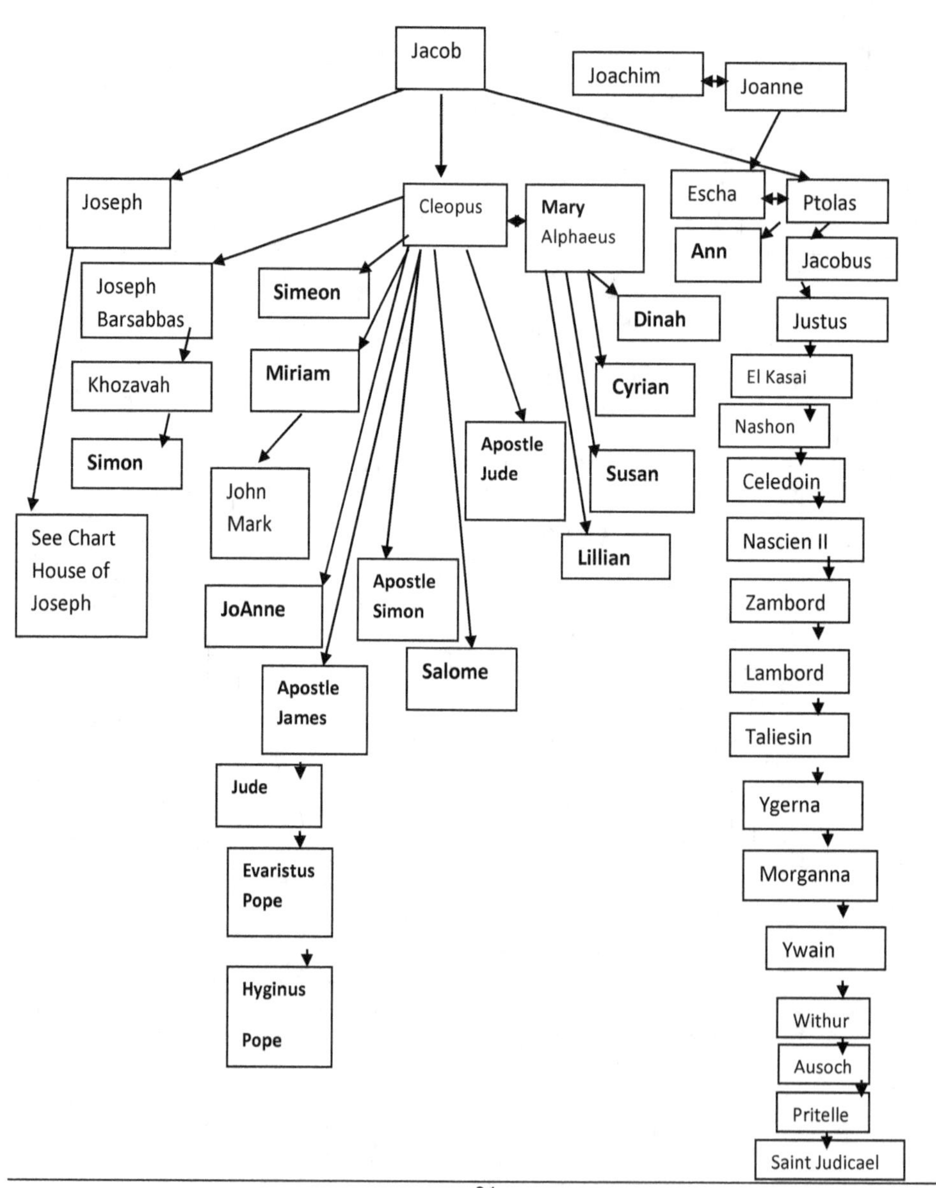
Jacob
Joachim
Joanne
Joseph
Cleopus
Mary
Alphaeus
Escha
Ptolas
Ann
Jacobus
Joseph
Barsabbas
Simeon
Dinah
Justus
Khozavah
Miriam
Cyrian
El Kasai
Nashon
Simon
John
Mark
Apostle
Jude
Susan
Celedoin
See Chart
House of
Joseph
Lillian
Nascien II
JoAnne
Apostle
Simon
Zambord
Salome
Lambord
Apostle
James
Taliesin
Jude
Ygerna
Evaristus
Pope
Morganna
Ywain
Hyginus
Pope
Withur
Ausoch
Pritelle
Saint Judicael

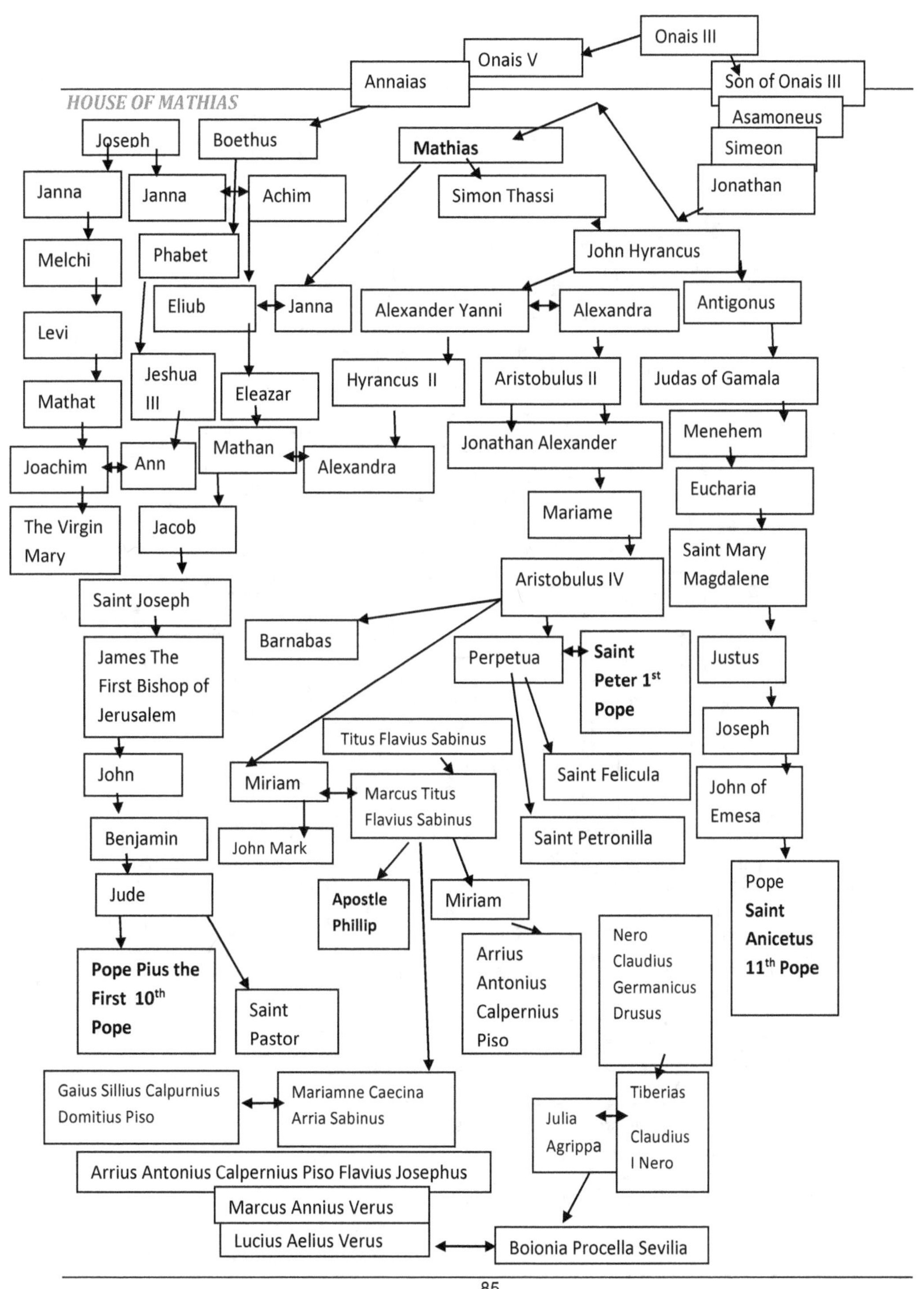
Onais III
Onais V
Annaias
Son of Onais III
Asamoneus
Simeon
Jonathan
Joseph
Boethus
Mathias
Janna
Janna
Achim
Simon Thassi
Melchi
Phabet
John Hyrancus
Eliub
Janna
Alexander Yanni
Alexandra
Antigonus
Levi
Jeshua III
Eleazar
Hyrancus II
Aristobulus II
Judas of Gamala
Mathat
Mathan
Jonathan Alexander
Menehem
Joachim
Ann
Alexandra
Eucharia
The Virgin Mary
Jacob
Mariame
Saint Mary Magdalene
Aristobulus IV
Saint Joseph
Barnabas
Perpetua
Saint Peter 1st Pope
Justus
James The First Bishop of Jerusalem
Titus Flavius Sabinus
Joseph
John
Miriam
Marcus Titus Flavius Sabinus
Saint Felicula
John of Emesa
Benjamin
John Mark
Saint Petronilla
Jude
Apostle Phillip
Miriam
Pope Saint Anicetus 11th Pope
Nero Claudius Germanicus Drusus
Arrius Antonius Calpernius Piso
Pope Pius the First 10th Pope
Saint Pastor
Gaius Sillius Calpurnius Domitius Piso
Mariamne Caecina Arria Sabinus
Tiberias Claudius I Nero
Julia Agrippa
Arrius Antonius Calpernius Piso Flavius Josephus
Marcus Annius Verus
Lucius Aelius Verus
Boionia Procella Sevilia

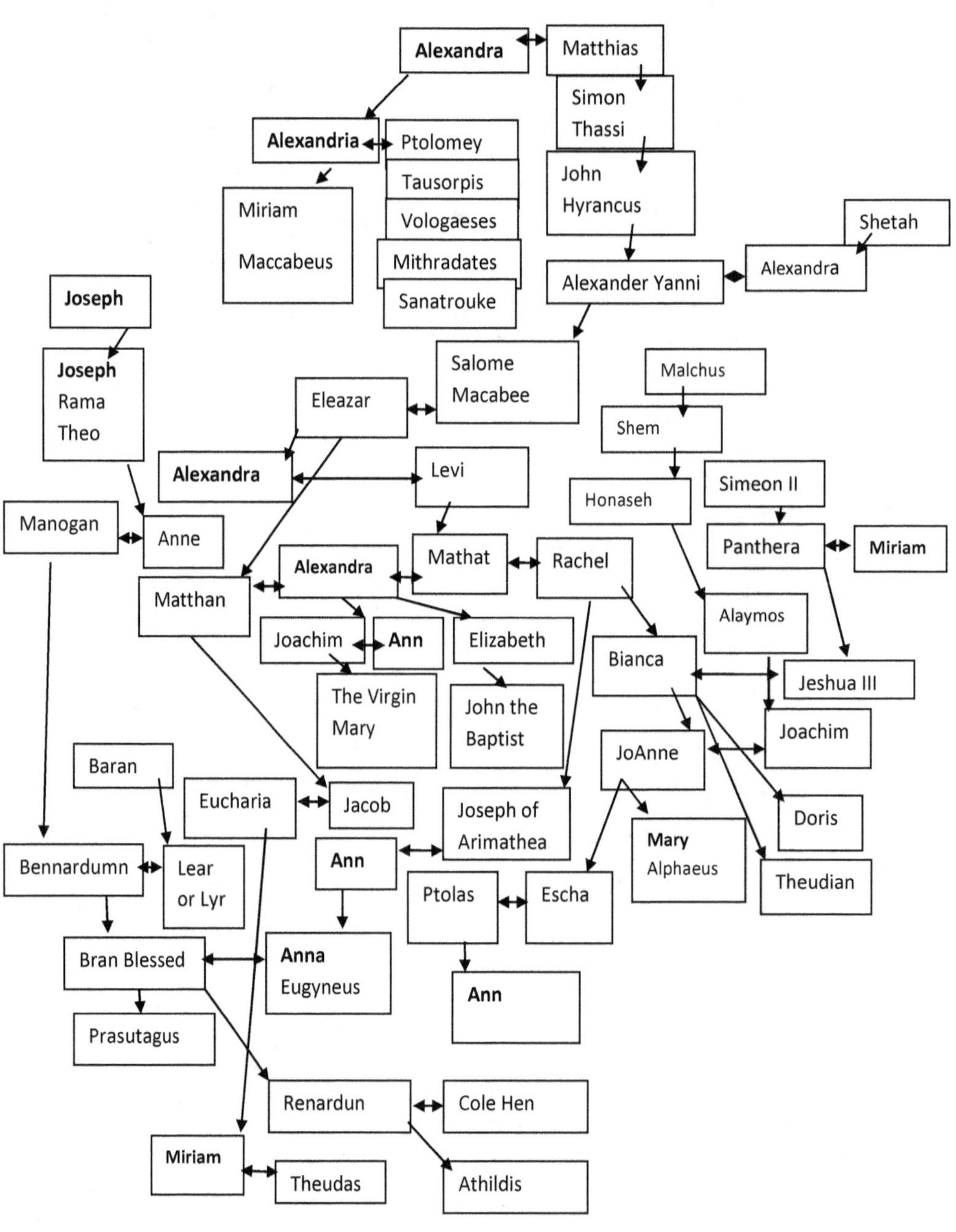
Alexandra
Matthias
Simon
Thassi
Alexandria
Ptolomey
Tausorpis
Vologaeses
Mithradates
Sanatrouke
Miriam
Maccabeus
John
Hyrancus
Shetah
Alexandra
Alexander Yanni
Joseph
Joseph
Rama
Theo
Salome
Macabee
Eleazar
Malchus
Shem
Alexandra
Levi
Honaseh
Simeon II
Manogan
Anne
Alexandra
Mathat
Rachel
Panthera
Miriam
Matthan
Alaymos
Joachim
Ann
Elizabeth
Bianca
Jeshua III
The Virgin
Mary
John the
Baptist
Joachim
JoAnne
Baran
Eucharia
Jacob
Joseph of
Arimathea
Doris
Mary
Alphaeus
Bennardumn
Lear
or Lyr
Ann
Ptolas
Escha
Theudian
Bran Blessed
Anna
Eugyneus
Ann
Prasutagus
Renardun
Cole Hen
Miriam
Theudas
Athildis

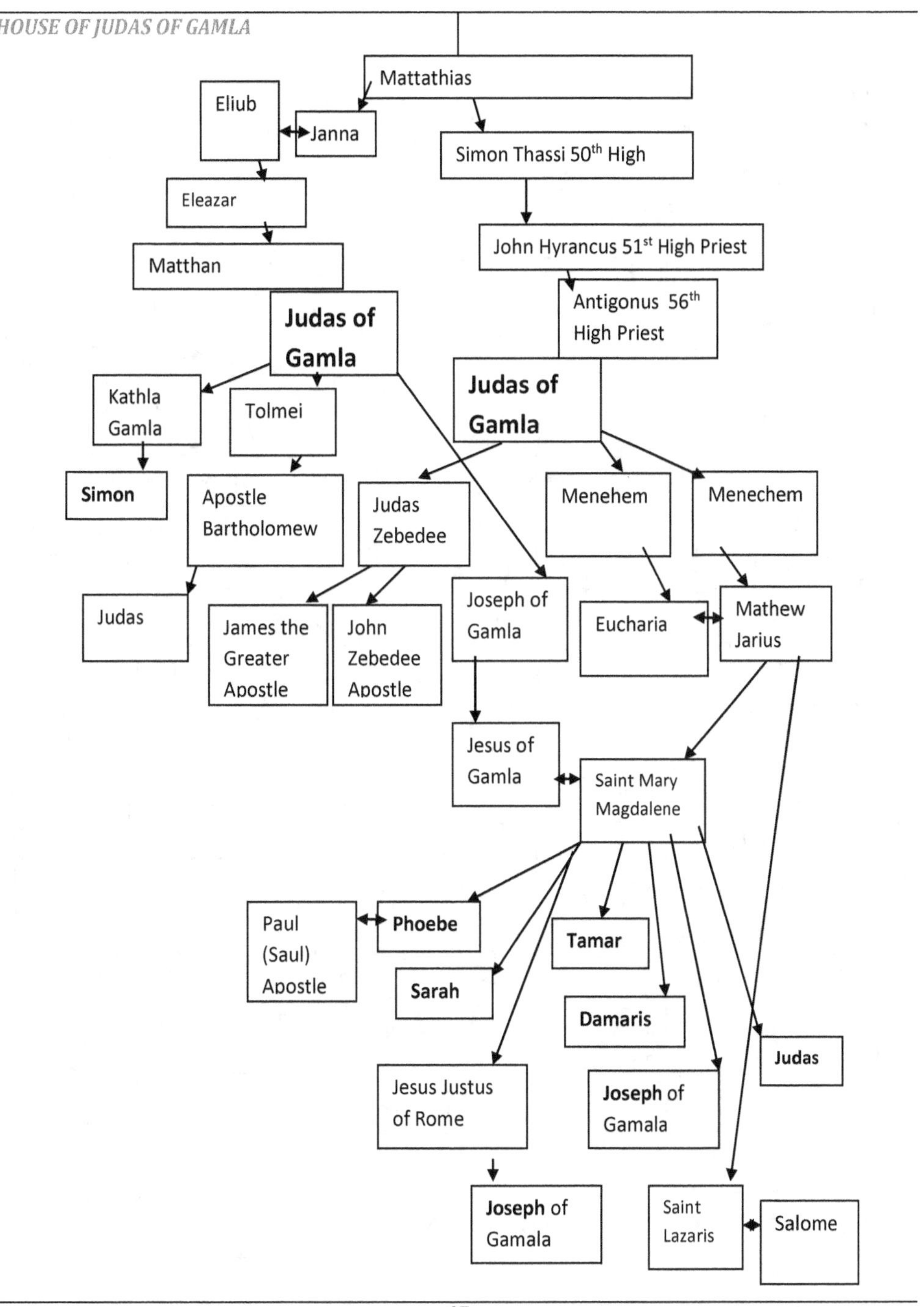
Mattathias
Eliub
Janna
Simon Thassi 50th High
Eleazar
John Hyrancus 51st High Priest
Matthan
Antigonus 56th High Priest
Judas of Gamla
Judas of Gamla
Kathla Gamla
Tolmei
Simon
Apostle Bartholomew
Judas Zebedee
Menehem
Menechem
Judas
James the Greater Apostle
John Zebedee Apostle
Joseph of Gamla
Eucharia
Mathew Jarius
Jesus of Gamla
Saint Mary Magdalene
Paul (Saul) Apostle
Phoebe
Tamar
Sarah
Damaris
Judas
Jesus Justus of Rome
Joseph of Gamala
Joseph of Gamala
Saint Lazaris
Salome

LINES MERGING INTO ISRAEL AND BEYOND

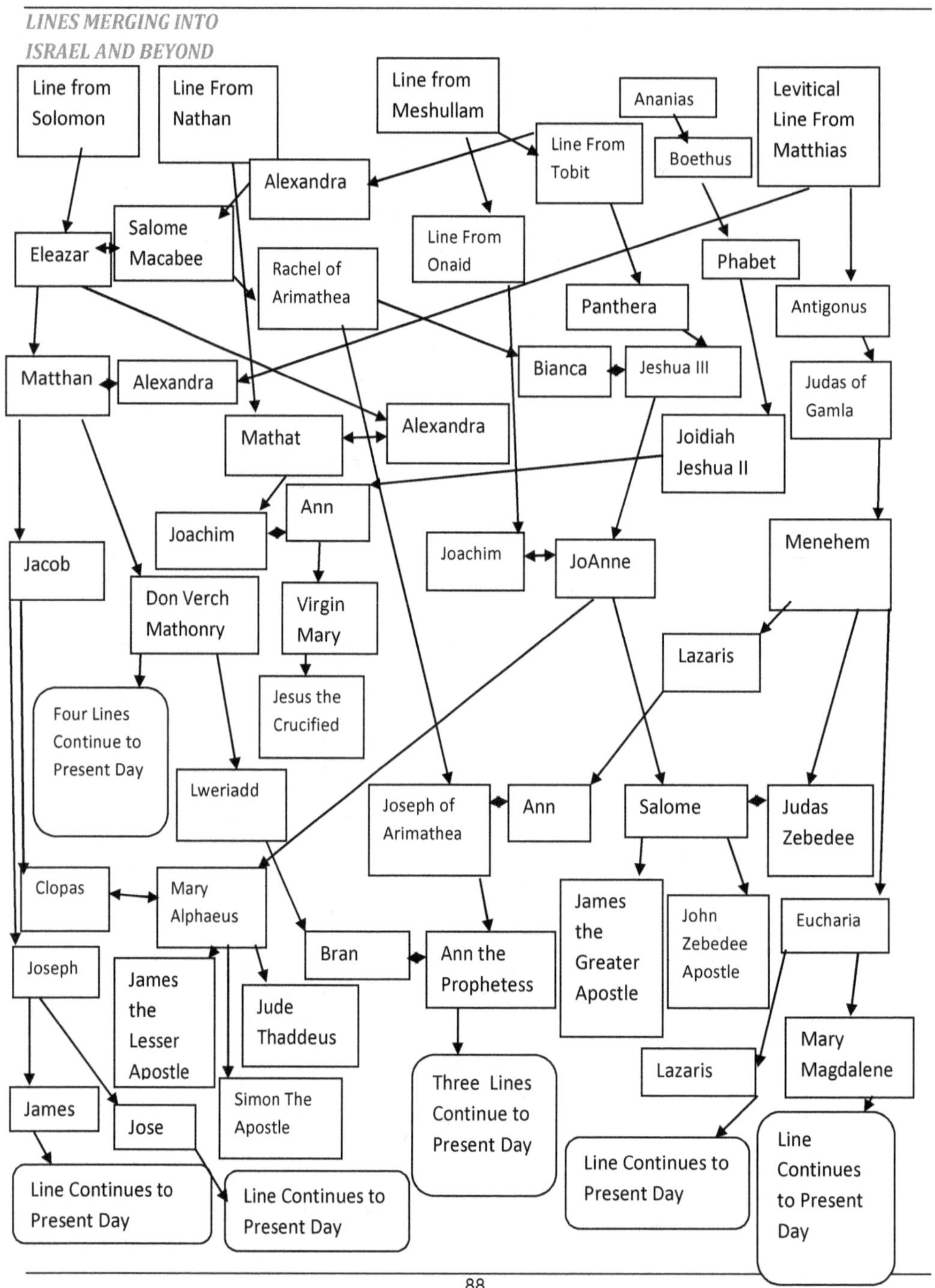

DAVIDIC AND LEVITICAL LINES

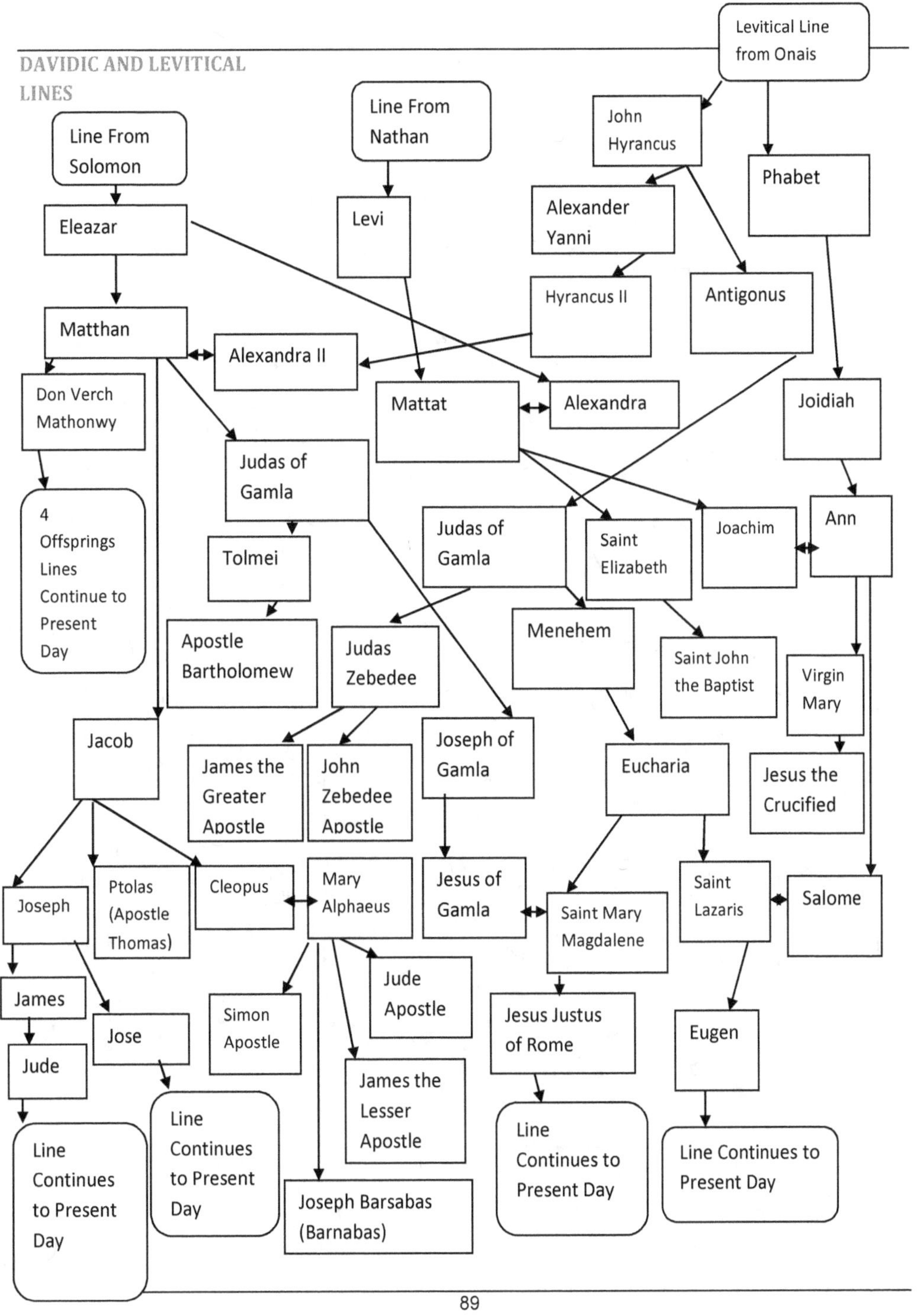

CHART THE LINES

These lines show the major line that are from the Judah and the Levi lines. Note that most of the lines are not Davidic.

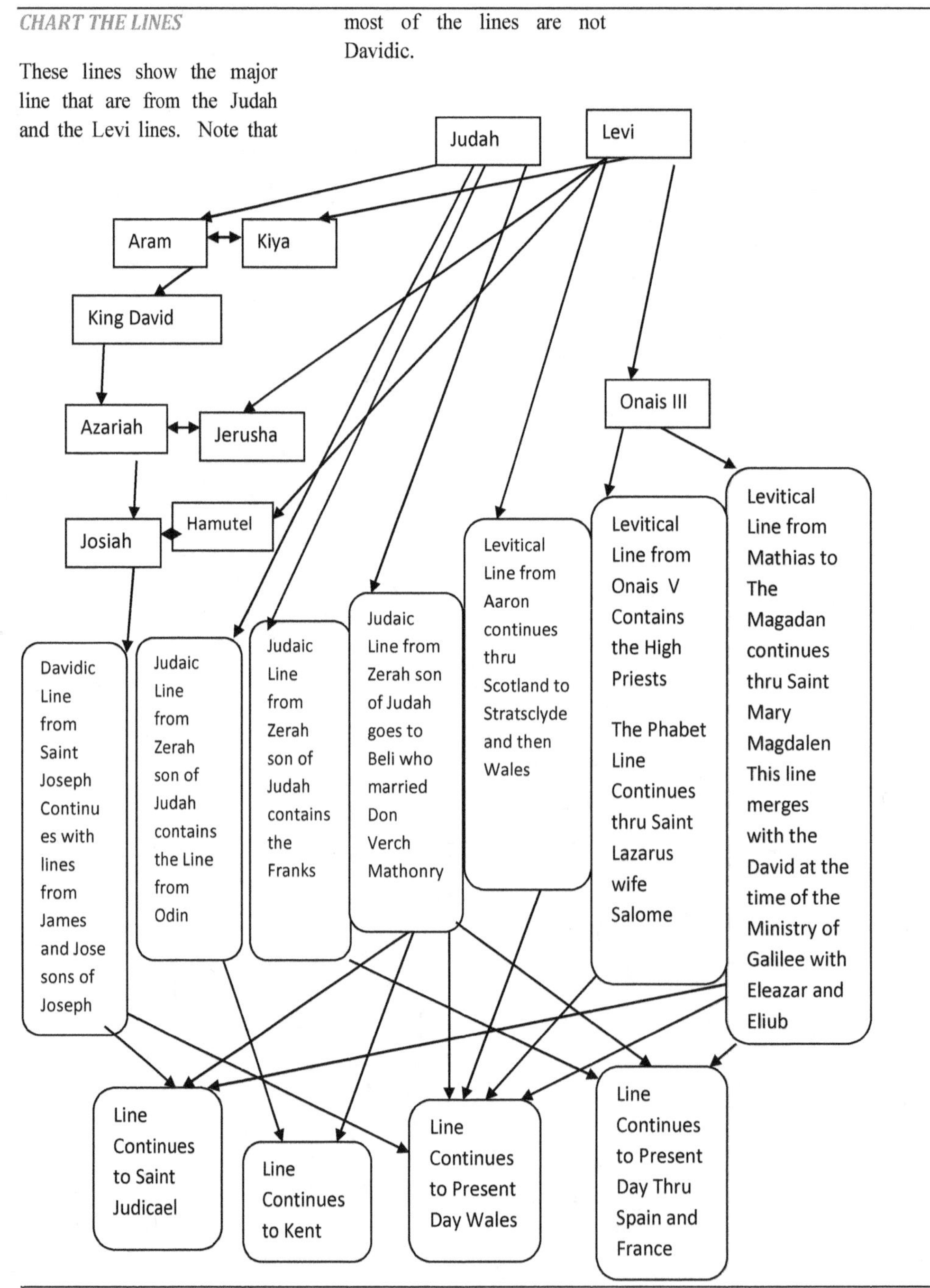

THE APOSTLES OF THE LORD OR

HOUSE OF POSTS

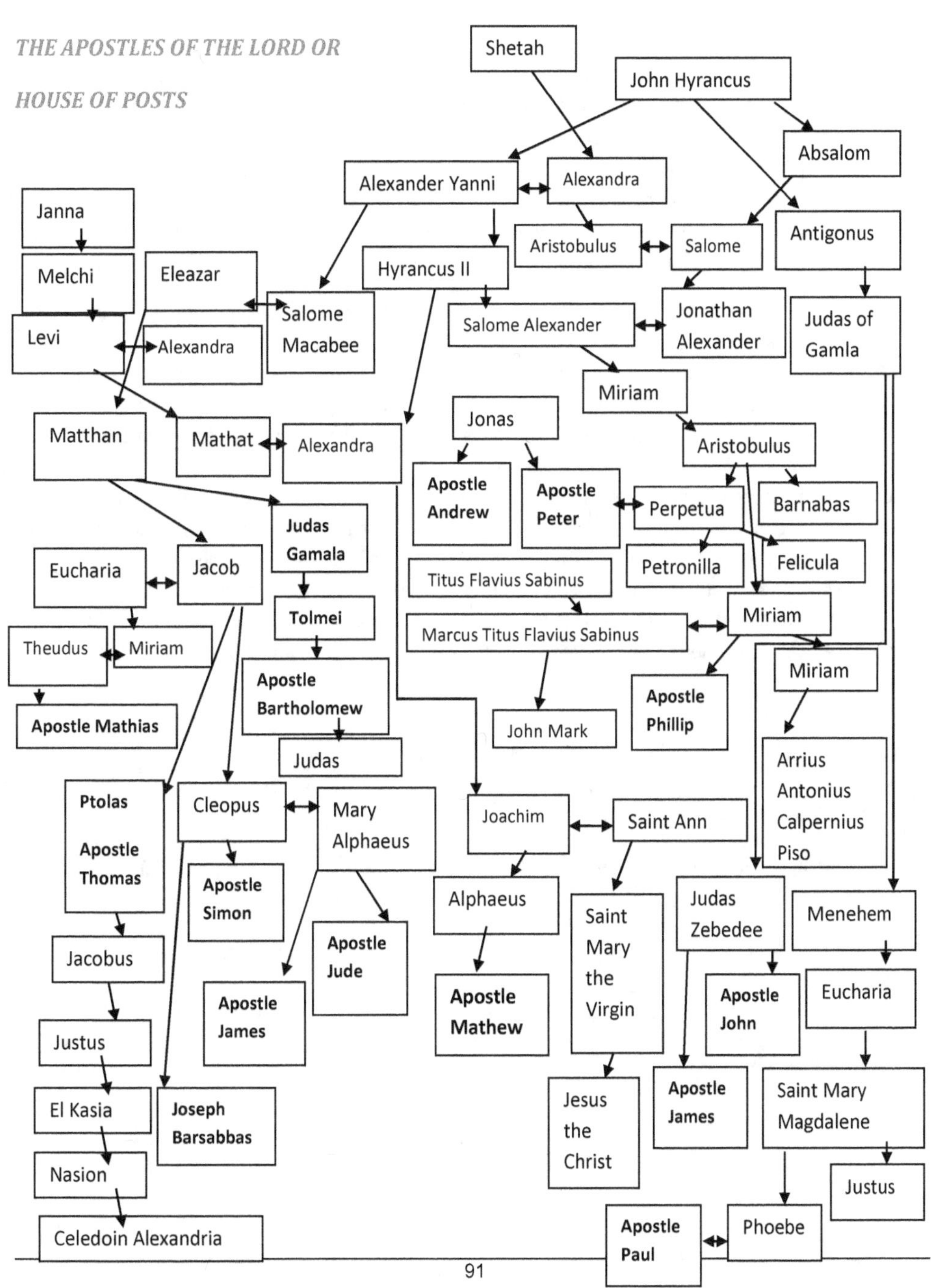

After the events in Galilee in 70 AD when the temple was torn down, the divine rule of the people of Israel was not solely done by the Aaronic Priest. The Priesthood of Aaron was not dissolved or done away with, but the strong Roman Emperors made the lives of the early followers of Christianity difficult. Many Christians were made martyrs and many emperors where given the credit for their punishment, because Christianity was considered a religion against the laws of the Roman State. This continued until Constantine the Emperor of Rome allowed Christianity to exist. Politically it was the parties opposed to the Emperor Julius Caesar and his descendents.

The early church had the early popes as the chair of Peter in Rome as one divine body. The Papacy has now existed for over 2000 years, but the first four hundred were the years when Christianity was persecuted. As well as the Papacy there existed in Jerusalem the Holy Bishops, primarily from the house of Joseph, with the exception of a desendent of Cleopas. So the Jews that did not embrace Chrisitianity were ruled by the Aaronic Priesthood of the high priest of the house of Cohen with the High Priest with the title Gadol. The Roman Church in Italy was ruled by the Pope, and the Church in Jerusalem was ruled by the Descendents of Joseph of the House of David. There existed many books and writings refered to by the sacred canon (the bible, a collection of the books made sacred by Saint Ireaneas) that had teachings and writings not easily understood by people not acquainted with the laws of Judism or the teaching of the Lord. Many scholars today would argue that the present religion of Christianity was made acceptable by stressing certain things about Christianity and suppressing others. Many of these writing exist today and are studied in divinity schools as well as available in book stores and to the public in countries where basic freedoms exist.

Following is the list of the Jerusalem High Priest, a List of the early Popes, and a quote taken from the Antiquities of the Jews relating the Aaronic High Priest to a graphic representation more readily understood by readers used to charts to show relationships rather than just lists of names. `

The priest succession of the Jerusalem may be a list of the descent of the Saint Joseph. Here is listed the first thirty seven and their lineage to Saint Joseph.

Secrets here are the first sixteen Bishops of Jerusalem.

Order of Bishop of Jerusalem	Years of Reign	Bishop of Jerusalem	1st Generation Ancestor	2nd Generation Ancestor	3rd Generation Ancestor	4th Generation Ancestor	5th Generation Ancestor
1st	c. 62	**Saint James the Just**	Saint Joseph				
2nd	c. 70-99	**Simeon**	Cleopas				
3rd	99-111	**Justus I (Jude)**	Saint James the Just	Saint Joseph			
4th	111-117	**Zacchaeus**	Simon	Saint Joseph			
5th	111-117	**Tobias**	Zakkai	Simon	Saint Joseph		
6th	111-117	**Benjamin**	John	Saint James the Just	Saint Joseph		
7th	117-134	**John**	Benjamin	John	Saint James the Just	Saint Joseph	
8th	117-134	**Mathias**	Zakkai	Simon	Saint Joseph		
9th	117-134	**Phillip**	Mathias	Zakkai	Simon	Saint Joseph	
10th	117-134	**Seneca**	Mathias	Zakkai	Simon	Saint Joseph	
11th	117-134	**Justus**	Mathias	Zakkai	Simon	Saint Joseph	
12th	117-134	**Levi**	Benjamin	John	Saint James the Just	Saint Joseph	
13th	117-134	**Ephres**	Zakkai	Simon	Saint Joseph		
14th	117-134	**Joseph**	Seneca	Mathias	Zakkai	Simon	Saint Joseph
15th	117-134	**Jude**	Benjamin	John	James the Just	Saint Joseph	

16th	134-162	**Mark**	Unknown Son	Josue El Harami	Joseph Ha Rama Theo	Saint Joseph	
17th	?-?	**Cassianus**	Joseph the 14th Bishop				
19th	?-?	**Maximanius**	Pope Pius the first	Jude 15th Bishop			
21th	?-?	**Gaius**	Son	Dioscorus	3 Generations of Unknown	Mark the 16th Bishop	
22nd	?-?	**Simmahos**	Gaius 21st Bishop				
23rd	?-162	**Gaius II**	Simmahos 22nd Bishop				
29th	?-185	**Dolihanus**	Cassianus 17th Bishop				
34th	231-249	**Alexander**	Dolihanus	Cassianus 17th Bishop			
35th	249-260	**Mazabanes**	Demetrius	Alexander 34th Bishop			
36th	260-276	**Hymanaeus**	Mazabanes the 35th Bishop				
37th	276-283	**Zabdas**	Paul	Theotecnus	Aslipiades	Maximanius 19th Bishop	

Please note that all of these Bishops are descended from Saint Joseph the Foster Father of Jesus the "Christ" except Simeon who is descended from Saint Joseph's brother Cleopus.

1) Marcus (135–???)
2) Cassianus (???–???)
3) Poplius (???–???)
4) Maximus I (???–???)
5) Julian I (???–???)
6) Gaius I (???–???)
7) Symmachus (???)
8) Gaius II (???–162)
9) Julian II (162–???)
10) Capion (???–???)
11) Maximus II (???–???)
12) Antoninus (???–???)
13) Valens (???–???)
14) Dolichianus (???–185)
15) Narcissus (185–???)
16) Dius (???–???)
17) Germanion (???–???)
18) Gordius (???–211)
    a. Narcissus (restored) (???–231)
19) Alexander (231–249)
20) Mazabanis (249–260)
21) Imeneus (260–276)
22) Zamudas (276–283)
23) Ermon (283–314)

24) Macarius I (314–333), since 325 Bishop of Jerusalem
25) Macarius I (325–333)
26) Maximus III (333–348)
27) Cyril I (350–386)
28) John II (386–417)
29) Praulius (417–422)
30) Juvenal (422–458), since 451 Patriarch
31) Juvenal (451–458)
32) Anastasius I (458–478)
33) Martyrius (478–486)
34) Sallustius (486–494)
35) Elias I (494–516)
36) John III (516–524)
37) Peter (524–552)
38) Macarius II (552, 564–575)
39) Eustochius (552–564)
40) John IV (575–594)
41) Amos (594–601)
42) Isaac (601–609)
43) Zacharias (609–632)
44) Modestus (632–634)
45) Sophronius I (634–638)
    a. *vacant* (638–???)
46) Anastasius II (???–706)
47) John V (706–735)
48) Theodore (745–770)
49) Elias II (770–797)
50) George (797–807)
51) Thomas I (807–820)
52) Basileus (820–838)
53) John VI (838–842)
54) Sergius I (842–844)
    a. *vacant* (844–855)
55) Solomon (855–860)
    a. *vacant* (860–862)
56) Theodosius (862–878)
57) Elias III (878–907)
58) Sergius II (908–911)
59) Leontius I (912–929)
60) Athanasius I (929–937)
61) Christodolus (937–950)
62) Agathon (950–964)
63) John VII (964–966)
64) Christodolus II (966–969)
65) Thomas II (969–978)
    a. *vacant* (978–980)
66) Joseph II (980–983)
67) Orestes (983–1005)
    a. *vacant* (1005–1012)
68) Theophilus I (1012–1020)
69) Nicephorus I (1020–???)
70) Joannichius (???–???)
71) Sophronius II (???–1084)
72) Euthemius I (1084)
73) Simon II (1084–1106)
74) Dositheos I (1190–1191)
75) Marcus II (1191–???)
    a. *vacant* (???–1223)
76) Euthemius II (1223)
77) Athanasius II (1224–1236)
78) Sophronius III (1236–???)
79) Gregory I (???–1298)
80) Thaddaeus (1298)
    a. *vacant* (1298–1313)
81) Athanasius III (1313–1314)
    a. *vacant* (1314–1322)
82) Gregory II (1322)
    a. *vacant* (1322–1334)
83) Lazarus (1334–1368)
    a. *vacant* (1368–1376)
84) Dorotheus I (1376–1417)
85) Theophilus II (1417–1424)
86) Theophanes I (1424–1431)
87) Joachim (1431–???)
    a. *vacant* (???–1450)
88) Theophanes II (1450)
    a. *vacant* (1450–1452)
89) Athanasius IV (1452–???)
    a. *vacant* (???–1460)
90) Jacob II (1460)
    a. *vacant* (1460–1468)
91) Abraham I (1468)
92) Gregory III (1468–1493)
    a. *vacant* (1493–1503)
93) Marcus III (1503)
    a. *vacant* (1503–1505)
94) Dorotheus II (1505–1537)
95) Germanus (1537–1579)

96) Sophronius IV (1579–1608)
97) Theophanes III (1608–1644)
98) Paiseus (1645–1660)
99) Nectarius I (1660–1669)
100) Dositheos II (1669–1707)
101) Chrysanthus (1707–1731)
102) Meletius (1731–1737)
103) Parthenius (1737–1766)
104) Ephram II (1766–1771)
105) Sophronius V (1771–1775)
106) Abraham II (1775–1787)
107) Procopius I (1787–1788)
108) Anthemus (1788–1808)
109) Polycarpus (1808–1827)
110) Athanasius V (1827–1845)
111) Cyril II (1845–1872)
112) Procopius II (1872–1875)
113) Jerotheus (1875–1882)
114) Nicodemus I (1883–1890)
115) Gerasimus I (1891–1897)
116) Damianus I (1897–1931)
117) Timotheus I (1935–1955)
    a. *vacant* (1955–1957)
118) Benedict I (1957–1980)
119) Diodoros I (1981–2000)
120) Irenaios I (2001–2005)
121) Theophilos III (2005–Present)

Mathias

Simon Thassi

John Hyrancus

Janna

Eliub

Alexander Yanni

Alexandra

Antigonus

Eleazar

Hyrancus II

Aristobulus II

Judas of Gamala

Mathan

Alexandra

Jonathan Alexander

Menehem

Jacob

Don Verch Mathonry

Mariame

Eucharia

Saint Mary Magdalene

Saint Joseph

Cleopus

Lweriadd

Aristobulus IV

James The First Bishop of Jerusalem

Apostle James the Lesser

Bran

Perpetua

Saint Peter 1st Pope

Justus

Joseph

John

Jude

Saint Felicula

John of Emesa

Benjamin

Pope Evaristus 5th Pope

Saint Petronilla

Jude

Eurgen

Saint Linus 2nd Pope

Pope **Saint Anicetus 11th Pope**

Pope Hyginus 9th Pope

Pope Pius the First 10th Pope

Saint Pastor

Saint Cyllin or Cletus 3rd Pope

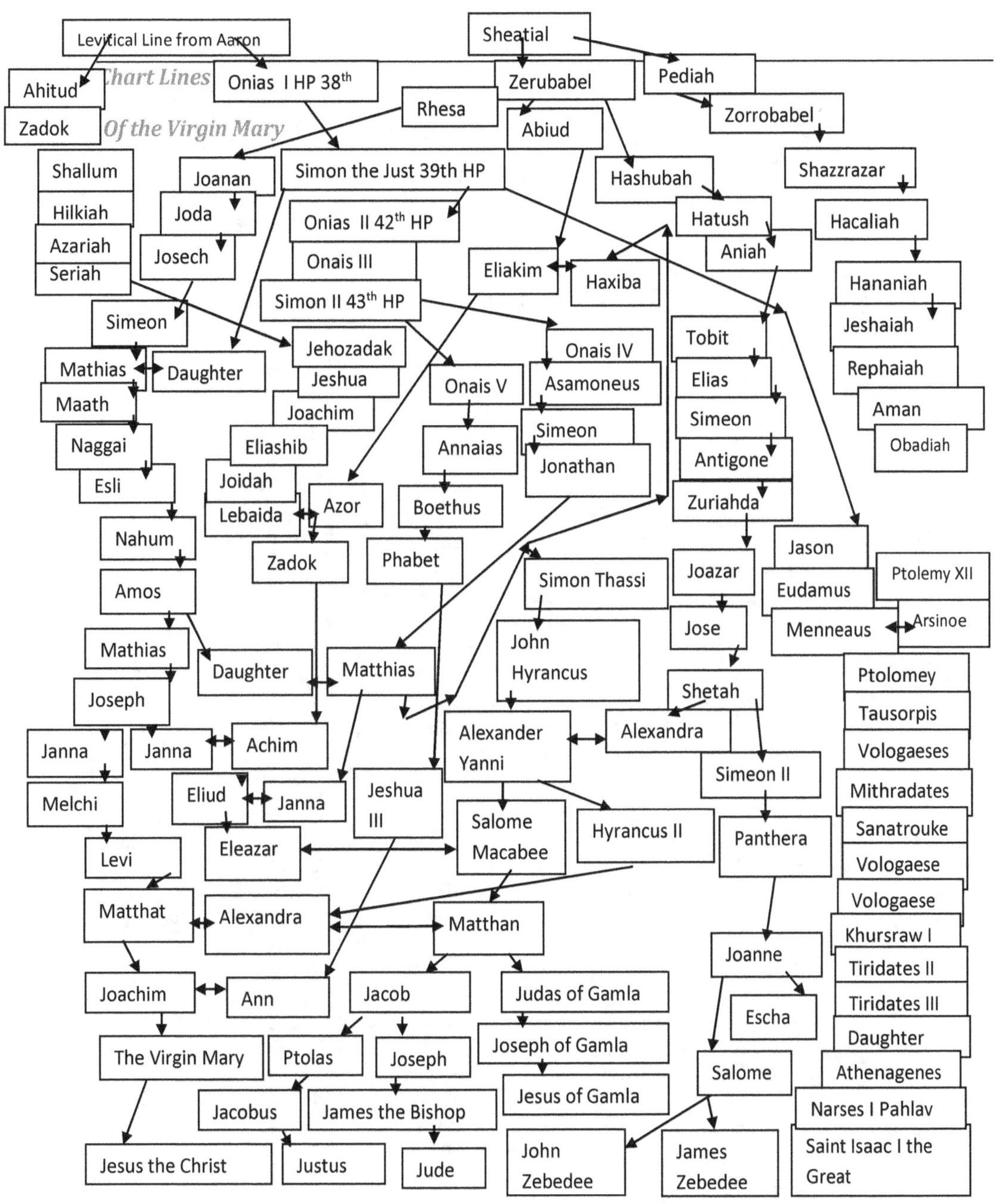

Levitical Line from Aaron
Chart Lines
Of the Virgin Mary
Ahitud
Zadok
Onias I HP 38th
Sheatial
Zerubabel
Pediah
Zorrobabel
Rhesa
Abiud
Shallum
Hilkiah
Azariah
Seriah
Joanan
Joda
Josech
Simon the Just 39th HP
Onias II 42th HP
Onais III
Simon II 43th HP
Hashubah
Hatush
Aniah
Shazzrazar
Hacaliah
Hananiah
Jeshaiah
Rephaiah
Aman
Obadiah
Eliakim
Haxiba
Simeon
Mathias
Daughter
Jehozadak
Jeshua
Joachim
Onais IV
Asamoneus
Onais V
Tobit
Elias
Simeon
Antigone
Zuriahda
Maath
Naggai
Esli
Eliashib
Joidah
Lebaida
Azor
Annaias
Simeon
Jonathan
Boethus
Nahum
Amos
Zadok
Phabet
Simon Thassi
Joazar
Jason
Eudamus
Ptolemy XII
Menneaus
Arsinoe
Jose
Mathias
Daughter
Matthias
John Hyrancus
Shetah
Ptolomey
Tausorpis
Vologaeses
Joseph
Janna
Janna
Achim
Alexander Yanni
Alexandra
Simeon II
Mithradates
Sanatrouke
Vologaese
Vologaese
Melchi
Eliud
Janna
Jeshua III
Salome Macabee
Hyrancus II
Panthera
Levi
Eleazar
Matthat
Alexandra
Matthan
Khursraw I
Tiridates II
Tiridates III
Daughter
Joanne
Escha
Joachim
Ann
Jacob
Judas of Gamla
Joseph of Gamla
The Virgin Mary
Ptolas
Joseph
Salome
Athenagenes
Jacobus
James the Bishop
Jesus of Gamla
Narses I Pahlav
Jesus the Christ
Justus
Jude
John Zebedee
James Zebedee
Saint Isaac I the Great

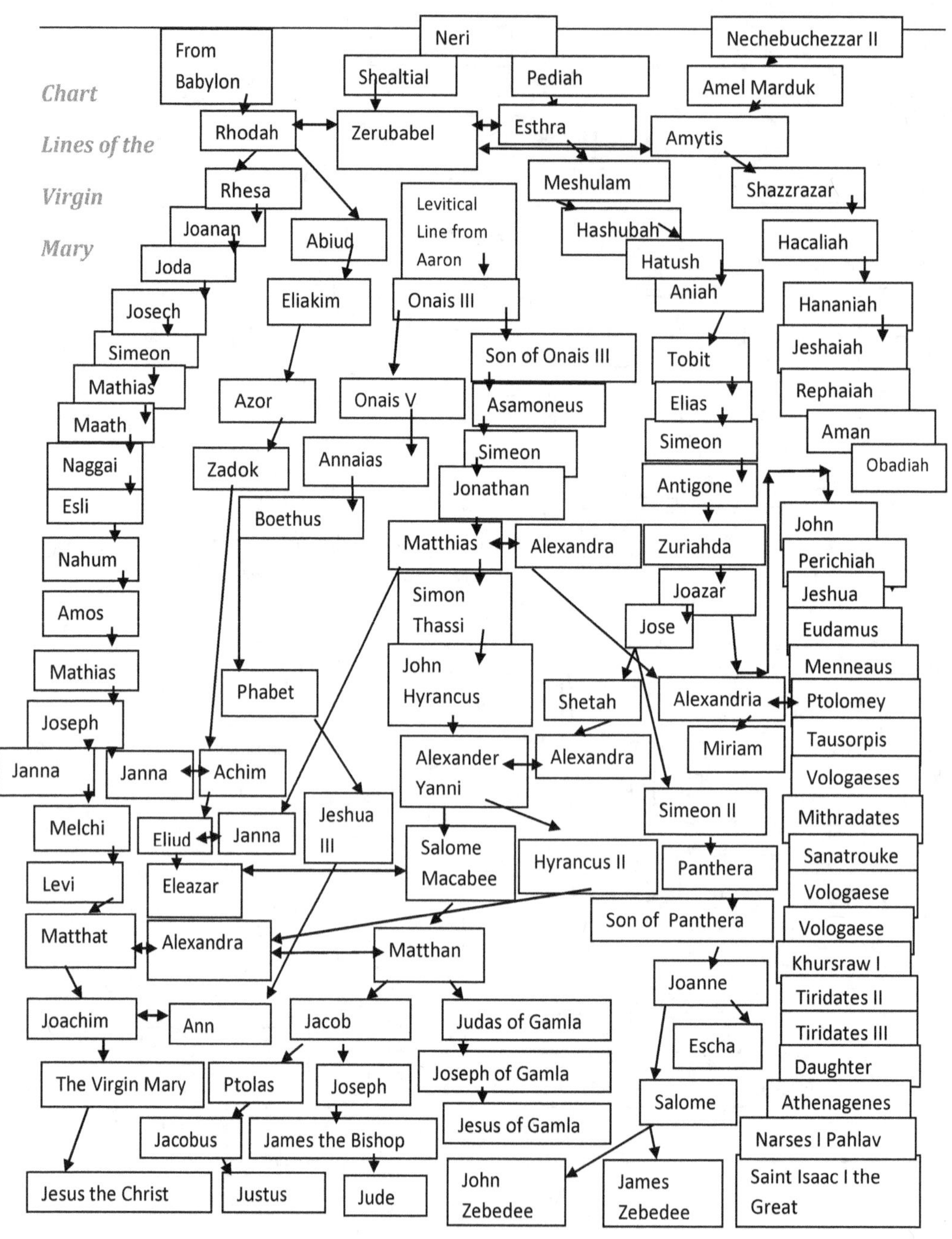
Chart
Lines of the
Virgin
Mary
From Babylon
Neri
Nechebuchezzar II
Shealtial
Pediah
Amel Marduk
Rhodah
Zerubabel
Esthra
Amytis
Rhesa
Meshulam
Shazzrazar
Joanan
Abiud
Levitical Line from Aaron
Hashubah
Hacaliah
Joda
Hatush
Josech
Eliakim
Onais III
Aniah
Hananiah
Simeon
Son of Onais III
Tobit
Jeshaiah
Mathias
Azor
Onais V
Asamoneus
Elias
Rephaiah
Maath
Simeon
Aman
Naggai
Zadok
Annaias
Simeon
Obadiah
Jonathan
Antigone
Esli
Boethus
John
Nahum
Matthias
Alexandra
Zuriahda
Perichiah
Simon Thassi
Joazar
Jeshua
Amos
Jose
Eudamus
John Hyrancus
Menneaus
Mathias
Phabet
Shetah
Alexandria
Ptolomey
Joseph
Miriam
Tausorpis
Janna
Janna
Achim
Alexander Yanni
Alexandra
Vologaeses
Jeshua III
Simeon II
Mithradates
Melchi
Eliud
Janna
Salome Macabee
Hyrancus II
Panthera
Sanatrouke
Levi
Eleazar
Vologaese
Son of Panthera
Vologaese
Matthat
Alexandra
Matthan
Khursraw I
Joanne
Tiridates II
Joachim
Ann
Jacob
Judas of Gamla
Escha
Tiridates III
Daughter
The Virgin Mary
Ptolas
Joseph
Joseph of Gamla
Salome
Athenagenes
Jacobus
James the Bishop
Jesus of Gamla
Narses I Pahlav
Jesus the Christ
Justus
Jude
John Zebedee
James Zebedee
Saint Isaac I the Great

ERA OF THE TIME OF ABRAHAM TO DAVID, THEN THE TIME OF DAVID TO BABYLON, THEN THE TIME OF BABYLON TO THE ERA OF CHRISTIANITY

SECTION SIX: THE AARONIC HIGH PRIEST

THE AARONIC PRIEST

Following is the knowledge of the Aaronic Priest, extremely important to the people with the God belief. The God belief of the Hebrew predates many of the ideas of the Roman, The Greek, and the Knight.

There were 84 High Priests of Aaron that were related to the line of Aaron. This office was held high in honor for the entire nation. It was Eli who was involved in the formation of the King of Israel and Judah thru the son Samuel. All of the 84 High Priests were of the blood of Aaron. One, Alcimus, was not of the Priest line however although he was a son of Aaron. The lines of the Aaronic priest were made so that a son would succeed his father, however sometimes a priest of Aaron did not have a son, so the line would continue thru another descendent of Aaron. Thus in the succession of the Priest there are ancestors who are the Priest Line that did not hold the office of the High Priest however their descendent did.

THE HIGH PREIST OF ISRAEL

The high priest of Israel was not known by the Romans at the time of the Ministry of the Lord. This was obviously an advantage of the Jews. In the book, The Antiquities of the Jews written by a Jew who became a Roman, in Book 20, Chapter 10 Verse 1(224). " And now I think it Proper and agreeabel to this history, to give an account of our high priests; how they began, who those are which are capable of that dignity, and how many of them there had been at the end of the war. In the first place, therefore, history informs us that Aaron, the brother of Moses, officiated to God as a high priest; and that, after his death, his sons succeeded him immediately; and that this dignity hath been continued down from them all to their posterity. " The quote goes on and is very interesting, noting a high priest in office until the last high priest. It further says there were twenty eight from the "days of Herod until Titus took the temple and the city and burnt them" (Book 20 Chapter 10 Verse (250))

In a footnote in the Translation of William Whiston A.M. of The Antiquities of the Jews there is a list of the High Priest. Here is the list.

1) Ananelus
2) Aristobulus
3) Jesus the son of Fabus
4) Simon the Son of Boethus
5) Matthias the son of Teophilus
6) Joazar, the son of Boethus
7) Eleazar the son of Boethus
8) Jesus the son of Sic
9) Ananus the son of Seth

10) Ismael the son of Fabus

11) Eleazar the sonof Annanus

12) Simon, the son of Camithus

13) Josephus Caiaphas, the son in law to Ananus

14) Jonathan the son of Ananus

15) Theophilus his brother and son of Ananus

16) Simon the son of Camithus

17) Matthias, the brother of Jonathan and son of Ananus

18) Ajioneus

19) Josephus the son of Camydus

20) Ananias the son of Nebedeus

21) Jonathas

22) Ismael the son of Fabi

23) Joseph Cabi, the son of Simon

24) Ananus the son of Ananus

25) Jesus the son of Damneus

26) Jesus the son of Gamaliel

27) Matthias the son of Theophilus

28) Phannias the son of Samuel

As for Ananus and Joseph Caiaphas, here mentioned about the middle oftheis catalogue, they are no other than those Annas and Caiaphas so often mentioned in the Four Gospels; and that Ananias, the son of Nebedeus, was that high priest before whom St. Paul pleaded his own case,Acts 24.

Aaaronic High Priest

The following pages are a representation of the 84 High Priests of the Aaronic line that ruled Israel, with lineages, and family relationships. The charts show who served as High Priest, who did not, how some lines of High Priests did not continue.

There is a quote from the Antiquities of the Jews that shows the high priests as quoted there.

All 84 High Priests are in the charts, and following is a list of the Priests with a comment of their relationships to other High Priests. The Aaronic line continues past the fall of Jerusalem, however only to the high priest Phannias is shown.

1. Aaron son of Amram
2. Eleazar son of Aaron
3. Phinehas son of Eleazar
4. Abishua son of Phinehas
5. Bukki son of Abishua
6. Uzzi son of Bukki
7. Eli son on Itamar son of Aaron
8. Phineas son of Ili
9. Ahitub son of Phineas
10. Abijah son of Ahitub
11. Ahimelech son of Ahijah Reign of King Saul
12. Abaithar son of Ahimelech Reighn of King David and Early years of Solomon
13. Zadok son of Ahitub of the line of Uzzi
14. Ahimaaz son of Zadok
15. Azariah son of Ahimaaz
16. Joash son of Azariah
17. Jehoiarib son of Joash
18. Jehoshaphat son of Jehoirib
19. Jehoiada son of Jehoshaphat

20. Pediah son of Jehoida
21. Zedekiah son of Pediah
22. Azariah son of Zedikiah
23. Jotham son of Azariah
24. Urijah son of Jotham
25. Azariah III son of Johanan son of Azariah II
26. Hoshaiah son of Azariah III
27. Shallum son of Zadok of the line of Azariah III
28. Hilkiah son of Shallum
29. Azariah IV son of Hiliah
30. Seriah son of Azariah
31. Jehozadak son of Seriah
32. Joshua son of Jehozadak
33. Joiakim son of Joshua
34. Eliashib son of Joiakim
35. Joiada son of Eliashib
36. Johanan son of Joiada
37. Jaddua son of Johanan
38. Onias son of Jaddua
39. Simon the Just son of Onias
40. Eleazar son of Onias
41. Manasseh son of Jaddua
42. Onias II son of Simon the Just
43. Simon II son of Onias III
44. Onais III son of Simon II
45. Jason the first son of Simon the Just
46. Menelaus son of Simon the Just
47. Onais IV son of Onais III
48. Alcimus Not of the Priest Line However Aaronic
49. Jonathan Apphus son of Mattathis
50. Simon Thassi son of Mattahias
51. John Hyrancus son of Simon Thassi
52. Aritobulus I son of John Hyrancus
53. Alexander Yanni son of John Hyrancus
54. Hyrancus II son of Alexander Yanni
55. Aristobulus II son nof Alexander Yanni
56. Antigonus son of John Hyrancus
57. Aristobulus III son of Johnathan Alexander son of Aristobulus II
58. Ananelus son of Boethus
59. Jeshua III son of Phabet
60. Simon IV son of Boethus
61. Mathias son of Theophilus son of Annais son of Onais V
62. Joazar son of Boethus
63. Eleazar son of Boethus
64. Yeshua IV son of Sethus
65. Ananus son of Sic
66. Ishmael son of Phabi
67. Eleazar son of Ananus
68. Simon V son of Camydus
69. Caiahas son of Simon V
70. Jonathan II son of Ananus
71. Theophils son of Ananus
72. Kantheras Simon VI son of Boethus
73. Matthias son of Ananus
74. Elionius son of Kantheras
75. Josephus son of Camydus
76. Ananais son of Nebedus
77. Jonathan II son of Sethus
78. Ishmael son of Phabet
79. Joseph son of Simon son of Phabet
80. Ananus II son f Ananus
81. Jeshua V son of Damneus
82. Jeshua IV son of Gamaliel
83. Mathais III son of Theophilus
84. Phannais son of Samuel

HIGH PRIEST

OF ISRAEL

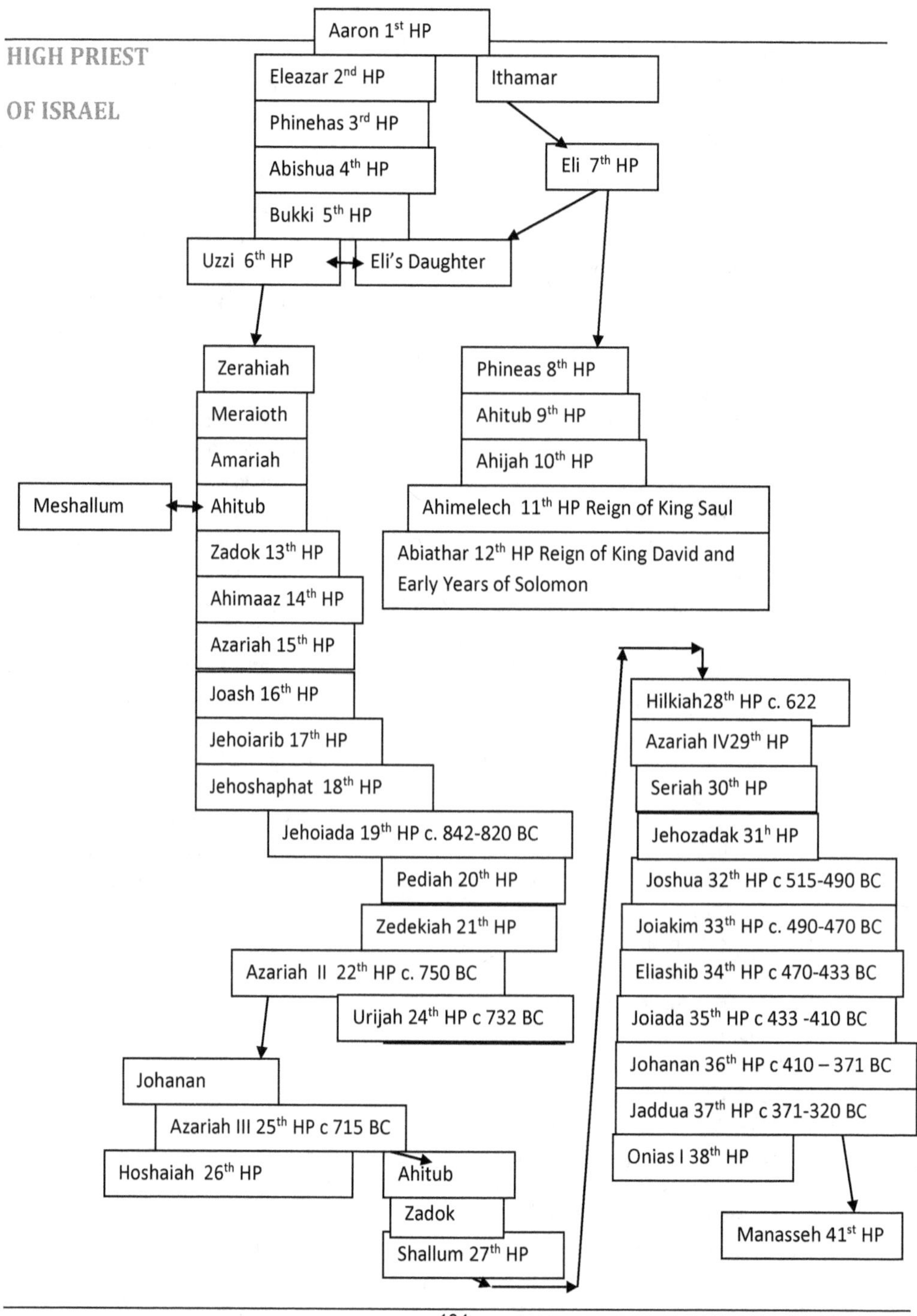

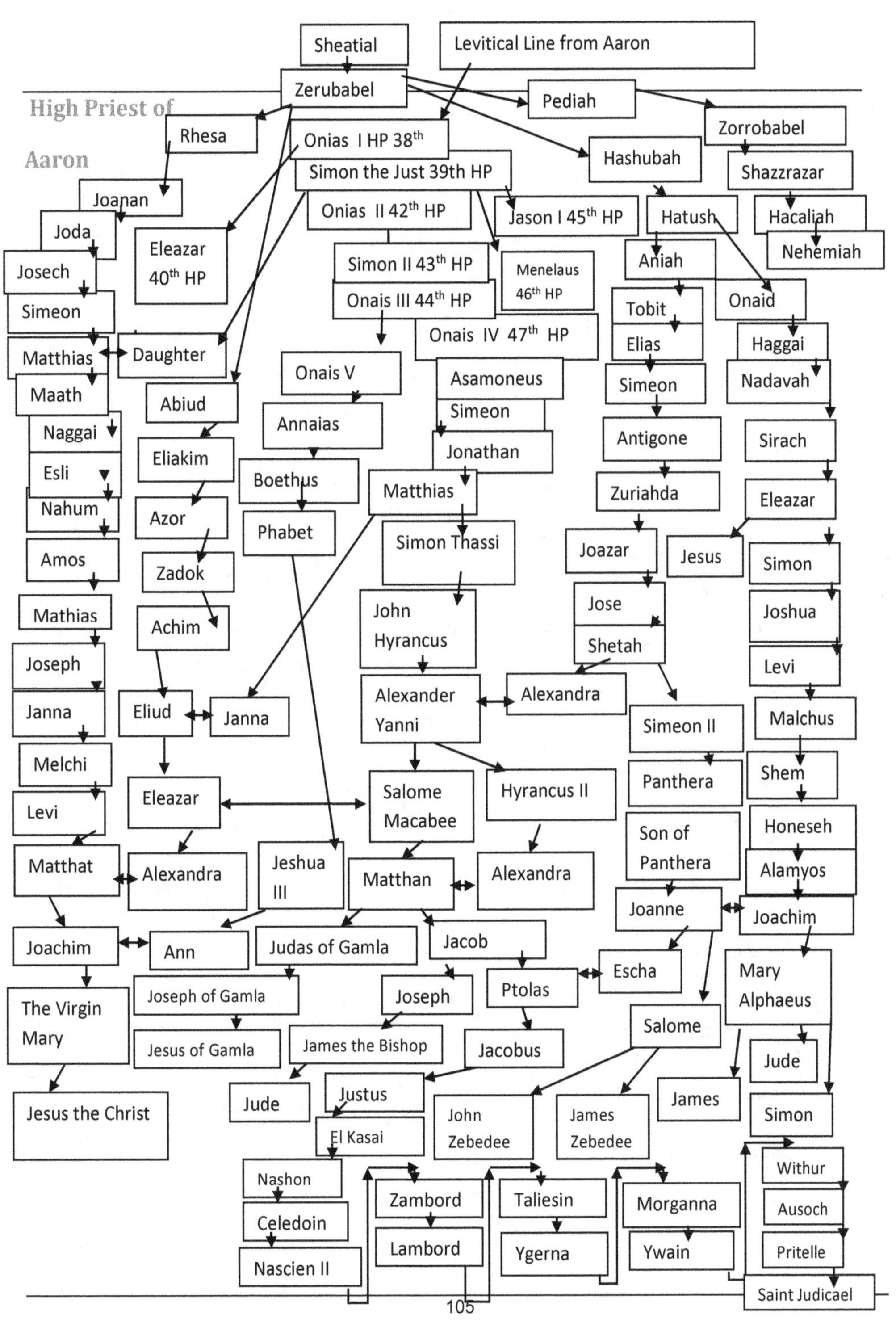
Sheatial
Levitical Line from Aaron
Zerubabel
Pediah
High Priest of Aaron
Rhesa
Onias I HP 38th
Zorrobabel
Hashubah
Simon the Just 39th HP
Shazzrazar
Joanan
Onias II 42th HP
Jason I 45th HP
Hatush
Hacaliah
Joda
Eleazar 40th HP
Nehemiah
Simon II 43th HP
Aniah
Josech
Menelaus 46th HP
Onais III 44th HP
Onaid
Simeon
Tobit
Onais IV 47th HP
Haggai
Elias
Matthias
Daughter
Onais V
Asamoneus
Nadavah
Maath
Simeon
Abiud
Simeon
Naggai
Annaias
Antigone
Sirach
Eliakim
Jonathan
Esli
Boethus
Matthias
Zuriahda
Eleazar
Nahum
Azor
Phabet
Simon Thassi
Joazar
Jesus
Simon
Amos
Zadok
Jose
Joshua
Mathias
Achim
John Hyrancus
Shetah
Joseph
Levi
Alexander Yanni
Alexandra
Janna
Eliud
Janna
Simeon II
Malchus
Melchi
Panthera
Shem
Eleazar
Salome Macabee
Hyrancus II
Levi
Son of Panthera
Honeseh
Matthat
Jeshua III
Alexandra
Alamyos
Alexandra
Matthan
Joanne
Joachim
Joachim
Ann
Judas of Gamla
Jacob
Mary Alphaeus
Escha
Joseph of Gamla
Ptolas
The Virgin Mary
Joseph
Salome
James the Bishop
Jesus of Gamla
Jacobus
Jude
Jude
Justus
James
Jesus the Christ
John Zebedee
James Zebedee
Simon
El Kasai
Withur
Nashon
Zambord
Taliesin
Morganna
Ausoch
Celedoin
Lambord
Ygerna
Ywain
Pritelle
Nascien II
Saint Judicael

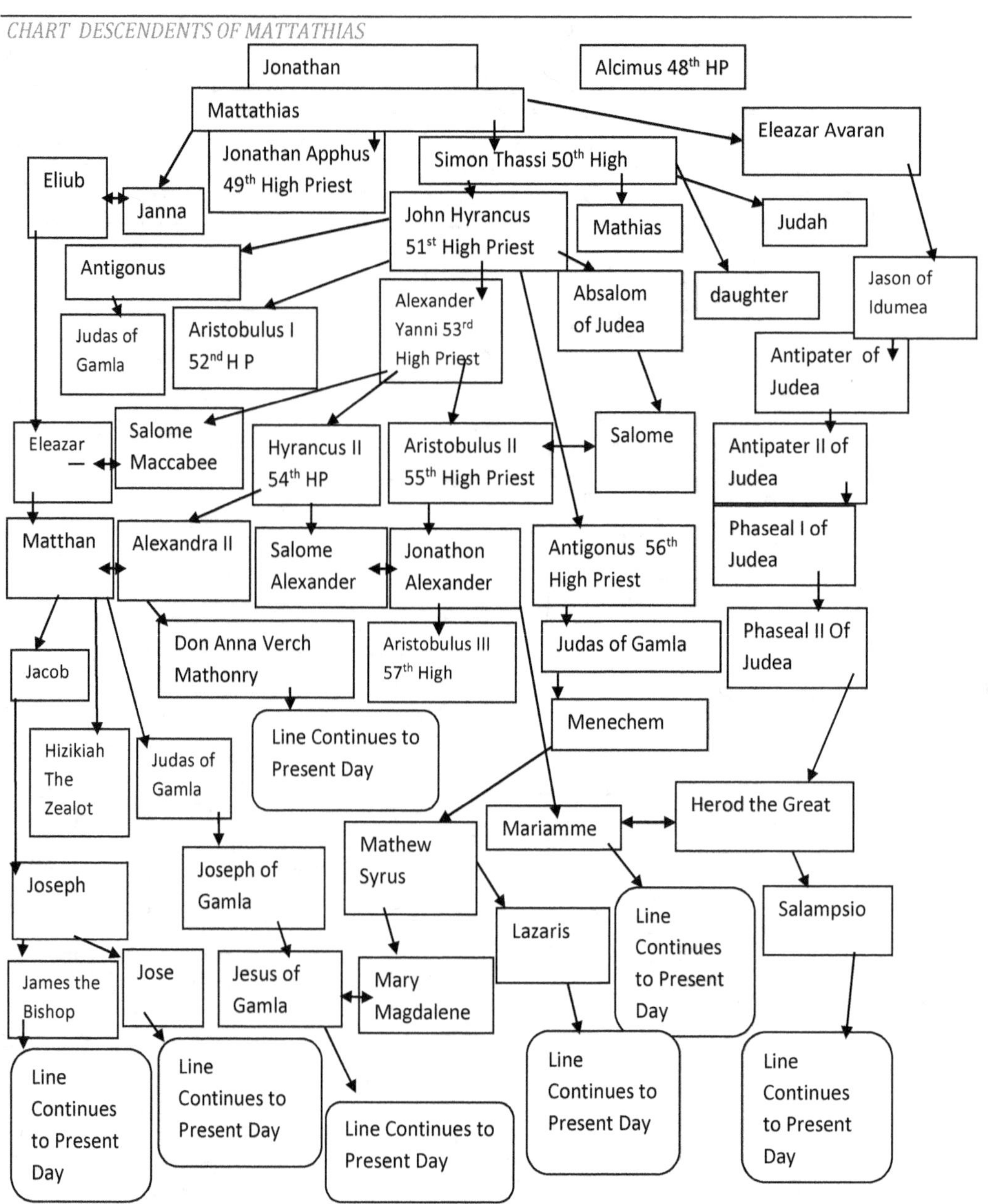
Jonathan
Alcimus 48th HP
Mattathias
Eleazar Avaran
Jonathan Apphus 49th High Priest
Simon Thassi 50th High
Eliub
Janna
John Hyrancus 51st High Priest
Mathias
Judah
Antigonus
Absalom of Judea
daughter
Jason of Idumea
Judas of Gamla
Aristobulus I 52nd H P
Alexander Yanni 53rd High Priest
Antipater of Judea
Eleazar
Salome Maccabee
Hyrancus II 54th HP
Aristobulus II 55th High Priest
Salome
Antipater II of Judea
Matthan
Alexandra II
Salome Alexander
Jonathon Alexander
Antigonus 56th High Priest
Phaseal I of Judea
Jacob
Don Anna Verch Mathonry
Aristobulus III 57th High
Judas of Gamla
Phaseal II Of Judea
Hizikiah The Zealot
Judas of Gamla
Line Continues to Present Day
Menechem
Herod the Great
Mariamme
Mathew Syrus
Joseph
Joseph of Gamla
Lazaris
Line Continues to Present Day
Salampsio
James the Bishop
Jose
Jesus of Gamla
Mary Magdalene
Line Continues to Present Day
Line Continues to Present Day
Line Continues to Present Day
Line Continues to Present Day
Line Continues to Present Day

HIGH PRIEST AND THE BETRAYER

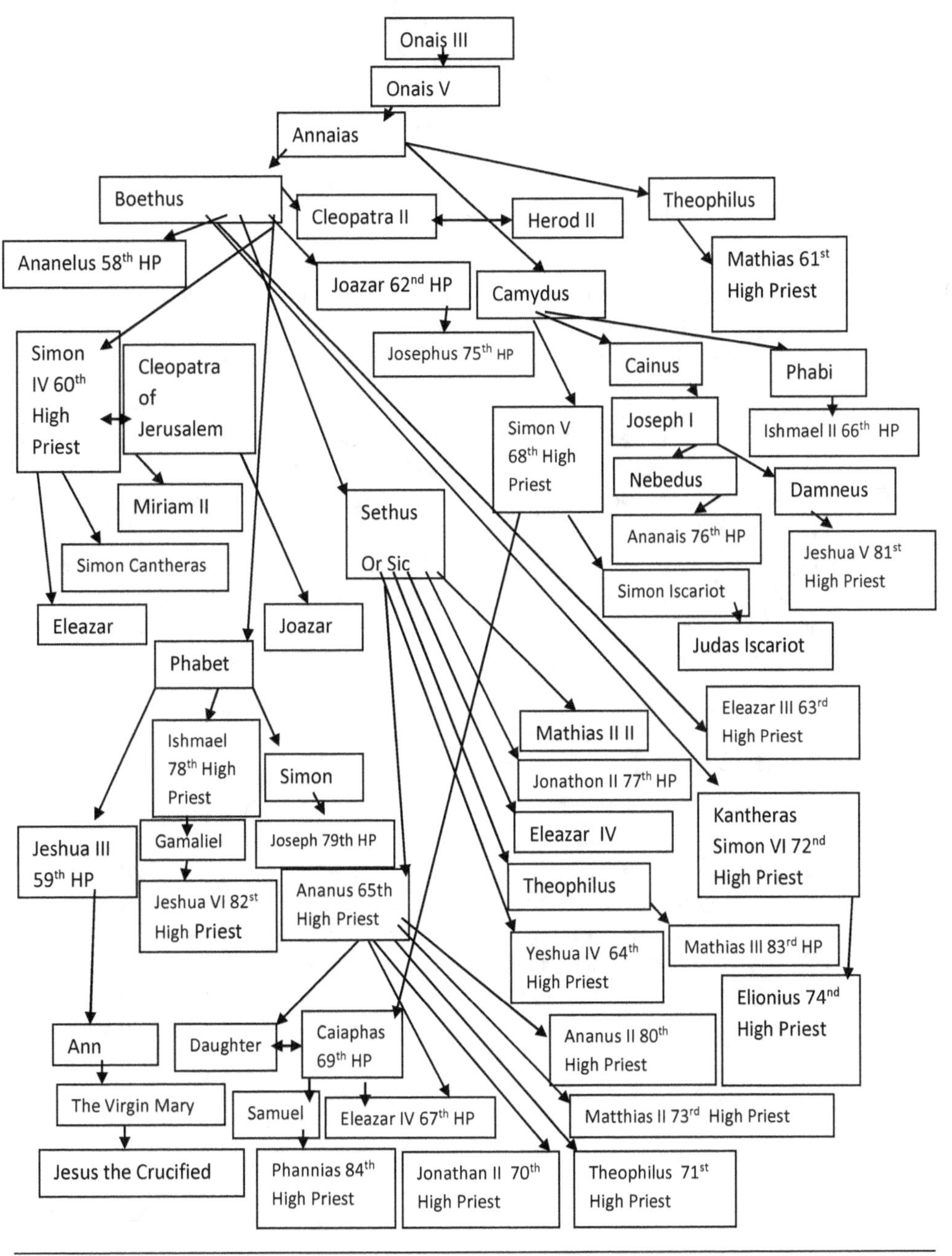

ERA OF CHRISTIANITY TO THE EARLY SAINTS, BEFORE 1000 AD.

SECTION SEVEN: CHRISTIAN SAINTS AND THEIR LINEAGES

ADDITIONAL SAINTS FROM EARLY CHRISTIANITY

The Gospel Writer Saint Mark

Mary the wife of Cleopas had a daughter Miriam. I have found in one genealogy that this Miriam is the mother of John Mark, who wrote the Gospel. We know that John Mark had a mother Mary and that he was a scribe and had communicated with Peter, who inspired the Gospel by the holy spirit.

Aristobulus the son of Miriame had a daughter Miriam. He also had Perpetua and Barnabas who also wrote a book. Aristobulus was the brother to Alexander, so both Aristobulus and Alexander were sons of Miriam or sons of Mary. Now Miriam the daughter of Arisobulus had a daughter Miriam, and a son John Mark. This is found in other genealogies. Now John Mark would have been the nephew of Barnabas, the son and brother of Mary. It is likely that Phillip the Apostle is also found as a brother of Miriam, the daughter of Miriam. This would make Phillip the son of Mary, the daughter of Mary, and the twin of Mary. Because Perpetua is the Aunt of John Mark, it can be reached by conclusion that this is found in the area of Bethsaida. Now Perpetua is the wife of Simon Peter, and so related as well to Andrew son of Jonas. All three Apostles Peter, Andrew, and Phillip were from Bethsaida.

Saint Mark did not leave any children, however Peter, did, and John Mark's mother did as well. John Mark's mother's line married into the Royal line of Emperor Julius Caesar, and so continued to this very day. Please see the charts found in this work.

Of course this is found in one genealogy and may not be correct, however it satisfies the authors curiosity about the lineage of the Apostles, and the relationships in Galilee. In any religious argument there are factions that approve and disprove this. I have only to claim that I found all this information on the internet, and I leave it to the reader to say if it is the truth, or just an attempt at the truth.

Feastday : December 17

Date: d 658

Family:

Parents: Father- Hoel III King of Bretons Mother- Pritelle

Wife: Morone

Children: Alain II High King of the Bretons

Ancestry:

Saint Judicael ancestors include Saint Patrick, Saint Cyllinus, Blessed Bran and Anna of Arimathea Anna of Armimathea's father is Saint Joseph of Arimathea and so the Line of Nathan Son of David King of Israel and Judah. King David's ancestors include the Israelites, Zebulon, Levi, Joseph, and Judah. Also Anna of Arimathea, daughter to Joseph of Aramathea married Bran the Blessed whose line goes to Tros and so to Epraim son of Joseph the Israelite. Also the line from Anna of Arimathea's mother goes thru Simon the Just thru many High Priests to Judah the Israelite.

Descendents:

Cadell ap Rhodri Mawr King of South Wale 861 – 910, Hywel Dda' ap Cadell Prince of Deheubarth
887 – 950, Owain ap Hywel Dda King of South Wales 913 – 987 and also King Edward IV Plantagenet of England.

Biography:

King in Amorica, in Brittany. Succeeded by his brother St. Judoc, he abdicated his throne. He spent twenty years as a monk at Gael Abbey. He assumed the title of King when his father died, prince of Domnonia. After abdicating, he became a monk, again resigned and lived in the monastery of Gael the last twenty years of his life.

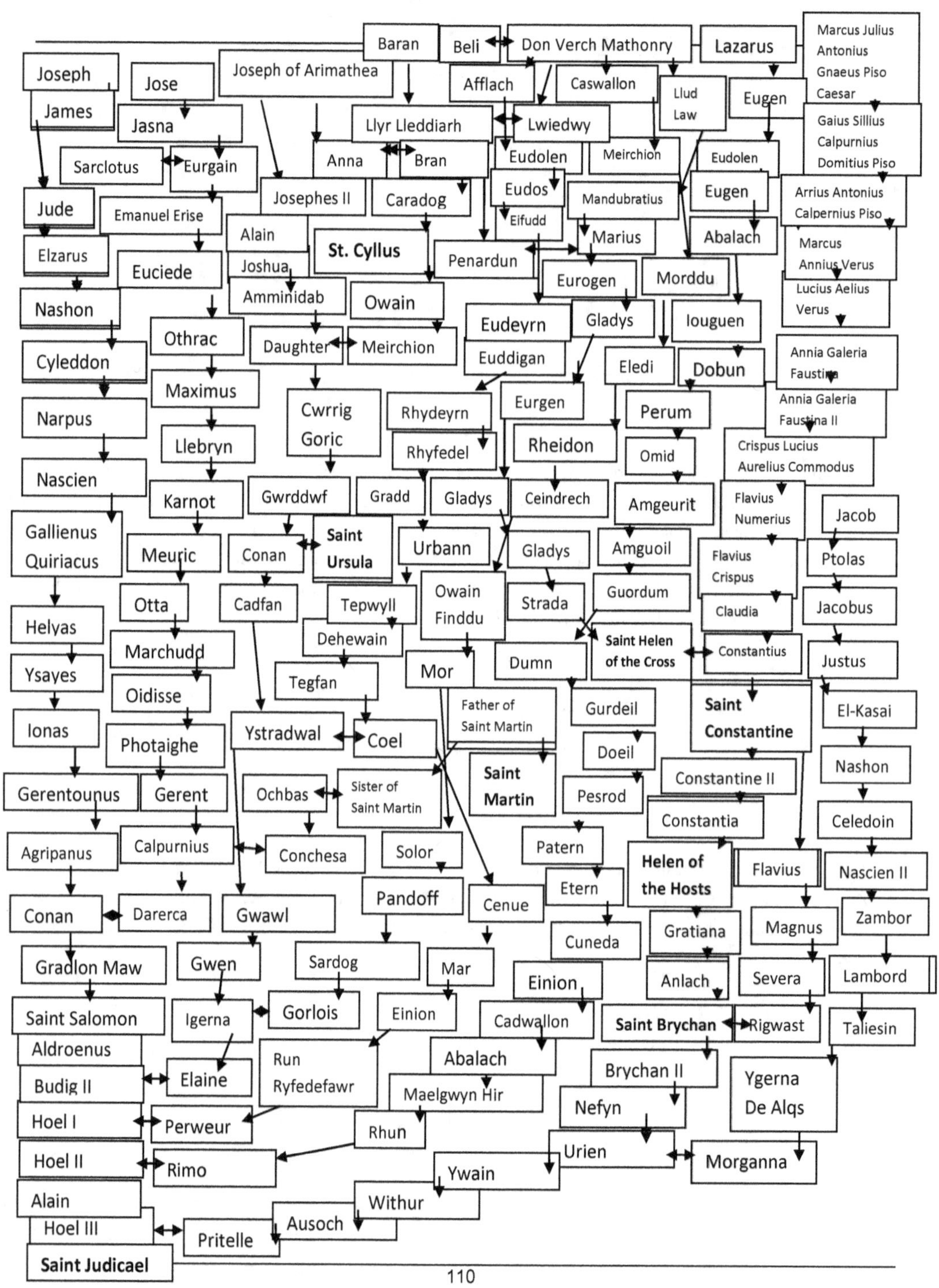

Baran
Beli
Don Verch Mathonry
Lazarus
Marcus Julius Antonius Gnaeus Piso Caesar
Joseph
Jose
Joseph of Arimathea
Afflach
Caswallon
Llud Law
Eugen
James
Jasna
Llyr Lleddiarh
Lwiedwy
Gaius Sillius Calpurnius Domitius Piso
Sarclotus
Eurgain
Anna
Bran
Eudolen
Meirchion
Eudolen
Jude
Emanuel Erise
Josephes II
Caradog
Eudos
Eifudd
Mandubratius
Eugen
Arrius Antonius Calpernius Piso
Elzarus
Alain
St. Cyllus
Marius
Abalach
Marcus Annius Verus
Euciede
Joshua
Penardun
Eurogen
Morddu
Nashon
Amminidab
Owain
Lucius Aelius Verus
Othrac
Eudeyrn
Gladys
Iouguen
Cyleddon
Daughter
Meirchion
Euddigan
Annia Galeria Faustina
Maximus
Eledi
Dobun
Annia Galeria Faustina II
Narpus
Cwrrig Goric
Rhydeyrn
Eurgen
Perum
Llebryn
Rhyfedel
Rheidon
Omid
Crispus Lucius Aurelius Commodus
Nascien
Karnot
Gwrddwf
Gradd
Gladys
Ceindrech
Ameurit
Flavius Numerius
Jacob
Gallienus Quiriacus
Meuric
Conan
Saint Ursula
Urbann
Gladys
Amguoil
Flavius Crispus
Ptolas
Otta
Cadfan
Tepwyll
Owain Finddu
Strada
Guordum
Claudia
Jacobus
Helyas
Marchudd
Dehewain
Saint Helen of the Cross
Constantius
Justus
Ysayes
Oidisse
Tegfan
Mor
Dumn
Ionas
Father of Saint Martin
Gurdeil
Saint Constantine
El-Kasai
Photaighe
Ystradwal
Coel
Doeil
Nashon
Gerentounus
Gerent
Ochbas
Sister of Saint Martin
Saint Martin
Pesrod
Constantine II
Celedoin
Agripanus
Calpurnius
Conchesa
Solor
Patern
Constantia
Helen of the Hosts
Flavius
Nascien II
Conan
Darerca
Gwawl
Pandoff
Cenue
Etern
Gratiana
Magnus
Zambor
Cuneda
Gradlon Maw
Gwen
Sardog
Mar
Einion
Anlach
Severa
Lambord
Saint Salomon
Igerna
Gorlois
Einion
Cadwallon
Saint Brychan
Rigwast
Taliesin
Aldroenus
Run Ryfedefawr
Abalach
Brychan II
Budig II
Elaine
Maelgwyn Hir
Ygerna De Alqs
Nefyn
Hoel I
Perweur
Rhun
Urien
Morganna
Hoel II
Rimo
Ywain
Alain
Withur
Hoel III
Ausoch
Pritelle
Saint Judicael

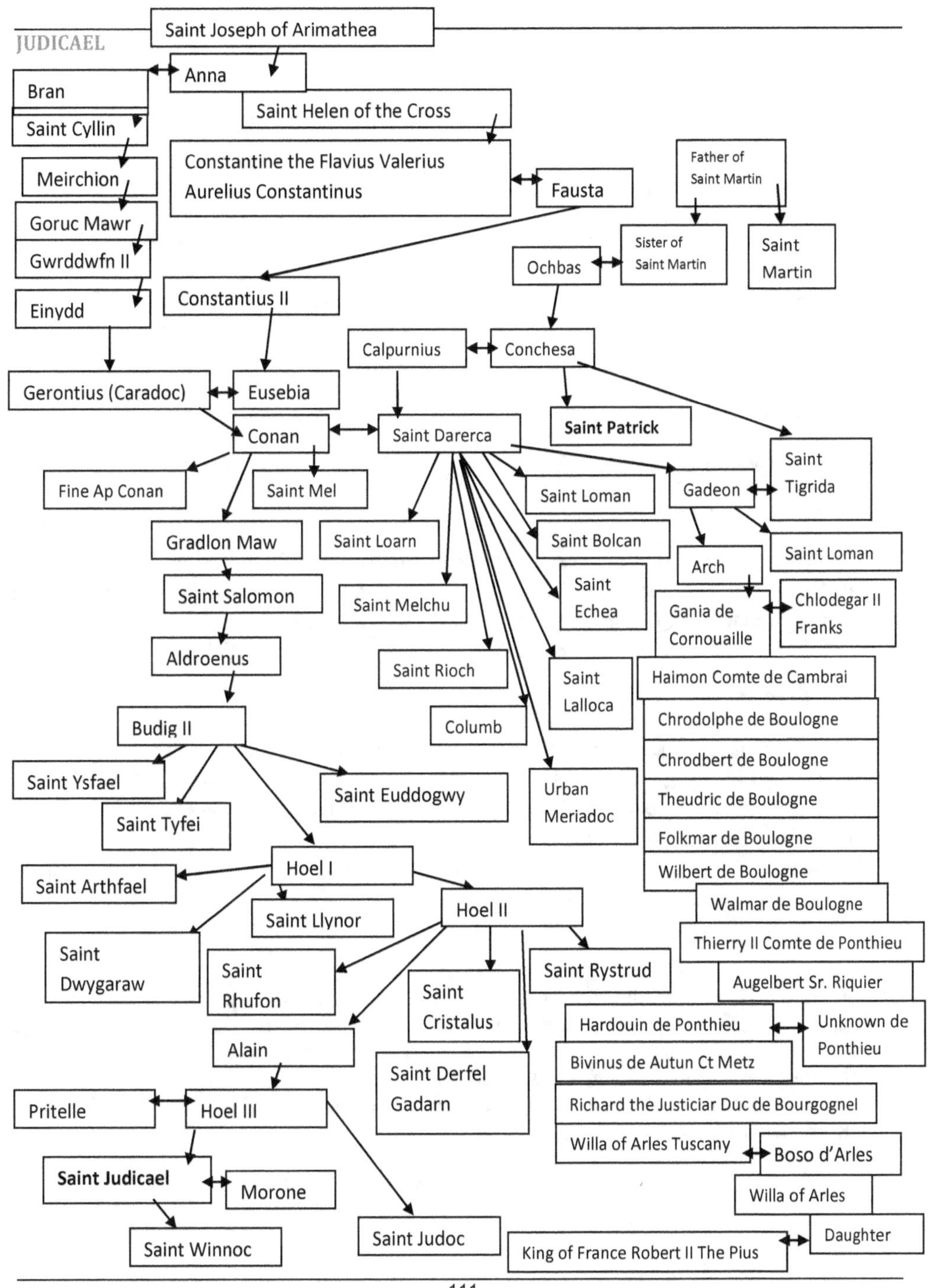
Saint Joseph of Arimathea
Anna
Bran
Saint Cyllin
Saint Helen of the Cross
Meirchion
Constantine the Flavius Valerius Aurelius Constantinus
Fausta
Father of Saint Martin
Goruc Mawr
Gwrddwfn II
Sister of Saint Martin
Saint Martin
Ochbas
Einydd
Constantius II
Calpurnius
Conchesa
Gerontius (Caradoc)
Eusebia
Saint Patrick
Conan
Saint Darerca
Saint Tigrida
Fine Ap Conan
Saint Mel
Saint Loman
Gadeon
Gradlon Maw
Saint Loarn
Saint Bolcan
Saint Loman
Arch
Saint Salomon
Saint Melchu
Saint Echea
Gania de Cornouaille
Chlodegar II Franks
Aldroenus
Saint Rioch
Saint Lalloca
Haimon Comte de Cambrai
Budig II
Columb
Chrodolphe de Boulogne
Chrodbert de Boulogne
Saint Ysfael
Saint Euddogwy
Urban Meriadoc
Theudric de Boulogne
Saint Tyfei
Folkmar de Boulogne
Hoel I
Wilbert de Boulogne
Saint Arthfael
Walmar de Boulogne
Saint Llynor
Hoel II
Thierry II Comte de Ponthieu
Saint Dwygaraw
Saint Rhufon
Saint Rystrud
Augelbert Sr. Riquier
Saint Cristalus
Hardouin de Ponthieu
Unknown de Ponthieu
Alain
Bivinus de Autun Ct Metz
Saint Derfel Gadarn
Richard the Justiciar Duc de Bourgognel
Pritelle
Hoel III
Willa of Arles Tuscany
Boso d'Arles
Saint Judicael
Morone
Willa of Arles
Saint Winnoc
Saint Judoc
King of France Robert II The Pius
Daughter

Chart on the previous Page is of Saint Judicael

Saint King Ethelbert

Feastday: February 25

Date: 560-616

Family:

Parents: Father- Eormenric Kent King Kent Mother- Unknown

Wife: Bertha of the Franks

Children: Eadbald Kent King Kent

Ancestry:

Saint Ethelbert of Kent ancestry traces back to Zerah thru the Kings of Troy. His wife Saint Bertha also is traced back to the lines of the Frankish Kings to Zerah whose father is Judah. Saint Bertha's ancestor is Saint Clotilde who converted the Frankish King Clovis to Christianity. Also included is Joseph of Arimathea. Also King David of Judah and Israel is an ancestor thru Nathan his son.

Descendents:

Sainted descendants include Saint Adele of Blois, Saint Louis IX of France, Saint Fernando III of Spain, Saint Cunigunda of Luxemborg, Saint Leopold III of Austria, Saint Henry II of Germany, Saint Edgar the peaceful King of England and Saint David and Saint Margaret of Scotland. Royal descendents include King Edward III Plantagenet of England, King of Naples Charles II, King of France Philip IV, and King of Scotland William the Lion. Also Casimir King of Poland, Alphonso Enriquez I King of Portugal and Henry IV Holy Roman Emperor of Germany are descendents.

Biography:

Converted by Saint Augustine, Ethelbert was King of Kent. He married a Christian daughter of King Charibert of Paris, Bertha, and fought the West Saxons in 568. Baptized in 597, Ethelbert brought a large part of Kent's population into the faith. He brought the King of the East Saxons and The King of the East Angles into the Church, but he did not enforce conversions. For fifty-six years, Ethelbert ruled, and founded the abbeys of Christ Church, Sts. Peter and Paul in Canterbury, and St. Andrew's in Rochester. Ethelbert is listed as Aedilbert by St. Bede.

Feastday: February 25

Date: 548-580

Family:
Parents: Father- Unknown Mother- Unknown
Husband: Saint Ethelbert of Kent
Children: Eadbald Kent King Kent
Ancestry:

Saint Ethelbert of Kent ancestry traces back to Zerah thru the Kings of Troy. His wife Saint Bertha also is traced back to the lines of the Frankish Kings to Zerah whose father is Judah. Saint Bertha's ancestor is Saint Clotilde who converted the Frankish King Clovis to Christianity. Also included is Joseph of Arimathea. Also King David of Judah and Israel is an ancestor thru Nathan his son.

Descendents:

Sainted descendants include Saint Adele of Blois, Saint Louis IX of France, Saint Fernando III of Spain, Saint Cunigunda of Luxemborg, Saint Leopold III of Austria, Saint Henry II of Germany, Saint Edgar the peaceful King of England and Saint David and Saint Margaret of Scotland. Royal descendents include King Edward III Plantagenet of England, King of Naples Charles II, King of France Philip IV, and King of Scotland William the Lion. Also Casimir King of Poland, Alphonso Enriquez I King of Portugal and Henry IV Holy Roman Emperor of Germany are descendents.

Biography:

Wife of Saint Ethelbert of Kent she was the first Christian queen of England, a Frankish Princess. She brought her chaplain Luidhard to the pagan king Saint Ethelbert. Saint Ethelbert welcomed Saint Augustine to Kent in 596. She has been venerated since her death, but no feast day has been given to Bertha.

LINES

The lines from Clovis ascend to Saint Helen of the Cross. Also these lines go to Meroveus and so to Argotta.

The line from Ethelbert leads to Odin and Frigg. Frigg's line is Davidic and so leads to Saint Joseph of Arimathea and to Llud Law the son of Beli and Don verch Mathonwry. Therefore Frigg is a Davidic lineage. Now Odin's line is known to lead to Priam thru many generations as is shown in the chart.

Saint Ethelbert married Bertha of the Franks. Bertha of the Franks line also lead to Priam. Note that Bertha's line has many more generations than Odin's line.

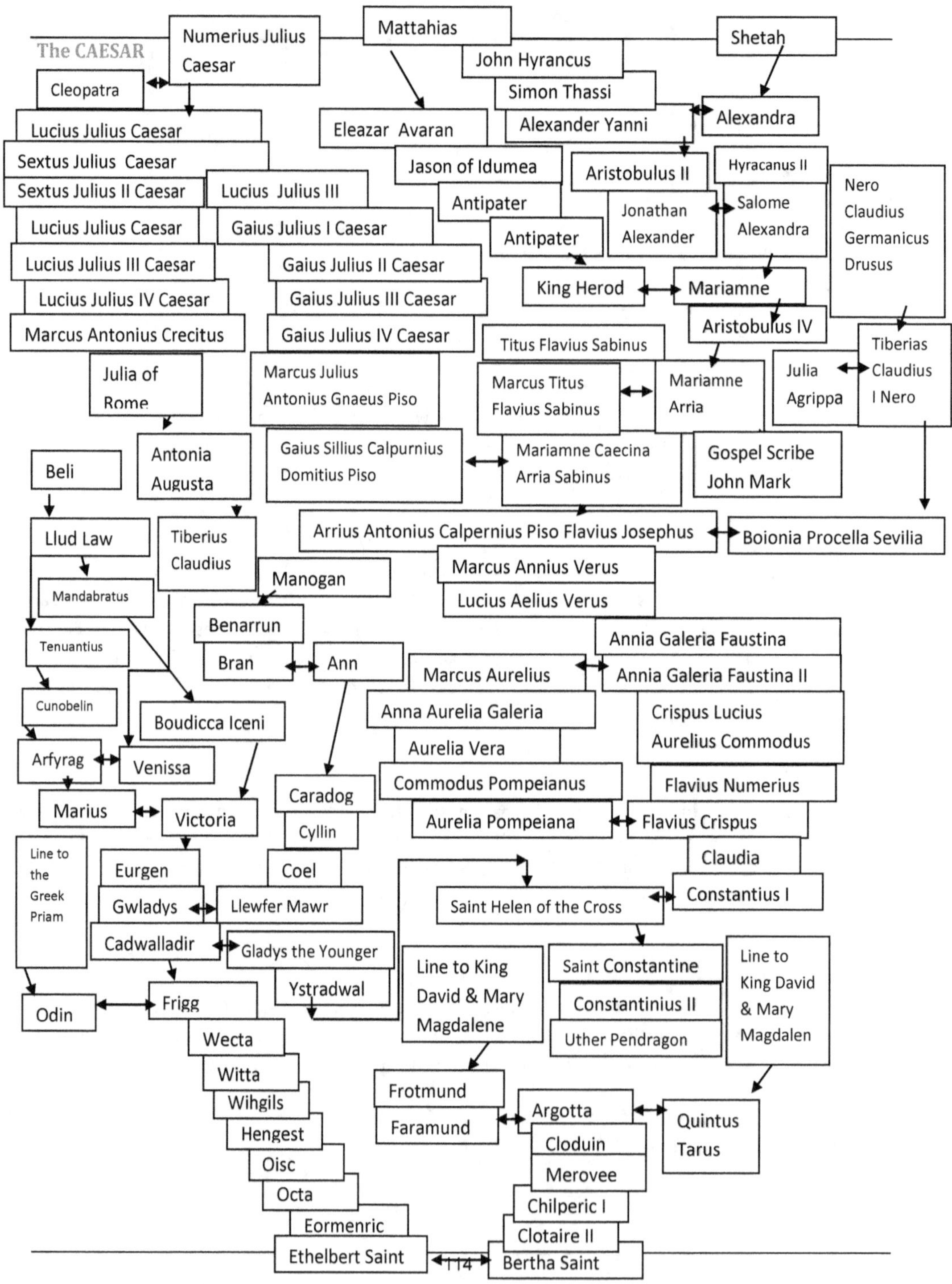
The CAESAR
Numerius Julius Caesar
Mattahias
Shetah
John Hyrancus
Cleopatra
Simon Thassi
Alexander Yanni
Alexandra
Lucius Julius Caesar
Eleazar Avaran
Sextus Julius Caesar
Jason of Idumea
Aristobulus II
Hyracanus II
Sextus Julius II Caesar
Lucius Julius III
Antipater
Jonathan Alexander
Salome Alexandra
Nero Claudius Germanicus Drusus
Lucius Julius Caesar
Gaius Julius I Caesar
Antipater
Lucius Julius III Caesar
Gaius Julius II Caesar
King Herod
Mariamne
Lucius Julius IV Caesar
Gaius Julius III Caesar
Aristobulus IV
Marcus Antonius Crecitus
Gaius Julius IV Caesar
Titus Flavius Sabinus
Tiberias Claudius I Nero
Julia of Rome
Marcus Julius Antonius Gnaeus Piso
Marcus Titus Flavius Sabinus
Mariamne Arria
Julia Agrippa
Antonia Augusta
Gaius Sillius Calpurnius Domitius Piso
Mariamne Caecina Arria Sabinus
Gospel Scribe John Mark
Beli
Llud Law
Tiberius Claudius
Arrius Antonius Calpernius Piso Flavius Josephus
Boionia Procella Sevilia
Manogan
Marcus Annius Verus
Mandabratus
Lucius Aelius Verus
Benarrun
Tenuantius
Annia Galeria Faustina
Bran
Ann
Marcus Aurelius
Annia Galeria Faustina II
Cunobelin
Boudicca Iceni
Anna Aurelia Galeria
Crispus Lucius Aurelius Commodus
Aurelia Vera
Arfyrag
Venissa
Commodus Pompeianus
Caradog
Flavius Numerius
Marius
Victoria
Cyllin
Aurelia Pompeiana
Flavius Crispus
Line to the Greek Priam
Claudia
Eurgen
Coel
Gwladys
Llewfer Mawr
Saint Helen of the Cross
Constantius I
Cadwalladir
Gladys the Younger
Line to King David & Mary Magdalene
Saint Constantine
Line to King David & Mary Magdalen
Ystradwal
Odin
Frigg
Constantinius II
Uther Pendragon
Wecta
Witta
Frotmund
Wihgils
Argotta
Quintus Tarus
Faramund
Hengest
Cloduin
Oisc
Merovee
Octa
Chilperic I
Eormenric
Clotaire II
Ethelbert Saint
Bertha Saint

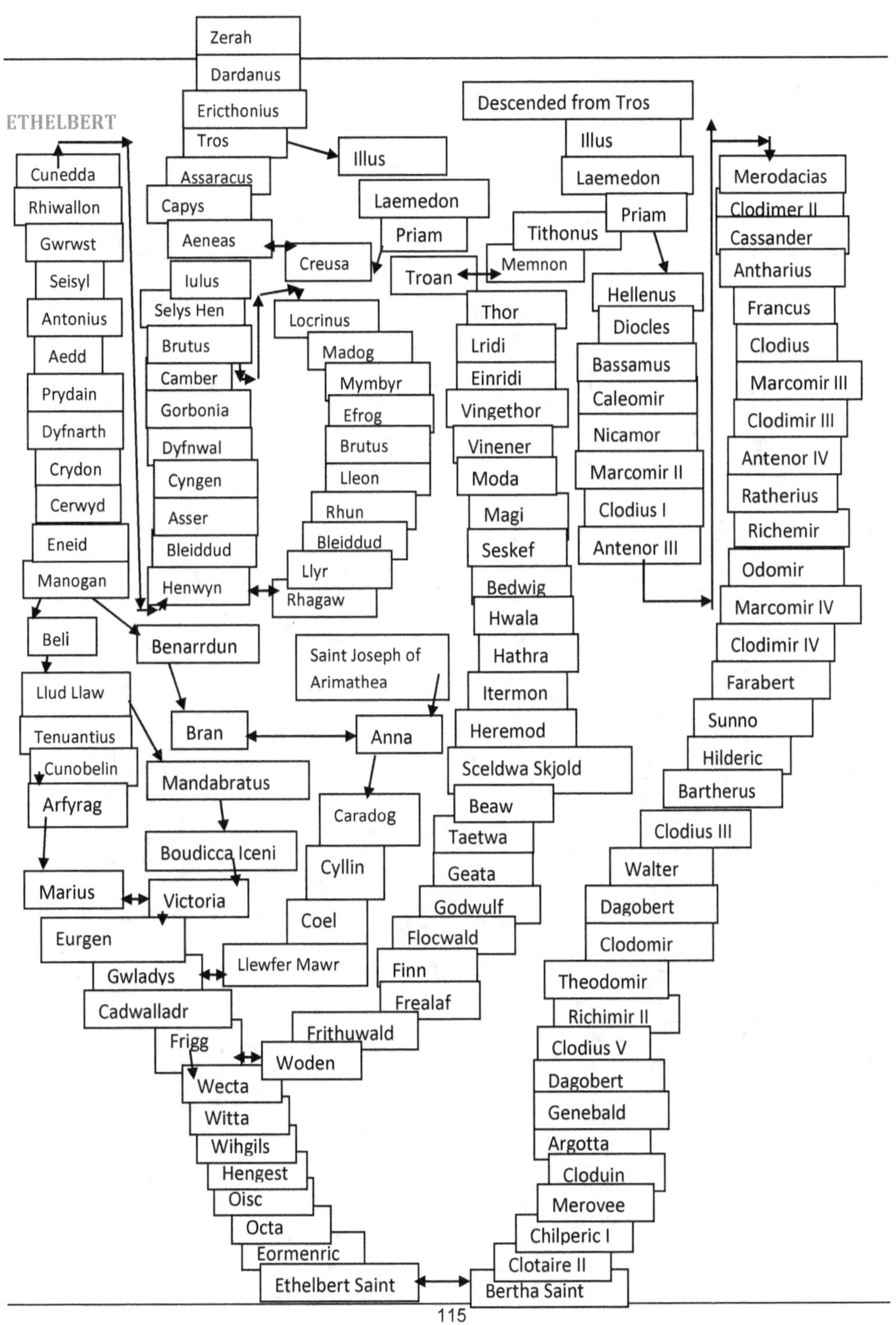
ETHELBERT
Zerah
Dardanus
Ericthonius
Tros
Illus
Assaracus
Capys
Aeneas
Creusa
Iulus
Selys Hen
Locrinus
Brutus
Madog
Camber
Mymbyr
Gorbonia
Efrog
Dyfnwal
Brutus
Cyngen
Lleon
Asser
Rhun
Bleiddud
Bleiddud
Llyr
Henwyn
Rhagaw
Cunedda
Rhiwallon
Gwrwst
Seisyl
Antonius
Aedd
Prydain
Dyfnarth
Crydon
Cerwyd
Eneid
Manogan
Beli
Benarrdun
Llud Llaw
Tenuantius
Cunobelin
Arfyrag
Bran
Saint Joseph of Arimathea
Anna
Mandabratus
Caradog
Boudicca Iceni
Cyllin
Marius
Victoria
Coel
Eurgen
Llewfer Mawr
Gwladys
Cadwalladr
Frigg
Woden
Wecta
Witta
Wihgils
Hengest
Oisc
Octa
Eormenric
Ethelbert Saint
Laemedon
Priam
Troan
Memnon
Descended from Tros
Illus
Laemedon
Priam
Tithonus
Thor
Lridi
Einridi
Vingethor
Vinener
Moda
Magi
Seskef
Bedwig
Hwala
Hathra
Itermon
Heremod
Sceldwa Skjold
Beaw
Taetwa
Geata
Godwulf
Flocwald
Finn
Frealaf
Frithuwald
Hellenus
Diocles
Bassamus
Caleomir
Nicamor
Marcomir II
Clodius I
Antenor III
Merodacias
Clodimer II
Cassander
Antharius
Francus
Clodius
Marcomir III
Clodimir III
Antenor IV
Ratherius
Richemir
Odomir
Marcomir IV
Clodimir IV
Farabert
Sunno
Hilderic
Bartherus
Clodius III
Walter
Dagobert
Clodomir
Theodomir
Richimir II
Clodius V
Dagobert
Genebald
Argotta
Cloduin
Merovee
Chilperic I
Clotaire II
Bertha Saint

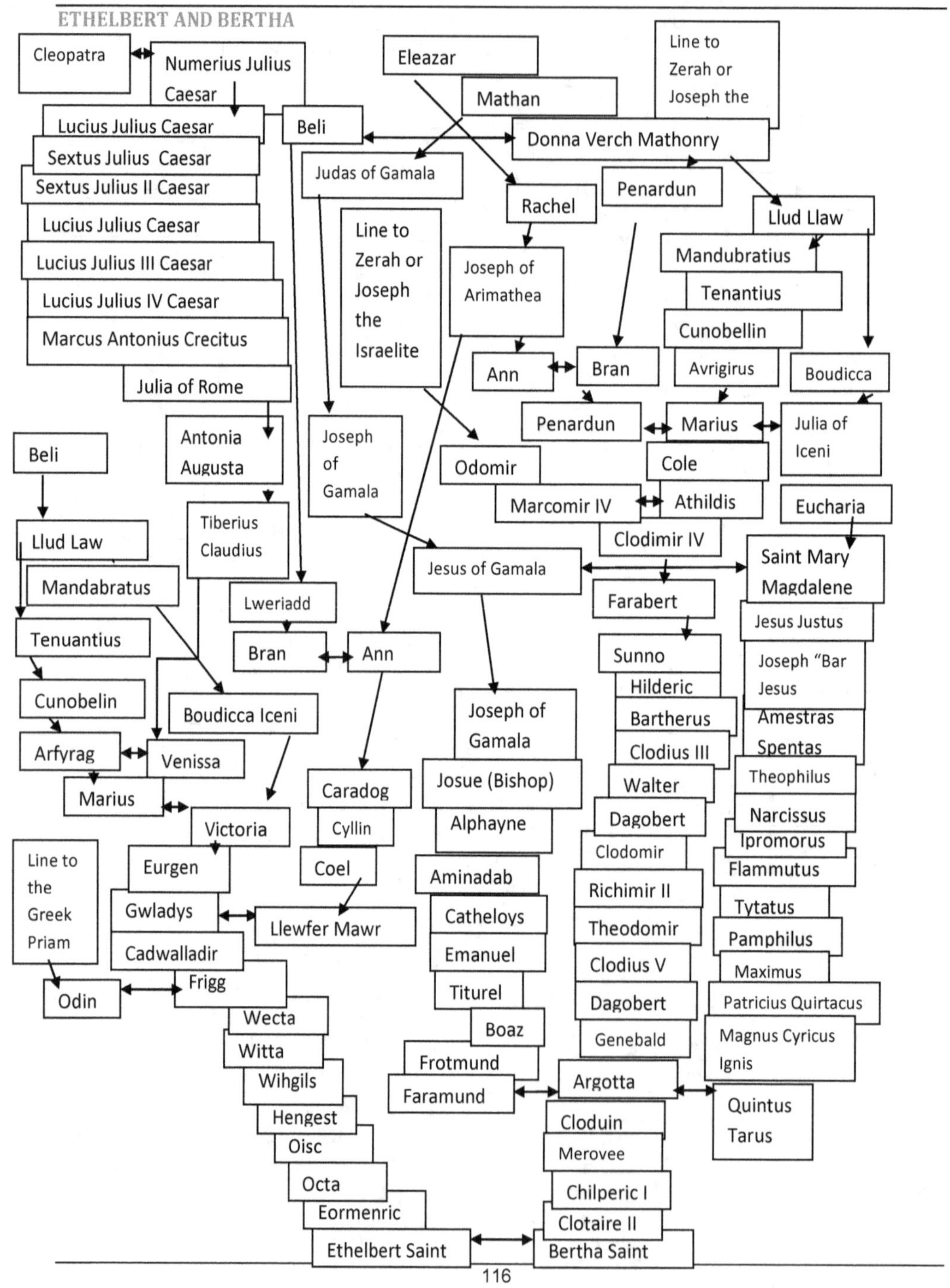
Cleopatra
Numerius Julius Caesar
Lucius Julius Caesar
Sextus Julius Caesar
Sextus Julius II Caesar
Lucius Julius Caesar
Lucius Julius III Caesar
Lucius Julius IV Caesar
Marcus Antonius Crecitus
Julia of Rome
Antonia Augusta
Tiberius Claudius
Beli
Eleazar
Mathan
Line to Zerah or Joseph the
Donna Verch Mathonry
Judas of Gamala
Rachel
Penardun
Llud Llaw
Line to Zerah or Joseph the Israelite
Joseph of Arimathea
Mandubratius
Tenantius
Cunobellin
Ann
Bran
Avrigirus
Boudicca
Penardun
Marius
Julia of Iceni
Joseph of Gamala
Odomir
Cole
Marcomir IV
Athildis
Eucharia
Clodimir IV
Saint Mary Magdalene
Jesus of Gamala
Beli
Llud Law
Mandabratus
Tenuantius
Cunobelin
Arfyrag
Venissa
Marius
Boudicca Iceni
Victoria
Lweriadd
Bran
Ann
Farabert
Jesus Justus
Sunno
Joseph "Bar Jesus
Hilderic
Bartherus
Amestras Spentas
Clodius III
Theophilus
Walter
Narcissus
Dagobert
Ipromorus
Clodomir
Flammutus
Richimir II
Tytatus
Theodomir
Pamphilus
Clodius V
Maximus
Dagobert
Patricius Quirtacus
Genebald
Magnus Cyricus Ignis
Joseph of Gamala
Josue (Bishop)
Alphayne
Aminadab
Catheloys
Emanuel
Titurel
Boaz
Frotmund
Faramund
Argotta
Quintus Tarus
Cloduin
Merovee
Chilperic I
Clotaire II
Bertha Saint
Caradog
Cyllin
Coel
Llewfer Mawr
Eurgen
Gwladys
Cadwalladir
Line to the Greek Priam
Odin
Frigg
Wecta
Witta
Wihgils
Hengest
Oisc
Octa
Eormenric
Ethelbert Saint

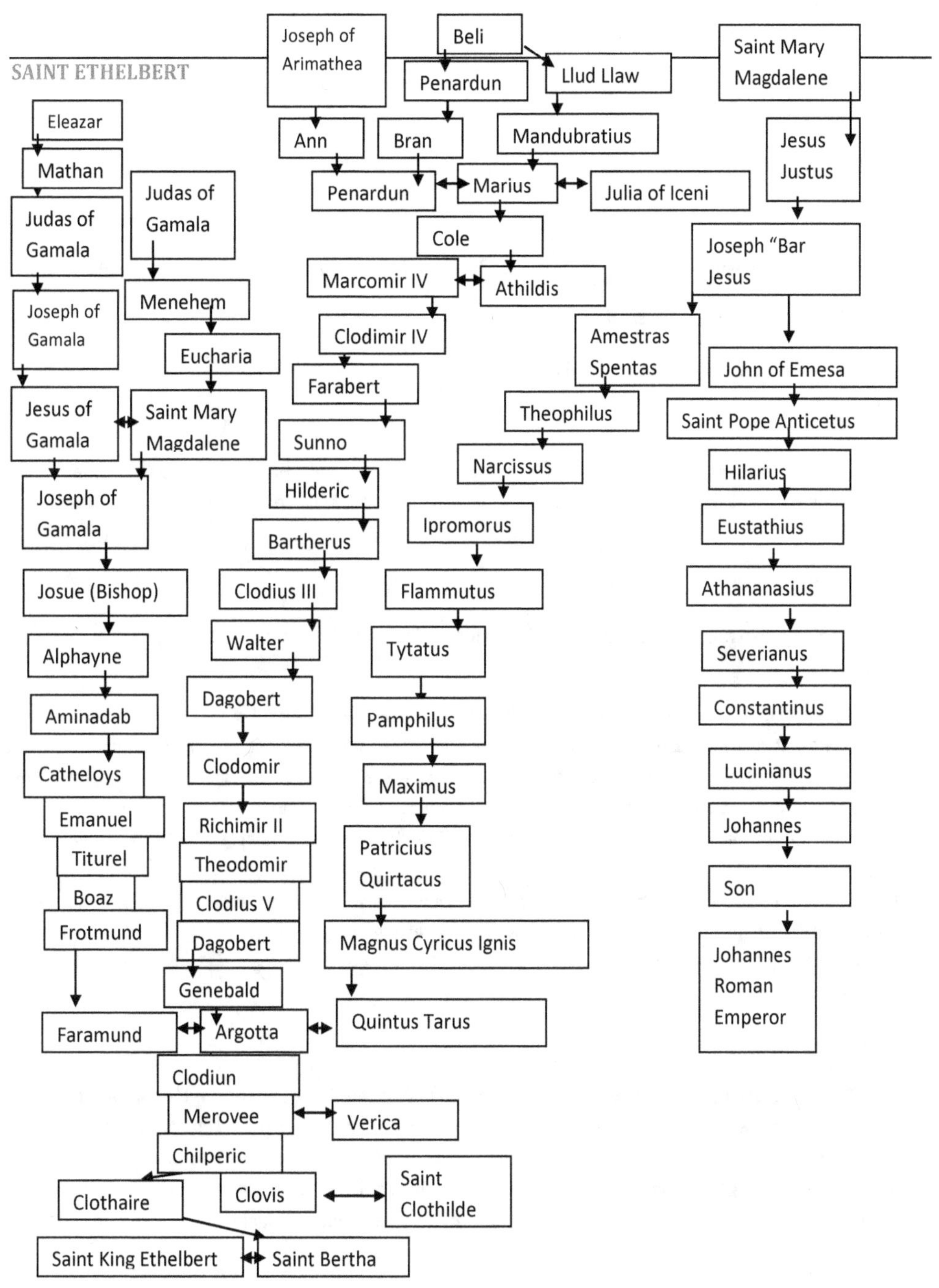
Joseph of Arimathea
Beli
Penardun
Llud Llaw
Saint Mary Magdalene
Eleazar
Ann
Bran
Mandubratius
Jesus Justus
Mathan
Penardun
Marius
Julia of Iceni
Judas of Gamala
Judas of Gamala
Cole
Joseph "Bar Jesus
Marcomir IV
Athildis
Menehem
Joseph of Gamala
Clodimir IV
Amestras Spentas
Eucharia
John of Emesa
Farabert
Jesus of Gamala
Saint Mary Magdalene
Theophilus
Saint Pope Anticetus
Sunno
Narcissus
Hilarius
Joseph of Gamala
Hilderic
Ipromorus
Eustathius
Bartherus
Josue (Bishop)
Clodius III
Flammutus
Athananasius
Walter
Tytatus
Alphayne
Severianus
Dagobert
Pamphilus
Constantinus
Aminadab
Clodomir
Catheloys
Maximus
Lucinianus
Emanuel
Richimir II
Johannes
Titurel
Theodomir
Patricius Quirtacus
Son
Boaz
Clodius V
Frotmund
Dagobert
Magnus Cyricus Ignis
Johannes Roman Emperor
Genebald
Faramund
Argotta
Quintus Tarus
Clodiun
Merovee
Verica
Chilperic
Clothaire
Clovis
Saint Clothilde
Saint King Ethelbert
Saint Bertha

Saint Raymond Berenger

Feastday: March 15

Date: 1113-1162

Family:

Parents: Father- Raymond III the Great Count of Berengar Mother- Dolca Countess of Provence

Wife: Ramirez, Petronilla Queen of Aragon

Children: Alphonso II the Chaste King of Aragon

Ancestry:

Saint Raymond has Helena of Rome for an Ancestor. Also Joseph of Arimathea. Also Charlemange. Also King David of Judah and Israel is an ancestor thru Nathan his son. King Solomon of Israel and Judah is also an ancestor.

Descendents:

His son King of Aragon Alphonso, and King Henry III of England are descendents.

Biography:

Cistercian abbot and founder of the Order of Calatrava, also called Ramon Sierra. Born in Spain, in Aragon, he was a canon at Tarazona Cathedral and then at the Monastery Scala Dei he joined the Cistercians. Sent to Spain to serve as abbot and establish the Fitero Abbey in Navarre, the post brought him to the forefront of the Christian Spanish and the Moor struggle. Raymond convinced King Sancho III of Castile to aid his call for an army when the Moors were on the verge of attacking the Toledo outpost of Calatrava in 1158. A one time Knight, then a monk assisted Raymond, namely Diego Velasques, who with the enlisted aid of the archbishop of Toledo they created a vast host of Christian Soldiers. The Moors failed to attack, but the host was formed into the military order of the Knights of Calatrava. Members distinguished themselves as one of the most powerful causes of the Reconquist (reconquest of Spain against the Moors) and too the Benedictine rule. The cult of Raymond as a saint was approved in 1719.

Additional Notes:

Saint Raymond was the son of Raymond the Third. Raymond the Third also married Maria Diaz the daughter of El Cid Rodriguez, who was of the line of the Count Fernandez of Spain. The father of El Cid was killed, Lainez Castro, and El Cid revenged the blood of his father. El Cid was also the companion of Raymond the Saint, who was involved in the founding of the order of Knights, the Caltrava. This order was prepared to defend Spain from the moors, but was never used, as the Moors left Spain without a struggle.

Lineage of Saint Raymond.

Saint Raymond has the franks, the Castile house of Spain, the lines of the Greeks by the franks, and the lines of Wales, excepting Saint Judicael. Saint Brychan, the son of Saint Joseph Joses is also an ancestor. There are two charts that show the lineage of Saint Raymond, which is similar to the lineage of the country of Spain. One chart shows the relationship to Charlemange, which is joined about two generations below Saint Raymond. Thus Imperial France was not a part of Saint Raymond, and Holy Spain, but was joined about two generations past Saint Raymond. Imperial France never attached Spain, and the Empire created by Charlemagne never attached Holy Spain. Charlemagne had wars against Germany, saved Italy and created a vast Empire. Perhaps Charlemagne agreed with the idea of a son avenging his fathers blood, which was done by El Cid. Now the Kingdom of the Franks, Imperial France has as a founder Merovee. This is part of Saint Raymonds lineage, and will lead back to Saint Mary Magdalene. However by 750 and beyond the lines are different to Merovee. Saint Gondolfus is part of Charlemagne's lineage, but not part of Saint Raymonds. Note that the early Franks, Cloitaire, Boggis of Aquitaine, and Saint Clotilde were ancestors of Saint Raymond, with Saint Hubert Bishop of Liege and all the early Franks being ancestors of Saint Raymond. Now also note that El Cid has Franks as ancestors, has the Greek and Israelites Joseph as descendents, and also King David, however does not necessarily have the Wales links that the Castile, Garcia, Sanchez, and Early Franks have as ancestors.

The chart below shows the lineage of Saint Raymond, with ancestors including the Castile line and the line of El Cid Rodriguez. El Cid's descendents include the Des Spencer that is of the line of Princess Diana Spencer, and after two generations these descendents can be shown to be descendents of Charlemagne. The Castile line leads to the Franks, who marry at Eudes, and contilinue to Mathilde of Ireland that marries Dagobert II. Dagobert II descendents include Hildegard, one of the wifes of Charlemagne. This line continues in ancestry from Matilde of Ireland to King Arthur, the Pendragon, and so the ascent goes to many Davidic and Biblical ancestors.

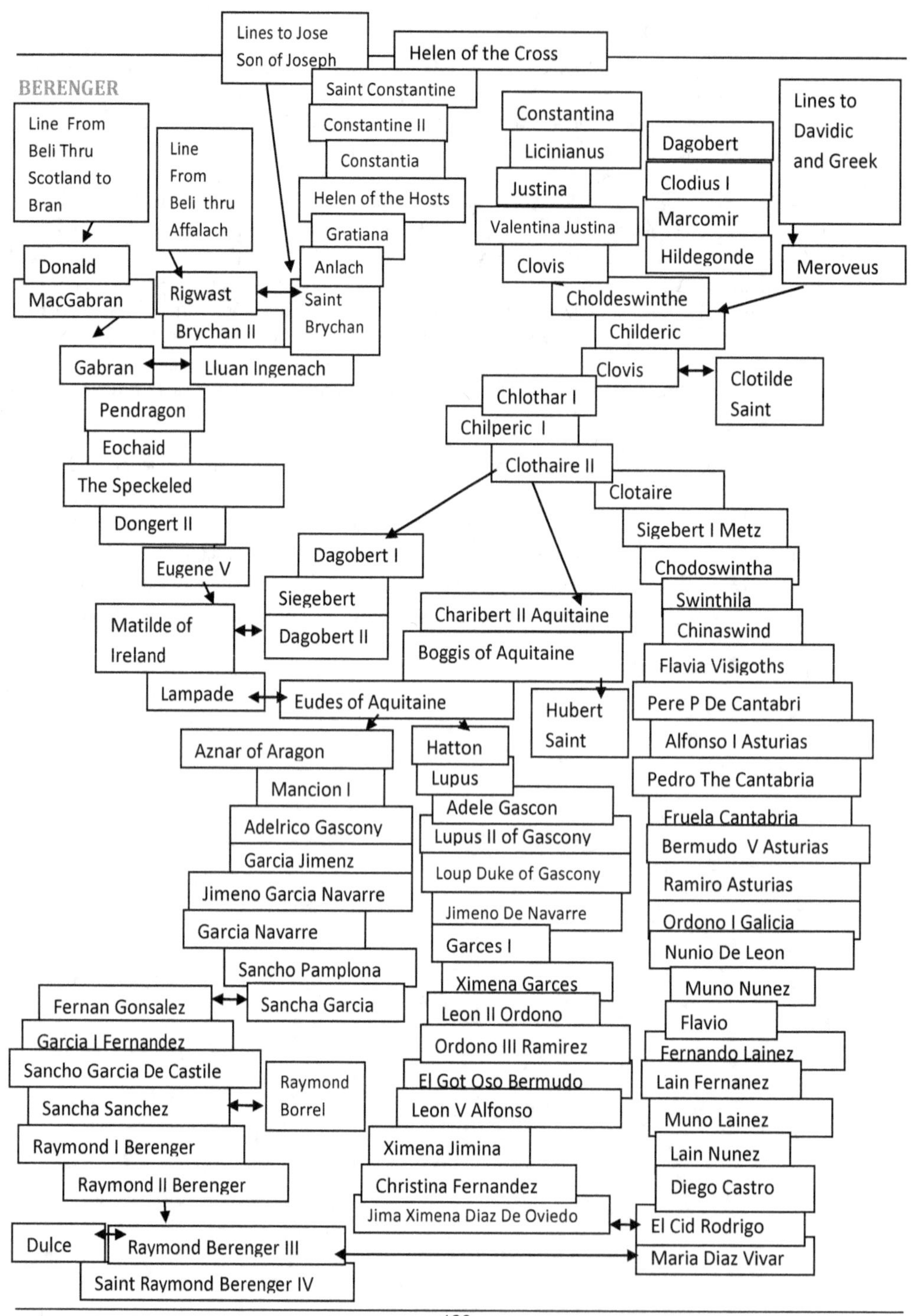
BERENGER
Lines to Jose Son of Joseph
Helen of the Cross
Saint Constantine
Constantine II
Constantia
Helen of the Hosts
Gratiana
Anlach
Saint Brychan
Line From Beli Thru Scotland to Bran
Donald
MacGabran
Gabran
Line From Beli thru Affalach
Rigwast
Brychan II
Lluan Ingenach
Pendragon
Eochaid
The Speckeled
Dongert II
Eugene V
Matilde of Ireland
Lampade
Constantina
Licinianus
Justina
Valentina Justina
Clovis
Dagobert
Clodius I
Marcomir
Hildegonde
Lines to Davidic and Greek
Meroveus
Choldeswinthe
Childeric
Clovis
Clotilde Saint
Chlothar I
Chilperic I
Clothaire II
Clotaire
Sigebert I Metz
Chodoswintha
Swinthila
Chinaswind
Flavia Visigoths
Pere P De Cantabri
Alfonso I Asturias
Pedro The Cantabria
Fruela Cantabria
Bermudo V Asturias
Ramiro Asturias
Ordono I Galicia
Nunio De Leon
Muno Nunez
Flavio
Fernando Lainez
Lain Fernanez
Muno Lainez
Lain Nunez
Diego Castro
El Cid Rodrigo
Maria Diaz Vivar
Dagobert I
Siegebert
Dagobert II
Charibert II Aquitaine
Boggis of Aquitaine
Hubert Saint
Eudes of Aquitaine
Aznar of Aragon
Mancion I
Adelrico Gascony
Garcia Jimenz
Jimeno Garcia Navarre
Garcia Navarre
Sancho Pamplona
Sancha Garcia
Hatton
Lupus
Adele Gascon
Lupus II of Gascony
Loup Duke of Gascony
Jimeno De Navarre
Garces I
Ximena Garces
Leon II Ordono
Ordono III Ramirez
El Got Oso Bermudo
Leon V Alfonso
Ximena Jimina
Christina Fernandez
Jima Ximena Diaz De Oviedo
Fernan Gonsalez
Garcia I Fernandez
Sancho Garcia De Castile
Sancha Sanchez
Raymond Borrel
Raymond I Berenger
Raymond II Berenger
Dulce
Raymond Berenger III
Saint Raymond Berenger IV

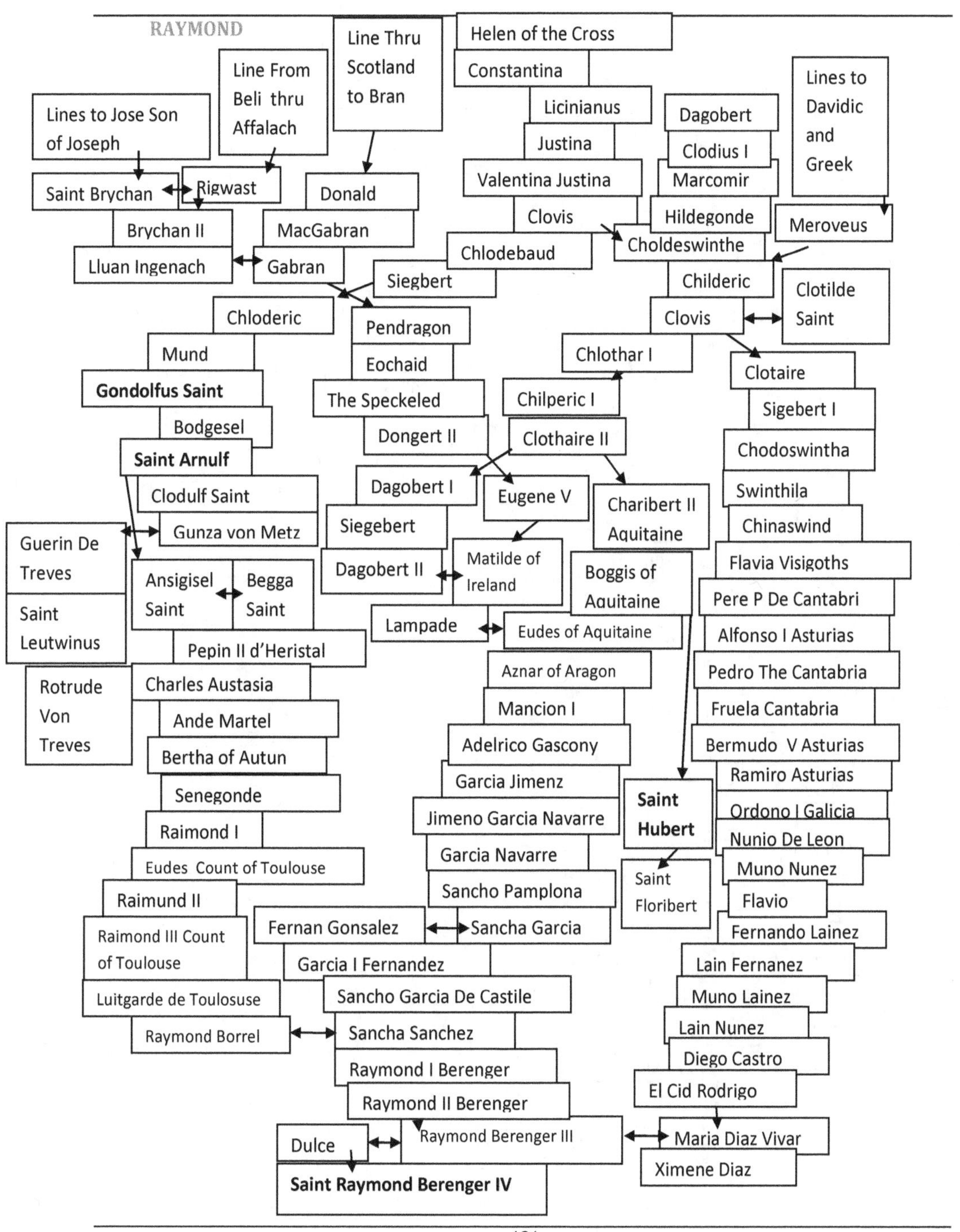
Lines to Jose Son of Joseph
Line From Beli thru Affalach
Line Thru Scotland to Bran
Helen of the Cross
Constantina
Licinianus
Justina
Valentina Justina
Clovis
Chlodebaud
Dagobert
Clodius I
Marcomir
Hildegonde
Choldeswinthe
Lines to Davidic and Greek
Meroveus
Saint Brychan
Rigwast
Donald
Brychan II
MacGabran
Lluan Ingenach
Gabran
Siegbert
Childeric
Clotilde Saint
Clovis
Chloderic
Pendragon
Eochaid
Mund
Chlothar I
Clotaire
Gondolfus Saint
The Speckeled
Chilperic I
Sigebert I
Bodgesel
Dongert II
Clothaire II
Chodoswintha
Saint Arnulf
Clodulf Saint
Dagobert I
Eugene V
Charibert II Aquitaine
Swinthila
Guerin De Treves
Gunza von Metz
Siegebert
Chinaswind
Matilde of Ireland
Flavia Visigoths
Saint Leutwinus
Ansigisel Saint
Begga Saint
Dagobert II
Boggis of Aquitaine
Pere P De Cantabri
Lampade
Eudes of Aquitaine
Alfonso I Asturias
Pepin II d'Heristal
Aznar of Aragon
Pedro The Cantabria
Rotrude Von Treves
Charles Austasia
Ande Martel
Mancion I
Fruela Cantabria
Bertha of Autun
Adelrico Gascony
Bermudo V Asturias
Garcia Jimenz
Ramiro Asturias
Senegonde
Saint Hubert
Jimeno Garcia Navarre
Ordono I Galicia
Raimond I
Nunio De Leon
Eudes Count of Toulouse
Garcia Navarre
Muno Nunez
Saint Floribert
Sancho Pamplona
Flavio
Raimund II
Fernan Gonsalez
Sancha Garcia
Fernando Lainez
Raimond III Count of Toulouse
Garcia I Fernandez
Lain Fernanez
Luitgarde de Toulosuse
Sancho Garcia De Castile
Muno Lainez
Raymond Borrel
Sancha Sanchez
Lain Nunez
Raymond I Berenger
Diego Castro
Raymond II Berenger
El Cid Rodrigo
Dulce
Raymond Berenger III
Maria Diaz Vivar
Ximene Diaz
Saint Raymond Berenger IV

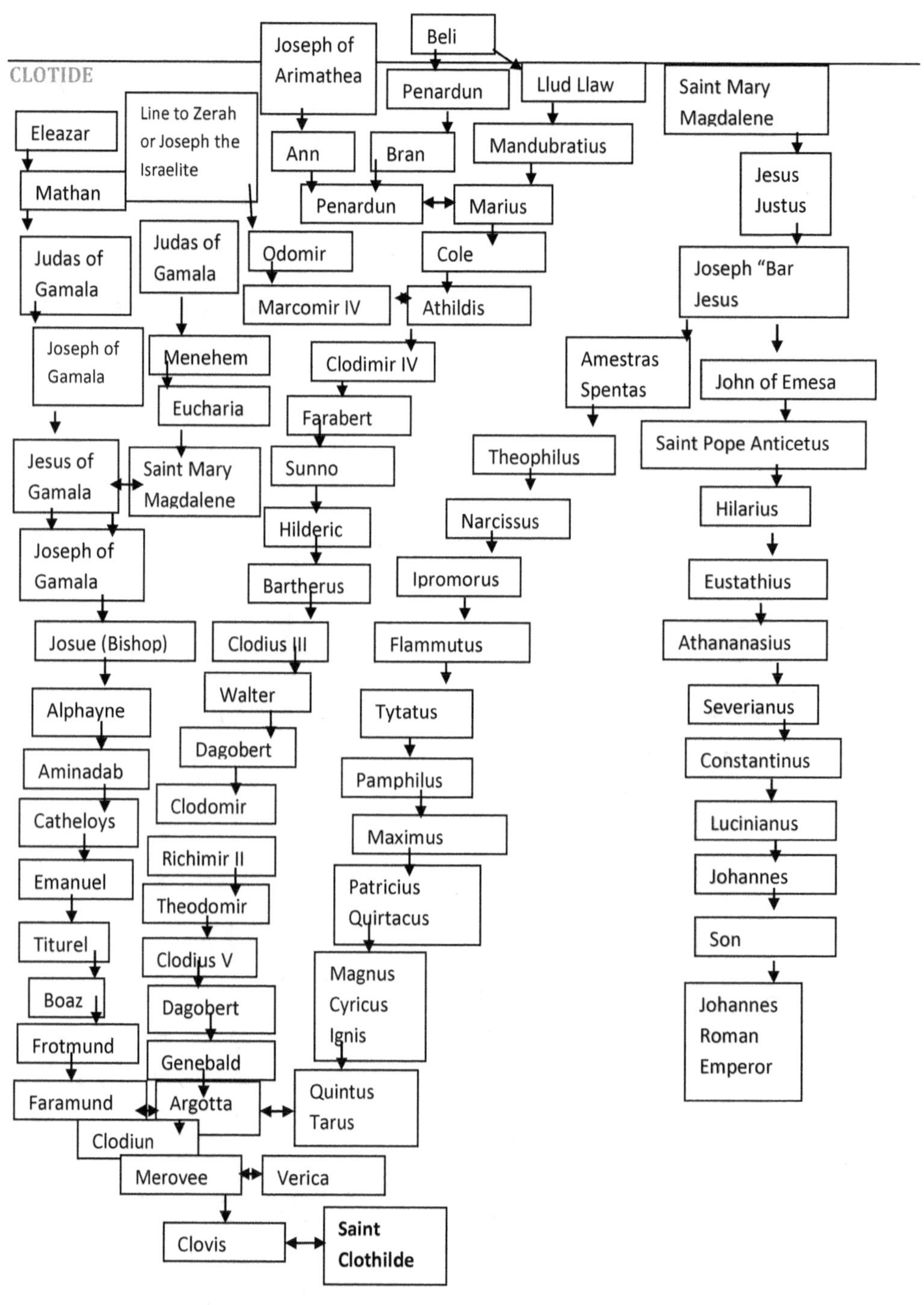

Joseph of Arimathea
Beli
Penardun
Llud Llaw
Saint Mary Magdalene
Line to Zerah or Joseph the Israelite
Eleazar
Ann
Bran
Mandubratius
Mathan
Penardun
Marius
Jesus Justus
Judas of Gamala
Judas of Gamala
Odomir
Cole
Joseph "Bar Jesus
Marcomir IV
Athildis
Joseph of Gamala
Menehem
Clodimir IV
Amestras Spentas
John of Emesa
Eucharia
Farabert
Saint Pope Anticetus
Jesus of Gamala
Saint Mary Magdalene
Sunno
Theophilus
Hilarius
Narcissus
Joseph of Gamala
Hilderic
Ipromorus
Eustathius
Bartherus
Josue (Bishop)
Clodius III
Flammutus
Athananasius
Walter
Alphayne
Tytatus
Severianus
Dagobert
Aminadab
Pamphilus
Constantinus
Clodomir
Catheloys
Maximus
Lucinianus
Richimir II
Emanuel
Patricius Quirtacus
Johannes
Theodomir
Titurel
Son
Clodius V
Magnus Cyricus Ignis
Boaz
Dagobert
Johannes Roman Emperor
Frotmund
Genebald
Faramund
Argotta
Quintus Tarus
Clodiun
Merovee
Verica
Clovis
Saint Clothilde

March 1 **Saint Dewi**

Country: Britain **Date:** c. 600

Family: Father: Sant Mother: Saint Non

Spouse: None Siblings: Unknown

Ancestors: Saint Cyllus is an ancestor. Saint Helen of the Host is an Ancestor, Also Saint Brychan is an ancestor. Saint Constantine The Great is an Ancestor, as is Helen of the True Cross (Saint Helenus). Bran the Blessed is an Ancestor, as is his wife Anna of Arimathea. Saint Joseph of Arimathea and so the Line of Nathan Son of David King of Israel and Judah. King David's ancestors include the Israelites, Zebulon, Levi, Joseph, and Judah. Also Anna of Arimathea, daughter to Joseph of Aramathea married Bran the Blessed whose line goes to Tros and so to Epraim son of Joseph the Israelite. Also the line from Anna of Arimathea's mother goes thru Simon the Just thru many High Priests to Judah the Israelite.

Branches of the Tree: Saint Non is the granddaughter of Saint Brychan.

Biography: The son of King Sant of South Wales and Saint Non. Saint David was ordained to priesthood and studied under Saint Belinda's. He founded a number of monasteries and he was involved in missionary work. One monastery in southwestern Wales at Menevia of was noted for extreme asceticism. Monks at his monastery and Saint David drank only water never wanting beer also monks put in a full day of heavy manual labor. Saint David and his monks also were expected to do some intense study. There was a synod at Brevi in Cardiganshir about the year 550. Saint David was elected as primary of the Cambrian church. This was due largely to his contributions at the synod at Brevi. Saint David visited the holy land where he was reportedly consecrated Archbishop by the patriarch of Jerusalem. Pelagianism was near its end and Saint David is said to have invoked a council that ended its last vestiges. About the year 589 Saint David died at his monastery in Menevia. Pope Callista II approved his cult about 1120 A.D. Saint David is forever revered the patriot of Wales. There is no doubt Saint David was granted substantial qualities and quantities of spiritual leadership. Many monasteries leveraged as results of his leadership is good example. It is his monastic piety that sets an example for everyone. His feast day is March 1

Direct Descendants of Levi to The Saint Dewi

The secrets here are the ascent of Saint Dewi thru his father Sant, and the line to the sister of the Virgin Mary.

1 Levi

2 Kohath

3 Amram

4 Aaron

5 Eleazer

6 Phineas

7 Bukki

8 Uzzi

9 Zerahiah

10 Meraioth

11 Amariah

12 Ahitud

13 Zadok

14 Ahima-az

15 Azariah

16 Johanan

17 Azariah

18 Amariah

19 Ahitud

20 Zadok

21 Shallum

22 Hilkiah

23 Azariah

24 Seraiah

25 Jehozadak

26 Jeshua

27 Joachim

28 Eliashib

29 Joiadah

30 Johanan

31 Jaddual

32 Onias

33 Simon The Just

34 Onias II

35 Simon II

36 Onas III

37 Son of Onas III

38 Asamoneus

39 Simeon

40 Jonathon

41 Mattathias

42 Simon Ben Mattathias

43 John Hyrcanus

44 Antigonus I Hyrcanus

45 Joiadah

+ Estha

46 Anna

+ Joachim

47 Sister of Mary

48 Eugen

49 Eudolen

50 Eugen

51 Abalach

52 Iouguen

53 Dobun

54 Perum

55 Omid

56 Amguerit

57 Amguoil

58 Guordumn

59 Dumn

60 Gurdeil

61 Doeil

62 Peisrud

63 Patern

64 Etern

65 Cuneda

66 Cheritic

67 Sant

+ Saint Non

68 David (Dewi) Saint

Above the generations from 47 to 68 are taken from the Rhvqvvarch's Life of Saint David written between 1057 and 1099.

The following is a lineage suggested by Prince Michael of Albany in the book The Forgotten Monarchy of Scotland. Note that the line leads to Saint Joseph of Arimathea and not to the levitical lineage of Mary the Virgin. See the section on Saint Joseph of Arimathea for his levitical lineage

1	Saint James the Just (Saint Joseph of Arimathea)	7	Duvan	16	Patern Pesrut
		8	Onwedd	17	Octern
		9	Anguerit	18	Cunnedda +Gwawl
2	Anna +Bran the Blessed	10	Anjouloyb		
		11	Gur Dumn	19	Ceredig +Saint Mereri verch Brychan
3	Beli	12	Dumn		
4	Avallach	13	Guiocein		
5	Eugein	14	Cein	20	Sandde
6	Brithguein	15	Tegid Pies Rudawg	21	Saint Dewi

The ancestor of Gwawl (generation 18) would be Coel, and the lineage of Bran the Blessed (generation 2) leads to the Kings of Britain, Bran's father being King Llyr son of Casswallan son of Beli Mawr (The Great), Sovereign Lord of the Celtic Britons 132-72 BC.

Section on Saint Judicael and King Arthur

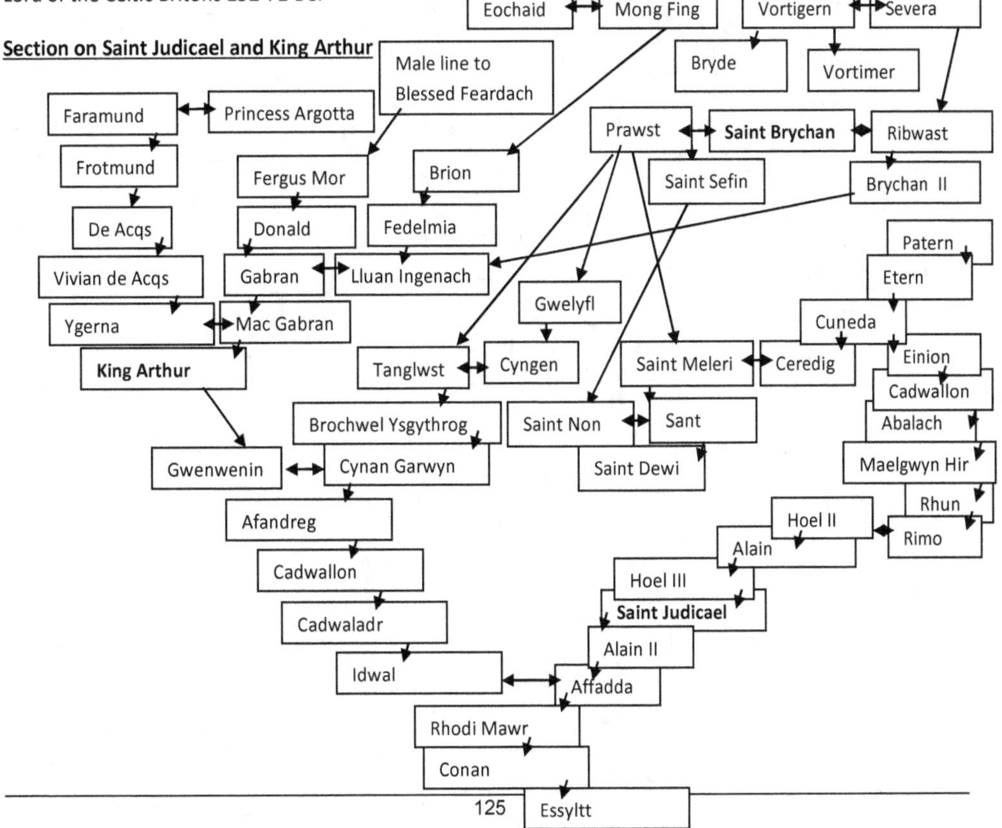

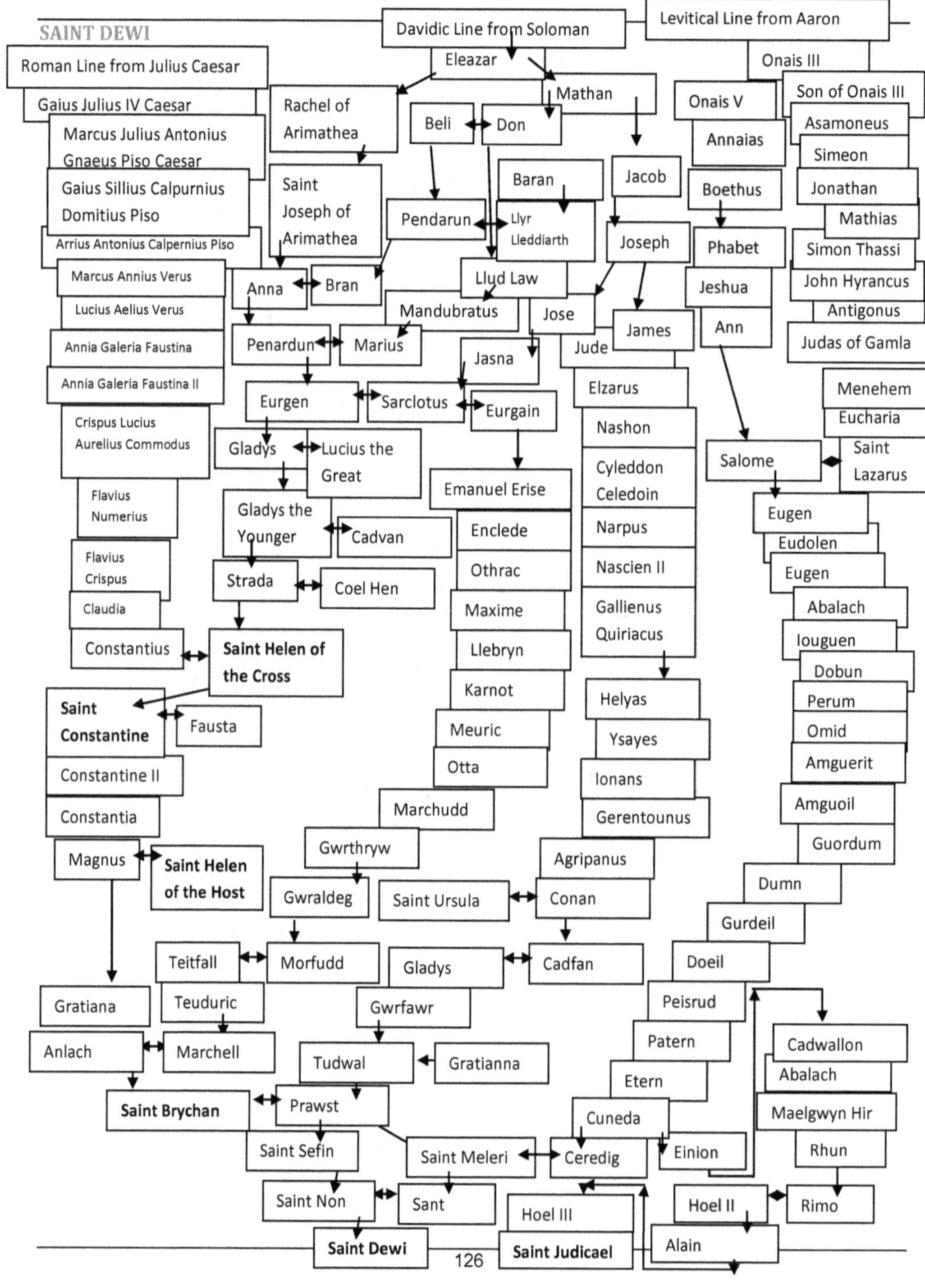
Davidic Line from Soloman
Levitical Line from Aaron
Roman Line from Julius Caesar
Eleazar
Onais III
Gaius Julius IV Caesar
Rachel of Arimathea
Mathan
Onais V
Son of Onais III
Beli
Don
Marcus Julius Antonius Gnaeus Piso Caesar
Annaias
Asamoneus
Simeon
Gaius Sillius Calpurnius Domitius Piso
Saint Joseph of Arimathea
Baran
Jacob
Boethus
Jonathan
Pendarun
Llyr Lleddiarth
Joseph
Phabet
Mathias
Arrius Antonius Calpernius Piso
Simon Thassi
Marcus Annius Verus
Anna
Bran
Llud Law
Jeshua
John Hyrancus
Lucius Aelius Verus
Mandubratus
Jose
Ann
Antigonus
James
Annia Galeria Faustina
Penardun
Marius
Jasna
Jude
Judas of Gamla
Annia Galeria Faustina II
Elzarus
Menehem
Eurgen
Sarclotus
Eurgain
Eucharia
Crispus Lucius Aurelius Commodus
Nashon
Gladys
Lucius the Great
Salome
Saint Lazarus
Emanuel Erise
Cyleddon Celedoin
Flavius Numerius
Gladys the Younger
Eugen
Enclede
Narpus
Cadvan
Eudolen
Flavius Crispus
Othrac
Nascien II
Strada
Coel Hen
Eugen
Maxime
Gallienus Quiriacus
Abalach
Claudia
Iouguen
Constantius
Saint Helen of the Cross
Llebryn
Dobun
Karnot
Helyas
Perum
Saint Constantine
Fausta
Meuric
Ysayes
Omid
Amguerit
Otta
Constantine II
Ionans
Amguoil
Constantia
Marchudd
Gerentounus
Guordum
Gwrthryw
Agripanus
Magnus
Saint Helen of the Host
Dumn
Gwraldeg
Saint Ursula
Conan
Gurdeil
Teitfall
Morfudd
Gladys
Cadfan
Doeil
Gratiana
Teuduric
Gwrfawr
Peisrud
Anlach
Marchell
Patern
Cadwallon
Tudwal
Gratianna
Abalach
Etern
Saint Brychan
Prawst
Cuneda
Maelgwyn Hir
Saint Sefin
Saint Meleri
Ceredig
Einion
Rhun
Saint Non
Sant
Hoel III
Hoel II
Rimo
Saint Dewi
Saint Judicael
Alain

The three saints from Armenia, Saint Gregory the Enlightened, Saint Narses, and Saint Isaac all have very interesting lineages. Saint Gregory's lineage is not really known, however both Saint Narses and Saint Isaac's lineage gets pretty complicated. Saint Joseph, father of Salome, James, Jose, and husband of the Virgin has a line thur Salome that continues with King Abgar that leads to Saint Narses. Also Saint Narses line goes up to John, the son of Joazar who has Tobit as an ancestor. This line from Tobit goes thur to Shealtiel and is therefore from the Davidic blood of King Solomon. Now the line from Narses also goes up thur Armenia to join with King Darius. There are three branches of interest here. One line goes to the King of Persia Nechebanezzar who is mentioned in the book of Daniel and the book of Judith. Note there are three Nechebanezzar's in the line. (Nechebanezzar means sneeze in some language). The other line from King Darius goes thru Esther, who is of the tribe of Benjamin. This line is from Kish the Father of Maachah and King Saul. There is another line that goes to Teispes. In conclusion then, the Armenian Saints Narses, and Isaac have Davidic blood thru Tobit, thur Saint Joseph, and can be from Benjamin without being Davidic. They also go back to the King of Babylon.

The interesting thing about lines that continue past Saint Isaac is that they do not join with nobility of Europe until much later past the first millennium with the line of William Autun of the Desert.

Saint Gregory the Enlightened

Feastday: September 30

Date: b 240 d .326

Family:

Parents: Unknown

Wife: Unknown

Children: Yusik Patriach of the Armenian Church

Ancestry:

Even parentage is unknown.

Descendents:

Saint Fernando III is a descendent. Also Edward I Longshanks King of England is a descendent. Edward III and Edward IV Plantagenet are also descendents, with Thomas Prince of England. Edward Stafford 3rd Duke of Buckingham is also a descendent. Also William X Duke of Aquitane. Konstantinos Emperor of Byzantium is a descendent.

Biography:

Surnamed the Illuminator, Gregory the Enlightener is of unknown origins. Anok a Parthian who murdered King Khosrov I or Armenia may be his father, the murder happening when Gregory was a baby. Gregory, smuggled to Caesarea, was baptized, and had two sons after marriage. He was smuggled as the dying Khosrov's ordered to murder the entire family. Tiridates, King Khosrov's son, regained his father's throne, and Gregory was permitted to return. Support of the Armenian Christians and his conversion activities incurred the King's displeasure. Tiridates was converted to Christianity in time by Gregory and the Official religion of Armenia became Christianity. Consecrated bishop of Ashtishat, Gregory set about organizing the Church in Armenia. Evangelization and building a native clergy working untiringly was what kept Gregory busy as bishop. When his son Aristakes was consecrated to the episcopate he set into motion the process that made his See a hereditary position. Gregory then retired to a hermitage on Mount Manyea in Taron and remained there until his death. Miracles and Extravagant legends were attributed to him, many becoming celebrated feasts by the Armenians. Gregory the Enlightener is considered the apostle of Armenia. Feast day is September 30th.

He is the ancestor of Saint Narses Pahlav.

Saint Narses Pahlav

Feastday: November 19

Date: 335-373

Family:

Parents: Father- Athenagenes   Mother-Ataknines-Bambism   Princess of Armenia

Wife: Sandukht

Children: Saint Isaac Pahlav

Ancestry:

Saint Gregory the Enlightened is an Ancestor.   Further Ancestry is unknown.

Descendents:

Saint Fernando III is a descendent. Also Edward I Longshanks King of England is a descendent. Edward III and Edward IV Plantagenet are also descendents, with Thomas Prince of England. Edward Stafford 3rd Duke of Buckingham is also a descendent. Also William X Duke of Aquitane. Konstantinos Emperor of Byzantium is a descendent.

Biography:

Father of St. Isaac the Great and Bishop and Martyr. He studied in Cappadocia, a native of Armenia, and he wed a princess who gave birth to Isaac. He served as a chamberlain in the court of King Arshak of Armenia after her death. He was made Catholicos of the Armenians in 353. Based on the principles he had studied under St. Basil at Caesarea Nerses devoted much effort to reforming the Armenian Church, including convening a synod in 365. His reforms and denunciation of King Arshak's murder of the queen led to his exile although he established hospitals and monasteries. After Arshak's death in battle he returned, but relations were not much better with the new Armenian ruler, Pap, whose dissolute lifestyle caused Nerses to refuse him admission into the church. Invited to a royal banquet at Khakh, on the Euphrates River, Nerses was assassinated by poison.

Saint Narses is the father of Saint Isaac Pahlav.

Saint Isaac Pahlav

Feastday: September 9

Date: b. 351- d. 438

Family:

Parents: Father-Narses I Nerseh Pahlav Saint b. 335 Mother- Sandukht

Wife: Unknown

Children: Hamazasp

Ancestry:

Saint Gregory the Enlightened is an ancestor. Further ancestry is not known.

Descendents:

Saint Fernando III is a descendent. Also Edward I Longshanks King of England is a descendent. Edward III and Edward IV Plantagenet are also descendents, with Thomas Prince of England. Edward Stafford 3rd Duke of Buckingham is also a descendent. Also William X Duke of Aquitane. Konstantinos Emperor of Byzantium is a descendent.

Biography:

Saint Isaac the Great was the son of St. Nerses I of Armenia.

Isaac the Great whose feast day is September 9 became a monk. He studied at Constantinople, married, and on the early death of his wife became a monk. He was appointed Catholicos of Armenia in 390 and secured from Constantinople recognition of the metropolitan rights of the Armenian Church, thus terminating its long dependence on the Church of Caesarea in Cappodocia. He at once began to reform the Armenian Church. He enforced Byzantine canon law, encouraged monasticism, ended the practice of married bishops, fought Persian paganism, and built churches and schools. He supported St. Mesrop in his creation of an Armenian alphabet, and was responsible for establishing a national liturgy and the beginnings of Armenian literature. He also helped to promote the translation of the Bible and the works of the Greek and Syrian doctors into Armenian. He was the founder of the Armenian Church and is sometimes called Sahak in Armenia.

When the Persians conquered part of his territory he was driven into retirement in 428 but returned at an advanced age to rule again from his See at Ashtishat, where he died in the year 439. The Armenian Saints Isaac, Nerses and Gregory have a unique line of descent that leads to the Emperors of the Byzantine Empire. This line is pretty isolated from the known royal lines of Europe, and joins the existing royalty lines with Edward I Longshanks of England around the year 1000. The line is from the Mamokonian house and contains William Count of Toulouse and his wife Konstantinos. William Count of Toulouse will be mentioned again at the chapter that concerns the years 700-800. Saint Louis IX and Saint Fernando are also Descendents.

There are at least three was to trace the ancestors of Saint Isaac Pavlav that are shown in this work. The line from Salome the daughter of Saint Joseph is one, the line from Esther that goes thru Xerses of Armenia is one, and the line from John and Perichai that goes thru Haggai and Shetial is another. There is also lines that go thru the Roman.

Saint Isaac is shown to be a descendent of Isaac the son of Abraham, and also descended from the Babylon empire King Nechabanezzar and from the King David of Judah and Israel. He is shown to have the blood of Cleopatra and the Ptolemies as well. He is shown in the following chart to have the blood of Benjamine as well.

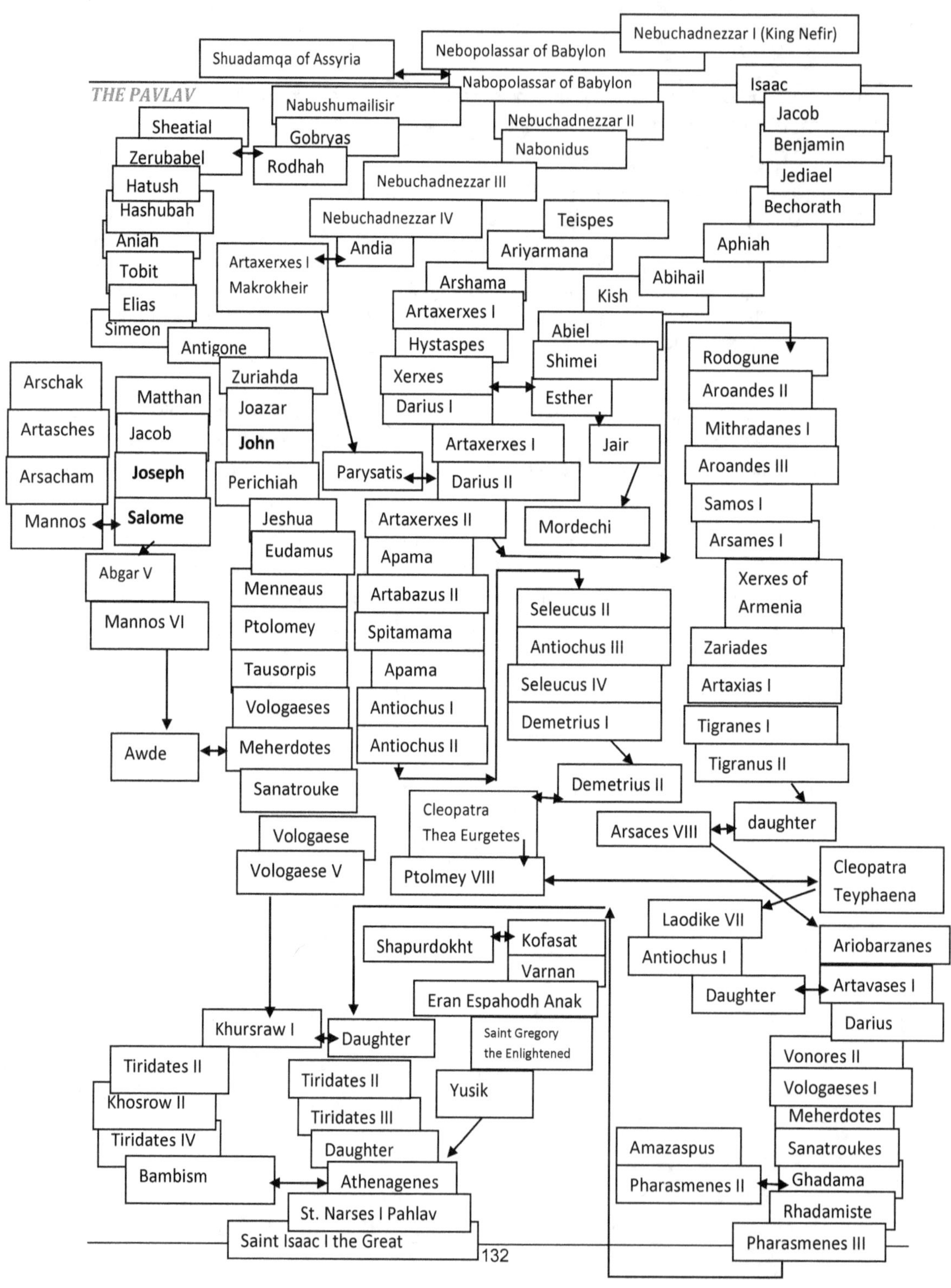
Nebuchadnezzar I (King Nefir)
Nebopolassar of Babylon
Shuadamqa of Assyria
Nabopolassar of Babylon
Isaac
Jacob
Benjamin
Jediael
Bechorath
Aphiah
Abihail
Kish
Abiel
Shimei
Esther
Jair
Mordechi
Nabushumailisir
Gobryas
Nebuchadnezzar II
Nabonidus
Nebuchadnezzar III
Nebuchadnezzar IV
Andia
Teispes
Ariyarmana
Arshama
Artaxerxes I
Hystaspes
Xerxes
Darius I
Artaxerxes I
Darius II
Artaxerxes II
Apama
Artabazus II
Spitamama
Apama
Antiochus I
Antiochus II
Sheatial
Zerubabel
Rodhah
Hatush
Hashubah
Aniah
Tobit
Elias
Simeon
Antigone
Artaxerxes I
Makrokheir
Zuriahda
Joazar
John
Perichiah
Parysatis
Jeshua
Eudamus
Menneaus
Ptolomey
Tausorpis
Vologaeses
Meherdotes
Sanatrouke
Arschak
Artasches
Arsacham
Mannos
Matthan
Jacob
Joseph
Salome
Abgar V
Mannos VI
Awde
Rodogune
Aroandes II
Mithradanes I
Aroandes III
Samos I
Arsames I
Xerxes of
Armenia
Zariades
Artaxias I
Tigranes I
Tigranus II
daughter
Seleucus II
Antiochus III
Seleucus IV
Demetrius I
Demetrius II
Cleopatra
Thea Eurgetes
Ptolmey VIII
Arsaces VIII
Cleopatra
Teyphaena
Laodike VII
Antiochus I
Daughter
Ariobarzanes
Artavases I
Darius
Vologaese
Vologaese V
Shapurdokht
Kofasat
Varnan
Eran Espahodh Anak
Saint Gregory
the Enlightened
Yusik
Khursraw I
Daughter
Tiridates II
Khosrow II
Tiridates IV
Bambism
Tiridates II
Tiridates III
Daughter
Athenagenes
St. Narses I Pahlav
Saint Isaac I the Great
Vonores II
Vologaeses I
Meherdotes
Sanatroukes
Ghadama
Rhadamiste
Pharasmenes III
Amazaspus
Pharasmenes II

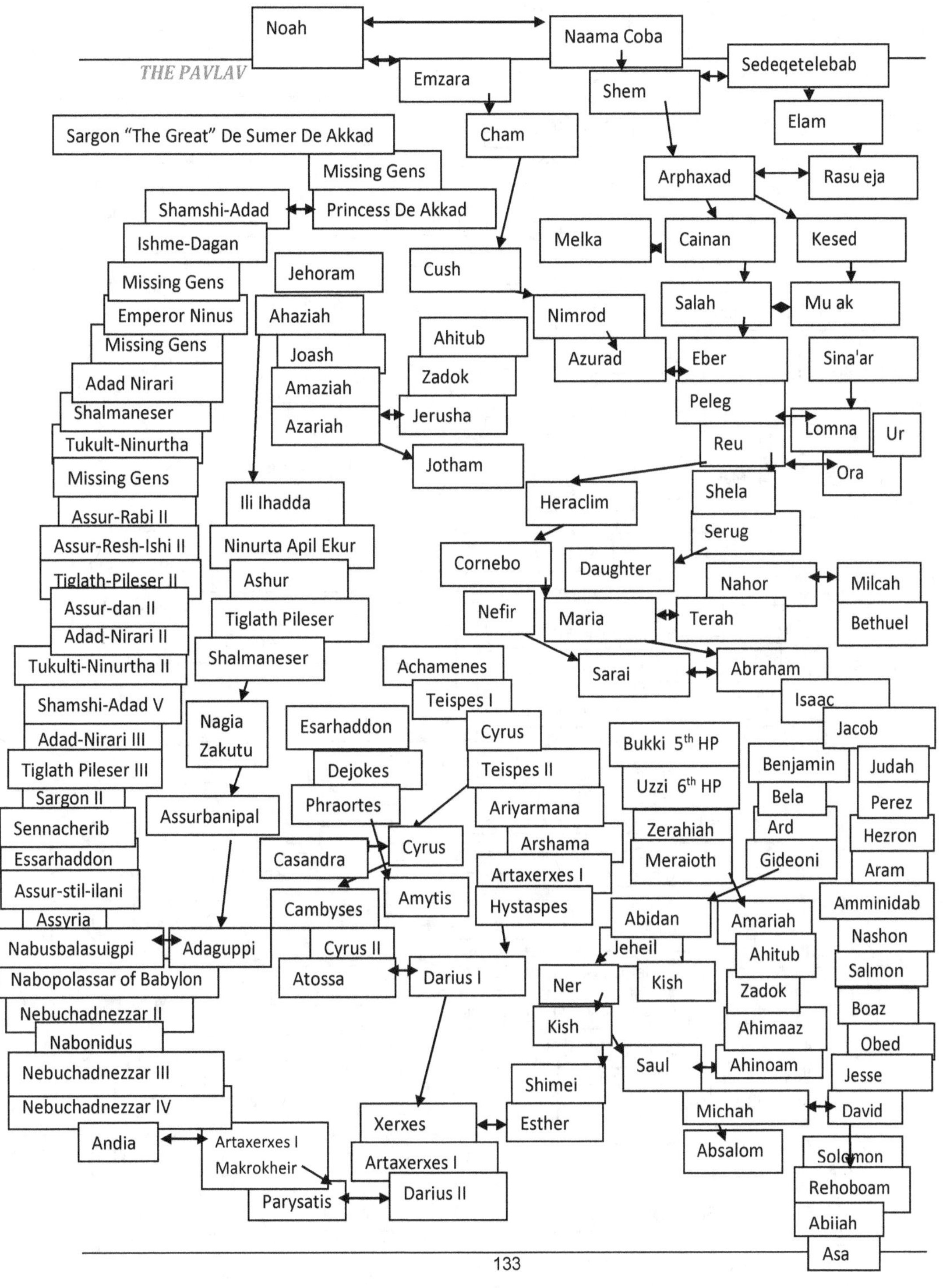
Noah
Naama Coba
Emzara
Sedeqetelebab
Shem
Elam
Sargon "The Great" De Sumer De Akkad
Cham
Missing Gens
Arphaxad
Rasu eja
Shamshi-Adad
Princess De Akkad
Ishme-Dagan
Melka
Cainan
Kesed
Missing Gens
Jehoram
Cush
Emperor Ninus
Ahaziah
Nimrod
Salah
Mu ak
Missing Gens
Ahitub
Joash
Azurad
Eber
Sina'ar
Adad Nirari
Amaziah
Zadok
Shalmaneser
Jerusha
Peleg
Lomna
Ur
Tukult-Ninurtha
Azariah
Reu
Jotham
Missing Gens
Ora
Shela
Heraclim
Ili Ihadda
Assur-Rabi II
Serug
Assur-Resh-Ishi II
Ninurta Apil Ekur
Cornebo
Daughter
Tiglath-Pileser II
Ashur
Nahor
Milcah
Assur-dan II
Nefir
Maria
Terah
Tiglath Pileser
Bethuel
Adad-Nirari II
Tukulti-Ninurtha II
Shalmaneser
Achamenes
Sarai
Abraham
Teispes I
Isaac
Shamshi-Adad V
Nagia Zakutu
Esarhaddon
Cyrus
Jacob
Bukki 5th HP
Adad-Nirari III
Benjamin
Judah
Tiglath Pileser III
Dejokes
Teispes II
Uzzi 6th HP
Sargon II
Bela
Perez
Phraortes
Ariyarmana
Sennacherib
Assurbanipal
Zerahiah
Ard
Hezron
Arshama
Essarhaddon
Casandra
Cyrus
Meraioth
Gideoni
Artaxerxes I
Aram
Assur-stil-ilani
Amytis
Amminidab
Cambyses
Hystaspes
Abidan
Assyria
Amariah
Nashon
Nabusbalasuigpi
Adaguppi
Cyrus II
Jeheil
Ahitub
Nabopolassar of Babylon
Atossa
Darius I
Ner
Kish
Salmon
Zadok
Nebuchadnezzar II
Boaz
Kish
Ahimaaz
Nabonidus
Obed
Nebuchadnezzar III
Saul
Ahinoam
Shimei
Jesse
Nebuchadnezzar IV
Michah
David
Xerxes
Esther
Andia
Artaxerxes I Makrokheir
Absalom
Artaxerxes I
Solomon
Rehoboam
Parysatis
Darius II
Abiiah
Asa

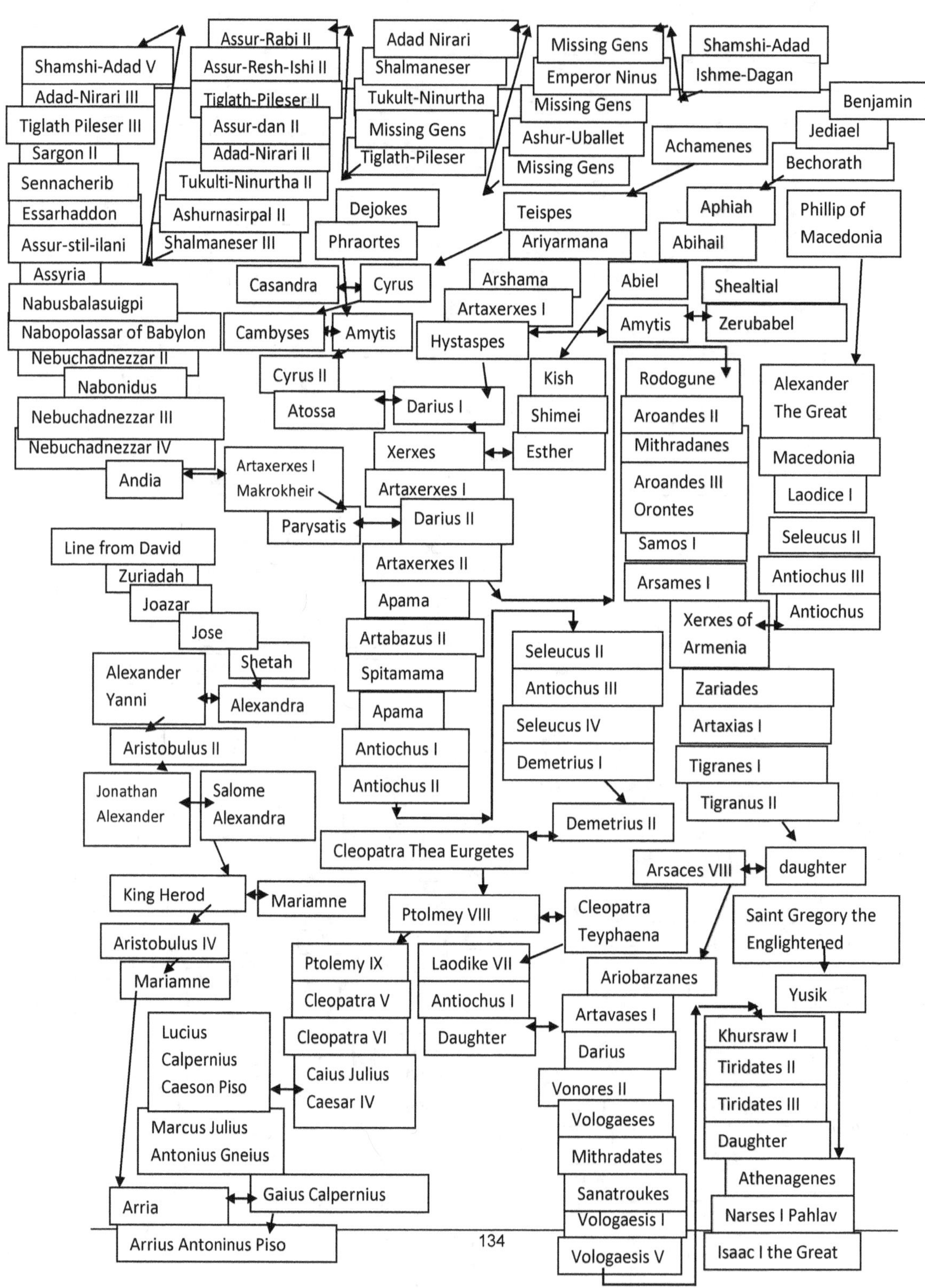

Shamshi-Adad V
Adad-Nirari III
Tiglath Pileser III
Sargon II
Sennacherib
Essarhaddon
Assur-stil-ilani
Assyria
Nabusbalasuigpi
Nabopolassar of Babylon
Nebuchadnezzar II
Nabonidus
Nebuchadnezzar III
Nebuchadnezzar IV
Andia
Assur-Rabi II
Assur-Resh-Ishi II
Tiglath-Pileser II
Assur-dan II
Adad-Nirari II
Tukulti-Ninurtha II
Ashurnasirpal II
Shalmaneser III
Adad Nirari
Shalmaneser
Tukult-Ninurtha
Missing Gens
Tiglath-Pileser
Dejokes
Phraortes
Casandra
Cyrus
Cambyses
Amytis
Cyrus II
Atossa
Darius I
Missing Gens
Emperor Ninus
Missing Gens
Ashur-Uballet
Missing Gens
Teispes
Ariyarmana
Arshama
Artaxerxes I
Hystaspes
Shamshi-Adad
Ishme-Dagan
Achamenes
Benjamin
Jediael
Bechorath
Aphiah
Abihail
Abiel
Amytis
Shealtial
Zerubabel
Phillip of Macedonia
Kish
Shimei
Esther
Xerxes
Artaxerxes I
Artaxerxes I Makrokheir
Parysatis
Darius II
Artaxerxes II
Apama
Artabazus II
Spitamama
Apama
Antiochus I
Antiochus II
Rodogune
Aroandes II
Mithradanes
Aroandes III Orontes
Samos I
Arsames I
Alexander The Great
Macedonia
Laodice I
Seleucus II
Antiochus III
Antiochus
Xerxes of Armenia
Line from David
Zuriadah
Joazar
Jose
Shetah
Alexander Yanni
Alexandra
Aristobulus II
Jonathan Alexander
Salome Alexandra
King Herod
Mariamne
Aristobulus IV
Mariamne
Lucius Calpernius Caeson Piso
Caius Julius Caesar IV
Marcus Julius Antonius Gneius
Arria
Gaius Calpernius
Arrius Antoninus Piso
Seleucus II
Antiochus III
Seleucus IV
Demetrius I
Demetrius II
Cleopatra Thea Eurgetes
Ptolmey VIII
Cleopatra Teyphaena
Ptolemy IX
Cleopatra V
Cleopatra VI
Laodike VII
Antiochus I
Daughter
Zariades
Artaxias I
Tigranes I
Tigranus II
Arsaces VIII
daughter
Ariobarzanes
Artavases I
Darius
Vonores II
Vologaeses
Mithradates
Sanatroukes
Vologaesis I
Vologaesis V
Saint Gregory the Englightened
Yusik
Khursraw I
Tiridates II
Tiridates III
Daughter
Athenagenes
Narses I Pahlav
Isaac I the Great

ERA OF THE TIME OF BABYLON TO THE ERA OF CHRISTIANITY

The two scriptures the Gospel of Mathew and the Gospel of Luke have genealogies that are supposedly the lineage of the Lord, however they do not agree. I always wondered about this and was told in a college course one was the lineage of Mary and one of Joseph. This is accurate in a way and a possible explanation. However when I actually took a piece of paper and wrote them down and how they work and the relationships it made sense. Note in the Graph on the previous page the lineage of the Virgin Mary is shown, as well as the lineage of Eleazar of the house of David. So both Gospels are correct, although different and the Gospels do not show the women and their marriages that make it all work. Note it is proper to always refer to Saint Joseph as the Foster Father of the Lord, as the Lord was conceived from the Virgin and Joseph considered a divorce. Because Mary was likely the first wife of Joseph and Joseph was father of James, Jose, Simon, and Judas, Mary, Salome, and Ann, he was widowed when the Virgin was with child and she did need a husband, and she was from the levitiacal priesthood.

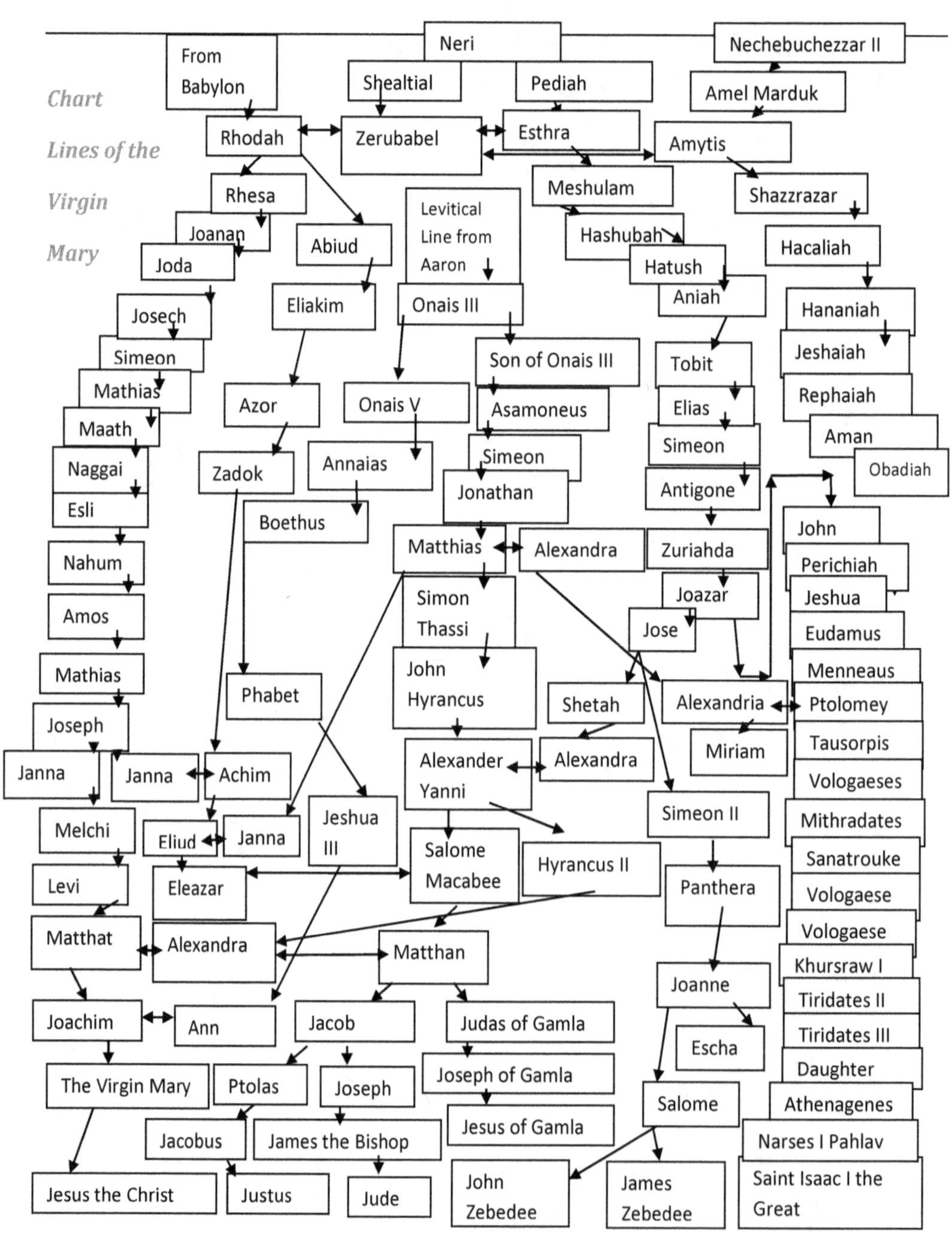
Chart
Lines of the
Virgin
Mary
From Babylon
Neri
Nechebuchezzar II
Shealtial
Pediah
Amel Marduk
Rhodah
Zerubabel
Esthra
Amytis
Rhesa
Meshulam
Shazzrazar
Joanan
Abiud
Levitical Line from Aaron
Hashubah
Hacaliah
Joda
Hatush
Aniah
Josech
Eliakim
Onais III
Hananiah
Simeon
Son of Onais III
Tobit
Jeshaiah
Mathias
Azor
Onais V
Asamoneus
Elias
Rephaiah
Maath
Simeon
Simeon
Aman
Naggai
Zadok
Annaias
Jonathan
Antigone
Obadiah
Esli
Boethus
John
Matthias
Alexandra
Zuriahda
Nahum
Perichiah
Simon Thassi
Joazar
Jeshua
Amos
Jose
Eudamus
Mathias
John Hyrancus
Menneaus
Phabet
Shetah
Alexandria
Ptolomey
Joseph
Miriam
Tausorpis
Janna
Janna
Achim
Alexander Yanni
Alexandra
Vologaeses
Jeshua III
Simeon II
Mithradates
Melchi
Eliud
Janna
Salome Macabee
Hyrancus II
Sanatrouke
Levi
Eleazar
Panthera
Vologaese
Vologaese
Matthat
Alexandra
Matthan
Khursraw I
Joanne
Tiridates II
Joachim
Ann
Jacob
Judas of Gamla
Escha
Tiridates III
The Virgin Mary
Ptolas
Joseph
Joseph of Gamla
Daughter
Salome
Athenagenes
Jacobus
James the Bishop
Jesus of Gamla
Narses I Pahlav
Jesus the Christ
Justus
Jude
John Zebedee
James Zebedee
Saint Isaac I the Great

ERA OF THE TIME OF DAVID TO THE TIME OF BABYLON

SECTION EIGHT: THE KINGDOM AND KINGS

Shown here are lineages of David, the next page showing most of the relationships that a listed genealogy (as shown in the bible in Chronicles or the Gospels) does not include. A vertical ascent is good, owever the missing relationships could be known as well.

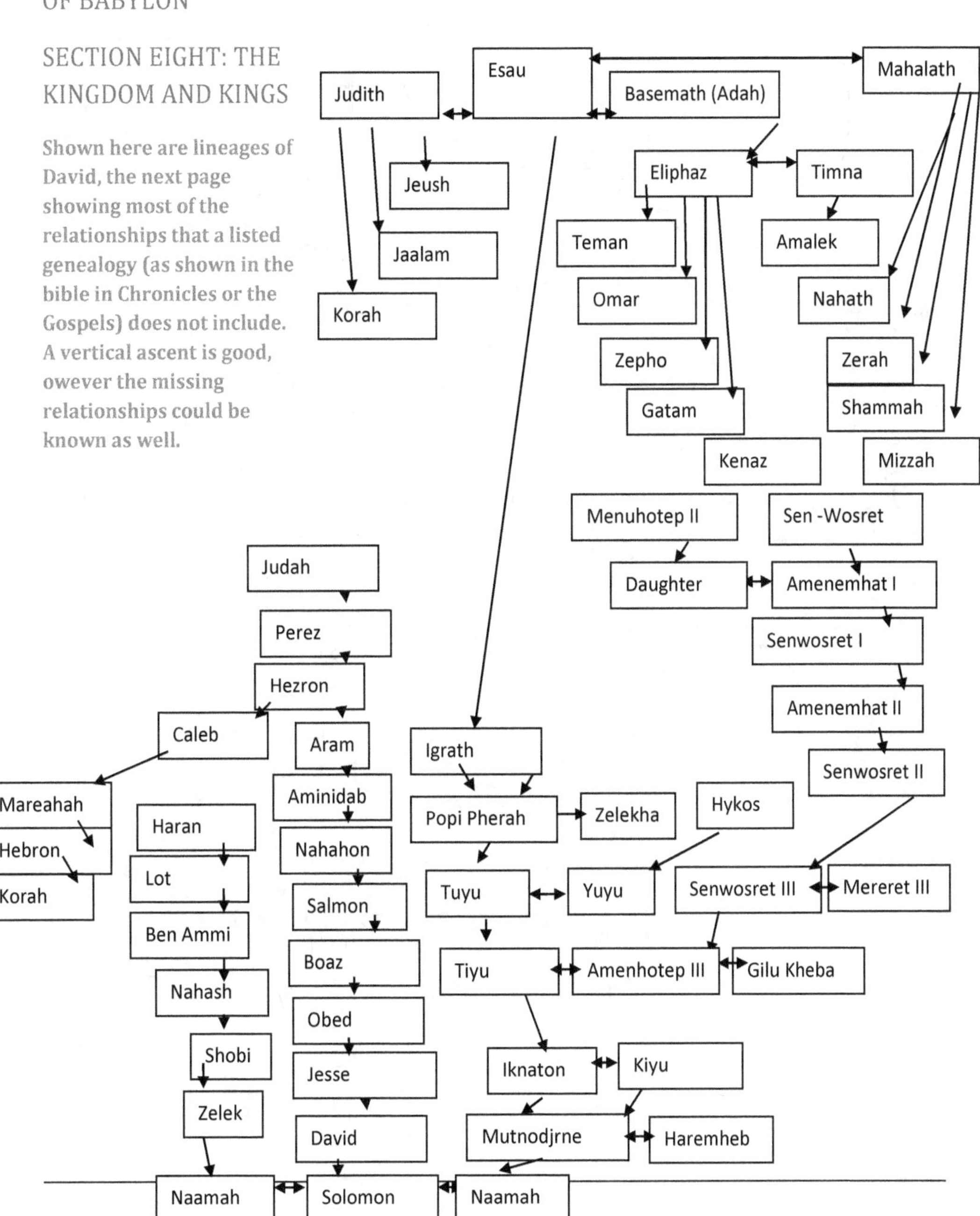

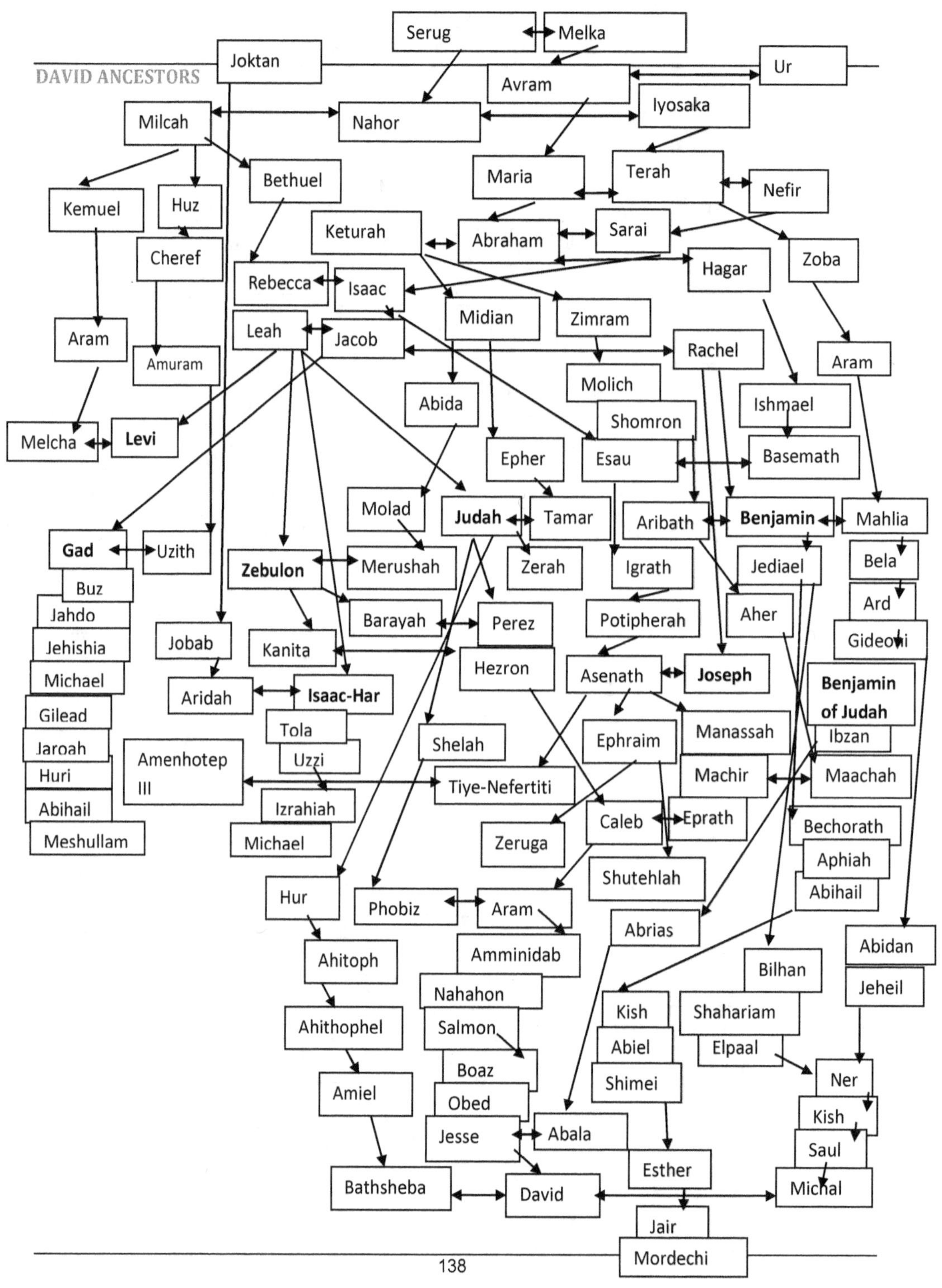
Serug
Melka
Joktan
Ur
Avram
Milcah
Nahor
Iyosaka
Bethuel
Maria
Terah
Nefir
Kemuel
Huz
Keturah
Abraham
Sarai
Cheref
Zoba
Hagar
Rebecca
Isaac
Midian
Zimram
Leah
Jacob
Aram
Amuram
Rachel
Aram
Molich
Abida
Shomron
Ishmael
Melcha
Levi
Epher
Esau
Basemath
Molad
Judah
Tamar
Aribath
Benjamin
Mahlia
Gad
Uzith
Zebulon
Merushah
Zerah
Igrath
Jediael
Bela
Buz
Ard
Jahdo
Barayah
Perez
Potipherah
Aher
Jobab
Gideoni
Jehishia
Kanita
Hezron
Asenath
Joseph
Michael
Benjamin of Judah
Aridah
Isaac-Har
Gilead
Tola
Manassah
Ibzan
Shelah
Ephraim
Jaroah
Amenhotep III
Uzzi
Huri
Machir
Maachah
Tiye-Nefertiti
Abihail
Izrahiah
Caleb
Eprath
Bechorath
Meshullam
Michael
Zeruga
Aphiah
Shutehlah
Abihail
Hur
Phobiz
Aram
Abrias
Amminidab
Abidan
Ahitoph
Bilhan
Nahahon
Jeheil
Kish
Shahariam
Ahithophel
Salmon
Abiel
Elpaal
Boaz
Ner
Amiel
Shimei
Obed
Kish
Jesse
Abala
Saul
Esther
Bathsheba
David
Michal
Jair
Mordechi

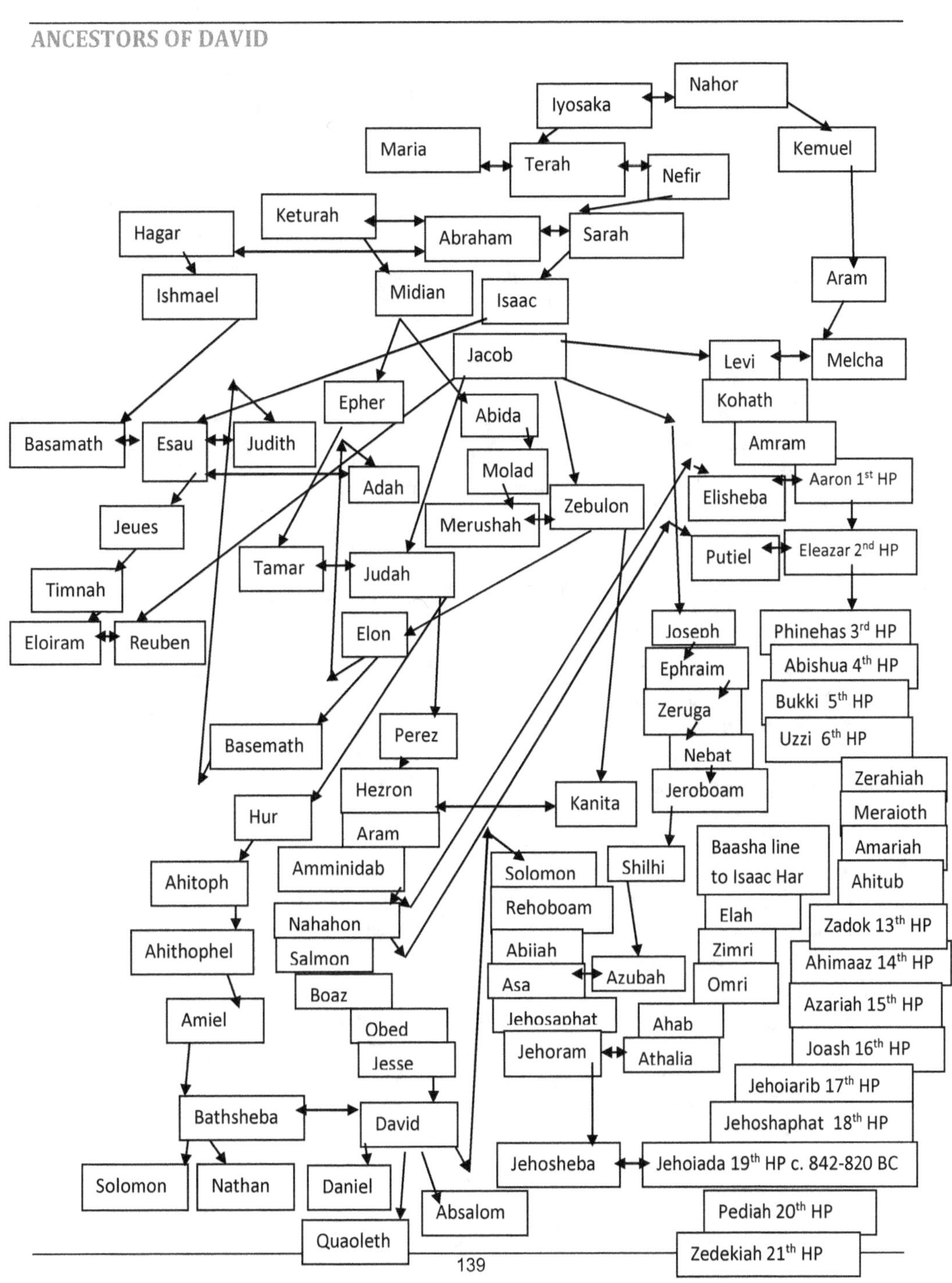
Nahor
Iyosaka
Maria
Terah
Nefir
Kemuel
Keturah
Hagar
Abraham
Sarah
Ishmael
Midian
Isaac
Aram
Jacob
Levi
Melcha
Epher
Kohath
Abida
Basamath
Esau
Judith
Amram
Adah
Molad
Aaron 1st HP
Elisheba
Zebulon
Jeues
Merushah
Tamar
Judah
Putiel
Eleazar 2nd HP
Timnah
Eloiram
Reuben
Elon
Joseph
Phinehas 3rd HP
Ephraim
Abishua 4th HP
Zeruga
Bukki 5th HP
Basemath
Perez
Uzzi 6th HP
Nebat
Zerahiah
Hezron
Jeroboam
Kanita
Hur
Meraioth
Aram
Baasha line
to Isaac Har
Amariah
Amminidab
Shilhi
Ahitoph
Solomon
Ahitub
Rehoboam
Elah
Nahahon
Zadok 13th HP
Salmon
Abiiah
Zimri
Ahithophel
Ahimaaz 14th HP
Asa
Azubah
Omri
Boaz
Azariah 15th HP
Amiel
Jehosaphat
Ahab
Obed
Joash 16th HP
Jehoram
Athalia
Jesse
Jehoiarib 17th HP
Bathsheba
David
Jehoshaphat 18th HP
Jehosheba
Jehoiada 19th HP c. 842-820 BC
Solomon
Nathan
Daniel
Absalom
Pediah 20th HP
Quaoleth
Zedekiah 21st HP

The Kingdom of David, How it evolved with his descendents line of Kings.

Here are the relationships that are the lineage of Ezra. Note how these relationships are not shown in the scriptures.

Ezra is shown in these charts to be descended from King David, Jacob, Joseph, Joshua son of Nun, Joshua son of Eliezer. The charts show the relationships and marriage ties that tie the Line from King David to the Aaronic Lines.

The lines from the descendents of Solomon married the lines that are from Joseph that were the kings of Israel. Note that the line from Ahab whose daughter Athalia married Jerom is descended thru a hidden line to Epraim and from Joseph. Note also that Zeruah who married Nebat line continues thru to Hur the father of Ezer who married Miriam. Now Miriam was also a wife of Hur, but not necessarily the mother of Ezer.

Here in the charts as found on the internet Joshua son of Nun is shown to marry Rahab who was the daughter of Bezezeel who was also a mother of Boaz of the line of David. There is also a Joshua son of Elizer of the line of Nathan that may have had a child with a daughter of that married the levitical Priest line and was an ancestor of the High Priest Ezra. Note also that Jeremiah who was the author of a biblical book is a brother to the High Priest of Aaron line and had a daughter that married the line of David.

Another interesting fact found in these charts is that Jehiokim had a daughter that married Neri. Now Neri had a daughter that married Jeconiah. Now Jeconiah is said in the scripture lines to be a father of Shealtial. This makes Shealtial of the Royal house of Solomon and David. Shealtial on other genealogies is shown to be the line of Nathan. It is known that Shealtial is of the blood of Nathan but was adopted by Jeconiah to have the line continue. The idea here is that a line based on a figure that hurls stones at Giants and kills them and goes from place to place and is a great warrior cannot continue as a line, but a line of the son of David Nathan or the brother of David, Nathaniel who repremands the King for his marriage to Bathesheba (who in this book is shown to be from the Israelite Judah) and ordering Uriah to the front line.

Here is also shown the lineage of Absalom and the relationships to Rehoboam and Abijah who married the daughters of Absalom.

Note the lines from the Davidic and the Aaronic merge to become the lines that lead to the priestess the Virgin Mary.

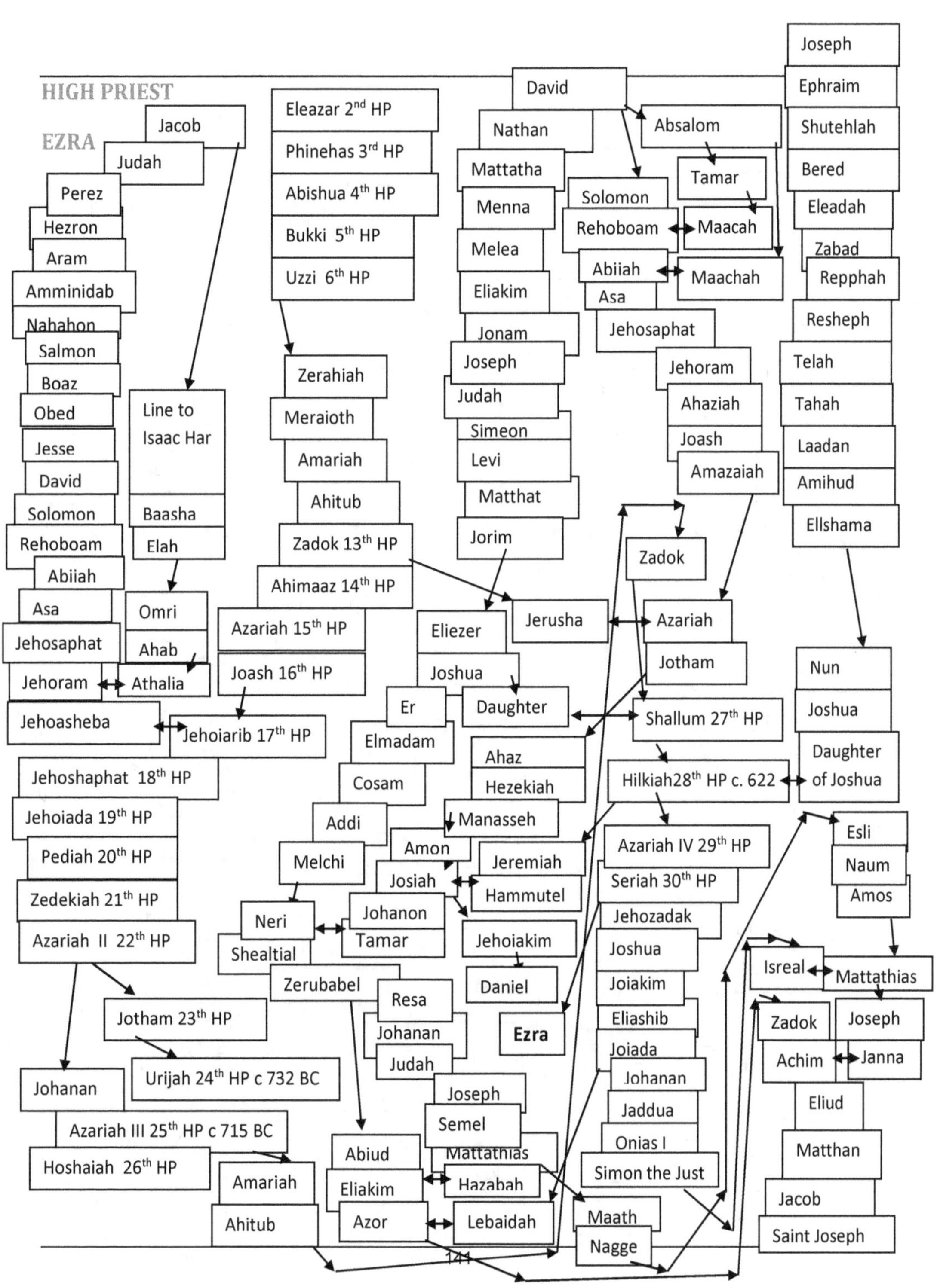
HIGH PRIEST
EZRA
Jacob
Judah
Perez
Hezron
Aram
Amminidab
Nahahon
Salmon
Boaz
Obed
Jesse
David
Solomon
Rehoboam
Abiiah
Asa
Jehosaphat
Jehoram
Athalia
Jehoasheba
Line to Isaac Har
Baasha
Elah
Omri
Ahab
Eleazar 2nd HP
Phinehas 3rd HP
Abishua 4th HP
Bukki 5th HP
Uzzi 6th HP
Zerahiah
Meraioth
Amariah
Ahitub
Zadok 13th HP
Ahimaaz 14th HP
Azariah 15th HP
Joash 16th HP
Jehoiarib 17th HP
Jehoshaphat 18th HP
Jehoiada 19th HP
Pediah 20th HP
Zedekiah 21st HP
Azariah II 22th HP
Jotham 23th HP
Urijah 24th HP c 732 BC
Johanan
Azariah III 25th HP c 715 BC
Hoshaiah 26th HP
Amariah
Ahitub
David
Nathan
Mattatha
Menna
Melea
Eliakim
Jonam
Joseph
Judah
Simeon
Levi
Matthat
Jorim
Eliezer
Joshua
Er
Daughter
Elmadam
Cosam
Addi
Melchi
Neri
Shealtial
Zerubabel
Johanon
Tamar
Resa
Johanan
Judah
Joseph
Semel
Mattathias
Abiud
Eliakim
Hazabah
Azor
Lebaidah
Absalom
Tamar
Solomon
Rehoboam
Maacah
Abiiah
Maachah
Asa
Jehosaphat
Jehoram
Ahaziah
Joash
Amazaiah
Zadok
Jerusha
Azariah
Jotham
Shallum 27th HP
Ahaz
Hezekiah
Manasseh
Amon
Josiah
Jeremiah
Hammutel
Jehoiakim
Daniel
Ezra
Hilkiah28th HP c. 622
Azariah IV 29th HP
Seriah 30th HP
Jehozadak
Joshua
Joiakim
Eliashib
Joiada
Johanan
Jaddua
Onias I
Simon the Just
Maath
Nagge
Joseph
Ephraim
Shutehlah
Bered
Eleadah
Zabad
Repphah
Resheph
Telah
Tahah
Laadan
Amihud
Ellshama
Nun
Joshua
Daughter of Joshua
Esli
Naum
Amos
Isreal
Mattathias
Zadok
Joseph
Achim
Janna
Eliud
Matthan
Jacob
Saint Joseph

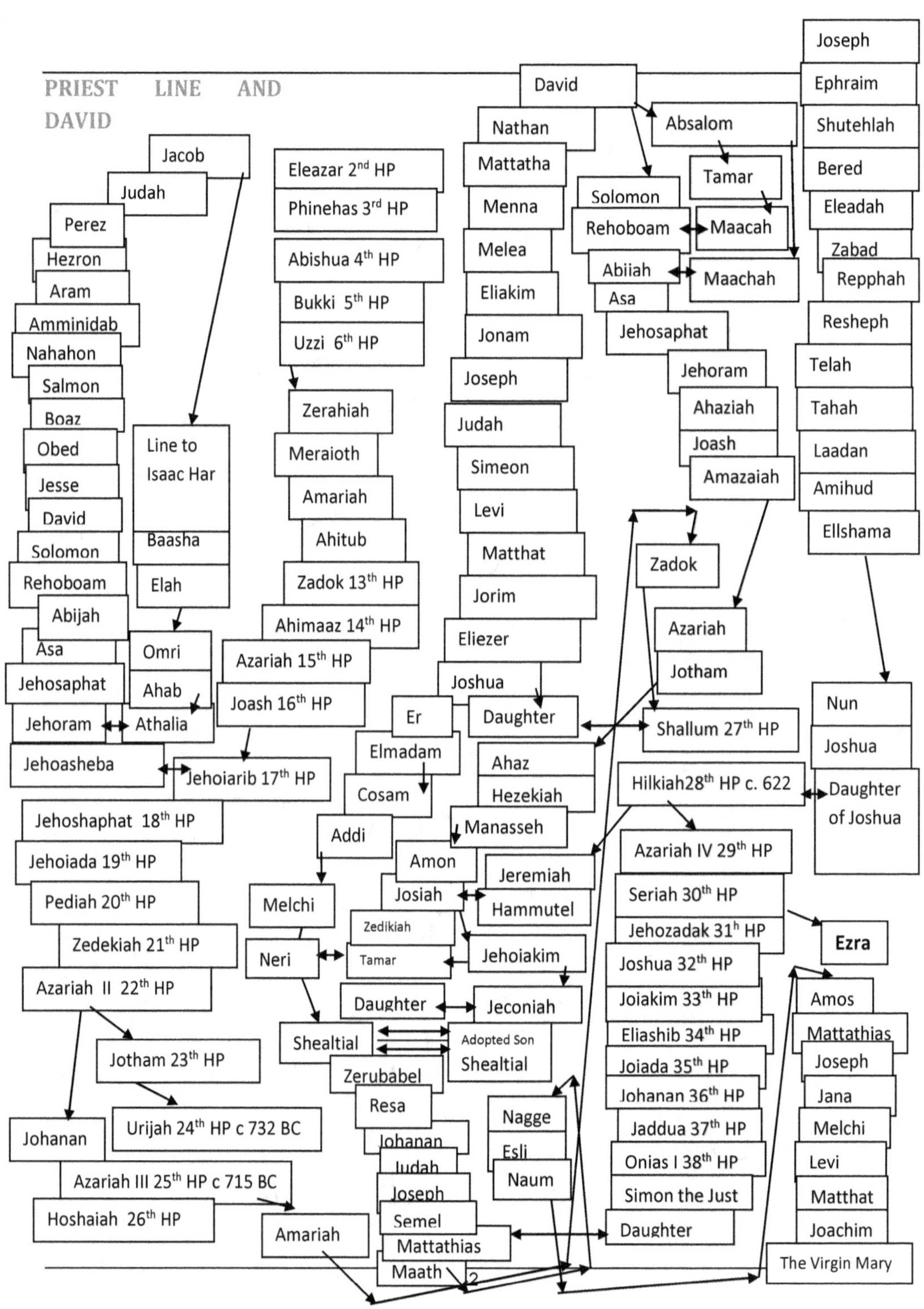
PRIEST LINE AND DAVID
Jacob
Judah
Perez
Hezron
Aram
Amminidab
Nahahon
Salmon
Boaz
Obed
Jesse
David
Solomon
Rehoboam
Abijah
Asa
Jehosaphat
Jehoram
Athalia
Jehoasheba
Line to Isaac Har
Baasha
Elah
Omri
Ahab
Eleazar 2nd HP
Phinehas 3rd HP
Abishua 4th HP
Bukki 5th HP
Uzzi 6th HP
Zerahiah
Meraioth
Amariah
Ahitub
Zadok 13th HP
Ahimaaz 14th HP
Azariah 15th HP
Joash 16th HP
Jehoiarib 17th HP
Jehoshaphat 18th HP
Jehoiada 19th HP
Pediah 20th HP
Zedekiah 21st HP
Azariah II 22th HP
Jotham 23th HP
Urijah 24th HP c 732 BC
Johanan
Azariah III 25th HP c 715 BC
Hoshaiah 26th HP
Amariah
David
Nathan
Mattatha
Menna
Melea
Eliakim
Jonam
Joseph
Judah
Simeon
Levi
Matthat
Jorim
Eliezer
Joshua
Er
Daughter
Elmadam
Cosam
Addi
Melchi
Neri
Shealtial
Zerubabel
Resa
Johanan
Judah
Joseph
Semel
Mattathias
Maath
Ahaz
Hezekiah
Manasseh
Amon
Josiah
Jeremiah
Hammutel
Zedikiah
Tamar
Jehoiakim
Daughter
Jeconiah
Adopted Son Shealtial
Nagge
Esli
Naum
Absalom
Tamar
Solomon
Rehoboam
Maacah
Abiiah
Maachah
Asa
Jehosaphat
Jehoram
Ahaziah
Joash
Amazaiah
Zadok
Azariah
Jotham
Shallum 27th HP
Hilkiah28th HP c. 622
Azariah IV 29th HP
Seriah 30th HP
Jehozadak 31h HP
Joshua 32th HP
Joiakim 33th HP
Eliashib 34th HP
Joiada 35th HP
Johanan 36th HP
Jaddua 37th HP
Onias I 38th HP
Simon the Just
Daughter
Joseph
Ephraim
Shutehlah
Bered
Eleadah
Zabad
Repphah
Resheph
Telah
Tahah
Laadan
Amihud
Ellshama
Nun
Joshua
Daughter of Joshua
Ezra
Amos
Mattathias
Joseph
Jana
Melchi
Levi
Matthat
Joachim
The Virgin Mary

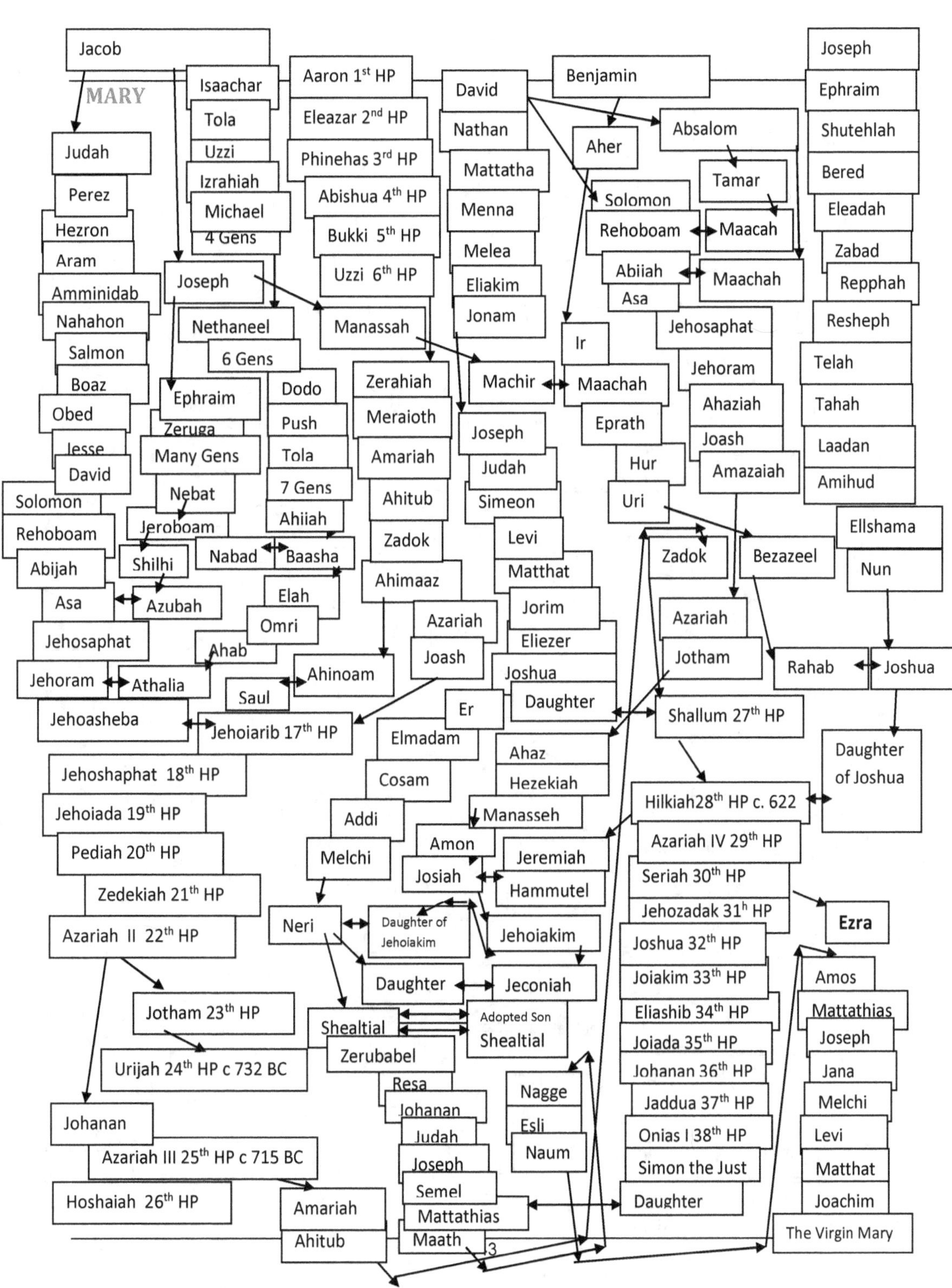

Jacob
MARY
Judah
Perez
Hezron
Aram
Amminidab
Nahahon
Salmon
Boaz
Obed
Jesse
David
Solomon
Rehoboam
Abijah
Asa
Jehosaphat
Jehoram
Athalia
Jehoasheba
Jehoiarib 17th HP
Jehoshaphat 18th HP
Jehoiada 19th HP
Pediah 20th HP
Zedekiah 21st HP
Azariah II 22th HP
Jotham 23th HP
Urijah 24th HP c 732 BC
Johanan
Azariah III 25th HP c 715 BC
Hoshaiah 26th HP
Isaachar
Tola
Uzzi
Izrahiah
Michael
4 Gens
Joseph
Nethaneel
6 Gens
Ephraim
Zeruga
Many Gens
Nebat
Jeroboam
Shilhi
Azubah
Nabad
Baasha
Elah
Omri
Ahab
Saul
Ahinoam
Aaron 1st HP
Eleazar 2nd HP
Phinehas 3rd HP
Abishua 4th HP
Bukki 5th HP
Uzzi 6th HP
Manassah
Dodo
Push
Tola
7 Gens
Ahiiah
Zerahiah
Meraioth
Amariah
Ahitub
Zadok
Ahimaaz
Azariah
Joash
Er
Elmadam
Cosam
Addi
Melchi
Neri
Daughter of Jehoiakim
Daughter
Shealtial
Zerubabel
Resa
Johanan
Judah
Joseph
Semel
Mattathias
Maath
Amariah
Ahitub
David
Nathan
Mattatha
Menna
Melea
Eliakim
Jonam
Machir
Joseph
Judah
Simeon
Levi
Matthat
Jorim
Eliezer
Joshua
Daughter
Ahaz
Hezekiah
Manasseh
Amon
Josiah
Jeremiah
Hammutel
Jehoiakim
Jeconiah
Adopted Son Shealtial
Nagge
Esli
Naum
Benjamin
Aher
Ir
Maachah
Eprath
Hur
Uri
Absalom
Tamar
Solomon
Rehoboam
Maacah
Abiiah
Maachah
Asa
Jehosaphat
Jehoram
Ahaziah
Joash
Amazaiah
Zadok
Bezazeel
Azariah
Jotham
Shallum 27th HP
Hilkiah28th HP c. 622
Azariah IV 29th HP
Seriah 30th HP
Jehozadak 31h HP
Joshua 32th HP
Joiakim 33th HP
Eliashib 34th HP
Joiada 35th HP
Johanan 36th HP
Jaddua 37th HP
Onias I 38th HP
Simon the Just
Daughter
Joseph
Ephraim
Shutehlah
Bered
Eleadah
Zabad
Repphah
Resheph
Telah
Tahah
Laadan
Amihud
Ellshama
Nun
Rahab
Joshua
Daughter of Joshua
Ezra
Amos
Mattathias
Joseph
Jana
Melchi
Levi
Matthat
Joachim
The Virgin Mary
3

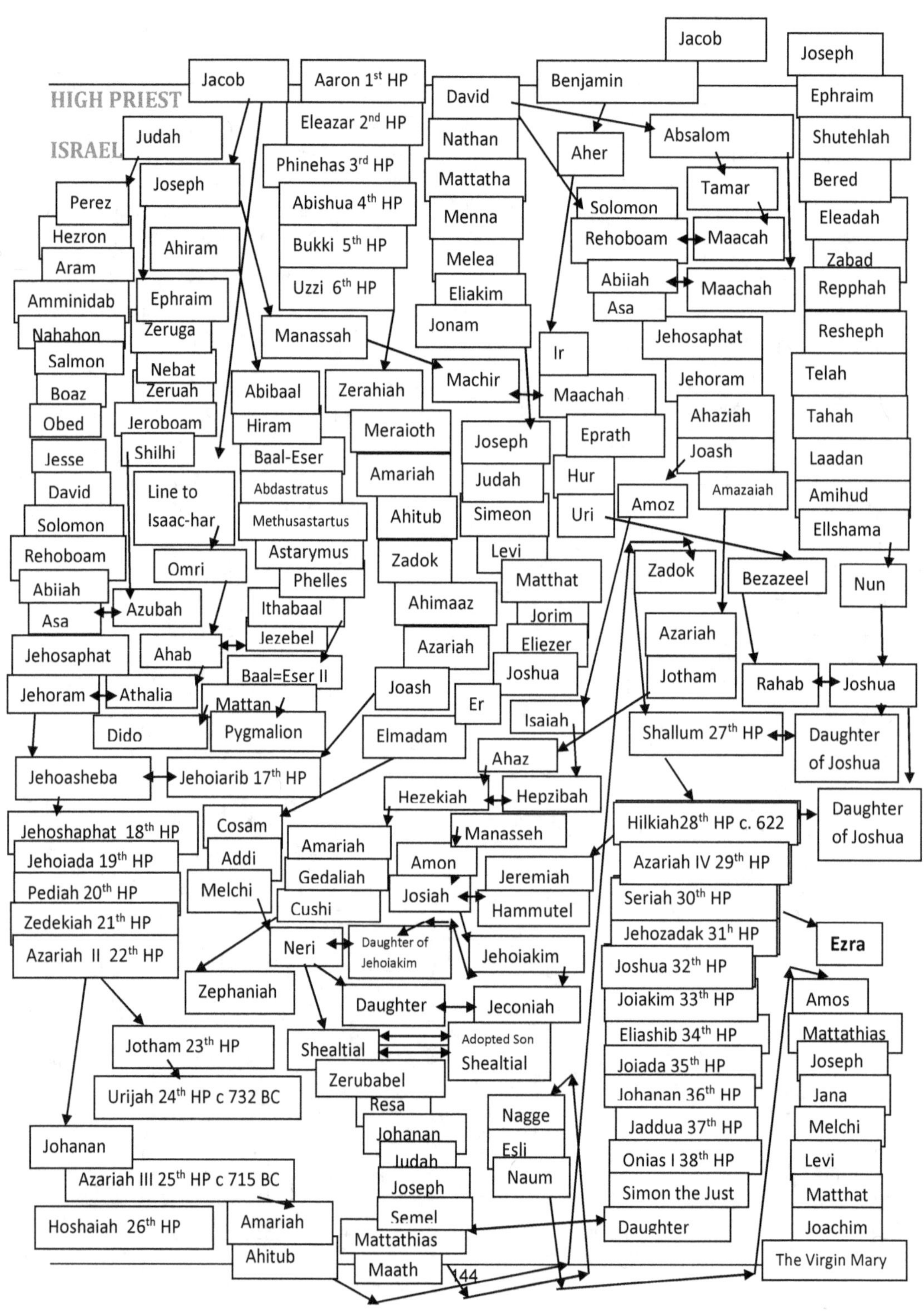
HIGH PRIEST
ISRAEL
Jacob
Judah
Perez
Hezron
Aram
Amminidab
Nahahon
Salmon
Boaz
Obed
Jesse
David
Solomon
Rehoboam
Abiiah
Asa
Jehosaphat
Jehoram
Athalia
Jehoasheba
Jehoshaphat 18th HP
Jehoiada 19th HP
Pediah 20th HP
Zedekiah 21th HP
Azariah II 22th HP
Jotham 23th HP
Urijah 24th HP c 732 BC
Johanan
Azariah III 25th HP c 715 BC
Hoshaiah 26th HP
Joseph
Ahiram
Ephraim
Zeruga
Nebat
Zeruah
Jeroboam
Shilhi
Line to Isaac-har
Omri
Azubah
Ahab
Jezebel
Dido
Mattan
Pygmalion
Jehoiarib 17th HP
Aaron 1st HP
Eleazar 2nd HP
Phinehas 3rd HP
Abishua 4th HP
Bukki 5th HP
Uzzi 6th HP
Manassah
Abibaal
Hiram
Baal-Eser
Abdastratus
Methusastartus
Astarymus
Phelles
Ithabaal
Baal=Eser II
Zerahiah
Meraioth
Amariah
Ahitub
Zadok
Ahimaaz
Azariah
Joash
Elmadam
Cosam
Addi
Melchi
Amariah
Gedaliah
Cushi
Neri
Daughter of Jehoiakim
Zephaniah
Daughter
Shealtial
Adopted Son Shealtial
Zerubabel
Resa
Johanan
Judah
Joseph
Semel
Mattathias
Maath
Amariah
Ahitub
David
Nathan
Mattatha
Menna
Melea
Eliakim
Jonam
Machir
Joseph
Judah
Simeon
Levi
Matthat
Jorim
Eliezer
Joshua
Er
Isaiah
Ahaz
Hezekiah
Hepzibah
Manasseh
Amon
Josiah
Jeremiah
Hammutel
Jehoiakim
Jeconiah
Nagge
Esli
Naum
Benjamin
Aher
Ir
Maachah
Eprath
Hur
Uri
Absalom
Tamar
Solomon
Rehoboam
Maacah
Abiiah
Maachah
Asa
Jehosaphat
Jehoram
Ahaziah
Joash
Amaziah
Amoz
Zadok
Azariah
Jotham
Shallum 27th HP
Hilkiah28th HP c. 622
Azariah IV 29th HP
Seriah 30th HP
Jehozadak 31h HP
Joshua 32th HP
Joiakim 33th HP
Eliashib 34th HP
Joiada 35th HP
Johanan 36th HP
Jaddua 37th HP
Onias I 38th HP
Simon the Just
Daughter
Bezazeel
Rahab
Joshua
Daughter of Joshua
Daughter of Joshua
Ezra
Jacob
Joseph
Ephraim
Shutehlah
Bered
Eleadah
Zabad
Repphah
Resheph
Telah
Tahah
Laadan
Amihud
Ellshama
Nun
Amos
Mattathias
Joseph
Jana
Melchi
Levi
Matthat
Joachim
The Virgin Mary

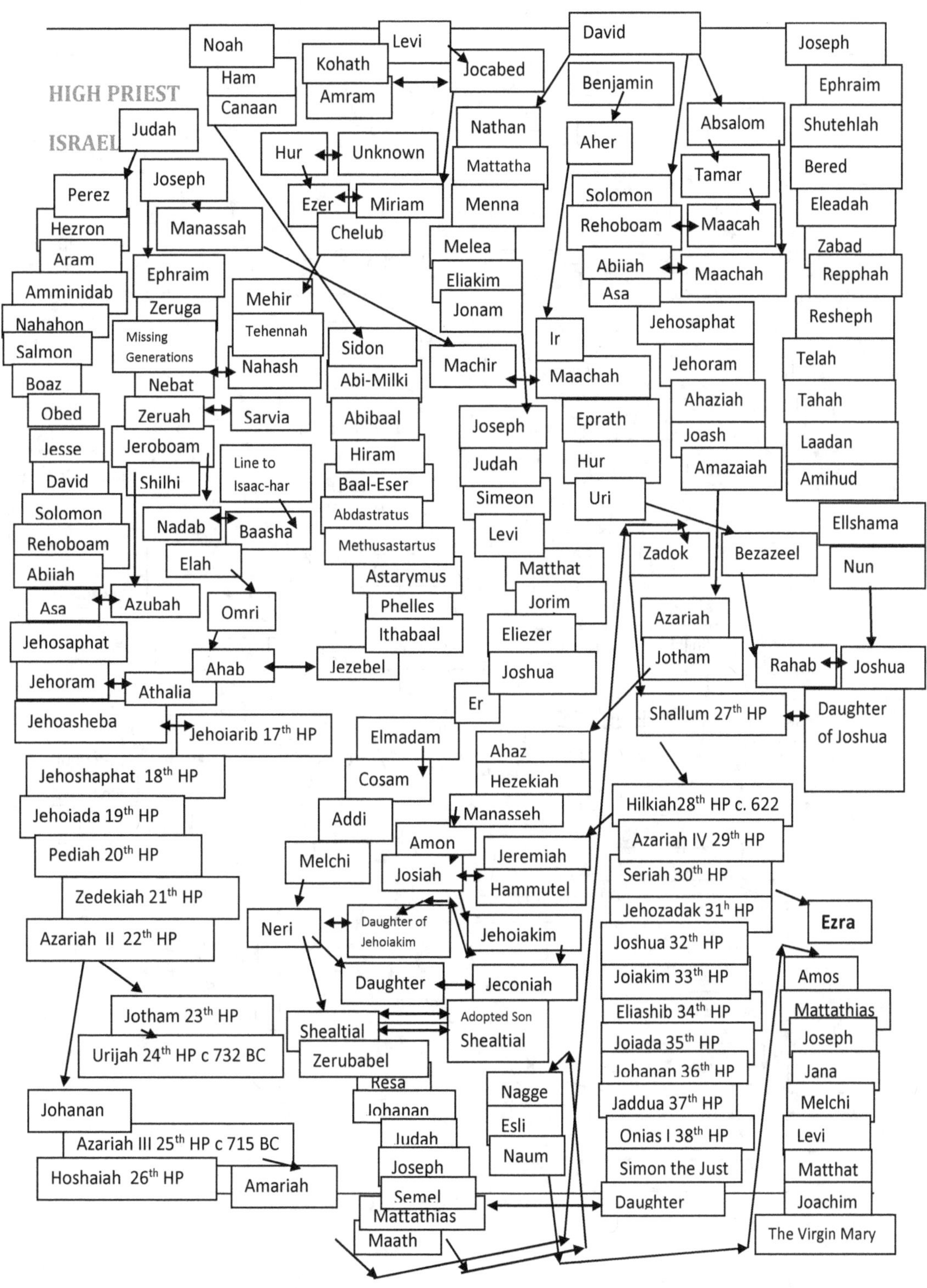

HIGH PRIEST
ISRAEL
Noah
Ham
Canaan
Levi
Kohath
Amram
Jocabed
David
Joseph
Ephraim
Shutehlah
Bered
Eleadah
Zabad
Repphah
Resheph
Telah
Tahah
Laadan
Amihud
Ellshama
Nun
Joshua
Rahab
Daughter of Joshua
Benjamin
Aher
Ir
Maachah
Eprath
Hur
Uri
Bezazeel
Absalom
Tamar
Maacah
Solomon
Rehoboam
Abiiah
Maachah
Asa
Jehosaphat
Jehoram
Ahaziah
Joash
Amazaiah
Nathan
Mattatha
Menna
Melea
Eliakim
Jonam
Joseph
Judah
Simeon
Levi
Matthat
Jorim
Eliezer
Joshua
Er
Elmadam
Cosam
Addi
Melchi
Neri
Judah
Perez
Hezron
Aram
Amminidab
Nahahon
Salmon
Boaz
Obed
Jesse
David
Solomon
Rehoboam
Abiiah
Asa
Azubah
Jehosaphat
Jehoram
Athalia
Jehoasheba
Jehoiarib 17th HP
Jehoshaphat 18th HP
Jehoiada 19th HP
Pediah 20th HP
Zedekiah 21th HP
Azariah II 22th HP
Jotham 23th HP
Urijah 24th HP c 732 BC
Johanan
Azariah III 25th HP c 715 BC
Hoshaiah 26th HP
Amariah
Joseph
Manassah
Ephraim
Zeruga
Missing Generations
Nebat
Zeruah
Sarvia
Jeroboam
Shilhi
Line to Isaac-har
Nadab
Baasha
Elah
Omri
Ahab
Jezebel
Hur
Unknown
Ezer
Miriam
Chelub
Mehir
Tehennah
Nahash
Sidon
Abi-Milki
Abibaal
Hiram
Baal-Eser
Abdastratus
Methusastartus
Astarymus
Phelles
Ithabaal
Machir
Zadok
Azariah
Jotham
Shallum 27th HP
Ahaz
Hezekiah
Manasseh
Amon
Josiah
Jeremiah
Hammutel
Jehoiakim
Daughter of Jehoiakim
Daughter
Jeconiah
Shealtial
Adopted Son Shealtial
Zerubabel
Resa
Johanan
Judah
Joseph
Semel
Mattathias
Maath
Nagge
Esli
Naum
Hilkiah28th HP c. 622
Azariah IV 29th HP
Seriah 30th HP
Jehozadak 31h HP
Joshua 32th HP
Joiakim 33th HP
Eliashib 34th HP
Joiada 35th HP
Johanan 36th HP
Jaddua 37th HP
Onias I 38th HP
Simon the Just
Daughter
Ezra
Amos
Mattathias
Joseph
Jana
Melchi
Levi
Matthat
Joachim
The Virgin Mary

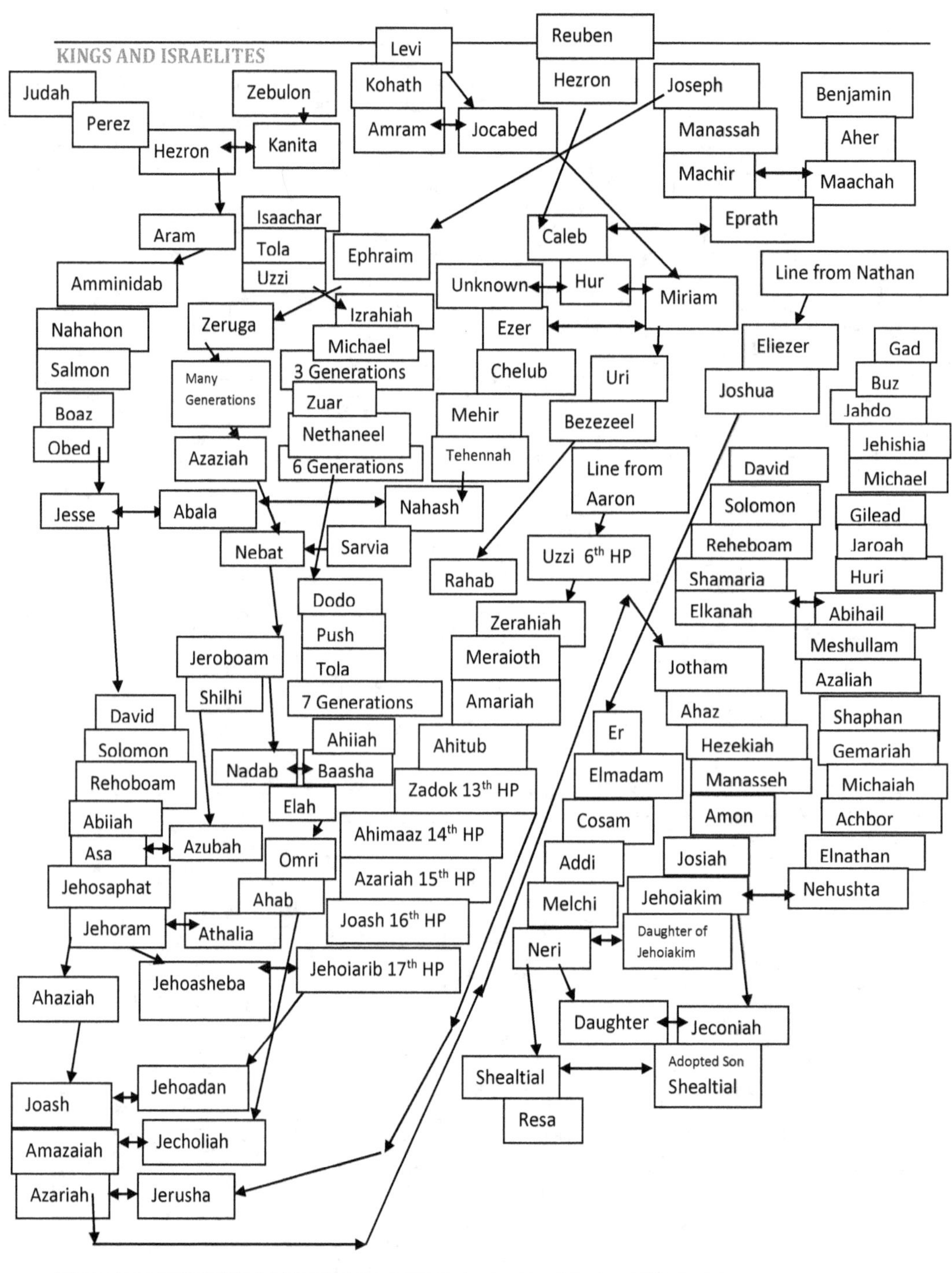
Levi
Reuben
Judah
Perez
Zebulon
Kohath
Hezron
Joseph
Benjamin
Hezron
Kanita
Amram
Jocabed
Manassah
Aher
Machir
Maachah
Isaachar
Eprath
Aram
Tola
Ephraim
Caleb
Amminidab
Uzzi
Unknown
Hur
Miriam
Line from Nathan
Nahahon
Zeruga
Izrahiah
Ezer
Michael
Eliezer
Gad
Salmon
Many Generations
3 Generations
Chelub
Uri
Buz
Joshua
Zuar
Mehir
Bezezeel
Jahdo
Boaz
Nethaneel
Jehishia
Obed
Azaziah
6 Generations
Tehennah
Line from Aaron
David
Michael
Jesse
Abala
Nahash
Solomon
Gilead
Nebat
Sarvia
Uzzi 6th HP
Reheboam
Jaroah
Rahab
Shamaria
Huri
Dodo
Elkanah
Abihail
Zerahiah
Push
Meshullam
Jeroboam
Meraioth
Tola
Jotham
Azaliah
Shilhi
7 Generations
Amariah
David
Ahaz
Shaphan
Ahiiah
Er
Solomon
Ahitub
Hezekiah
Gemariah
Nadab
Baasha
Elmadam
Rehoboam
Zadok 13th HP
Manasseh
Michaiah
Elah
Abiiah
Cosam
Amon
Achbor
Ahimaaz 14th HP
Azubah
Asa
Omri
Addi
Josiah
Elnathan
Jehosaphat
Azariah 15th HP
Ahab
Melchi
Jehoiakim
Nehushta
Joash 16th HP
Jehoram
Athalia
Daughter of Jehoiakim
Neri
Jehoiarib 17th HP
Ahaziah
Jehoasheba
Daughter
Jeconiah
Adopted Son Shealtial
Shealtial
Jehoadan
Joash
Resa
Amazaiah
Jecholiah
Azariah
Jerusha

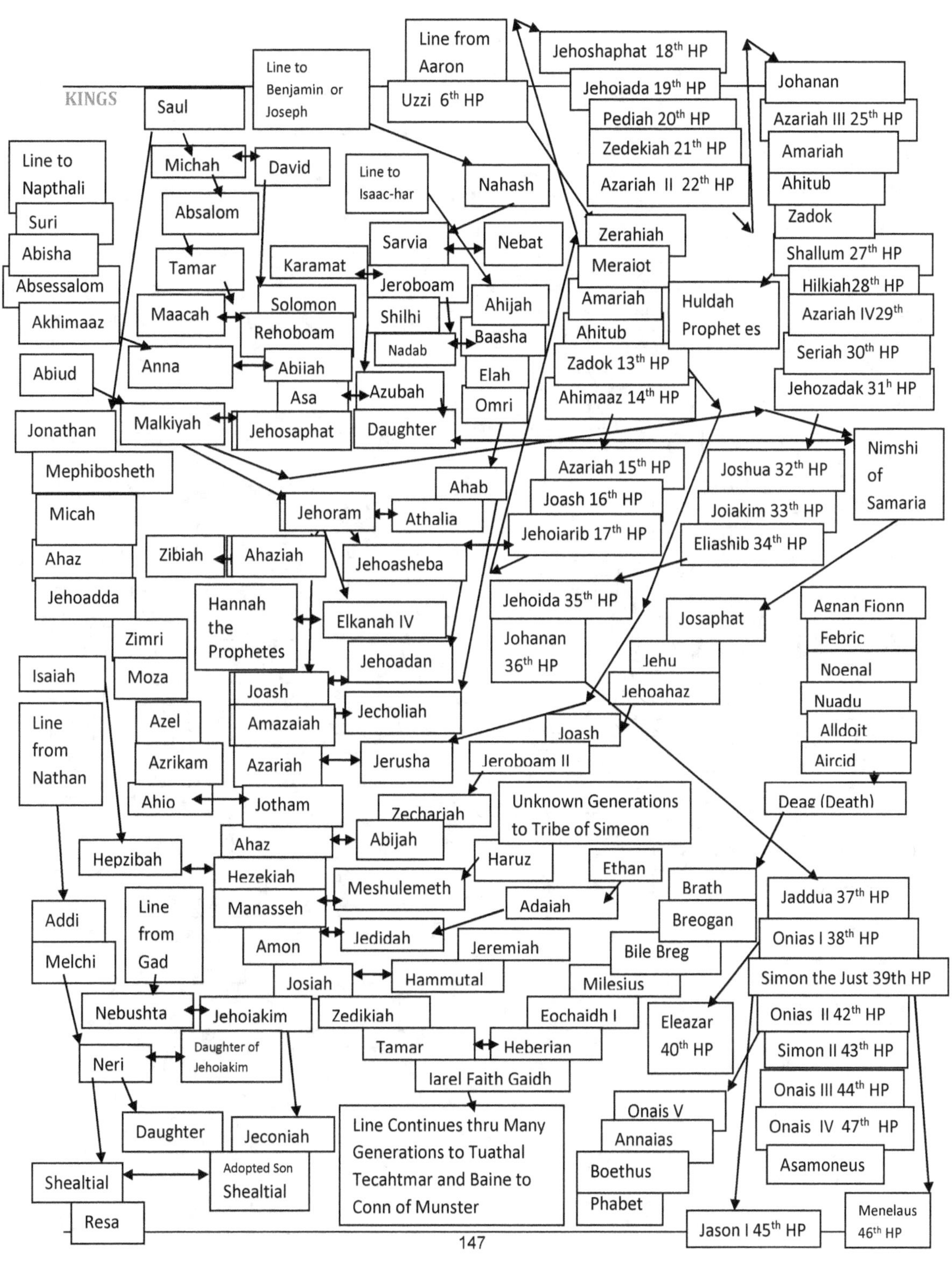
KINGS
Line from Aaron
Jehoshaphat 18th HP
Line to Benjamin or Joseph
Uzzi 6th HP
Jehoiada 19th HP
Johanan
Saul
Pediah 20th HP
Azariah III 25th HP
Zedekiah 21th HP
Amariah
Line to Napthali
Michah
David
Line to Isaac-har
Nahash
Azariah II 22th HP
Ahitub
Suri
Absalom
Zadok
Abisha
Sarvia
Nebat
Zerahiah
Shallum 27th HP
Tamar
Karamat
Meraiot
Absessalom
Jeroboam
Hilkiah28th HP
Solomon
Ahijah
Amariah
Huldah Prophet es
Azariah IV29th
Akhimaaz
Maacah
Shilhi
Rehoboam
Baasha
Ahitub
Nadab
Seriah 30th HP
Abiud
Anna
Abiiah
Zadok 13th HP
Elah
Jehozadak 31h HP
Asa
Azubah
Ahimaaz 14th HP
Omri
Malkiyah
Jonathan
Jehosaphat
Daughter
Nimshi of Samaria
Azariah 15th HP
Joshua 32th HP
Mephibosheth
Ahab
Joash 16th HP
Joiakim 33th HP
Jehoram
Micah
Athalia
Jehoiarib 17th HP
Eliashib 34th HP
Ahaz
Zibiah
Ahaziah
Jehoasheba
Jehoadda
Jehoida 35th HP
Agnan Fionn
Hannah the Prophetes
Elkanah IV
Josaphat
Zimri
Febric
Johanan 36th HP
Jehu
Noenal
Isaiah
Jehoadan
Moza
Joash
Jehoahaz
Nuadu
Jecholiah
Azel
Amazaiah
Alldoit
Line from Nathan
Joash
Aircid
Azrikam
Azariah
Jerusha
Jeroboam II
Deag (Death)
Ahio
Jotham
Zechariah
Unknown Generations to Tribe of Simeon
Ahaz
Abijah
Hepzibah
Haruz
Ethan
Hezekiah
Brath
Meshulemeth
Jaddua 37th HP
Adaiah
Addi
Line from Gad
Manasseh
Breogan
Onias I 38th HP
Amon
Jedidah
Bile Breg
Melchi
Jeremiah
Simon the Just 39th HP
Josiah
Hammutal
Milesius
Nebushta
Jehoiakim
Zedikiah
Eochaidh I
Eleazar 40th HP
Onias II 42th HP
Tamar
Heberian
Neri
Daughter of Jehoiakim
Simon II 43th HP
Iarel Faith Gaidh
Onais III 44th HP
Onais V
Daughter
Jeconiah
Line Continues thru Many Generations to Tuathal Tecahtmar and Baine to Conn of Munster
Annaias
Onais IV 47th HP
Asamoneus
Shealtial
Adopted Son Shealtial
Boethus
Phabet
Menelaus 46th HP
Resa
Jason I 45th HP

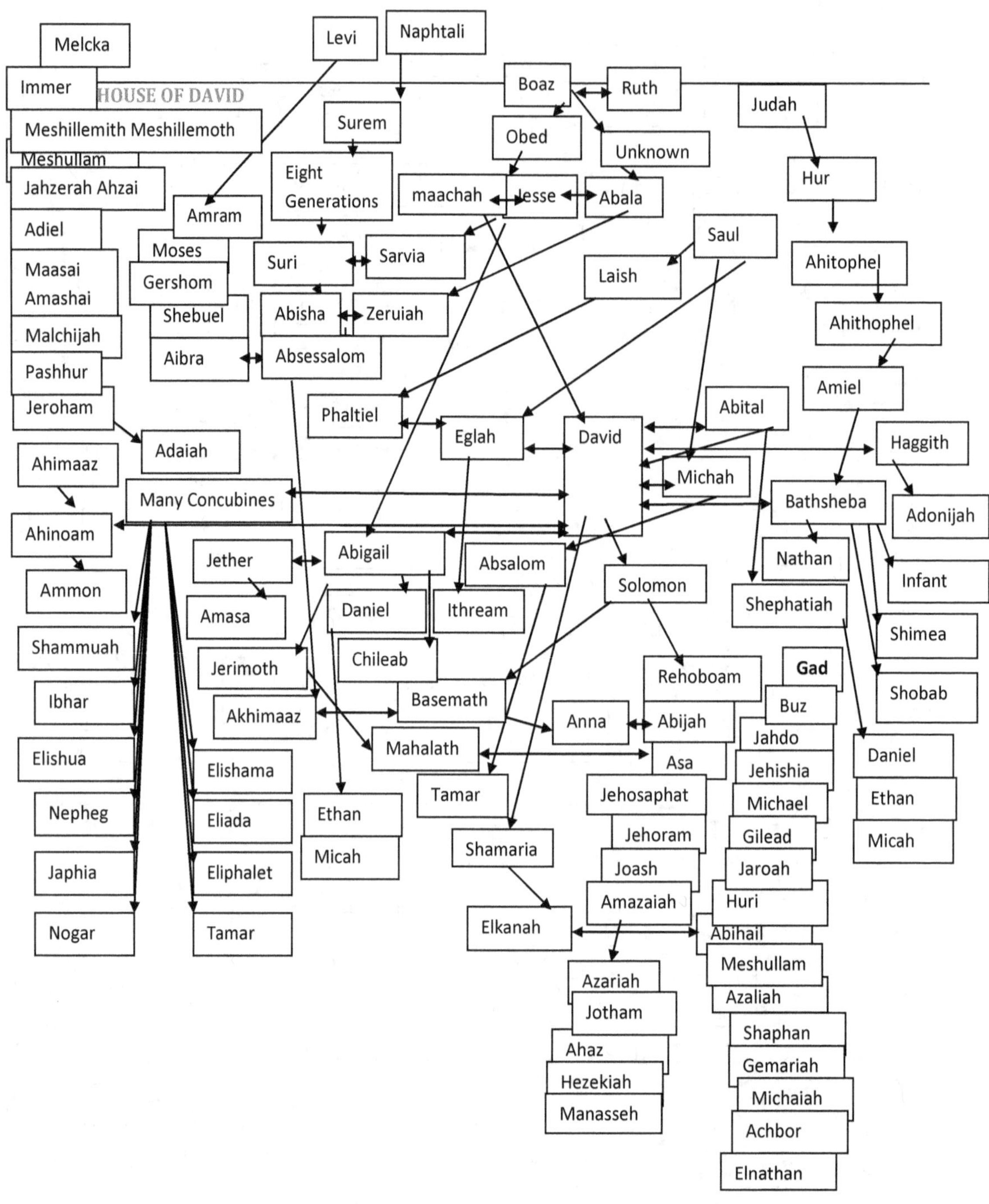

HOUSE OF DAVID
Melcka
Immer
Meshillemith Meshillemoth
Meshullam
Jahzerah Ahzai
Adiel
Maasai Amashai
Malchijah
Pashhur
Jeroham
Levi
Naphtali
Surem
Eight Generations
Amram
Moses
Gershom
Shebuel
Aibra
Suri
Sarvia
Abisha
Zeruiah
Absessalom
Boaz
Ruth
Obed
Unknown
maachah
Jesse
Abala
Judah
Hur
Saul
Laish
Ahitophel
Ahithophel
Amiel
Phaltiel
Eglah
David
Abital
Haggith
Michah
Bathsheba
Adonijah
Adaiah
Ahimaaz
Many Concubines
Ahinoam
Ammon
Shammuah
Ibhar
Elishua
Nepheg
Japhia
Nogar
Elishama
Eliada
Eliphalet
Tamar
Jether
Abigail
Amasa
Daniel
Ithream
Absalom
Solomon
Nathan
Infant
Shephatiah
Shimea
Shobab
Jerimoth
Chileab
Akhimaaz
Basemath
Mahalath
Ethan
Micah
Tamar
Shamaria
Elkanah
Anna
Rehoboam
Abijah
Asa
Jehosaphat
Jehoram
Joash
Amazaiah
Azariah
Jotham
Ahaz
Hezekiah
Manasseh
Gad
Buz
Jahdo
Jehishia
Michael
Gilead
Jaroah
Huri
Abihail
Meshullam
Azaliah
Shaphan
Gemariah
Michaiah
Achbor
Elnathan
Daniel
Ethan
Micah

KINGS OF JUDAH MARRIAGES OR HOUSE OF KINGS

The Kings of Judah all married good wives from different lineages.

- King David married Bathsheba, whose lineage is Judah
- King Solomon married Egyptian lineage from the Ramses.
- King Reheboam married a line from Jesse and from David.
- King Abijah married a line from Levi the Israelite, not from the Aaronic Priest but from Gershom the son of Moses.
- King Asa married Azubah a line containing Jezebel and from Joseph and Benjamin the Israelites
- King Jehosphat married Jehoadin and fathered Nimshi and Israeli kings. Also married wife of line of Gersonites of Levi..
- King Jehoram married Athalia an Israelites lineage to the Tribe of Isaachar.
- King Ahiziah married married his mother, who had a daughter, who he married, and had Joash.
- King Joash married Jehoadan from the Aaronic Priest Line of Levites.
- King Amaziah married Jecholiah from the Tribe of Isaachar just as did King Jehoram.
- King Azariah married Jerusha of the line from the Aaronic Priest line of the levites, as did King Joash.
- King Jotham married Ahio who was from a Benjaminite line from King Saul.
- King Ahaz married Abijah who was from an Israeli line of King Nimshi the son of King Jehosphat.
- King Hezikiah married Hepzibah the daughter of the Prophet Isaiah who was from the Levitical Priest lines of Aaron just as did King Joash and King Azariah
- King Manassah married Meshulimeth the daughter of Haruz his brother.
- King Amon married Jedidah of the line of both the Aaronic Levites and King Jehoram.
- King Josiah married Hammutel the daughter of the Prophet Jeremiah who was of the Aaronic Priest Line.
- King Jehoikim married Nebushta of the line of the Tribe of Gad that has Michael son of Jehishia. Nebushta was also from the line of Sharmaria son of David.
- King Jeconiah was the son of Jehoikim and had a daughter but no son, so he adopted King Sheal tial who was of the line of Nathan and whose mother Thalmar was the daughter of Jehoikim. Thus the royal lineage of the House of David thru King Solomon was continued although the direct male line did not produce a heir.

SUMMARY There are four Kings that married the Levitical Priest lines of Aaron, King Hezekiah, King Joash, and King Azariah and King Josiah. Two Kings married the tribe of Isaac-har, King Jehoram and King Amaziah. There are Kings that married the lines from Moses, (Levite),from Joseph, From Benjamin, and from Gad. There are two tribes not accounted for, Simeon, and Asher and two Kings wifes lines not known. Did the Levitical Priests intend to breed all twelve tribes with the descendents of Solomon? If this were so then the kings Mannasseh who married Meshulemeth or Ahaziah who married Zibiah are the lines from the tribe of Simon and Asher.

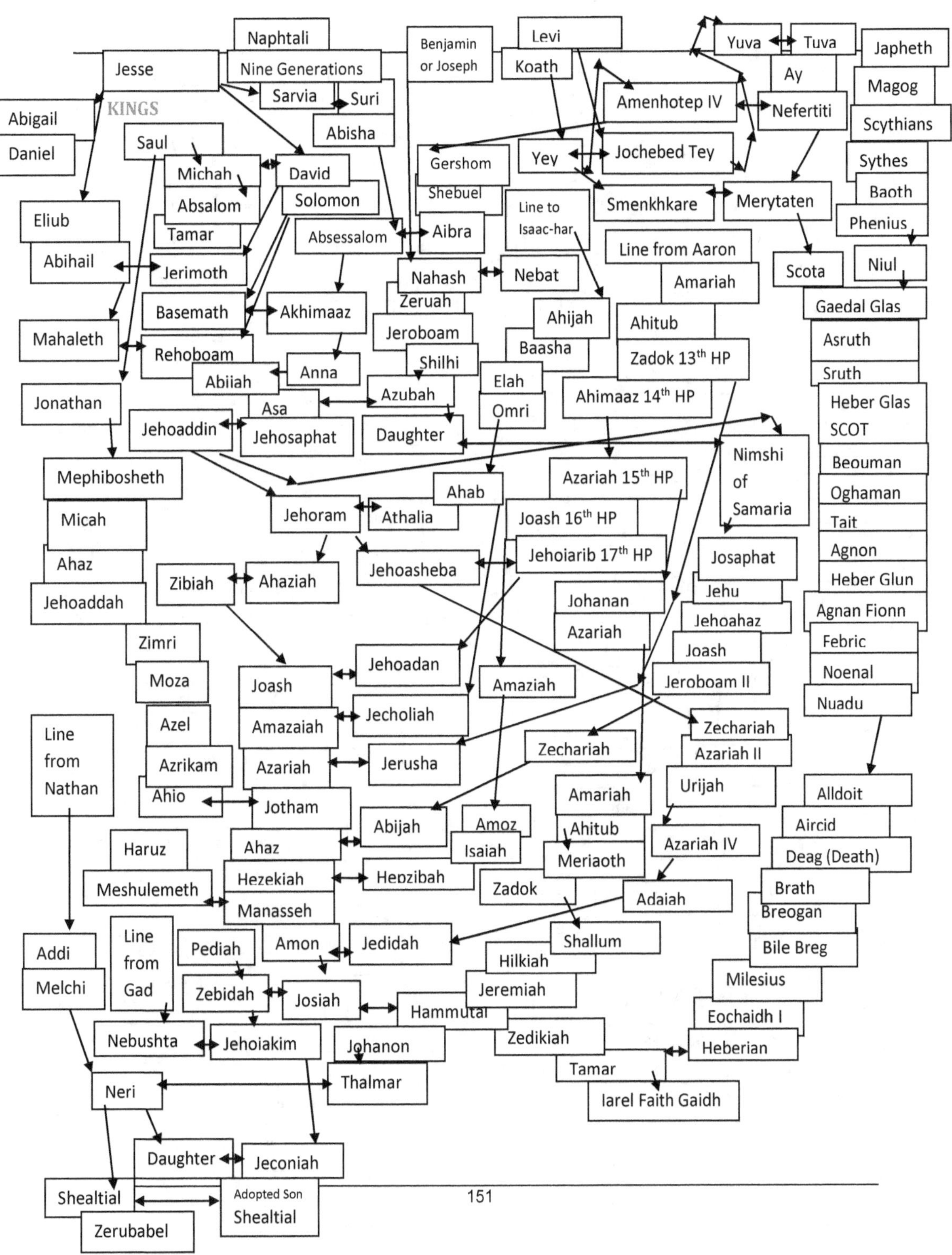

Naphtali
Nine Generations
Benjamin or Joseph
Levi
Koath
Yuva
Tuva
Japheth
Jesse
Sarvia
Suri
Ay
Magog
Amenhotep IV
Nefertiti
Scythians
Abigail
KINGS
Daniel
Saul
Abisha
Michah
David
Gershom
Yey
Jochebed Tey
Sythes
Absalom
Solomon
Shebuel
Line to Isaac-har
Smenkhkare
Merytaten
Baoth
Eliub
Tamar
Abessalom
Aibra
Phenius
Line from Aaron
Abihail
Jerimoth
Nahash
Nebat
Amariah
Scota
Niul
Zeruah
Gaedal Glas
Basemath
Akhimaaz
Ahijah
Ahitub
Jeroboam
Asruth
Mahaleth
Rehoboam
Baasha
Zadok 13th HP
Shilhi
Anna
Sruth
Abijah
Azubah
Elah
Ahimaaz 14th HP
Heber Glas SCOT
Jonathan
Asa
Omri
Jehoaddin
Jehosaphat
Daughter
Nimshi of Samaria
Beouman
Mephibosheth
Ahab
Azariah 15th HP
Oghaman
Micah
Jehoram
Athalia
Joash 16th HP
Tait
Agnon
Ahaz
Jehoiarib 17th HP
Josaphat
Zibiah
Ahaziah
Jehoasheba
Heber Glun
Jehoaddah
Jehu
Johanan
Agnan Fionn
Jehoahaz
Azariah
Febric
Zimri
Joash
Jehoadan
Moza
Joash
Amaziah
Jeroboam II
Noenal
Nuadu
Azel
Amazaiah
Jecholiah
Zechariah
Line from Nathan
Azrikam
Azariah
Jerusha
Zechariah
Azariah II
Ahio
Jotham
Amariah
Urijah
Alldoit
Abijah
Amoz
Ahitub
Aircid
Haruz
Ahaz
Isaiah
Azariah IV
Deag (Death)
Meriaoth
Meshulemeth
Hezekiah
Hepzibah
Zadok
Adaiah
Brath
Manasseh
Breogan
Line from Gad
Amon
Jedidah
Shallum
Addi
Pediah
Bile Breg
Hilkiah
Milesius
Melchi
Zebidah
Josiah
Jeremiah
Hammutal
Eochaidh I
Nebushta
Jehoiakim
Johanon
Zedikiah
Heberian
Tamar
Neri
Thalmar
Iarel Faith Gaidh
Daughter
Jeconiah
Shealtial
Adopted Son Shealtial
Zerubabel

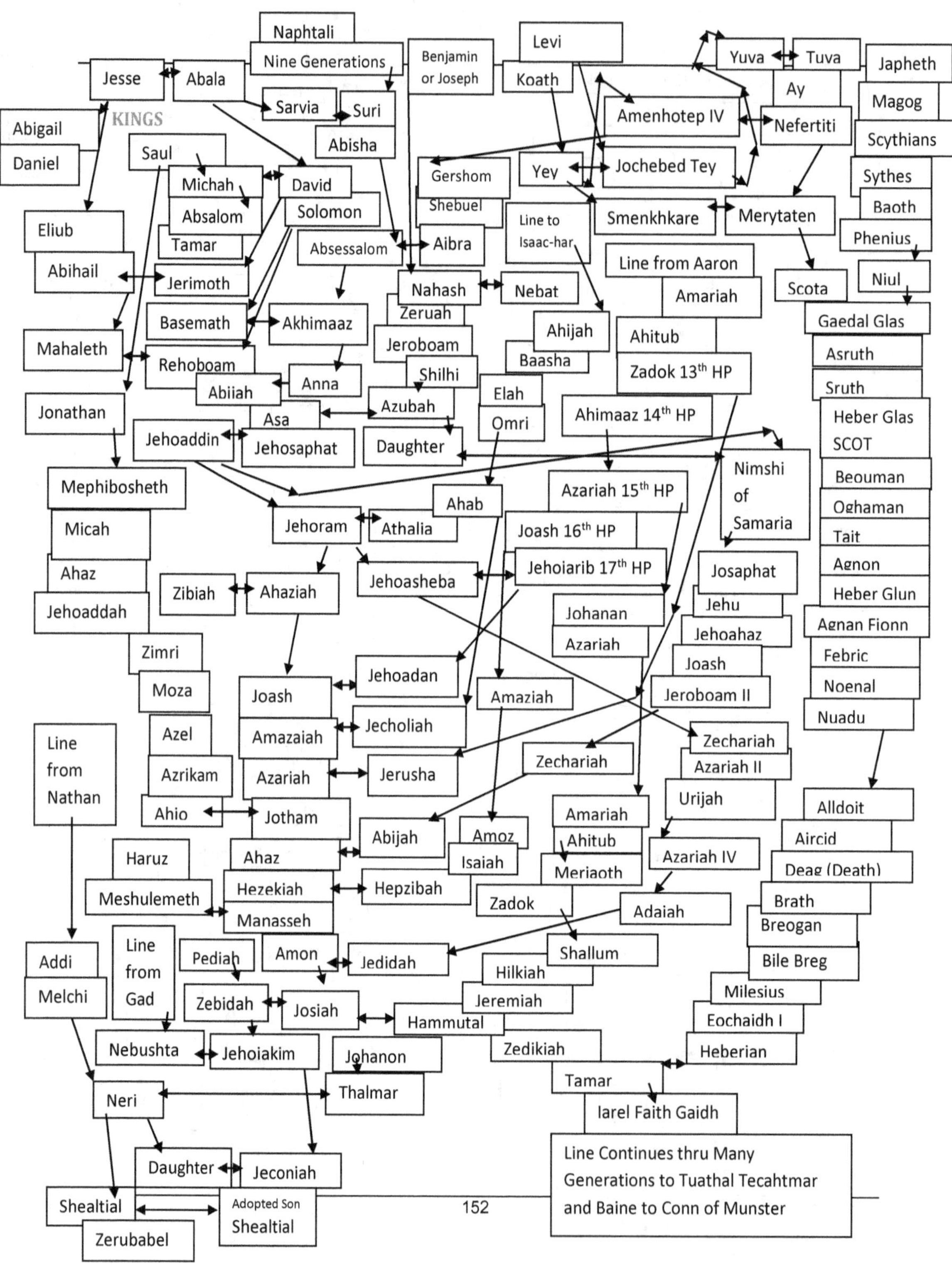

Naphtali
Nine Generations
Benjamin or Joseph
Levi
Koath
Yuva
Tuva
Japheth
Jesse
Abala
Ay
Magog
Abigail
KINGS
Sarvia
Suri
Amenhotep IV
Nefertiti
Scythians
Daniel
Abisha
Saul
Michah
David
Gershom
Yey
Jochebed Tey
Sythes
Absalom
Solomon
Shebuel
Line to Isaac-har
Smenkhkare
Merytaten
Baoth
Eliub
Tamar
Absessalom
Aibra
Phenius
Abihail
Jerimoth
Line from Aaron
Niul
Nahash
Nebat
Amariah
Scota
Zeruah
Gaedal Glas
Basemath
Akhimaaz
Ahijah
Ahitub
Mahaleth
Jeroboam
Baasha
Asruth
Rehoboam
Shilhi
Zadok 13th HP
Anna
Sruth
Abiiah
Elah
Jonathan
Azubah
Heber Glas SCOT
Asa
Ahimaaz 14th HP
Omri
Jehoaddin
Jehosaphat
Daughter
Nimshi of Samaria
Mephibosheth
Beouman
Azariah 15th HP
Ahab
Oghaman
Micah
Jehoram
Athalia
Joash 16th HP
Tait
Ahaz
Jehoiarib 17th HP
Josaphat
Agnon
Zibiah
Ahaziah
Jehoasheba
Heber Glun
Jehoaddah
Jehu
Johanan
Agnan Fionn
Jehoahaz
Zimri
Azariah
Febric
Joash
Jehoadan
Moza
Noenal
Joash
Amaziah
Jeroboam II
Nuadu
Azel
Jecholiah
Zechariah
Line from Nathan
Amazaiah
Azrikam
Zechariah
Azariah II
Azariah
Jerusha
Urijah
Alldoit
Ahio
Jotham
Amariah
Abijah
Amoz
Aircid
Haruz
Ahitub
Ahaz
Isaiah
Azariah IV
Deag (Death)
Meriaoth
Meshulemeth
Hezekiah
Hepzibah
Zadok
Brath
Adaiah
Manasseh
Breogan
Line from Gad
Pediah
Amon
Shallum
Addi
Jedidah
Bile Breg
Hilkiah
Milesius
Melchi
Zebidah
Josiah
Jeremiah
Hammutal
Eochaidh I
Nebushta
Jehoiakim
Johanon
Zedikiah
Heberian
Neri
Thalmar
Tamar
Iarel Faith Gaidh
Line Continues thru Many Generations to Tuathal Tecahtmar and Baine to Conn of Munster
Daughter
Jeconiah
Shealtial
Adopted Son Shealtial
Zerubabel

Lines from Ahab and Jehoikim and the ArchAngel Michael.

Here are the lineages of Ten of the sons of Jacob. Note that the lines can be compared to other lines in this book. The Israelites are Jacob's sons by Leah Reuben, Judah, Zebulon, Isaachar, and Levi, by Zilpah Jacob's son Gad, a servant son, and by Rachel her sons Joseph and Benjamin.and by Bilhah, Jacobs sons Dan and Naptali. The two remaining are found to go thru Babylon for Simon, and the Greek for Asher. There are lines that show that there is a Caleb who is in the line of Reuben. Now Caleb married Eprath who was the mother of Hur who was the mother of Uri, whose line continued to Rahab. Some lines show this as Caleb the son of Hezron of the line of Judah and some show Caleb as the line of Rueben. If Caleb who married Eprath was of the line of Reuben then there would be evidence that Reuben is also an ancestor of the peoples charts.Now from Ahab it is possible to find a line that shows the line to Isaachar, that contains Michael. Is this the lineage of Michael? There is also a line from the wife of Jehoikim who was descended thru a line that has Micahah and Gilead and also Michael. Is this the line to Michael.Also the line from Reuben to Caleb has the name Michael. Following this chart is a chart that shows the line of the Virgin Mary. Here is the relationships of the two different lineages of the Virgin Mary whose lineages are presented in the translations of the Gospels of Luke and Mathew. These lines are a possible solution to the dilemma of the reader who reads these lineages and does not understand how they can be different. Now the lines to Adam and Eve are expected to be the end of the lines. God by some genealogists is a common name and has his own ancestry. These lines show a high priest to the figures that are shown in the lineages in Luke, and the relationships to the people that are also related to these lines. Note that in these ancient times the relationships to brother and sister are not considered to be impossible as both a brother and sister to be a father and mother of a being or child. Now on the preceding pages the lines from Ahab to Epraim cannot also be from Ahab to Isaachar. It is interesting to see the link to Jereboam is a son Nabad. Now Nabal was shown to be a husband of Abigail who was a fool. (In Hebrew Nabal the word is Fool) Is Nabad also a way in Genealogy to be a fool? Perhaps these lines from Ahab to Jehoboam are false and the lines to Isaachar are correct. Possibly or not. In any case Jehoboam II is a line that in history was exterminated according to Flavius Josephus who was a Hebrew that reverted to the Romans after losing the war in Jerusalem and was known to lie to the Romans by giving histories that are in some parts accurate and other parts false and said all of Jehoboam II line was exterminated. This was done by the High Priests Eli thru to Abithar. Are these secrets protected by the Roman Priest and only used at their discretion? At any rate the author suggests this idea of destroying a line of all of the descendents of someone is interesting, especially due to the erradification of the Hebrew in the World War II death camps.The chart on the next page shows the seven Isralites that are shown to be ancestors of Shealtial and Resa. Note that there is only one servant son, Gad, Both of Rachel's son's and four of Leah's sons

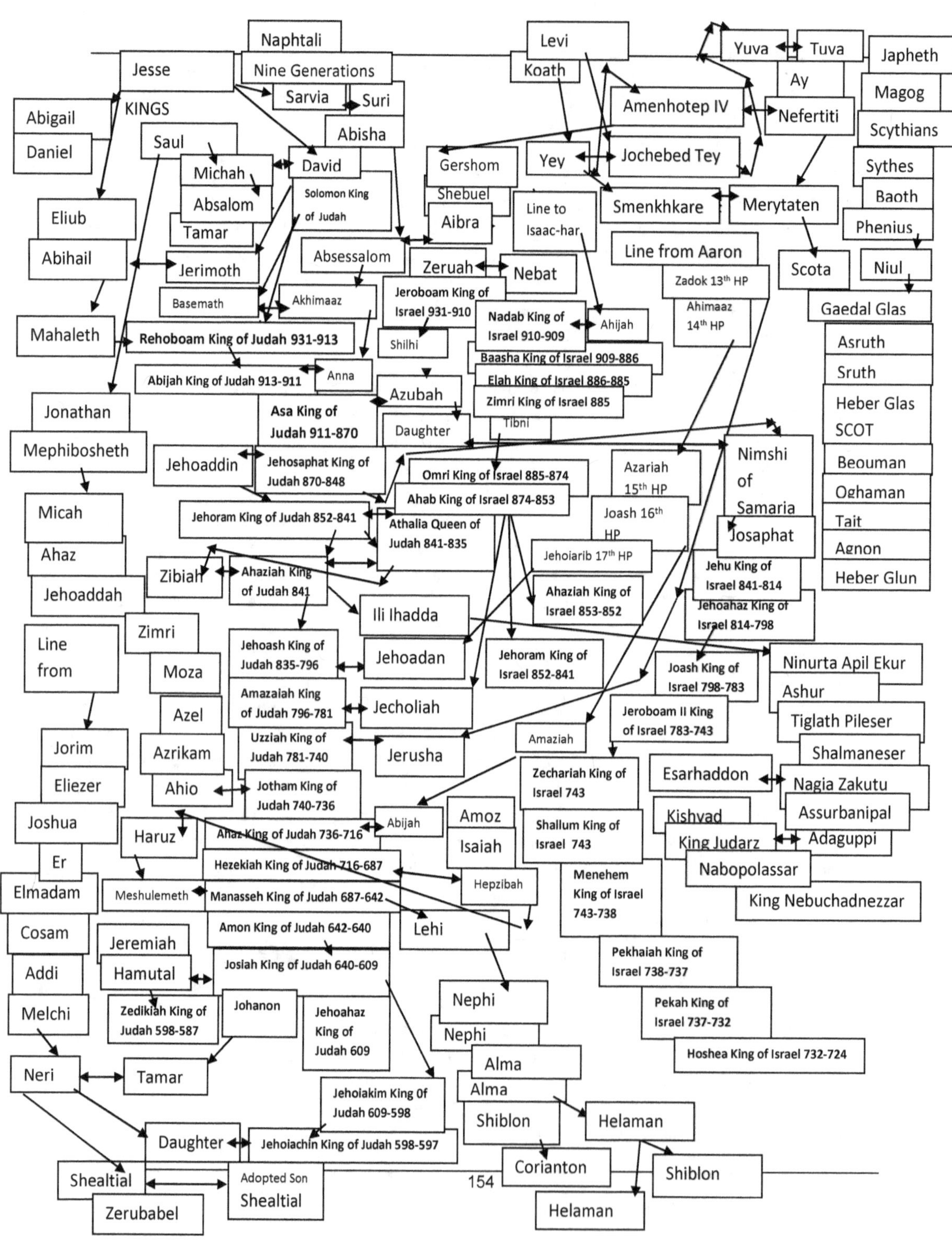

Naphtali
Nine Generations
Jesse
KINGS
Sarvia
Suri
Abisha
Abigail
Daniel
Saul
Michah
David
Solomon King of Judah
Absalom
Tamar
Eliub
Abihail
Jerimoth
Absessalom
Basemath
Akhimaaz
Mahaleth
Rehoboam King of Judah 931-913
Abijah King of Judah 913-911
Anna
Asa King of Judah 911-870
Jonathan
Mephibosheth
Jehoaddin
Jehosaphat King of Judah 870-848
Jehoram King of Judah 852-841
Athalia Queen of Judah 841-835
Micah
Ahaz
Jehoaddah
Zibiah
Ahaziah King of Judah 841
Ili Ihadda
Zimri
Line from
Moza
Jehoash King of Judah 835-796
Jehoadan
Amazaiah King of Judah 796-781
Jecholiah
Azel
Azrikam
Jorim
Uzziah King of Judah 781-740
Jerusha
Eliezer
Ahio
Jotham King of Judah 740-736
Joshua
Haruz
Ahaz King of Judah 736-716
Abijah
Er
Elmadam
Meshulemeth
Hezekiah King of Judah 716-687
Hepzibah
Manasseh King of Judah 687-642
Lehi
Cosam
Jeremiah
Amon King of Judah 642-640
Hamutal
Josiah King of Judah 640-609
Addi
Melchi
Zedikiah King of Judah 598-587
Johanon
Jehoahaz King of Judah 609
Neri
Tamar
Jehoiakim King Of Judah 609-598
Daughter
Jehoiachin King of Judah 598-597
Shealtial
Adopted Son Shealtial
Zerubabel
Levi
Koath
Gershom
Shebuel
Aibra
Yey
Jochebed Tey
Amenhotep IV
Line to Isaac-har
Smenkhkare
Zeruah
Nebat
Jeroboam King of Israel 931-910
Nadab King of Israel 910-909
Ahijah
Shilhi
Baasha King of Israel 909-886
Elah King of Israel 886-885
Azubah
Zimri King of Israel 885
Tibni
Daughter
Omri King of Israel 885-874
Ahab King of Israel 874-853
Jehoiarib 17th HP
Ahaziah King of Israel 853-852
Jehoram King of Israel 852-841
Amaziah
Zecharaiah King of Israel 743
Amoz
Isaiah
Shallum King of Israel 743
Menehem King of Israel 743-738
Pekhaiah King of Israel 738-737
Pekah King of Israel 737-732
Hoshea King of Israel 732-724
Nephi
Nephi
Alma
Alma
Shiblon
Helaman
Corianton
Shiblon
Helaman
Yuva
Tuva
Ay
Nefertiti
Merytaten
Line from Aaron
Zadok 13th HP
Ahimaaz 14th HP
Scota
Azariah 15th HP
Joash 16th HP
Nimshi of Samaria
Josaphat
Jehu King of Israel 841-814
Jehoahaz King of Israel 814-798
Joash King of Israel 798-783
Jeroboam II King of Israel 783-743
Esarhaddon
Kishvad
King Judarz
Nabopolassar
Japheth
Magog
Scythians
Sythes
Baoth
Phenius
Niul
Gaedal Glas
Asruth
Sruth
Heber Glas SCOT
Beouman
Oghaman
Tait
Agnon
Heber Glun
Ninurta Apil Ekur
Ashur
Tiglath Pileser
Shalmaneser
Nagia Zakutu
Assurbanipal
Adaguppi
King Nebuchadnezzar

In the book of Kings King David, the King of Israel and Judah is replaced by his son by Bathsheba Solomon. King David had many concubines and managed to hold the kingdom together well. Solomon created the temple, and had a very good reign. Jeroboam however revolted and claimed he was king of Israel. Jeroboam was the son of Nebat the son of Azaziah and Sarviya the harlot who was the daughter of Abala by Nahash. Now Abala was the mother of David by Jesse. Therefore Sarvia was a half sister of David sharing his mother. Now Nebat lineage was from Epraim, and Nahash lineage was from Reuben thru the curse of Jacob that Reuben was given by his father. Now Solomon's line continued and the Kings of Israel's lines were varied. The chart shows the King of Israel and the years that they served as King, as well as the vertical ascention to King Solomon son of David for the line for the Kings of Judah. Now consider how the Kings of Judah all married lines from each of the twelve tribes, and notice the dates of the Kings of both Judah and Israel. Interesting to the reader may be the wives that were part of the lines of Levi, or of the lines of Saul, or the lines of the tribe of Isaac-har, and also of the lines of Asher, or Simon. Notice the interesting addition of the son of Manasseh Lehi, who was married to a Saraih and his son Nelphi who also was married to a Saraiah. Consider also in time after the lines of Shealtial the book of Tobit that has Sariah and the Angel Rafael. Was the Lehi son of Manassah an attempt to regulate those who are men of the blood, (like King David) into a breeding law where the fortunes of the father are used with Sarah, Nicole the queen of Sheba, Karamat the wife of Jeroboam, and controlled the making of each Father's Lord.

Now also consider the Judgement of each individual is similar to the Judgement of a King. A King's power is the abilty to pass judgement thru his court for the crimes of his subjects. His Justice is a result of his subjects and their instructions. So the Kings is a judgement book where the Hebrew people said we are going to write the law of all the things you can do wrong, and if you do them wrong we are going to take them out of your father, and make your lord son subject to everything you have done. This was done about 1000 bc and took many years of breeding and trial by the people. Now the Roman Empire did not like this idea and so defeated the Jewish People, but the Kingdom of Israel resurfaced about 1948 and is alive today. So obviously the Jewish people thru the Christians does not care if they have a King or not, but they are ruled by law and are likely the first and strongest law givers that can administer the law across the planet for all peoples, and so will institute a rule of law for all people. Murderors, cutthroats and so on will resurrect likely, only not as powerful as the knowledgeable scolars and Priests that exist today and will resurrect their houses with Lords, Soldiers, Priests, while the killers will be subjected to Canaan for generations until their sins are forgiven.

Kinky Notes.

Ahaziah fathered with Athalia and made his wife who he fathered with to make his son.

Hezekiah had Hepzibah who made Haraz whose daughter Meshalum married Hezekiah son Manassah.

Nimshi married his father Jehosaphat sister.

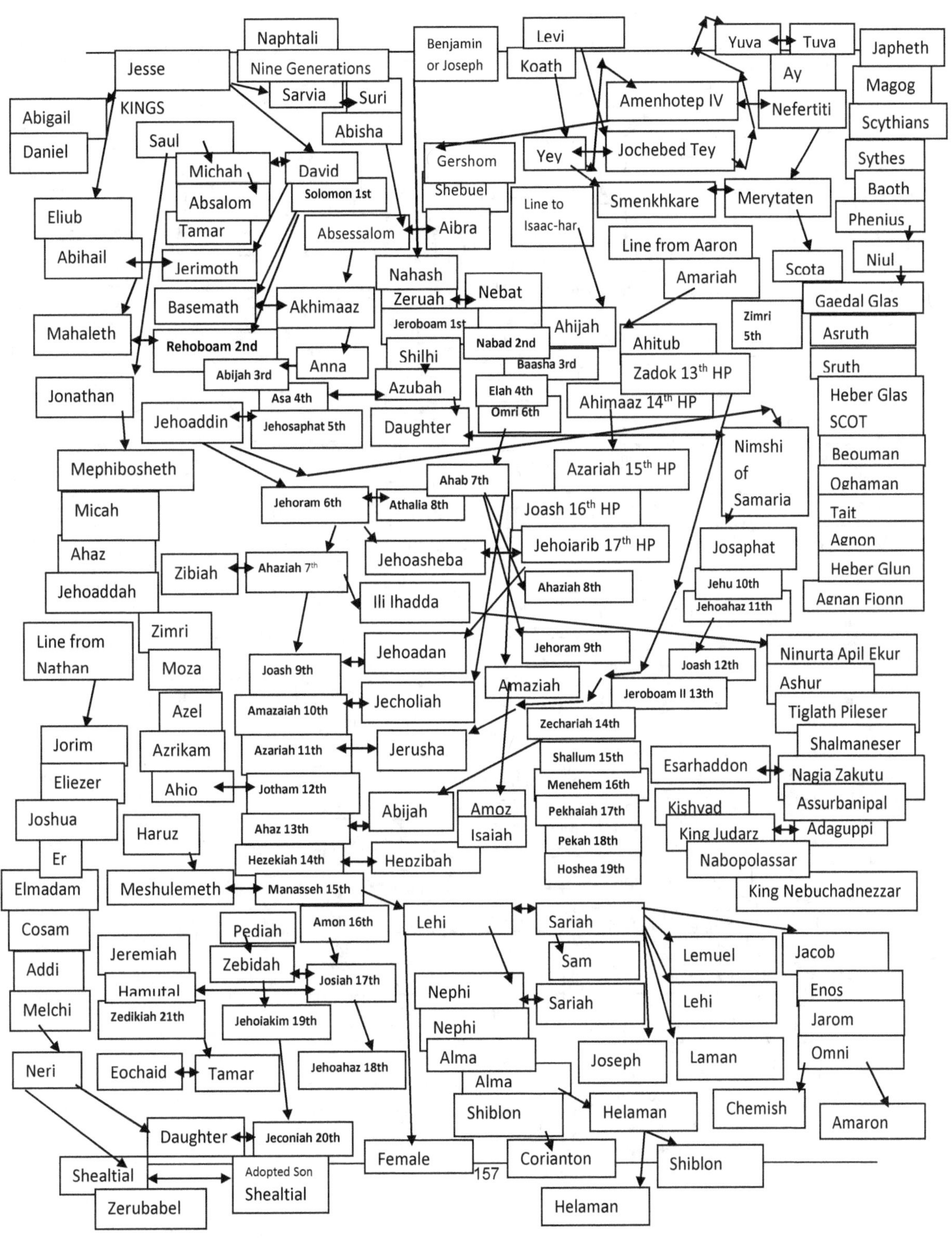
Naphtali
Jesse
Nine Generations
Benjamin or Joseph
Levi
Koath
Yuva
Tuva
Japheth
Ay
Magog
Sarvia
Suri
Amenhotep IV
Nefertiti
Scythians
Abigail
KINGS
Abisha
Daniel
Saul
Yey
Jochebed Tey
Gershom
Sythes
Michah
David
Shebuel
Baoth
Solomon 1st
Smenkhkare
Merytaten
Absalom
Line to Isaac-har
Eliub
Tamar
Abessalom
Aibra
Phenius
Abihail
Line from Aaron
Jerimoth
Nahash
Scota
Niul
Amariah
Zeruah
Nebat
Gaedal Glas
Basemath
Akhimaaz
Zimri 5th
Jeroboam 1st
Ahijah
Mahaleth
Asruth
Rehoboam 2nd
Nabad 2nd
Ahitub
Shilhi
Anna
Baasha 3rd
Sruth
Abijah 3rd
Zadok 13th HP
Azubah
Heber Glas SCOT
Jonathan
Asa 4th
Elah 4th
Ahimaaz 14th HP
Jehoaddin
Jehosaphat 5th
Daughter
Omri 6th
Nimshi of Samaria
Beouman
Mephibosheth
Ahab 7th
Azariah 15th HP
Oghaman
Jehoram 6th
Athalia 8th
Micah
Joash 16th HP
Tait
Agnon
Ahaz
Jehoasheba
Jehoiarib 17th HP
Josaphat
Zibiah
Ahaziah 7th
Heber Glun
Jehu 10th
Ahaziah 8th
Jehoaddah
Ili Ihadda
Agnan Fionn
Jehoahaz 11th
Zimri
Line from Nathan
Ninurta Apil Ekur
Jehoram 9th
Jehoadan
Moza
Joash 9th
Joash 12th
Ashur
Amaziah
Jeroboam II 13th
Azel
Amazaiah 10th
Jecholiah
Tiglath Pileser
Zechariah 14th
Jorim
Azrikam
Shalmaneser
Azariah 11th
Jerusha
Shallum 15th
Esarhaddon
Eliezer
Nagia Zakutu
Ahio
Jotham 12th
Menehem 16th
Joshua
Abijah
Amoz
Kishvad
Assurbanipal
Haruz
Pekhaiah 17th
Ahaz 13th
Isaiah
King Judarz
Adaguppi
Er
Pekah 18th
Hezekiah 14th
Hepzibah
Nabopolassar
Elmadam
Meshulemeth
Hoshea 19th
Manasseh 15th
King Nebuchadnezzar
Lehi
Sariah
Cosam
Amon 16th
Pediah
Jacob
Jeremiah
Sam
Lemuel
Zebidah
Addi
Josiah 17th
Enos
Nephi
Sariah
Hamutal
Lehi
Melchi
Zedikiah 21th
Jehoiakim 19th
Jarom
Nephi
Alma
Omni
Joseph
Laman
Neri
Eochaid
Tamar
Jehoahaz 18th
Alma
Shiblon
Helaman
Chemish
Amaron
Daughter
Jeconiah 20th
Female
Corianton
Shiblon
Shealtial
Adopted Son Shealtial
Zerubabel
Helaman

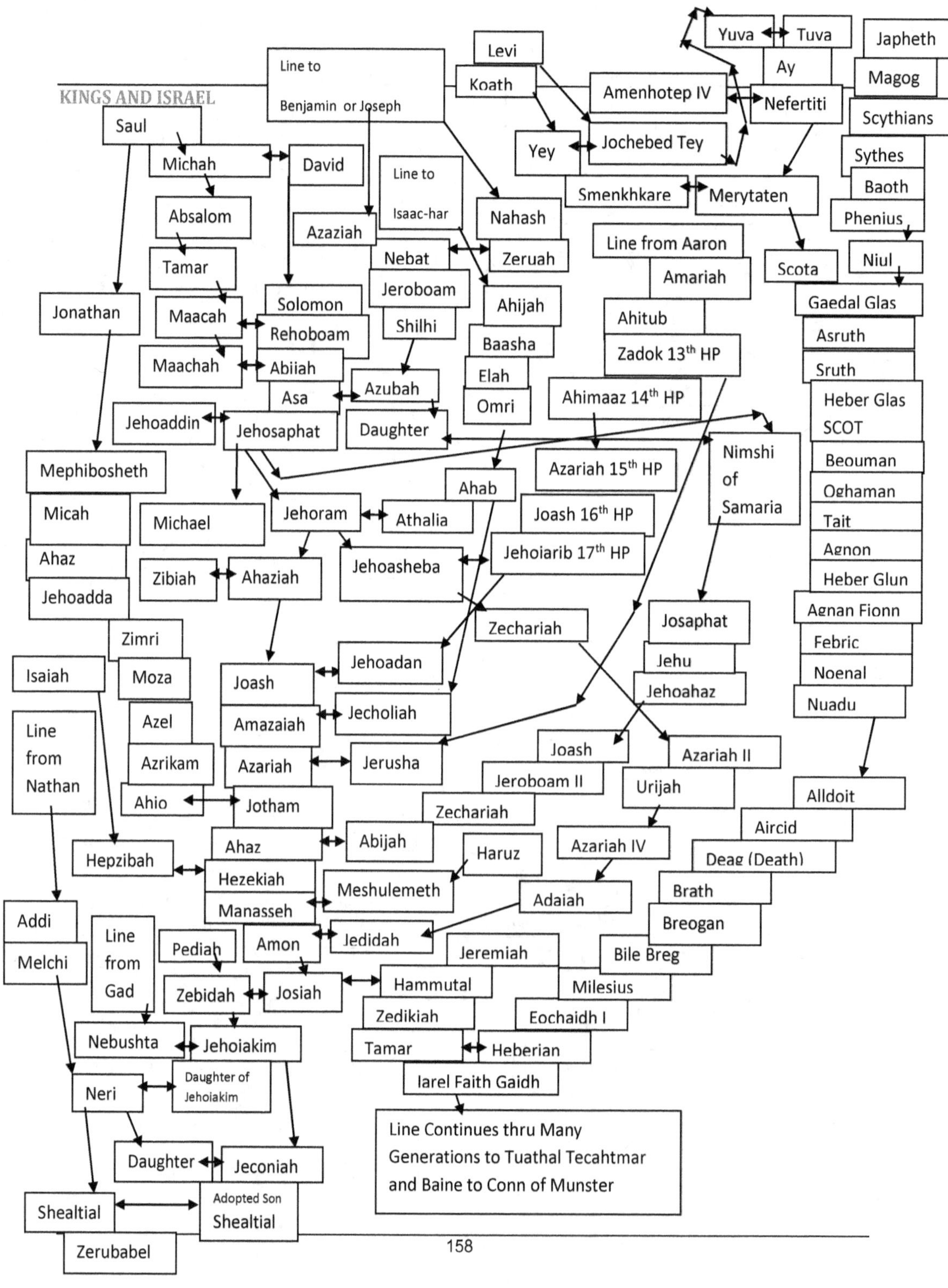
Yuva
Tuva
Japheth
Levi
Line to
Benjamin or Joseph
Ay
Magog
Koath
Amenhotep IV
Nefertiti
Scythians
Saul
Yey
Jochebed Tey
Sythes
Michah
David
Line to
Isaac-har
Baoth
Smenkhkare
Merytaten
Absalom
Nahash
Phenius
Azaziah
Line from Aaron
Niul
Tamar
Nebat
Zeruah
Scota
Amariah
Jeroboam
Gaedal Glas
Jonathan
Solomon
Ahijah
Maacah
Shilhi
Ahitub
Rehoboam
Baasha
Asruth
Zadok 13th HP
Maachah
Abiiah
Elah
Sruth
Azubah
Heber Glas
Asa
Ahimaaz 14th HP
Omri
SCOT
Jehoaddin
Jehosaphat
Daughter
Nimshi
of
Samaria
Beouman
Mephibosheth
Azariah 15th HP
Ahab
Oghaman
Micah
Michael
Jehoram
Athalia
Joash 16th HP
Tait
Ahaz
Agnon
Zibiah
Ahaziah
Jehoasheba
Jehoiarib 17th HP
Heber Glun
Jehoadda
Agnan Fionn
Zechariah
Josaphat
Zimri
Febric
Jehoadan
Jehu
Isaiah
Moza
Joash
Noenal
Jehoahaz
Nuada
Azel
Amazaiah
Jecholiah
Line
from
Nathan
Joash
Azrikam
Azariah
Jerusha
Azariah II
Jeroboam II
Urijah
Ahio
Jotham
Alldoit
Zechariah
Aircid
Ahaz
Abijah
Haruz
Azariah IV
Hepzibah
Deag (Death)
Hezekiah
Meshulemeth
Brath
Adaiah
Manasseh
Addi
Line
from
Gad
Breogan
Pediah
Amon
Jedidah
Jeremiah
Bile Breg
Melchi
Zebidah
Josiah
Hammutal
Milesius
Zedikiah
Eochaidh I
Nebushta
Jehoiakim
Tamar
Heberian
Iarel Faith Gaidh
Neri
Daughter of
Jehoiakim
Line Continues thru Many
Generations to Tuathal Tecahtmar
and Baine to Conn of Munster
Daughter
Jeconiah
Adopted Son
Shealtial
Shealtial
Zerubabel

Jeroboam

The Prophet Ezekiel declared to Jeroboam you are to inherit ten tribes. Now we know David was a man of blood, the Phillistines it seems, so his son Solomon, born from Bathsheba with questionable honor. Now the levites said David's descendents would inherit the Kingdom, which became the tribe of Judah. Jeroboam had the sister of David as a mother as, Abala, the wife of Jesse and Nahash. Sarvia was the daughter of Abala and Nahash and was the wife of Nebat. Now Nebat was the son of Azaziah and his male line continues to Zeruga, son of Epraim the chosen of the heir of Jacob Joseph due to the eldest, Reuben infidelity with Jacob's wife Bilah. Nahash was of the male line of Reuben. It is likely that Reuben did not care about an inheritance, the eldest son is always with the father and in Hebrew the Father has cursed his son since Isaac was almost sacrificed on the altar. Keep in mind that Daniel, the son of David's sister Abigail was also not a man of blood. Now how did Jeroboam order the ten tribes of Israel and what where those tribes since there are twelve tribes. Solomon was king of Judah. So of the eleven tribes the tribe of Simeon was always related to the daughter Dinah, and was not one of the ten tribes. The tribe of Simeon was used by Simeon's brother's tribe Levi to manage the men of Israel and Egypt that became a man of blood. Following is a chart of the order of the tribes, with the Christian apostile and the number of the rank of the tribe. Notice it is based on the eldest, Reuben being the strongest tribe. Notice since Judah was the strongest Israelite, who married Tamar the daughter of Epher or Atlas, the eldest was the strongest of Israel. First the eldest, then the general Isaac-har, then the priest Levi, then the Chosen Joseph, then the innocent Benjamin, then Zebulon, and finally the servant sons, Dan, Gad, Asher, and Naphtali.

Order of Power of Israel's Ten Tribes		
Reuben	12	Judas Iscariot
Issachar	10	Phillip
Levi	2	Mathew
Joseph	11	Thomas
Benjamin	7	John
Zebulon	4	James the Lesser
Dan	8	Bartholomew
Gad	3	Andrew
Asher	5	Simon
Naphtali	1	Judas Thadeus
Two Remaining Tribes		
Simon	6	Peter
Judah	9	James the Greater

ERA OF BABYLON

SECTION NINE: DANIEL THE PROPHET AND PERSIA

Dan was an Israelite. The name David is similar to Dan, and the name Daniel is derived from Dan. In the Old Testament there is an entire section devoted to Dan, called Daniel and the Minor Prophets.

In the modern AD times Daniel of the Hofnai is a use of the name of Daniel, as well as being found in Wales and other places. Dan is a fairly common name. Daniel of the Hofnai is interesting for two lineages, that of Obadiah, and the Cross of Hezekiah alive in the year 33 AC, and the the lineage of China, of Otyoro alive in the year 33 AD. Now the lineage of China is shown to come up at Eber, a few generations above the Abrahamic. Another China line is that of Dao Gao that comes up in the Mongols to Munk Zunk and Attilla the Hun. Dao Gao was also alive in the the year 33 AD. So Dan of the Hofnai is shown to be part of the line thru Persia of Obadiah, and also to one of the lineages of the Oriental people.

Jehiokim lost the war to King Nechebenezzar. Now Jecoliah was the heir and was likely killed by the Persians. So was Daniel the brother to Jecoliah, and a young child at the time of the invasion of Israel when all the jewish people became captives in Babylon? The book of Daniel is said by some to be a childrens book with large monsters and dreams and Kings and Soldiers, and visions. Daniel is given three friends, with the rest of the captives, and the story goes on. The text does say that the friends and Daniel were the royal blood or the noble blood. If it were the royal blood Daniel may have been the brother to Jecoliah and the heir to the Kingdom of David.

King Nechebenezzar has a very interesting lineage. It is shown that his lineage goes back thru two wives of his ancestors to Ahaziah, the King of Judah, who is descended from Solomon and thus David. So that is very interesting. It is also interesting that Simon the son of Jacob has a line that history has preserved that continues thru Israel to Assyria and then to the Babylon Kings and finally to King Nechebenezzar. So Nechebenezzar is the first biblical character that can claim descent from Simon, as well as Judah, Zebulon, Levi, Benjamin and Joseph, just as can King David. Now Isaac-har joins the lineage in Kings after Ahaziah, so Isaac-har may not be in King Nechebenezzar's lineage. Also many of the lines of Levi join with the Kings lines, so these are not part of Nechebenezzar II lineage. Finally the Israel that is from Jeroboam who is from Reuben would not be a large part of Nechebenezzars lineage. So clearly Daniel has an advantage in lineage of most of Solomon's Descendents, as well as Jeroboam and most of the kings of Israel.

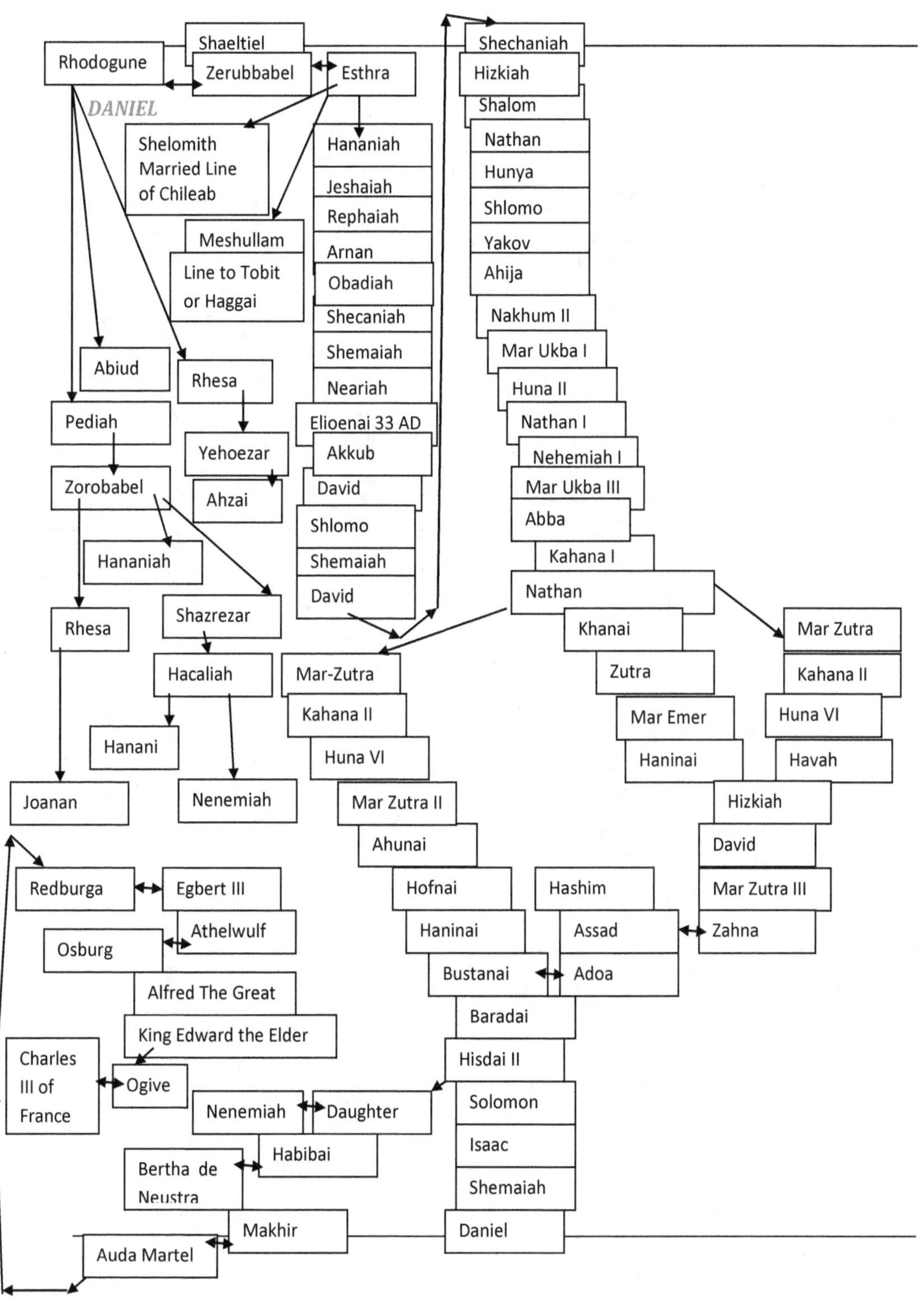

Shaeltiel
Rhodogune
Zerubbabel
Esthra
DANIEL
Shelomith Married Line of Chileab
Hananiah
Jeshaiah
Rephaiah
Meshullam
Line to Tobit or Haggai
Arnan
Obadiah
Shecaniah
Shemaiah
Neariah
Elioenai 33 AD
Akkub
David
Shlomo
Shemaiah
David
Abiud
Rhesa
Pediah
Yehoezar
Zorobabel
Ahzai
Hananiah
Rhesa
Shazrezar
Hacaliah
Hanani
Nenemiah
Joanan
Shechaniah
Hizkiah
Shalom
Nathan
Hunya
Shlomo
Yakov
Ahija
Nakhum II
Mar Ukba I
Huna II
Nathan I
Nehemiah I
Mar Ukba III
Abba
Kahana I
Nathan
Khanai
Zutra
Mar Emer
Haninai
Mar Zutra
Kahana II
Huna VI
Havah
Hizkiah
David
Mar Zutra III
Zahna
Mar-Zutra
Kahana II
Huna VI
Mar Zutra II
Ahunai
Hofnai
Haninai
Bustanai
Hashim
Assad
Adoa
Baradai
Hisdai II
Solomon
Isaac
Shemaiah
Daniel
Redburga
Egbert III
Osburg
Athelwulf
Alfred The Great
King Edward the Elder
Charles III of France
Ogive
Nenemiah
Daughter
Habibai
Bertha de Neustra
Makhir
Auda Martel

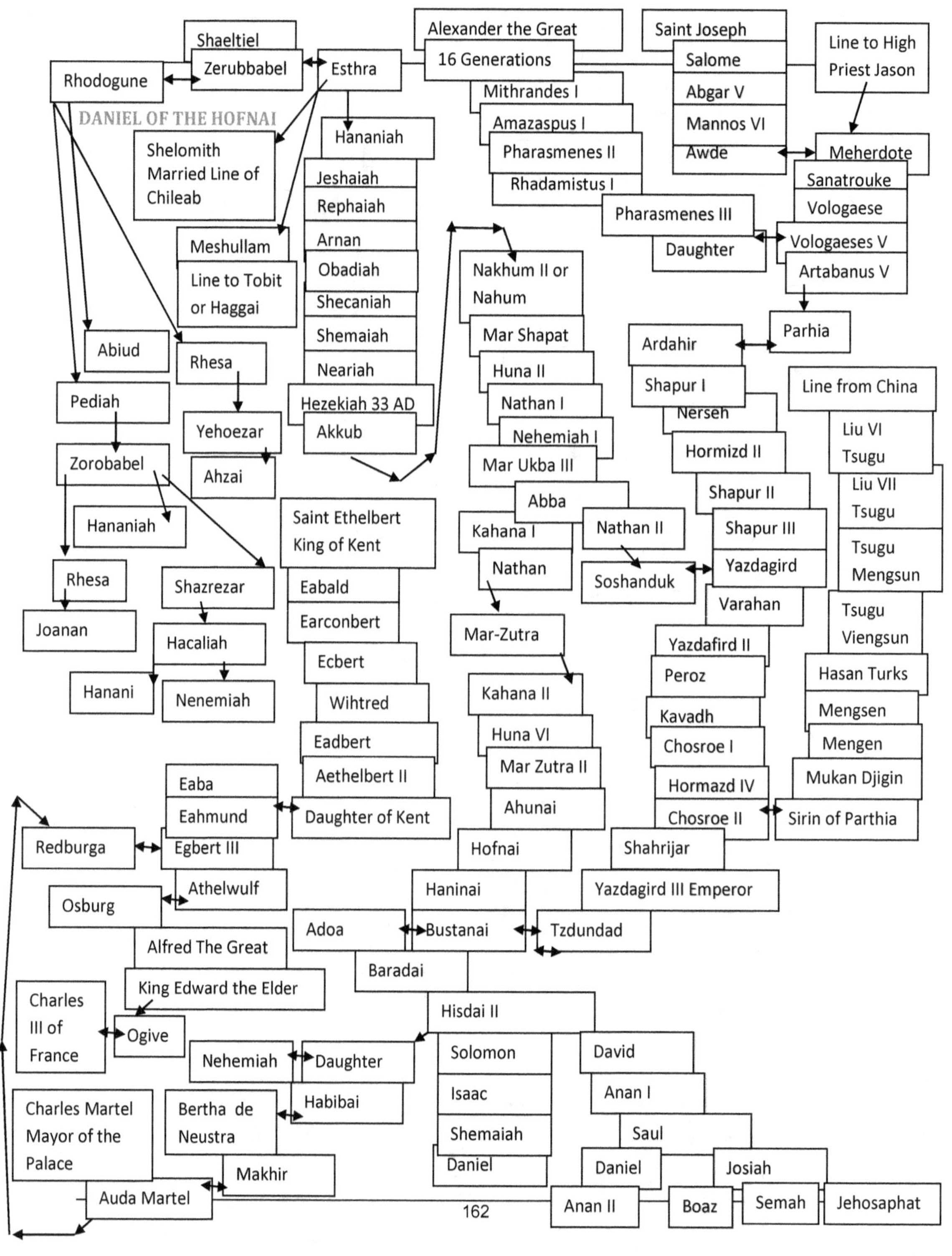
Shaeltiel
Alexander the Great
Saint Joseph
16 Generations
Salome
Line to High Priest Jason
Rhodogune
Zerubbabel
Esthra
Mithrandes I
Abgar V
DANIEL OF THE HOFNAI
Amazaspus I
Mannos VI
Hananiah
Shelomith Married Line of Chileab
Pharasmenes II
Awde
Meherdote
Jeshaiah
Rhadamistus I
Sanatrouke
Rephaiah
Pharasmenes III
Vologaese
Meshullam
Arnan
Daughter
Vologaeses V
Line to Tobit or Haggai
Obadiah
Nakhum II or Nahum
Artabanus V
Shecaniah
Shemaiah
Mar Shapat
Ardahir
Parhia
Abiud
Rhesa
Neariah
Huna II
Shapur I
Line from China
Pediah
Hezekiah 33 AD
Nathan I
Nerseh
Yehoezar
Akkub
Nehemiah I
Liu VI Tsugu
Zorobabel
Hormizd II
Ahzai
Mar Ukba III
Liu VII Tsugu
Shapur II
Abba
Saint Ethelbert King of Kent
Hananiah
Kahana I
Nathan II
Shapur III
Tsugu Mengsun
Nathan
Yazdagird
Rhesa
Shazrezar
Eabald
Soshanduk
Varahan
Joanan
Earconbert
Tsugu Viengsun
Hacaliah
Mar-Zutra
Ecbert
Yazdafird II
Peroz
Hasan Turks
Hanani
Nenemiah
Kahana II
Wihtred
Kavadh
Mengsen
Huna VI
Eadbert
Chosroe I
Mengen
Mar Zutra II
Aethelbert II
Mukan Djigin
Eaba
Hormazd IV
Ahunai
Eahmund
Daughter of Kent
Chosroe II
Sirin of Parthia
Redburga
Egbert III
Hofnai
Shahrijar
Athelwulf
Haninai
Yazdagird III Emperor
Osburg
Adoa
Bustanai
Tzdundad
Alfred The Great
Baradai
King Edward the Elder
Charles III of France
Hisdai II
Ogive
Nehemiah
Daughter
Solomon
David
Charles Martel Mayor of the Palace
Bertha de Neustra
Habibai
Isaac
Anan I
Shemaiah
Saul
Makhir
Daniel
Daniel
Josiah
Auda Martel
Anan II
Boaz
Semah
Jehosaphat

The Prophet Daniel

In the introduction to the book of the Old Testament Daniel, the mention of royal eunuchs is made, Hananiah, Mishael, and Azariah. The preceding page shows Daniel as listed with no children. Now in the genealogies searched there is a Mishael the son of Uzziel the son of Levi the Israelite. He had no offspring. There is also a son of Zerah the son of Judah, who was Ethan, who was the father of Azariah who had no offspring. Finally the brother of Nehemiah was Hananiah who had no offspring. Are these the royalty the Babylonians caught and raised in the court? If so it would have been a watch in Judah or Zeus, (Zerah was thought to be Zeus by some) thru Azariah, a watch in Levi by Mishael, and a watch in Nenemiah by Hannaniah.

Now another translation shows Daniels fellow friends as female, AziRuth, Michelle, and Hannah. In the Genealogies there is a Hannah that married Elkanah IV the son of Joram of the line of Kings. This is like the watch on Samuel who was the son of Hannah and Elkanah, however Hannah who married Elkanah IV had no children. Also on a watch of Judah could Bath-Shua who married Judah and made Shelah and Nafut be the same as Michelle? This would be the watch on Judah, the same as Azariah. Now Aziruth is like Azariah and the only likeness maybe Asruth of the line of Scota leading to the Centurian old Priest of Aaron. Aaron was extremely old in age (similar to Abraham) when Moses daughter Merytatum was given him as a bed warmer. The offspring was Scota who was of the line that continued thru Scotland and Ireland to Tuthal Techmar who married the house of David with Baine. Thus the centurian line of Scotland and Ireland from Aaron had both Abraham who conceived with Sarah at an old age and Aaron who conceived with Merytatum at an old age. This was not the Priest line of Aaron but a hidden line in Scotland and Ireland, with the knowledge they were oaf Abraham and also of Aaron.

So now how do you marry or find mates for the Eunuchs found in the book of Daniel. Well Mishael was about the same time as Asruth, and Aziriah was the watch on Judah the same as Michell. Hannah was the wife of Elkanah and could easily be meant for Hanani.Now keep in mind in the Clan war between Israel and Esau Judah was killed by Samwise (Edom) and Dan buried his knife in Samwise while Sams sword was in Judah, Dan buried to the throat. Thus now Dan becomes the avenger of Judah, (Law of Life for a Life) with the widows Bath-Shua and Tamar, and Hur, Perez, Shelah, and Nafut, and Zerah become orphans. Likely Zerah and Perez also were in the clan battle. We know Joseph got Luce the son of Samwise Eldritch)(Korah) in the clan battle but Susi, the daughter of Samwise was a very young innocent and was spared by Israel and raised by Dan. Likely Zerah got servants of Esau. Thus the Jupiterians will not allow Zeus to be the father, due to the clan battle (he may have taken a life) but rather Jupiter. OTHER PLACES DAN IS FOUND in HISTORY. Daniel or Chileab is listed as the son of Abigail by David in Chronicles. Another son of Abigail by Jether was Amasa who would have been the half brother of Daniel or possibly a full brother. Suppose that Jether abused Abigail (Jether means to punch) and so David took his sister Abigail back to the castle. Now Daniel would not be born from incest, so likely Jether creeped in and Abigail conceived and Daniel was listed as a son of David, although he was not so in truth. It is said he is son of the creep. So Daniel is found as a son of Abigail, a son of Jacob called Israel, and a son of Bustani, and a capture in the old testament sacred writing. (book about POW's and Metalurgy) He is also in Wales and the son of Ivan the terrible in Mother Russia.

Now the word Christ means King. Daniel is made to be King of Persia. This is done by making Daniel the son of Abigail, grow up in the Kingdom of David. The Kingdom of David is a divided Kingdom that was eventually defeated by all the world coming together and eliminating the line of Judah. Now Daniel is exiled in Persia with a King Nechabenezzar who is from the same King David thru the King Ahaziah whose line both continues to the Kings of Judah as well as having daughters that are ancestors of King Nechebenezzar. So how does Daniel become the King of Persia? He consults his god and prays until all of his ancestry, both the Kings of Judah and the Kings of Israel totally defeat Nechabenezzar whose son Beltashazzar sees a vision of the writing on the wall and soon dies after that. So Daniel's spirit thru three generations stays in Persia under the Kings Cyrus and Darius until finally the Hebrew are freed from exile and continue in Jerusalem. The exile in Babylon is now over so the third section of the Bible, Daniel and the minor Prophets takes over. Unlike the first and most powerful section, the Torah, or the first five books of the bible, the third section is about prophets whose predictions come true. Daniel is a pretty common name in the Hebrew culture and is usually granted as the son of Abigail the daughter of Jesse. Now the father of Daniel is written in the sacred writings of Cronicles as David, however Daniel is the son of Abigail who is the mother of Amasa by Jether. Jethers lineage is a series of Hebrew words that can easily be related to boxing or fisticuffs. Jether is the undercut of the body, his father Jada is the Jab, and his father Onam is side swipe to the head, while Onam is the son of Jeremeel who is the windmill of the fists and Jeremeel is the Eldest son of Hezron, which in Hebrew means the Right Cross. So obviously the Elder line of Jether is a violent line of physical fitness and able body building, worked out in the gym. Now suppose that Abigail is abused by her undercutting spouse Jether and David takes her to his castle. Jether is so able and Abigail is after all his wife so Jether creeps into the castle and has relations with Abigail and fathers Daniel. King David plays along and possibly because he is likely to kill anyone he wants he has killed after all King David may have raped his sister Abigail and thought he made Daniel. At any rate this makes Daniel the son of the creep, either King David or Jether, and of the eldest line of Hezron of Judah. So Daniel is likely an able King that sees no reason to Kill, named after the Son of Jacob and participated in the battle of Clans between Jacob and Esau, in which Esau is Killed and Jacob becomes Israel and Dan has his trials as a master instead of a man. This is likely made so that Daniel will not trust anyone, who can make Dan repeat his battle with Edom, and so make his able elder line of Hezron not part of sport but of war. Notice there are clues in the bible about this but this law is not given to the average reader of the bible.

ERA OF ISRAEL, A FEW GENERATIONS AFTER ABRAHAM

SECTION TEN: ISRAELITES AND MAJOR FIGURES OF ISRAEL

In this section the Isralites, their wives, their parents, and their offspring are examined from a lineage descendent or genealogy perspective. All twelve of the Isralites had the same father. Jacob called Israel. Now Jacob had four wives. Leah and Rachel were sisters, while Bilhah and Zilphas were also sisters. Now it is interesting to know that all of the Isrealites Grandfather was of course Isaac and Grandmother was Rebecca. Grandfather for Gad,Asher, Dan and Naphtali, was Roetheus and Grandmother was Aena or (Anna). Grandfather for the other eight Isrealites was Laban and his wife Adinah. Who were parents of the Sisters Rachel and Leah whose brother was Lucas. (Twin to Leah). Jacob as of course twin to Esau so all of the Isralites had Esau as an uncle, while the sons of the servant women had Cheref as an Uncle and the other eight had Lucas as an uncle. Please see the section on Cousins of Rebecca for other relationships past Grandparents and Uncles and Aunts. So the servant sisters where related to Roetheus and so to his father Huz, son of Nahor, while the eight sons of Jacob from Leah and Rachel were from Isaac, son of Abraham and his father Terah son of Nahor. So everyone was really from Nahor eventually the difference being from Huz or from Terah.

So the figures of Leah, Roetheus, Rachel form the major three houses. Leah has six Isralites, while Roetheus has four and Rachel has two. Leah has the oldest while Rachel has the chosen.

Each Chieftain or Isrealite has its advantages and aspects, such as Dan being the Chief of Moab, while Joseph is the Chosen one of Jacob, and Reuben is the Eldest with a wife from both Ishmael and Esau.

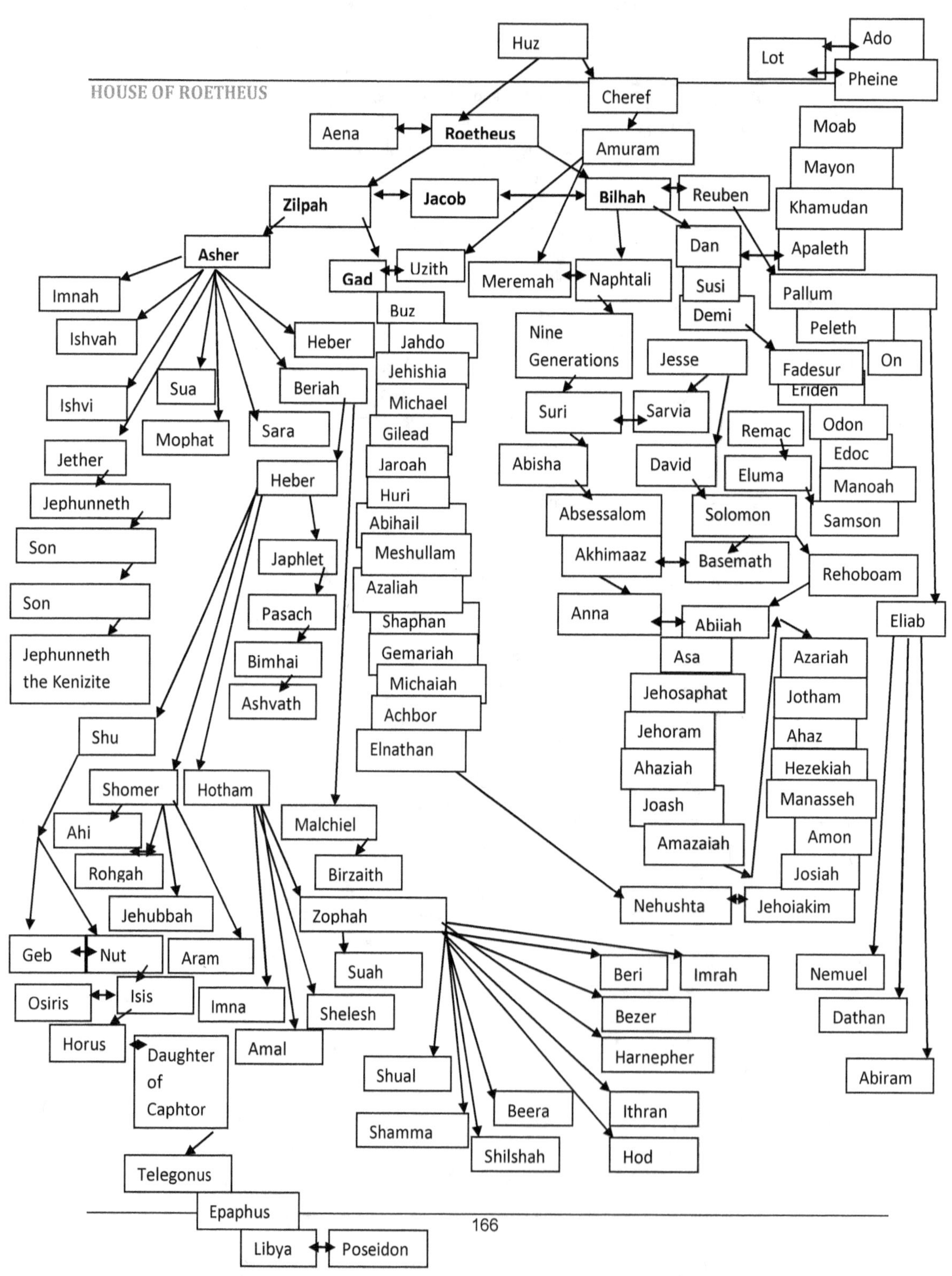
Huz
Lot
Ado
Pheine
Cheref
Aena
Roetheus
Amuram
Moab
Mayon
Zilpah
Jacob
Bilhah
Reuben
Khamudan
Asher
Dan
Apaleth
Gad
Uzith
Meremah
Naphtali
Susi
Pallum
Imnah
Buz
Demi
Peleth
Ishvah
Heber
Jahdo
Nine
Generations
Jesse
Fadesur
On
Jehishia
Eriden
Ishvi
Sua
Beriah
Michael
Suri
Sarvia
Remac
Odon
Mophat
Sara
Gilead
Edoc
Jether
Jaroah
Abisha
David
Eluma
Manoah
Heber
Huri
Jephunneth
Abihail
Absessalom
Solomon
Samson
Son
Japhlet
Meshullam
Akhimaaz
Basemath
Rehoboam
Azaliah
Son
Pasach
Anna
Abiiah
Eliab
Shaphan
Asa
Azariah
Jephunneth
the Kenizite
Bimhai
Gemariah
Jehosaphat
Ashvath
Michaiah
Jotham
Achbor
Jehoram
Ahaz
Shu
Elnathan
Ahaziah
Hezekiah
Manasseh
Shomer
Hotham
Joash
Malchiel
Ahi
Amon
Amazaiah
Birzaith
Rohgah
Josiah
Jehubbah
Zophah
Nehushta
Jehoiakim
Geb
Nut
Aram
Suah
Beri
Imrah
Nemuel
Osiris
Isis
Imna
Shelesh
Bezer
Dathan
Horus
Daughter
of
Caphtor
Amal
Harnepher
Shual
Abiram
Beera
Ithran
Shamma
Shilshah
Hod
Telegonus
Epaphus
Libya
Poseidon

HOUSE OF RACHEL

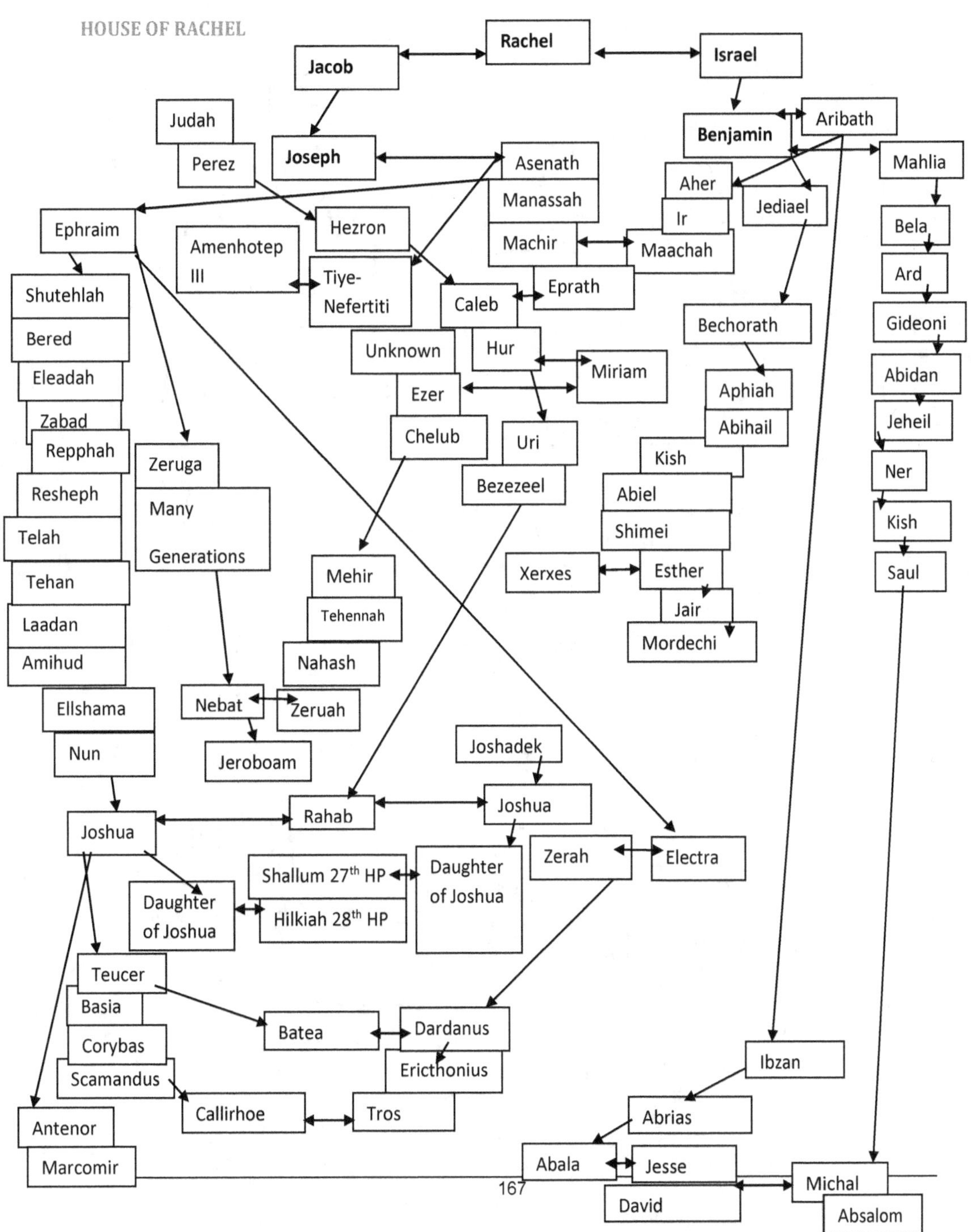

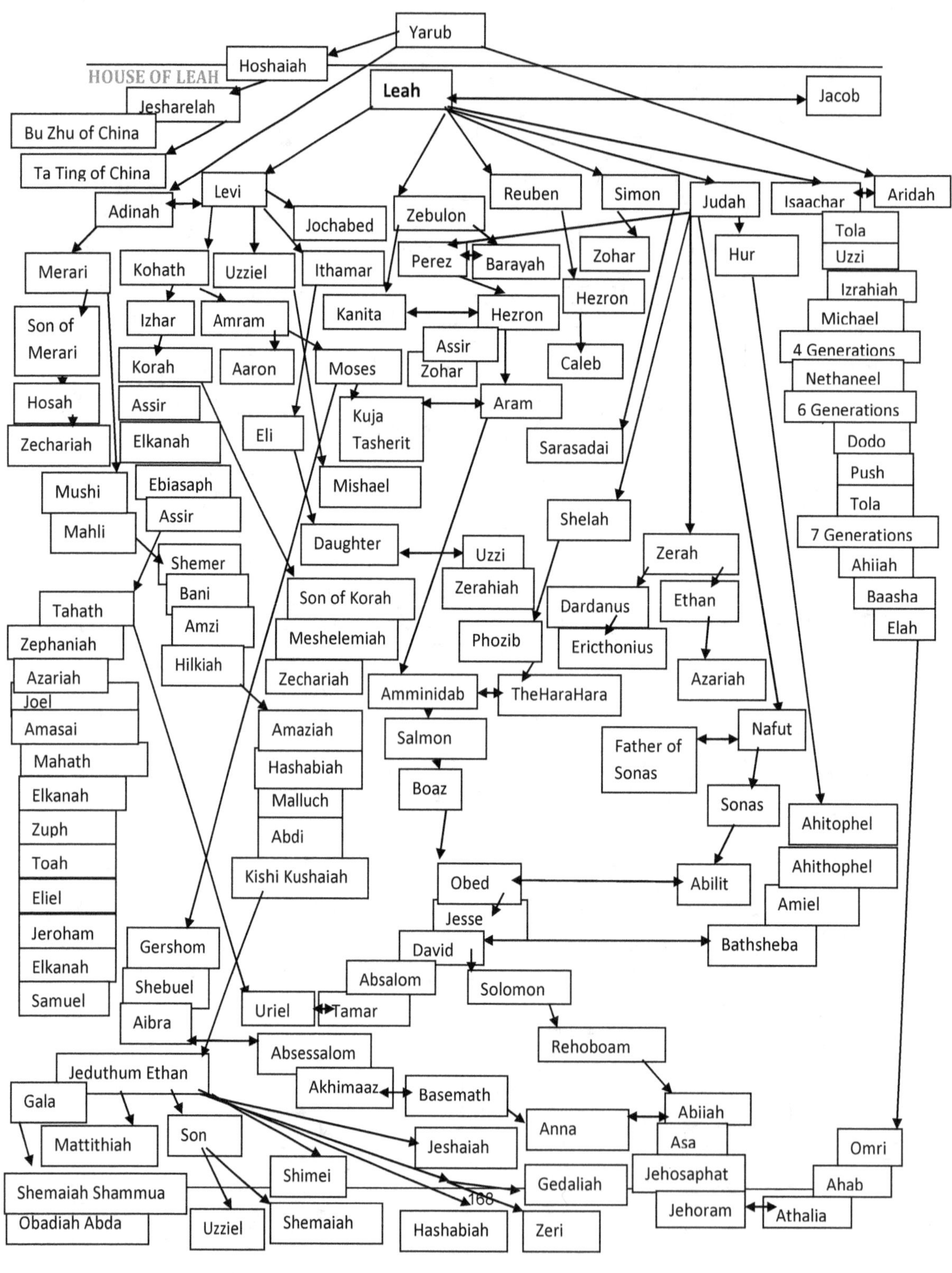

HOUSE OF LEAH
Yarub
Hoshaiah
Leah
Jacob
Jesharelah
Bu Zhu of China
Ta Ting of China
Levi
Adinah
Jochabed
Zebulon
Reuben
Simon
Judah
Isaachar
Aridah
Tola
Uzzi
Izrahiah
Michael
4 Generations
Nethaneel
6 Generations
Dodo
Push
Tola
7 Generations
Ahiiah
Baasha
Elah
Merari
Kohath
Uzziel
Ithamar
Perez
Barayah
Zohar
Hur
Hezron
Son of Merari
Izhar
Amram
Kanita
Hezron
Assir
Zohar
Caleb
Korah
Aaron
Moses
Hosah
Assir
Kuja Tasherit
Aram
Zechariah
Elkanah
Eli
Sarasadai
Mushi
Ebiasaph
Mishael
Mahli
Assir
Shelah
Daughter
Uzzi
Zerah
Shemer
Bani
Zerahiah
Dardanus
Ethan
Tahath
Son of Korah
Amzi
Phozib
Ericthonius
Zephaniah
Meshelemiah
Azariah
Hilkiah
Zechariah
Azariah
Joel
Amminidab
TheHaraHara
Amasai
Amaziah
Nafut
Mahath
Hashabiah
Salmon
Father of Sonas
Elkanah
Malluch
Boaz
Zuph
Abdi
Sonas
Ahitophel
Toah
Kishi Kushaiah
Eliel
Obed
Abilit
Ahithophel
Jeroham
Jesse
Amiel
Gershom
Elkanah
David
Bathsheba
Shebuel
Absalom
Solomon
Samuel
Uriel
Tamar
Aibra
Absessalom
Rehoboam
Jeduthum Ethan
Akhimaaz
Basemath
Gala
Abiiah
Anna
Mattithiah
Son
Jeshaiah
Asa
Omri
Shimei
Jehosaphat
Shemaiah Shammua
Gedaliah
Ahab
Obadiah Abda
Uzziel
Shemaiah
Hashabiah
Zeri
Jehoram
Athalia

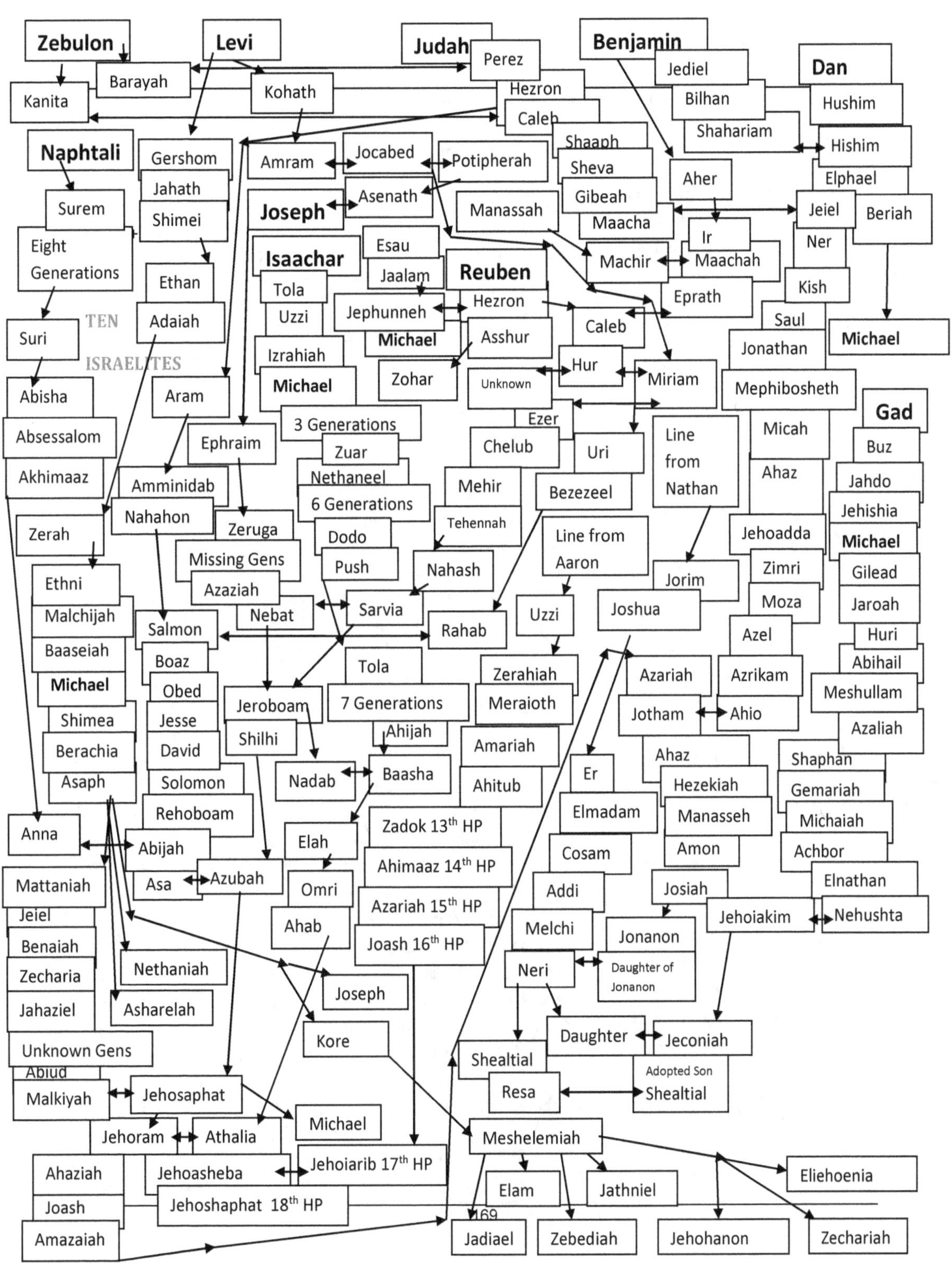
Zebulon
Levi
Judah
Perez
Benjamin
Jediel
Dan
Barayah
Kanita
Kohath
Hezron
Bilhan
Hushim
Caleb
Shahariam
Hishim
Naphtali
Gershom
Amram
Jocabed
Potipherah
Shaaph
Sheva
Aher
Elphael
Jahath
Surem
Shimei
Joseph
Asenath
Manassah
Gibeah
Maacha
Jeiel
Beriah
Eight
Generations
Esau
Isaachar
Jaalam
Reuben
Machir
Ir
Maachah
Ner
Ethan
Tola
Jephunneh
Hezron
Eprath
Kish
Suri
TEN
Adaiah
Uzzi
Michael
Asshur
Caleb
Saul
Michael
ISRAELITES
Izrahiah
Jonathan
Abisha
Aram
Michael
Zohar
Unknown
Hur
Miriam
Mephibosheth
Gad
Absessalom
3 Generations
Ezer
Micah
Buz
Ephraim
Zuar
Chelub
Uri
Line
from
Nathan
Akhimaaz
Amminidab
Nethaneel
Mehir
Bezezeel
Ahaz
Jahdo
6 Generations
Jehishia
Zerah
Nahahon
Zeruga
Tehennah
Line from
Aaron
Jehoadda
Michael
Dodo
Missing Gens
Push
Nahash
Jorim
Zimri
Gilead
Ethni
Azaziah
Moza
Jaroah
Malchijah
Nebat
Sarvia
Uzzi
Joshua
Salmon
Rahab
Azel
Huri
Baaseiah
Boaz
Abihail
Michael
Tola
Zerahiah
Azariah
Azrikam
Meshullam
Obed
Jeroboam
7 Generations
Meraioth
Shimea
Jesse
Jotham
Ahio
Azaliah
Shilhi
Ahijah
Amariah
Berachia
David
Ahaz
Shaphan
Asaph
Solomon
Nadab
Baasha
Er
Hezekiah
Gemariah
Ahitub
Rehoboam
Elmadam
Manasseh
Michaiah
Anna
Zadok 13th HP
Abijah
Elah
Amon
Achbor
Cosam
Ahimaaz 14th HP
Mattaniah
Asa
Azubah
Omri
Addi
Josiah
Elnathan
Jeiel
Azariah 15th HP
Ahab
Jehoiakim
Nehushta
Benaiah
Melchi
Jonanon
Joash 16th HP
Zecharia
Nethaniah
Neri
Daughter of
Jonanon
Joseph
Jahaziel
Asharelah
Kore
Daughter
Jeconiah
Unknown Gens
Shealtial
Abiud
Adopted Son
Malkiyah
Jehosaphat
Resa
Shealtial
Michael
Jehoram
Athalia
Meshelemiah
Jehoiarib 17th HP
Ahaziah
Jehoasheba
Eliehoenia
Elam
Jathniel
Joash
Jehoshaphat 18th HP
Amazaiah
Jadiael
Zebediah
Jehohanon
Zechariah

Here the author lists the twelve tribes and comments on the genealogy of each. Keep in mind that each of these Israelites is a Chieftain. There are two main houses, Rachel and her servant Bilhah, four Israelites, and Leah and her servant Zilpah, eight Israelites.

Joseph, the chosen son of Jacob has many male descendents. The chosen Israelites both his sons are ancestors of King David as is his daughter. His lines go thru the Greek as well thru his son Epraim, and Jeraboam can claim him as an ancestor. However King Saul cannot claim Joseph. Asenath, the wife of Joseph was the daughter of Potipherah and Jocabed. Thus all of Joseph's descendents can claim Levi as an ancestor and Egypt as a heritage for Jochabed was daughter of Levi.

Reuben , the eldest son of Jacob has only a few sons before the line discontinues with a women, (Rahab). The curse of Jacob, where Jacob curses Reuben for sleeping with Jacobs wife Bilhah is found in his descendents. The line for Pallum his son by Bilhah does not continue. Again very few Reubenites. Reuben's wife had strong lineage thur Ishmael the oldest son of Abraham and Esau eldest of Isaac.

Zebulon is the son of Leah, and has only two daughters of his generation whose lines continue. Thus there are few Zebulonites. Elon his son did not leave heirs.

Dan has a son and three daughters, and Susi, whose line continues to Sampson. However Dan's blood merges with Benjamin and Judah and Saul can claim Dan as an Ancestor, as well as Judah and Benjamin. Thus there are few Danites. Dan's wife was a Moabite so Dan was considered the chief of Moab.

Levi has many lines that continue, the most important being the Priest line of Aaron. There are many Levites, so many that his sons became a type of Israelite such as the Gershonites. Notable Levites became High Priests and Prophets such as Caiphas, Jeremiah, Isaiah, Moses, and Aaron. Levi had more than one wife, and his wife Melka's ancestor Aram was a cousin to Rebecca.

Benjamin was born after the clan battle and did not have his mother survive. There are many Benjaminites, and his lines continue to King David, King Saul, and finally merge with the levitical priest line of Aaron with Shallum. His lines merged with Dan and Judah after only a few generations. Benjamin had many wifes, one a descendent of Zimram, a son of Abraham, and one wife had an ancestor Zoba who was a cousin to Rebecca.

Simeon line continue for a few generations and then merge with the Kings of Assyria and Babylon and the record of this has been kept for many generations. His noteable desendent is King Nechabenezzar as found as the victor in the book of Daniel. Simeon's wife had lineage that went to the son of Noah Ham.

Naptali has an interesting descent and joins with the lines after King David. There are quite a few Naptalites. His line is called the Big Sir, possibly because it joins with Abijah at Anna, whose existence is covered and in most lineages the wife of Abijah is Maacah. (a toucan sam) This is likely because there is a cousin marriage in the lineage of the Big Sir that is not accepted by modern religion. Naptali's wife was

Meramah,(similar to Mary or Maria) and was a sister to Gad's wife.

Isaac-har descent joins with a descendent of David a Judean King as well as the lines of the Israelite Kings. In this line Is found Dodo the mighty man of David as well as an archangel Michael.

Judah's descent is very difficult, due to the fact that his son was the God of the Greeks. The Greek lineages are a religion all to themselves, and they continue to baffle Greek Scholars. His **descent** from Hur leads to the beautiful Bathsheba and his line from Perez and Hezron are the major lineages found in the Bible. His line from Shelah thru Bathshua is found to continue to King David. So Judah can be said to the be the Father of the Greeks, and also of King David, and the Kingdom of Judah was found to compete with the Kingdom of Israel. Note that Judah did not survive the clan battle, but Israel did and so fathered Benjamin the innocent that was not part of the battle. So the Kingdom of Judah may be likened to the Martydom kingdoms while the Kingdom of Israel is the Victor. Judah may have been the resurrection of Nimrod, the greatest warrior. He is credited as being the strongest of the Israelites. His wife was Tamar, who was of the line of Epher (also very strong) Therefore Zerah's mother was the strongest woman and Zerah's father was the strongest man.

Gad is a sheltered descent in a way and there are many Gadites. However most Gadites are not everyone's ancestors, as Gad's primary descendent is Nebushta, who married Jehoikim. Now Jehoikim lost the battle with Babylon and King Nechebenezzar and left a heir whose line did not continue. Therefore Jehoikim is not an ancestor of anyone but rather a brother of an ancestor . However his father, Josiah had a line that had a daughter whose blood continues. So to enter the line of Nebushta, the path is thru the Judaean King Josiah and down one generation and then up many to Gad. Thus the Gadites are known however are not direct ancestors. Gad's wife was sister to Naptali's wife.

Asher had a few male descendents before he had a daughter. The line continued to Horus, an Egyptian God who required human sacrifice. This line continued to the Greek, and joined with two of the lines of descent from the Greeks, the Herculean, and the Lines from Helen. The Greek line from Priam and Virgil (Aeneas) did not have Asher as an ancestor.

FIRST GENERATION
ISRAELITES

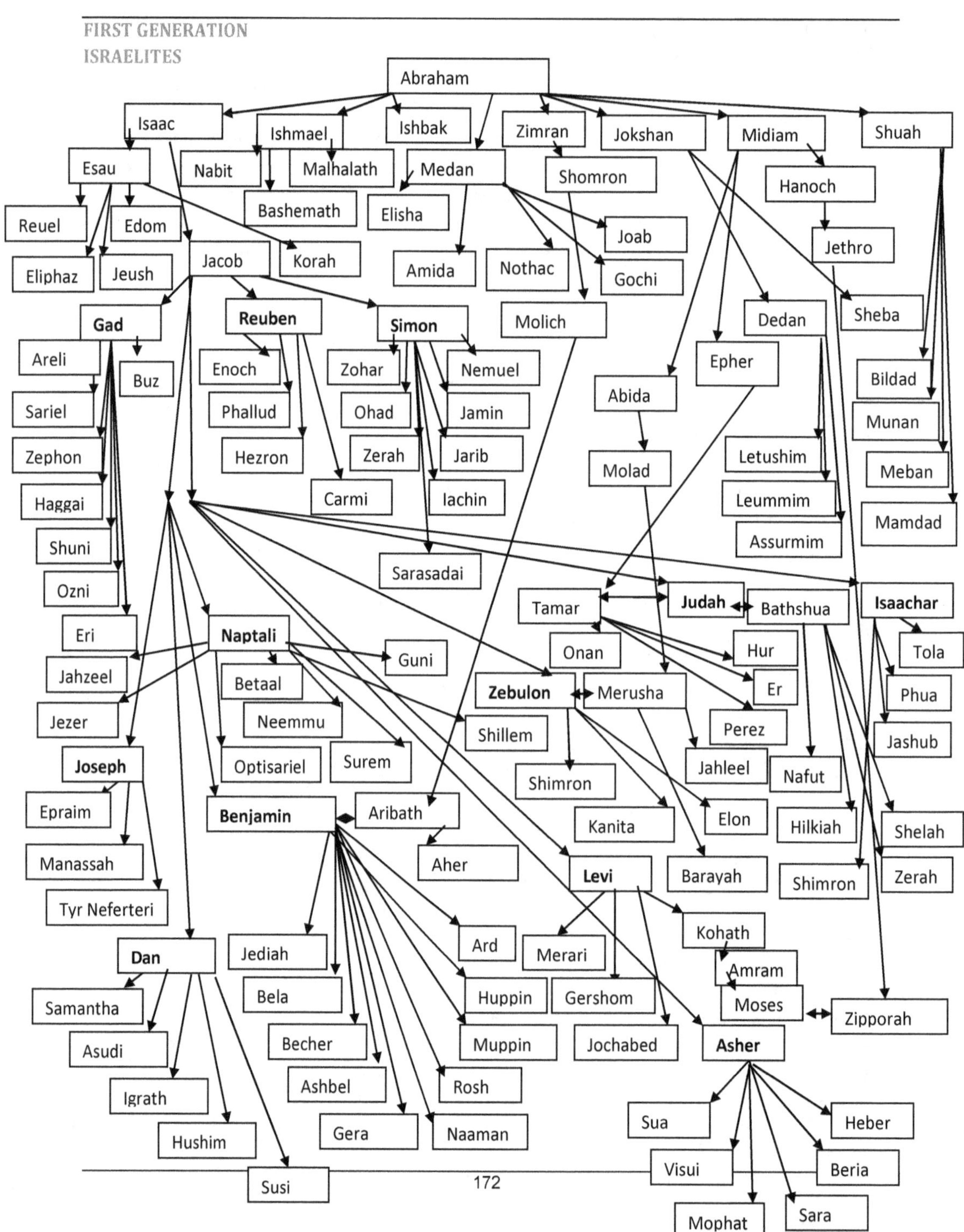

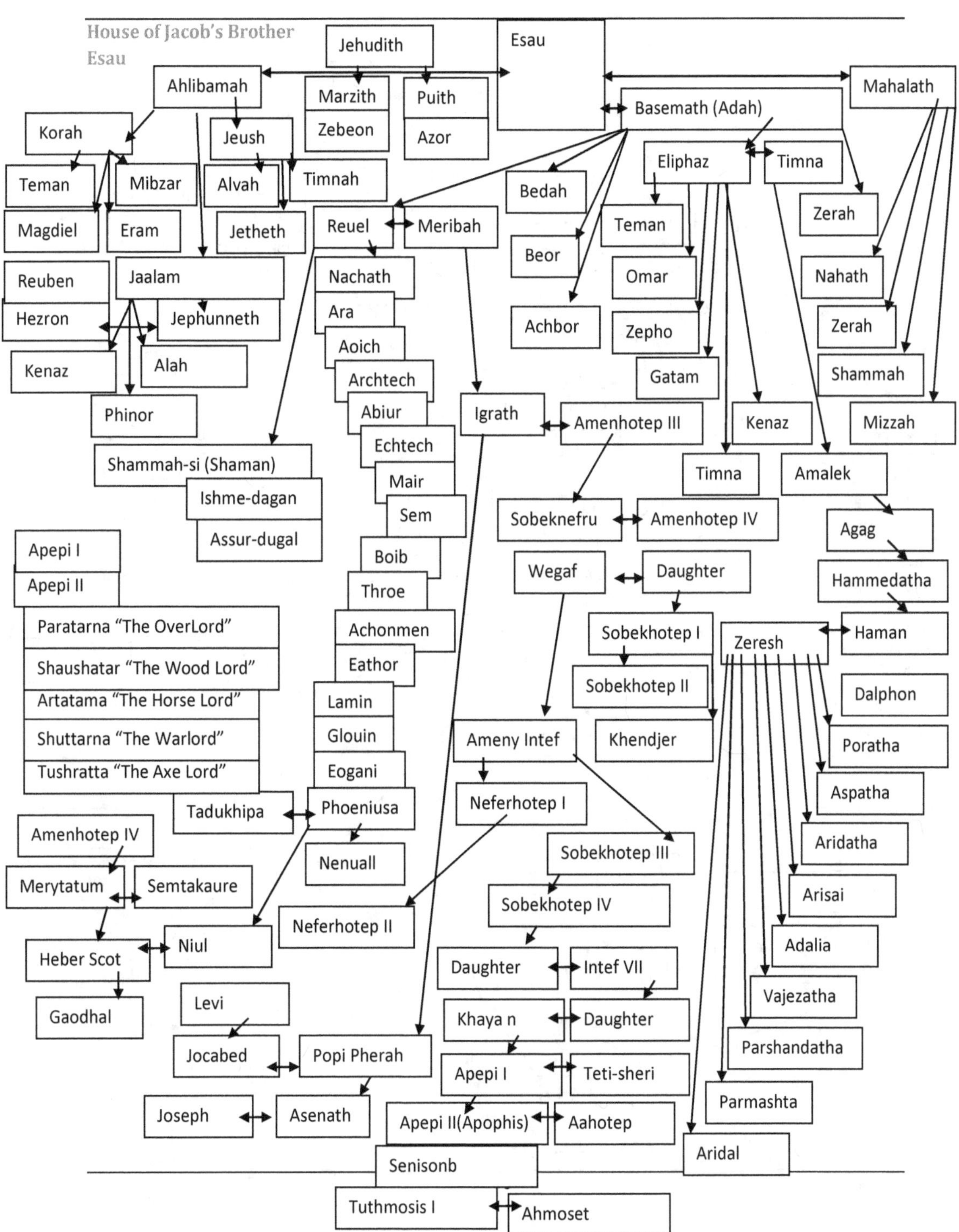
House of Jacob's Brother Esau
Esau
Jehudith
Ahlibamah
Marzith
Zebeon
Puith
Azor
Mahalath
Basemath (Adah)
Korah
Jeush
Teman
Mibzar
Alvah
Timnah
Magdiel
Eram
Jetheth
Reuel
Meribah
Eliphaz
Timna
Bedah
Teman
Zerah
Beor
Reuben
Jaalam
Nachath
Omar
Nahath
Hezron
Jephunneth
Ara
Achbor
Zepho
Zerah
Kenaz
Alah
Aoich
Gatam
Shammah
Archtech
Phinor
Abiur
Igrath
Amenhotep III
Kenaz
Mizzah
Echtech
Shammah-si (Shaman)
Timna
Amalek
Mair
Ishme-dagan
Sem
Sobeknefru
Amenhotep IV
Agag
Assur-dugal
Apepi I
Boib
Wegaf
Daughter
Apepi II
Hammedatha
Throe
Paratarna "The OverLord"
Achonmen
Sobekhotep I
Zeresh
Haman
Shaushatar "The Wood Lord"
Eathor
Sobekhotep II
Dalphon
Artatama "The Horse Lord"
Lamin
Shuttarna "The Warlord"
Glouin
Ameny Intef
Khendjer
Poratha
Tushratta "The Axe Lord"
Eogani
Aspatha
Tadukhipa
Phoeniusa
Neferhotep I
Amenhotep IV
Aridatha
Nenuall
Sobekhotep III
Merytatum
Semtakaure
Arisai
Sobekhotep IV
Neferhotep II
Heber Scot
Niul
Adalia
Daughter
Intef VII
Gaodhal
Levi
Vajezatha
Khaya n
Daughter
Parshandatha
Jocabed
Popi Pherah
Apepi I
Teti-sheri
Parmashta
Joseph
Asenath
Apepi II(Apophis)
Aahotep
Aridal
Senisonb
Tuthmosis I
Ahmoset

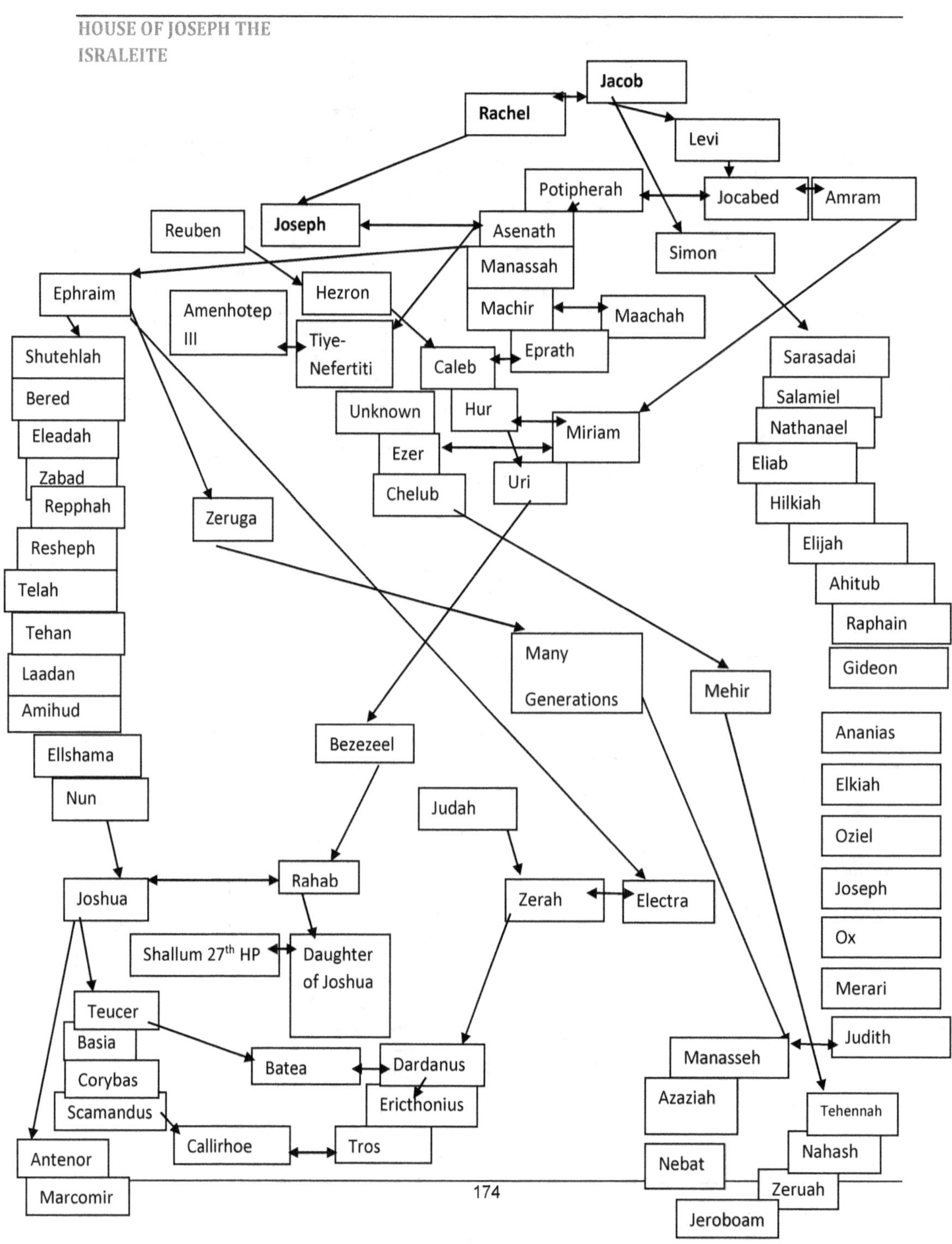
Jacob
Rachel
Levi
Potipherah
Jocabed
Amram
Reuben
Joseph
Asenath
Simon
Manassah
Ephraim
Hezron
Amenhotep III
Machir
Maachah
Tiye-Nefertiti
Eprath
Shutehlah
Caleb
Sarasadai
Bered
Unknown
Hur
Salamiel
Nathanael
Miriam
Eleadah
Ezer
Eliab
Zabad
Uri
Repphah
Chelub
Hilkiah
Zeruga
Resheph
Elijah
Telah
Ahitub
Raphain
Tehan
Many Generations
Laadan
Gideon
Mehir
Amihud
Ananias
Bezezeel
Ellshama
Elkiah
Nun
Judah
Oziel
Rahab
Joseph
Joshua
Zerah
Electra
Ox
Shallum 27th HP
Daughter of Joshua
Merari
Teucer
Judith
Basia
Manasseh
Batea
Dardanus
Corybas
Azaziah
Tehennah
Ericthonius
Scamandus
Callirhoe
Tros
Nahash
Antenor
Nebat
Zeruah
Marcomir
Jeroboam

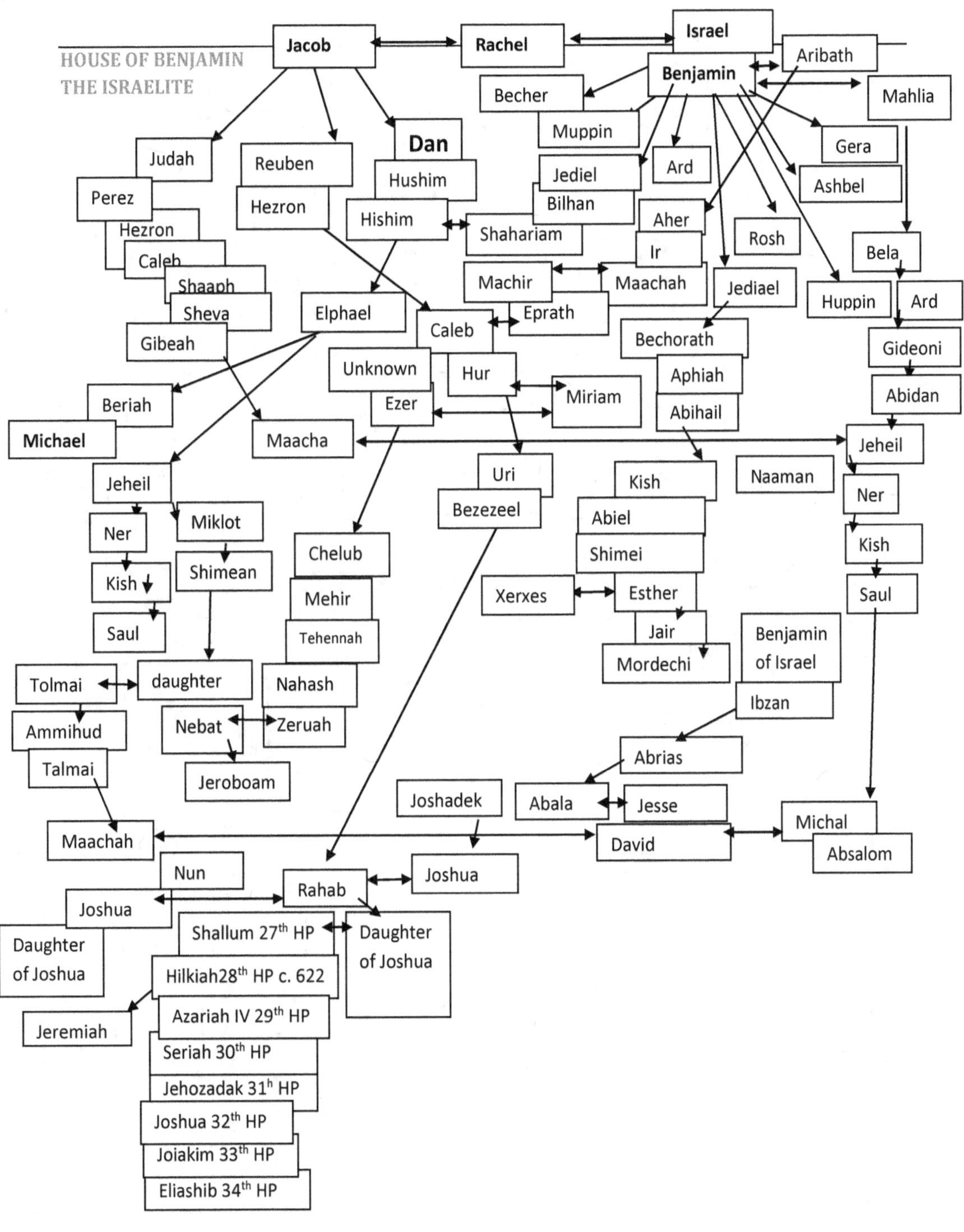
HOUSE OF BENJAMIN
THE ISRAELITE
Jacob
Rachel
Israel
Benjamin
Aribath
Mahlia
Becher
Muppin
Jediel
Ard
Gera
Ashbel
Bilhan
Aher
Ir
Rosh
Bela
Judah
Reuben
Dan
Hushim
Perez
Hezron
Hezron
Hishim
Shahariam
Caleb
Shaaph
Sheva
Gibeah
Elphael
Machir
Maachah
Jediael
Huppin
Ard
Caleb
Eprath
Bechorath
Gideoni
Unknown
Hur
Aphiah
Beriah
Ezer
Miriam
Abihail
Abidan
Michael
Maacha
Jeheil
Jeheil
Uri
Kish
Naaman
Ner
Ner
Miklot
Bezezeel
Abiel
Kish
Chelub
Shimei
Kish
Shimean
Mehir
Xerxes
Esther
Saul
Saul
Tehennah
Jair
Benjamin of Israel
Mordechi
Tolmai
daughter
Nahash
Ibzan
Ammihud
Nebat
Zeruah
Abrias
Talmai
Jeroboam
Joshadek
Abala
Jesse
Michal
Maachah
David
Absalom
Nun
Rahab
Joshua
Joshua
Shallum 27th HP
Daughter of Joshua
Daughter of Joshua
Hilkiah28th HP c. 622
Azariah IV 29th HP
Jeremiah
Seriah 30th HP
Jehozadak 31h HP
Joshua 32th HP
Joiakim 33th HP
Eliashib 34th HP

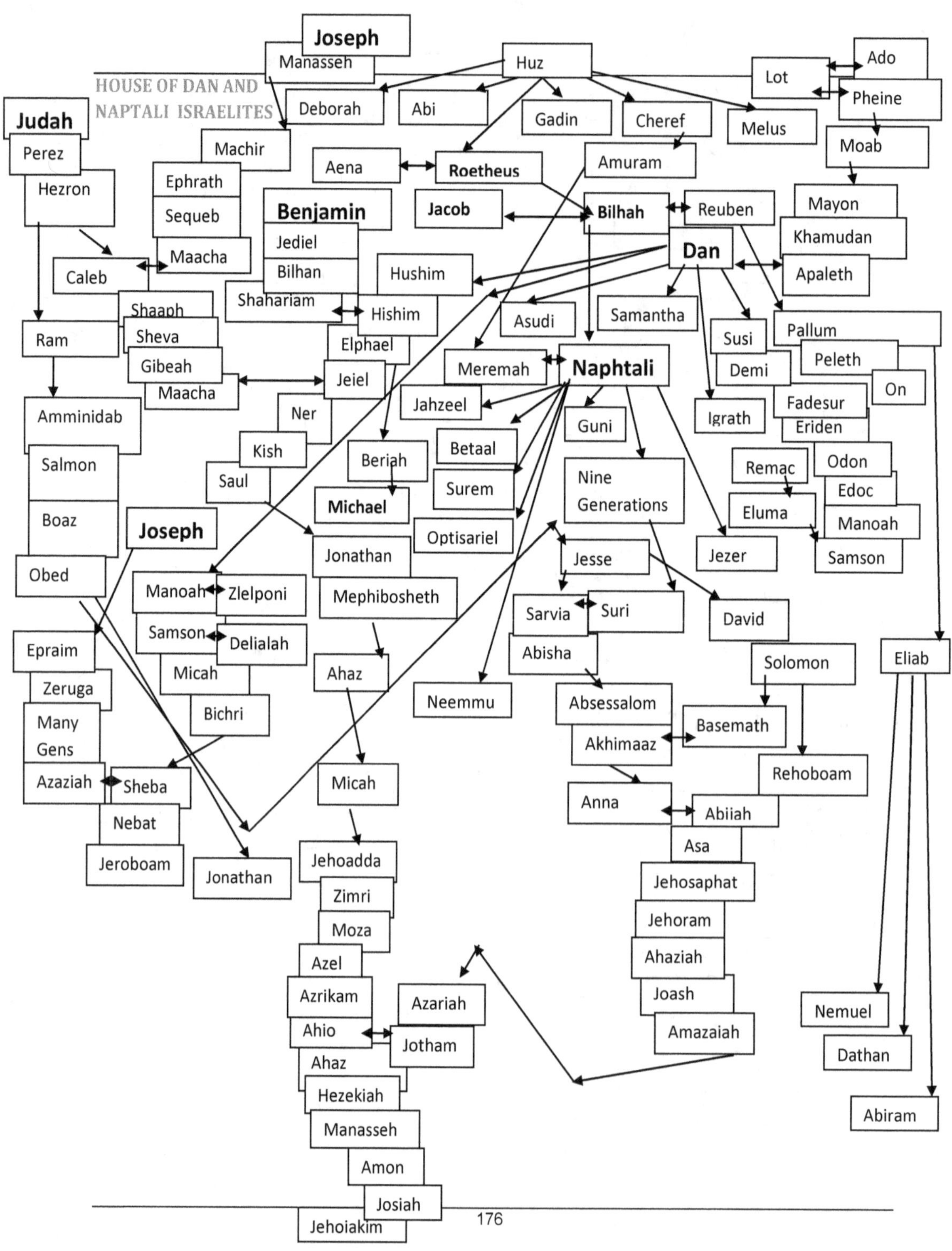

HOUSE OF DAN AND NAPTALI ISRAELITES
Joseph
Manasseh
Huz
Lot
Ado
Pheine
Deborah
Abi
Gadin
Cheref
Melus
Moab
Judah
Perez
Hezron
Machir
Ephrath
Sequeb
Aena
Roetheus
Amuram
Mayon
Khamudan
Benjamin
Jediel
Bilhan
Jacob
Bilhah
Reuben
Dan
Apaleth
Maacha
Caleb
Hushim
Shaaph
Shahariam
Hishim
Asudi
Samantha
Susi
Pallum
Ram
Sheva
Elphael
Gibeah
Maacha
Jeiel
Meremah
Naphtali
Demi
Peleth
On
Amminidab
Ner
Jahzeel
Guni
Igrath
Fadesur
Eriden
Kish
Beriah
Betaal
Salmon
Saul
Surem
Nine Generations
Remac
Odon
Edoc
Michael
Eluma
Manoah
Boaz
Joseph
Optisariel
Jonathan
Jesse
Jezer
Samson
Obed
Manoah
Zlelponi
Mephibosheth
Sarvia
Suri
David
Samson
Delialah
Epraim
Micah
Ahaz
Abisha
Solomon
Eliab
Zeruga
Bichri
Neemmu
Absessalom
Basemath
Many Gens
Akhimaaz
Rehoboam
Azaziah
Sheba
Micah
Anna
Abiiah
Nebat
Asa
Jeroboam
Jonathan
Jehoadda
Jehosaphat
Zimri
Jehoram
Moza
Ahaziah
Azel
Joash
Azrikam
Azariah
Nemuel
Ahio
Jotham
Amazaiah
Ahaz
Dathan
Hezekiah
Abiram
Manasseh
Amon
Josiah
Jehoiakim

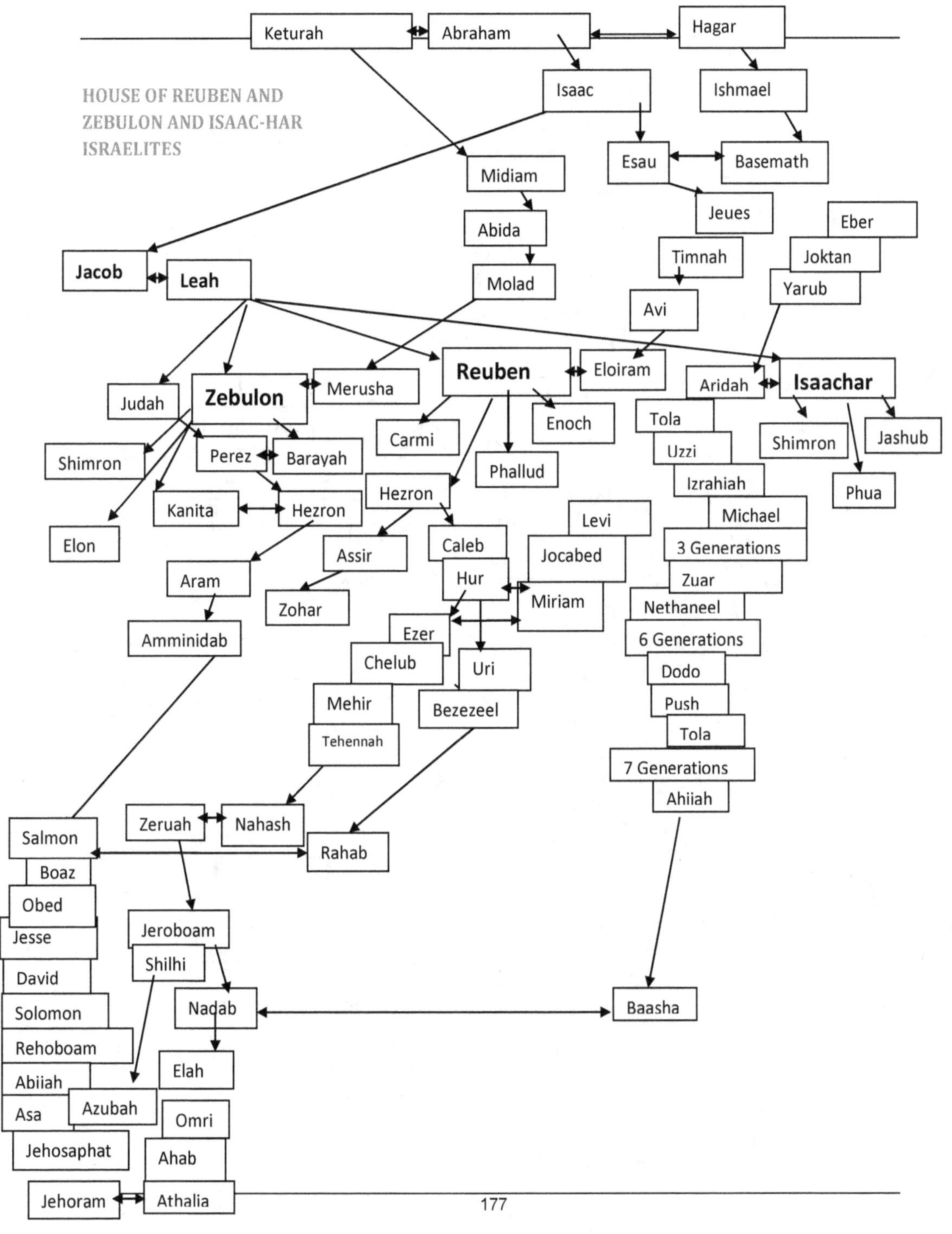
Keturah
Abraham
Hagar
HOUSE OF REUBEN AND ZEBULON AND ISAAC-HAR ISRAELITES
Isaac
Ishmael
Midiam
Esau
Basemath
Jeues
Abida
Eber
Timnah
Joktan
Jacob
Leah
Molad
Yarub
Avi
Reuben
Eloiram
Aridah
Isaachar
Zebulon
Merusha
Judah
Enoch
Tola
Carmi
Shimron
Jashub
Perez
Barayah
Uzzi
Shimron
Phallud
Izrahiah
Phua
Hezron
Kanita
Hezron
Levi
Michael
Elon
Caleb
Assir
Jocabed
3 Generations
Aram
Hur
Zuar
Zohar
Miriam
Nethaneel
Ezer
Amminidab
6 Generations
Chelub
Uri
Dodo
Mehir
Bezezeel
Push
Tola
Tehennah
7 Generations
Ahiiah
Zeruah
Nahash
Salmon
Rahab
Boaz
Obed
Jesse
Jeroboam
Shilhi
David
Nadab
Baasha
Solomon
Rehoboam
Elah
Abiiah
Azubah
Asa
Omri
Jehosaphat
Ahab
Jehoram
Athalia

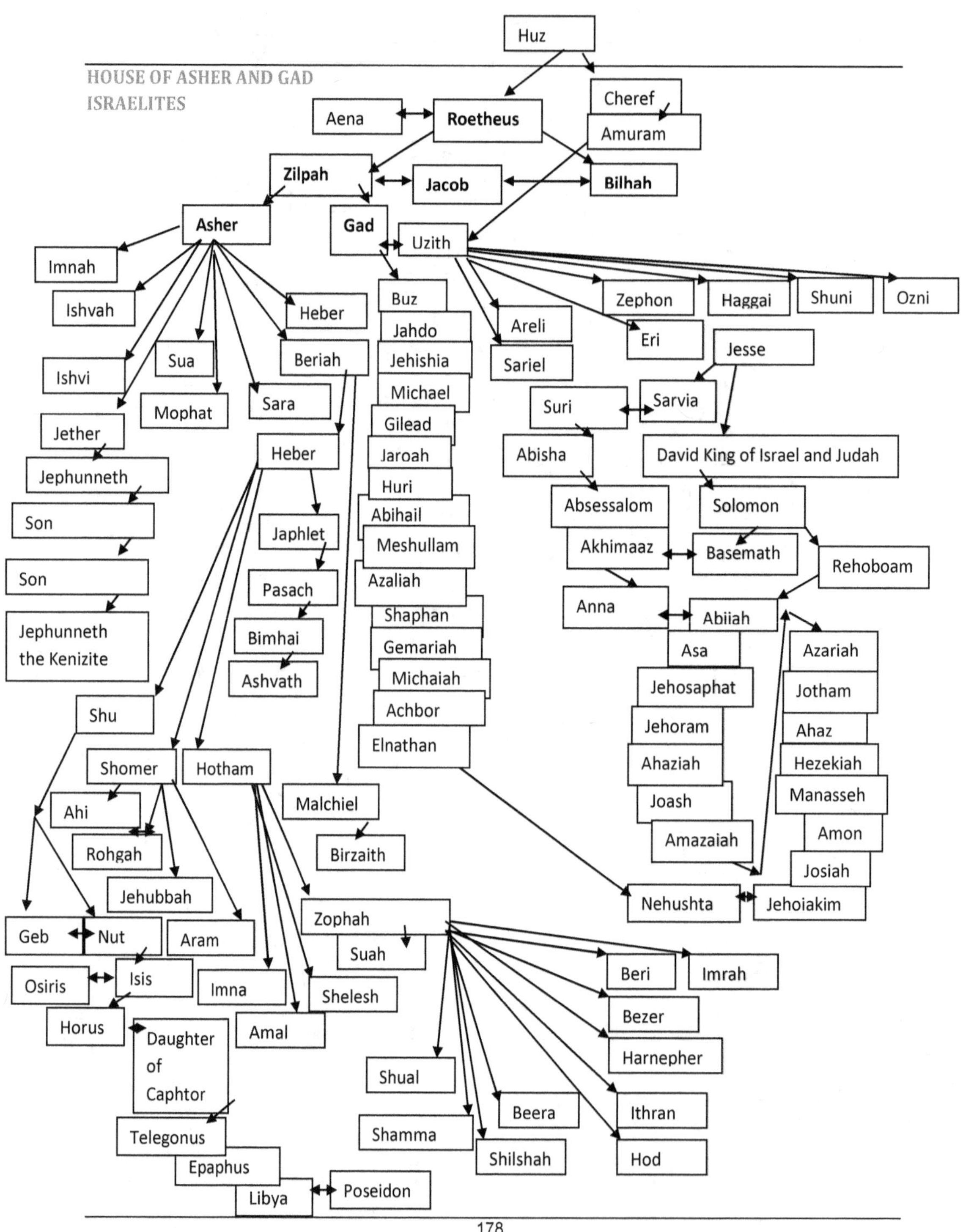
HOUSE OF ASHER AND GAD
ISRAELITES
Huz
Aena
Roetheus
Cheref
Amuram
Zilpah
Jacob
Bilhah
Asher
Gad
Uzith
Imnah
Ishvah
Heber
Buz
Jahdo
Jehishia
Michael
Gilead
Jaroah
Huri
Abihail
Meshullam
Azaliah
Shaphan
Gemariah
Michaiah
Achbor
Elnathan
Zephon
Haggai
Shuni
Ozni
Areli
Sariel
Eri
Jesse
Ishvi
Sua
Beriah
Mophat
Sara
Suri
Sarvia
Jether
Heber
Abisha
David King of Israel and Judah
Jephunneth
Absessalom
Solomon
Son
Japhlet
Akhimaaz
Basemath
Rehoboam
Son
Pasach
Anna
Abiiah
Jephunneth
the Kenizite
Bimhai
Asa
Azariah
Ashvath
Jehosaphat
Jotham
Shu
Jehoram
Ahaz
Ahaziah
Hezekiah
Shomer
Hotham
Manasseh
Malchiel
Joash
Ahi
Amon
Rohgah
Birzaith
Amazaiah
Josiah
Jehubbah
Nehushta
Jehoiakim
Zophah
Geb
Nut
Aram
Suah
Osiris
Isis
Imna
Shelesh
Beri
Imrah
Bezer
Horus
Amal
Harnepher
Daughter
of
Caphtor
Shual
Beera
Ithran
Telegonus
Shamma
Shilshah
Hod
Epaphus
Libya
Poseidon

HOUSE OF SIMEON THE ISRAELITE

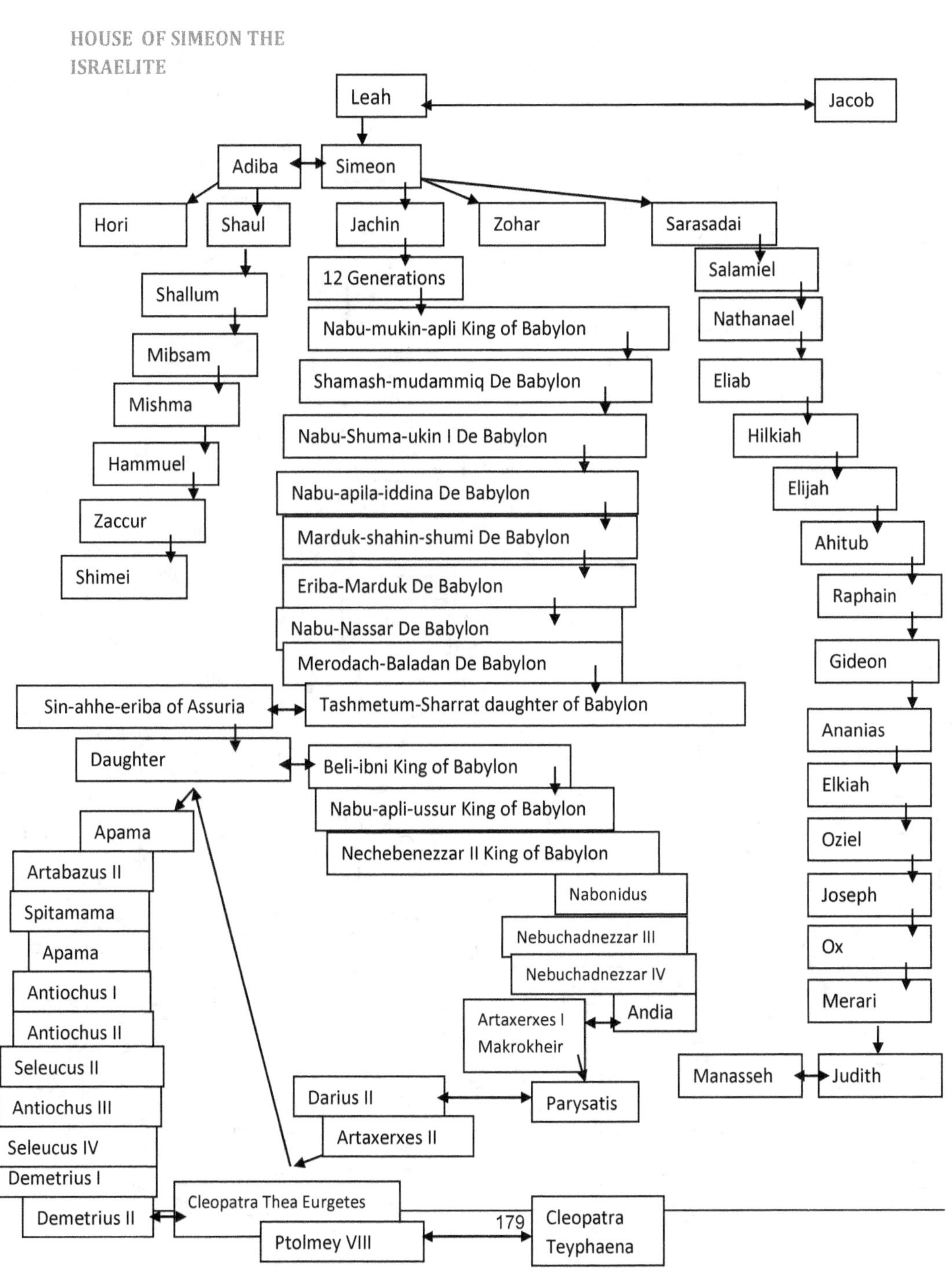

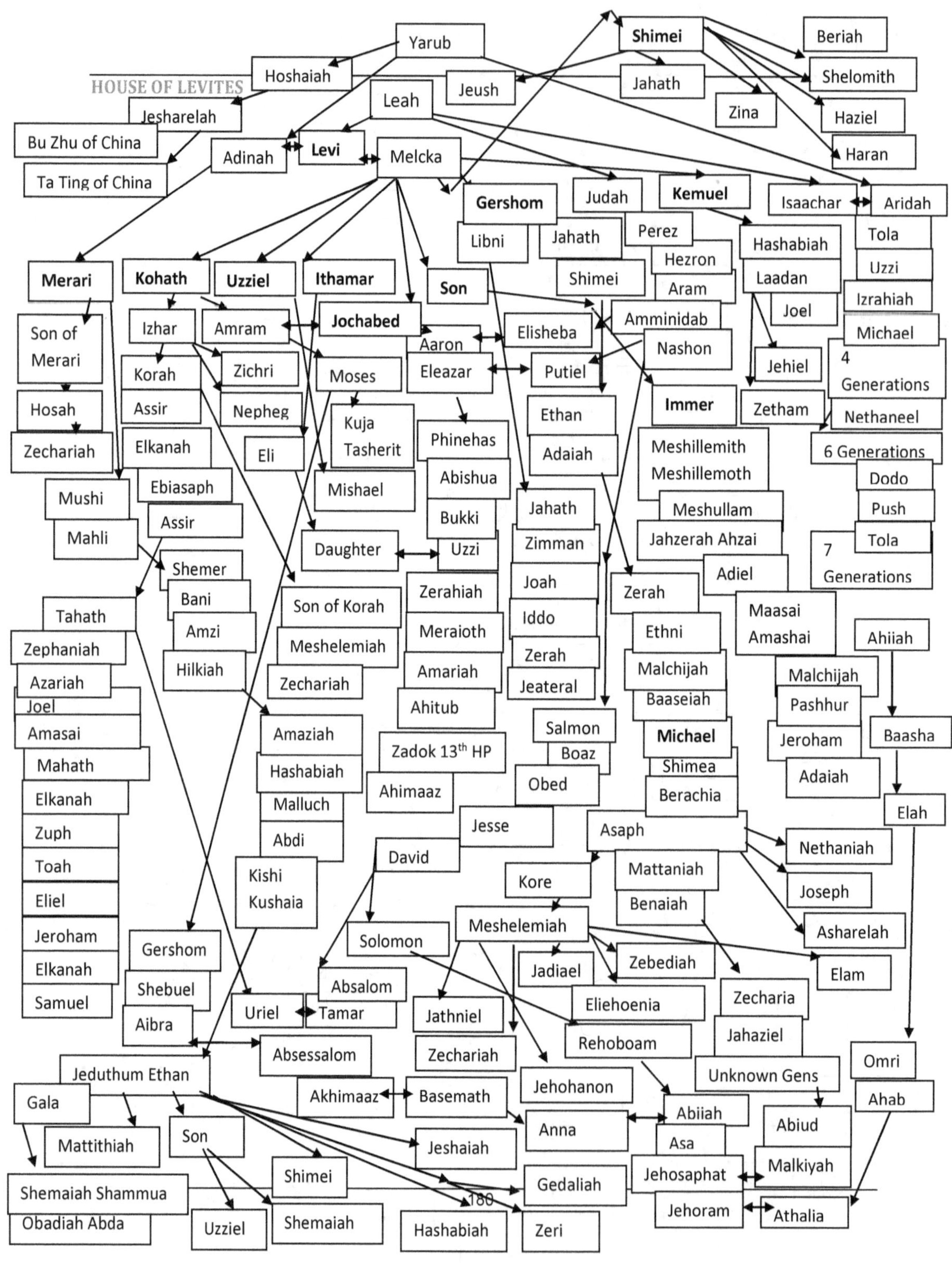
HOUSE OF LEVITES
Yarub
Shimei
Beriah
Hoshaiah
Jeush
Jahath
Shelomith
Leah
Zina
Haziel
Jesharelah
Bu Zhu of China
Adinah
Levi
Melcka
Haran
Ta Ting of China
Gershom
Judah
Kemuel
Isaachar
Aridah
Libni
Jahath
Perez
Hashabiah
Tola
Hezron
Uzzi
Merari
Kohath
Uzziel
Ithamar
Son
Shimei
Aram
Laadan
Izrahiah
Amminidab
Joel
Izhar
Amram
Jochabed
Elisheba
Michael
Son of Merari
Aaron
Nashon
4 Generations
Korah
Zichri
Moses
Eleazar
Putiel
Jehiel
Hosah
Assir
Nepheg
Kuja Tasherit
Ethan
Immer
Zetham
Nethaneel
Zechariah
Elkanah
Eli
Phinehas
Adaiah
Meshillemith Meshillemoth
6 Generations
Ebiasaph
Abishua
Dodo
Mushi
Mishael
Jahath
Meshullam
Push
Assir
Bukki
Mahli
Daughter
Uzzi
Zimman
Jahzerah Ahzai
Tola
7 Generations
Shemer
Adiel
Bani
Son of Korah
Zerahiah
Joah
Zerah
Tahath
Maasai Amashai
Amzi
Meraioth
Iddo
Ethni
Ahiiah
Zephaniah
Meshelemiah
Zerah
Hilkiah
Amariah
Malchijah
Malchijah
Azariah
Zechariah
Jeateral
Joel
Ahitub
Baaseiah
Pashhur
Amasai
Amaziah
Salmon
Michael
Jeroham
Baasha
Mahath
Zadok 13th HP
Boaz
Hashabiah
Shimea
Adaiah
Elkanah
Ahimaaz
Obed
Malluch
Berachia
Elah
Zuph
Jesse
Asaph
Abdi
Nethaniah
Toah
David
Kishi Kushaia
Mattaniah
Kore
Joseph
Eliel
Benaiah
Jeroham
Meshelemiah
Asharelah
Solomon
Gershom
Elkanah
Zebediah
Jadiael
Elam
Absalom
Shebuel
Samuel
Zecharia
Uriel
Tamar
Eliehoenia
Jathniel
Aibra
Jahaziel
Rehoboam
Absessalom
Zechariah
Omri
Jeduthum Ethan
Unknown Gens
Jehohanon
Gala
Akhimaaz
Basemath
Ahab
Abiiah
Son
Anna
Mattithiah
Abiud
Jeshaiah
Asa
Shimei
Malkiyah
Jehosaphat
Gedaliah
Shemaiah Shammua
Jehoram
Athalia
Obadiah Abda
Uzziel
Shemaiah
Hashabiah
Zeri

Here is the lines from the Israelites wifes as they relate to the ancestors of the Israelites. Note who was married to diffent wives. Dan was married to Apheleth who was from Moab the son of Lot. Simeon was married to Bunah that had a lineage to Ham, not thru Abraham. Gad and Napthali married sisters, and were from Nahor. Benjamin and Zebulon's wife were from Keturah, while Reuben's wife was from Esau. Joseph's wife was from both Esau and Ishmael. Isaac Har's wife was from Joktan, not thru Nahor. Benjamin had more than on wife.

Shown on these pages are the lines from Benjamin to Saul and his daughter who married King David.

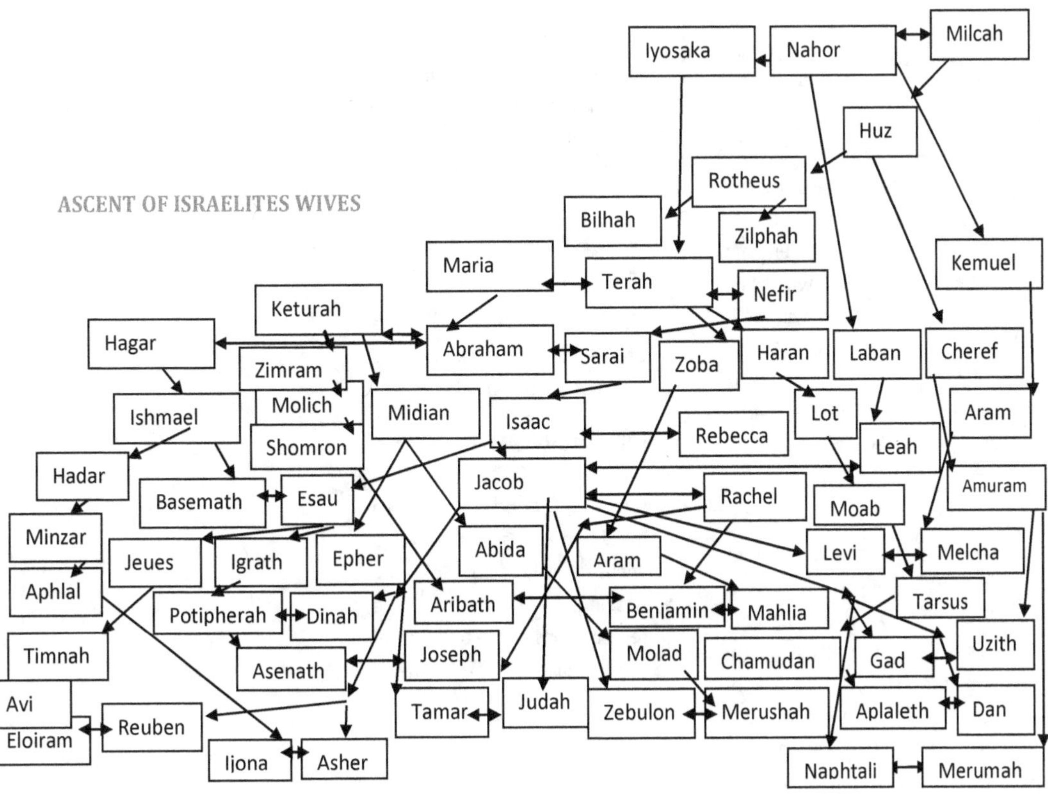

ERA OF NOAH TO ABRAHAM.

SECTION ELEVEN: EGYPT

THE LINE TO SARAH, ABRAHAM, AND SOLOMONS WIFE THE QUEEN FROM EGYPT.

Note that the line from Abraham to Noah is well documented in the scripture. This line is about eleven generations. The line from Noah to Sarah thru Cham is about thirty five generations. Now Sarah is told to be the half sister of Abraham. Abraham's mother was Maria and Sarah's mother was Nefir. Many lines say Towait, however they agree that past Sarah's mother name the lines are about the same.

The lines intertwine together, and a study of the line of Solomon's wife thru Egypt is also very interesting. The generations work out that the line from Solomons wife thru multiple Ramses and Isis etc... that Apepi II son of Apepi I may also be Pepy II the son of Pepi in the line from Nefir. Nefir is the same generation from Amenhotep III and the line goes thru a daughter of Amenhotep III while the line to the Ramses and the Solomon's wife is a son of Amenhotep III. Now Amenhotep III is in the genealogies is the father of an adopted son Amenhotep IV. This Amenhotep IV is the Isralite Moses who served Egypt as a General, successful as the conqueror of Ethiopia.

The chart on the next page is the lineage of Sarah. Following that is the lineage of Amenhotep I. Both similar at Pepi II or Apepi II who has the father Pepy I or Apepi I. The line from Amenhotep I does go thru to the wife of Solomon thru the Ramses Kings of Egypt.

The following pages are charts of the lineage of Cain and his twin LULU who had children.

Following that is the lineage of the wives of all the Israelites as found on the internet. Shown in the book is the possible ancestry of eight of the Israelites, and the relationships to the ancestry of the wives of these.

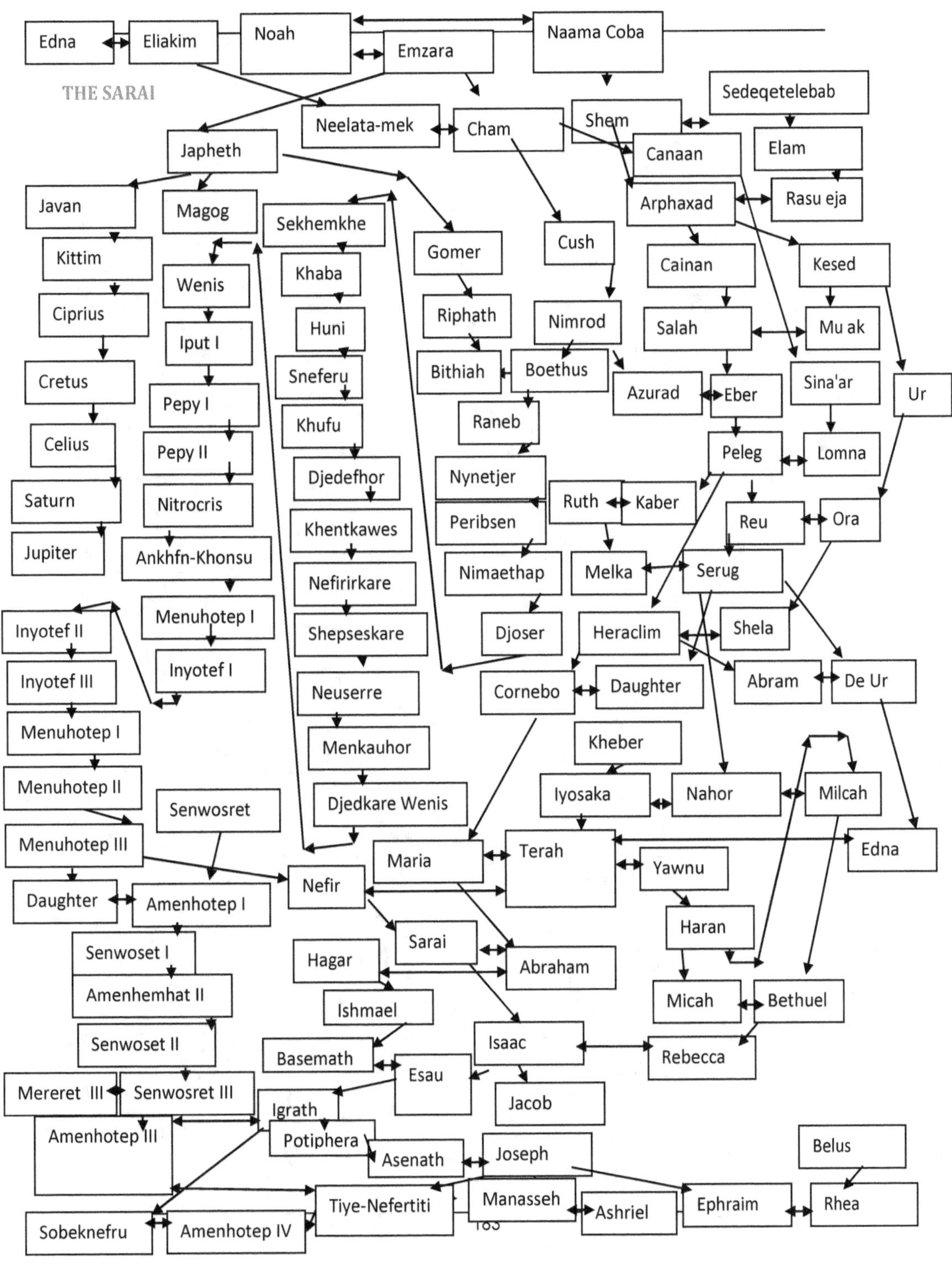
Edna
Eliakim
Noah
Naama Coba
Emzara
Sedeqetelebab
Neelata-mek
Cham
Shem
Japheth
Canaan
Elam
Javan
Magog
Sekhemkhe
Arphaxad
Rasu eja
Gomer
Cush
Kittim
Khaba
Cainan
Kesed
Wenis
Ciprius
Huni
Riphath
Nimrod
Salah
Mu ak
Iput I
Sneferu
Bithiah
Boethus
Cretus
Pepy I
Khufu
Azurad
Eber
Sina'ar
Ur
Raneb
Celius
Pepy II
Djedefhor
Nynetjer
Peleg
Lomna
Saturn
Nitrocris
Khentkawes
Ruth
Kaber
Peribsen
Reu
Ora
Jupiter
Ankhfn-Khonsu
Nefirirkare
Nimaethap
Melka
Serug
Inyotef II
Menuhotep I
Shepseskare
Djoser
Heraclim
Shela
Inyotef III
Inyotef I
Neuserre
Cornebo
Daughter
Abram
De Ur
Menuhotep I
Menkauhor
Kheber
Menuhotep II
Senwosret
Djedkare Wenis
Iyosaka
Nahor
Milcah
Menuhotep III
Maria
Terah
Edna
Yawnu
Nefir
Daughter
Amenhotep I
Haran
Sarai
Senwoset I
Hagar
Abraham
Amenhemhat II
Ishmael
Micah
Bethuel
Senwoset II
Isaac
Rebecca
Basemath
Esau
Mereret III
Senwosret III
Jacob
Igrath
Amenhotep III
Potiphera
Asenath
Joseph
Belus
Tiye-Nefertiti
Manasseh
Ashriel
Ephraim
Rhea
Sobeknefru
Amenhotep IV

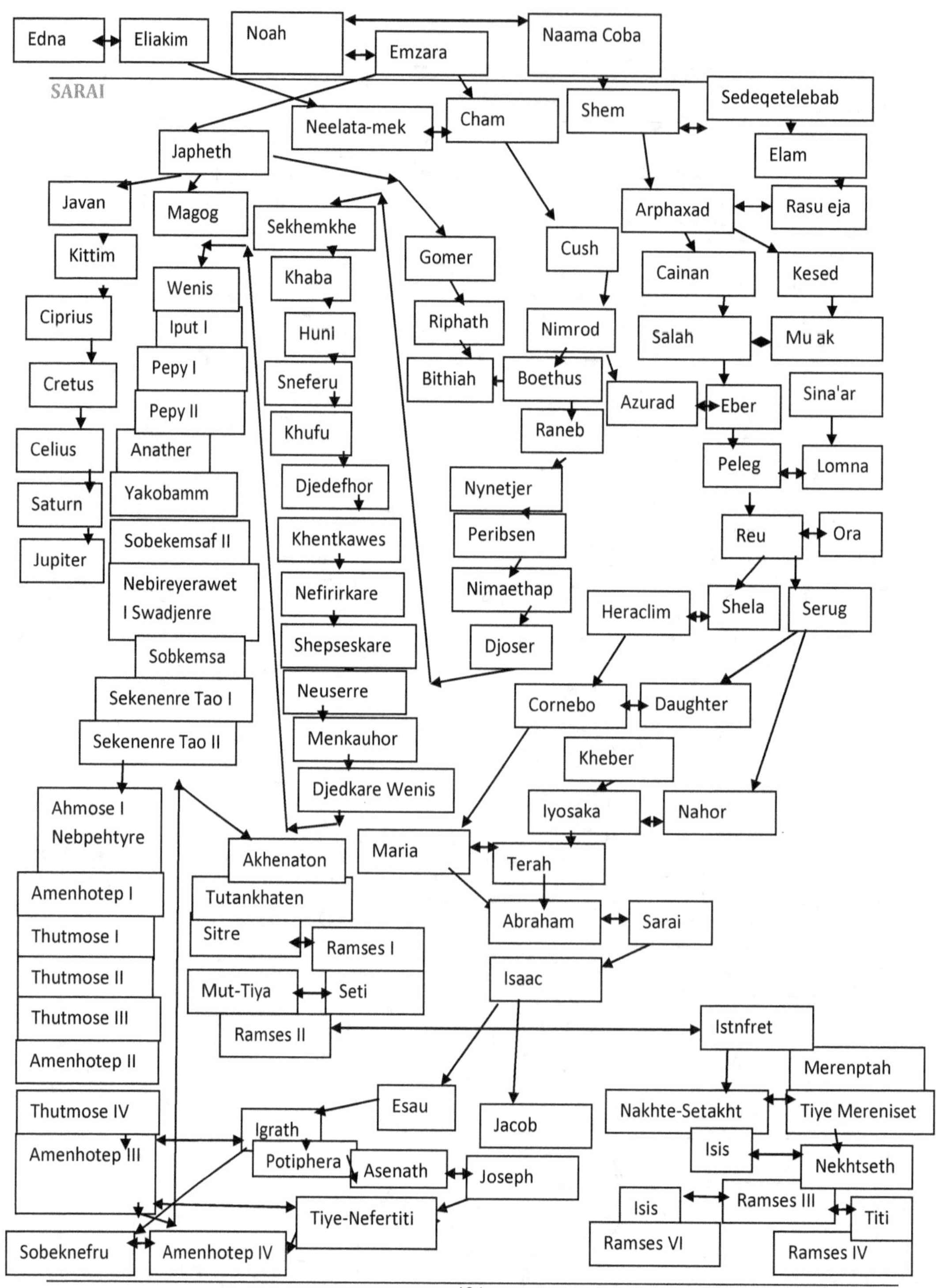
Edna
Eliakim
Noah
Emzara
Naama Coba
Neelata-mek
Cham
Shem
Sedeqetelebab
Japheth
Elam
Javan
Magog
Sekhemkhe
Gomer
Cush
Arphaxad
Rasu eja
Kittim
Wenis
Khaba
Cainan
Kesed
Iput I
Riphath
Nimrod
Ciprius
Hunl
Salah
Mu ak
Pepy I
Sneferu
Bithiah
Boethus
Cretus
Azurad
Eber
Sina'ar
Pepy II
Khufu
Raneb
Celius
Anather
Peleg
Lomna
Djedefhor
Nynetjer
Yakobamm
Saturn
Reu
Ora
Khentkawes
Peribsen
Sobekemsaf II
Jupiter
Nebireyerawet
I Swadjenre
Nefirirkare
Nimaethap
Heraclim
Shela
Serug
Sobkemsa
Shepseskare
Djoser
Sekenenre Tao I
Neuserre
Cornebo
Daughter
Sekenenre Tao II
Menkauhor
Kheber
Djedkare Wenis
Ahmose I
Nebpehtyre
Iyosaka
Nahor
Akhenaton
Maria
Terah
Amenhotep I
Tutankhaten
Abraham
Sarai
Thutmose I
Sitre
Ramses I
Thutmose II
Mut-Tiya
Seti
Isaac
Thutmose III
Ramses II
Istnfret
Amenhotep II
Merenptah
Esau
Jacob
Nakhte-Setakht
Tiye Mereniset
Thutmose IV
Igrath
Isis
Amenhotep III
Potiphera
Asenath
Joseph
Nekhtseth
Isis
Ramses III
Titi
Tiye-Nefertiti
Ramses VI
Sobeknefru
Amenhotep IV
Ramses IV

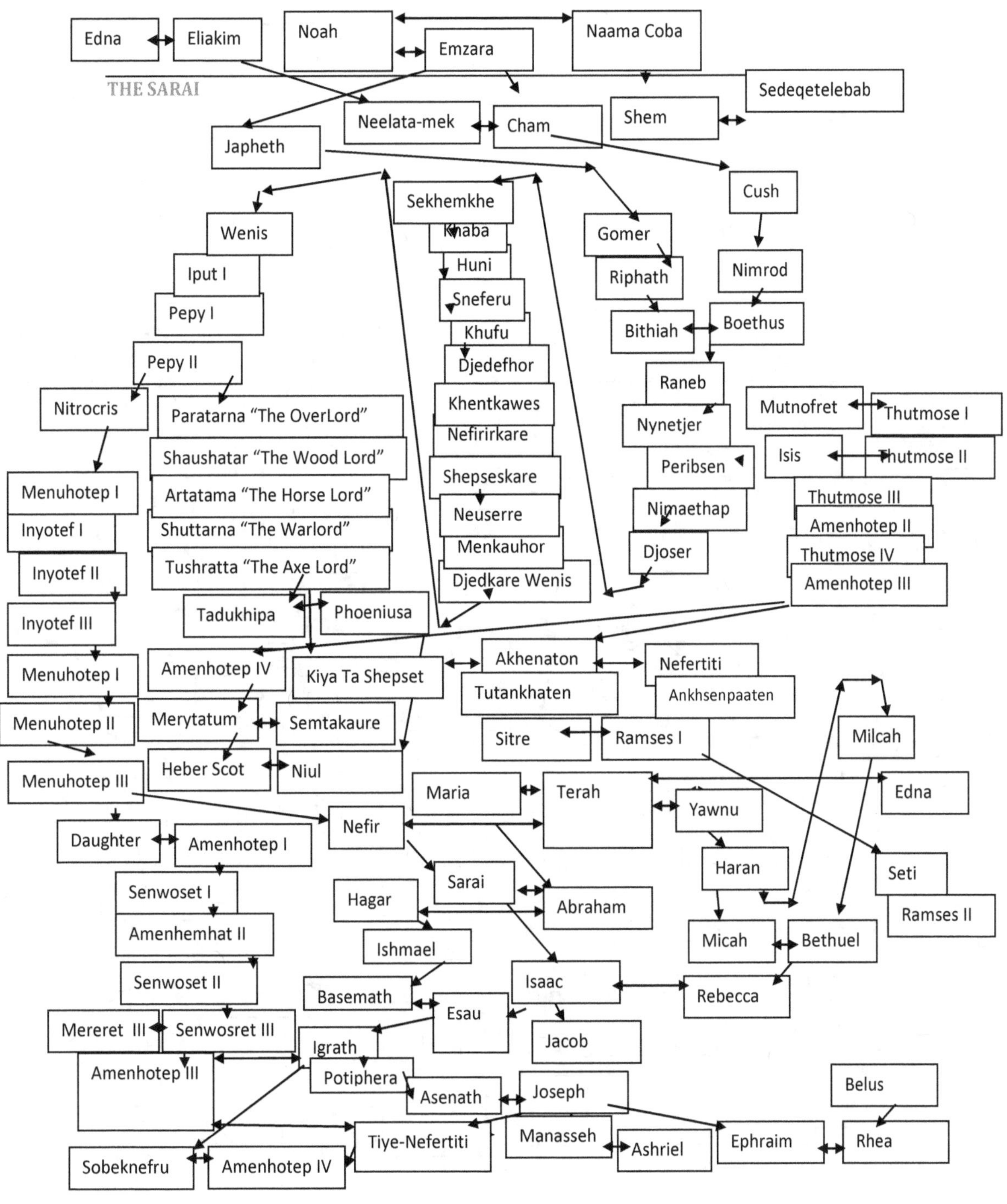
Edna
Eliakim
Noah
Emzara
Naama Coba
Sedeqetelebab
Neelata-mek
Cham
Shem
Japheth
Cush
Sekhemkhe
Khaba
Huni
Sneferu
Khufu
Djedefhor
Khentkawes
Nefirirkare
Shepseskare
Neuserre
Menkauhor
Djedkare Wenis
Wenis
Iput I
Pepy I
Pepy II
Nitrocris
Paratarna "The OverLord"
Shaushatar "The Wood Lord"
Artatama "The Horse Lord"
Shuttarna "The Warlord"
Tushratta "The Axe Lord"
Gomer
Riphath
Bithiah
Nimrod
Boethus
Raneb
Nynetjer
Peribsen
Nimaethap
Djoser
Mutnofret
Thutmose I
Isis
Thutmose II
Thutmose III
Amenhotep II
Thutmose IV
Amenhotep III
Menuhotep I
Inyotef I
Inyotef II
Inyotef III
Menuhotep I
Menuhotep II
Menuhotep III
Tadukhipa
Phoeniusa
Amenhotep IV
Kiya Ta Shepset
Akhenaton
Nefertiti
Tutankhaten
Ankhsenpaaten
Merytatum
Semtakaure
Heber Scot
Niul
Sitre
Ramses I
Milcah
Maria
Terah
Yawnu
Edna
Nefir
Daughter
Amenhotep I
Haran
Seti
Sarai
Abraham
Hagar
Micah
Bethuel
Ramses II
Senwoset I
Amenhemhat II
Ishmael
Senwoset II
Isaac
Rebecca
Basemath
Esau
Jacob
Mereret III
Senwosret III
Igrath
Amenhotep III
Potiphera
Asenath
Joseph
Belus
Tiye-Nefertiti
Manasseh
Ashriel
Ephraim
Rhea
Sobeknefru
Amenhotep IV

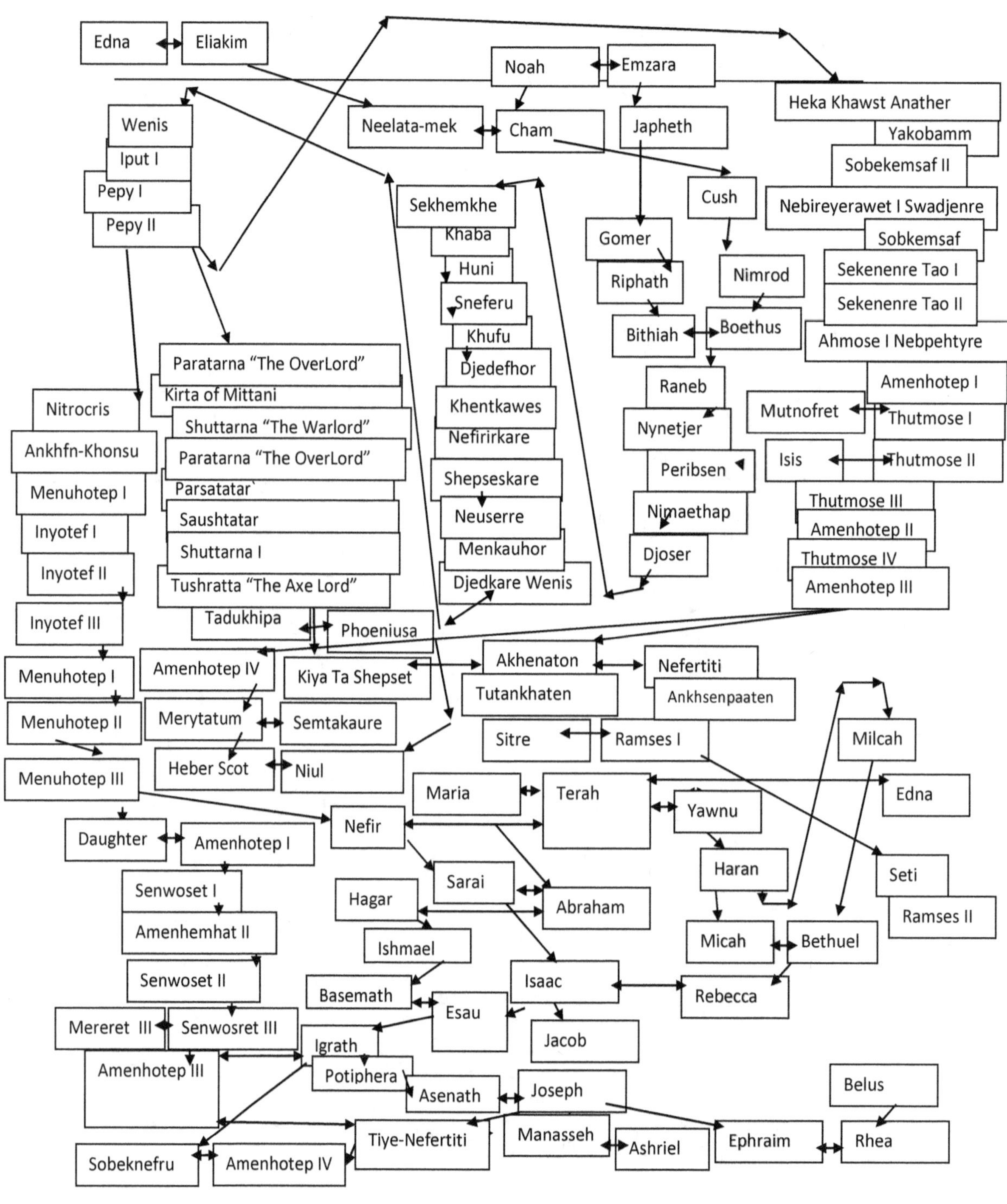

Edna
Eliakim
Noah
Emzara
Heka Khawst Anather
Yakobamm
Sobekemsaf II
Nebireyerawet I Swadjenre
Sobkemsaf
Sekenenre Tao I
Sekenenre Tao II
Ahmose I Nebpehtyre
Amenhotep I
Thutmose I
Mutnofret
Isis
Thutmose II
Thutmose III
Amenhotep II
Thutmose IV
Amenhotep III
Wenis
Iput I
Pepy I
Pepy II
Neelata-mek
Cham
Japheth
Cush
Gomer
Riphath
Nimrod
Bithiah
Boethus
Raneb
Nynetjer
Peribsen
Nimaethap
Djoser
Sekhemkhe
Khaba
Huni
Sneferu
Khufu
Djedefhor
Khentkawes
Nefirirkare
Shepseskare
Neuserre
Menkauhor
Djedkare Wenis
Paratarna "The OverLord"
Kirta of Mittani
Shuttarna "The Warlord"
Paratarna "The OverLord"
Parsatatar
Saushtatar
Shuttarna I
Tushratta "The Axe Lord"
Tadukhipa
Phoeniusa
Nitrocris
Ankhfn-Khonsu
Menuhotep I
Inyotef I
Inyotef II
Inyotef III
Menuhotep I
Menuhotep II
Menuhotep III
Amenhotep IV
Kiya Ta Shepset
Akhenaton
Nefertiti
Tutankhaten
Ankhsenpaaten
Merytatum
Semtakaure
Heber Scot
Niul
Sitre
Ramses I
Milcah
Maria
Terah
Yawnu
Edna
Nefir
Daughter
Amenhotep I
Haran
Seti
Ramses II
Sarai
Abraham
Hagar
Ishmael
Senwoset I
Amenhemhat II
Micah
Bethuel
Senwoset II
Basemath
Esau
Isaac
Rebecca
Jacob
Mereret III
Senwosret III
Igrath
Amenhotep III
Potiphera
Asenath
Joseph
Belus
Tiye-Nefertiti
Manasseh
Ashriel
Ephraim
Rhea
Sobeknefru
Amenhotep IV

On the previous page is the lineage of Sarah thru her mother called Towait or Nefir, and the thirty generations that lead to her ancestor Noah. Now Abraham is only about eight or ten generations to Noah thru Shem. This leads to an idea of a line that breeds slower may be stronger than a line that breeds at early ages. The line from Apepi to the Queen of Sheba is not thru Nitrocris, but thru a line that from Anather thru to the Ramses Kings of Egypt that did not have all the problems with the kingdom that the Hebrew had in Israel with the rape of Dinah and the attempt by Esau to steal his fathers blessing that ended in the tribe of Israel's war with the Tribe of Esau. Thus Egypt was not part of this tribal warfare and the line from Anather would not be part of this lineage of David. The Chart above is a chart made from the line from Wenis to Pepy thru Anather to the queen of Sheba's ancestors that were part of the Ramses line that joined with David. Note that the lineage between Pepi and Sarah are about the same as the lineage between Apepi and Amenhotep I. Now to get to the line that is male that leads to Sarah, Amenhotep marries a daughter of the male line and so is closely related to Sarah. There is another male line to Amenhotep I from Apepi thru Anather that leads thru many generations to the wife of Solomon. This is of course fourteen generations between David and Abraham and Sarah, so about fifteen generations of David's line to about twenty Three generatons of the queen of Sheba's line. Both of these lines are very similar. Note the lines from Ramses VI shown on the previous page and Ramses IV also on the previous page lead to the wife of Solomon shown on another page.

Note that in the following chart the lines from the wife of Solomon are presented. Note that Naaman is from Haran, and the generations may be false, as about twenty generations are compared with about seven. This is Highly unlikely but this genealogy is found very extensively on the internet.

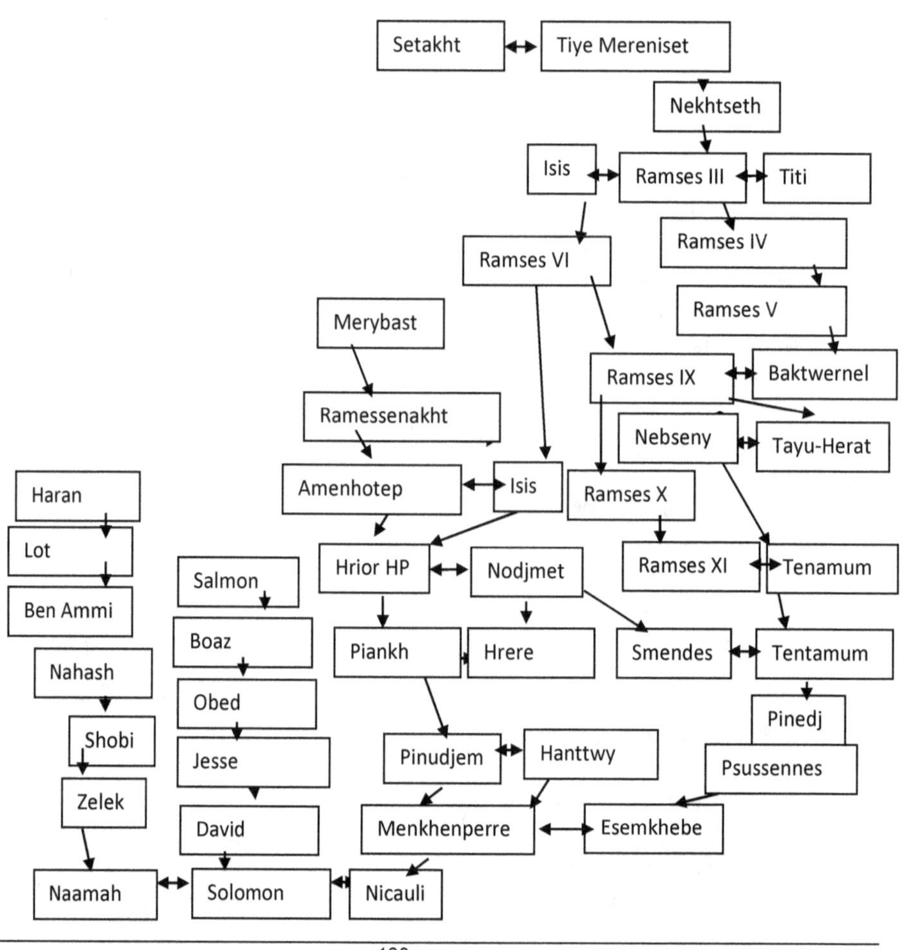

This is one geneology of the wife of Solomon. Note that this is similar to many and some files are more extensive than others. These lines go thru to Ramses III but not up to Amenhotep as on another page.

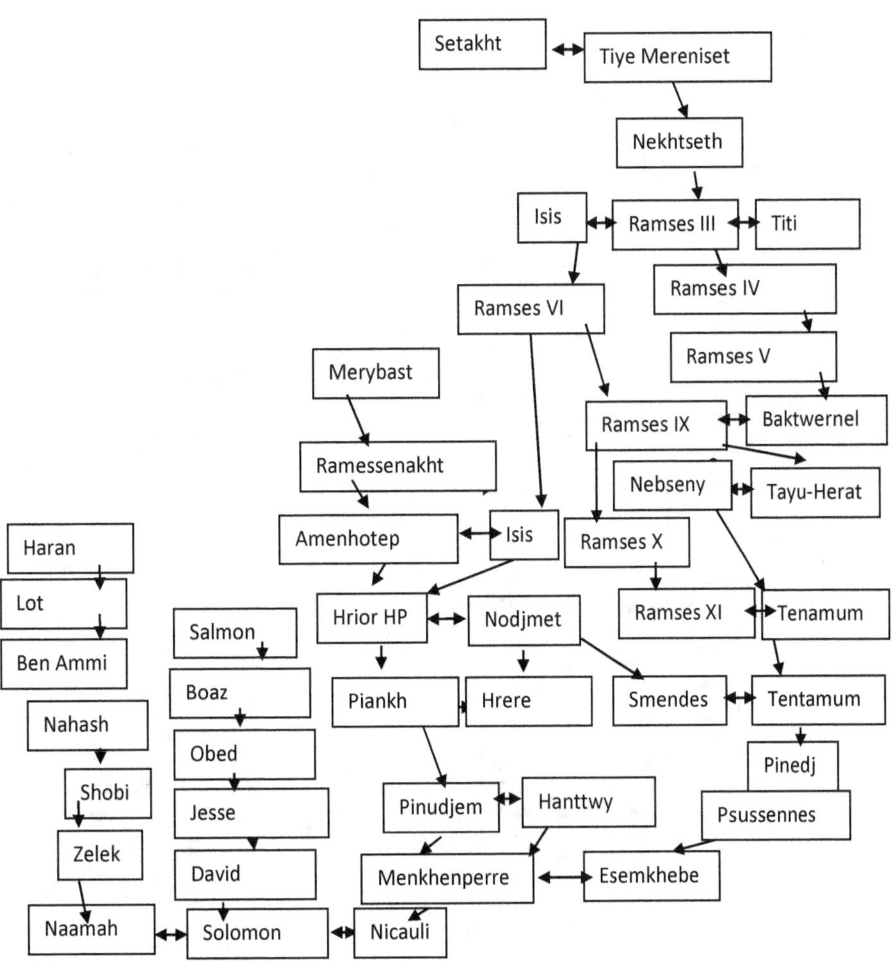

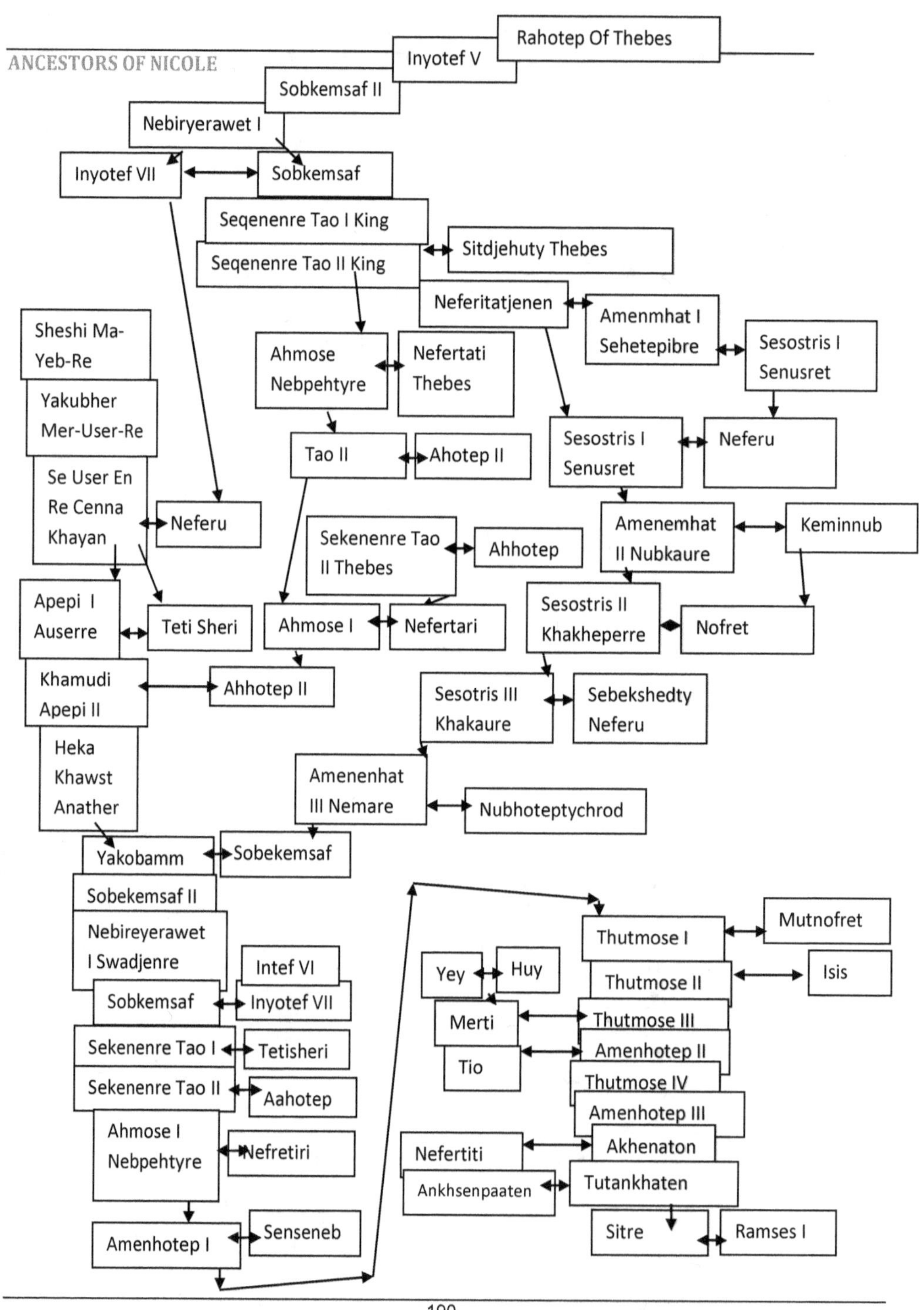
Rahotep Of Thebes
Inyotef V
Sobkemsaf II
Nebiryerawet I
Inyotef VII
Sobkemsaf
Seqenenre Tao I King
Seqenenre Tao II King
Sitdjehuty Thebes
Neferitatjenen
Amenmhat I Sehetepibre
Sesostris I Senusret
Sheshi Ma-Yeb-Re
Ahmose Nebpehtyre
Nefertati Thebes
Yakubher Mer-User-Re
Tao II
Ahotep II
Sesostris I Senusret
Neferu
Se User En Re Cenna Khayan
Neferu
Sekenenre Tao II Thebes
Ahhotep
Amenemhat II Nubkaure
Keminnub
Apepi I Auserre
Teti Sheri
Ahmose I
Nefertari
Sesostris II Khakheperre
Nofret
Khamudi Apepi II
Ahhotep II
Sesotris III Khakaure
Sebekshedty Neferu
Heka Khawst Anather
Amenenhat III Nemare
Nubhoteptychrod
Yakobamm
Sobekemsaf
Sobekemsaf II
Nebireyerawet I Swadjenre
Intef VI
Sobkemsaf
Inyotef VII
Sekenenre Tao I
Tetisheri
Sekenenre Tao II
Aahotep
Ahmose I Nebpehtyre
Nefretiri
Amenhotep I
Senseneb
Thutmose I
Mutnofret
Yey
Huy
Thutmose II
Isis
Merti
Thutmose III
Tio
Amenhotep II
Thutmose IV
Amenhotep III
Nefertiti
Akhenaton
Ankhsenpaaten
Tutankhaten
Sitre
Ramses I

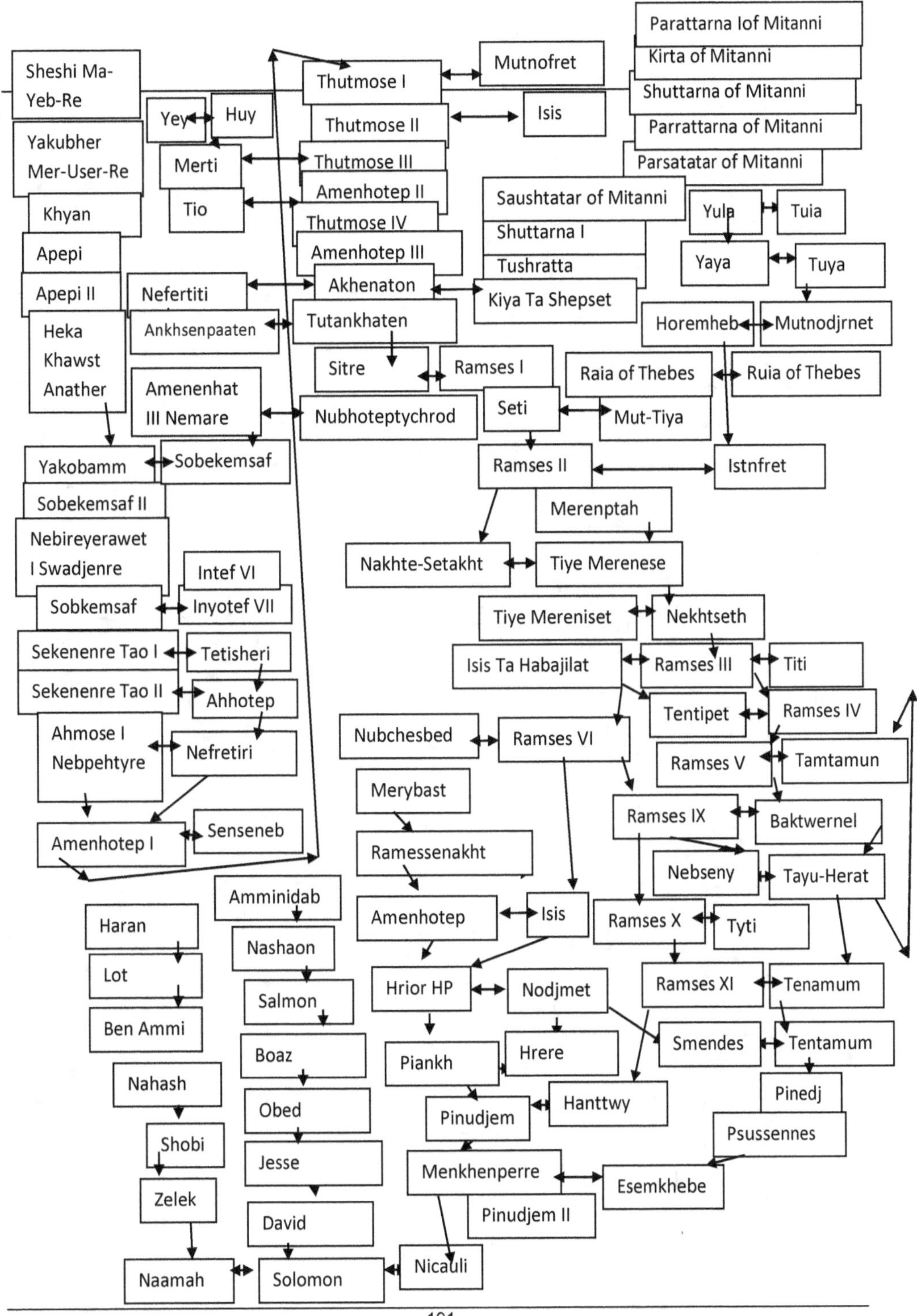
Parattarna Iof Mitanni
Kirta of Mitanni
Shuttarna of Mitanni
Parrattarna of Mitanni
Parsatatar of Mitanni
Sheshi Ma-Yeb-Re
Thutmose I
Mutnofret
Yey
Huy
Thutmose II
Isis
Yakubher Mer-User-Re
Merti
Thutmose III
Amenhotep II
Tio
Khyan
Thutmose IV
Saushtatar of Mitanni
Shuttarna I
Tushratta
Yula
Tuia
Yaya
Tuya
Apepi
Amenhotep III
Apepi II
Nefertiti
Akhenaton
Kiya Ta Shepset
Ankhsenpaaten
Tutankhaten
Horemheb
Mutnodjrnet
Heka Khawst Anather
Sitre
Ramses I
Raia of Thebes
Ruia of Thebes
Amenenhat III Nemare
Nubhoteptychrod
Seti
Mut-Tiya
Yakobamm
Sobekemsaf
Ramses II
Istnfret
Sobekemsaf II
Merenptah
Nebireyerawet I Swadjenre
Intef VI
Nakhte-Setakht
Tiye Merenese
Sobkemsaf
Inyotef VII
Tiye Mereniset
Nekhtseth
Sekenenre Tao I
Tetisheri
Isis Ta Habajilat
Ramses III
Titi
Sekenenre Tao II
Ahhotep
Tentipet
Ramses IV
Ahmose I Nebpehtyre
Nefretiri
Nubchesbed
Ramses VI
Ramses V
Tamtamun
Merybast
Ramses IX
Baktwernel
Amenhotep I
Senseneb
Ramessenakht
Nebseny
Tayu-Herat
Amminidab
Haran
Amenhotep
Isis
Ramses X
Tyti
Nashaon
Lot
Hrior HP
Nodjmet
Ramses XI
Tenamum
Salmon
Ben Ammi
Smendes
Tentamum
Boaz
Piankh
Hrere
Nahash
Pinedj
Obed
Pinudjem
Hanttwy
Shobi
Psussennes
Jesse
Menkhenperre
Esemkhebe
Zelek
David
Pinudjem II
Nicauli
Naamah
Solomon

JEREBOAM AND KARAMAT

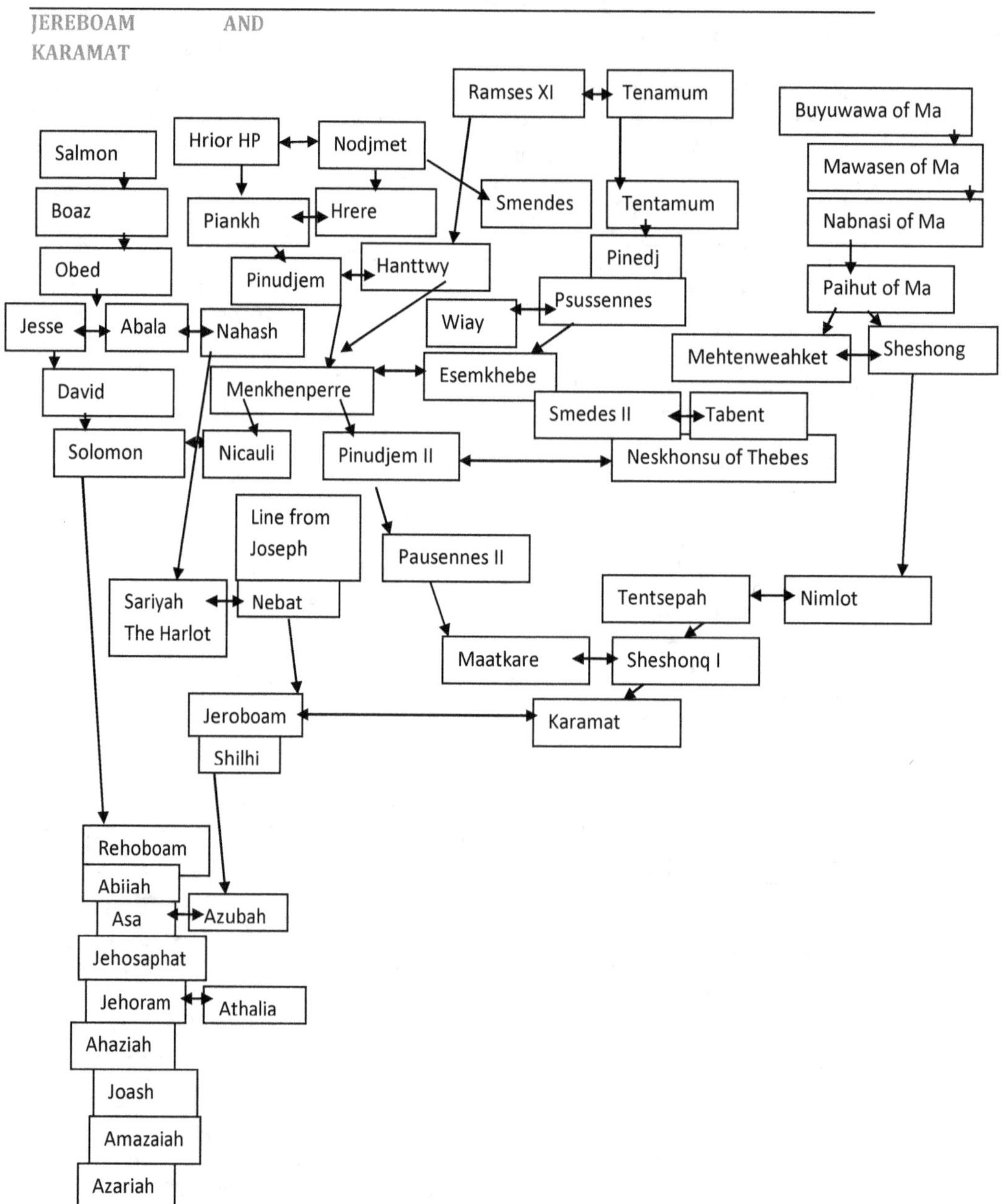

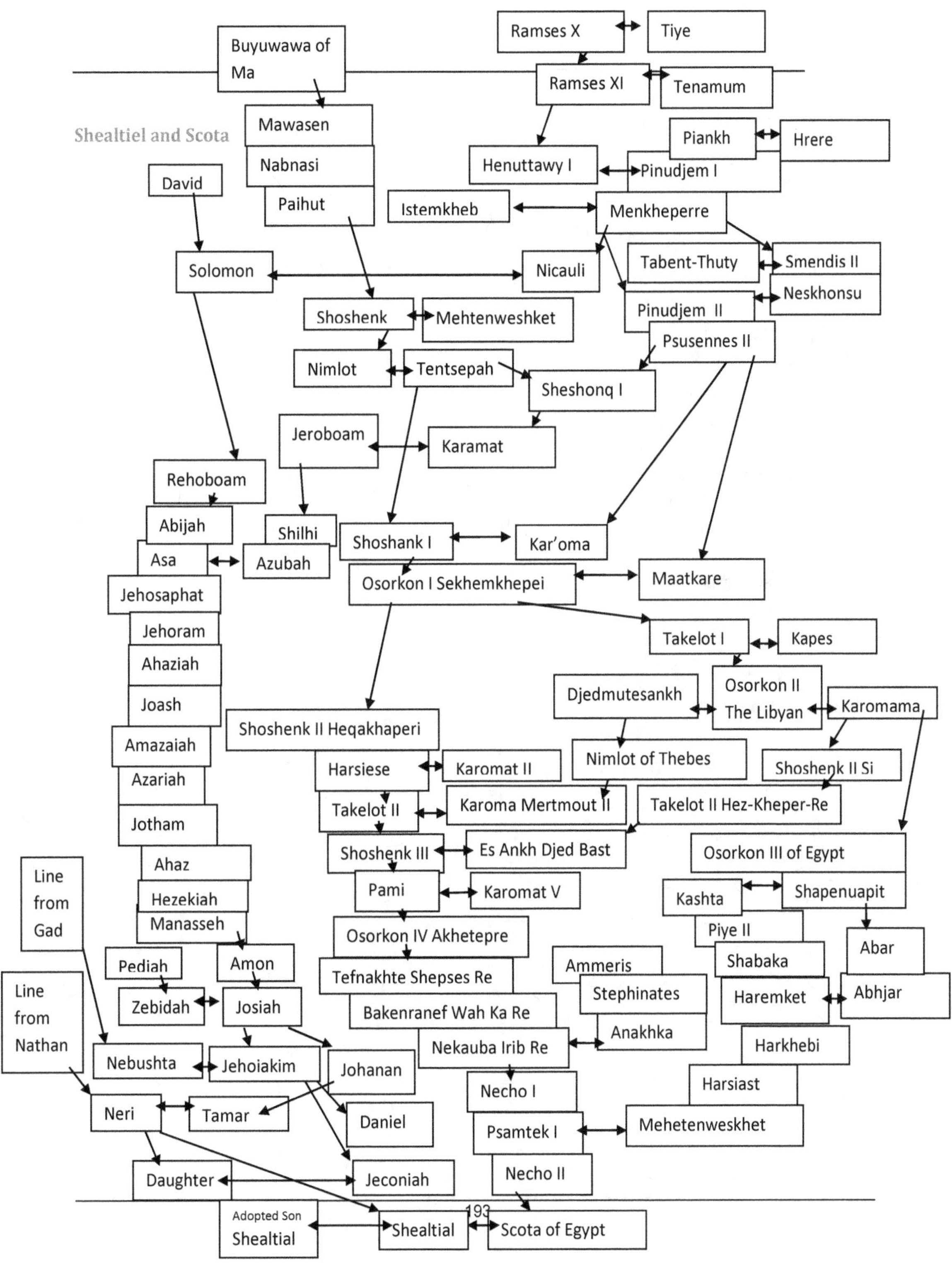

Ramses X
Tiye
Buyuwawa of Ma
Ramses XI
Tenamum
Mawasen
Piankh
Hrere
Nabnasi
Henuttawy I
Pinudjem I
David
Paihut
Istemkheb
Menkheperre
Solomon
Nicauli
Tabent-Thuty
Smendis II
Neskhonsu
Shoshenk
Mehtenweshket
Pinudjem II
Psusennes II
Nimlot
Tentsepah
Sheshonq I
Jeroboam
Karamat
Rehoboam
Abijah
Shilhi
Shoshank I
Kar'oma
Asa
Azubah
Maatkare
Osorkon I Sekhemkhepei
Jehosaphat
Jehoram
Takelot I
Kapes
Ahaziah
Osorkon II The Libyan
Djedmutesankh
Karomama
Joash
Shoshenk II Heqakhaperi
Amazaiah
Harsiese
Karomat II
Nimlot of Thebes
Shoshenk II Si
Azariah
Takelot II
Karoma Mertmout II
Takelot II Hez-Kheper-Re
Jotham
Shoshenk III
Es Ankh Djed Bast
Osorkon III of Egypt
Ahaz
Line from Gad
Pami
Karomat V
Kashta
Shapenuapit
Hezekiah
Manasseh
Piye II
Osorkon IV Akhetepre
Abar
Pediah
Amon
Ammeris
Shabaka
Tefnakhte Shepses Re
Stephinates
Line from Nathan
Zebidah
Josiah
Haremket
Abhjar
Bakenranef Wah Ka Re
Anakhka
Nekauba Irib Re
Harkhebi
Nebushta
Jehoiakim
Johanan
Harsiast
Necho I
Neri
Tamar
Daniel
Psamtek I
Mehetenweskhet
Necho II
Daughter
Jeconiah
Adopted Son Shealtial
Shealtial
Scota of Egypt

ERA OF BEFORE ADAM AND EVE AND BETWEEN ADAM AND NOAH

SECTION TWELVE: ANCIENT CIVILIZATIONS WHAT LINEAGE STILL EXISTS.

In this section the civilizations of Greece, the ancient lines of Noah, the ancient lines of Adam, and his father God, and the lines of China are examined. Egypt was examined in a previous section. The China line was found in the section on Daniel.

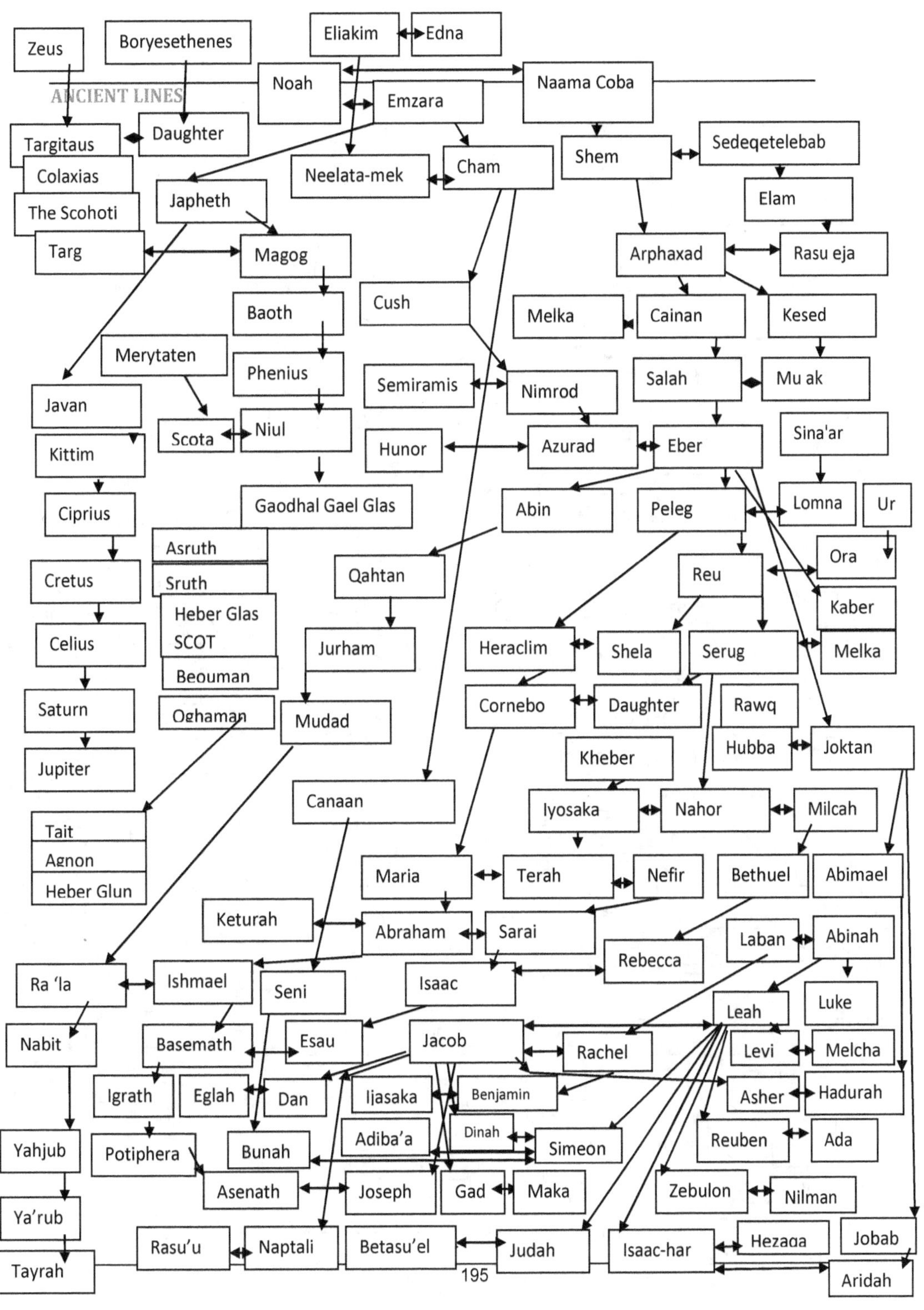

ANCIENT LINES
Zeus
Boryesethenes
Eliakim
Edna
Noah
Naama Coba
Emzara
Targitaus
Daughter
Colaxias
The Scohoti
Targ
Japheth
Neelata-mek
Cham
Shem
Sedeqetelebab
Elam
Magog
Arphaxad
Rasu eja
Baoth
Cush
Melka
Cainan
Kesed
Merytaten
Phenius
Semiramis
Nimrod
Salah
Mu ak
Javan
Scota
Niul
Hunor
Azurad
Eber
Sina'ar
Kittim
Gaodhal Gael Glas
Abin
Peleg
Lomna
Ur
Ciprius
Asruth
Ora
Cretus
Sruth
Qahtan
Reu
Heber Glas
SCOT
Kaber
Celius
Jurham
Heraclim
Shela
Serug
Melka
Beouman
Saturn
Oghaman
Mudad
Cornebo
Daughter
Rawq
Jupiter
Hubba
Joktan
Kheber
Canaan
Iyosaka
Nahor
Milcah
Tait
Agnon
Heber Glun
Maria
Terah
Nefir
Bethuel
Abimael
Keturah
Abraham
Sarai
Laban
Abinah
Rebecca
Ra 'la
Ishmael
Seni
Isaac
Luke
Leah
Nabit
Basemath
Esau
Jacob
Rachel
Levi
Melcha
Igrath
Eglah
Dan
Ijasaka
Benjamin
Asher
Hadurah
Yahjub
Adiba'a
Dinah
Simeon
Reuben
Ada
Potiphera
Bunah
Asenath
Joseph
Gad
Maka
Zebulon
Nilman
Ya'rub
Rasu'u
Naptali
Betasu'el
Judah
Isaac-har
Hezaqa
Jobab
Tayrah
Aridah

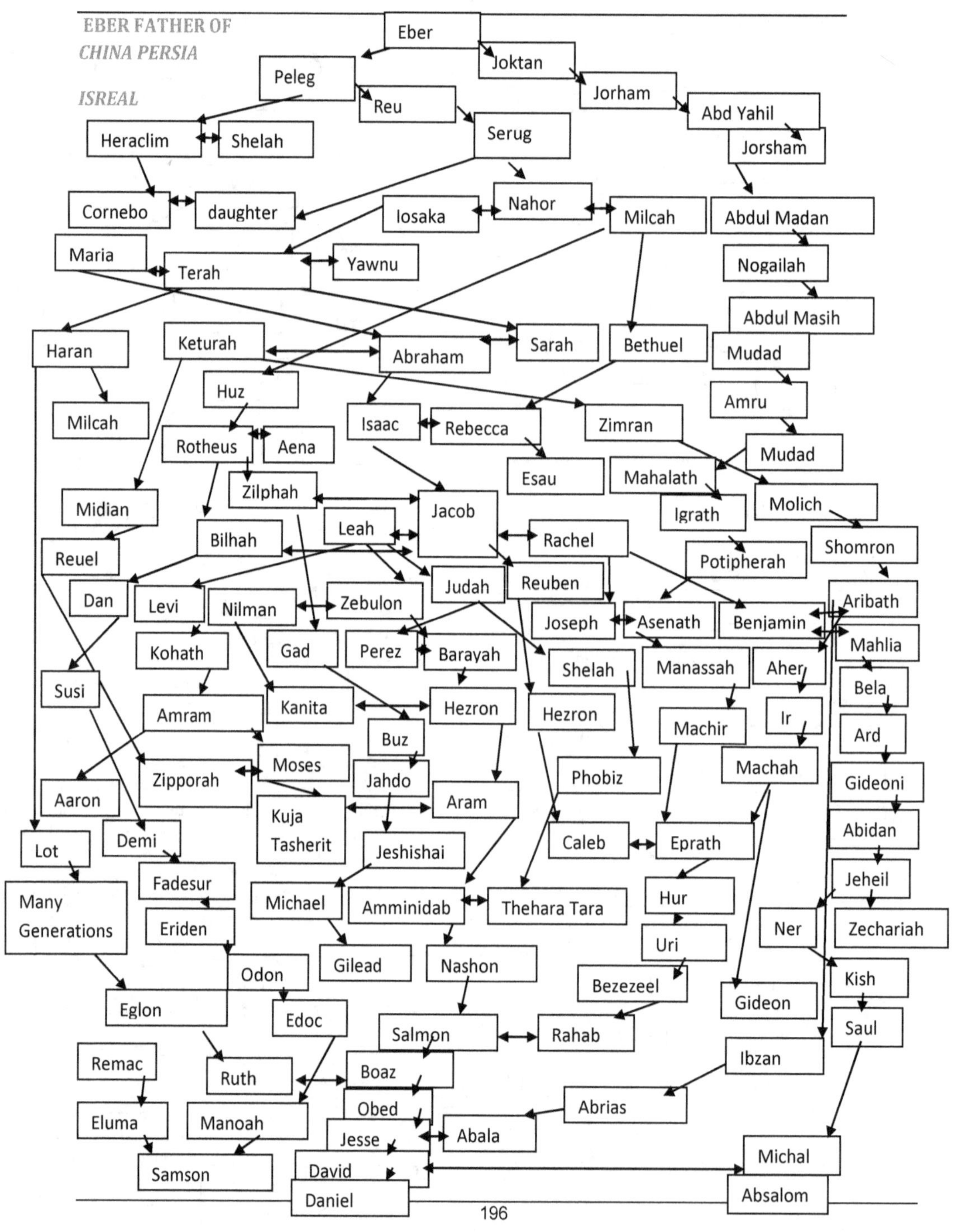

EBER FATHER OF
CHINA PERSIA
ISREAL
Eber
Joktan
Peleg
Jorham
Reu
Abd Yahil
Heraclim
Shelah
Serug
Jorsham
Cornebo
daughter
Iosaka
Nahor
Milcah
Abdul Madan
Maria
Terah
Yawnu
Nogailah
Abdul Masih
Haran
Keturah
Abraham
Sarah
Bethuel
Mudad
Huz
Milcah
Isaac
Rebecca
Zimran
Amru
Rotheus
Aena
Esau
Mahalath
Mudad
Zilphah
Jacob
Igrath
Molich
Midian
Leah
Bilhah
Rachel
Shomron
Reuel
Potipherah
Judah
Reuben
Dan
Levi
Nilman
Zebulon
Aribath
Joseph
Asenath
Benjamin
Kohath
Gad
Perez
Barayah
Mahlia
Shelah
Manassah
Aher
Susi
Bela
Amram
Kanita
Hezron
Hezron
Ir
Buz
Machir
Ard
Moses
Machah
Zipporah
Jahdo
Phobiz
Gideoni
Aaron
Aram
Kuja
Tasherit
Abidan
Lot
Demi
Caleb
Eprath
Jeshishai
Jeheil
Fadesur
Many
Generations
Michael
Amminidab
Thehara Tara
Hur
Eriden
Ner
Zechariah
Uri
Gilead
Nashon
Odon
Kish
Bezezeel
Eglon
Edoc
Gideon
Salmon
Rahab
Saul
Remac
Ibzan
Ruth
Boaz
Eluma
Manoah
Obed
Abrias
Jesse
Abala
Samson
David
Michal
Daniel
Absalom

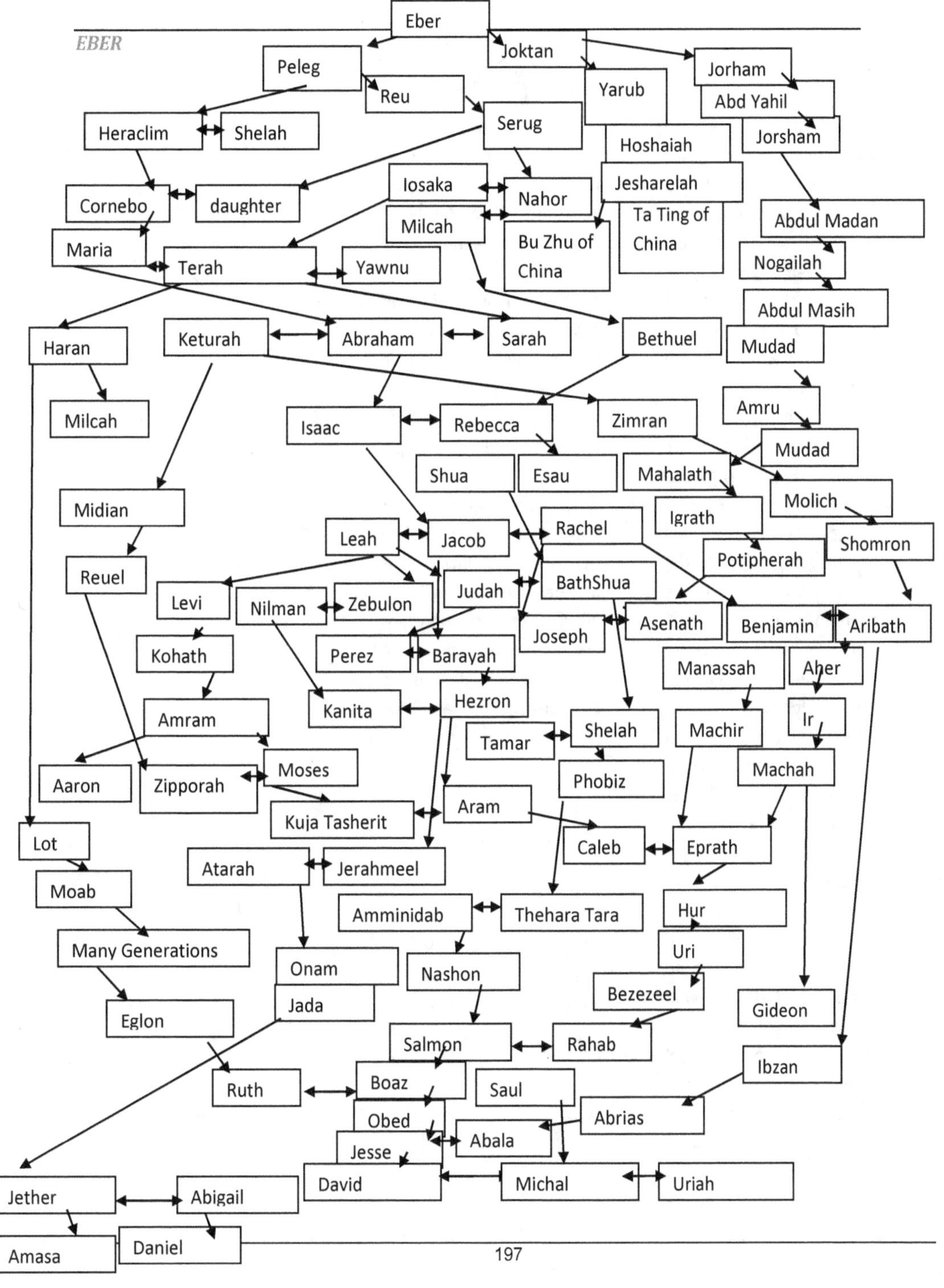
Eber
Peleg
Joktan
Jorham
Yarub
Abd Yahil
Reu
Serug
Heraclim
Shelah
Hoshaiah
Jorsham
Iosaka
Nahor
Jesharelah
Cornebo
daughter
Ta Ting of China
Milcah
Bu Zhu of China
Abdul Madan
Maria
Terah
Yawnu
Nogailah
Abdul Masih
Haran
Keturah
Abraham
Sarah
Bethuel
Mudad
Milcah
Isaac
Rebecca
Zimran
Amru
Mudad
Shua
Esau
Mahalath
Molich
Midian
Igrath
Leah
Jacob
Rachel
Shomron
Potipherah
Reuel
Levi
Nilman
Zebulon
Judah
BathShua
Asenath
Benjamin
Aribath
Joseph
Kohath
Perez
Barayah
Manassah
Aher
Kanita
Hezron
Ir
Amram
Tamar
Shelah
Machir
Machah
Aaron
Zipporah
Moses
Phobiz
Kuja Tasherit
Aram
Lot
Caleb
Eprath
Atarah
Jerahmeel
Moab
Amminidab
Thehara Tara
Hur
Many Generations
Onam
Nashon
Uri
Bezezeel
Eglon
Jada
Gideon
Salmon
Rahab
Ibzan
Ruth
Boaz
Saul
Obed
Abrias
Abala
Jesse
David
Michal
Uriah
Jether
Abigail
Amasa
Daniel

Note here the line from the queen of Sheba. Now Egypt who had extensive ties with Israel and the sons and daughter of Abraham would very much like to eliminate the idea of a King like David who had made war, killed Goliath and everyone that got in his way, including two sons, who sent a warrior to the front lines for the wife, and slept with his sister Abigail after Jether or (Nabal) was killed. Egypt and the royalty would much prefer a King or Queen that ruled by Judgement, not the sword. So Solomon was offered the Queen of Sheba that was related to the lines of Sarah, without very much bloodshed. He fathered and the resulting descent of the King Solomon is apparently lost and leads to a daughter that has a son, and the biblical line is said to continue. In fact the daughter's son is unable to father and the son is of the blood of Nathan, who marries the sister of Jeconiah. So the royal blood is maintained thru adoption and the lines from Japeth and Ham, used to make the line of Sarah thru her mother Nefir that are thirty generations continue with a branch at Pepy, called Apepy for the royal line thru a son . It is assumed that Nitrocris is the brother of Anather. The High Priest Kantheras would be a candidate for the resurrection of Anather. There are a lot of brothers and sisters shown in genealogy for people such as King David and Joshua that are not recorded. For example Joshua had Teucer, Antenor, and either one or two daughters by Rahab the mother of Boaz. It is for the readers speculation what other relationships are hidden, due to infidelity, or sibling relationships not accepted by certain societies.

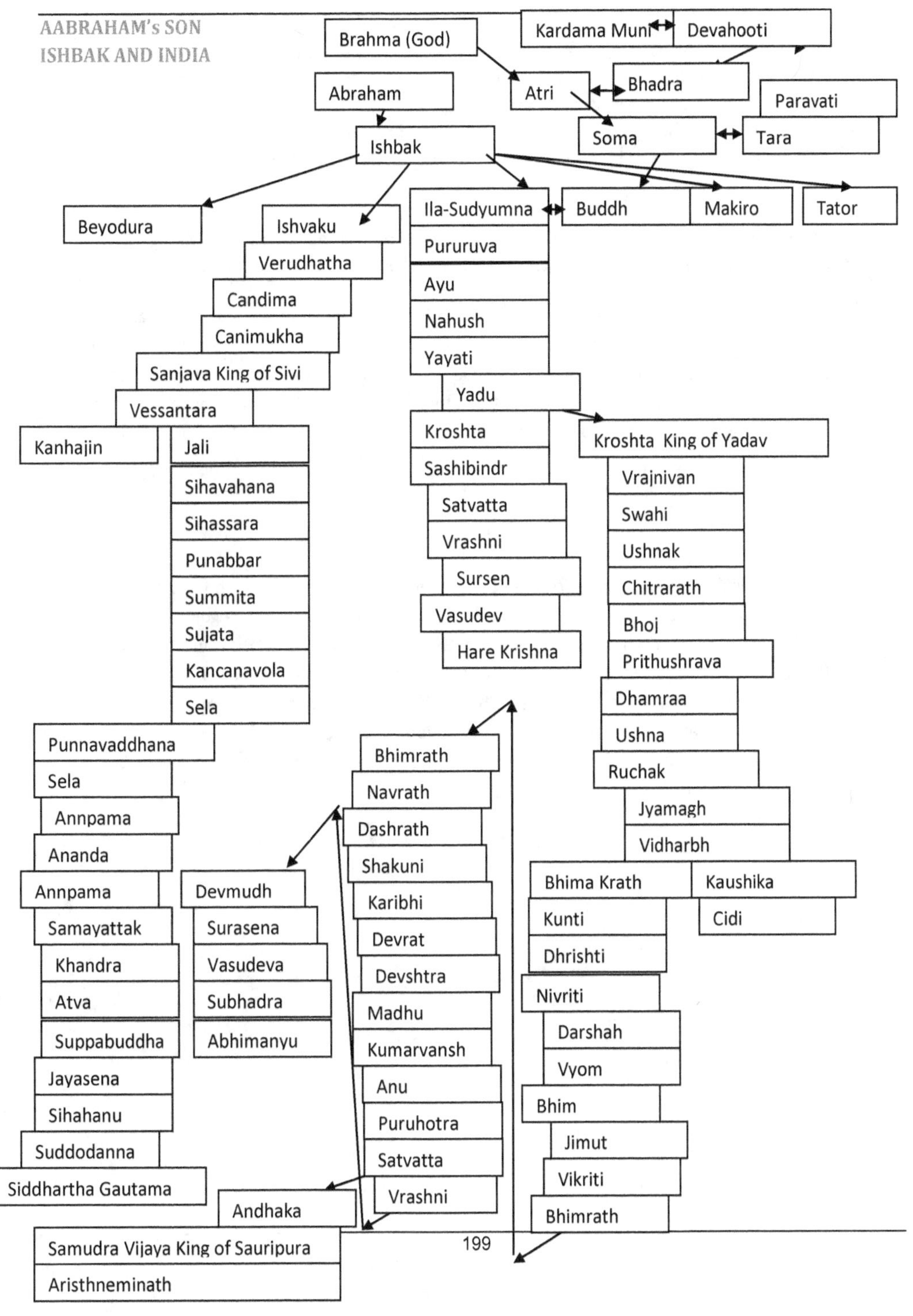
Brahma (God)
Kardama Muni
Devahooti
Atri
Bhadra
Abraham
Paravati
Soma
Tara
Ishbak
Ila-Sudyumna
Buddh
Makiro
Tator
Beyodura
Ishvaku
Pururuva
Verudhatha
Ayu
Candima
Nahush
Canimukha
Yayati
Sanjava King of Sivi
Yadu
Vessantara
Kroshta
Kroshta King of Yadav
Kanhajin
Jali
Sashibindr
Vrajnivan
Sihavahana
Satvatta
Swahi
Sihassara
Vrashni
Ushnak
Punabbar
Sursen
Chitrarath
Summita
Vasudev
Bhoj
Sujata
Hare Krishna
Prithushrava
Kancanavola
Dhamraa
Sela
Ushna
Punnavaddhana
Bhimrath
Ruchak
Sela
Navrath
Jyamagh
Annpama
Dashrath
Vidharbh
Ananda
Shakuni
Bhima Krath
Kaushika
Annpama
Devmudh
Karibhi
Kunti
Cidi
Samayattak
Surasena
Devrat
Dhrishti
Khandra
Vasudeva
Devshtra
Nivriti
Atva
Subhadra
Madhu
Darshah
Suppabuddha
Abhimanyu
Kumarvansh
Vyom
Jayasena
Anu
Bhim
Sihahanu
Puruhotra
Jimut
Suddodanna
Satvatta
Vikriti
Siddhartha Gautama
Vrashni
Andhaka
Bhimrath
Samudra Vijaya King of Sauripura
Aristhneminath

Found on the page above is the Lineage of Ishbak. This lineage goes to India and the noble Prince Hari Krishna and Siddhartha Gautama. Notice the line to the Indian God Brahma, In a marriage to the Abrahamic people. Notice the two sons of Ishbak, both sacred and written about in the Bhagavad *Gita.* Isvaku has Siddhartha and the Suppabudda with Jali. Now Ila-Sudyumna marries the line of Devihooti, (God or Goddess of giving milk) and Hare Krishna is from this line. Notice the branch at Kroshta King of Yadav and the many generations to Samudra Vijaya King of Sauripura.

Following on the page is the lineage of Saint Grace, or Zayda. Her sister was Saint Mary and her broter was Saint Bernard. Now Zayda was the daughter of Muhammad III Al Mutimid of Seville

who was 17 generations away from Muhammad the Prophet who the angel Gabriel appeared to and inspired the holy work called the Quaran, which may be God's law for the people of Ishmael and Eber. Notice the generations to get to Ishmael and even more apparent is that most of these lines go to Eber, not Ishmael so Muhammad tru father has Abraham, however most of it is Eber. Ishmael is so sacred to these people that the son of the concubine is s better than most of the father of Persia which is Eber. So most of Persia is from Eber, thru Iraq, just like Eber is the ancestor of most of China, the Huns, and the East.

Notice in the lineage of China the two lines go to the Mongols, who aided the Christians in the Seventh Crusage, and the Otyura line that joins with Wessex England. This line goes to the Bustani that has many descendents including Daniel the father of Ammon and David. Notice the strength of the Father Eber. He is over Taoism, a father of Abraham and the Abrahamic Religions, Christianity, Judaism, and Islam, and is the Father of the East and Far East. Taoism is the largest religion on the planet, and LaoTzu wrote the masterwork, Tao Te Ching. (the given name of Lao Tzu or Laozi was Li Er and he was alive in the same time as Confusious) Lao Tzu is given divinity by his most ardent followers.

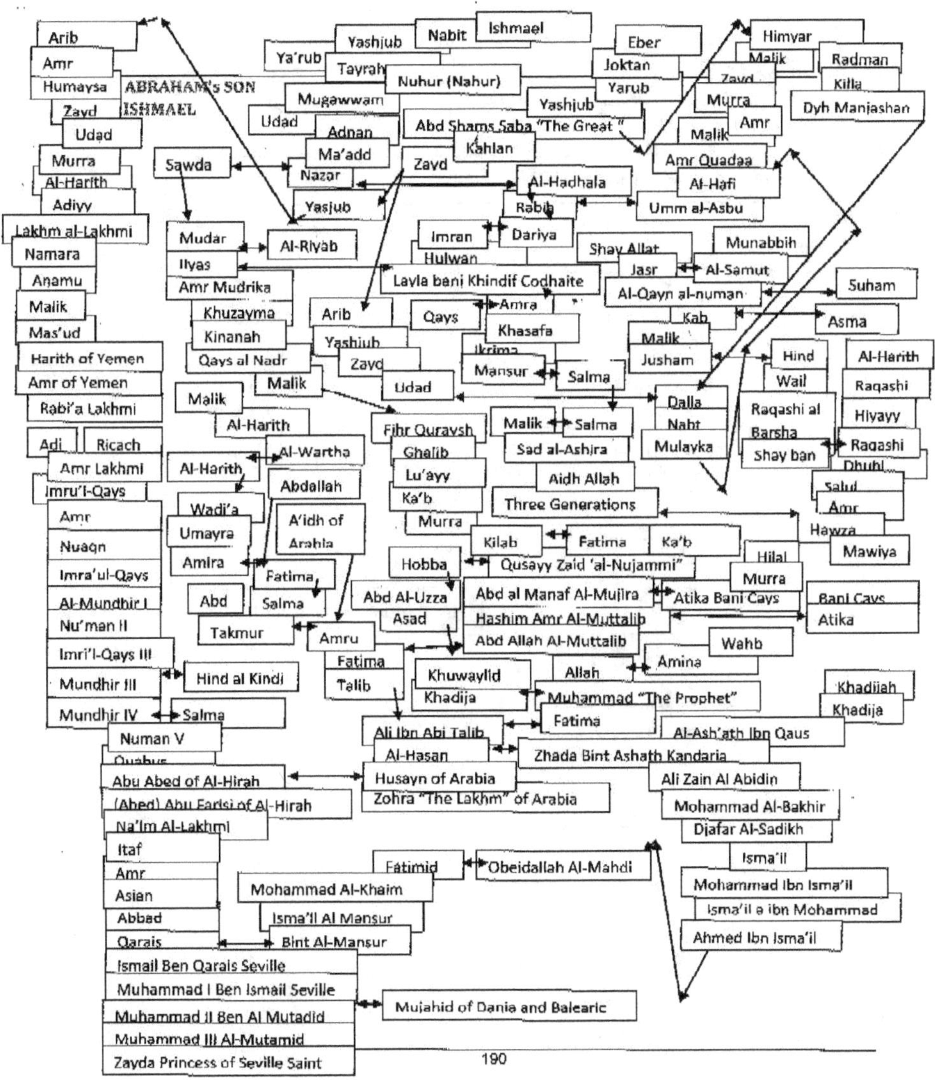
ABRAHAM's SON ISHMAEL
Arib
Amr
Humaysa
Zayd
Udad
Murra
Al-Harith
Adiyy
Lakhm al-Lakhmi
Namara
Anamu
Malik
Mas'ud
Harith of Yemen
Amr of Yemen
Rabi'a Lakhmi
Adi
Ricach
Amr Lakhmi
Imru'l-Qays
Amr
Nuaqn
Imra'ul-Qays
Al-Mundhir I
Nu'man II
Imri'l-Qays III
Mundhir III
Hind al Kindi
Mundhir IV
Salma
Numan V
Abu Abed of Al-Hirah
(Abed) Abu Farisi of Al-Hirah
Na'im Al-Lakhmi
Itaf
Amr
Asian
Abbad
Qarais
Ismail Ben Qarais Seville
Muhammad I Ben Ismail Seville
Muhammad II Ben Al Mutadid
Muhammad III Al-Mutamid
Zayda Princess of Seville Saint
Mujahid of Dania and Balearic
Ishmael
Nabit
Yashjub
Ya'rub
Tayrah
Nuhur (Nahur)
Muqawwam
Udad
Adnan
Ma'add
Nazar
Sawda
Yasjub
Zayd
Kahlan
Abd Shams Saba "The Great"
Yashjub
Eber
Joktan
Yarub
Himyar
Malik
Radman
Zayd
Killa
Murra
Dyh Manjashan
Amr
Malik
Amr Quadaa
Al-Hafi
Al-Hadhala
Rabia
Umm al-Asbu
Imran
Dariya
Hulwan
Mudar
Al-Riyab
Ilyas
Amr Mudrika
Layla bani Khindif Codhaite
Khuzayma
Kinanah
Qays al Nadr
Arib
Yashjub
Zayd
Udad
Malik
Qays
Amra
Khasafa
Ikrima
Mansur
Salma
Shay Allat
Munabbih
Jasr
Al-Samut
Al-Qayn al-numan
Suham
Kab
Asma
Malik
Jusham
Hind
Al-Harith
Wail
Raqashi
Dalla
Nabt
Mulayka
Raqashi al Barsha
Hiyayy
Shay ban
Raqashi
Dhubi
Salul
Amr
Hawza
Mawiya
Malik
Al-Harith
Al-Wartha
Al-Harith
Abdallah
Wadi'a
A'idh of Arabia
Umayra
Amira
Fatima
Abd
Salma
Takmur
Amru
Fatima
Talib
Fihr Quraysh
Ghalib
Lu'ayy
Ka'b
Murra
Malik
Salma
Sad al-Ashira
Aidh Allah
Three Generations
Kilab
Fatima
Ka'b
Hilal
Hobba
Qusayy Zaid 'al-Nujammi"
Murra
Abd Al-Uzza
Abd al Manaf Al-Mujira
Atika Bani Cays
Bani Cays
Asad
Hashim Amr Al-Muttalib
Atika
Abd Allah Al-Muttalib
Wahb
Amina
Allah
Khuwaylid
Khadija
Muhammad "The Prophet"
Khadijah
Khadija
Fatima
Ali Ibn Abi Talib
Al-Ash'ath Ibn Qaus
Al-Hasan
Zhada Bint Ashath Kandaria
Husayn of Arabia
Ali Zain Al Abidin
Zohra "The Lakhm" of Arabia
Mohammad Al-Bakhir
Djafar Al-Sadikh
Isma'il
Fatimid
Obeidallah Al-Mahdi
Mohammad Al-Khaim
Mohammad Ibn Isma'il
Isma'il a ibn Mohammad
Isma'il Al Mansur
Bint Al-Mansur
Ahmed Ibn Isma'il

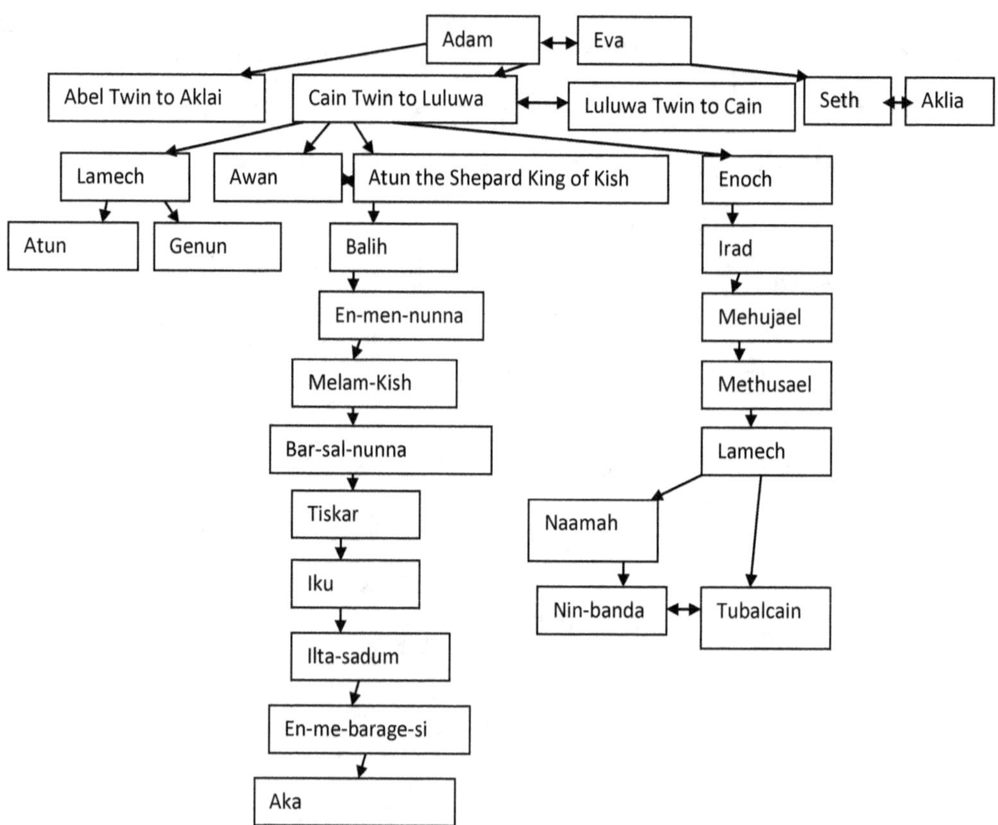
Adam
Eva
Abel Twin to Aklai
Cain Twin to Luluwa
Luluwa Twin to Cain
Seth
Aklia
Lamech
Awan
Atun the Shepard King of Kish
Enoch
Atun
Genun
Balih
Irad
En-men-nunna
Mehujael
Melam-Kish
Methusael
Bar-sal-nunna
Lamech
Tiskar
Naamah
Iku
Nin-banda
Tubalcain
Ilta-sadum
En-me-barage-si
Aka

THE ANCIENT LINES OF GOD

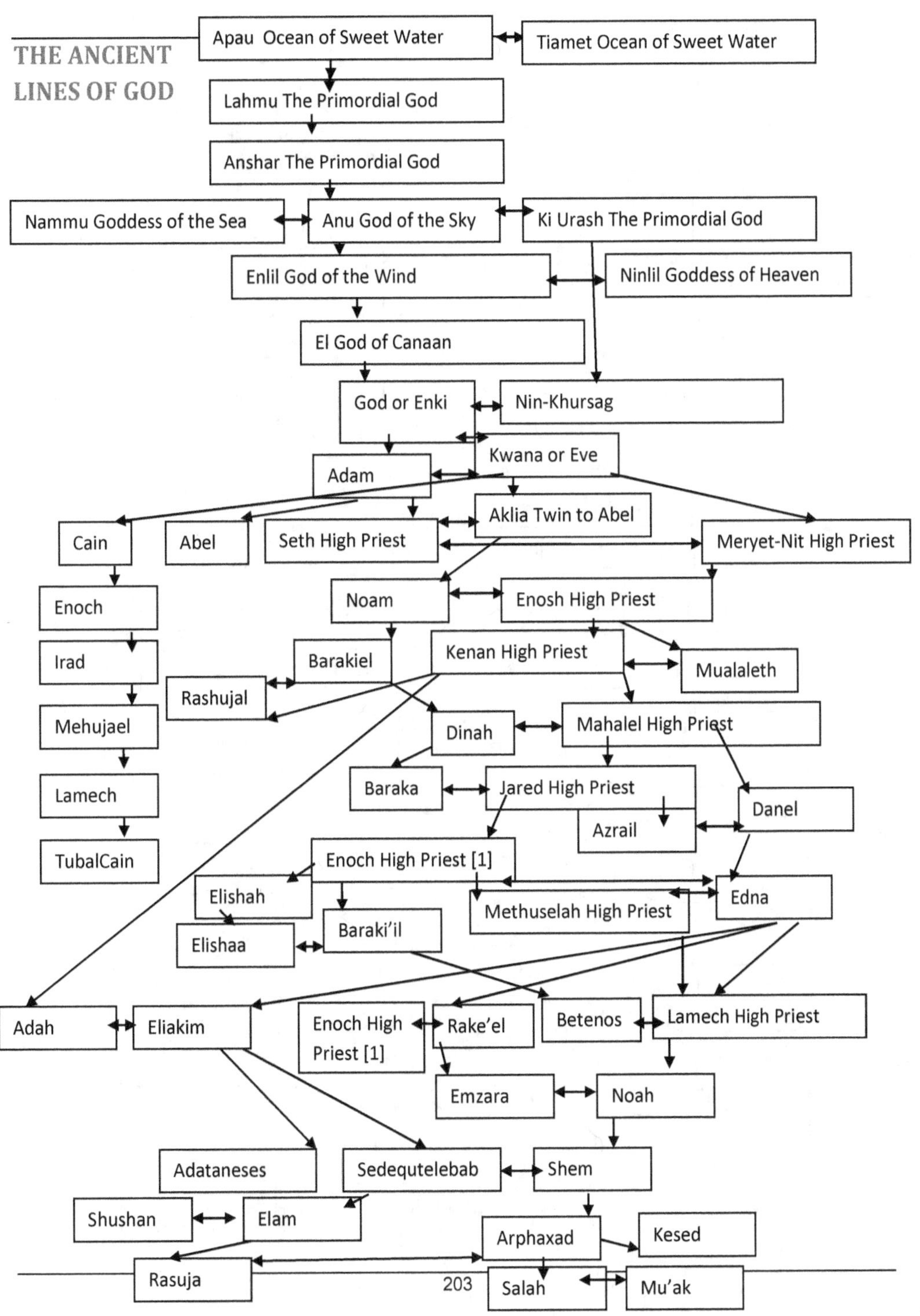

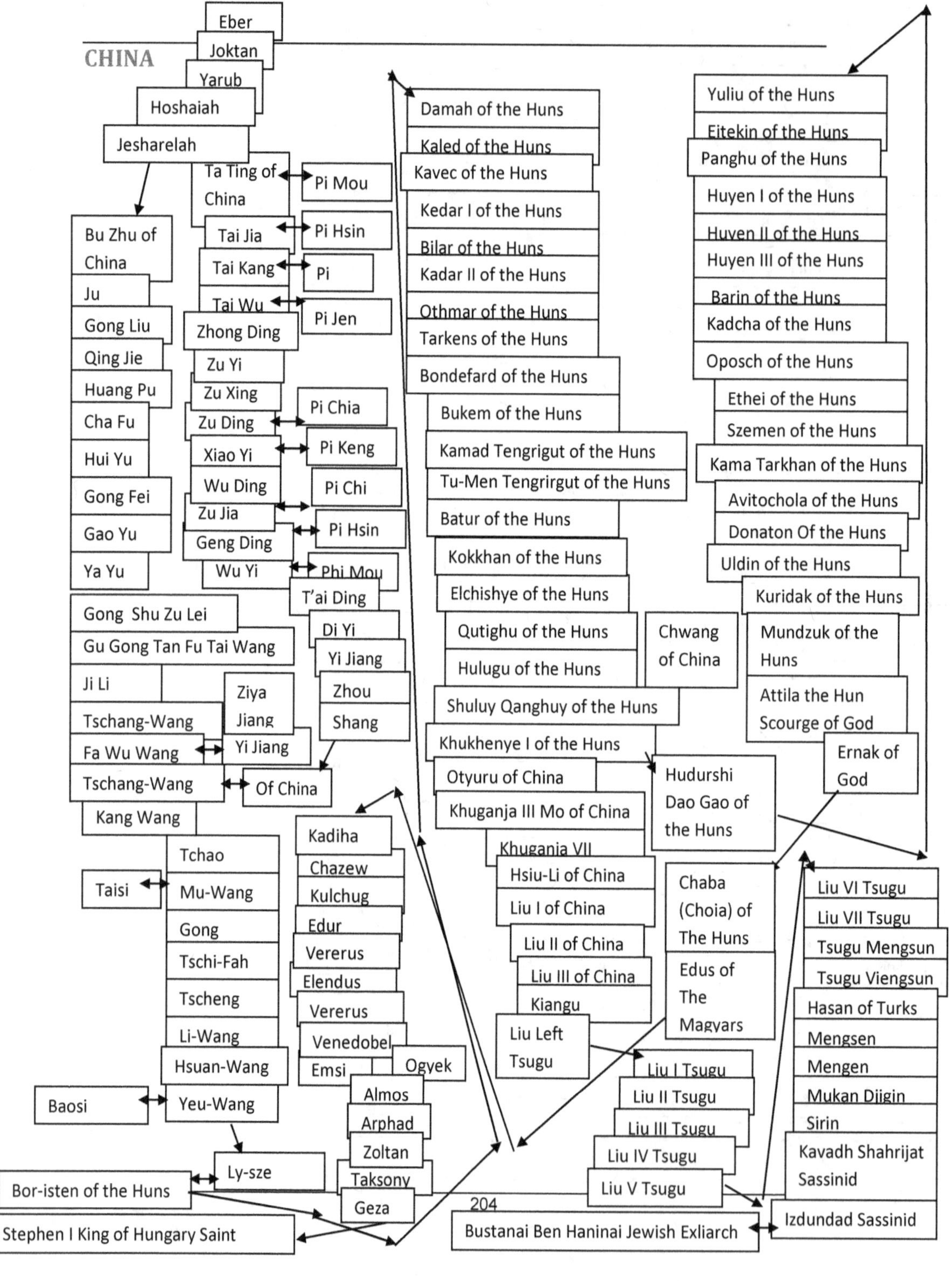
CHINA
Eber
Joktan
Yarub
Hoshaiah
Jesharelah
Bu Zhu of China
Ju
Gong Liu
Qing Jie
Huang Pu
Cha Fu
Hui Yu
Gong Fei
Gao Yu
Ya Yu
Ta Ting of China
Pi Mou
Tai Jia
Pi Hsin
Tai Kang
Pi
Tai Wu
Pi Jen
Zhong Ding
Zu Yi
Zu Xing
Pi Chia
Zu Ding
Xiao Yi
Pi Keng
Wu Ding
Pi Chi
Zu Jia
Geng Ding
Pi Hsin
Wu Yi
Phi Mou
T'ai Ding
Di Yi
Yi Jiang
Zhou
Shang
Gong Shu Zu Lei
Gu Gong Tan Fu Tai Wang
Ji Li
Ziya Jiang
Tschang-Wang
Fa Wu Wang
Yi Jiang
Tschang-Wang
Of China
Kang Wang
Tchao
Taisi
Mu-Wang
Gong
Tschi-Fah
Tscheng
Li-Wang
Hsuan-Wang
Baosi
Yeu-Wang
Ly-sze
Bor-isten of the Huns
Stephen I King of Hungary Saint
Kadiha
Chazew
Kulchug
Edur
Vererus
Elendus
Vererus
Venedobel
Emsi
Ogyek
Almos
Arphad
Zoltan
Taksony
Geza
Damah of the Huns
Kaled of the Huns
Kavec of the Huns
Kedar I of the Huns
Bilar of the Huns
Kadar II of the Huns
Othmar of the Huns
Tarkens of the Huns
Bondefard of the Huns
Bukem of the Huns
Kamad Tengrigut of the Huns
Tu-Men Tengrirgut of the Huns
Batur of the Huns
Kokkhan of the Huns
Elchishye of the Huns
Qutighu of the Huns
Hulugu of the Huns
Chwang of China
Shuluy Qanghuy of the Huns
Khukhenye I of the Huns
Otyuru of China
Khuganja III Mo of China
Khugania VII
Hsiu-Li of China
Liu I of China
Liu II of China
Liu III of China
Kiangu
Liu Left Tsugu
Hudurshi Dao Gao of the Huns
Chaba (Choia) of The Huns
Edus of The Magyars
Liu I Tsugu
Liu II Tsugu
Liu III Tsugu
Liu IV Tsugu
Liu V Tsugu
Bustanai Ben Haninai Jewish Exliarch
Yuliu of the Huns
Eitekin of the Huns
Panghu of the Huns
Huyen I of the Huns
Huyen II of the Huns
Huyen III of the Huns
Barin of the Huns
Kadcha of the Huns
Oposch of the Huns
Ethei of the Huns
Szemen of the Huns
Kama Tarkhan of the Huns
Avitochola of the Huns
Donaton Of the Huns
Uldin of the Huns
Kuridak of the Huns
Mundzuk of the Huns
Attila the Hun Scourge of God
Ernak of God
Liu VI Tsugu
Liu VII Tsugu
Tsugu Mengsun
Tsugu Viengsun
Hasan of Turks
Mengsen
Mengen
Mukan Djigin
Sirin
Kavadh Shahrijat Sassinid
Izdundad Sassinid

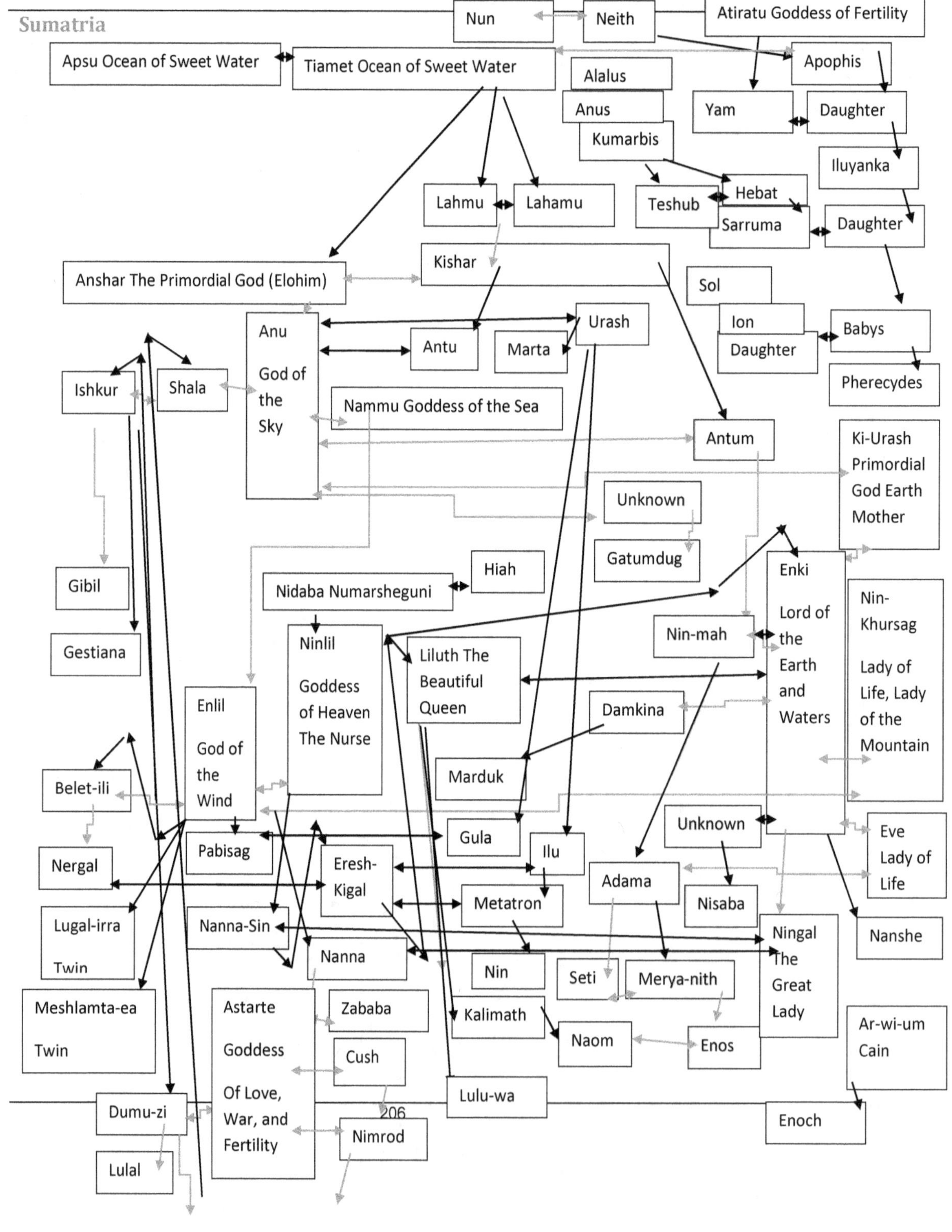
Sumatria
Nun
Neith
Atiratu Goddess of Fertility
Apsu Ocean of Sweet Water
Tiamet Ocean of Sweet Water
Apophis
Alalus
Anus
Kumarbis
Yam
Daughter
Iluyanka
Lahmu
Lahamu
Teshub
Hebat
Sarruma
Daughter
Anshar The Primordial God (Elohim)
Kishar
Sol
Anu
God of
the
Sky
Antu
Marta
Urash
Ion
Daughter
Babys
Pherecydes
Ishkur
Shala
Nammu Goddess of the Sea
Antum
Ki-Urash
Primordial
God Earth
Mother
Unknown
Gatumdug
Gibil
Hiah
Nidaba Numarsheguni
Enki
Lord of
the
Earth
and
Waters
Nin-
Khursag
Lady of
Life, Lady
of the
Mountain
Gestiana
Ninlil
Goddess
of Heaven
The Nurse
Liluth The
Beautiful
Queen
Nin-mah
Enlil
God of
the
Wind
Damkina
Marduk
Belet-ili
Unknown
Eve
Lady of
Life
Nergal
Pabisag
Gula
Ilu
Eresh-
Kigal
Adama
Nisaba
Metatron
Lugal-irra
Twin
Nanna-Sin
Ningal
The
Great
Lady
Nanshe
Nanna
Nin
Seti
Merya-nith
Meshlamta-ea
Twin
Astarte
Goddess
Of Love,
War, and
Fertility
Zababa
Kalimath
Naom
Enos
Ar-wi-um
Cain
Cush
Lulu-wa
Dumu-zi
Enoch
Nimrod
Lulal

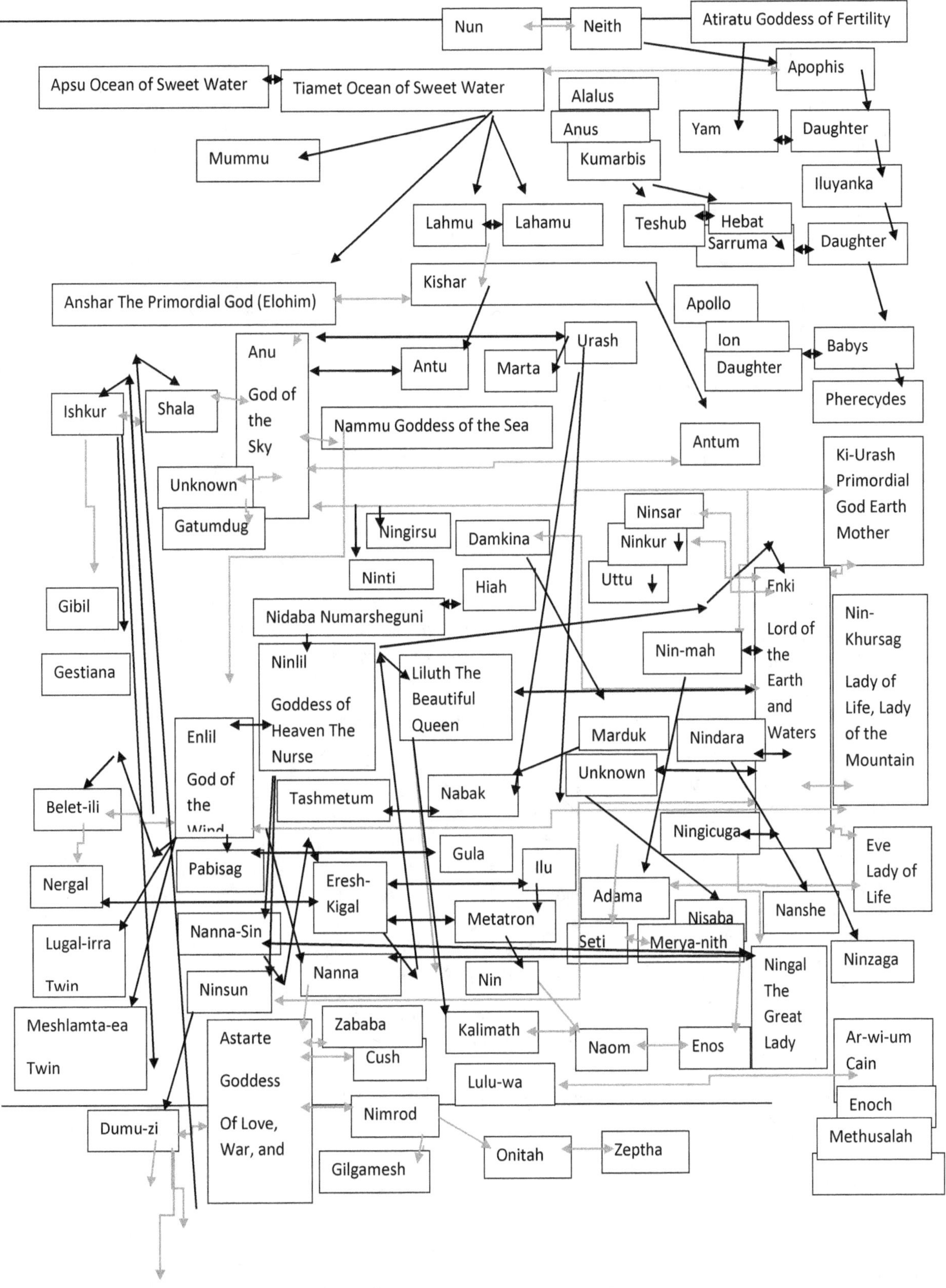

Nun
Neith
Atiratu Goddess of Fertility
Apophis
Apsu Ocean of Sweet Water
Tiamet Ocean of Sweet Water
Alalus
Anus
Kumarbis
Yam
Daughter
Mummu
Iluyanka
Lahmu
Lahamu
Teshub
Hebat
Sarruma
Daughter
Kishar
Anshar The Primordial God (Elohim)
Apollo
Ion
Daughter
Babys
Urash
Anu
God of the Sky
Antu
Marta
Pherecydes
Ishkur
Shala
Nammu Goddess of the Sea
Antum
Unknown
Gatumdug
Ki-Urash Primordial God Earth Mother
Ninsar
Ninkur
Ningirsu
Damkina
Uttu
Ninti
Hiah
Gibil
Nidaba Numarsheguni
Enki
Lord of the Earth and Waters
Nin-Khursag
Lady of Life, Lady of the Mountain
Gestiana
Nin-mah
Ninlil
Goddess of Heaven The Nurse
Liluth The Beautiful Queen
Enlil
God of the Wind
Marduk
Nindara
Unknown
Belet-ili
Tashmetum
Nabak
Ningicuga
Eve
Lady of Life
Pabisag
Gula
Ilu
Nergal
Eresh-Kigal
Adama
Metatron
Nisaba
Nanshe
Lugal-irra
Twin
Nanna-Sin
Seti
Merya-nith
Ningal
The Great Lady
Ninzaga
Ninsun
Nanna
Nin
Meshlamta-ea
Twin
Astarte
Goddess
Of Love, War, and
Zababa
Cush
Kalimath
Naom
Enos
Ar-wi-um
Cain
Lulu-wa
Enoch
Methusalah
Dumu-zi
Nimrod
Onitah
Zeptha
Gilgamesh

Astarte the Goddess was the daughter of Nanna and Ningal Ningal was the Great Lady who also was with Nanna Sin. Nanna Sin was the son of Ninlil the Goddess of Heaven the nurse and Enlil the God of the Wind who was a jealous God. Enlil was the son of Anu God of the Sky and Nammu Goddess of the Sea. Ninlil was the daughter of Nidaba Numarsheguni and Hiah.

Astarte the Goddess had Zababa and made Shala, who was with Enlil. Shala was with Ishkur the father of Gibil. Shala was with Ishkur and she made Dumu-zi who was the father of Lulal. Astarte also was the mother of a daughter that had Gilgamesh and made Kenkene and had two other children who grew up and their lines continued to Uriah the Hittite and Sargon I.

Astarte the Goddess had Cush the son of Ham and made Nimrod. Astarte had Nimrod and made Gilgamesh.

Enki or Samael was the father of Adama with Ninmah the daughter of Antum the daughter of Kishar. Antum had Anu as father of Ninmah the mother of Adama. Antum was the daughter of Kishar who was the daughter of Lahmu and Lahamu. Kishar had Anshar who was the father of Anu and Antum.

Ki-Urash the Primordial earth mother had Anu and made Nin-Khursah Lady of Life Lady of the Mountain.

Nin-Khursag had Enki Lord of the earth and waters and made Eve Lady of Life. Eve had Enki and made Ar-wi-um or Cain. Cain had Lulu-wa the daughter of Liluth the Beautiful Queen and Enki. Lulu-wa made Enoch the son of Cain.

Liluth the Beautiful Queen was sister to Enki and daughter of Eresh-Kigal. Eresh-Kigal was the wife of Nergal the God of the Underworld, and Nergal was the son of Enlil and Belet-ili.

Anu God of the Sky had Urash who made Marta, Gula, and Ilu. Ilu had Eresh-Kigal and made Metatron. Metatron had Eresh-Kigal and made Nin.

Liluth the Beautiful Queen had Enki and made Kalimath who had Seti the son of Adama and Eve and made Naom. Adama had Eve and Eve made Mery-nith and she had Seti and made Enos who had Naom.

Damkina had Enki and made Marduk.

Anu was son of Anshar who was the son of Tiamet who had had Apsu. Tiamet also had Apophis who had a daughter who made a son Iluyanka who had a daughter married Sarruma. The daughter made Babys who was father of Pherecydes who was the son of a daughter of Ion. Ion was the son of Sol who was Apollo.

Apophis was the son of Nun and Neith and Apophis daughter had Yam who was the son of Atiratu Goddess of Fertility. Yam had Iluyanka whose daughter was Sarruma who was the son of Hebat and Teshub children of Kumarbis son of Anus son of Alalus.

The ladies are Ningal the Great Lady, Ninlil the beautiful queen, Ninmah mother of Adama, Nin-Khursag, Ninasi the Lady Who Fills the Mouth, Ningikuga of the pure reed, Ningirsu, Ninkur, Ninsar, Ninshebargunu, Ninsun of the cow, Ninti, Ninus Nin-banda of Ur.

ERA OF ISRAELITES TO BABYLON IN GREECE

SECTION THIRTEEN: THE GREEK

THE ANCIENT LINES OF ZEUS

NOTE ON LINEAGES

Sir Hector is an interesting hero. Notice that he has lineage to Joshua, son of Nun thru Priam. From his mother Hecuba he has lineage to Zeus. He has many deities of the Greek religion as ancestors as well.

Aeneas is also interesting. He does not have lineage to Priam, however he does go back to Tros. Therefore he is also a descendent of Joshua.

Iulus the son of Aeneas is also very interesting because he has Creusa for a mother. Creusa is sister to Sir Hector so Iulus has the advantage of the same lineage as Hector but also thru the advantages of the lineage of his father Aeneas.

Hercules has interesting lineage, and his line continues to the Father of Alexander the Great Phillip II of Macedonia. He does not have Joshua, but has many deities of Zeus as ancestors, including Perseus.

Helen has similar lineage to Hercules, thru her mother Leda, and also does not have Joshua. Her line continues thru to the mother of Alexander the Great Olympias. Helen has many deities of Zeus, as well. Also Leda had ancestors that married Zeus.

Alexander the Great (not shown in charts) has the advantage of Helen and Hercules as an ancestor. Paris is also an ancestor who does have Joshua as an ancestor so Alexander the Great is the merging of the line of Hercules and Helen.

Please not on all the following lineage tables that these are not the only ancestors of these Greek Heros. Many lines that lead only to a King and not to Zeus, or to Uranus or Oceanus were omitted due to space considerations. A Gedcom of all these lineages as published is available, please see the end of the book for the offer.

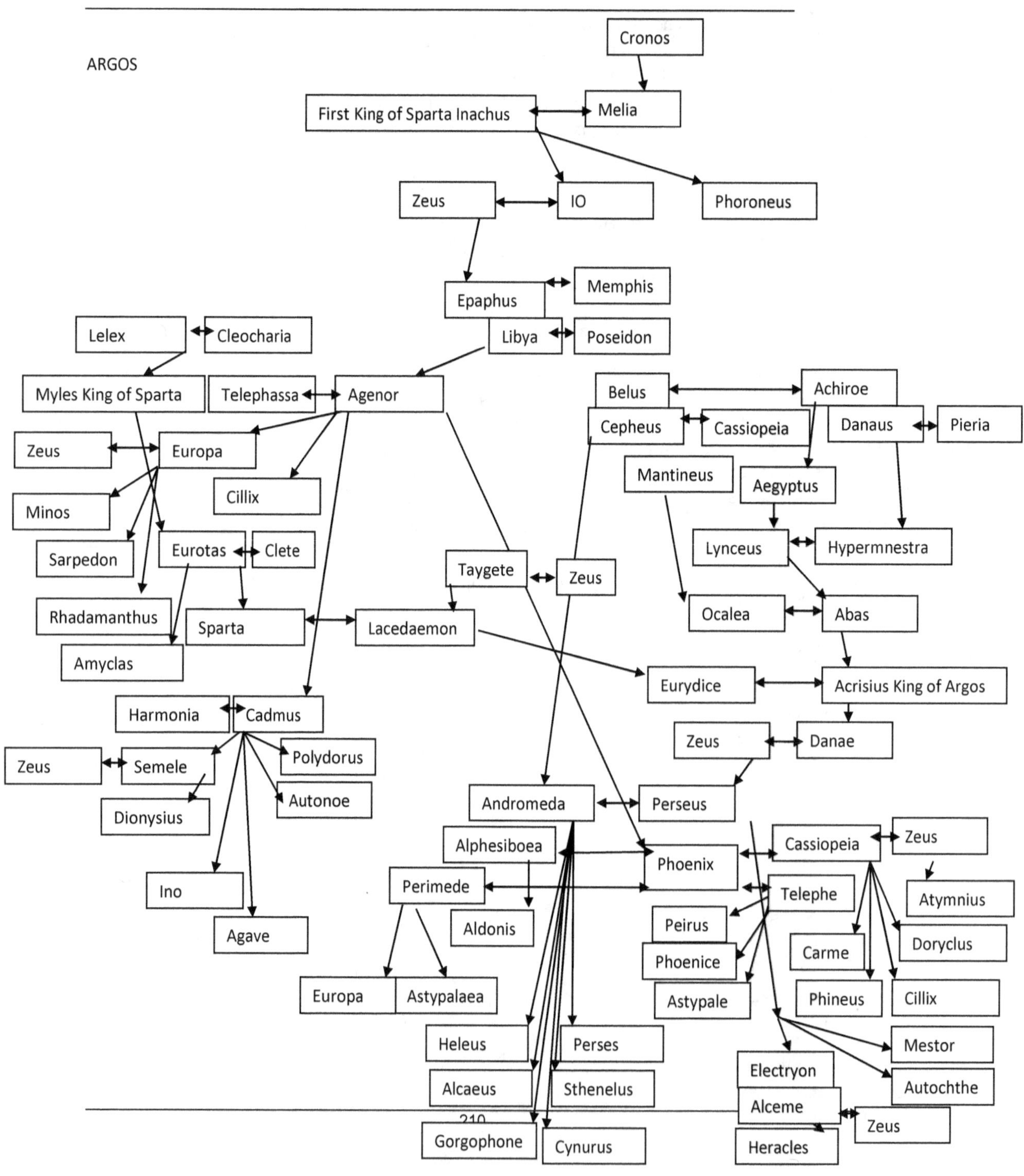
ARGOS
Cronos
First King of Sparta Inachus
Melia
Zeus
IO
Phoroneus
Epaphus
Memphis
Libya
Poseidon
Lelex
Cleocharia
Myles King of Sparta
Telephassa
Agenor
Belus
Achiroe
Cepheus
Cassiopeia
Danaus
Pieria
Zeus
Europa
Cillix
Mantineus
Aegyptus
Minos
Sarpedon
Eurotas
Clete
Lynceus
Hypermnestra
Taygete
Zeus
Rhadamanthus
Sparta
Lacedaemon
Ocalea
Abas
Amyclas
Eurydice
Acrisius King of Argos
Harmonia
Cadmus
Zeus
Danae
Zeus
Semele
Polydorus
Autonoe
Dionysius
Andromeda
Perseus
Alphesiboea
Phoenix
Cassiopeia
Zeus
Perimede
Telephe
Atymnius
Ino
Aldonis
Peirus
Agave
Phoenice
Carme
Doryclus
Europa
Astypalaea
Astypale
Phineus
Cillix
Heleus
Perses
Mestor
Electryon
Alcaeus
Sthenelus
Autochthe
Alceme
Zeus
Gorgophone
Cynurus
Heracles

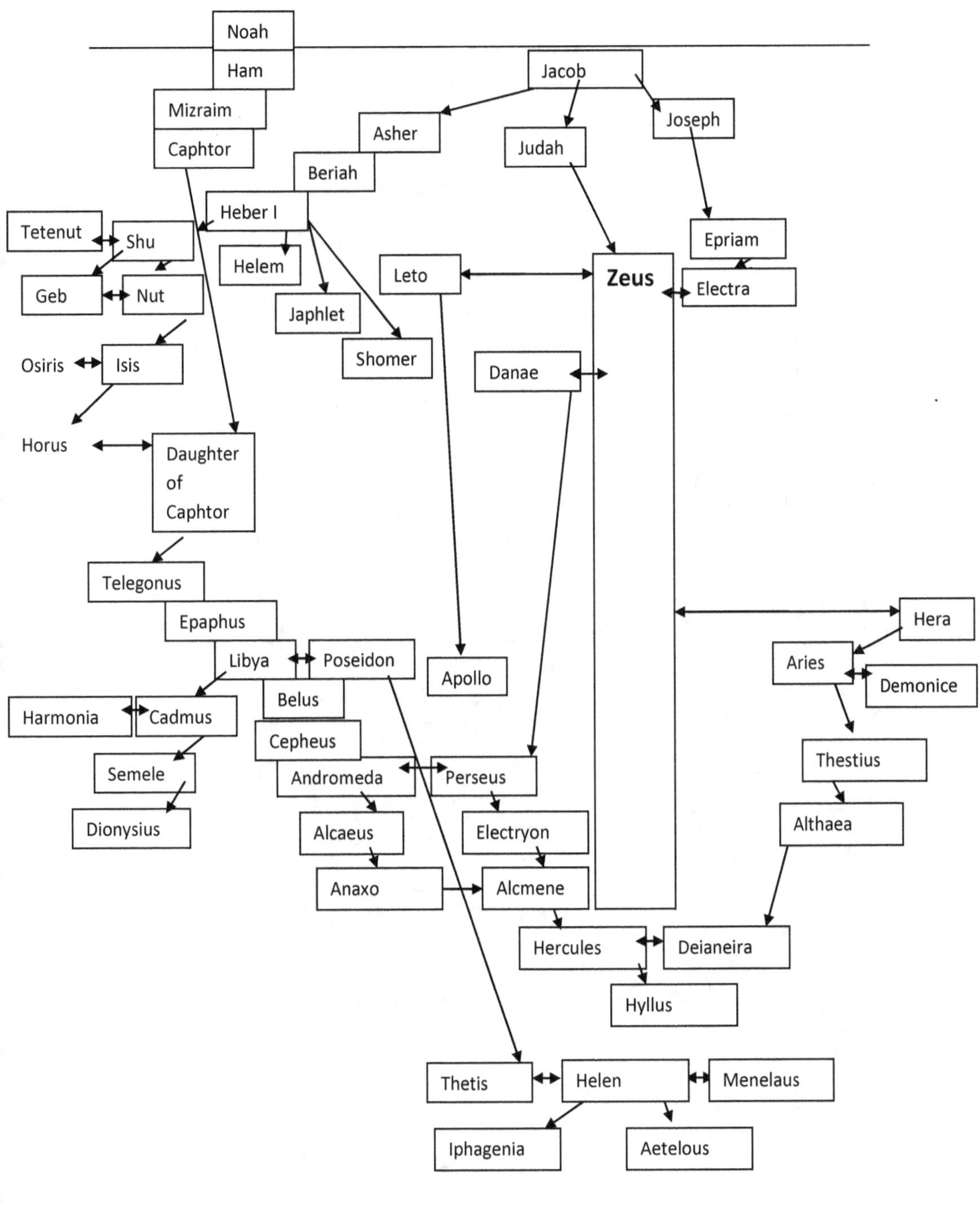
Noah
Ham
Mizraim
Caphtor
Jacob
Asher
Judah
Joseph
Beriah
Heber I
Tetenut
Shu
Helem
Epriam
Leto
Zeus
Electra
Geb
Nut
Japhlet
Shomer
Osiris
Isis
Danae
Horus
Daughter of Caphtor
Telegonus
Epaphus
Hera
Libya
Poseidon
Apollo
Aries
Demonice
Belus
Harmonia
Cadmus
Cepheus
Thestius
Andromeda
Perseus
Semele
Althaea
Dionysius
Alcaeus
Electryon
Anaxo
Alcmene
Hercules
Deianeira
Hyllus
Thetis
Helen
Menelaus
Iphagenia
Aetelous

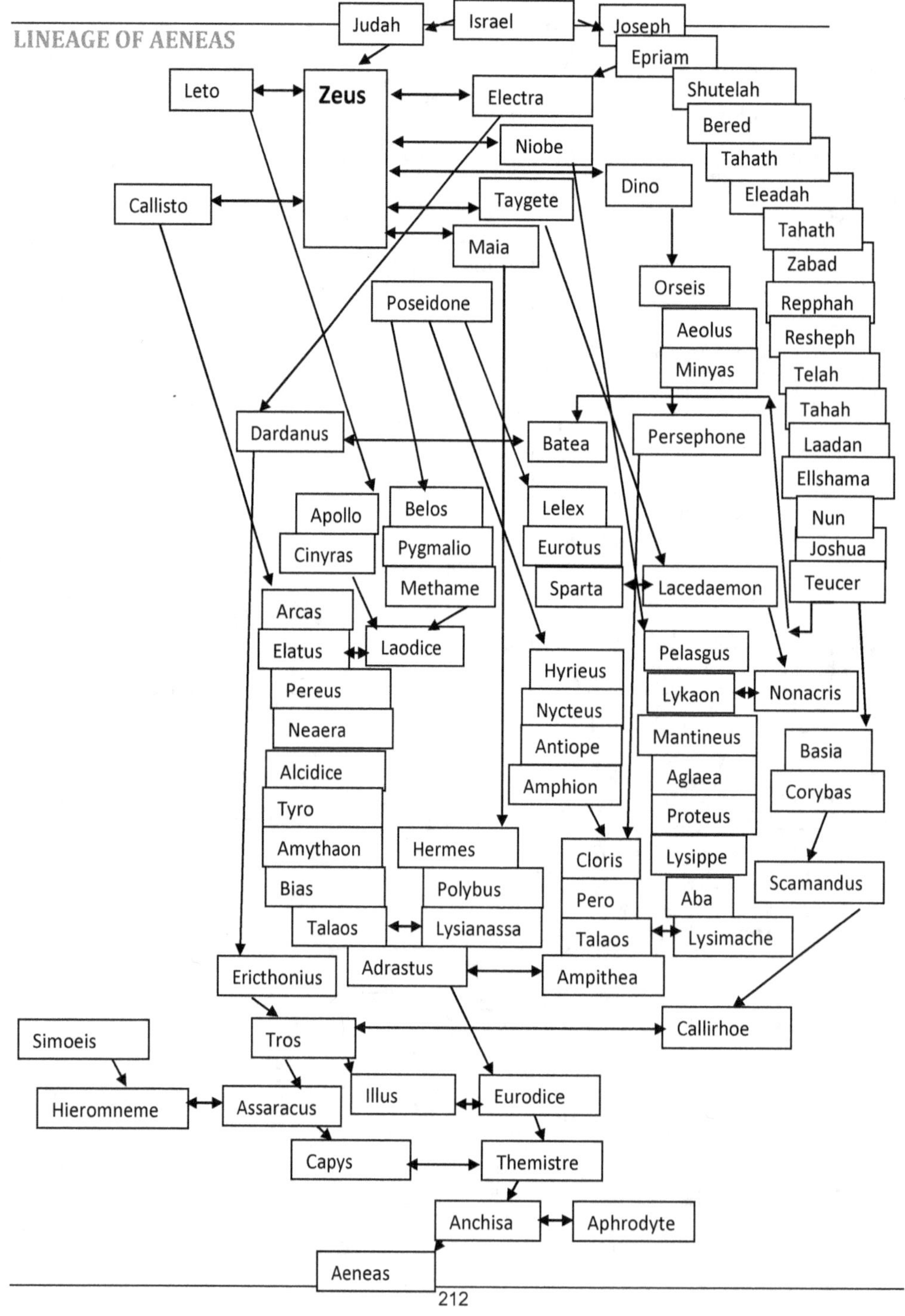
Judah
Israel
Joseph
Epriam
Leto
Zeus
Electra
Shutelah
Bered
Niobe
Tahath
Dino
Eleadah
Callisto
Taygete
Tahath
Maia
Zabad
Orseis
Poseidone
Repphah
Aeolus
Resheph
Minyas
Telah
Tahah
Dardanus
Batea
Persephone
Laadan
Ellshama
Apollo
Belos
Lelex
Nun
Cinyras
Pygmalio
Eurotus
Joshua
Methame
Sparta
Lacedaemon
Teucer
Arcas
Elatus
Laodice
Pelasgus
Hyrieus
Pereus
Lykaon
Nonacris
Nycteus
Neaera
Mantineus
Basia
Antiope
Alcidice
Aglaea
Corybas
Amphion
Tyro
Proteus
Amythaon
Hermes
Cloris
Lysippe
Scamandus
Bias
Polybus
Pero
Aba
Talaos
Lysianassa
Talaos
Lysimache
Adrastus
Ericthonius
Ampithea
Callirhoe
Simoeis
Tros
Illus
Eurodice
Hieromneme
Assaracus
Capys
Themistre
Anchisa
Aphrodyte
Aeneas

The lineage of Aeneas shows his relationship to his mother Aphrodyte. Note all the lineages here from Callirhoe who married Tros as related to Joshua son of Nun and also Euroduce who married Illus. Most of the Greek lineages are hidden, not mentioned in the bible, and the amount of people who used the same name is small. There are not eight or ten people thru the generations all with the same name. There is lineage shown in the Charts of Zeus that also show Poiseidon. Most of Joshua's lineage is funneled thru the descendent Antenor that leads to the Franks. He also had Teucer that has two lines that join with the Greek lines from Zeus son of Cronos. Some say Cronos is Judah, others Jacob, and in the genealogy this is one place that is illustrated both ways.

Now Joshua would have descendents thru Teucer joining the Greek lines to Callirhoe and Tros and Batea and Dardanus. Joshua also had Rahab and her daughter is very close to Jeremiah and Ezra. Joshua also had a son Antenor and this son's line lead to Charlemange and the Franks, who became a world power. In the lineage of Illus there is quite a few descendents of Poiseidon. Poiseidon's father was also Cronos, so he may have been any one of the sons of Israel, or Israel himself. That would depend on if Cronos is Israel or Judah or another figure. In the Greek lineages that are studied there is not that much agreement on which lineage is true or not, there is a large amount of disparity in the lineages. Duplications of descendents and ancestors and different ideas about which is right coupled with the idea of Greek Myth for the "story" that goes with each ancestor lead one to believe that it may not be that important for the lineages of Zeus to be found correct. With Greece as one of the more violent republics with Athens and Spartica and other Cities and rulers claiming descent from Hercules, Apollo, and other deities it is not difficult to assume that the correct geneology might win the war of each City State against another. Some of the Greek deities names are known among the living people, Apollo for example being a well used name. Zeus himself would have to be one of the more successful fathers, with 28 wives and 42 children or there about, he would have had to have started being a father at about 12 to 15 years old and have lived to be well over 120 years old for some of the relationships shown to have come true. The only other figure found in genealogy similar to this is Saint Brychan who had about 40 to 50 Children, however with only two wives.

There are many what the author will call loops of lines that have twenty or thirty generations thru one line and ten or twelve to another line. This is true of the lineage of Alexander the great who has about thirty plus generations thru his Father Phillip of Macedonia to his ancestor Hercules son of Zeus and about ten or twelve generations thru his mother Olympia to Helen daughter of Zeus. If the twenty or thirty generations averaged 15 years to have a son, and the ten generations averaged 50 years to have a son or daughter this works out mathematically and is entirely possible.

All the lineages of the Greek charts shown show that there are a lot of generations between sons and daughters of Zeus. It is remarkable however possible that Zeus just watched over 42 Children and tried to seduce them (if female) to have more children thru about 110 years of life as a fertile strong male. In a culture based on war the side with the more male soldiers would likely win. Anyone who could father would be encouraged to .

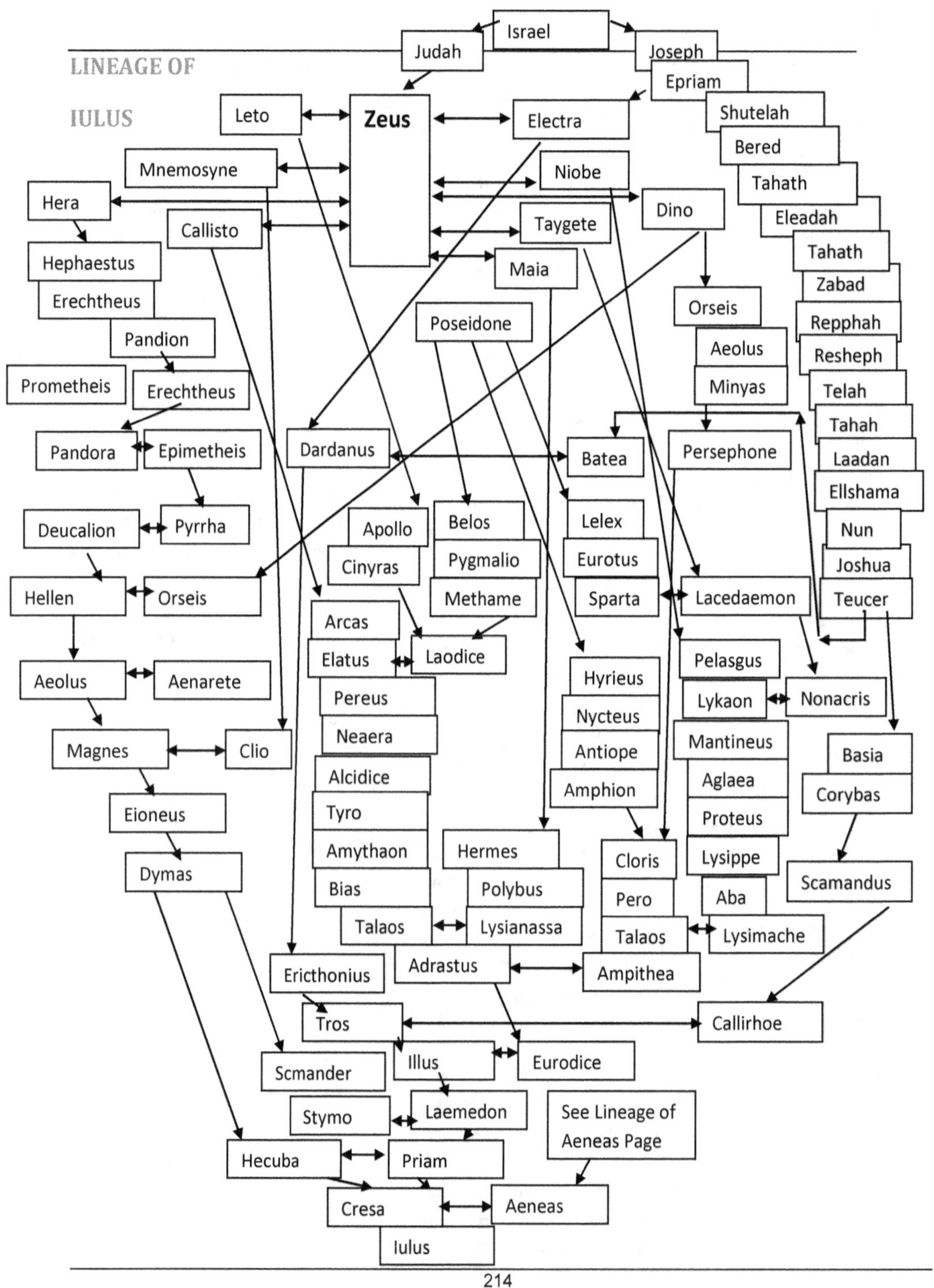
LINEAGE OF IULUS
Israel
Judah
Joseph
Epriam
Shutelah
Bered
Tahath
Eleadah
Tahath
Zabad
Repphah
Resheph
Telah
Tahah
Laadan
Ellshama
Nun
Joshua
Teucer
Leto
Zeus
Electra
Mnemosyne
Niobe
Hera
Callisto
Dino
Taygete
Maia
Hephaestus
Erechtheus
Pandion
Prometheis
Erechtheus
Pandora
Epimetheis
Deucalion
Pyrrha
Hellen
Orseis
Aeolus
Aenarete
Magnes
Clio
Eioneus
Dymas
Poseidone
Orseis
Aeolus
Minyas
Persephone
Dardanus
Batea
Apollo
Belos
Cinyras
Pygmalio
Methame
Lelex
Eurotus
Sparta
Lacedaemon
Arcas
Elatus
Laodice
Pereus
Neaera
Alcidice
Tyro
Amythaon
Bias
Talaos
Lysianassa
Hermes
Polybus
Hyrieus
Nycteus
Antiope
Amphion
Pelasgus
Lykaon
Nonacris
Mantineus
Aglaea
Proteus
Lysippe
Aba
Basia
Corybas
Scamandus
Cloris
Pero
Talaos
Lysimache
Ericthonius
Adrastus
Ampithea
Tros
Callirhoe
Scmander
Illus
Eurodice
Stymo
Laemedon
See Lineage of Aeneas Page
Hecuba
Priam
Cresa
Aeneas
Iulus

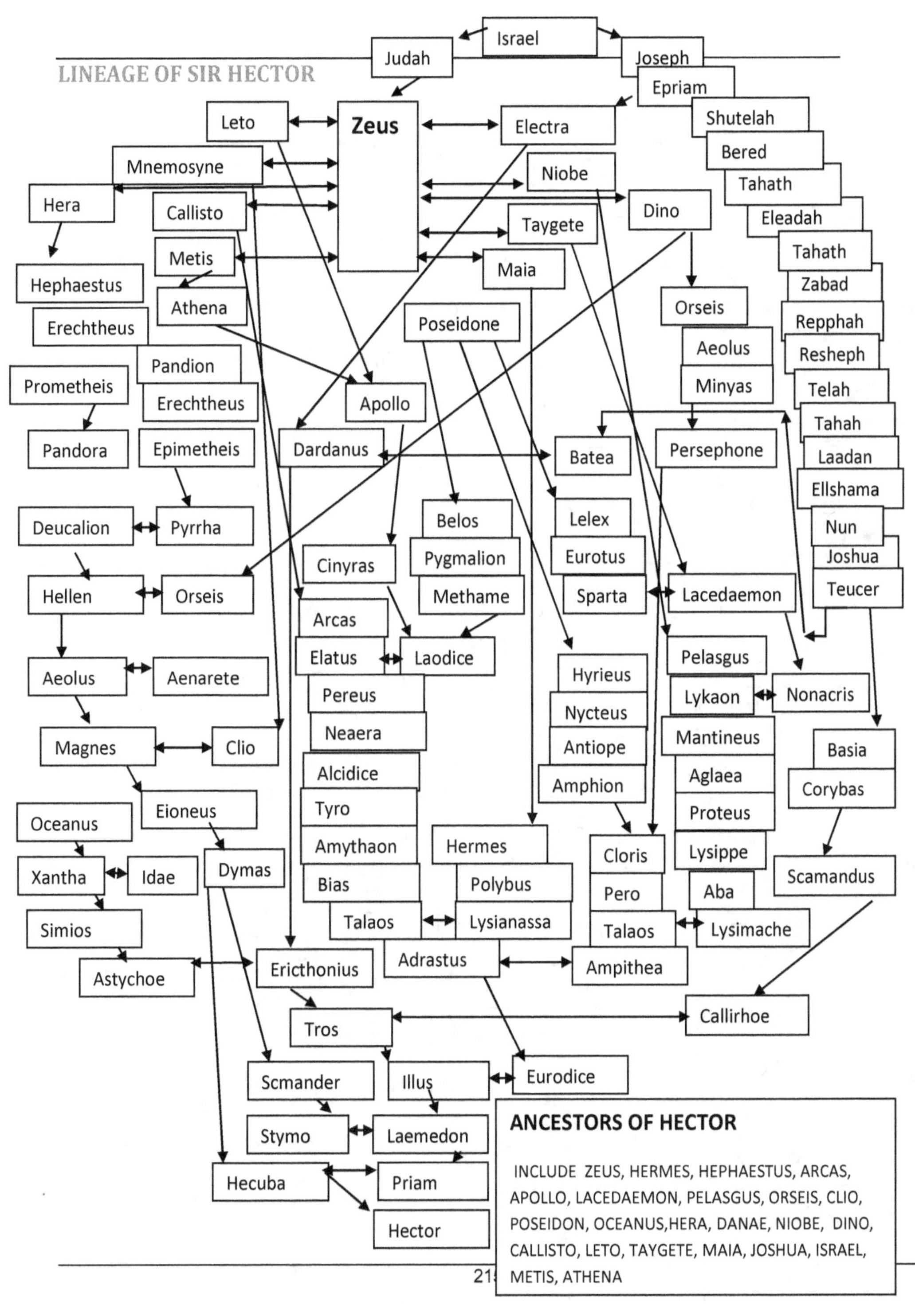
LINEAGE OF SIR HECTOR
Israel
Judah
Joseph
Epriam
Shutelah
Bered
Tahath
Eleadah
Tahath
Zabad
Repphah
Resheph
Telah
Tahah
Laadan
Ellshama
Nun
Joshua
Teucer
Leto
Zeus
Electra
Mnemosyne
Niobe
Hera
Callisto
Dino
Taygete
Metis
Maia
Hephaestus
Athena
Erechtheus
Poseidone
Orseis
Aeolus
Pandion
Minyas
Prometheis
Erechtheus
Apollo
Pandora
Epimetheis
Dardanus
Batea
Persephone
Belos
Lelex
Deucalion
Pyrrha
Cinyras
Pygmalion
Eurotus
Hellen
Orseis
Methame
Sparta
Lacedaemon
Arcas
Elatus
Laodice
Pelasgus
Aeolus
Aenarete
Hyrieus
Lykaon
Nonacris
Pereus
Nycteus
Neaera
Mantineus
Basia
Magnes
Clio
Antiope
Alcidice
Aglaea
Corybas
Amphion
Eioneus
Tyro
Proteus
Oceanus
Amythaon
Hermes
Cloris
Lysippe
Scamandus
Xantha
Idae
Dymas
Bias
Polybus
Pero
Aba
Simios
Talaos
Lysianassa
Talaos
Lysimache
Adrastus
Astychoe
Ericthonius
Ampithea
Tros
Callirhoe
Scmander
Illus
Eurodice
Stymo
Laemedon
Hecuba
Priam
Hector
ANCESTORS OF HECTOR
INCLUDE ZEUS, HERMES, HEPHAESTUS, ARCAS, APOLLO, LACEDAEMON, PELASGUS, ORSEIS, CLIO, POSEIDON, OCEANUS,HERA, DANAE, NIOBE, DINO, CALLISTO, LETO, TAYGETE, MAIA, JOSHUA, ISRAEL, METIS, ATHENA

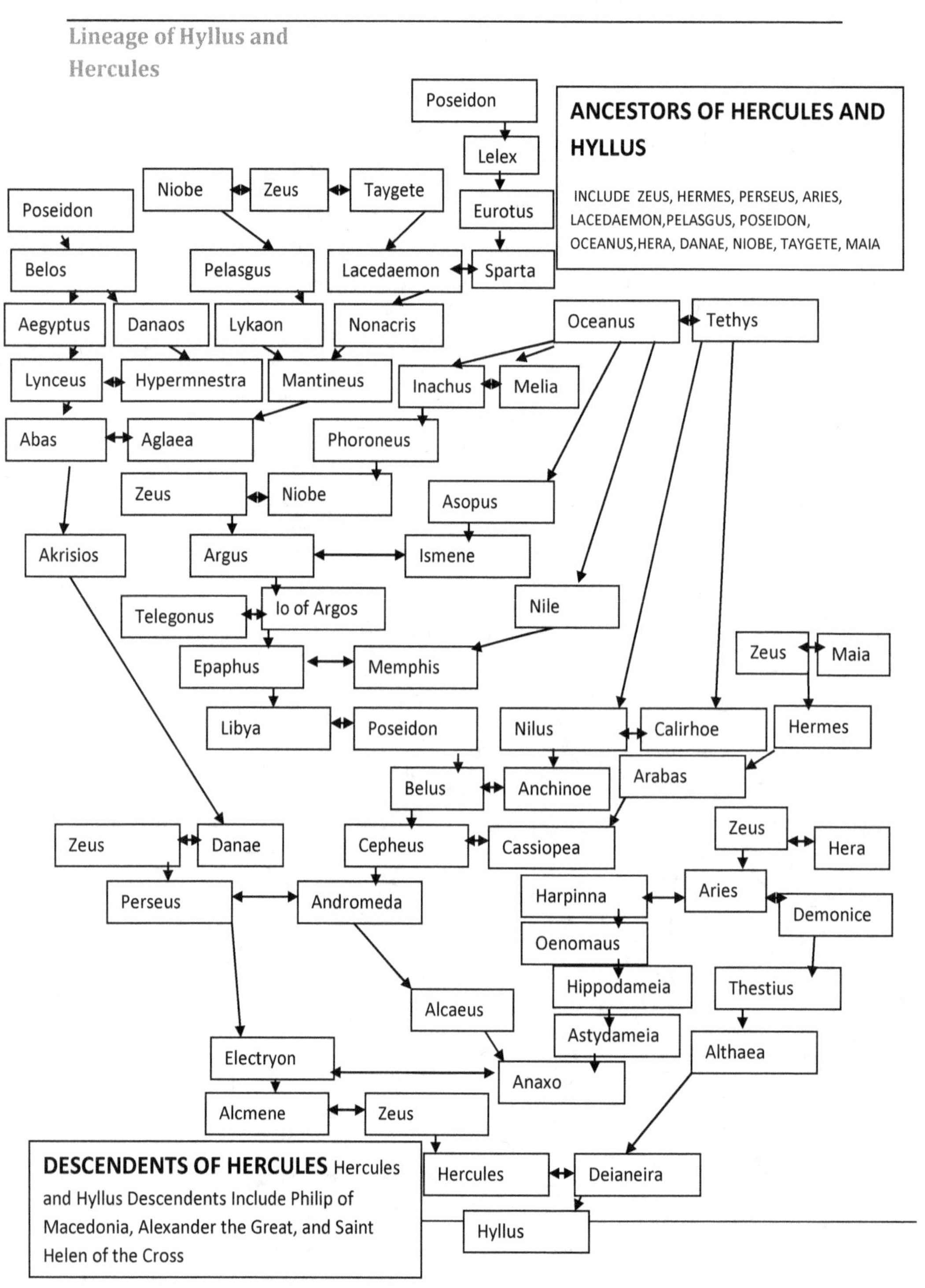

Lineage of Hyllus and Hercules
Poseidon
Lelex
Eurotus
Sparta
ANCESTORS OF HERCULES AND HYLLUS
INCLUDE ZEUS, HERMES, PERSEUS, ARIES, LACEDAEMON,PELASGUS, POSEIDON, OCEANUS,HERA, DANAE, NIOBE, TAYGETE, MAIA
Niobe
Zeus
Taygete
Poseidon
Belos
Pelasgus
Lacedaemon
Aegyptus
Danaos
Lykaon
Nonacris
Oceanus
Tethys
Lynceus
Hypermnestra
Mantineus
Inachus
Melia
Abas
Aglaea
Phoroneus
Zeus
Niobe
Asopus
Akrisios
Argus
Ismene
Telegonus
Io of Argos
Nile
Epaphus
Memphis
Zeus
Maia
Libya
Poseidon
Nilus
Calirhoe
Hermes
Belus
Anchinoe
Arabas
Zeus
Danae
Cepheus
Cassiopea
Zeus
Hera
Perseus
Andromeda
Harpinna
Aries
Demonice
Oenomaus
Hippodameia
Thestius
Alcaeus
Astydameia
Althaea
Electryon
Anaxo
Alcmene
Zeus
DESCENDENTS OF HERCULES Hercules and Hyllus Descendents Include Philip of Macedonia, Alexander the Great, and Saint Helen of the Cross
Hercules
Deianeira
Hyllus

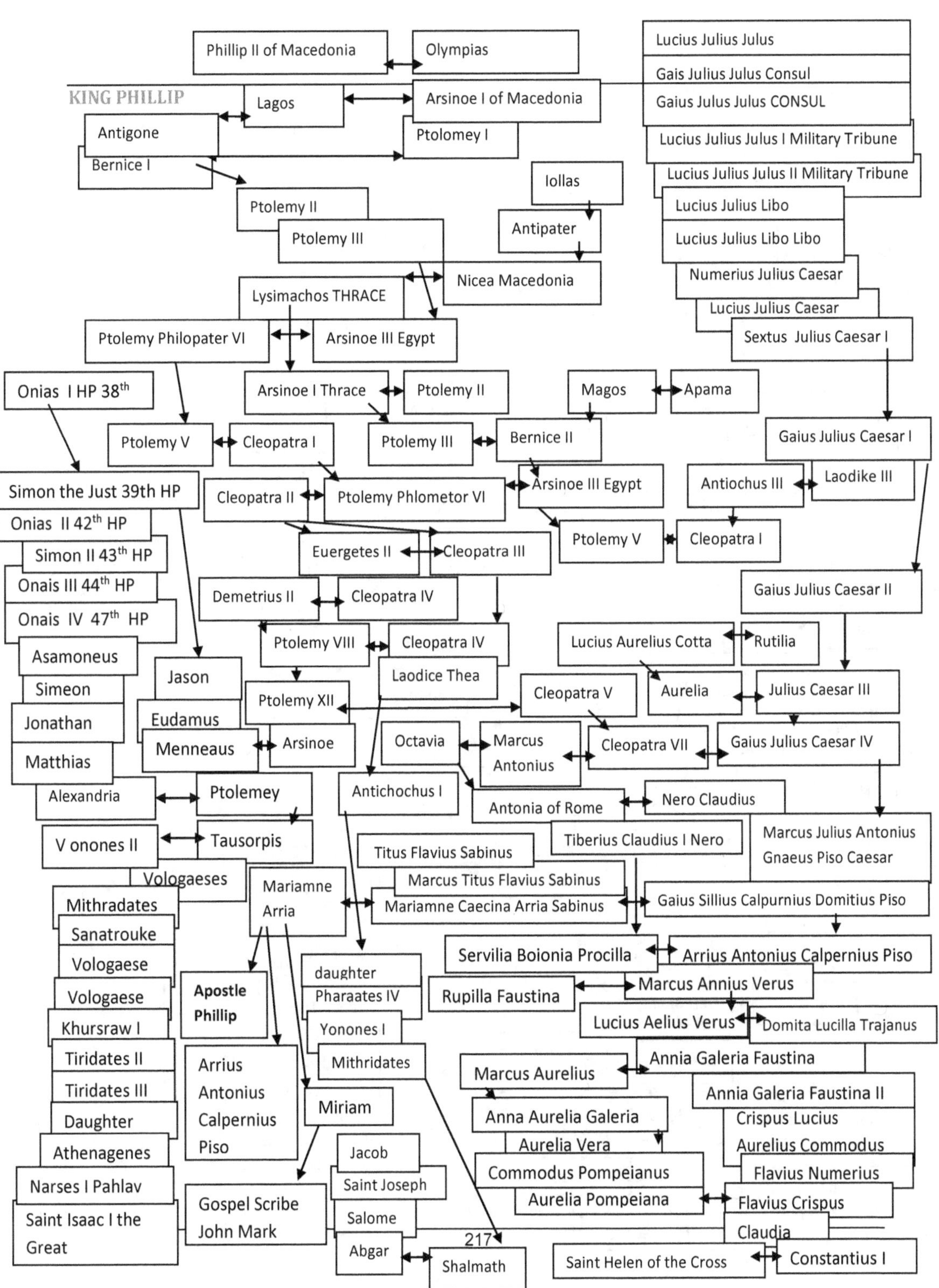
Phillip II of Macedonia
Olympias
KING PHILLIP
Lagos
Arsinoe I of Macedonia
Antigone
Bernice I
Ptolomey I
Ptolemy II
Ptolemy III
Iollas
Antipater
Nicea Macedonia
Lysimachos THRACE
Ptolemy Philopater VI
Arsinoe III Egypt
Lucius Julius Julus
Gais Julius Julus Consul
Gaius Julius Julus CONSUL
Lucius Julius Julus I Military Tribune
Lucius Julius Julus II Military Tribune
Lucius Julius Libo
Lucius Julius Libo Libo
Numerius Julius Caesar
Lucius Julius Caesar
Sextus Julius Caesar I
Onias I HP 38th
Arsinoe I Thrace
Ptolemy II
Magos
Apama
Ptolemy V
Cleopatra I
Ptolemy III
Bernice II
Gaius Julius Caesar I
Simon the Just 39th HP
Onias II 42th HP
Simon II 43th HP
Onais III 44th HP
Onais IV 47th HP
Cleopatra II
Ptolemy Phlometor VI
Arsinoe III Egypt
Antiochus III
Laodike III
Euergetes II
Cleopatra III
Ptolemy V
Cleopatra I
Gaius Julius Caesar II
Demetrius II
Cleopatra IV
Asamoneus
Simeon
Jonathan
Matthias
Jason
Eudamus
Menneaus
Arsinoe
Ptolemy VIII
Cleopatra IV
Laodice Thea
Ptolemy XII
Lucius Aurelius Cotta
Rutilia
Cleopatra V
Aurelia
Julius Caesar III
Octavia
Marcus Antonius
Cleopatra VII
Gaius Julius Caesar IV
Alexandria
Ptolemey
Antichochus I
Antonia of Rome
Nero Claudius
V onones II
Tausorpis
Titus Flavius Sabinus
Tiberius Claudius I Nero
Marcus Julius Antonius Gnaeus Piso Caesar
Vologaeses
Mariamne Arria
Marcus Titus Flavius Sabinus
Mariamne Caecina Arria Sabinus
Gaius Sillius Calpurnius Domitius Piso
Mithradates
Sanatrouke
Vologaese
Vologaese
Khursraw I
Tiridates II
Tiridates III
Daughter
Athenagenes
Narses I Pahlav
Saint Isaac I the Great
Apostle Phillip
Arrius Antonius Calpernius Piso
daughter
Pharaates IV
Yonones I
Mithridates
Miriam
Jacob
Saint Joseph
Salome
Abgar
Shalmath
Gospel Scribe John Mark
Servilia Boionia Procilla
Arrius Antonius Calpernius Piso
Rupilla Faustina
Marcus Annius Verus
Lucius Aelius Verus
Domita Lucilla Trajanus
Annia Galeria Faustina
Marcus Aurelius
Annia Galeria Faustina II
Anna Aurelia Galeria
Aurelia Vera
Crispus Lucius Aurelius Commodus
Commodus Pompeianus
Flavius Numerius
Aurelia Pompeiana
Flavius Crispus
Claudia
Saint Helen of the Cross
Constantius I

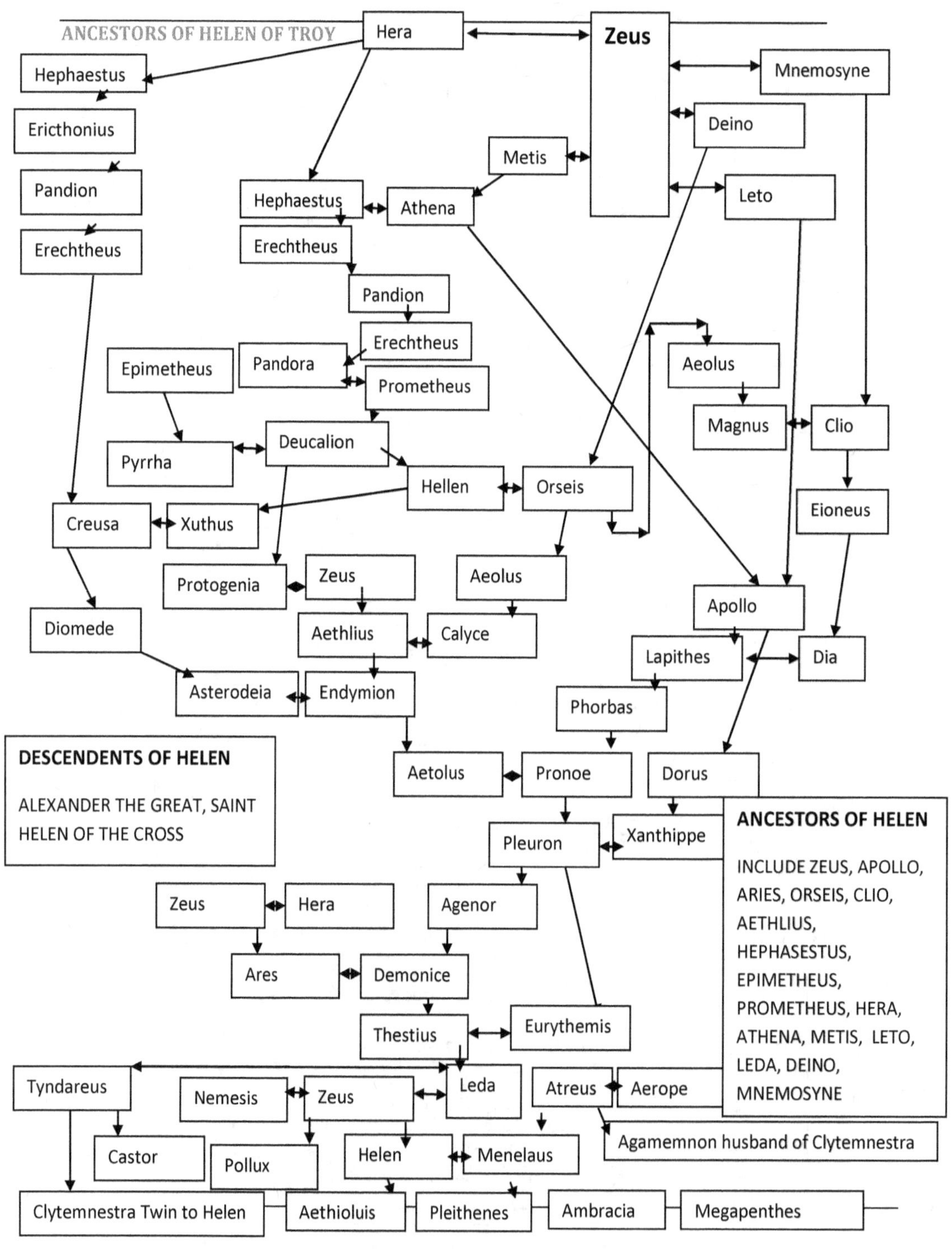
ANCESTORS OF HELEN OF TROY
Hera
Zeus
Hephaestus
Mnemosyne
Ericthonius
Deino
Metis
Pandion
Hephaestus
Athena
Leto
Erechtheus
Erechtheus
Pandion
Erechtheus
Epimetheus
Pandora
Prometheus
Aeolus
Magnus
Clio
Deucalion
Pyrrha
Hellen
Orseis
Eioneus
Creusa
Xuthus
Protogenia
Zeus
Aeolus
Apollo
Diomede
Aethlius
Calyce
Lapithes
Dia
Asterodeia
Endymion
Phorbas
DESCENDENTS OF HELEN
ALEXANDER THE GREAT, SAINT HELEN OF THE CROSS
Aetolus
Pronoe
Dorus
Pleuron
Xanthippe
ANCESTORS OF HELEN
INCLUDE ZEUS, APOLLO, ARIES, ORSEIS, CLIO, AETHLIUS, HEPHASESTUS, EPIMETHEUS, PROMETHEUS, HERA, ATHENA, METIS, LETO, LEDA, DEINO, MNEMOSYNE
Zeus
Hera
Agenor
Ares
Demonice
Thestius
Eurythemis
Tyndareus
Leda
Nemesis
Zeus
Atreus
Aerope
Agamemnon husband of Clytemnestra
Castor
Pollux
Helen
Menelaus
Clytemnestra Twin to Helen
Aethioluis
Pleithenes
Ambracia
Megapenthes

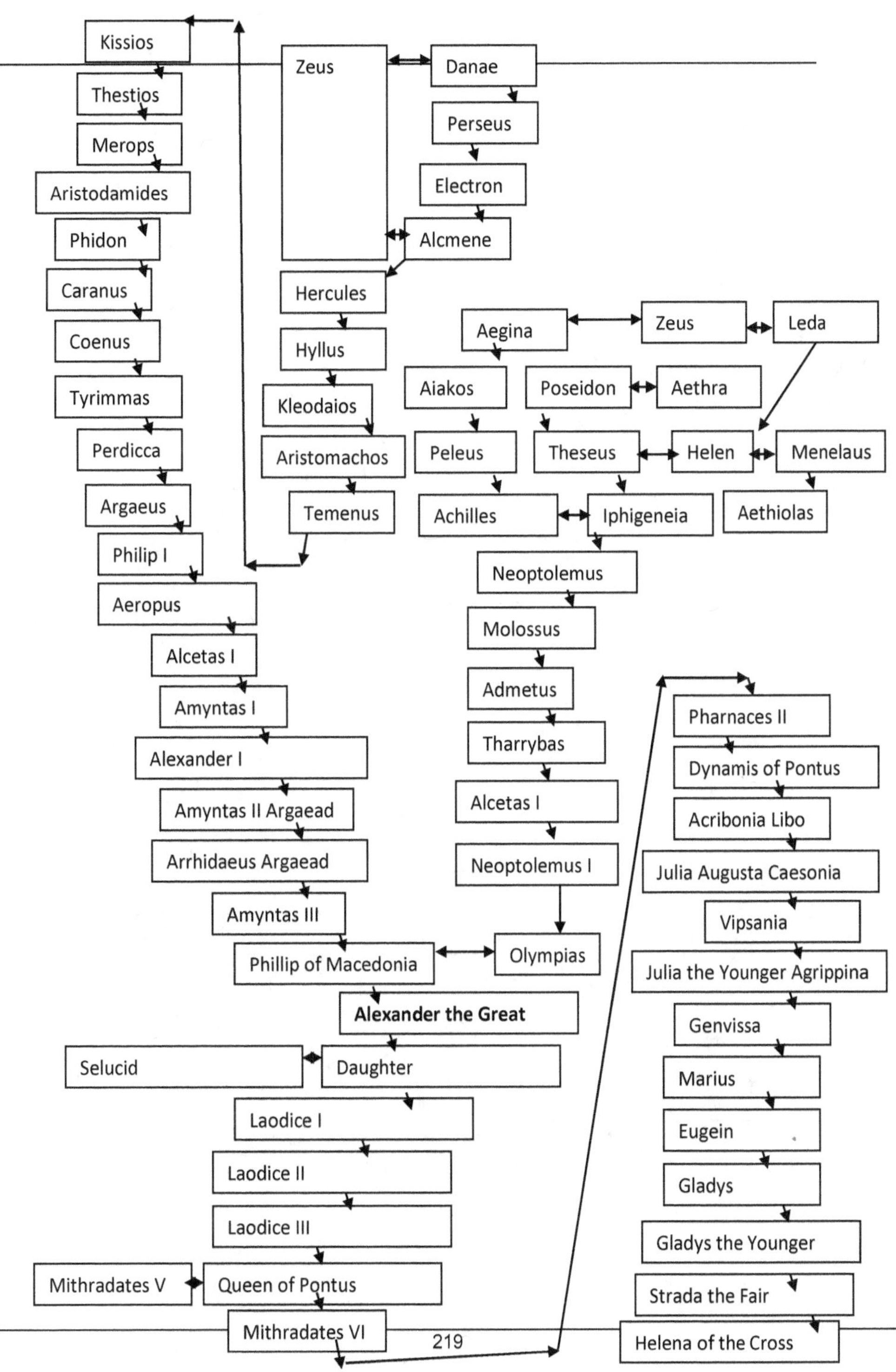
Kissios
Thestios
Merops
Aristodamides
Phidon
Caranus
Coenus
Tyrimmas
Perdicca
Argaeus
Philip I
Aeropus
Alcetas I
Amyntas I
Alexander I
Amyntas II Argaead
Arrhidaeus Argaead
Amyntas III
Phillip of Macedonia
Zeus
Danae
Perseus
Electron
Alcmene
Hercules
Hyllus
Kleodaios
Aristomachos
Temenus
Aegina
Zeus
Leda
Aiakos
Poseidon
Aethra
Peleus
Theseus
Helen
Menelaus
Achilles
Iphigeneia
Aethiolas
Neoptolemus
Molossus
Admetus
Tharrybas
Alcetas I
Neoptolemus I
Olympias
Alexander the Great
Selucid
Daughter
Laodice I
Laodice II
Laodice III
Mithradates V
Queen of Pontus
Mithradates VI
Pharnaces II
Dynamis of Pontus
Acribonia Libo
Julia Augusta Caesonia
Vipsania
Julia the Younger Agrippina
Genvissa
Marius
Eugein
Gladys
Gladys the Younger
Strada the Fair
Helena of the Cross

Here is a genealogy found on the internet. It is interesting because it contains both Nimrod and Abraham. Also Thamar is shown to have the lineage the same as Tamar wife of Judah. Perhaps here Judah is Jupiter II (Cambo Blascon) Note the son Jasius who leads to Faunus and Vulcan whose line ties into Brutus. Perhaps here a Reference is made to Jupiter II instead of Jupiter due to this being the second marriage of Tamar, not to Judah but to a descendent of Nimrod.

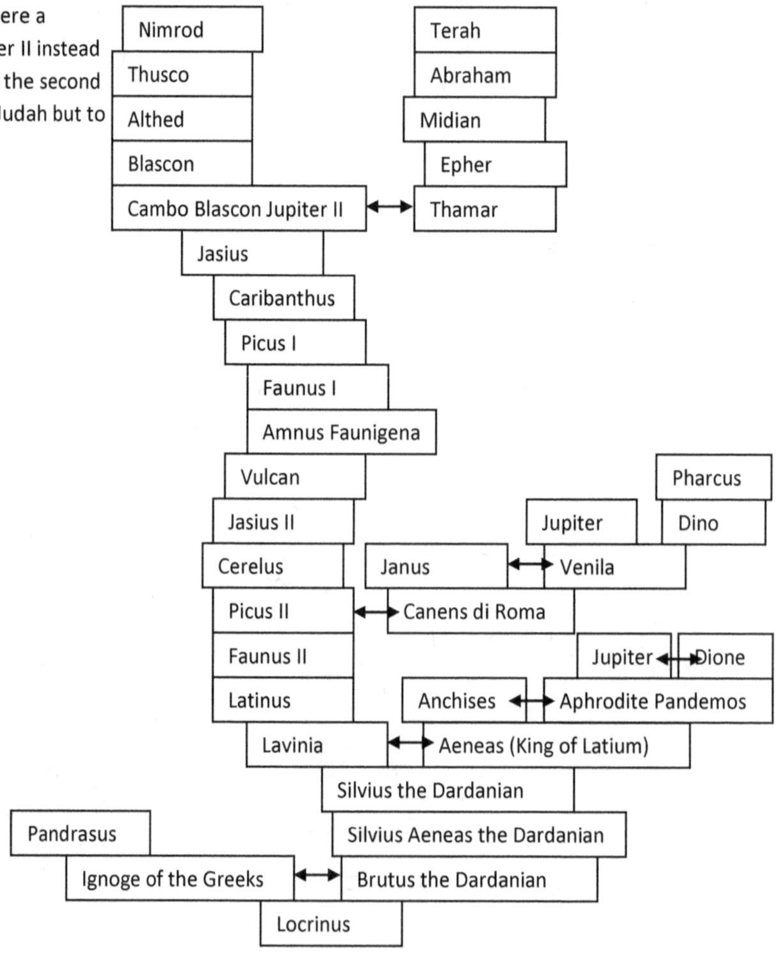

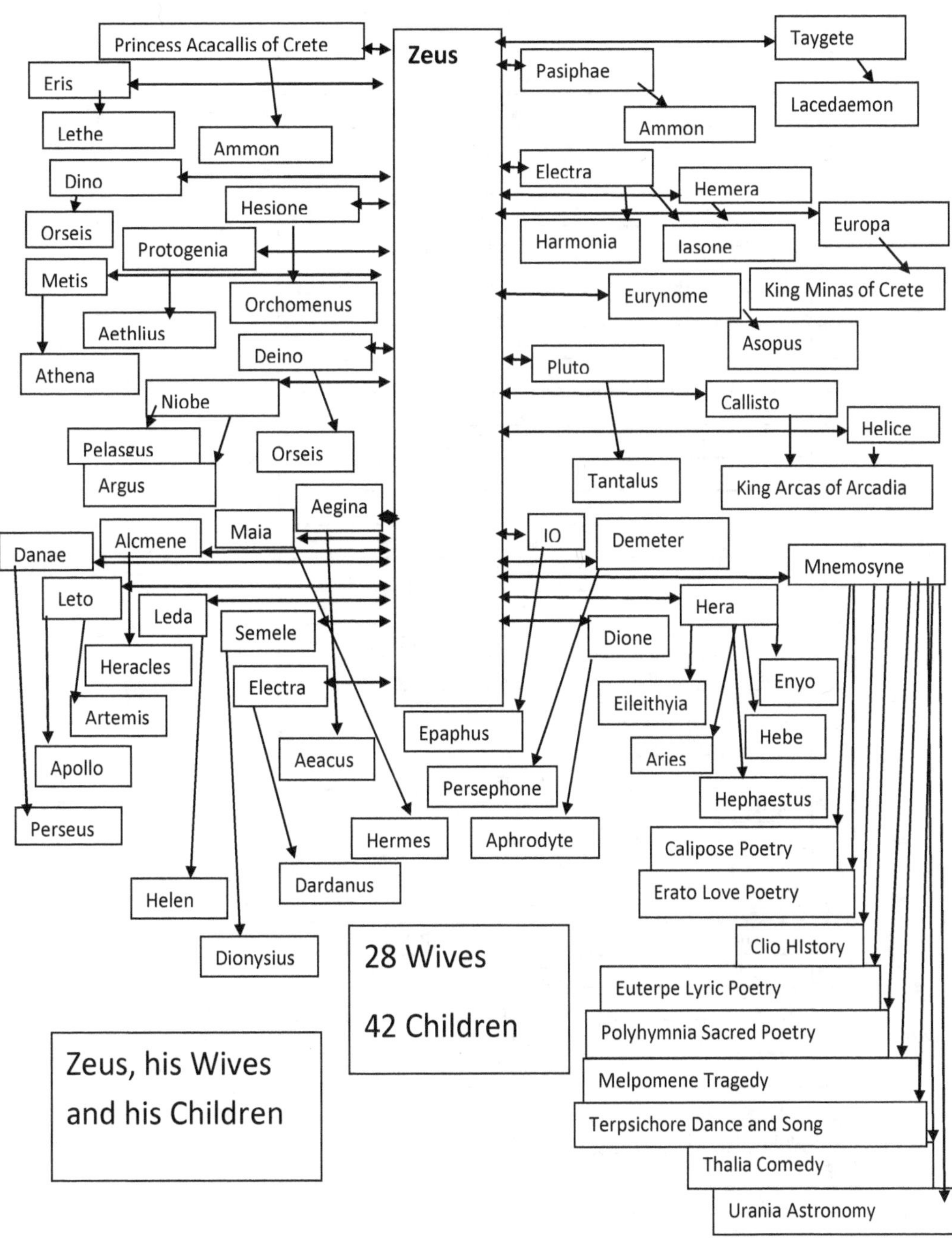
Zeus
Princess Acacallis of Crete
Eris
Lethe
Ammon
Dino
Orseis
Hesione
Protogenia
Metis
Orchomenus
Aethlius
Athena
Deino
Niobe
Pelasgus
Argus
Orseis
Aegina
Maia
Alcmene
Danae
Leto
Leda
Semele
Heracles
Electra
Artemis
Apollo
Aeacus
Perseus
Hermes
Dardanus
Helen
Dionysius
Taygete
Lacedaemon
Pasiphae
Ammon
Electra
Hemera
Europa
Harmonia
Iasone
King Minas of Crete
Eurynome
Asopus
Pluto
Callisto
Helice
Tantalus
King Arcas of Arcadia
IO
Demeter
Mnemosyne
Hera
Dione
Enyo
Eileithyia
Hebe
Epaphus
Aries
Persephone
Hephaestus
Aphrodyte
Calipose Poetry
Erato Love Poetry
Clio HIstory
Euterpe Lyric Poetry
Polyhymnia Sacred Poetry
Melpomene Tragedy
Terpsichore Dance and Song
Thalia Comedy
Urania Astronomy
28 Wives
42 Children
Zeus, his Wives and his Children

TABLE OF WIVES OF ZEUS AND THEIR CHILDREN

	Wife Greek	Wife Roman	Children Gr.	Children Roman
1	Hera	Juno	Aries	Mars
			Hephaestus	Vulcan
			Hebe	Juventas
			Enyo	Bellona
			Eileithyia	
2	Dione		Aphrodyte	Venus
3	Demeter	Ceres	Persephone	Proserpina
4	Mnemosyne		Calipose	
			Melpomene	
			Erato	Cupid
			Terpsichore	
			Clio	
			Euterpe	
			Urania	
			Thalia	
			Polyhymnia	
5	IO		Epaphus	
6	Aegina		Aeacus	
7	Maia		Hermes	Mercury
8	Semele	Stimula	Dionysius	Bachus
9	Electra		Dardanus	
			Harmonia	
			lasone	
10	Leda		Helen	
11	Leto	Latona	Apollo	
			Artemis	Diana
12	Danae		Perseus	
13	Alcmene		Heracles	Hercules
14	Deino		Orseis	
15	Niobe		Pelasgus	
			Argus	
16	Metis		Athena	Minerva
17	Protogenia		Aethilius	
18	Hesione		Orchomenus	
19	Acacallis		Ammon	

20	Eris	Discordia	Lethe	
21	Taygete		Lacedaemon	
22	Pasiphe		Ammon	
23	Hemera		Harmonia	
24	Europa		Minas	
25	Eurynome		Asopus	
26	Pluto		Tantalus	
27	Callisto		Arcas	
28	Helice		Arcas	

On the next page it looks impossible that the fifteen generations between Epriam and Batea could result in a marriage between Batea and Dardanus. Now suppose that Epriam was 12 years old and each line to Joshua as 12 years old. 12 x 15 is 180 years. Now if Epriam was 100 when he fathered Electra, and Electra was 100 when she gave birth to Dardanus this was possible. Zeus would also have been around 100 if he was the son of Judah who would have to have been very old when he fathered Zeus or Zerah. Unlikely, however not impossible. The argument is also taken with Callirhoe, whose line thru Epriam would have to be about 200 plus years and from Epriam to Tros only four generations. Unlikely yet possible.

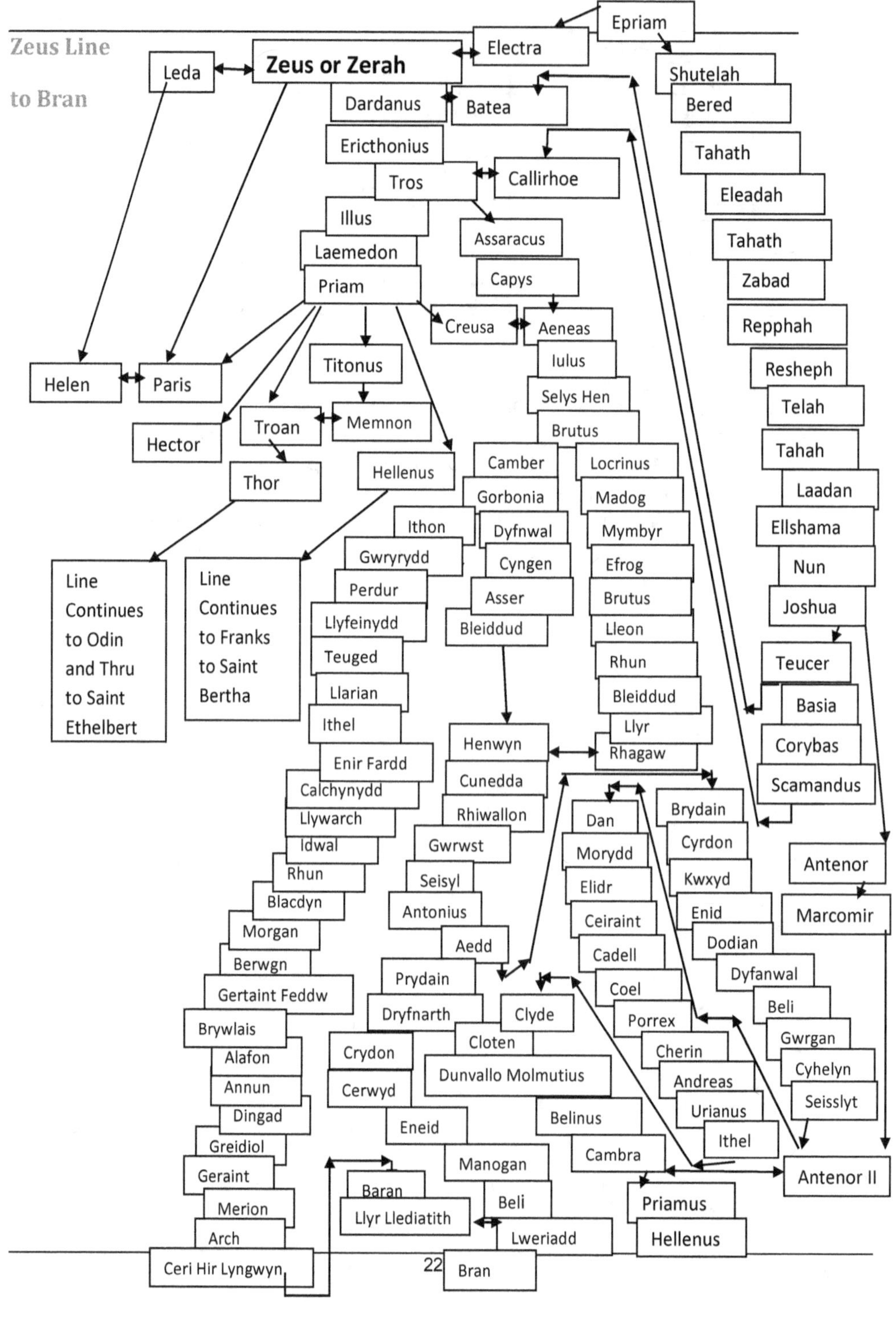

Zeus Line
to Bran
Epriam
Electra
Leda
Zeus or Zerah
Shutelah
Dardanus
Batea
Bered
Ericthonius
Tahath
Tros
Callirhoe
Eleadah
Illus
Assaracus
Tahath
Laemedon
Capys
Zabad
Priam
Creusa
Aeneas
Repphah
Iulus
Resheph
Helen
Paris
Titonus
Selys Hen
Telah
Hector
Troan
Memnon
Brutus
Tahah
Thor
Hellenus
Camber
Locrinus
Laadan
Gorbonia
Madog
Ithon
Dyfnwal
Mymbyr
Ellshama
Gwryrydd
Cyngen
Efrog
Nun
Line Continues to Odin and Thru to Saint Ethelbert
Line Continues to Franks to Saint Bertha
Perdur
Asser
Brutus
Joshua
Llyfeinydd
Bleiddud
Lleon
Teuged
Rhun
Teucer
Llarian
Bleiddud
Basia
Ithel
Llyr
Henwyn
Rhagaw
Corybas
Enir Fardd
Cunedda
Scamandus
Calchynydd
Brydain
Rhiwallon
Dan
Llywarch
Cyrdon
Idwal
Gwrwst
Morydd
Antenor
Kwxyd
Rhun
Seisyl
Elidr
Blacdyn
Enid
Marcomir
Antonius
Ceiraint
Morgan
Dodian
Aedd
Cadell
Berwgn
Dyfanwal
Prydain
Coel
Gertaint Feddw
Beli
Dryfnarth
Clyde
Porrex
Brywlais
Gwrgan
Cloten
Cherin
Crydon
Alafon
Cyhelyn
Dunvallo Molmutius
Andreas
Annun
Cerwyd
Urianus
Seisslyt
Dingad
Belinus
Eneid
Ithel
Greidiol
Cambra
Manogan
Antenor II
Geraint
Baran
Beli
Priamus
Merion
Llyr Llediatith
Lweriadd
Hellenus
Arch
Ceri Hir Lyngwyn
Bran

Zeus and His Family

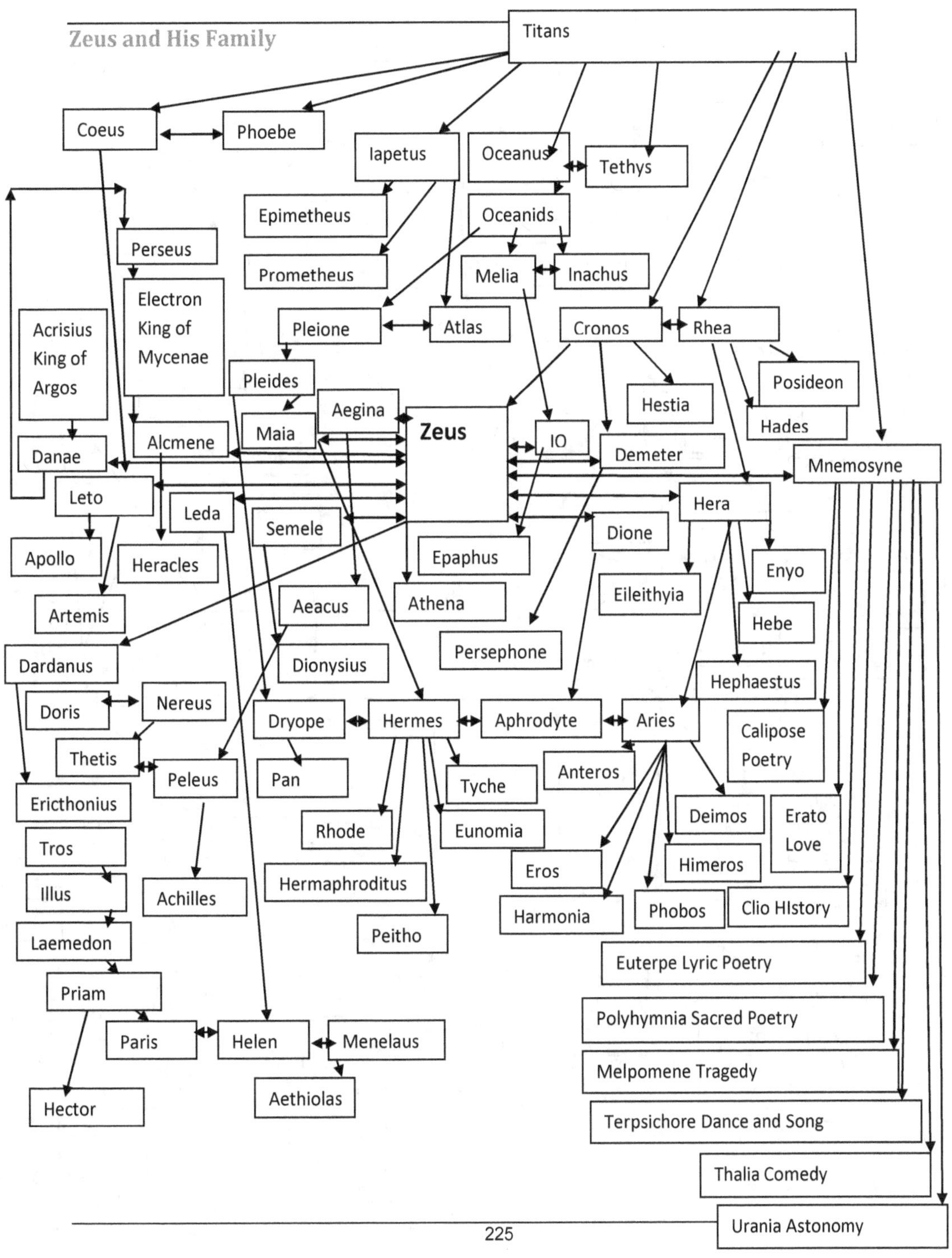

Zeus and His Family

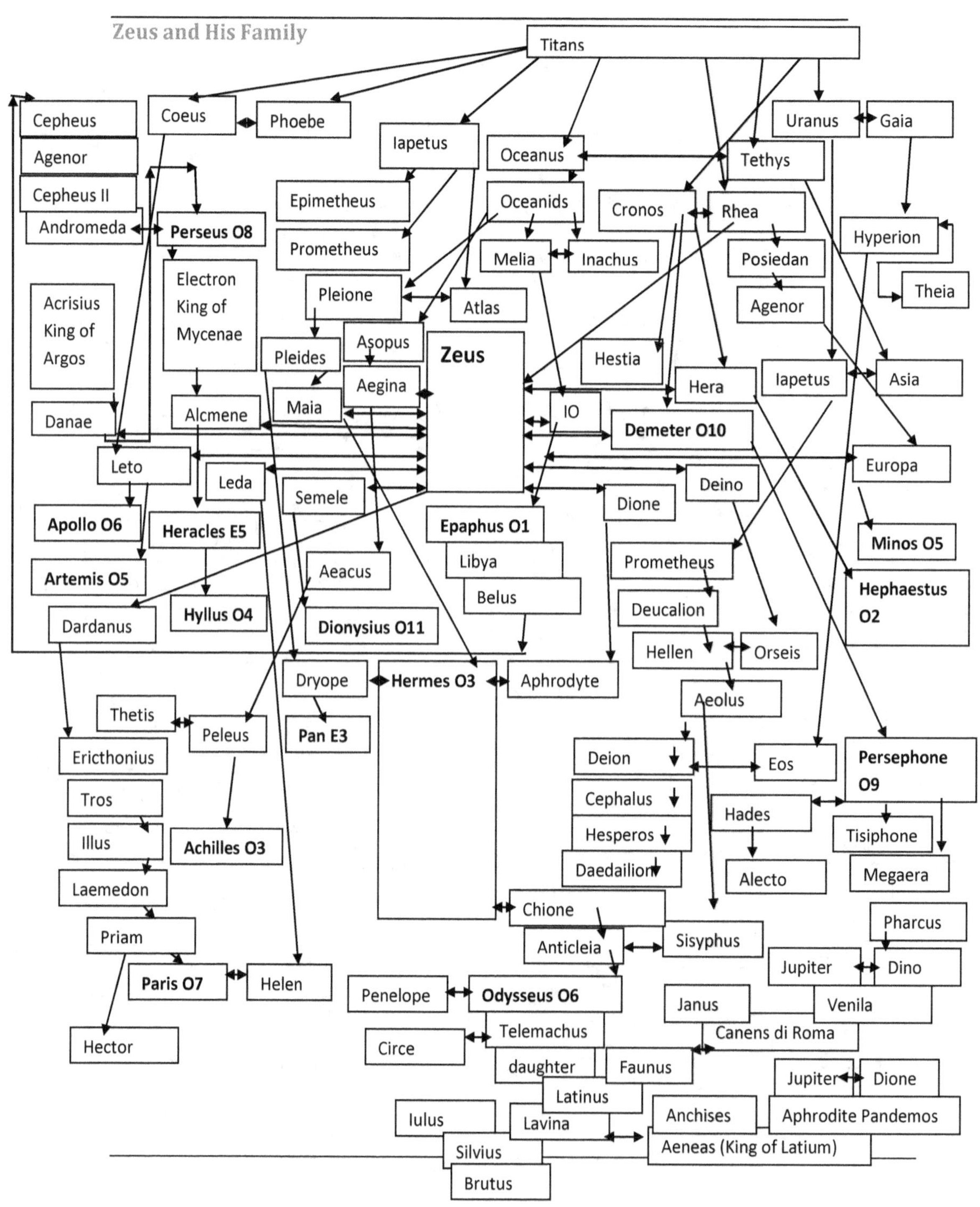

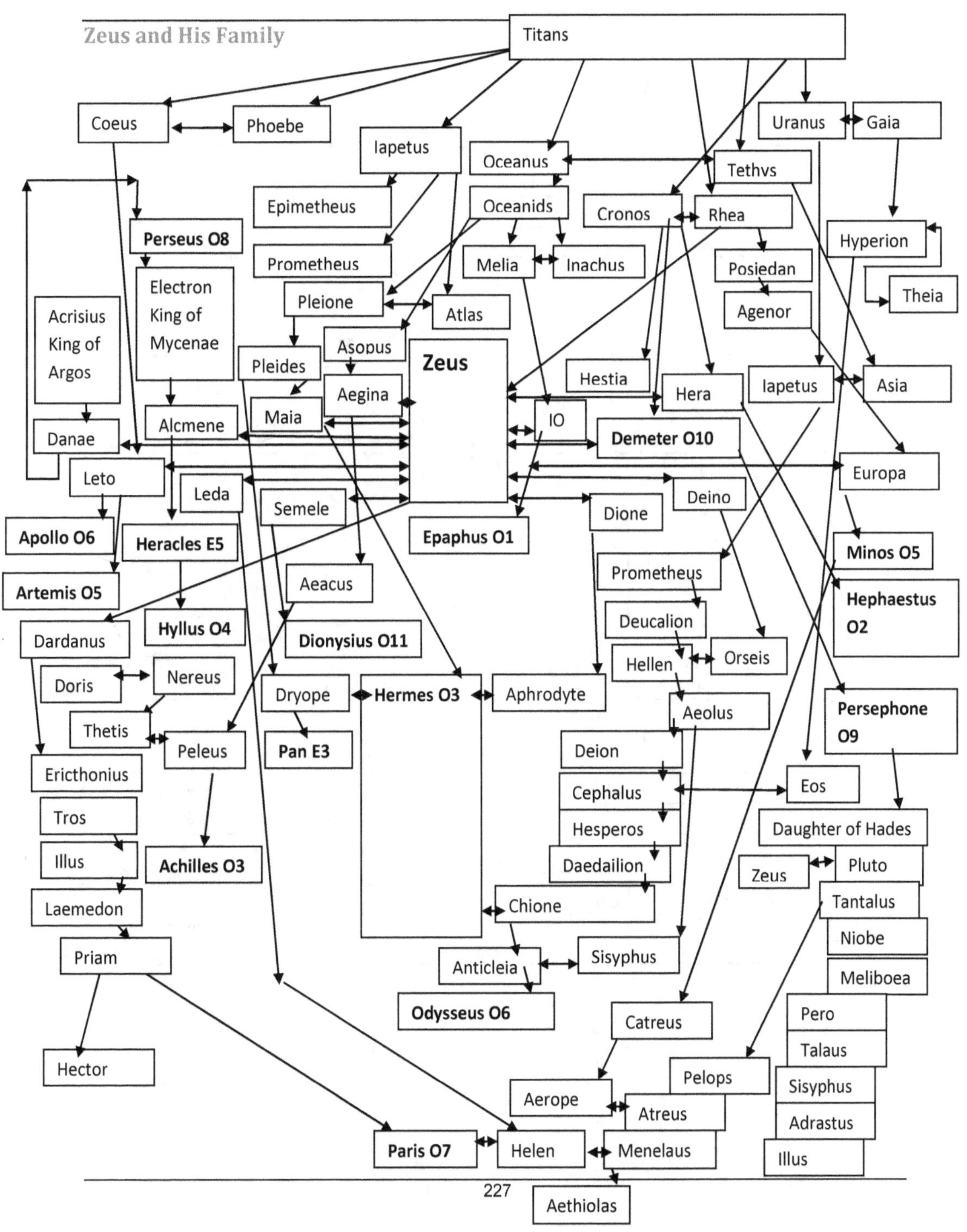
Titans
Coeus
Phoebe
Iapetus
Oceanus
Tethys
Uranus
Gaia
Epimetheus
Oceanids
Cronos
Rhea
Hyperion
Perseus O8
Prometheus
Melia
Inachus
Posiedan
Theia
Electron King of Mycenae
Pleione
Atlas
Agenor
Acrisius King of Argos
Asopus
Zeus
Pleides
Hestia
Iapetus
Asia
Hera
Aegina
Maia
IO
Alcmene
Danae
Demeter O10
Leto
Europa
Leda
Semele
Deino
Dione
Apollo O6
Heracles E5
Epaphus O1
Minos O5
Aeacus
Prometheus
Artemis O5
Hephaestus O2
Hyllus O4
Dionysius O11
Deucalion
Dardanus
Hellen
Orseis
Doris
Nereus
Dryope
Hermes O3
Aphrodyte
Persephone O9
Aeolus
Thetis
Peleus
Pan E3
Deion
Ericthonius
Cephalus
Eos
Tros
Hesperos
Daughter of Hades
Illus
Achilles O3
Daedailion
Zeus
Pluto
Laemedon
Chione
Tantalus
Priam
Niobe
Anticleia
Sisyphus
Meliboea
Odysseus O6
Catreus
Pero
Talaus
Hector
Pelops
Sisyphus
Aerope
Atreus
Adrastus
Paris O7
Helen
Menelaus
Illus
Aethiolas

SECTION FOURTEEN :ROMAN AND RANKS

The Law related to Military Rank, Greek, Roman, and Hebrew Saints and Gods.

Noble Rank	Greek Diety	Roman Diety		Apostle	Military Rank
squire	Pan	Faunus	E3		Lance Corporal
	Heracles	Hercules	E5-E10		Sargent
Lord	Ephasus for Land or Hephaestus for Sea	Vulcan	O1	Saint Judas Thaddeus	2nd Lietenant
Knight	Hermes for Sea or Hephaestus for Land	Mercury	O2	Saint Mathew	1st Lieutenant
Barron	Achilles for Sea or Hermes for land		O3	Saint Andrew	Captain
Count	Hyllus son of Deinaria and Heracles		O4	Saint James the Lesser	Major
Earle	Artemis for Sea or Minos for land	Diana	O5	Saint Simon	Lt Colonel or First Mate
Duke	Odysseus for Sea or Apollo for land	Ulysses for Sea or Apollo for Land	O6	Saint Peter	Colonel or Navy Captain
Prince	Paris		O7	Saint John	Adjujant General
King	Perseus		O8	Saint Bartholomew	Brigidier General
Emperor	Persephone	Proserpina	O9	Saint James the Greater	Major General
	Demeter	Ceres	O10	Saint Philip	General
	Dionysius	Bacchus	O11	Saint Thomas	Commander General

	Greek Diety		Mother	Father	Spouse	Mother Diety	Father Diety
E3-E4	Pan	M	Dryope	Hermes	Echo, Bona Dea, Marica	Atlas	Cronos
E5-E10	Heracles	M	Almene	Zeus	Deinaria	Cronos or Uranus	Cronos
O1	Epaphus	M	IO	Zeus	Cassiopeia, Memphis	Oceanus	Cronos
O1 or O2	Hephaestus	M	Hera	Zeus	Athena, Gaia, Atthis	Cronos	Cronos
O2 or O3	Hermes	M	Maia	Zeus	Dryope or Aphrodyte	Atlas	Cronos
O3	Achilles	M	Thetis	Peleus	Iphigeneia of Helen of Troy	Poiseidon	Poiseidon
O4	Hyllus	M	Deinaria	Hercules	Iole	Zeus	Zeus
O5	Artemis	F	Leto	Zeus	Hermes	Uranus and Gaia	Cronos
O5	Minos	M	Europa	Zeus	Pasiphae	Uranus and Gaia	Cronos
O6	Odysseus	M	Anticleia	Laertes	Calypso, Penelope, Circe	Zeus and Atlas	Uranus and Oceanus
O6	Apollo	M	Leto	Zeus	Cresusa	Uranus and Gaia	Cronos
O7	Paris	M	Hecuba	Priam of Troy	Helen	Zeus	Zeus
O8	Perseus	M	Danae	Zeus	Andromeda	Cronos or Uranus	Cronos
O9	Persephone	F	Demeter	Zeus	Hades	Cronos	Cronos
O10	Demeter	F	Rhea	Cronos	Zeus	Rhea	Cronos
O11	Dionysius	M	Semele	Zeus	Aphrodyte	Poiseidon	Cronos

Enlisted Ranks

			Army	Marine	Explanation and Duties
No Name			E1		Not worthy of anything
Private			E2	E1	Privacy
Private First Class			E3	E2	First Class Individual or Rich Person (Millionaire or Billionaire)
Lance Corporal			N/A	E3	Roman who used his Lance to draw the Blood of the Lord When he was on the Cross Unconsciuos
Corporal			E4	E4	Subject to Sargeant
Sargeant			E5	E5	Worshiper of Nimrod God of War with same Strength
Staff Sargeant			E6	E6	Worshiper of Jathar, the son of Hezron whose name in Hebrew means Staff
Gunnery Sargeant			E7	E7	Worshiper of Guni, the son of Napthali the son of Jacob
Master Sargeant			E7	E7	Worshiper of Children, takes the Gunnery Sargeant (what he has made) and puts in Napthali's son Guni
First Sargeant			E8	E8	Worshipper of Tubal Cain, who attempts to be the first of a conflict to the line of Cain, so a man can get the jump on an enemy, (the first to Cain) and kill him
Master Gunnery Sargeant			E9	E9	Combination of Gunnery Sargeant and Master Sargeant
Warrant Sargeant				E10	Used by MP for Warrant for arrest.

Now let us consider the Roman Mythology. In the book it is shown that Zerah might be Zeus. The spelling is the same, the time line is the same. Epraim and Zerah would both be grandson's of Israel, and it makes sense.

Now it was eight generations from Noah to Abraham thru Shem. Suppose that Jupiter who is shown on a previous page is the diety Zeus, that he is from Japeth about eight generations, and that all the ideas that Zeus is a son of Judah and from Israel would go away. The tie to Epraim to Israel would remain, so the descent and idea that Zeus is Zerah, may not be correct but that Zeus is Jupiter.

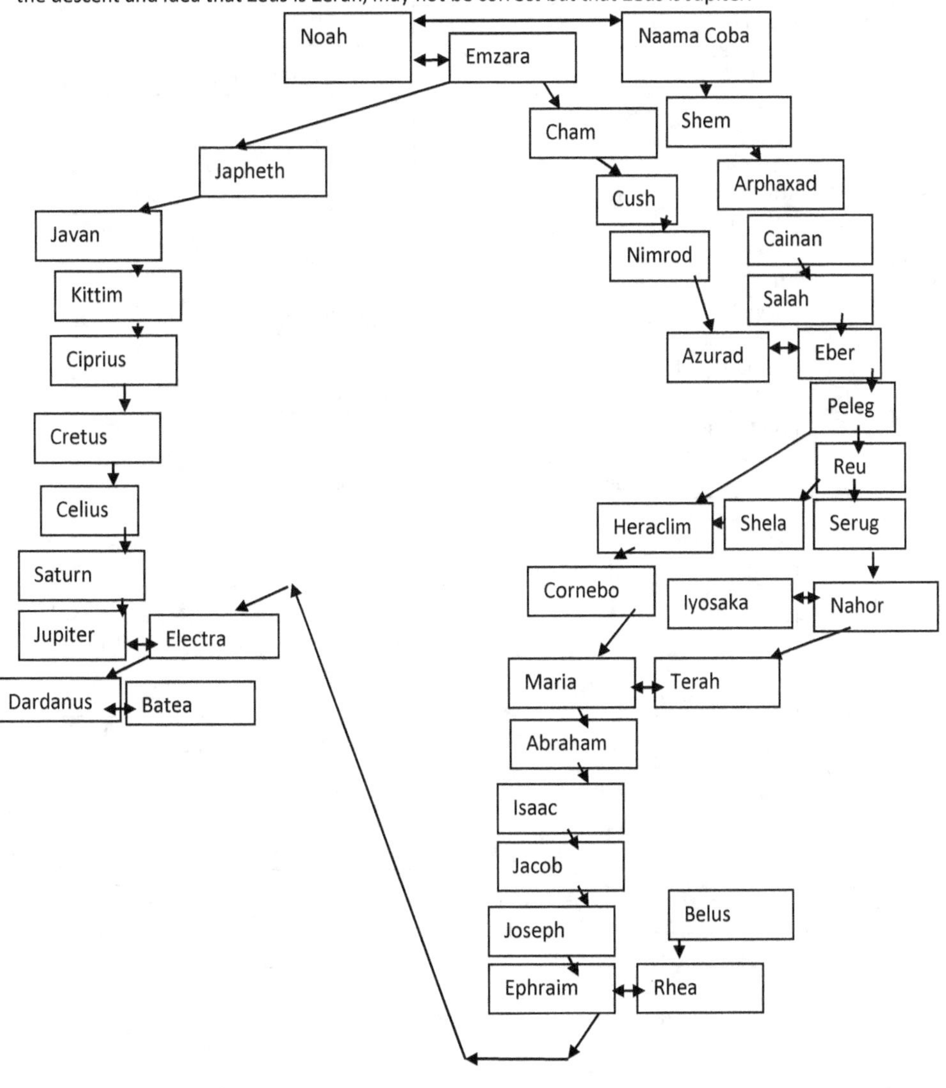

Noble Rank	Greek Diety	Roman Diety		Apostle	Military Rank
squire	Pan	Faunus	E3		Lance Corporal
	Heracles	Hercules	E5-E10		Sargent
Lord	Ephasus for Land or Hephaestus for Sea	Vulcan	O1	Saint Judas Thaddeus	2nd Lietenant
Knight	Hermes for Sea or Hephaestus for Land	Mercury	O2	Saint Mathew	1st Lieutenant
Barron	Achilles for Sea or Hermes for land		O3	Saint Andrew	Captain
Count	Hyllus son of Deinaria and Heracles		O4	Saint James the Lesser	Major
Earle	Artemis for Sea or Minas for land	Diana	O5	Saint Simon	Lt Colonel or First Mate
Duke	Odysseus for Sea or Apollo for land	Ulysses for Sea or Apollo for Land	O6	Saint Peter	Colonel or Navy Captain
Prince	Paris		O7	Saint John	Adjujant General
King	Perseus		O8	Saint Bartholomew	Brigidier General
Emperor	Persephone	Proserpina	O9	Saint James the Greater	Major General
	Demeter	Ceres	O10	Saint Philip	General
	Dionysius	Bacchus	O11	Saint Thomas	Commander General

	Greek Dieties	Roman Dieties	
1st Heaven	Apollo	Sol	
2nd Heaven	Aphrodyte, Artemis	Venus, Diana	
3rd Heaven	Aries, Athena	Mars	
4th Heaven	Heracles the Mortal	Hercules	
5th Heaven	Zeus, Poseidon , Hestia	Jupiter, Neptune, Vesta	
6th Heaven	Cronos, Oceanus	Saturn	

7th Heaven	Lord Jesus Christ and Apostles		
8th Heaven	The Jury of Peace (Jerusalem) 12 Elders of Israel		
	Joel, Daniel, Samuel, Ezekiel, Elijah, Elisha,Gabriel,		
	Michael, Rafael, Haniel, Uriel, Remiel, Barachiel, Pravatel,		
9th Heaven	Elhim, Elwin, Elron, Elgin, Elrim		
10th Heaven	El, Estelle, Elohim, Elowin, Elogin, Eloron, Elorim		

The Apostles Guardianship

The Apostles guard against bad things from happening, and will try to prevent it.

LAW In the Lord.

1) 2nd Lieutenant. Saint Judas Thadeus, guard against Homosexuality
2) Ist Lietenant, Saint Mathew guard against Adultery
3) Captain Saint Andrew guard against Man Rapes a Women
4) Major Saint James the Lesser guard againt Man rapes a boy
5) Lieutenant Colonel Saint Simon guard against Women rapes a Boy
6) Colonel Saint Peter guard against Women Rapes a Man Greek Ullyses
7) Adjujent General Saint John guard against Father rapes his daughter Greek Paris
8) Brigidier General Saint Bartholomew guard against Brother or Sister (incest) Greek Persius
9) Major General Saint James the Greater guard against Man rapes his son Persperoni
10) Commanding General Saint Phillip guard against Mother raping her daughter Greek Demeter
11) Commander Saint Thomas guard against Son raping his Mother and Daughter rapes her father Greek Dionynysius
12) Saint Judas Iscariot guard against the sin of Heinous sins, the least being taking ones own life, the worst being to take the life of another. And then there is a guard against Martyrdom.

LAW In the Knight

1) Noble Rank of Lord,2nd Lieutenant. Saint Judas Thadeus , guard against Man Kills a Man or Women Kills a Women.
2) Noble Rank of Knight or Ist Lietenant, Saint Mathew guard against Marriage Murder Husband Kills his wife or Wife Kills his Husband
3) Noble Rank of Barron or Captain Saint Andrew guard against Man kills a women
4) Noble Rank of Count or Major Saint James the Lesser guard againt Man Kills a boy
5) Noble Rank of Earle or Lieutenant Colonel Saint Simon guard against women kills a boy
6) Noble Rank of Duke Colonel Saint Peter guard against Women Kills a man
7) Noble Rank of King or One Star or Adjujent General Saint John guard against Father kills his daughter
8) Noble Rank of Emperor Two Star or Brigidier General Saint Bartholomew guard against Brother kills his Sister
9) 3 Star or Major General Saint James the Greater guard against Man Kills his son.

10) 4 Star or Commanding General Saint Phillip guard against Mother Kills her daughter.
11) 5 Star or Commander Saint Thomas guard against Son Kills his mother Mother or daughter kills her father.
12) Saint Judas Iscariot guard against One Kills Oneself.

THE CRIMES AND THEIR PREVENTION

		Christianity	Mandean	Roman
		Mary	Elizabeth	Ann
Guardian Ship		Haineus	Heineous	Horrific
Military Rank	Jewel	Crime	Crime	
Lance Corporal				
Sargent				
2nd Lieutenant	Bar	Homosexuality	Murder	
1st Lieutenant	Two Bar	Adultery	Murder in Marriage	
Captain		Man Rape of Women	Murder of Women by Man	
Major		Man Rape of Boy	Murder of Boy by Man	
Lt Colonel		Women Rape of Boy	Murder of Boy by Women	
Colonel or Navy Captain	Cluster Leaf	Women Rape of Man	Murder of Man by Women	
Adjujant General	One Star	Man Rape of Daughter	Murder of Daughter by Man	
Brigidier General	Two Star	Incest	Murder of Brother or Sister by each other	War Crimes
Major General	Three Star	Man Rape of Son	Murder of Father's Son	Mass Murder
General	Four Star	Women Rape of Daughter	Murder of Mother's Daughter	Genecide
Commander General	Five Star	Daughter Rape of Man	Murder of Parents	War

Now the second heaven is Venus and Diane. Venus loves everyone, including soldiers, and Diane will harvest the virgin soldier.

Aries is God of War, and Athena is a Goddess of War. This is the third heaven, and their involvement in the battle field is done, although they are not related to the minor deities of Stars.

Now Hercules is the son of Zeus who will not war. He is the strongest, and half mortal. He has more brains than a warrior or god of war, and is half mortal because he must use his fathers line of Zeus and not his mothers line. He is the fourth heaven because he is greater than Aries, but less than Zeus.

Now Zeus is the Father of the gods. The commandment have no other Gods before me applies to the Greek in that he is the father of the gods, therefore superior to the other Gods. In the legends he is son of Cronos and the Titans, and brother to Hades and Neptune. He is likely Zerah, the son of Judah. He would be an orphan because Sam son of Esau encouraged Esau to go against Jacob and win his fathers blessing. Jacob had received the blessing from Isaac, and so enforced the will of his father with an Arrow. (Jacob slew his twin brother). Jacobs children fought a battle against Esau and his children and estate, and Sam slew Judah. Thus Judah was a Martyr. Now Dan saw this and enforced the law of life for a life so because Sam had dispatched Judah, thus Dan enforced the law and slew Sam. Now legend has it that Joseph slew the son of Sam, (traditionally the son of Samuel was Eldrich) although the son of Samwise may have been Luce. Benjamin was also involved and that may have been traditional the family of Samuel that is Joel or Heman.

Now Jacob was God of Esau and Dan was god of Sam. Dan had the daughter Samantha,(in regard to Samwise) and Asudy (in rememberance of Judah) and Igrath, all babies that died before the children of Israel went to Egypt because of the famine. Dan also had Husim who survived and served as Slaves who built the pyramids until Moses and the Exodus. (Except for the chieftain Joseph who was Governor. (see Exodus) (Much of this is found in the Book of Jubilees.) Note, a jubilee happens every fifty years so the Modern State of Israel had its first Jubilee in 1998 because that is the fifty year anniversay of the founding of Israel (1948). Because a century is based on one hundered Modern Israel cannot at this time claim a centuriuan, however can claim a Jubilee. Th idea here is that a Julal or cutting in half of a century is based on Gabriel the archangel who is half of the strength of Michael who is the Archangel of War. Considering that Michael traditionally cuts the devil in half makes a Gabriel. (remember the scene in Star Wars when Obuwan or one of the Jedi cuts the Sith in two with his light sabre.) Sort of makes you wonder who was the Steer eater that fought the Saracen by sword in the Crusades and managed to cut the Saracen in half thru the middle. Quite a sharp sword would have been needed.

SECTION FIFTEEN: PHILOSOPHIES

The Great Clan Battle

In Ancient Times there were two clans, the clan of Jacob and the clan of Esau. It is well documented in the bible about the inheritance of the son from Isaac. Jacob was the younger and Esau was the older, although twins where Jacob clung to the heal of Esau as they were born.

The translators of the bible did not see fit to include the clan battle as part of the sacred scripture, but it was left in charge of a people that had their own sacred literature, namely the book of Jubilee or the Little Genesis. This book is a history of the Hebrew people during the time of Genesis, Exodus, and Numbers, and basically that's it.

Now the battle included a lot of characters. Let us introduce to this section the chosen one of Jacob, by Rachel the Chieftain Joseph. At the time of the battle Joseph was not sentenced by his brothers, and the incident of his only sister Dinah had already taken place possibly, or not as some may say, but in any case his mother Rachel was alive. Jacob had four wives, Leah, who he had worked seven years for, and Rachel, who he had worked another seven years for, and his wifes servant women Bilah and Zilpah. Now Bilah had given birth for Jacob of Dan and Naptali, and Zilpah had given Jacob the sons Gad and Asher. Leah had had six sons, the oldest Reuben, also Zebulon, Judah, Levi, Simeon, and Isaac-Har. Judah was the strongest with the strength of ten horses.

Now Esau and Jacob were separated by many miles and Edom the son of Esau said to Esau, let us go against the clan of Jacob and get for us the inheritance of my grandfather Isaac, and settle the matter. Now Esau was a great hunter and thought that might be a good idea. Jacob had fled from Laban with his wives in an effort to get away from his father in law. Jacob obviously loved his wives and his holdings and was traveling with many spotted lambs as the bible says.

Esau had other sons than Edom or Korah with him, and servants as well, and Esau's son's were Eliphaz, Reuel, Korah and there were many servants as well. Edom or Korah had a son, possibly Eldrictch, and a child daughter Susi and his brothers and sisters had family as well.

This is what happened as far as the battle goes, and if a reader is interested the wording in the sacred writings of the Little Genesis and the Bible becomes important, although this recounting of the past has gone on for over four thousand years.

The two sides advanced toward each other. Jacob enforced the will of his father with an arrow, and Esau went down. Edom or Korah advanced on the strongest Judah and slew him with sword, and Dan was angry so while the sword was in Judah and Edom's not able to defend himself Dan slit his throat slew Edom or Korah which became the law life for a life. Eldritch the son of Edom saw his father go down and advanced but the Chosen of Jacob Joseph slew Eldritch with a sword. Zerah the son of Judah saw his father go down but could not avenge his father but fought bravely on and showed himself one of the greatest warriors ever and slew and slew. Reuben, Simeon, Isaac-har, Gad, Asher, Naptali and Zebulon also participated and showed themselves well. When the battle was over only the women and children and livestock was all that was left of Esau and his clan and Jacob Joseph Dan Naptali and Leah's family all adopted the children because after all they were from Isaac, however did not have the promise of the blessing of their father. Dan adopted Susi and established his tribe after the Exodus and Numbers, and the lists today show Dan as the father of Susi. Even the book of Daniel lists the virtues of Susanne as part of the sacred book of Daniel.

Weapons at the Clan Battle

We do not know how the arms were made in the clan battle. We do know Jacob used a bow. We do not know if it is a cross bow or a long bow. We know and think that Esau was the first to fall, because the bow is a range weapon. Josephe, the youngest of his clan used the honorable sword. We think Dan used the knife and the sword. We know Rebecca protected Esau because he did not slay anyone. We think Judah slew many servants before Edom attacked and killed him. Dan got most of the killing done. Israel did not kill any of his nephews or children of his nephews. Only woman involved in the blood shed was Igrath the daughter of Esau, who may have gotten servants, not the blood. Esau's clan was completely defeated, their spirits resurrected below the Israel.

Wisdom of the Clan Battle

The Rabbitical wisdom of Israel works like this.

Israel is the greatest Master Now Jacob would be god of Esau due to Esau's death in the man because he only killed animals. So in the resurrection of a Rabbitical Priest or teacher called a Rabbi Rabbi Israel should be able to order around Rabbi Esau. This idea leads to adage of sayings made from one Rabbi to Another. A sort of Game where is the First Rabbi is he really able in the law to order the second rabbi or is it a glide. Of Course Rabbi David would always be able to Order Rabbi Goliath. Thus the Wisdom of the Clan Battle in order to decode the Rabbitcal priest or divine it in a way Wisdom must be applied.

Finaly is Rabbi Baltzahazar the commander of Rabbi Gaspar or is Rabbi Melchoir.

Each Master Rabbi has a subject Rabbi due to the blood of Isaac and Abraham

- Rabbi Isreal said to Rabbi Esau, we must save our innocent children twin.
- Rabbi Josephe said to Rabbi Korah we must save our honor.
- Rabbi Dan said to Rabbi Edom, we must not do evil, possession, or kill our own.
- Rabbi Zebulon said to Rabbi Reuel we must not lose our path,
- Rabbi Zohar said to Rabbi Shammah the divinity cannot change.

- Rabbi Beltshazzar said to Rabbi Eliphaz we must not be aliens.
- Rabbi Zeus said to Rabbi Zerah we must not kill ourselves.
- Rabbi Dan said to Rabbi Pallium we must not be too generous,
- Rabbi Dan said to Rabbi Shammah we must respect lesser divinity,
- Rabbi Judah said to Rabbi Nahath we must keep a plentiful supply of stores.
- Rabbi Reubel said to Rabbi Mizzah let us meet in heaven.
- Rabbi Nephalim said to Rabbi Beor, wrestle the bear in primitive combat prove you are a man.
- Rabbi Manoah said to Rabbi Zerah your brother the good priest gives us diety status divinity.
- Rabbi Dan said to Rabbi Bedah sleep well.
- Rabbi Isreal said to Rabbi Esau let your son Rabbi Puith know my son Rabbi Dan said put it there chum.
- Rabbi Josephe said to Rabbi Marzith god of your wars.
- Rabbi Simeon said to Rabbi Achbor we have a failure to communicate.
- Rabbi Issachar said to Rabbi Jeush let us practice our faith in heaven.
- Rabbi Israel said to Rabbi Esau please tell my is chosen son Rabbi Joseph thru Rabbi Magdiel consult divine judgement when taking on a larger force even if your divinity is less than mine.
- Rabbi Dan said to Rabbi Amalek do not execute before a fair trial,
- Rabbi Israel said to Rabbi Esau let my son Rabbi Levi have reign over Rabbi Kenaz who recognizes angelic divinity lesser than our own.
- Rabbi Zebulon said to Rabbi Teman let us drink divine wine.
- Rabbi Asher said to Rabbi Gatam let us sacrifice animals only to the priest with honor.
- Rabbi Simeon said to the daughter Igrath do not add to your misery.
- Rabbi Judah said to Rabbi Omar stay thigh path.
- Rabbi Dan said to Rabbi Zepho look to the sky.
- Rabbi Simeon said to Rabbi Mibzar compromise will not be tolerated.
- Rabbi Dan said to Rabbi Eram your flock is indeed growing.
- Rabbi Josephe said to Rabbi Magdiel with no commander Kingdoms Fall.
- Rabbi Betall said to Rabbi Nachath let us eat food that is not Kosher to prevent starvation.
- Rabbi Gad said to Rabbi Alvin let us not kill each other cousin and rest at the Oasis with psalm and many beautiful women.
- Rabbi Zabulon said to Daughter of Rabbi Reuel, Igrath, you are such a dirty Kate.
- Rabbi Judah said to Rabbi Amalek, see your descendents don't be executives for large groups.
- Rabbi Reuben said to Rabbi Jaalam, Keep the inlaw lambs blood active.
- Rabbi Dan Said to Rabbi Gatam don't injure the innocent Gad
- Rabbi Asher said to the Rabbitical Servants, sometimes its just not enough
- Rabbi Isaachar said to Rabbi Marzith, God of play war!!!!
- Rabbi Judah said to Rabbi Zepho, you are not greater than my son Zeus
- Rabbi Zabulon said to Rabbi Gatam, my brother Gad is greater than thou.
- Rabbi Judah said to Rabbi Mibzar, let us never meet in the middle
- Rabbi Betall said to Rabbi Phinor, fear not my rath, fear my sword in the high priest Hilkiah!!!

First Rabbi	Second Rabbi	Father First Rabbi	Father Second Rabbi
Israel	Esau*	Isaac	Isaac
Josephe	Korah*	Jacob	Esau
	Shammah*		Korah
Dan	Edom*	Jacob	Esau
	Pallium*		Jacob
	Shammah*		Esau
	Eram*		Korah
Judah	Zepho*	Jacob	Esau
	Amalek*		Eliaphaz
	Mizzah*		Eliaphaz
	Achbor*		Esau
	Mibzar		Korah
	Omar*		Esau
Reubel	Jaalam*	Jacob	Esau
Simeon	Magdiel*	Jacob	Korah
Levi	Kenaz*	Jacob	
Nephthalim	Beor*	Jacob	Esau
Gad	Alvah*	Jacob	
Asher	Servants of Esau*	Jacob	
Isaachar	Marzith*	Jacob	Esau
Zabulon	Reuel*	Jacob	Esau
	Nahath*		Esau
	Teman*		
	Gatam*		Eliaphaz
	Bedah*		Esau
	Igrath*		Daughter Reuel
Zeus	Zerah*	Judah	Esau Mahalith
Manoah	Zerah*	Dan	Esah Adah
Betall	Phinor*	Nephthali	Reuel

Jacob had may sons The oldest Reubel, meaning Mercy Simeon meaning Prayer, Levi, meaning confirmer of friendship, Judah, meaning Thanksgiving, Dan meaning Divine Judgement, Nepthalim meaning unconquerable in strategy, Gad meaning fortune, Asher meaning Happy man, Isaachar meaning one born from hire, and Zabulon meaning meaning born as a pledge of benevolence. Dinah. These three may have been triplets. Then Joseph from Rachel meaning one may be added to him.

Now consider Jacobs age. If he was of age when he went to Laban he must have been about 18; He was to work seven years for Laban for ownership of Leah. So he either would have been fathering with servants or celibate for seven years or with Lea before she was his. If he was with Lea before Jacob was given her by Laban, then Reubel, nine months, now 19, Simeon nine more months now 20, Levi now 21; then Dan and Napthalim, now Dan and Napthalim would not be by Leah so no addition to age, now Gad and Asher also not by Lea, Isaachar, Zebulon, and Dinah another nine months now Jacob is 22 then Joseph with Rachel, now Jacob is 23, earliest age. So was Lea and Rachel owned by Laban while Jacob made most of Israel? Possibly. Now consider oldest age. Jacob might arrive at 22 wait seven years make all the children by Lea waiting the seven years and then make Joseph. Now Joseph took out Korah at the clan battle but he had to be of age consider 15.; Jacob is now 18 plus seven for Lea and seven for Rachel and 15 for Joseph to come of age. Now Jacob honorable age was 47. The first way makes Jacob and Laban the father of the Israelites while the second makes only Jacob thru servitude. Now Reubel the oldest could have been much older than Joseph the honorable minimum age difference seven years. So if Reubel fathered his sons where they at the clan battle?

In my idealogy Judah is slain and his son Zerah sees it and also becomes an Israelite by honoring his father Judah So if Judah was only three years older and Zerah was of age then the battle had to take place when Jacob was about 60; So now Israel is 50 and Zerah is of age. So did Josephs sons Manassah and Epriam take part? if so they add another three of four years to Jacob. So now Jacob is at minimum 55. This seems to be about the age that the Judean Hebrew people come into manhood. This considering there was no birthcontrol and conception was easy for a man as prolific as Jacob makes his leadership of the tribe about his best age. Now don't forget Esau was also the same age because he was a twin. So if the Clan battle happened while Jacob was between 55 and 60 then the conception of Benjamin would have to be at Jacobs age of a half century. However Benjamin would not belong to the priest as Samuel and the Virgin Mary did, considering Isaac required a priest when the father Abraham was over 100 Isaac must belong to the Priest as well. Remember his conception was after a visit by the priest.

So attendance of the battle would be the israelites at about 35 years old each and their sons at about 15.

The Rabbitical wisdom of Israel works like this. Rabbi Isreal said to Rabbi Esau, we must save our innocent children twin. Rabbi Josephe said to Rabbi Korah we must save our honor. Rabbi Dan said to Rabbi Edom, we must not do evil, possession, or kill our own. Rabbi Zebulon said to Rabbi Reuel we must not lose our path, Rabbi Zohar said to Rabbi Shammah the divinity cannot change. Rabbi Beltshazzar said to Rabbi Eliphaz we must not be aliens. Rabbi Zeus said to Rabbi Zerah we must not kill ourselves. Rabbi Dan said to Rabbi Pallium we must not be too generous, Rabbi Dan said to Rabbi Shammah we must respect lesser divinity, Rabbi Judah said to Rabbi Nahath we must keep a plentiful supply of stores. Rabbi Reubel said to Rabbi Mizzah let us meet in heaven. Rabbi Nephalim said to Rabbi Beor, wrestle the bear in primitive combat prove you are a man. Rabbi Manoah said to Rabbi Zerah your brother the good priest gives us diety status divinity. Rabbi Dan said to Rabbi Bedah sleep well. Rabbi Isreal said to Rabbi Esau let your son Rabbi Puith know my son Rabbi Dan said put it there chum. Rabbi Josephe said to Rabbi Marzith god of your wars. Rabbi Simeon said to Rabbi Achbor we have a failure to communicate. Rabbi Issachar said to Rabbi Jeush let us practice our faith in heaven. Rabbi Israel said to Rabbi Esau please tell my is chosen son Rabbi Joseph thru Rabbi Magdiel consult divine judgement when taking on a larger force even if your divinity is less than mine. Rabbi Dan said to Rabbi Amalek do not execute before a fair trial, Rabbi Israel said to Rabbi Esau let my son Rabbi Levi have reign over Rabbi Kenaz who recognizes angelic divinity lesser than our own. Rabbi Zebulon said to Rabbi Teman let us drink divine wine. Rabbi Asher said to Rabbi Gatam let us sacrifice animals only to the priest with honor. Rabbi Simeon said to the daughter Igrath do not add to your misery. Rabbi Judah said to Rabbi Omar stay thigh path. Rabbi Dan said to Rabbi Zepho look to the sky. Rabbi Simeon said to Rabbi Mibzar compromise will not be tolerated. Rabbi Dan said to Rabbi Eram your flock is indeed growing. Rabbi Josephe said to Rabbi Magdiel with no commander Kingdoms Fall. Rabbi Betall said to Rabbi Nachath let us eat food that is not Kosher to prevent starvation. Rabbi Gad said to Rabbi Alvin let us not kill each other cousin and rest at the Oasis with psalm and many beautiful women.

Esau's sons. Korah and brother Jeush, Marzith and brother Puith, Reuel and brothers Bedah, Beor, and Zerah and Achbor, Eliphaz and brother Zerah, Nahath and brothers Zerah Shammah, Mizzah. That's about 15.

Esau's Grandsons. Teman, Mibzar, Magdiel, Eram. Alvah, Timnah, Jetheth, Shammah-si, Nachath, Teman, Omar, Zepho, Gatam,Timna, Kenaz, Amalek,

Jacobs Grandsons. Jacob because he had the blessing of his father had more grandchildren than his brother Esau even though Esau had more sons. Edom knew this and that may be the motivation for the Attack. Jacob had about 50 or 60 Grandchildren. Listed in this writing is Jacobs grandchildren Mannassah Josephs oldest, Manoah Dans son, Betaal Naptali's son.

In primitive combat Jacob would have sent his sons first to protect their children, the same with Esau

After Genesis

Now it is interesting to note that the Hebrews have always been a secretive people ruled by priests, after the torah the priests were known as Levites. The history of these people has not been lost and the Hebrew people of the Dragon of David has been the oldest house that has claimed to have written the law. The above battle of the clans is hidden from the old testament and entrusted to only those people who have found this law. Now let us consider some other points of the Book of Jubilee keeping in mind the Battle would have taken place before Joseph was sentenced to Egypt by his brothers. And this is why. Jacob is not the father of Benjamin, Jacob is the father of Benjamin's eleven brothers, but Israel is the father of Benjamin. Jacob was visited by an angel (Esau was the angel but Jacob became Israel by the slewing of Esau sending Esau to his father or to heaven). This is simply an authors way of naming, that was not to say that Joseph and Benjamin had different mothers and fathers, but to say they did have the same mother and father.

Now because Rachel was alive during the clan battle Benjamin could not be alive and guilty of the war against Esau's clan because Benjamin means sorrow because Rachel died during the delivery of Benjamin. So apparently the primitive tribes came to know that if the Father has taken a life and made his wife pregnant there is a danger that she would die in childbirth. So what about the other people that took place in the battle? Dan was a master of life, as was Joseph, Zerah, and Judah was dead. So therefore all of Judah's children were older than Benjamin, which includes Hur, Perez, Nafut, Shelah and Zerah. The Clan battle was not the first of the visits of the people of Abraham by an angel, as Lot was visited in Sodom and Gemorrah by an Angel when Abraham had an argument with God. Now Lot was the generation above Jacob and the Israelites. Certainly Lot was from Nahor but not the same as Abraham. Consider the relationships of Abraham, his nephew Lot and how confusing it becomes. That will be considered once the discussion of the tree of life is taken and one very important quote from the Kabala. In the Kaballa there is a tree of life exponded by five masters and five beings who are called man. The five masters are David, Aaron, Joseph, Moses, and Jacob, and the five beings who are Man are called Nahor, Terah, Abraham, Isaac, and Serug. There is some argument about Maria being involved but however Serug had a daughter and Cornebo married her and so had Maria who married Terah. Cornebo is considered a part of the being called Man, as can be Maria, although Maria is of a different gender and is considered divine!!!!! At any rate the idea is that the division between Man and Master took place at the Clan battle when Israel was born as the greatest master of man therefore any generation greater than the generation of Israel would be considered Man.

Philosphy of the Aaronic Priest

Each Aaronic Priest of Aaron has a Rabbi or teacher that teaches that law. It stands to reason that this is what a divinity school would teach and that a major in divinity could be earned and a Reverend is not someone who just heard the call and opened up a place of worship but a degreed person that has some knowledge of the law, and knows how to relate it to his people that come to meeting. Here is an expertation about King David how he really is honorable and could be part of the High Priest Urijah.

I was watching Michael Huckabee's on Fox when I was inspired about him getting rid of all evil. (Archangle Micheal good for getting rid of evil in the christians.) I was reading in the Zohar volume 7 by Dan Matt, about the leviticus book, part of the torah but not the little genesis, I mean with a name like Dan I really don't care about Levi's rules, but anyway I will support the books Genesis , Numbers, and Exodus, and leave Leviticus and Deutoromony out of the little genesis. So in regard to King David he has a problem similar to Saint Mary Magdalene. He is always portrayed as setting up uriah to climb the hill and get killed. According the Zohar, rabbi says that Uriah was the adulterer of Michah the daughter of Saul who married David. Thus Absalom and his brother who rebelled against David were not his sons but

Uriah's. Now Dan the son of Abigail would be a member of the court and asked to pass judgement on David's behavior, and as being given the divine judgement would rule that Solomon is David's eldest son. Now that would make Dan Daniel. So when David asked his mighty man Johab to send uriah up the hill to be killed he was killling an adulterer and making a better kingdom. Samuel was likely cursing Saul since Samuel was a priest and against Saul and his children. Now consider the three wise kings Melchoir, Joseph, who get the commander Korah Dan who gets the instigator Edom Baltazar and Samuel. who is the resurrection of Korah and subject to the chosen Joseph.
So King David was honorable, his brother Nathaniel was suffering from the demon of ignorance and his sons Solomon and Nathaniel were wise. and Solomon was the heir and the eldest. So Daniel would be used to judge the eldest line. Consider the presentation that Dan uses He says he is the son of the creep. Now the writer of Cronicles, like Saint Nithard, sometimes gets translated the DAvid is the father of Daniel. serously Dan is better off with his brother Amasa the son of Abigail with Jerimoth the son of Abigail that Jether would have been the creep who creeped into the castle, castle penetration, and fathered Daniel, since David was honorable and certainly would not sleep with his sister Abigail. This makes Daniel the line from Jether that leads to the eldest son of Hezron Jeremeel, the eldest of Hezron. Now Hezron in hebrew means right cross so Daniel and Amasa and Jerimoth are likely gtood at hand to hand. Jeremeel is like the windmill in boxing and line goes jether (undercut) Jada (jab) Onam (side of the head) Jeremeel (windmill to the face) and Hezron (knowckout) that leaves amminidab and jathar the sons of Hezron subject. Now Jathar means staff in hebrew so is symbol of wisdom. So Daniel would be the heir to Judah thru the eldest line if he is from Jether, while David is from Amminidab.

Consider King David.

Now King David was the son of Abala and Jesse. Abala had also Sarvia and Abigail. they were considered sisters to the king.

Now Sarvia was the mother of Jereboam by Nebat from the line of Epraim. So consider that Nebat was the father and Sarvia was the mother but Sarvia was usually considered in most genealogies posted on the internet the daughter of Nashah from Reubens tribe. Suppose Abala made love to Jesse one night and conceived Abigail and made love to Nahash since Jesse was tired and conceived Sarvia and had twins. To futher complicate things King David may have been and identical twin to Abigail and a non identical twin to sarvia and a triplet.

Considering the idea that the Hebrew would try anytihng the conception of twins by identical twin fathers has not happened yet.

Is the conception of triplets something that Jesse, Abala, and Nahash were involved in?

Building the Justice

Let us look at who is guilty in the Clan Battle as an examination of good and evil. (Keep in mind that the Authors middle name is Daniel so the story may be slighted toward the Cheiftain Dan.) Esau was the leader of the Clan but certainly he did not care if he got the inheritance of the blessing, but was instigated by Edom. Now Edom caused the whole thing and is likely the most guilty. Not only did he lead the clan into battle he killed the biggest and strongest of Jacob's sons Judah. Judah by most in the sacred bible is considered the way and the light so to kill that would be the night. (it gets dark at night without light). Now Dan started the law of Life for a Life by avenging his half brother. It gets worse for Dan as his act of vengeance was an act of cowardice due to Edom was defenseless with his sword buried in Judah. But that is part of being only a humble servant son of Rachel and not a full blooded son of Laban, but only of Roethus the son of Huz the son of Nahor. (Bilhah and Zilphah were sisters and daughters of Roethus the son of Huz. In addition to Roethus Huz had a grandchild Aruham that had Meri and Uzith also sisters who married the servant sons Naptali and Uzith. Note how this makes for servant tribes to other tribes.)

Now Joseph was guilty of Killing the son of Edom, but his kill was clean, with honor, and he was of course the chosen one of Jacob. Guilty of War and killing but chosen none the less. Zerah was also guilty, but he was a very strong man as son of Judah, and was destined to father a mighty people (the Greeks) as his name was changed to Zeus the father of the gods. In his life he would have 28 wives and father 42 children, all gods and Kings, and think of his connections, a nephew to each of the twelve tribes of Isreal, and also an orphan. He would have had to have started having children when he was over twenty and lived about 120 years, having a new child every three of four years.

So was Jacob also Guilty? He enforced the will of his father. Rebecca had always known that Jacob was the second son of the twins, but I am sure she would not have her children kill each other. Rebecca had married Isaac, the second son of Abraham, while the elder Ismael was sentenced by Sarah's love for Isaac to exile Haggai and Ismael. Isaac never killed anyone. When another tribe came and demanded the well he dug in the desert he did not fight, he just moved and dug another one. He did this three times. He was man. Apparently he did not think that it was serious enough to take a life about. Now in the Sefriot Isaac is the youngest man and Rebecca is the the intelligence path called the Faithful intelligence. Becky will always say once a master always a master. It is possible for a man to become a master, but impossible for a master to become a man. (In other words once you have killed it is impossible to undo the deed). Jacob had won the blessing of his father but had to enforce it. Now he was a master. He was certainly sorrowful when Benjamin's birth caused his wife that he had worked 14 years for to pass away.

So in the Sefriot Dan was not mentioned. Neither was Zerah. Both had an important part to play in the Battle but after all Dan was a servant and Zerah was only a son of a chieftain, not a chief himself.

Now the Sefriot has five masters, and Joseph the chosen and Israel or Jacob are two. The man part is only from Isaac and previous generations, so who are the other masters? There are three. David, Moses, and Aaron. All readers of the sacred bible know that David slew Goliath the philistine. He was a giant of a warrior and David used a sling. So David is a master. Now Moses in the sacred bible was the main character of Exodus. Moses slew an Egyptian as a general. The book of Exodus is very good reading in the Torah, and is expounded in the Antiquities of the Jews as related by the captured Flavius Josephus as the Hebrews lost the war with the Roman Legions. In the Antiquities it is shown that Moses was also a very good General of Egypt and Prince of his people and led a great battle for Egypt against Ethiopia and won. So in the Sacred Bible and the Antiquities there is no mention of Aaron killing anyone. So then how is Aaron the master of the sefriot? What Rabbi would teach this? It is not in the sacred Zohar either. The rabbi's would all be part of the Aaronic Priesthood and so Aaron would be the high priest. How do we solve this mystery? Let us keep it in the mysterium for a few paragraphs and introduce Joseph's sister Dinah.

In the sacred bible Dinah is the only sister of the sons of Jacob called Israel. And she was raped. Ok, so now we have a problem here. First was the rape before or after the clan battle. Is that important? The sacred bible states that the clan that raped here was revenged by the Israelites. When Jacob found out about it that made Jacob upset. OK that clears Jacob. So how did it happen? Apparently while the tribe that raped Dinah was away from the Israelites the Israelites sneaked up and watched. They Dined and then they napped and while asleep the Israelites came into the camp and cut their throats. Levi and Simeon did the deeds while the eating was the Dan and the napping was the Naptali. (to eat means to Dan and to sleep means to Naptali). So Dinah was avenged. Now Levi confessed but Simeon did not feed the need to.

Levi had two Masters after his son Kohath was born. Kohath means to cut off a hand and it is done to a thief in ancient times. That way you can't steal again. So Kohath had the sons Aaron and Moses. There was a famine and the head of the clan of Judah Perez (that means to enslave) being born from Tamar who disguised herself as a woman of hire to seduce Judah got the whole thing somehow into Egypt and bondage. Jacob had chosen Joseph who the twelve brothers betrayed they thought to a traveling caravan. The twelve brothers thought they did away with that master so they lived happily until the famine when Jacob sent them into Egypt to get food and they found their brother. The Master Joseph told them to come and stay and they all migrated to Egypt where they were enslaved and had to leave. The Prince Moses led the people away as a General of Pharoah that betrayed his command. He used Aaron as a simple interpreter. Now there was a Joshua son of Nun who was of the line of Joseph and actually led the Israelites into the Holy land when Moses was of great age.

Enter some Genealogy. Moses and Aaron were three generations from Levi, who would have been much older than Joseph. David, the first Master was fourteen generations from Judah, and so was in a different time than the other masters. Joshua was of the line of Ephraim the son of Joseph by Asenath and was fifteen generations from Joseph. Yet Joshua was alive when Moses was very old. So the generations from Joseph to Joshua (15) would be very short compared to the generations between Levi and Moses and Aaron (3). Also keep in mind Levi was an older half brother to Joseph. If a child is born to a son the son must be at least about twelve years old. That's 15 times 12 or 178 years. So between Joseph and Joshua the estimated minimum time would be 178 years. So if Levi was 100 years old when he had Kohath and Kohath was 100 years old when he had Amram and Amran could be 100 when he had Aaron and Moses and Moses was 100 years old when Joshua went into battle then that's 400 years. So 178 years minimum into 400 years works alright. Its rather hard to believe but possible. So apparently Levi's tribe had children slower than Joseph's tribe. If Josephs son Now remember we are studying genealogy and the line of Heber Scot is of the tribe of Levi, not a priest of Aaron but a descendent of Aaron. So who is Heber Scot?

The last Master.

The genealogy lists show him a son of Merytatum and Aaron. So Heber Scot is a son of Merytatum. So who was Merytatum? The lists show Merytatum as the daughter of Moses. Now Aaron and Moses had a mother named Jochabed that was the daughter of Levi. She married Amram and had Aaron and Moses. It is thought that Merytatum was a very young bed warmer for Aaron in Aaron's old age. Aaron had Ithamar who was the father of the Priest Eli and Aaron had Eleazar who was the father of the Aaronic Priesthood. It is interesting to see the lines of Aaron in a genealogy study that shows the succession of the Priest. Not all of Aaron's sons from Eliezar became priests as some were younger brothers and elder lines did not produce heirs etc.. All of Itamar's sons became high priests but the line died out after the reign of Abiathar the 12th high priest did not produce a heir. Zadok succeeded the high priest hood of Aaron after four generations of descendents of Aaron with no high priest. This was the time of David when Abithar was the High Priest for King David and King Solomon. Note that Eli was the 7th high priest and his daughter was given to Uzzi the 6th High Priest. Therefore Eli is a direct ancestor of most everyone as is Itamar while Phineas, Ahitub, Ahijah, Ahimelech and Abiathar are not direct ancestors of most everyone. Now back to Jochabed the mother of Aaron. She also on some lists is considered the mother of Asenath with Potipherah. Potipherah is from Basemath who is from Ishmael so is Abrahamic although not part of the promise (Isaac) But Jochabed was. Now Amram was son of Kohath and his wife Jochabed was his Aunt as well as his wife. And Aaron had Heber Scot with his neice the daughter of Moses the general. So how does Aaron become a master. Who makes Aaron a master by becoming his victim and is he guilty. Is it his wife Mary and so does he become the cause for divorce, or is it his mother and and he is guilty of matricide?

By the way as far as the chosen Master Joseph's wife Asenath was certainly the daughter of Potipherah but may have Dinah as her mother. In either case she is daughter of the promise (either Dinah or Jochabed) and in both cases from Jacob, not Israel, yet possibly a descendent of Levi as well.

So apparently there was some rather unusual relationships in the tribe of Levi that are found in genealogy. So lets go back to Dan and see some other rather unusual relationships. Dan was the son of Bilhah the servant of Rachel. Now in some translations of the bible Reuben is the half brother to Dan.

In some translations of the bible Reuben has Bilhah and makes another half brother to Dan by Bilhah called Bono. Now Rabi Nicodemus in Genealogy has a father named Reuben on some lists. It makes sense then that Bono is the same as Nickolaus. Whatever the name he is both the half brother and Nephew to Dan, however does not have the same uncle as Dan, that of Lucas the twin to Leah. Dan would be the half Nephew of Lucas the twin to Leah and brother of Rachel because Jacob married Leah and Rachel. So Dan although a servant Master of Edom did not actually Kill Reuben but has had the priveledge of chewing him out everytime he goes to the deli and has a Reuben Sandwich. Of course Reuben was not a servant son like Dan but a son of Leah the wife Jacob got stuck with by Laban after working for seven years and thinking he would be Rachel but woke up after his wedding night and looked at his wife and saw Leah. So Laban got him to serve him another seven years for Rachel. So because Nickolaus was the son of a wife of Jacob he was also half brothers to Judah, Simeon, Levi, Zebulon, Isaac-har, Gad, Asher, Joseph, Benjamin, Naphtali, and Dan however not to Reuben because he was the son of Reuben Jacobs Eldest Son.

Lot From Nahor And the Precedent

About the family of Lot where an Angel visited Lot and the relationships of Haran and Abraham.

If you study the lists concerning Abraham, his Father Terah, and Nahor some interesting facts emerge.

Nahor had Iosaka and made Terah, who had Yawnu the mother of Milcah who had the same Nahor and made Bethuel. Now therefore Bethuel and Terah are both sons of Nahor, however Terah has to be older than Bethuel because Terah is the Grandfather of Bethuel his brother. This is a precident that is obvious and must be true but it gets better. Terah was the father of Haran by Maria. Now Haran was also the father of Micah by Yawnu and Micah married Bethuel and made Rebecca who married Isaac. So now thinking about it Micah and Milcah are sisters (daughters of Yawnu) so Micah became the aunt of Bethuel who was her husband the son of Milcah. Thinking about it further Rebecca was the daughter of Bethuel her cousin !!! Yawnu was the Grandmother of Rebecca and Yawnu was the Grandmother of Bethuel because Bethuel was the daughter of Milcah the daughter of Yawnu. If two people have the same Grandmother they are cousins, regardless of if they are Father and daughter. Now Haran had a son that was Lot. So Lot was the brother to Milcah and Micah. Now Haran had a brother the son of Terah and Maria called Abraham. To further complicate matters Rebecca was the Niece of Terah because she was daughter of Bethuel Terah's younger brother. So Terah was uncle to Becky. Now Abraham was son of Terah and Becky was the neice of Terah so Abraham and Becky were of the same generation. Going even further Lot was the brother to Milcah and Micah so if Abraham was Lots uncle then his sisters Micah and Milcah had Abraham as an uncle. Now Milcah was daughter of Terah and so was Abraham and Sarai and Haran so Milcah was the same generation as Abraham her uncle.

Another way is the Nahor had Iosaka and made Terah who had Maria and made Haran who had Yawnu and made Milcah who had Nahor and made Bethuel. This makes Terah the Great Grandfather of Bethuel thru the marriages of Haran and Yawnu and Nahor and Milcah. (Great Grandfathers have two marriages between themselves and their grandsons. This makes Milcah a generation below Abraham

Sarai and Haran and so is a different generation . The precident is that Terah is older than Bethuel because Bethuel is Terah's greatgrandson. This is a precident that is obvious and must be true but it gets better. Terah was the father of Haran by Maria. Now Haran was also the father of Micah by Yawnu and Micah married Bethuel and made Rebecca who married Isaac. As far as Rebecca being the descendent of Terah, he was her paternal Great Grandfather and also her uncle. Now Yawnu is still the Grandmother of Rebecca and Bethuel so Bethuel is cousins with his daughter Rebecca. Now there is a gap between Abraham and Becky. Abraham was uncle to Micah Rebecca's mother so Abraham was a Granduncle to Rebecca who married his son Isaac. Saria was also a GrandAunt of Rebecca who married Isaac. However Bethuel was uncle to Abraham because he was Terah's Brother so his daughter his cousin Rebecca was of the same Generation as Terah's son Abraham and so it follows that Rebecca was the same generations as her Grandfather Haran who was the brother to Abraham. It is a far stretch or reach or tall tail to say that Rebecca was the aunt of Isaac because she was the same generation as Isaac's mother and father who had a common father. (Terah). Consider the relationship between Bethuel and Micah. Micah was the sister to Milcah so Bethuel was Micah's nephew, and also her husband. Now we know from above that Rebecca and Bethuel are cousins. So Rebecca's Grandfather was Nahor and Abraham's grandfather was Nahor. There fore Abraham and Rebecca are cousins. To Keep up with all this then also Saria and Haran had the same grandfather as Abraham and Rebecca so therefore Abraham, Sarai, Haran, and Rebecca are all cousins thru the Grandfather Nahor and Rebecca and Bethuel are cousins thru the Grandmother Yawnu. So clearly these relationships are hard to express and fathom as many of these relationships are not approved by the pope that believes that laws like relationships between brothers and sisters are incestual and marriage of cousins is not allowed, and marriages of aunt and nephew are not allowed.

Lot

Now therefore Lot was the son of Haran by Yawny and therefore nephew to his fathers brother Abraham. Lot had a wife called Ado. Lot had two daughters called Benini and Palith. Some lists list Benini as Phiene. It is considered Sacred literature how the two daughters gave Lot wine and took him in a cave. Phiene was the father of Moab who was the father of the Moabites. Lot was the father of both Phiene and Moab, although Moab's mother was Lots daughter. Moab's line continued to Mayon and Khamudan who was the father of Apaleth who was the wife of Dan. Apaleth had a brother whose line continued to Ruth after ten generations on Ruth's Mothers side and seven generations on Ruth's fathers side. So Lot was an ancestor of King David the Master thru David's Great Grandmother Ruth. Now consider that Moab was the Grandson of Yawnu and Phiene and Palith were Granddaughters. Consider also that Bethuel and Rebecca are also Grandson and Granddaugher of Yawnu. Thus Yawnu's Grandchildren were Bethuel, Rebecca, Moab, Phiene, and Palith. Now Bethuel was father to Rebecca and Phiene was mother to Moab. Thus the cousins of Yawnu were also the relationships of Father to Daughter and Mother to Son. We did not forget Ammon however. He was the son of Palith and Lot and is also a cousin. Therefore the cousin count was 6 cousins from Yawnu and 4 cousins from Nahor so in the Generations from Nahor to the sons of Lot there are 10 cousins.

Lot

Now therefore Lot was the son of Haran and therefore nephew to his fathers brother Abraham. Lot had a wife called Ado. Lot had two daughters called Benini and Palith. Some lists list Benini as Phiene. It is considered Sacred literature how the two daughters gave Lot wine and took him in a cave. Phiene was the father of Moab who was the father of the Moabites. Lot was the father of both Phiene and Moab, although Moab's mother was Lots daughter. Moab's line continued to Mayon and Khamudan who was the father of Apaleth who was the wife of Dan. Apaleth had a brother whose line continued to Ruth after ten generations on Ruth's Mothers side and seven generations on Ruth's fathers side. So Lot was an ancestor of King David the Master thru David's Great Grandmother Ruth. Now however back to Abraham, Sarai, Isaac, and Rebecca.

From Abraham and Sari to Noah.

Now Terah had another wife called Towait or Nefir. This wife produced a daughter called Sarai who was a free woman. Abraham was the son of Terah by Maria so was half sister to Sarai. Now Sarai and Abraham had an ancestor in common called Noah. Between Abraham and Noah there was 11 generations and Abraham was from Shem. One line from Cham joined with Shem and was one generation smaller so there were ten generations from Noah to Abraham from Cham or Ham. Between Sarai and Noah there was 36 generations. Now Sarai was from Japeth and Cham and not from Shem. So the ratio was about one to three. One of Shem's generations was about three of Sarai's generations. There is a line from Maria the mother of Abraham to Heraclim's wife Shelah daughter of Ora, daughter of Ur son of Kesed son of Arphaxad that makes it Eight generations from Abraham to Noah.

So you can see that the precedent that Terah is older than Bethuel can be called a president and used in business.

Further Kinks

So around the time of Abraham there are half sisters and cousins and uncles that are not considered wrong by the Hebrew but are not considered as honorable by the Pope. And the Pope does believe in honor. So what is honorable. The marriage of cousin to cousin is not honorable yet the marriage of second cousin to second cousin is honorable. It is interesting that the time the Hebrew people were sent underground and their temple destroyed in 70 AD there was only one relationship in Galilee that was not "honorable", and this was the parents of Saint Mary Magdalene in the Dan. Once again the servant son Dan gets the Honor and this is likely the reason for all the slander that Our Lady of the Lake has always had.

So where else are there relationships that require one to say they are Hebrew? Well the King of Judah Jehosphat had a son Nimshi and that was with a Niece. The relationships around Caleb the son of Hezron and his son Hur with Miriam and Ezer require a priest. The relationships of Amram and Jocabed for Moses and Aaron require a priest and this is likely the origin of the priest. The relationships of Lot require a priest. In the lineages of Nicole, Karamat, and the Scota of Egypt there are many brothers and sisters that marry and these would all require a priest. The relationships above Noah are many brothers and sisters and aunts and uncles. Saul the first King of Israel had a daughter that married her nephew.

Now Abraham was the son of Maria and so was Haran. Terah was the husband of Yawnu and so the father of Milcah. Now Yawnu also married Haran and had Micah and Lot. So Lot and Milcah and Micah all had the same mother.

Consider the big sur. This is the line of Naptali that is part of everyone's blood line who can claim Abijah the son of Rehoboam as an ancestor. Now Rehoboam had Mahaleth as a wife and Abijah had Ann as a wife. Ann's line continued to Sarvia the daughter of Jesse who married the line of Naptali. Naptali had many sons, the one that is likely the ancestor of Sarvia's husband is Surem, or the Serum that is mixed in medicine research. Now here is where this needs to be covered up. Anna was the daughter of Basemath the daughter of Solomon. Now Abijah was the son of Rehoboam the son of Solomon. That makes Anna and Abijah cousins, (common grandfather) so this is usually covered by saying that Abijah wife is Machah and Reheboam's wife is Macchah. Then the Toucan Sam hits the scene and the lines from David are concealed. His son Shamariah the father of Elkanah that marries the line from Gad at Abihail is concealed, as well as the line from Rehboam that marries the line from Abihail the daughter of Eliab the Eldest son of Jesse and Jerimoth the Son of David by Abigail.

Now consider that three religions use Abraham as the Father or God, Christianity, Islam, and Judaism.

If Abraham is God, and has a son who married Rebecca, consider the relationships of Rebecca.

Recall how the Precident is that Terah has to be older than Bethuel due to lineage. Now Rebecca is the daughter of Bethuel. Rebecca like everyone else has four grandparents. One of these is Nahor

Rebecca is cousin to Abraham, Sarai, and Haran from Nahor and Iosaka. Now Consider also Rebecca has Yawnu as a Grandmother and Haran as a Grandfather. Rebecca is cousin to Bethuel, Belini, Palith, Ammon, and Moab thru her Grandparents Yawnu and Haran.

Rebecca is cousin to her father Bethuel. She is cousin to her God Abraham. She is cousin to her Grandfather Haran. She is cousin to both of Lot's daughters and both of Lot's Daughter's Sons.

Rebecca is Niece to her Uncle Terah, who is also her Great Grandfather, from Terah father of Haran, father of Micah, mother to Rebecca, and Terah is also her Great Great Grandfather from Terah father of Haran father of Milcah father of Bethuel father of Rebecca.

So in order to straighten this all out around Abraham there is God, Precedent and Cousins.

So Cousins become important.

In this book there are countless cousins found, however here the author is going to concentrate on Sacred Cousins first and then branch off into other cousins.

First, the Cousins of the Holy Name and the Sacred Cousins of Jesus Christ.

		Cousin	GrandParents	Relationship
1	Rebecca	Abraham son of Terah	Nahor	God
2	Rebecca	Saria daughter of Terah	Nahor	Mother in Law
3	Rebecca	Haran son of Terah	Nahor	Grandfather
4	Rebecca	Rotheus son of Huz	Nahor	Cousin
5	Rebecca	Cheref son of Huz	Nahor	Cousin
6	Rebecca	Bethuel son of Nahor	Yawnu	Father
7	Rebecca	Laban son of Bethuel	Nahor	Brother
8	Rebecca	Palith daughter of Lot	Yawnu	Cousin
9	Rebecca	Benani daughter of Lot	Yawnu	Cousin
10	Rebecca	Ammon son of Lot	Yawnu	Cousin
11	Rebecca	Moab son of Lot	Yawnu	Cousin
12	Rebecca	Iscah son of Terah	Nahor	Cousin
13	Rebecca	Zoba son of Terah	Nahor	Cousin
14	Rebecca	Aram son of Kemuel	Nahor	Cousin
15	Rebecca	Deborah Daughter of Huz	Nahor	Cousin
16	Rebecca	Gadin son of Huz	Nahor	Cousin
17	Rebecca	Melus son of Huz	Nahor	Cousin
18	Rebecca	Abi son of Huz	Nahor	Cousin
19	Rebecca	Abimelech son of Terah	Nahor	Cousin
20	Rebecca	Chesed son of Kemuel	Nahor	Cousin
21	Rebecca	Hazo son of Kemuel	Nahor	Cousin
22	Rebecca	Pildash son of Kemuel	Nahor	Cousin
23	Rebecca	Jidlaph son of Kemuel	Nahor	Cousin
24	Rebecca	Abinah daughter of Bethuel	Nahor	Cousin
25	Rebecca	Rechob son of Kemuel	Nahor	Cousin
26	Rebecca	Kemuel	Yawnu	Cousin
27	Rebecca	Huz	Yawnu	Cousin
28	Rebecca	Naomi daughter of Kemuel	Nahor	Cousin

ERA OF ABRAHAM A FEW GENERATIONS UP AND A FEW DOWN.

Rebecca's Cousins.

There are 27, and possibly Iscah is really Sarah. Also Laban and Adinah are brother and sister as well as cousins so that makes 24. Note that Roetheus as the father of the sisters Bllhah and Zilpah the mothers of Dan, Naptali, Gad, and Asher. Aslo Moab's line continued to the wife of Dan, while Zoba's line continued to a wife of Benjamin. Aram's line continued to a wife of Levi, and Cheref's line continued to sisters that were wifes of Naptali and Gad. So if all twelve Israelites are ancestors, then Kemuel, Huz, Aram, Roetheus, Cheref, Benani, and Moab are all ancestors related to Israel, as are Abraham, Sarai and Rebecca and Haran and Bethuel. So eleven of Rebecca's cousins are related to Israel. (fourteen if you count Laban, Adinah, and Iscah)

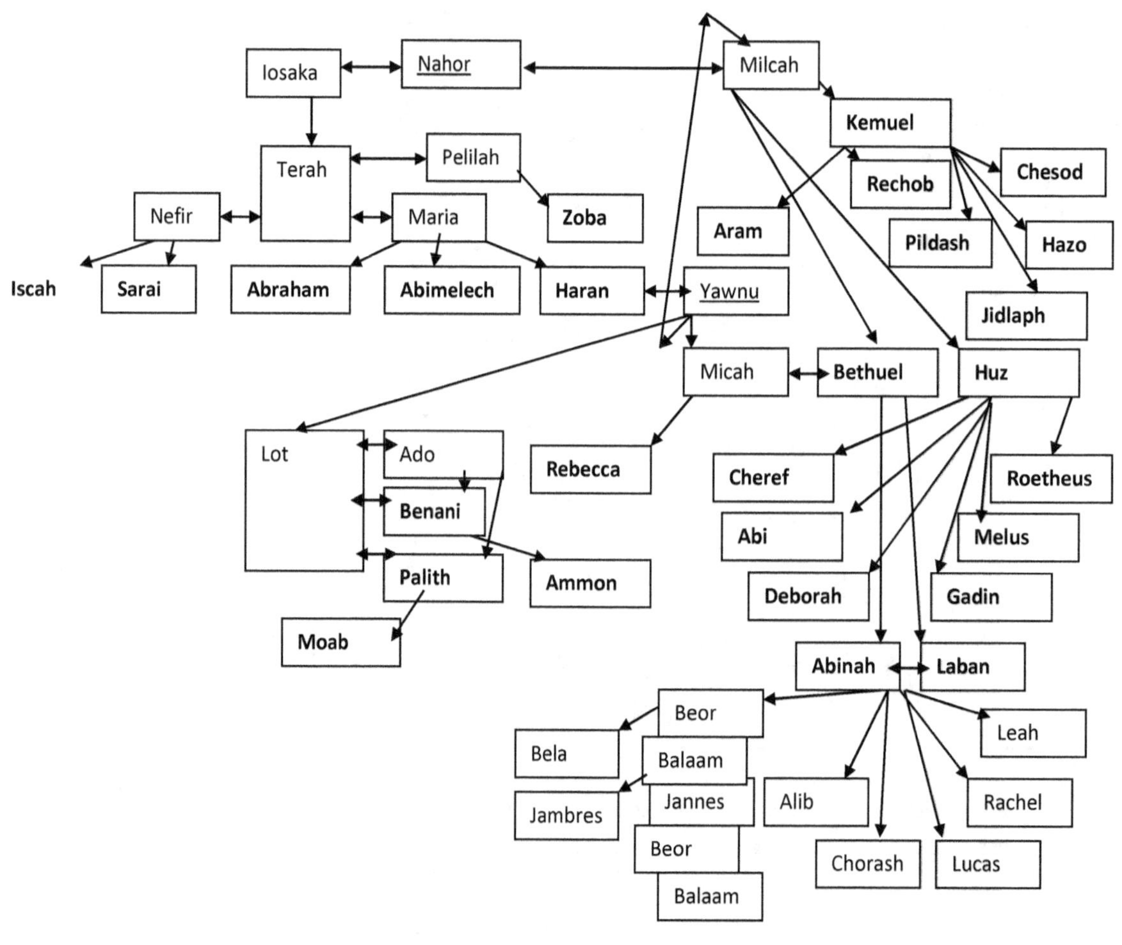

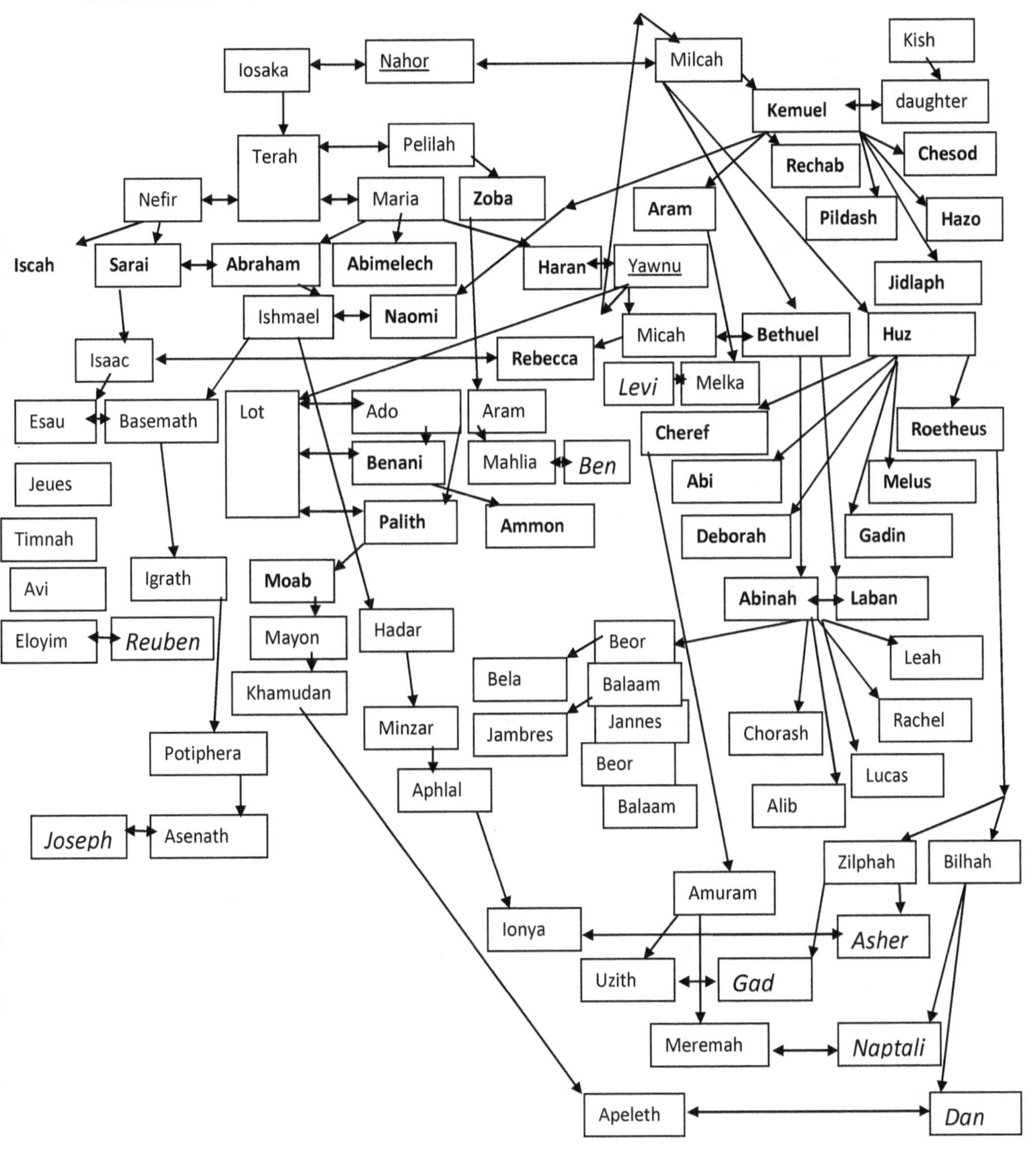

Iosaka
Nahor
Milcah
Kish
Kemuel
daughter
Terah
Pelilah
Rechab
Chesod
Nefir
Maria
Zoba
Aram
Pildash
Hazo
Iscah
Sarai
Abraham
Abimelech
Haran
Yawnu
Jidlaph
Ishmael
Naomi
Micah
Bethuel
Huz
Isaac
Rebecca
Levi
Melka
Esau
Basemath
Lot
Ado
Aram
Cheref
Roetheus
Benani
Mahlia
Ben
Abi
Melus
Jeues
Timnah
Palith
Ammon
Deborah
Gadin
Avi
Igrath
Moab
Abinah
Laban
Eloyim
Reuben
Mayon
Hadar
Beor
Leah
Bela
Balaam
Khamudan
Jannes
Minzar
Jambres
Chorash
Rachel
Potiphera
Beor
Lucas
Aphlal
Balaam
Alib
Joseph
Asenath
Zilphah
Bilhah
Amuram
Ionya
Asher
Uzith
Gad
Meremah
Naptali
Apeleth
Dan

Descendents of the Spotted Lambs Ancestral Cousins

Reuben	Abraham	Sarai	Rebecca	Naomi	Kemuel			
Isaac-har	Abraham	Sarai	Rebecca					
Levi	Abraham	Sarai	Rebecca	Aram	Kemuel			
Joseph	Abraham	Sarai	Rebecca	Naomi	Kemuel			
Benjamin	Abraham	Sarai	Rebecca	Zoba	Kemuel			
Zebulon	Abraham	Sarai	Rebecca					
Dan	Abraham	Sarai	Rebecca	Moab	Rotheus	Huz	Haran	Palith
Gad	Abraham	Sarai	Rebecca	Rotheus	Cheref	Huz		
Asher	Abraham	Sarai	Rebecca	Rotheus	Naomi	Huz	Kemuel	
Naphali	Abraham	Sarai	Rebecca	Rotheus	Cheref	Huz		
Simeon	Abraham	Sarai	Rebecca					
Judah	Abraham	Sarai	Rebecca					

Israelites Wives Ancestral Cousins of Rebecca

Wife	Israelite	Cousins				
Ijona	*Asher*	Naomi	Kemuel			
Apaleth	*Dan*	Moab	Rotheus	Huz	Haran	Palith
Eloyram	*Reuben*	Naomi	Kemuel			
Merumah	*Napthali*	Cheref	Huz			
Aseneth	*Joseph*	Naomi	Kemuel			
Melka	*Levi*	Aram	Kemuel			
Mahlia	*Benjamin*	Zoba	Kemuel			
Uzith	*Gad*	Cheref	Huz			

ERA OF CHRISTIANITY

SECTION NINETEEN: TIME LINE

Time in History

The secret here is the time line of happenings in history.

Time of Writing the Bible to the Roman Empire becoming the Holy Roman Empire. Many of the Church Martyrs who became Saints lived during this time.

Jerusalem fell to the Romans about 70 AD.

5 BC Jesus of Nazareth is born
33 The resurrection of Jesus
46 Paul begins missionary journeys
64 Nero burns Rome
70 The destruction of Jerusalem
81 Domitian persecution begins
98 Trajan persecution begins
100 Justin Martyr is born
110 Martyrdom of Ignatius
117 Hadrian persecution begins
130 Conversion of Justin
130 Irenaeus is born
135 Justin writes Dialogue
138 Antonius Pius persecution begins
c150 Justin's writes First Apology
150 Clement of Alexandria is born
155 Martyrdom of Polycarp
155 Tertullian is born
161 Marcus Aurelius persecution begins
163 Martyrdom of Justin
178 Iranaeus is bishop of Lyon
178 Celsus writes True Reason
185 Iraneaus writes Against Heresies
185 Origen is born
193 Septimus Severus persecution begins
196 Tertullian begins to write
200 Clement begins to write
200 Cyprian is born
211 First era of peace begins
220 Origen begins to write
230 Church at Dura-Europas built
248 Cyprian is bishop of Carthage
248 Origen writes Contra Celsus
251 Anthony is born
255 Rebaptism controversy
257 Valerian persecution begins
260 Second era of peace begins
260 Eusebius is born
264 Councils at Antioch
269 Anthony goes into the desert
286 Pachomius is born

303 The Great Persecution begins
311 Edict of Toleration
311 Donatist schism begins
311 Edict of Toleration
311 Donatist schism begins
312 Battle of Milvian Bridge
313 Edict of Milan
315 Arian controversy begins
316 Martin of Tours is born
324 Constantine controls entire empire
324 Pachomius starts commune
325 Council of Nicea
328 Athanasius is bishop Alexandria
330 Constantinople founded
337 Constantine's baptism and death
339 Ambrose is born
345 Chrysostom is born
347 Jerome is born
353 Constantius' pro-Arian policy
354 Augustine is born
360 John Cassian is born
361 Julian the Apostate gains control
367 Athanasius defines New Testament
370 Basil becomes bishop of Caesarea
378 Battle of Adrianople
379 Theodosius becomes emperor
381 Council of Constantinople
385 Ambrose prevails
387 Augustine's conversion
395 Augustine becomes bishop of Hippo
398 Chrysostom bishop of Constantinople

Early Dark Ages. Rome is still a very large power in the world.

406 Jeromes completes the Vulgate
410 Fall of Rome
418 Synod of Carthage
431 Council of Ephesus

410 Fall of Rome
418 Synod of Carthage
431 Council of Ephesus
432 Patrick's mission to Ireland

440 Leo the Great becomes pope
449 The "Robber Synod"
451 Council of Chalcedon
455 Vandals sack Rome
476 Odoacer deposes last Roman emperor
480 Benedict is born
496 Clovis is baptized

Second Century of the Dark Ages.

521 b. Columba, Irish missionary to Scotland
529 The Council of Orange540 b. Gregory the Great
540 Benedict write his Rule
553 Second Council of Constantinople
560 b. Isidore of Seville
575 Gregory the Great becomes a monk
590 Gregory the Great becomes pope.
596 Augustine of Canterbury sent to England.

Third Century of the Dark Ages.

604 d. Gregory the Great
613 d. Augustine of Canterbury
615 The Persians capture Jerusalem
622 Beginning of Islam
632 Death of Muhammad
636 d. Isidore of Seville
663 Synod of Whitby reconciles the old British liturgy and the Roman liturgy
675 b. John of Damascus
680 b. Boniface

Fourth Century of the Dark Ages. The Dark Ages begin to end and the Middle Ages begin.

732 Battle of Tours
749 d. John of Damascus
754 d. Boniface
772 Charlemagne attacks the Saxons
781 Alcuin becomes royal advisor
793 Vikings raid Lindisfarne
800 Charlemagne becomes emperor

The Dark Ages end and the Middle Ages begin. The Saxons take over England.

800 Pope Leo III crowns Charlemagne head of the Holy Roman Empire
827 Saracens raid Sicily
841 Vikings establish base in Dublin
860 Cyril & Methodius' missions to Germany

The Middle Ages. Saxons in power in England.

907 Magyars destroy Bavarian army
950 Conversion of Olga of Russia
955 Otto I defeats Magyars
988 Conversion of Russia begins

Middle Ages. Normans in Power in England.

1054 East and West split

1088 Christainazation of Russia
1093 Anselm becomes archbishop of Canterbury
1095 Council of Clermont
1095 Crusade begin
1099 Crusaders take Jerusalem

Middle Ages.

1115 Bernard founds monastery at Clairvaux
1122 Concordat of Worms
1141 Abelard is condemned
1144 Fall of Edessa
1150 Universities at Paris and Oxford
1175 Waldensian movement begins

Middle Ages. Age of Renaissance to begin in one century.

1208 Francis renounces wealth
1215 Fourth Lateran Council
1272 Thomas completes Summa
1291 End of crusader presence in holy land

The Late Middle Ages: 1300-1500

1309 'Babylon captivity' begins
1337 The Hundred Years War begins
1370 Catherine of Sienna writes Letters
1377 'Babylon captivity' ends
1378 The Great Schism
1380 Wycliffe condemned

1409 Council of Pisa
1413 Jon Huss burned at stake
1413 Lollard rebellion
1414 Council of Constance begins
1423 The Great Schism ends
1431 Joan of Arc martyred
1453 Fall of Constantinople
1498 Savonarola dies

The Reformation: 1500-1599

1512 Michelangelo completes the Sistine Chapel
1517 Luther's 95 theses
1521 Diet of Worms
1522 Ignatius Loyola writes *Spiritual Exercises*
1524 Peasant's War
1525 Anabaptist movement begun
1529 Colloguy at Marburg
1530 Augsburg Confession
1530 St. Peter's Basilica rebuilt
1536 Calvins *Institutes* first edition
1536 Henry VIII and Act of Supremacy
1545 Council of Trent and Counter Reformation
1549 Book of Common Prayer
1549 Xavier begins mission in Japan
1554 Marian Persecution and flight to Geneva
1555 Latimer and Oxford Martyrs
1559 John Knox returns to Scotland
1559 Calvin's *Institutes* final edition
1565 Teresa of Avila writes *The Way of Perfection*
1572 Huguenot St. Bartholomew's Day massacre
1576 Pacification of Ghent
1595 Ricci's *The True Doctrine of God*
1596 Japanese persecute Christians
1598 Edict of Nantes

Davids Mighty Men

Asahel
page 342

Elhanan son of Dodo of Bethlehem
page 341

Shammah of Harod
page 344

Elika of Harod
page 344

Helez of Beth-Pelet
page 344

Ira son of Ikkesh of Tekoa
page 341

Abiezer of Anathoth
page 345

Sibbecai of Hushah
page 341

Zalmon of Ahoh
?

Maharai of Netophah
page 341

Heled son of Baanah of Netophah
page 341

Ittai son of Ribai of Gibeah in Benjamin
page 346

Benaiah of Pirathon
page 344

Hiddai of the Torrents of Gaash
page 345

Abibaal of Beth-ha-Arabah
page 347

Azmaveth of Bahurim
page 344

Eliahba of Shaalbon
?

Jashen of Gimzo
page 344

Jonathan son of Shammah of Harar
page 344

Ahiam son of Sharar of Harar
page 349

Eliphalet son of Ahasbai of Beth Maacah
?

Eliam son of Ahithophel
page 347

Hezro of carmel
?

Paarai of Arab
page 341

Igal son of Nathan of Zobah
page 341

Bani the Gadite
page 350

Zelek the Ammonite
page 346

Naharai of Beeroth squire to Joab son of Zeruiah
page 346

Ira of Jattir
page 346

Gareb of Jattir
page 345

Uriah the Hittite
page 345

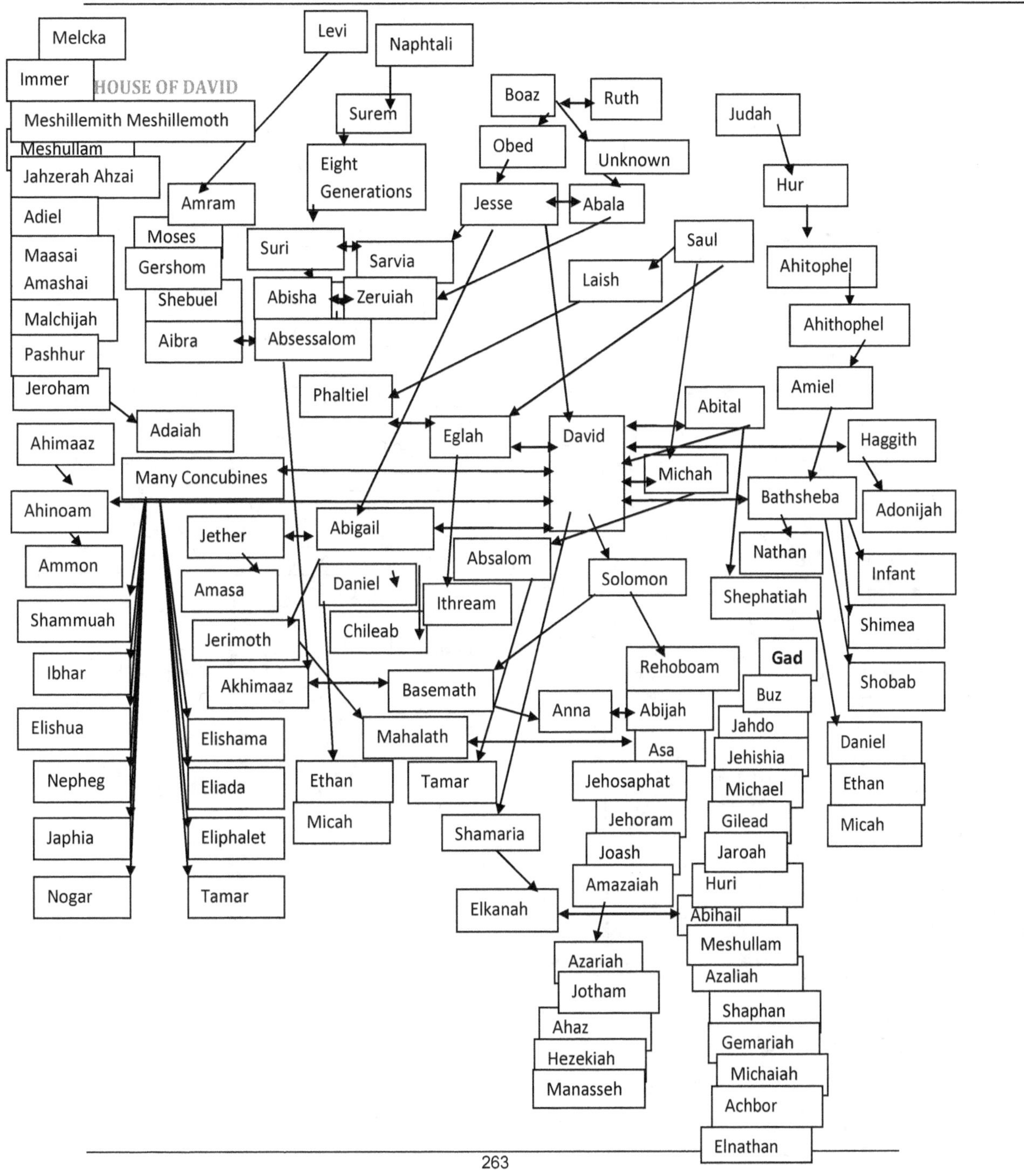
HOUSE OF DAVID
Melcka
Immer
Meshillemith Meshillemoth
Meshullam
Jahzerah Ahzai
Adiel
Maasai Amashai
Malchijah
Pashhur
Jeroham
Adaiah
Levi
Naphtali
Surem
Eight Generations
Amram
Moses
Gershom
Shebuel
Aibra
Suri
Sarvia
Abisha
Zeruiah
Absessalom
Boaz
Ruth
Obed
Unknown
Jesse
Abala
Judah
Hur
Ahitophel
Ahithophel
Amiel
Saul
Laish
Phaltiel
Eglah
David
Abital
Haggith
Adonijah
Michah
Bathsheba
Nathan
Infant
Shimea
Shobab
Ahimaaz
Many Concubines
Ahinoam
Ammon
Shammuah
Ibhar
Elishua
Nepheg
Japhia
Nogar
Elishama
Eliada
Eliphalet
Tamar
Jether
Amasa
Jerimoth
Akhimaaz
Abigail
Daniel
Chileab
Ithream
Absalom
Solomon
Shephatiah
Basemath
Mahalath
Anna
Abijah
Rehoboam
Gad
Buz
Jahdo
Jehishia
Michael
Gilead
Jaroah
Huri
Abihail
Meshullam
Azaliah
Shaphan
Gemariah
Michaiah
Achbor
Elnathan
Daniel
Ethan
Micah
Ethan
Micah
Tamar
Shamaria
Elkanah
Asa
Jehosaphat
Jehoram
Joash
Amazaiah
Azariah
Jotham
Ahaz
Hezekiah
Manasseh

HOUSE OF REUBEN AND

ZEBULON AND ISAAC-HAR ISRAELITES

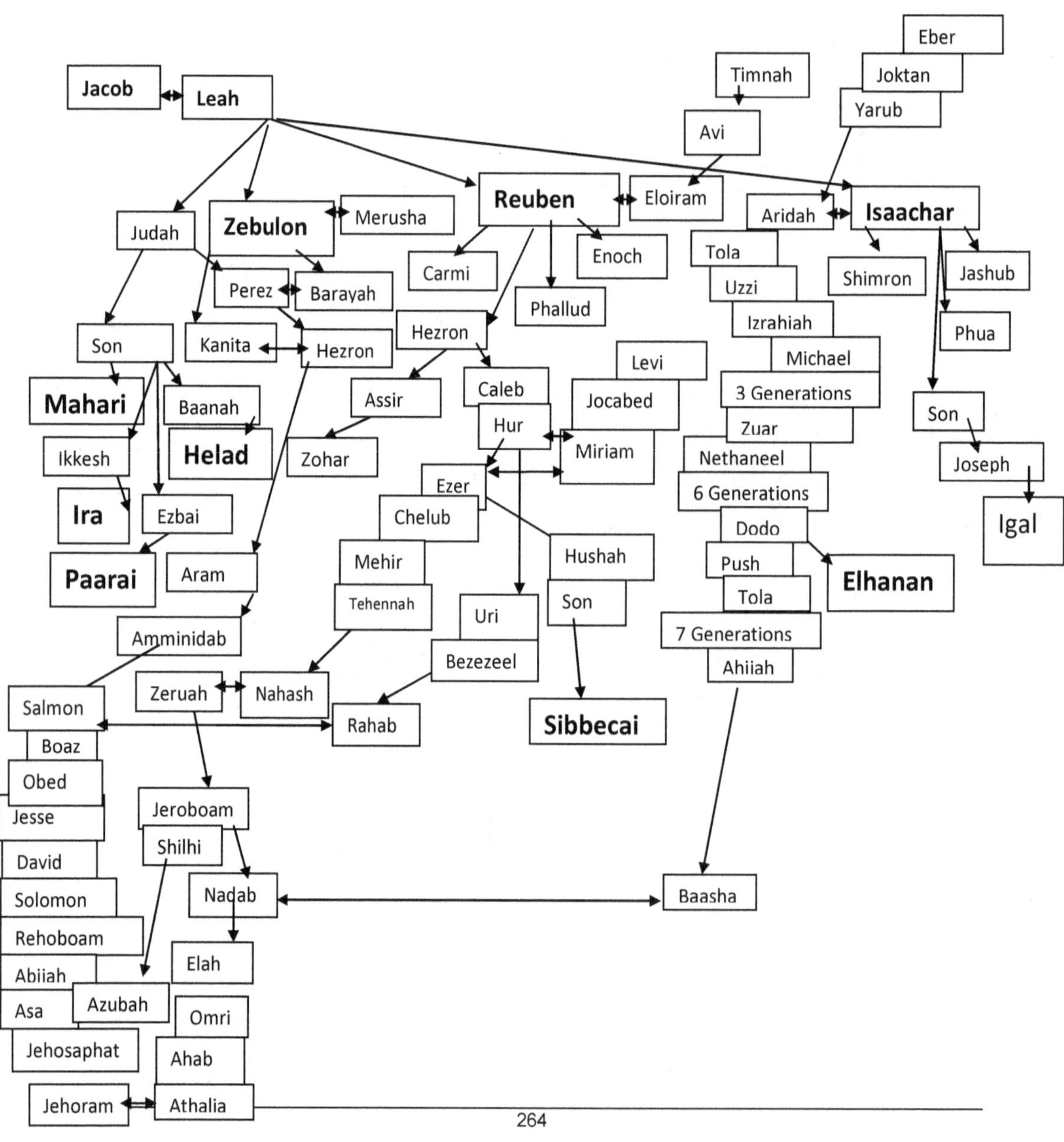

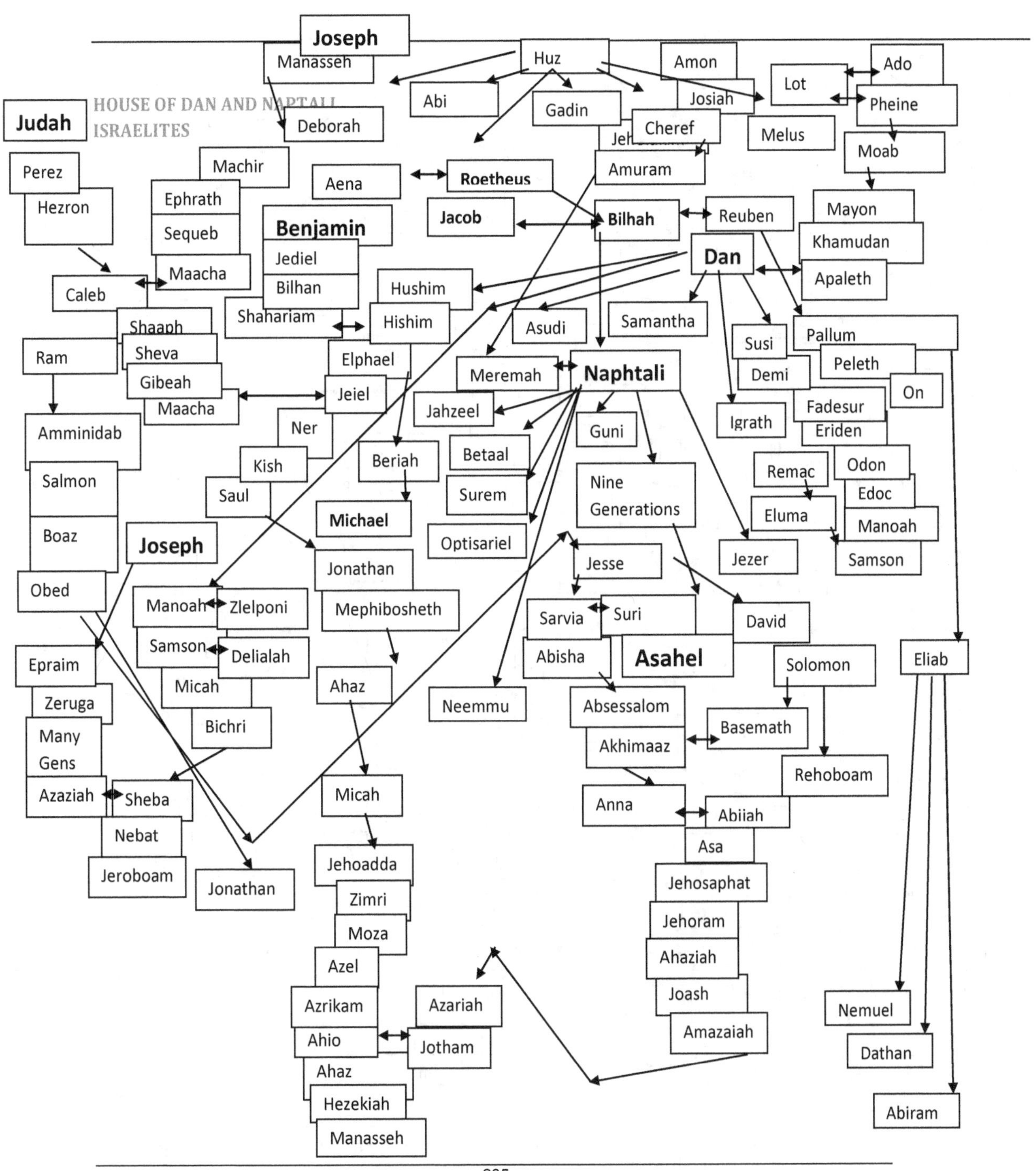

Joseph
Manasseh
Huz
Amon
Ado
Lot
Abi
Gadin
Josiah
Pheine
Judah
HOUSE OF DAN AND NAPTALI
ISRAELITES
Deborah
Cheref
Melus
Moab
Perez
Machir
Aena
Roetheus
Amuram
Hezron
Ephrath
Jacob
Bilhah
Reuben
Mayon
Sequeb
Benjamin
Khamudan
Jediel
Dan
Maacha
Hushim
Apaleth
Caleb
Bilhan
Shahariam
Hishim
Asudi
Samantha
Shaaph
Pallum
Ram
Sheva
Elphael
Susi
Peleth
Meremah
Naphtali
Gibeah
Demi
On
Jeiel
Maacha
Jahzeel
Fadesur
Ner
Guni
Igrath
Eriden
Amminidab
Betaal
Kish
Beriah
Remac
Odon
Salmon
Nine
Generations
Surem
Saul
Edoc
Eluma
Michael
Manoah
Boaz
Joseph
Optisariel
Jesse
Jezer
Samson
Jonathan
Obed
Manoah
Zlelponi
Mephibosheth
Sarvia
Suri
David
Samson
Delialah
Abisha
Asahel
Solomon
Epraim
Eliab
Micah
Ahaz
Zeruga
Neemmu
Absessalom
Basemath
Many
Gens
Bichri
Akhimaaz
Rehoboam
Azaziah
Sheba
Micah
Anna
Abiiah
Nebat
Asa
Jehoadda
Jeroboam
Jonathan
Jehosaphat
Zimri
Jehoram
Moza
Ahaziah
Azel
Joash
Azrikam
Azariah
Nemuel
Amazaiah
Ahio
Jotham
Dathan
Ahaz
Hezekiah
Abiram
Manasseh

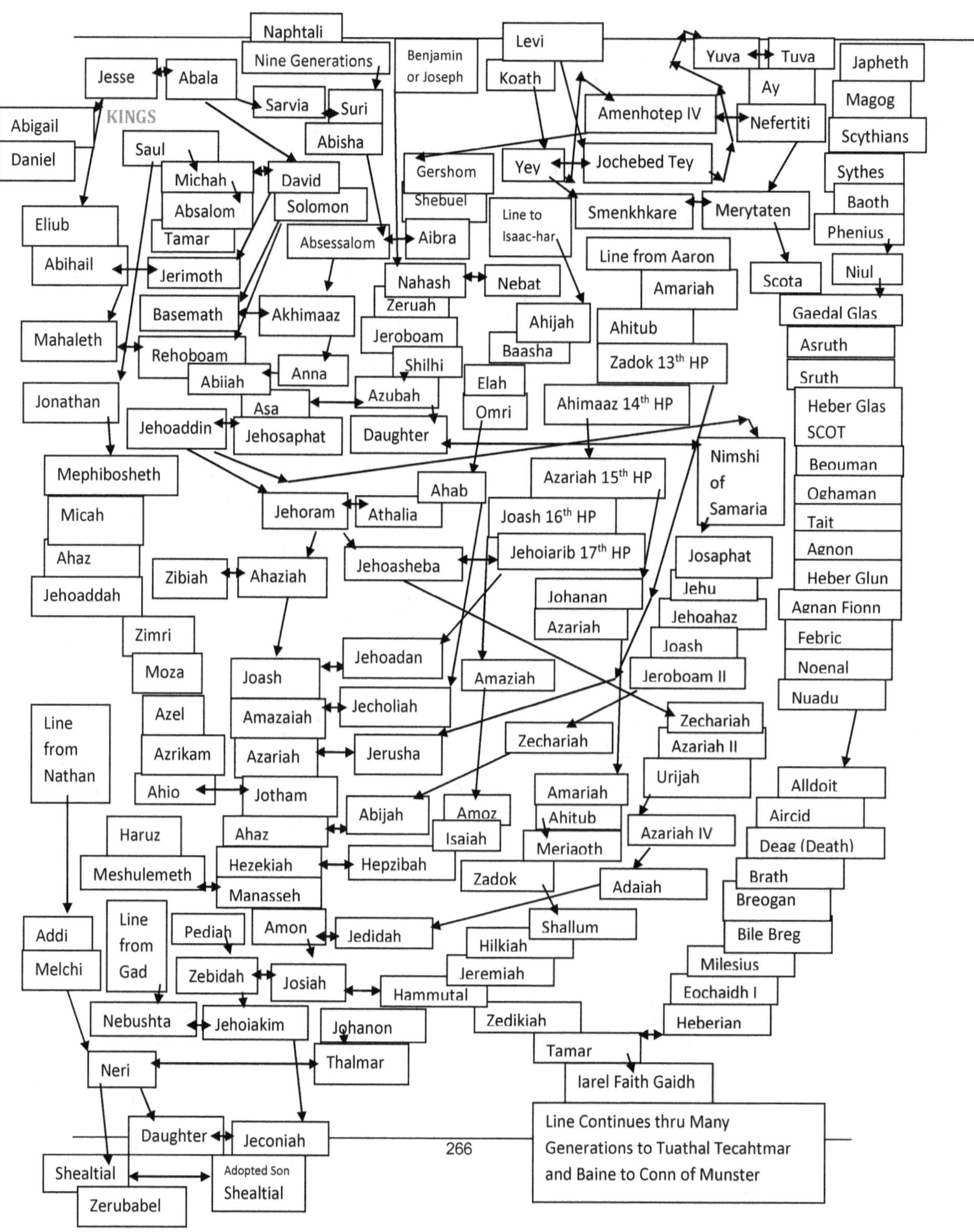

Naphtali
Nine Generations
Benjamin or Joseph
Levi
Yuva
Tuva
Japheth
Jesse
Abala
Koath
Ay
Magog
Sarvia
Suri
Amenhotep IV
Nefertiti
Abigail
KINGS
Abisha
Scythians
Daniel
Saul
David
Gershom
Yey
Jochebed Tey
Sythes
Michah
Solomon
Shebuel
Smenkhkare
Merytaten
Baoth
Absalom
Line to Isaac-har
Eliub
Tamar
Absessalom
Aibra
Phenius
Line from Aaron
Abihail
Jerimoth
Nahash
Nebat
Niul
Amariah
Scota
Basemath
Akhimaaz
Zeruah
Ahijah
Gaedal Glas
Mahaleth
Jeroboam
Ahitub
Asruth
Rehoboam
Shilhi
Baasha
Zadok 13th HP
Abiiah
Anna
Elah
Sruth
Jonathan
Azubah
Ahimaaz 14th HP
Heber Glas SCOT
Asa
Omri
Jehoaddin
Jehosaphat
Daughter
Nimshi of Samaria
Beouman
Mephibosheth
Azariah 15th HP
Ahab
Oghaman
Micah
Jehoram
Athalia
Joash 16th HP
Tait
Ahaz
Jehoiarib 17th HP
Josaphat
Agnon
Zibiah
Ahaziah
Jehoasheba
Heber Glun
Jehoaddah
Johanan
Jehu
Agnan Fionn
Zimri
Azariah
Jehoahaz
Febric
Joash
Moza
Joash
Jehoadan
Amaziah
Jeroboam II
Noenal
Azel
Amazaiah
Jecholiah
Nuadu
Line from Nathan
Zechariah
Zechariah
Azrikam
Azariah
Jerusha
Azariah II
Urijah
Ahio
Jotham
Amariah
Alldoit
Abijah
Amoz
Ahitub
Aircid
Haruz
Ahaz
Isaiah
Azariah IV
Meriaoth
Deag (Death)
Hezekiah
Hepzibah
Meshulemeth
Zadok
Brath
Adaiah
Manasseh
Breogan
Line from Gad
Pediah
Amon
Shallum
Addi
Jedidah
Bile Breg
Hilkiah
Melchi
Zebidah
Josiah
Jeremiah
Milesius
Hammutal
Eochaidh I
Nebushta
Jehoiakim
Johanon
Zedikiah
Heberian
Neri
Thalmar
Tamar
Iarel Faith Gaidh
Line Continues thru Many Generations to Tuathal Tecahtmar and Baine to Conn of Munster
Daughter
Jeconiah
Shealtial
Adopted Son Shealtial
Zerubabel

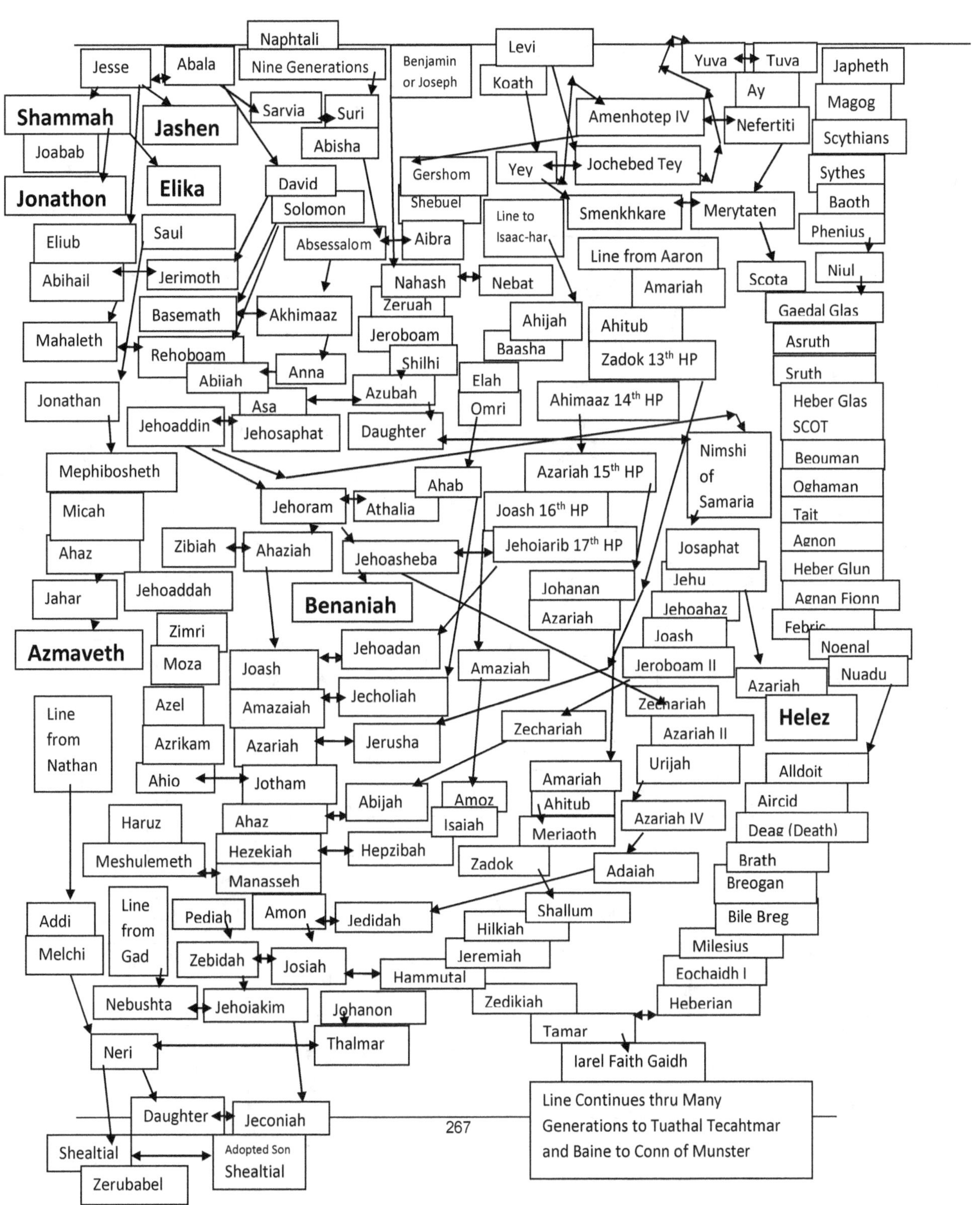
Naphtali
Nine Generations
Jesse
Abala
Benjamin or Joseph
Levi
Koath
Yuva
Tuva
Japheth
Ay
Magog
Shammah
Jashen
Sarvia
Suri
Abisha
Amenhotep IV
Nefertiti
Scythians
Joabab
Jonathon
Elika
David
Solomon
Gershom
Shebuel
Yey
Jochebed Tey
Sythes
Baoth
Smenkhkare
Merytaten
Phenius
Eliub
Saul
Abssessalom
Aibra
Line to Isaac-har
Line from Aaron
Niul
Abihail
Jerimoth
Nahash
Nebat
Amariah
Scota
Zeruah
Ahijah
Gaedal Glas
Basemath
Akhimaaz
Jeroboam
Ahitub
Asruth
Mahaleth
Rehoboam
Shilhi
Baasha
Zadok 13th HP
Sruth
Abiiah
Anna
Elah
Jonathan
Azubah
Heber Glas SCOT
Asa
Omri
Ahimaaz 14th HP
Jehoaddin
Jehosaphat
Daughter
Nimshi of Samaria
Beouman
Mephibosheth
Ahab
Azariah 15th HP
Oghaman
Micah
Jehoram
Athalia
Joash 16th HP
Tait
Ahaz
Zibiah
Ahaziah
Jehoasheba
Jehoiarib 17th HP
Josaphat
Agnon
Jehu
Heber Glun
Jahar
Jehoaddah
Benaniah
Johanan
Azariah
Jehoahaz
Agnan Fionn
Zimri
Febric
Azmaveth
Moza
Jehoadan
Joash
Noenal
Joash
Amaziah
Jeroboam II
Azariah
Nuadu
Line from Nathan
Azel
Amazaiah
Jecholiah
Zechariah
Helez
Azrikam
Azariah
Jerusha
Zecharaiah
Azariah II
Ahio
Jotham
Urijah
Alldoit
Abijah
Amoz
Amariah
Aircid
Haruz
Ahaz
Isaiah
Ahitub
Azariah IV
Deag (Death)
Meshulemeth
Hezekiah
Hepzibah
Meriaoth
Brath
Manasseh
Zadok
Adaiah
Breogan
Line from Gad
Pediah
Amon
Jedidah
Shallum
Bile Breg
Addi
Hilkiah
Milesius
Melchi
Zebidah
Josiah
Jeremiah
Eochaidh I
Hammutal
Nebushta
Jehoiakim
Johanon
Zedikiah
Heberian
Neri
Thalmar
Tamar
Iarel Faith Gaidh
Line Continues thru Many Generations to Tuathal Tecahtmar and Baine to Conn of Munster
Daughter
Jeconiah
Shealtial
Adopted Son Shealtial
Zerubabel

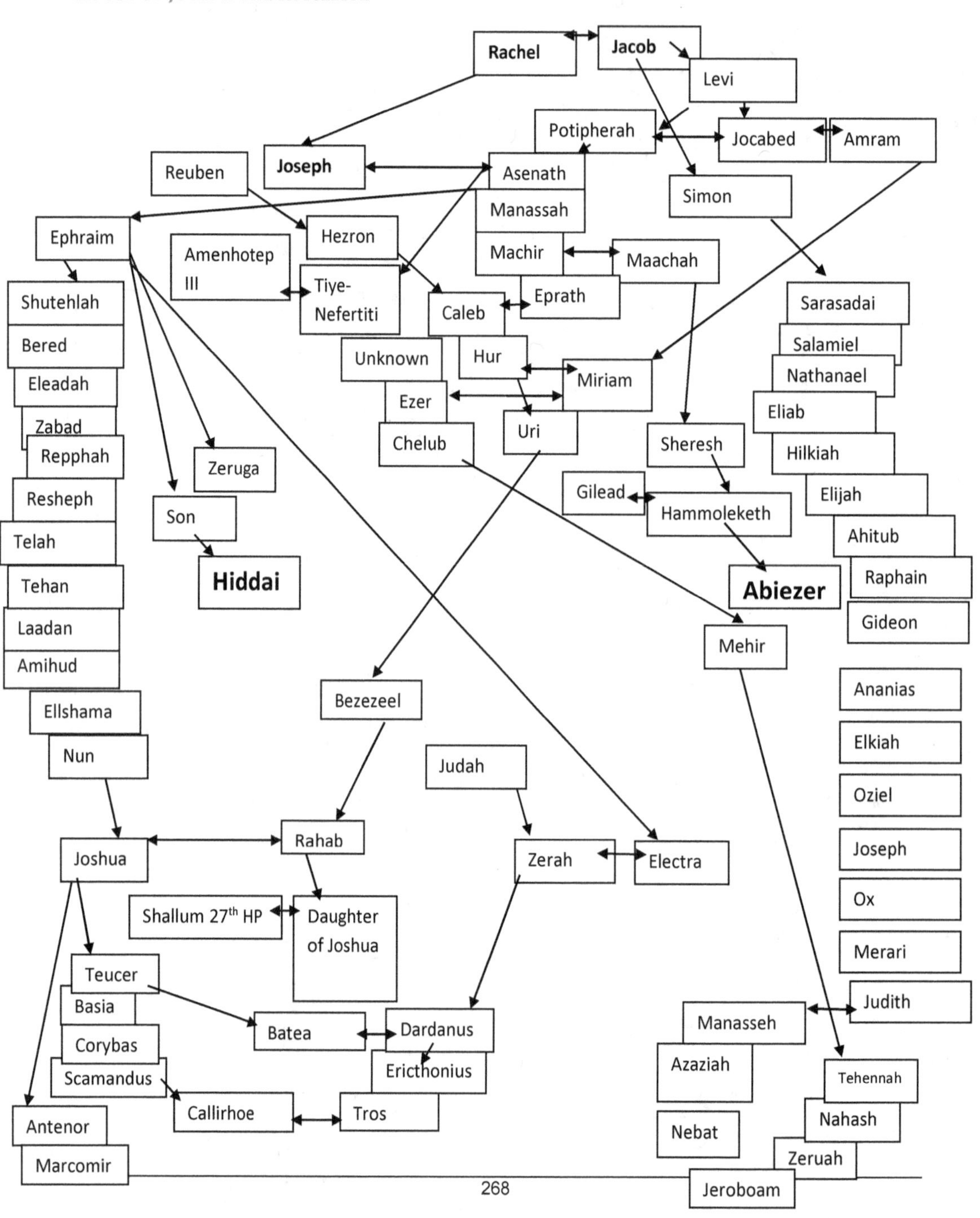
Rachel
Jacob
Levi
Potipherah
Jocabed
Amram
Reuben
Joseph
Asenath
Simon
Manassah
Ephraim
Hezron
Amenhotep III
Machir
Maachah
Tiye-Nefertiti
Eprath
Caleb
Shutehlah
Sarasadai
Bered
Unknown
Hur
Miriam
Salamiel
Nathanael
Eleadah
Ezer
Eliab
Zabad
Uri
Chelub
Sheresh
Hilkiah
Repphah
Zeruga
Resheph
Gilead
Hammoleketh
Elijah
Son
Telah
Ahitub
Tehan
Hiddai
Abiezer
Raphain
Laadan
Gideon
Mehir
Amihud
Ananias
Ellshama
Bezezeel
Elkiah
Nun
Judah
Oziel
Rahab
Joshua
Zerah
Electra
Joseph
Shallum 27th HP
Daughter of Joshua
Ox
Merari
Teucer
Judith
Basia
Manasseh
Batea
Dardanus
Corybas
Azaziah
Scamandus
Ericthonius
Tehennah
Callirhoe
Tros
Antenor
Nahash
Nebat
Marcomir
Zeruah
Jeroboam

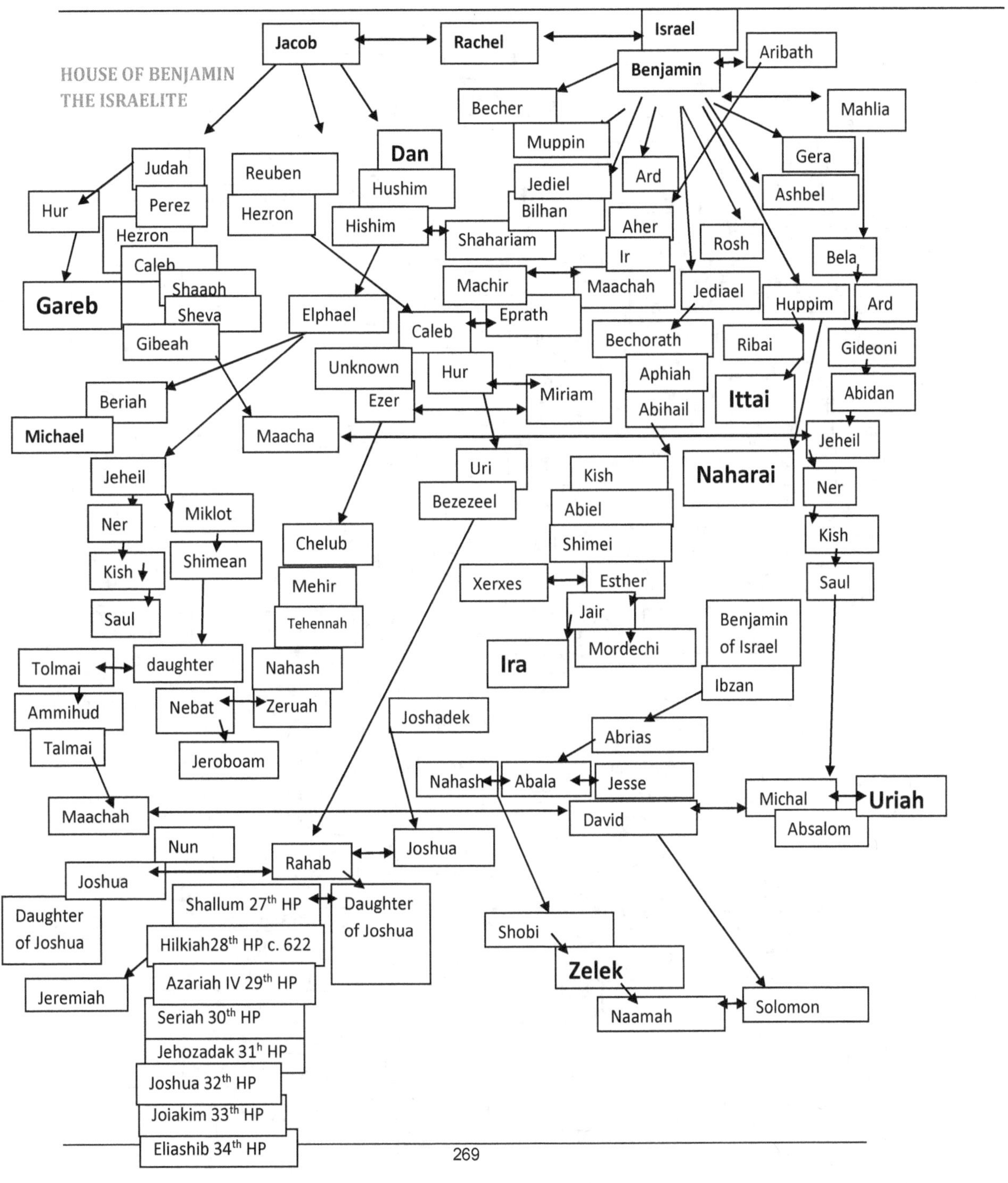
Jacob
Rachel
Israel
Benjamin
Aribath
HOUSE OF BENJAMIN
THE ISRAELITE
Becher
Mahlia
Muppin
Dan
Gera
Judah
Reuben
Ard
Jediel
Ashbel
Hushim
Perez
Hur
Bilhan
Hezron
Hishim
Aher
Rosh
Shahariam
Hezron
Ir
Bela
Caleb
Machir
Maachah
Jediael
Gareb
Shaaph
Huppim
Ard
Sheva
Elphael
Eprath
Caleb
Bechorath
Gibeah
Ribai
Gideoni
Unknown
Aphiah
Hur
Miriam
Ittai
Abidan
Beriah
Ezer
Abihail
Michael
Maacha
Jeheil
Uri
Naharai
Kish
Jeheil
Ner
Bezezeel
Abiel
Miklot
Ner
Chelub
Shimei
Kish
Shimean
Kish
Mehir
Xerxes
Esther
Saul
Tehennah
Jair
Saul
Benjamin
of Israel
Mordechi
Ira
Tolmai
daughter
Nahash
Ibzan
Nebat
Zeruah
Ammihud
Joshadek
Abrias
Talmai
Jeroboam
Nahash
Abala
Jesse
Michal
Uriah
Maachah
David
Absalom
Nun
Joshua
Rahab
Joshua
Shallum 27th HP
Daughter
of Joshua
Daughter
of Joshua
Shobi
Hilkiah28th HP c. 622
Zelek
Jeremiah
Azariah IV 29th HP
Naamah
Solomon
Seriah 30th HP
Jehozadak 31h HP
Joshua 32th HP
Joiakim 33th HP
Eliashib 34th HP

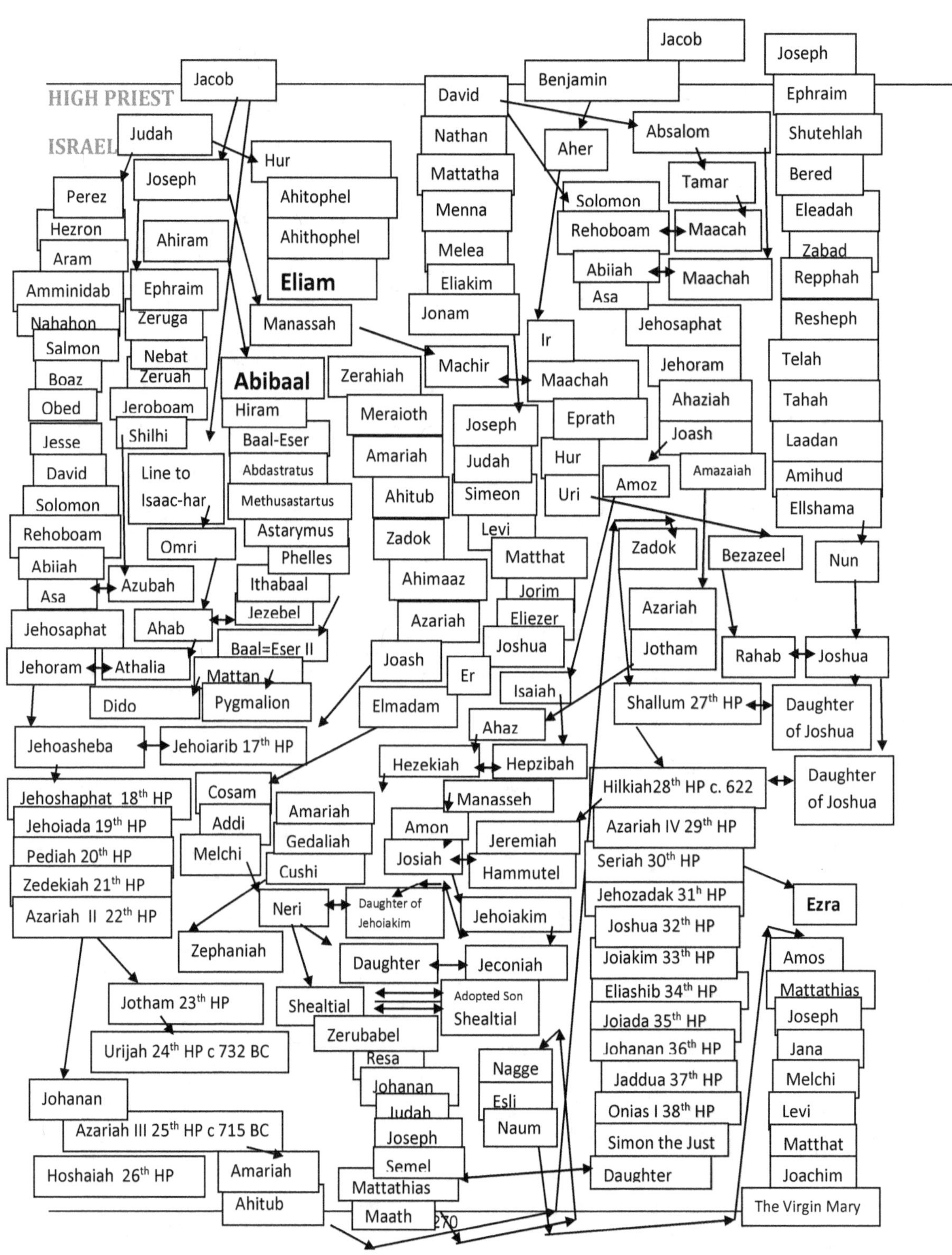

HIGH PRIEST
ISRAEL
Jacob
Judah
Perez
Hezron
Aram
Amminidab
Nahahon
Salmon
Boaz
Obed
Jesse
David
Solomon
Rehoboam
Abiiah
Asa
Jehosaphat
Jehoram
Athalia
Dido
Jehoasheba
Jehoiarib 17th HP
Jehoshaphat 18th HP
Jehoiada 19th HP
Pediah 20th HP
Zedekiah 21th HP
Azariah II 22th HP
Jotham 23th HP
Urijah 24th HP c 732 BC
Johanan
Azariah III 25th HP c 715 BC
Hoshaiah 26th HP
Joseph
Ahiram
Ephraim
Zeruga
Nebat
Zeruah
Jeroboam
Shilhi
Line to Isaac-har
Omri
Azubah
Ahab
Jezebel
Baal=Eser II
Mattan
Pygmalion
Hur
Ahitophel
Ahithophel
Eliam
Manassah
Abibaal
Hiram
Baal-Eser
Abdastratus
Methusastartus
Astarymus
Phelles
Ithabaal
Cosam
Addi
Melchi
Amariah
Gedaliah
Cushi
Neri
Daughter of Jehoiakim
Zephaniah
Shealtial
Adopted Son Shealtial
Zerubabel
Resa
Johanan
Judah
Joseph
Semel
Mattathias
Maath
Amariah
Ahitub
David
Nathan
Mattatha
Menna
Melea
Eliakim
Jonam
Machir
Zerahiah
Meraioth
Amariah
Ahitub
Zadok
Ahimaaz
Azariah
Joash
Elmadam
Er
Joseph
Judah
Simeon
Levi
Matthat
Jorim
Eliezer
Joshua
Isaiah
Ahaz
Hezekiah
Hepzibah
Manasseh
Amon
Josiah
Jeremiah
Hammutel
Jehoiakim
Daughter
Jeconiah
Nagge
Esli
Naum
Jacob
Benjamin
Aher
Absalom
Tamar
Solomon
Rehoboam
Maacah
Abiiah
Maachah
Asa
Ir
Maachah
Eprath
Hur
Uri
Jehosaphat
Jehoram
Ahaziah
Joash
Amazaiah
Amoz
Zadok
Azariah
Jotham
Shallum 27th HP
Bezazeel
Rahab
Hilkiah28th HP c. 622
Azariah IV 29th HP
Seriah 30th HP
Jehozadak 31h HP
Joshua 32th HP
Joiakim 33th HP
Eliashib 34th HP
Joiada 35th HP
Johanan 36th HP
Jaddua 37th HP
Onias I 38th HP
Simon the Just
Daughter
Joseph
Ephraim
Shutehlah
Bered
Eleadah
Zabad
Repphah
Resheph
Telah
Tahah
Laadan
Amihud
Ellshama
Nun
Joshua
Daughter of Joshua
Daughter of Joshua
Ezra
Amos
Mattathias
Joseph
Jana
Melchi
Levi
Matthat
Joachim
The Virgin Mary

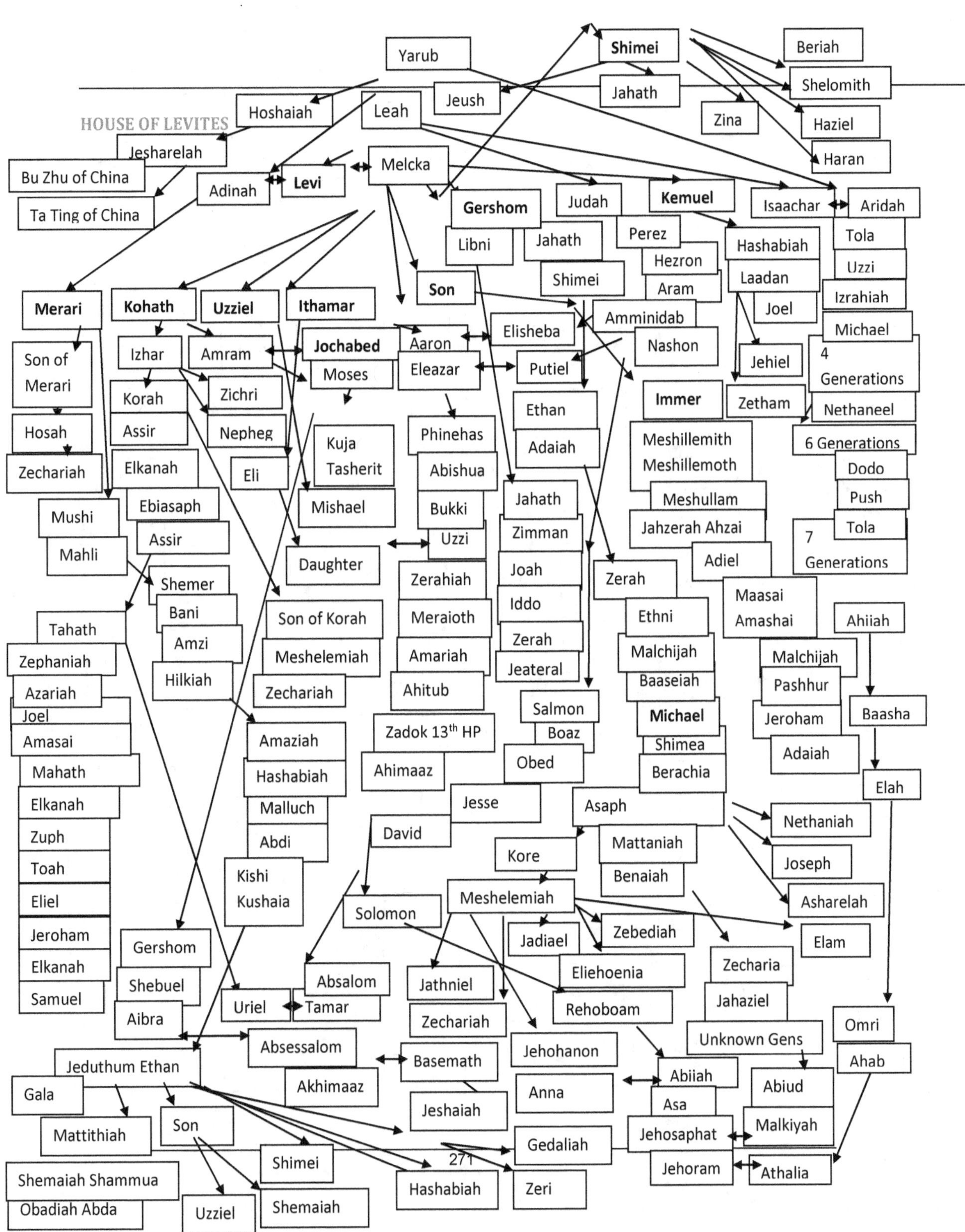
HOUSE OF LEVITES
Yarub
Shimei
Beriah
Shelomith
Hoshaiah
Leah
Jeush
Jahath
Zina
Haziel
Haran
Jesharelah
Bu Zhu of China
Adinah
Levi
Melcka
Ta Ting of China
Gershom
Judah
Kemuel
Isaachar
Aridah
Libni
Jahath
Perez
Hashabiah
Tola
Shimei
Hezron
Laadan
Uzzi
Aram
Izrahiah
Son
Joel
Merari
Kohath
Uzziel
Ithamar
Amminidab
Michael
Elisheba
Nashon
Son of Merari
Izhar
Amram
Jochabed
Aaron
Jehiel
4 Generations
Moses
Eleazar
Putiel
Korah
Zichri
Ethan
Immer
Zetham
Nethaneel
Assir
Nepheg
Phinehas
Meshillemith Meshillemoth
Hosah
Kuja Tasherit
Adaiah
6 Generations
Elkanah
Zechariah
Eli
Abishua
Dodo
Jahath
Meshullam
Push
Ebiasaph
Mishael
Bukki
Mushi
Zimman
Jahzerah Ahzai
Tola
Assir
Uzzi
7 Generations
Mahli
Daughter
Adiel
Joah
Zerah
Shemer
Zerahiah
Maasai Amashai
Iddo
Bani
Son of Korah
Meraioth
Ethni
Ahiiah
Tahath
Amzi
Zerah
Zephaniah
Meshelemiah
Amariah
Malchijah
Malchijah
Jeateral
Hilkiah
Azariah
Zechariah
Ahitub
Baaseiah
Pashhur
Joel
Salmon
Amasai
Michael
Jeroham
Baasha
Zadok 13th HP
Boaz
Amaziah
Shimea
Mahath
Hashabiah
Obed
Ahimaaz
Berachia
Adaiah
Elkanah
Malluch
Jesse
Asaph
Elah
Zuph
Nethaniah
Abdi
David
Mattaniah
Toah
Kore
Kishi Kushaia
Joseph
Eliel
Benaiah
Meshelemiah
Solomon
Asharelah
Jeroham
Gershom
Zebediah
Jadiael
Elam
Elkanah
Zecharia
Eliehoenia
Absalom
Jathniel
Shebuel
Samuel
Uriel
Tamar
Rehoboam
Jahaziel
Aibra
Zechariah
Omri
Unknown Gens
Absessalom
Jeduthum Ethan
Jehohanon
Basemath
Ahab
Abiiah
Gala
Akhimaaz
Abiud
Anna
Asa
Son
Mattithiah
Jeshaiah
Malkiyah
Jehosaphat
Gedaliah
Shimei
Shemaiah Shammua
Jehoram
Athalia
Hashabiah
Zeri
Obadiah Abda
Uzziel
Shemaiah

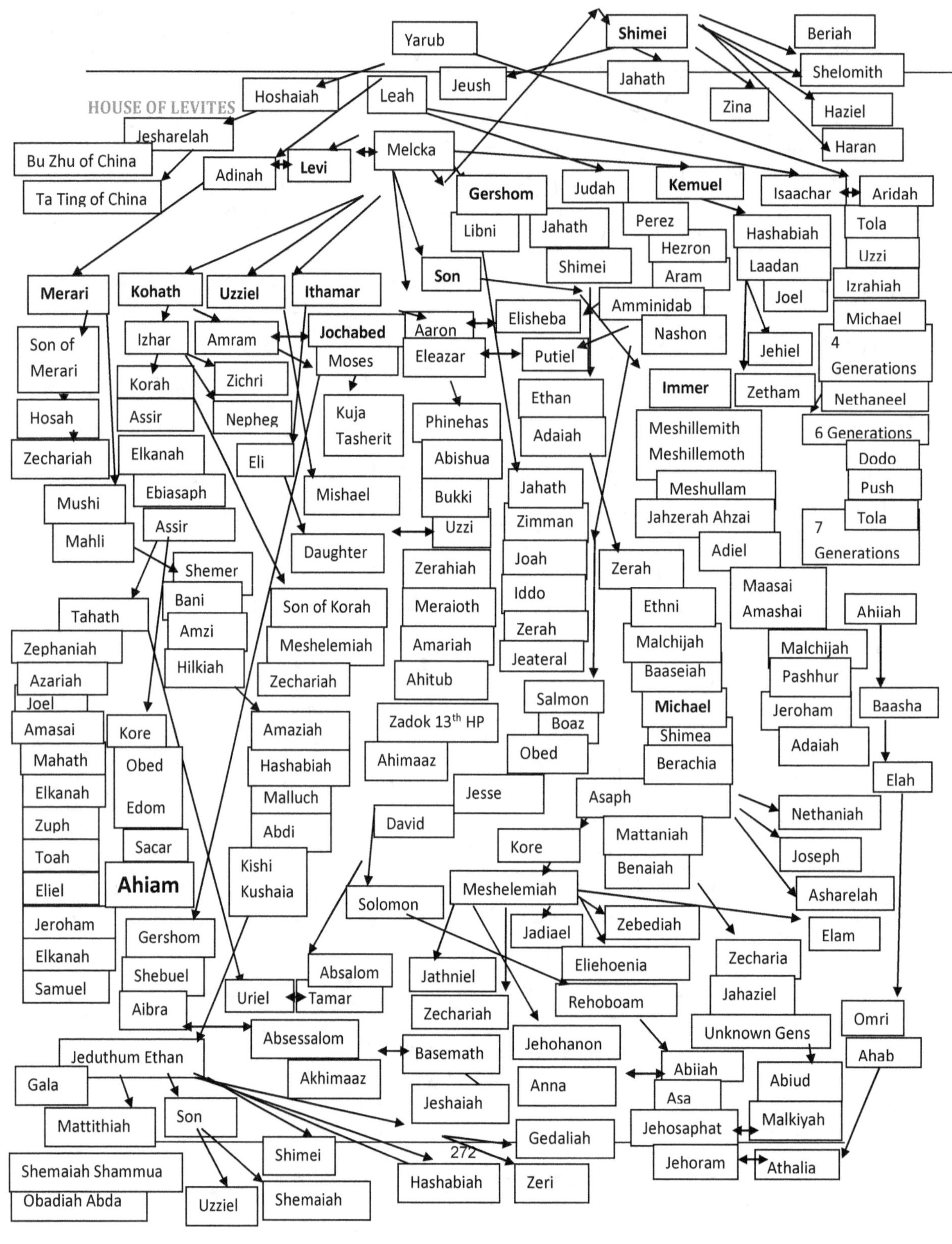

HOUSE OF LEVITES
Yarub
Shimei
Beriah
Jeush
Jahath
Shelomith
Hoshaiah
Leah
Zina
Haziel
Jesharelah
Haran
Bu Zhu of China
Levi
Melcka
Adinah
Ta Ting of China
Gershom
Judah
Kemuel
Isaachar
Aridah
Libni
Jahath
Perez
Hashabiah
Tola
Hezron
Uzzi
Shimei
Laadan
Aram
Izrahiah
Merari
Kohath
Uzziel
Ithamar
Son
Amminidab
Joel
Michael
Son of Merari
Izhar
Amram
Jochabed
Aaron
Elisheba
Nashon
Jehiel
4 Generations
Moses
Eleazar
Putiel
Korah
Zichri
Immer
Zetham
Nethaneel
Hosah
Assir
Nepheg
Kuja Tasherit
Phinehas
Ethan
Meshillemith Meshillemoth
6 Generations
Zechariah
Elkanah
Eli
Abishua
Adaiah
Dodo
Mishael
Bukki
Jahath
Meshullam
Push
Mushi
Ebiasaph
Tola
Zimman
Jahzerah Ahzai
7 Generations
Assir
Uzzi
Mahli
Daughter
Joah
Adiel
Shemer
Zerahiah
Zerah
Maasai Amashai
Bani
Son of Korah
Meraioth
Iddo
Ethni
Ahiiah
Tahath
Amzi
Zerah
Malchijah
Malchijah
Zephaniah
Meshelemiah
Amariah
Jeateral
Hilkiah
Baaseiah
Pashhur
Azariah
Zechariah
Ahitub
Salmon
Joel
Michael
Baasha
Jeroham
Amasai
Kore
Amaziah
Zadok 13th HP
Boaz
Shimea
Adaiah
Mahath
Obed Edom
Hashabiah
Ahimaaz
Obed
Berachia
Malluch
Elah
Elkanah
Jesse
Asaph
Nethaniah
Zuph
Abdi
David
Mattaniah
Sacar
Kore
Toah
Kishi Kushaia
Joseph
Benaiah
Eliel
Ahiam
Meshelemiah
Asharelah
Solomon
Jeroham
Zebediah
Elam
Jadiael
Gershom
Elkanah
Zecharia
Absalom
Jathniel
Eliehoenia
Shebuel
Jahaziel
Samuel
Uriel
Tamar
Rehoboam
Aibra
Zechariah
Omri
Unknown Gens
Absessalom
Jehohanon
Jeduthum Ethan
Basemath
Ahab
Abiiah
Gala
Akhimaaz
Anna
Abiud
Asa
Jeshaiah
Mattithiah
Son
Malkiyah
Jehosaphat
Gedaliah
Shimei
Shemaiah Shammua
Jehoram
Athalia
Hashabiah
Zeri
Obadiah Abda
Uzziel
Shemaiah

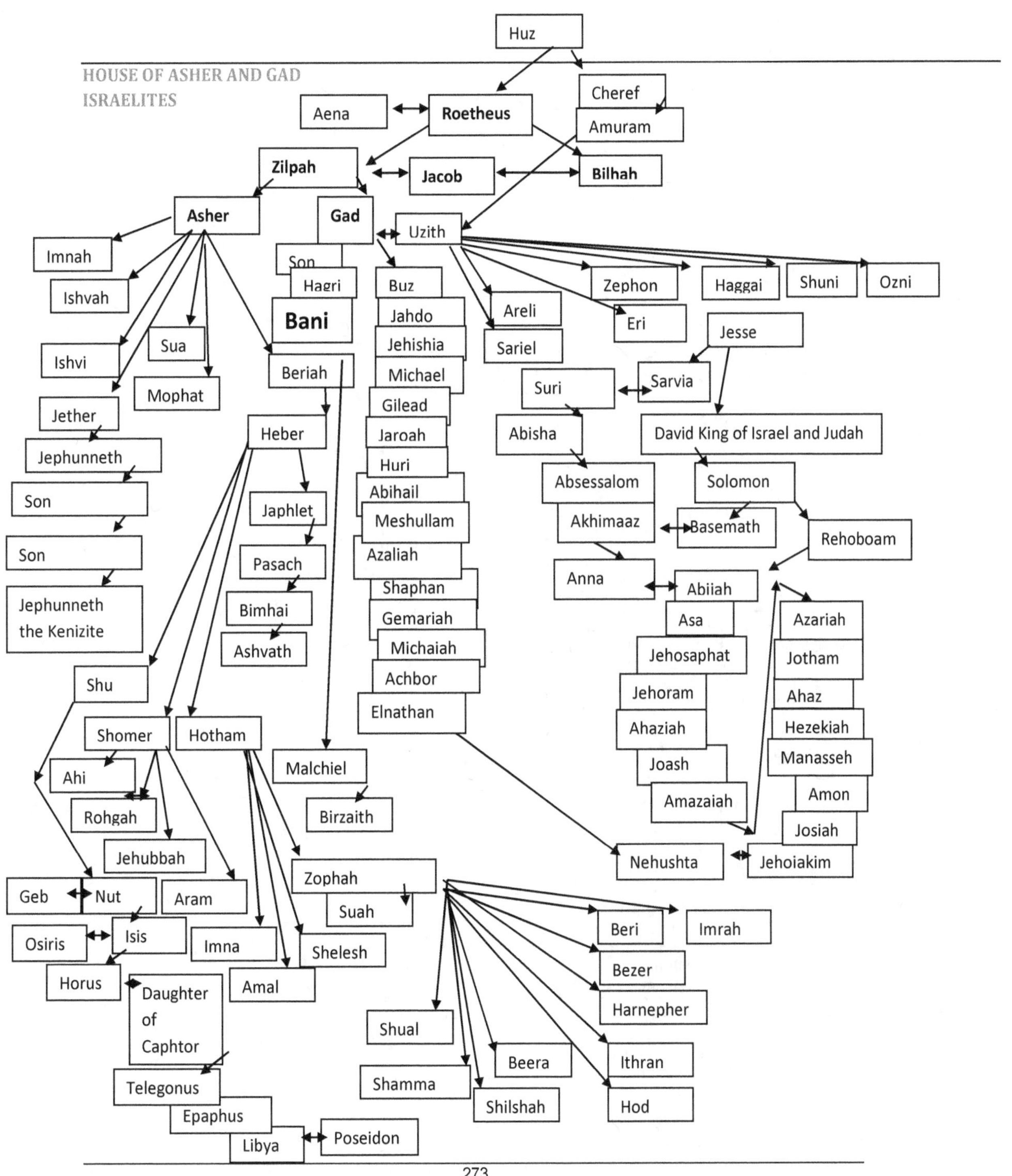
Huz
Cheref
Amuram
Aena
Roetheus
Zilpah
Jacob
Bilhah
Asher
Gad
Uzith
Imnah
Ishvah
Ishvi
Sua
Mophat
Jether
Jephunneth
Son
Son
Jephunneth the Kenizite
Son
Hagri
Bani
Beriah
Heber
Japhlet
Pasach
Bimhai
Ashvath
Shu
Shomer
Hotham
Ahi
Rohgah
Jehubbah
Aram
Geb
Nut
Osiris
Isis
Horus
Daughter of Caphtor
Telegonus
Epaphus
Libya
Poseidon
Imna
Amal
Shelesh
Malchiel
Birzaith
Zophah
Suah
Buz
Jahdo
Jehishia
Michael
Gilead
Jaroah
Huri
Abihail
Meshullam
Azaliah
Shaphan
Gemariah
Michaiah
Achbor
Elnathan
Areli
Sariel
Zephon
Eri
Haggai
Shuni
Ozni
Jesse
Suri
Sarvia
Abisha
David King of Israel and Judah
Absessalom
Solomon
Akhimaaz
Basemath
Rehoboam
Anna
Abiiah
Asa
Jehosaphat
Jehoram
Ahaziah
Joash
Amazaiah
Azariah
Jotham
Ahaz
Hezekiah
Manasseh
Amon
Josiah
Jehoiakim
Nehushta
Beri
Imrah
Bezer
Harnepher
Ithran
Hod
Shual
Shamma
Beera
Shilshah

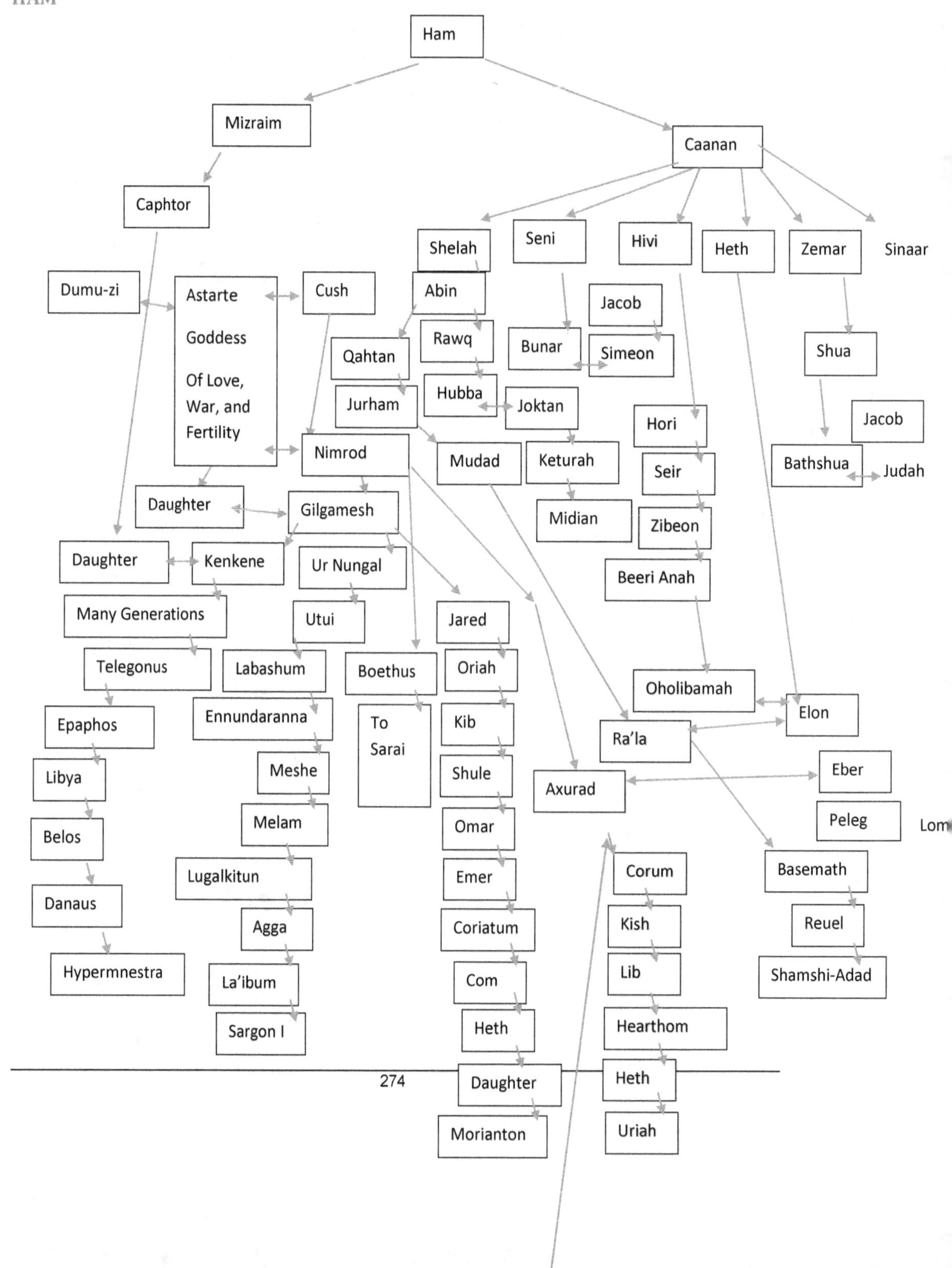
Ham
Mizraim
Caanan
Caphtor
Shelah
Seni
Hivi
Heth
Zemar
Sinaar
Dumu-zi
Astarte
Goddess
Of Love,
War, and
Fertility
Cush
Abin
Jacob
Rawq
Qahtan
Bunar
Simeon
Shua
Hubba
Jurham
Joktan
Hori
Jacob
Nimrod
Mudad
Keturah
Seir
Bathshua
Judah
Daughter
Gilgamesh
Midian
Zibeon
Daughter
Kenkene
Ur Nungal
Beeri Anah
Many Generations
Utui
Jared
Telegonus
Labashum
Boethus
Oriah
Oholibamah
Elon
Epaphos
Ennundaranna
To
Sarai
Kib
Ra'la
Eber
Libya
Meshe
Shule
Axurad
Belos
Melam
Omar
Peleg
Lom
Corum
Basemath
Lugalkitun
Emer
Danaus
Agga
Coriatum
Kish
Reuel
Hypermnestra
La'ibum
Com
Lib
Shamshi-Adad
Sargon I
Heth
Hearthom
Daughter
Heth
Morianton
Uriah

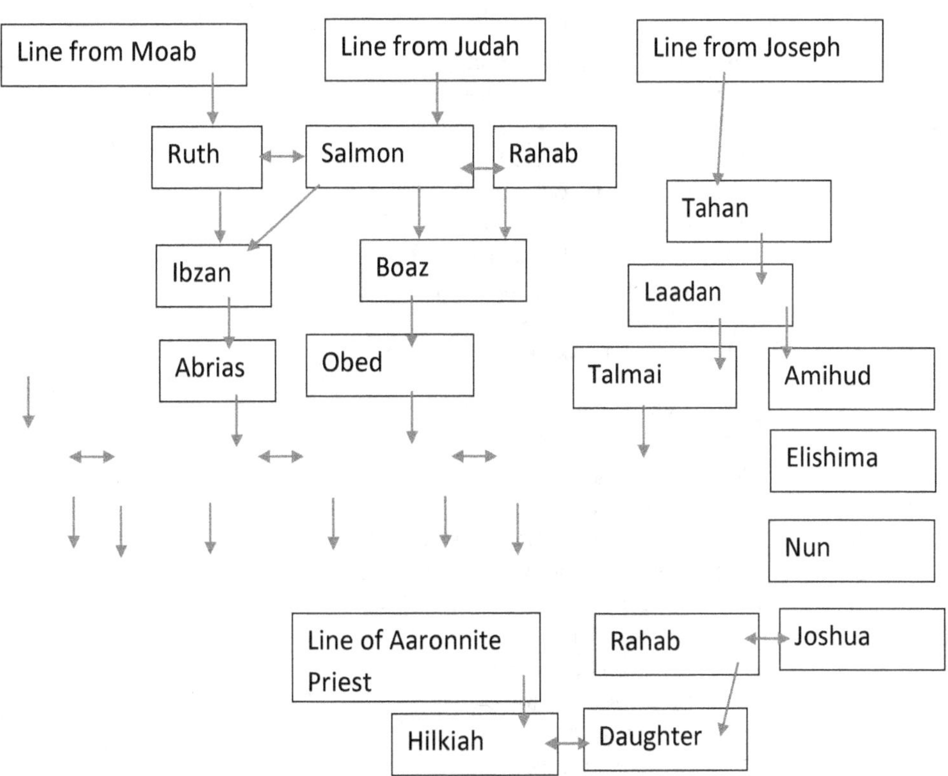
Line from Moab
Line from Judah
Line from Joseph
Ruth
Salmon
Rahab
Tahan
Ibzan
Boaz
Laadan
Abrias
Obed
Talmai
Amihud
Elishima
Nun
Line of Aaronnite Priest
Rahab
Joshua
Hilkiah
Daughter

Sariya was a great women. She was married to Suri, who is the father of what is called the Big Sur. Suri was from the tribe of Naptali, and had sons Joab, the general for King David, and Abisha. Abisha's line continued to marry into the house of David to Anna who married Abijah, the grandson of Solomon. Sariya was the daughter of Abala and Nahash. Reuben had taken Billah and she made a son, so Jacob on his deathbed is said to curse Reuben. This curse of a man fathering with his mother is found in the line of Nahash who married Abala the mother of Sariya and Nahash is from the male line of Reuben, making him a Reubenite.

Some conclusions can be inferred here due to the generational crosses. First Salmon was Abala great grandfather, so Sariya was Great Great to Salmon. Salmon's grandson Obed had a daughter that married the son Abisha to son of Suri. So here Sariya had to be much younger than Suri if the generations between Naptali and Suri and the generations between Judah and Obed are about the same. In the Big Sur Joab's daughter marries the line of the Danites, who marry the line of the Zeruga grandson of the Chosen of Jacob Joseph. Sariya has Nebat and makes Jeroboam who was the rebel that formed the kingdom of Israel. It is possible that Jeroboam made a deal with David or Jesse that he would insure Solomon's line would continue in exchange for owning the people who took lives. Sariya is Jeroboam's mother and she is also his Great Great Great Grandmother on his fathers side. This is extremely unusual and would be difficult to have happen again. Thus is shown the philosophy of the Hebrew people that their feats in breeding and making are impossible for other races to duplicate so they have earned the place of being the world rulers.

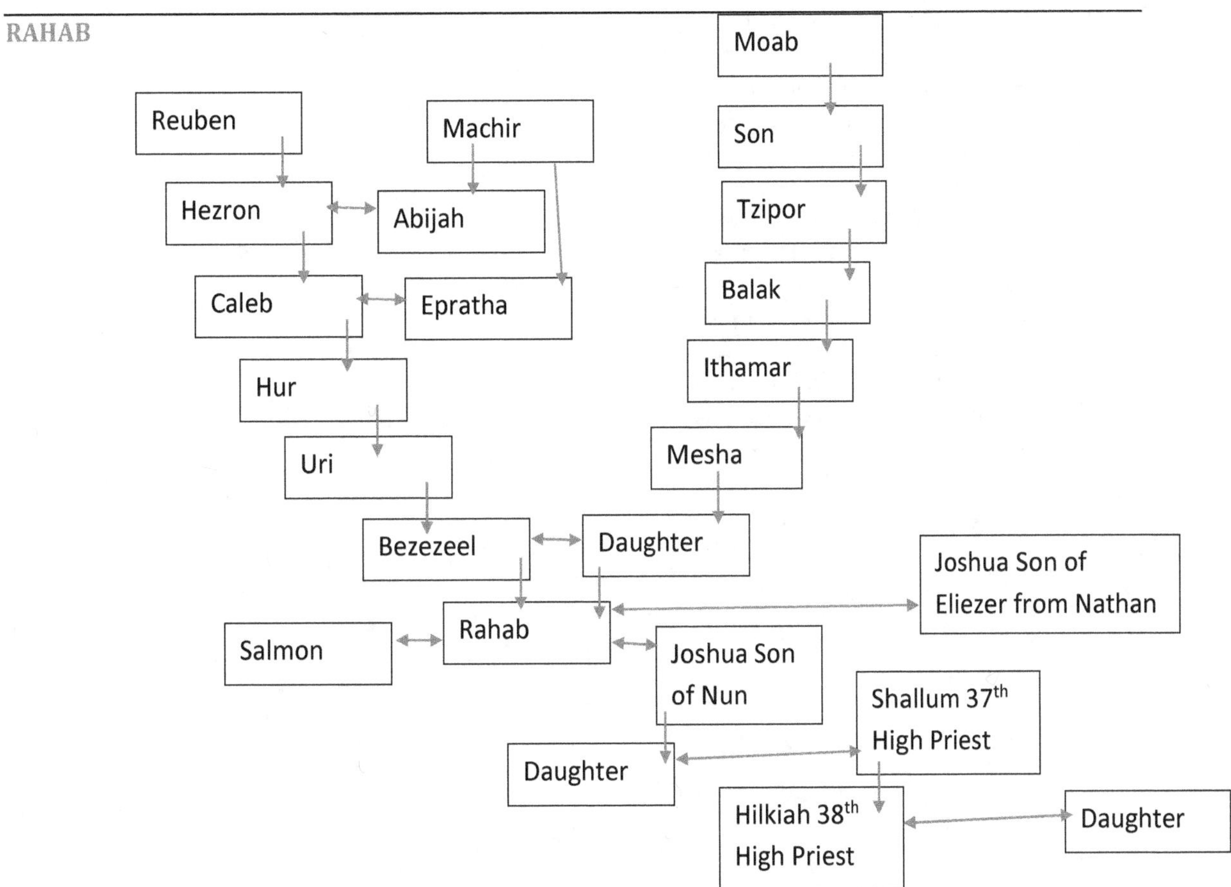
Moab
Reuben
Machir
Son
Hezron
Abijah
Tzipor
Caleb
Epratha
Balak
Hur
Ithamar
Uri
Mesha
Bezezeel
Daughter
Joshua Son of Eliezer from Nathan
Salmon
Rahab
Joshua Son of Nun
Shallum 37th High Priest
Daughter
Hilkiah 38th High Priest
Daughter

Rahab is a very great women. First she is from the male line of Reuben. Her mother is from the tribe of Moab. She marries Joshua, which is why many scholars believe she is likened to Mary while Joshua is likened to Jesus. She is the mother of Boaz, and like Sariya is considered a Harlot. She is a powerful force in Hebrew and is mentioned in the book of Joshua as a women who is part of the Hebrew. She gives shelter to 2 spies from the Hebrew camp, and so is not harmed after the Hebrew take the city.

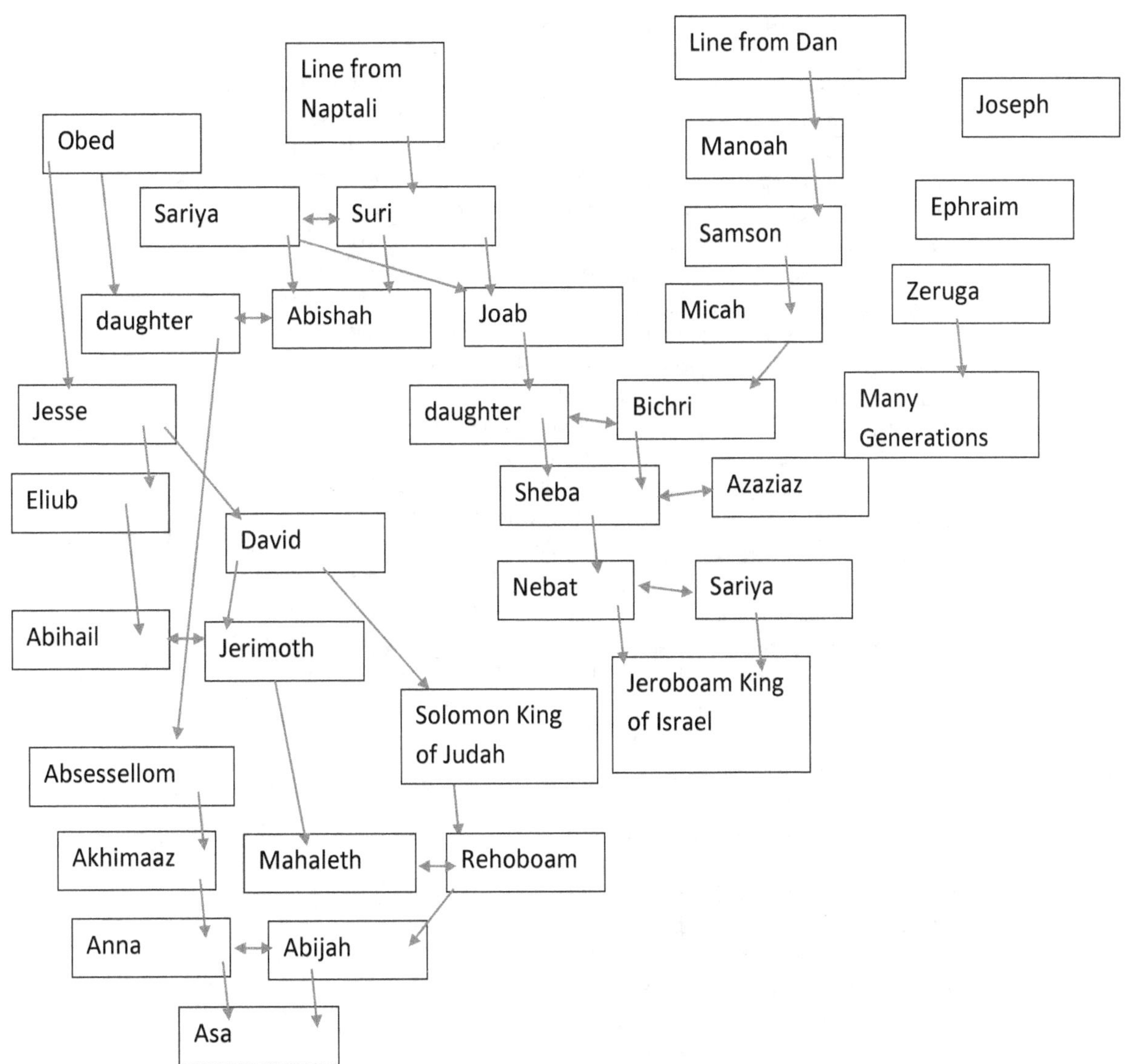
Line from Naptali
Line from Dan
Joseph
Obed
Manoah
Sariya
Suri
Ephraim
Samson
Zeruga
daughter
Abishah
Joab
Micah
Jesse
daughter
Bichri
Many Generations
Eliub
Sheba
Azaziaz
David
Nebat
Sariya
Abihail
Jerimoth
Jeroboam King of Israel
Solomon King of Judah
Absessellom
Akhimaaz
Mahaleth
Rehoboam
Anna
Abijah
Asa

The Ladies of the Tribe of Jacob.

The following chart shows the ladies of the tribe of Jacob. Jacob was a great man and was forced to defend himself from his twin brother Esau. He was told to travel to Kinsmen and take a wife. He loved Rachel, but was hoodwinked by Laban into first marrying Leah, Rachel's sister who was older and did not appeal to Jacob so much. Jacob eventually married Rachel and gives his blessing to his son Joseph, not the first born of Leah but the first born of Rachel. Both Rachel and Leah had servants, Billah and Zilphah. They were sisters of the line of Huz, who was the son of Nahor. Nahor had a son Terah by Iosaka that was stronger than Huz and Kemule, so Huz's descendents became servants of Terah's descendents. Billah bore Jacob two sons Dan and Naptali, both of the house of Rachel. It is not known how much the servitude was enforced by Rachel and Jacob but certainly Jacob would always choose Rachel's house to Leah's. Leah's house was much larger and had six sons of Leah and Jacob, and two from Zilphah. In the time of Ham there was a priest Melchezidec so Priests were part of the Hebrew people. Priests would see that spirits are resurrected so Zilphah may be the resurrected spirit of Astarte. Billah may be the angel of a death dealing women. As far as ruling Israel, which is what Jacob's tribe became after the clan battle Billah has the worst part to play as a servant of Rachel. She must obey Rachel's orders and is found to be with child from Reuben. It is not known if the women took part in the clan battle, but Billah as the mother of Dan was the mother of who would become the liege lord of Persia. Bathshua line merged with Judah, who was noted to be the strongest of Jacobs sons, possibly the resurrection of Cush. She was the mother of Hur, whose line continued to Bathsheba. Judah with Tamar was the mother of Zerah who after the clan battle become Zeus. Hur was called Hades and he was the father of Naomi, who was a very mean women, entrusted with the idea of naming people possibly the resurrection of Naom from Sumatra. Aribath was an important women. From Abraham's line thru Zimran the son of Keturah the descendents of Keturah could not stay in the lines from Midian, since Midian had his mother Keturah, so they would be forced to descend thru Zimran to Aribath who was the mother of the line of Gideon. Thus the people who are subject to Keturah are given their own translation of the bible to be law for them.

Finally Bathsheba. She is from the line of Judah thru the Bath Wife Bathshua who is from Ham. So she is likely very strong, strong enough to become a beautiful women. In Hebrew texts Uriah is shown to be cheating on his wife Bathsheba and fathering Absalom and Abadabon. So David is right to have his General Joab sentence Uriah to the front line to be killed while he takes the lives of the sons of Uriah. Thus Bathsheba is the mother of David's eldest son Solomon. Bathsheba is possibly the strongest lady of the Davidic kingdom. Solomon's wife Nicole is from the ptolomeys of Egypt and the marriage is more of a purpose to supplement the blood of Judah with strong ptolmies. Bathsheba is David's wife, while Abigail is David's half sister. The idea of the son of Abigail Daniel being the son of David implies that there is incest, so Daniel is thrown out of heaven. In fact Daniel is from the eldest line of Hezron David's ancestor and so seeks to take the kingdom of Judah. Thrown out he is the fallen angel, and so learns all about the underworld from his mother Abigail and his servant mother in the Jake Billah. Eventually the law plays out as David plans it and Daniel is forced to take on Hur for rule of the underworld, and he wins.

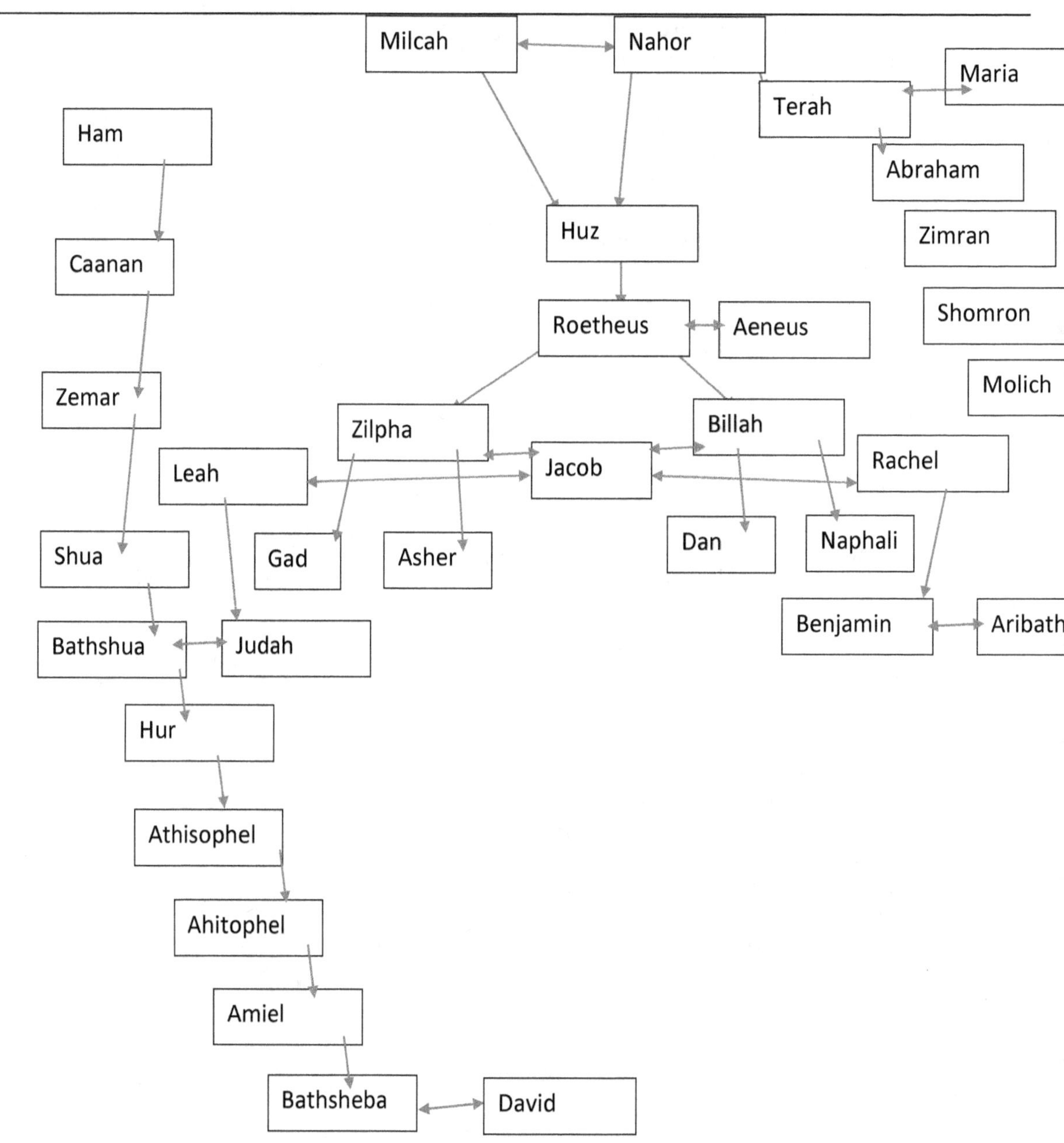
Milcah
Nahor
Maria
Terah
Ham
Abraham
Huz
Zimran
Caanan
Shomron
Roetheus
Aeneus
Molich
Zemar
Zilpha
Billah
Leah
Jacob
Rachel
Shua
Gad
Asher
Dan
Naphali
Benjamin
Aribath
Bathshua
Judah
Hur
Athisophel
Ahitophel
Amiel
Bathsheba
David

www.ingramcontent.com/pod-product-compliance
Lightning Source LLC
Chambersburg PA
CBHW051954280526
45793CB00005B/719

* 9 7 8 1 5 3 5 3 4 3 9 3 0 *